EIGHTH EDITION

Managerial Economics

Analysis, Problems, Cases

Lila J. Truett

Professor of Economics
The University of Texas at San Antonio

Dale B. Truett

Professor of Economics
The University of Texas at San Antonio

WILEY

John Wiley & Sons, Inc.

Acquisitions Editor	Leslie Kraham
Project Editor	Cindy Rhoads
Editorial Assistant	Jessica Bartlelt
Production Editor	Sandra Dumas
Senior Marketing Manager	Charity Robey
Senior Designer	Karin Kincheloe
Production Management Services	Hermitage Publishing Services

This book was typeset in Palatino by Hermitage and printed and bound by R. R. Donnelley(Crawfordsville). The cover was printed by Phoenix Color Corp.

The paper in this book was manufactured by a mill whose forest management programs include sustained yield harvesting of its timberlands. Sustained yield harvesting principles ensure that the number of trees cut each year does not exceed the amount of new growth.

This book is printed on acid-free paper. ∞

Truett, Lila, J., Truett, Dale, B.
Managerial Economics: Analysis, Problems Cases, Eighth Edition

ISBN 0-471-44466-9
ISBN 0-471-45223-8 (Wiley International Edition)

Printed in the United States of America.

10 9 8 7 6 5 4 3 2 1

Preface

The eighth edition marks a milestone for this book—over 25 years in the marketplace. We are happy that many thousands of students have learned from the book and are extremely grateful to all those who have taught from it for their acceptance of our work. Over the years, we have made many adjustments in our coverage and presentation of materials in order to keep the book current, concise, and clear. This edition is significantly changed, as we will outline for you below. As before, the book is designed primarily for use by business administration students who have done some introductory-level work in economics. Our main objective is to enhance students' understanding of the application of economic analysis to *managerial decisions.* We believe this goal can best be accomplished by providing a clear and brief statement of the principles of microeconomic decision making and supplementing this material with problems, examples, and cases that illustrate how such principles are applied.

Throughout each chapter, you will find numerical examples, applications, and mini-cases dispersed among discussions of decision criteria and rules. Each chapter ends with questions and problems related to the materials covered. In addition, we have provided Integrating Cases at the ends of the book's five major parts. Each case is somewhat longer than the typical end-of-chapter problem and integrates a number of concepts developed in the preceding chapters.

EIGHTH EDITION FEATURES AND CHANGES

In this edition, *Managerial Economics* has undergone some reorganization and improvement. Here is a list of some important changes and key features:

- *New Introductory Chapter.* Thoroughly revised, this chapter now presents students with ten *principles of managerial economics* that will both help them to understand what the field is about and serve as a guide to the analytical techniques they will meet in subsequent chapters. In addition, the material on basic demand and supply analysis (formerly in an appendix) has been moved into the body of the chapter.

- *New Treatment of Linear Demand Curve and Marginal Revenue.* A noncalculus explanation of why the marginal revenue *(MR)* curve for a linear demand curve is also a straight line with twice the negative slope has been added to Chapter 2. This approach is intended not only to enhance students' understanding of the relationship of the demand curve to *MR* and total revenue but also to improve their skills for problem-solving in later chapters that use these concepts.

- *New Chapter on Games, Information, and Strategy.* This chapter (Chapter 10) responds to the desire of many instructors for increased coverage of these important areas. It incorporates what were formerly two appendixes (9A and 9B) with a much-expanded discussion of the economics of information. We have taken a great deal of care to make this material both interesting and easily accessible to students.

- *Applications Boxes.* Two pedagogical devices introduced in a previous edition—*Managerial Perspectives* and *Numerical Examples*—have been retained and updated. The Managerial Perspectives are high-interest illustrations of how real-world firms have grappled with the kinds of issues and decision problems discussed in the book. The Numerical Examples call attention to the steps that must be taken to solve specific types of problems (arc elasticity, cost minimization, profit maximization, game strategy, present value, etc.) that students will encounter repeatedly in the end-of-chapter and *Study Guide* problems. Students can much improve their problem-solving skills if they take time to work through the numerical examples.

- *International Applications.* International applications of managerial economics are now more important than ever. Over the past fifteen or so years, we have had the good fortune to be able to travel, study, and participate in economics conferences in a number of countries, ranging from Russia and China to England, Australia, Korea, and South Africa. These experiences, coupled with research and consulting related to a broad range of industries in the United States, Canada, and Mexico, have much enhanced our understanding of business and public sector operations and decision making. We hope that what we have learned from these activities has helped to make this a better book, one that provides a unique, global perspective. That perspective is reinforced in the book's strategically-placed *International Capsules,* designed to make students think about how operating in a global environment affects economic decision making.

- *Glossary and Marginal Definitions.* As in previous editions, we have provided a Glossary at the end of the book. This one is somewhat expanded, partially as a result of our decision to style the text with running definitions in the body of each chapter. The aim of the running definitions, of course, is to make it easier for students to learn the precise economic terminology so necessary to understanding the analytical methods of our discipline.

- *Mathematical Appendix.* A Mathematical Appendix at the end of the text will serve as an important learning tool for many students. It also allows instructors to take a more math-intensive approach to the course if they so desire.

- *End-of-Chapter Problems.* Always an important feature of the book, these highly student-accessible problems have been retained and somewhat expanded. Experience tells us that students enhance their understanding greatly by working numerical problems that give tangible results. Answers to selected odd-numbered problems are provided at the end of the book.

COURSE DESIGN

Our own experience in teaching managerial economics leads us to caution both students and professors that this book contains more material than can normally be covered in a three credit-hour, one-semester course. Where students can be expected to have no more than an average level of preparation in economic principles, it may not be possible to cover more than Chapters 1 and 2, and 5 through 11 in a one-term course. Students with more advanced backgrounds may progress swiftly enough to allow inclusion of Chapters 3 and 4 in the preceding list.

The book allows for some variation in emphasis. For example, to orient a course toward both private and public sector capital project analysis, Chapters 13, 14, and 15 could be substituted for the materials on demand estimation, forecasting, and complex pricing problems covered in Chapters 3, 4, and 11. For this kind of course, probably all of Part 5 should be covered.

For a two-course sequence, we suggest coverage of the basic materials (Chapters 1 through 3, 5 through 10, and 16) in the first course. The second course, which might well be launched as an elective if it is not possible to include it in the core requirements of a program, could include economic forecasting (Chapter 4), linear programming (Appendix 7), advanced topics in pricing (Chapter 11 and its appendices), project analysis (Chapter 13, its appendix, and Chapter 14), and public sector decision making (Chapter 15). Chapter 12 on factor markets could be covered in either term.

APPENDICES

As mentioned earlier, at the end of the book, we have provided a Mathematical Appendix that can be used either for student review or to give the course a more quantitative slant. The appendices to Chapters 2 and 5 provide compact coverage, respectively, of indifference curves and constrained optimization in production analysis. The Appendix following Chapter 7 contains a concise introduction to linear programming. Those following Chapter 11 deal with expanded modeling of transfer pricing and price discrimination. The final appendix is on compounding and discounting and follows Chapter 13.

STUDY GUIDE, INSTRUCTOR'S MANUAL, AND TEST BANK

Student analytical skills in managerial economics can be enhanced by using the *Study Guide*, a learning tool that complements the problem-solving approach employed in the text. Virtually all of the *Study Guide* problems have been classroom tested, and step-by-step solutions are provided at the back of the guide. A unique feature of the guide is a prompting device called "Getting Started" that verbally walks the student through the steps that must be taken to solve a specific type of problem. The *Study Guide* is closely tied to the book by means of a cross-referencing system that indicates the specific end-of-chapter problem or problems that are similar to a given *Study Guide* problem. Finally, for most chapters, the *Study Guide* contains a set of Hand-In Problems that can be used as out-of-class or homework assignments.

Solutions for the Hand-In Problems are found in the *Instructor's Manual*. Many of the Hand-In Problems are set up in a way that allows the instructor to change the value of a key number to generate a variety of different answers. This allows instructors to vary the solutions from section to section of a given course or from one semester to another. The *Instructor's Manual* explains how to use this feature and provides some of the alternative values for the key numbers. The *Instructor's Manual* also contains step-by-step solutions to the end-of-chapter problems and all cases that appear in the book. We hope that instructors and students will use the problems and cases to the fullest possible extent: in our opinion, problem-solving experiences constitute the best way to develop an understanding of managerial economics.

This edition of *Managerial Economics* is accompanied by an improved and updated *Test Bank* revised by Nancy Retynski. The *Test Bank* includes a substantial number of problems that are similar to those found in the text and the *Study Guide,* as well as multiple choice and true/false questions. Note that the Hand-In Problems in the *Study Guide* can also be used as testing materials by changing key instructor-supplied numbers as explained here and in the *Instructor's Manual*.

A significant addition to the teaching support materials for this edition is a set of PowerPoint slides prepared by Jim Witsmeer. Jim has introduced some very innovative animation into his slide show. Thus, in using the PowerPoint materials, be sure to select the "Slide Show" mode. The slides should prove especially useful to instructors whose classes are large. The PowerPoint slides and other support materials can be downloaded from the the book's website (www.wiley.com/college/truett).

ACKNOWLEDGMENTS

We owe debts of gratitude to many teachers and mentors, some of whom have passed on. Those we especially wish to mention are James Jeffers and Gerald Nordquist of the University of Iowa, H. H. Liebhafsky and Wendell C. Gordon of The University of Texas at Austin, and Cliff Lloyd. Our colleagues, Robert E. Langley and the late Vincent DiMartino, are to be commended for their diligent work on various editions of the *Test Bank* and certain other materials. Vince DiMartino passed away when he was just starting to work on the *Test Bank* for this edition. Vince was our student over twenty years ago and, thereafter, became a treasured colleague and friend. The *Test Bank* will always reflect both his talents and his good humor. We certainly miss him deeply. We are grateful to Nancy Retynski for cheerfully stepping in to revise the *Test Bank* for this edition and also to Jim Witsmeer for both his fine work on the Power-Point slides and his suggestions regarding corrections and improvements in the text. Thanks are due as well to our reviewers and all of the instructors at other institutions who have taken the time to provide their comments on previous editions. Reviewers for the eighth edition were:

Steven Rock, Western Illinois University

Robert McComb, Texas Tech University

Tomotaka Ishimine, California State University-Long Beach

Paul Schoofs, Ripon College

Neal H. Hooker, Ohio State University

Harold Elder, University of Alabama

Krishna Rao Akkina, Kansas State University

Bijan Vasigh, Embry-Riddle University

Jodey S. Lingg, City University

Stanko Racic, University of Pittsburgh

We have tried to incorporate numerous of their suggestions in this revision.

Lila J. Truett
Dale B. Truett

Note to Students

In the short run (the present), playing your cards right gets you good grades. Over the long run (in the future), playing them right can get you success. We want to help you do both, and we wrote this book with that in mind.

Your immediate problem is going to be to cope with the course that goes with this book. Here's how.

1. Read your assignments *before* your instructor covers them in class. (If at first you do not understand the material, read through it again.)

2. Pay attention to the Numerical Examples that occasionally appear in the chapters. Work your way through them step by step with pencil and paper to make sure you understand them. It will help you to solve end-of-chapter, *Study Guide,* and exam problems.

3. Go down the list of questions at the end of each chapter. If there are some that you cannot answer, *review* the chapter and find the answer. Ask your instructor if you still are not sure.

4. Work *all* of the problems you are assigned, and do this *before* your instructor solves them for you.

5. When you think you understand a concept or method, make up a problem of your *own* (like the ones at the end of each chapter) and solve it.

We hope this book will help you develop useful skills for solving business or public economic problems or at least for evaluating the solutions or advice of others. These kinds of skills will likely be important to you long after your present course is over.

Much of what we discuss here is not too difficult if you put some thought into your study of it. One way to sharpen your economic I.Q. is to keep an eye on the news and on business periodicals such as *The Wall Street Journal* or *Business Week.* You will find, as we have, that the success or failure of many business undertakings hinges on how well management has understood many of the concepts we discuss in the chapters to follow. In fact we cite some experiences of real businesses in almost every chapter, and as you work your way through the book, we expect that you will develop some definite opinions about which firms have played their cards wisely and which ones have not. All of this, we hope, will help you to play yours well in the future.

About the Authors

Professors Lila J. Truett and Dale B. Truett teach managerial economics and a number of other economics courses at The University of Texas at San Antonio (UTSA). Lila Truett (Ph.D., University of Iowa) served an unusually long tenure as Director of the Division of Economics and Finance at UTSA and has also served on the Governing Board of the Southern Economic Association. Dale Truett received his Ph.D. from The University of Texas at Austin and has served as an academic administrator both at UTSA and at Florida International University, where he was founding chairman of the Department of Economics. From 1997–2002 he held an Ashbel Smith Professorship, the highest distinction for scholarship and research at UTSA. The Truetts have a great deal of consulting experience, including work with a number of Fortune 500 and Fortune 100 firms.

Lila and Dale Truett have contributed many articles to scholarly journals, among them the *American Economic Review*, the *Southern Economic Journal*, *Applied Economics*, the *Journal of Productivity Analysis*, the *Journal of Risk and Insurance*, the *Journal of Development Economics*, and the *Journal of Economic Education*. In addition to managerial economics and economic theory, their research interests include industrial development and international trade. These have taken them to more than 30 countries in the past 15 to 20 years and given them an especially broad perspective on business and economic problem solving.

Brief Contents

PART 4   ANALYSIS OF PROJECT DECISIONS

PART 5   THE FIRM AND THE PUBLIC SECTOR

Contents

PART 2   PRODUCTION, COST, AND PROFIT MAXIMIZATION

PART 3   MARKETS AND THE BEHAVIOR OF THE FIRM

PART 5   THE FIRM AND THE PUBLIC SECTOR

CHAPTER ONE

Introduction, Basic Principles, and Methodology

MANAGERIAL DECISIONS AND PRINCIPLES IN TODAY'S ECONOMY

Mariel is working at home between consulting jobs in Illinois and Italy when her computer suffers yet another crash. She gets on her spare line and calls the manufacturer's toll-free help number. Why does the technician who answers her call have such a brogue? Answer: Because his name is Shamus, and he's in Dublin! Dublin? Dublin *Ireland?* An American computer manufacturer has someone in Dublin who provides technical service to consumers in the United States? Why? The answer is that it was one of the myriad choices available to the company, and managers, once they analyzed its economic consequences, selected it. What made it both feasible and an economic winner were two important considerations. First, highly skilled, computer-literate people were available in Ireland at very attractive wage rates. Second, new communications technologies made telephone linkage to Ireland inexpensive.

Managers are constantly reminded by the choices in front of them that, in this new century, all types of business activities are becoming more complex and, frequently, more global. Most current discussions of how business is changing tend to focus on the significant increase in the number and types of decisions managers have come to face in recent years. Something as ordinary as the production of the book you are now reading has gone through major changes because of new technologies for activities ranging from data input, to imaging, to distribution. In fact, if for any course you have a textbook that is in its 7th, 8th, or higher edition, it is most likely that personal computers did not even *exist* when the first edition of that book was in production.

While technological changes and globalization of economic activity have become increasingly important sources of change, institutional arrangements (the rules that societies, individually and collectively, fashion to regulate their economic and political lives) have also increased both the interdependence of nations and the efficiency with which we produce goods and services. Thus, today we find non-U.S. firms, like Toyota, with multiple manufacturing plants in the United States. At the same time, U.S. firms are having computer codes written both at home and in India.

The hallmark of our new and vastly broader economy is that managers face many more opportunities and many more choices than they have had in the past. These choices are not limited to the question of what product to produce or how to produce it. For example, to be an efficient producer, a business firm must now, more than ever, determine not only what kinds of inputs to use but where to obtain both its inputs (labor, equipment, parts and materials, etc.) and its technology. While the United States, Japan, and Western Europe are technological giants, cutting-edge technologies have been developed and are available from such places as Mexico (directly reduced iron), Brazil (high-tech automobile plants, regional jet aircraft), and Russia (radial keratotomy, laser surgery equipment, rocket technology).[1]

Firms must also be concerned about the broadening of opportunities to *sell* their products. The analysis of consumer demand has become increasingly complex as demographics have changed in older markets and as new markets, frequently with very different characteristics, have opened up. Many of these developments have to do with the changing age structure of the population; others with the reorientation of a product line toward changing preferences. (An example is General Motors 2002–03 redesign of the Cadillac line to target younger buyers.)[2] While domestic markets are changing, new ones are opening up overseas, and both product design and mar-

---

[1] "Stantec and Hylsa Sign Alliance Agreement to Install and Promote Goodfellow EFSOP Technology," Corporate News Release, Stantec Global Technologies, January 11, 2001; "Why Detroit is Going to Pieces, *Business Week Online,* September 3, 2001 www.businessweek.com/magazine/content/01_36b3747100.htm, September 5, 2002; "Embraer Agrees Jet Aircraft Order Worth $510 Mln," *Forbes.com,* online, July 23, 2002 www.forbes.com, September 5, 2002; "MEDI Opthamologists Achieved Unique Result," online, September 7, 2001 www.emedi.ru/eng_laser/superlasik.html, September 5, 2002; and Michael A. Dornheim, "Rocket Technology Prevails Over Politics," *Aviation Week and Space Technology,* Vol. 147, No. 3 (August 14, 1995), pp. 51–52.

[2] G. Chambers Williams, III, "Cadillac Plans V-8 for CTS," *San Antonio Express-News,* July 6, 2002, p. J-1.

keting frequently have to be adapted for them. All of this requires research, analysis, and, most importantly, decision making. That is where managerial economics fits into the picture.

Managerial economics focuses on the types of choices described above. Its central themes are:

1. Identifying problems and opportunities.
2. Analyzing alternatives from which choices can be made.
3. Making choices that are best from the standpoint of the firm or organization.

The function of managerial economics is to provide a set of tools for analyzing decision problems and developing criteria for choosing the best possible solution to such problems.

Because managers are always confronted with situations involving choosing from among alternative policies or strategies (whether to go into a new product line, whether or not to employ a new technology, whether to consider production in a foreign market, and many other types of choices), the decision-making tools of managerial economics are important to them. It is certainly not true that all managers must be managerial economists, any more than it is true that all managers should have a degree in management. However, managers who understand the *economic* dimensions of business problems and apply economic analysis to the specific problems they encounter often choose more wisely than those who do not. This is increasingly the case as developments both at home and on the international scene broaden our opportunities and our range of choices.

Ten Economic Principles for Managers

Although the three central themes above broadly define what managerial economics is about, we can be more specific about the economic principles that capable managers understand and employ. Of course, any list such as the one that follows can be debated and modified, but we believe the 10 principles below capture the essence of what economic analysis holds for managers.

Principle No. 1: *The Role of Managers Is to Make Decisions* Business firms come in all sizes. Some are small—for example, an independent hairstyling salon or a "screwdriver shop" that assembles personal computers. Others can be very large, such as an automobile manufacturer or a major steel producer. Small and large firms differ greatly in the number of managers they have and in the magnitude of resources they command, but one thing is certain: *no firm has unlimited resources*. Because of this, managers must make decisions about how the resources available to the firm are employed.

The firm's resources are material, human, and financial. Managers must decide how and where plant and equipment will be employed, what kinds of labor will be hired and how much, and how to utilize available funds, including those that are borrowed or raised by selling shares in the firm (equity financing). They must also decide how many managers there will be and how much decision authority will exist at each level of management. Some decisions are very short run in nature, such as whether to be open or closed on Memorial Day or whether to buy new or recharged cartridges for the firm's laser printers. Others are long run, such as whether to build a new plant or develop a new line of product. Inevitably, then, managers make choices. Thus, the real issue is how to make decisions that make sense for the operation of the firm. To analyze this process, we need to consider the nature of choosing in general, and that brings us to our second managerial economics principle.

Principle No. 2: *Decisions Are Always Among Alternatives* Notice that in the previous paragraph the word "whether" appeared a number of times. That is because choices are always among alternatives. If there were no alternative to an action, there would be no choice. Sometimes a choice is between changing and not changing something. However, other choices may be between or among different types of changes. Think about buying a new computer. You may first consider the difference between keeping your old computer and, in general, upgrading to a newer generation machine. That turns out to be a "no brainer" if your old machine is obsolete. You are sure you will be able to do more with the new computer than with the old one. But then you must decide *what kind* of new computer to buy. There may be a large array of alternatives to consider at that point. Many will do the job, but some may be better at it than others, and their costs may differ. This brings us to our third managerial economics principle.

Principle No. 3: *Decision Alternatives Always Have Costs and Benefits* When faced with a managerial decision, an individual acts in much the same way he or she would if faced with a personal decision. We can take an example from student life. If Sandra decides to study for two hours, she gives up the opportunity of watching television for two hours. (She may have other alternatives to studying, such as exercising or playing her harp, but she views watching TV as the next best alternative.) What does she consider when making her decision? The first thing is the benefit gained from studying, whether she views it as increasing her own knowledge and capabilities or just improving her grade point average. The second is the cost of giving up two hours of television. If she chooses to study, her evaluation is that the additional benefit gained from two hours of study exceeds the additional cost to her of the next best alternative (two hours of television given up).

Opportunity cost is cost as measured by the next best alternative given up when a choice is made.

We can also say that the measure of what the two hours of study is worth to Sandra is what she gave up to do it—two hours of watching TV. Economists would say that the **opportunity cost** of two hours of study for Sandra is two hours of watching TV. The opportunity cost of any choice is measured by the foregone (next best) alternative. Los Angeles Lakers star Kobe Bryant decided to forego college and went directly to pro basketball from high school. Similarly, Tiger Woods dropped out of his undergraduate program at Stanford to pursue professional golf. Would they have been able to make as much money if they had obtained college degrees? You may view it as unlikely, but you really do not know. What you do know is that they viewed the alternative they chose as being more valuable than the one they decided to forego.

We all make the kinds of decisions Sandra made above, and so do the managers of firms. Even a simple decision about whether to increase output of a product by one unit has the same nature as Sandra's decision. There will be an additional cost and an additional benefit. The additional cost is the amount the firm must spend to produce one more unit of output, and the additional benefit is the change in the firm's sales revenue that it will get from selling one more unit of output. Economists would say that increasing output would be a rational decision if the *additional* benefit exceeds the *additional* cost. This is known as the **marginal or incremental approach** to decision making. It permeates economic life, and people who have never studied it often learn to use it from everyday experience. (Those who have learned it frequently become better decision makers for their trouble.)

We can safely assume that if Sandra chooses to study rather than watch TV, she believes that course of action will best fulfill her objective, whether it be shining up her grade point average or adding to her store of knowledge. Just like Sandra, firm managers will value alternatives based on their objective, but what is that objective? This brings us to a fourth principle of managerial economics.

> The **marginal or incremental approach** involves analyzing changes associated with a decision and making the decision based on the difference between the changes in benefits and the changes in costs.

Principle No. 4: *The Anticipated Objective of Management Is to Increase the Firm's Value* What makes a firm valuable to its owners is the firm's ability to generate profits. For any given time period, the firm's profit is the difference between its total revenue from sales *(TR)* and its total cost of producing and selling output *(TC)*. An individually owned firm (called a *sole proprietorship*) that will generate a profit stream of $2 million per year over the next five years is worth more than one that will generate only $1.5 million yearly profit over the same period (assuming equal risk). An investor would pay more to buy the firm that generates $2 million per year than to buy the one that yields only $1.5 million annually.

Of course, a firm may be owned by a group rather than an individual. Many of our largest firms are corporations whose shares are publicly traded and whose shareholders are the firm's owners. While general economic conditions, speculation, risk, and a host of other variables affect the prices of corporations' stocks, it is widely accepted that share values reflect the value of the firm as measured by its ability to profit from its activities.

Notice that the heading for this section says that the *anticipated* objective of managers is to increase the firm's value. The reason the word "anticipated" is inserted there is that corporate managers often have been criticized for not behaving in the interests of the firm's shareholders. This happens because it is not always in the managers' personal interest to do what is best for shareholders. A simple example can be found in the matter of executive perquisites or "perks." Executives of a firm may like to fly around in chartered or firm-owned jets, when they could as easily and more cheaply use scheduled airlines. This behavior may have a negative effect on profits and on the value of the firm, thereby harming shareholders.

Negative impacts like the one above stem from what economists call the **principal-agent problem.** In a corporation, the shareholders are the principals, and the managers are the agents who act on the shareholders' behalf. If the objectives of these two groups do not coincide, the firm may not be run in a way that maximizes its value. A glaring example occurred in the case of Enron Corporation in 2001–2002, where executives apparently made decisions that would initially run up the price of the company's stock when they held many shares but would later bankrupt the company. Shareholders in general were left with worthless stock, but certain managers who sold when the stock price was high profited handsomely. Cases like this one make it clear that we cannot always assume that a firm's managers will behave in a way that maximizes shareholder value.

> The **principal-agent problem** occurs when one party acts on behalf of another in a situation where the parties may have conflicting goals.

Principle No. 5: *The Firm's Value Is Measured by Its Expected Profits*
Although we have said that greater profits translate into greater value of the firm, it is clear that investors cannot know the size of actual profits before they occur. Thus, it is *expected* profits that determine, at any given point in time, what the value of the firm is.

Consider the following data:

Year	Expected Profit Corporation A (million dollars)	Expected Profit Corporation B (million dollars)
2007	12	15
2008	13	16
2009	13	20
2010	18	21
2011	19	22

If both corporations are about the same size, operate in the same industry, have equal numbers of shares outstanding, and face equal risks, which would you expect to have the highest share price in 2006? We hope you said B, since its expected profit for each future year is higher than that of Corpo-

precision using quantitative techniques. Even when they step outside their formal disciplines, they tend to analyze problems in terms of alternatives and expected outcomes. Thus, a CEO with this type of background seems always to be looking for the best alternative solution to a problem and, not surprisingly, expecting fellow managers and co-workers to provide the substantive input required to find that solution.

Role of Managerial Economics in Problem Solving

We can expect that only a few students of managerial economics will become either managerial economists or CEOs, but whether one's major field is accounting, marketing, information systems, finance, or some other specialization, the analytical abilities that are sharpened by a familiarity with applied economics are extremely valuable. Take, for example, the issue of pricing. Suppose you are considering whether or not to reduce the price of a given product. What is the most fundamental question one can ask in this regard? It has to be "will sales revenue *increase* or *decrease* as a result of this change in price?" Managerial economics can help to answer that question, and, in a business, someone who has skills similar to those of a managerial economist will be able to answer it, given the appropriate data. When they answer it, they will probably refer to the *elasticity of demand* (discussed in Chapter 2), as relevant to the outcome. Anyone else in the business, whether above or below that person on the organization chart, will need to have some idea what this technical relation is. It certainly can be very important. For example, Herbert Kelleher, the (now retired) CEO of Southwest Airlines and a lawyer by training, understood elasticity well and built a very strong firm on what he believed about it. (See "Managerial Perspective: Building a Business on E_p" in Chapter 2.)

Of course, even if lowering price increases sales revenue, the effect of increased sales volume on *cost* must also be considered. Thus, managerial economics not only looks at problems in pricing, but also in such areas as production, input use, cost, profit, and investment decisions. The tools and techniques it offers in analyzing these questions carry over into many others. They help people to communicate their own thoughts as well as to understand what others in a firm or an organization are trying to tell them.

The desired output of both research and managerial activities in a firm or organization is a set of decisions that are best for it, given its environment and the resources it has to work with. These are called "optimizing decisions." How managerial economics is related to the process of generating such decisions, as well as how it supplies tools to other areas in businesses and other entities is described graphically in Figure 1-1. The figure should be read from the upper left, then clockwise and downward. Managerial economics is one of three basic analytical areas that supply decision techniques to people working in what are sometimes called "functional areas" in busi-

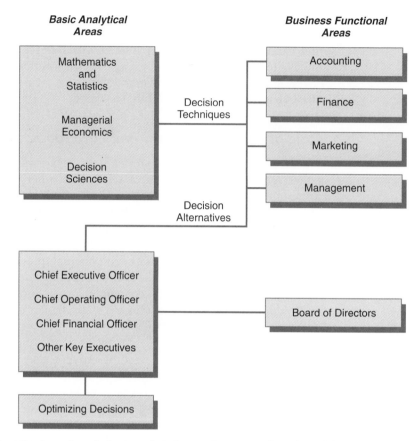

FIGURE 1-1

Relation of Managerial Economics to Decision Making in Firms and Other Organizations

Read this figure from the basic analytical areas, then over to the right and down. Managerial economics is a key area in basic business analysis, along with mathematics, statistics, and decision sciences. All three provide quantitative techniques that are essential to decision makers in the firm or organization. People working in the business functional areas use the tools provided by the basic analytical areas to advise executives and board members who make key decisions. Information flows in both directions along the paths connecting the boxes in the figure.

ness: accounting, finance, marketing, and management. (The latter are defined by the functions they perform, for example: accounting—keeping the firm's records; marketing—promoting the firm's product, etc.) The two other basic analytical areas are mathematics/statistics and decision sciences. All of these analytical areas have certain tools and techniques in common: algebra, calculus, and linear algebra, for example. Likewise, each of the basic analytical areas has a different focus. For example, managerial economics is more concerned with how markets for products and inputs behave than is statistics or mathematics. Yet, a managerial economist may draw on a widely used statistical technique, multiple regression analysis, to analyze a particular market. Together, the basic analytical areas supply decision-making techniques to persons working in the functional areas of business and, ultimately, to the firm or organization's managers.

It is certainly reasonable to think of Figure 1-1 as a two-way street, since the organization's chief executives often either develop alternatives to be analyzed or identify problems to be solved and then ask people in the functional and basic analytical areas for input regarding both the development of additional alternatives and the nature of the best or optimal decision. Thus, Figure 1-1 is not saying that everything depends on the basic analytical areas or on managerial economics, simply that decision making in the firms and other organizations can be much enhanced by those who have good basic analytical tools. Persons employing those tools may be located in a variety of different departments or divisions within the organization. (Figure 1-1 is *not* an organization chart.) For example, someone in the marketing department may have the skills required to answer our earlier-posed question about the impact of a price change on sales revenue, and the question may have been asked by the chief financial officer. The answer, however, can be obtained using techniques often studied in managerial economics. When all is said and done, these decision makers and researchers will communicate better if all of them have some managerial economics in their backgrounds to help them more fully understand the pricing issue.

Macroeconomics, Microeconomics, and the Corporate Economist

Macroeconomics is the branch of economic analysis that deals with aggregate economic variables such as the economy's total output, central government spending and tax policy, and money supply and interest rates.

Microeconomics is the study of individual economic units such as consumers, business firms, or specific government agencies.

Economists generally divide their discipline into two branches, *macroeconomics* and *microeconomics*. **Macroeconomics** focuses on the study of the economy as a whole and deals with issues such as the level of overall activity (gross domestic product or GDP), interest rates, federal budgets, international trade and currency questions, and federal taxes. **Microeconomics,** on the other hand, deals with the behavior of individual economic units, such as a consumer or a business firm. In this book we deal primarily with microeconomics, since we are addressing how economic analysis can be used to make decisions within a firm or an organization. Nonetheless, corporate economists are frequently asked to prepare research and suggest strategies relating to both macro- and microeconomic issues. This was underscored some years ago by the results of a survey conducted by the economics organization of American Telephone and Telegraph Company (AT&T). Respondents to the survey were 32 large corporations with identifiable economics organizations, including such well-known firms as American Cyanamid, IBM, Phillips Petroleum, and Weyerhauser Company. Macro and industry-level forecasting were singled out as areas where a large percentage of the time of economists working in these organizations is spent. However, the economists were also called upon to do research on specific products and markets, to evaluate potential investments, to provide environmental impact studies, and to assist in litigations.[5]

Many firms and public sector organizations are not large enough to have their own economics group and must either rely on consultants or in-house staff with some economics training to apply economic principles to decision problems. Generally, managers in these firms and organizations are interested in economic analysis only to the extent that it has something to say about questions that directly impact performance or profits. Thus, they are even more likely to ask questions of a microeconomic nature than are certain managers of larger corporations or organizations.

An intensifying emphasis on the microeconomic side of economic analysis for businesses was noted over three decades ago, when *Business Week* stated that

> companies across the country are now demanding less of the old-style corporate economist who churned out sweeping economic forecasts, which often were swept into the wastebasket, and are turning instead to the new-style economist who can ply his skills in such fields as econometrics and industrial economics to help shape company policy. Indeed, an increasing number of them have joined the team of top-level executives who map business strategy.[6]

Business Week's observation remains true today. Corporate economists are increasingly relied upon for input on issues that are specific to the performance of the firm. Their role has been redefined so that they spend less time providing general information and more time helping to analyze managerial decision problems. In fact, in a 1996 article, Walter E. Hoadley, a senior research fellow at the Hoover Institution, noted that a call is rising "for a new breed of business economists who think and act like decision makers, broaden the multidisciplined dimensions of their work, and serve as scouts and shields for senior policy executives."[7] This is a further indication that the techniques provided by managerial economics have broad applicability to problem solving within firms and other organizations. Thus, even if one does not plan to become a managerial economist, being familiar with the techniques they employ can yield many benefits both in helping to solve problems and in communicating with other decision makers.

---

[5] The results of the study are described in Dennis K. Hoover, "Business Economists: Not Just Forecasters," *Business Economics,* 27 (July 1992): 56–59.

[6] "Executive Clout for Economists," *Business Week* (February 13, 1978), pp. 58, 60.

[7] Walter E. Hoadley, "Who Needs Business Economists?—The Future of the Profession," *Business Economics* 31, No. 1 (January 1996): 14. For more, see David Fettig, "Business Economists: Can't Live with 'em, Can't Live without 'em," *Federal Reserve Bank of Minneapolis: The Region* 8, No. 4 (December 1994): 21–25.

Managers and Their Objectives

The managers of a firm are responsible for making most of the economic decisions—the type of product produced, its price, the production technology utilized, and the financing of production—that will ultimately result in profits or losses for the firm. We have already noted that managerial behavior is characterized by the existence of a principal-agent problem. The firm's manager or managers may or may not be its owner or owners; therefore, the goals of the managers may not be quite the same as those of owners. There may be an incentive for the managers to act in ways that are not in the best interests of the shareholders. In the United States there has been a great deal of concern about the compensation of corporate chief executives, which to many observers seems to have increased beyond all reason, especially in cases where companies are either losing money or not recording outstanding increases in profits. In 1992, it took an annual compensation of over $22 million to be among the top 10 U.S. CEOs, and the number one package came to over $125 million. *Business Week* reported in 2002 that the highest paid CEO in the United States (Lawrence J. Ellison, Oracle Corporation) received compensation in 2001 totaling over $700 million, in the form of stock options exercised. Another CEO, Thomas J. Engibous (Texas Instruments), lost his bonus but received a 5 percent salary increase and an increase in his options grant from 700,000 to 842,000 shares. He received these payments even though Texas Instruments had posted a loss of $201 million for the year.[8]

As a result of the furor over what many have viewed as excessive rewards, a growing number of firms are revamping their executive compensation plans so that high-level managers will have incentives to maximize profits. Changes that have been undertaken include linking stock option awards to stock performance, requiring stock prices to rise a specified percentage before stock options can be exercised, improving disclosure of executive salaries to shareholders, and providing executive compensation committees with independent consultants. It is clearly in the interest of shareholders to structure executive compensation programs in ways that ensure that the firm maintains a satisfactory level of profits and, preferably, a high rate of profit growth. Thus, more changes that tie managerial rewards to company performance are quite likely to take place.

The recent debate over managerial compensation is related to various hypotheses about the objectives of managers and business firms. We have already focused on the hypothesis that firms will be operated in a way that leads to *profit maximization*. Although this seems to be reasonable, it *is* open to question. Economists and specialists in organizational management have derived other hypotheses about the behavior of firms and have done a great

---

[8] "Even CEOs Get the Blues—Sort Of," *Business Week Online,* March 25, 2002 www.business-week.com/magazine/content/02_12b3775068.htm, September 7, 2002.

deal of research aimed at testing these hypotheses. The following are some of the alternative hypotheses.

1. *Market share maximization:* Firms will behave in a way that maximizes market share (as measured by sales revenue, or perhaps, proportion of quantity sold to total market).

2. *Growth maximization:* Increasing the size of the firm over time will take precedence over other objectives. Profit may be sacrificed to attain higher rates of growth in other variables.

3. *Maximization of managerial returns:* Managers will make choices that maximize their own interest, subject to generating sufficient profit to keep their jobs.

The results of empirical testing of these hypotheses, as well as tests of the profit-maximization hypothesis, have been mixed.[9] At different points in time and under different states of the economy (expansion, recession), one or another of the hypotheses seems to have empirical support. However, economists have generally favored the profit-maximization hypothesis for a variety of reasons.

First and foremost among the reasons economists lean toward the profit-maximization hypothesis is that a firm is unlikely to survive in the long run if it is not profitable. Second, although at some points in time and in some firms managerial rewards may be more closely correlated with sales or growth than with profit, as we have seen, shareholders and government regulators alike are interested in designing compensation packages that are tied to profit performance. Third, profit maximization requires careful study of factors, such as demand and cost, that will remain important even when the firm has another main objective or a set of more complex objectives. Finally, and perhaps most importantly, *if one does not know what result a profit-maximizing strategy will yield, it is not possible to assess the cost to the firm of pursuing alternatives to it.* For all of these reasons, in this book we will generally assume that the firm is a profit maximizer. This will give us an important benchmark from which we can assess any alternative behaviors that may present themselves. We will assume that in a business firm, the chief decision makers are interested enough in profit to want to know what strategy will maximize it. When we deal with a public sector or not-for-profit organization, the usual assumption will be that the

---

[9] A very thorough survey of the literature on goals and objectives of the firm and its managers can be found in Donald A. Hay and Derek J. Morris, *Industrial Economics and Organization* (New York: Oxford University Press, 1991), esp. Ch. 9. The relationship between market share and profitability is examined in N. Venkatraman and John E. Prescott, "The Market Share–Profitability Relationship: Testing Temporal Stability across Business Cycles," *Journal of Management* 16, No. 4 (1990): 783–805.

organization wishes to use its resources efficiently, thereby maximizing the stream of net benefits it produces.

In large, private sector corporations, along with the CEO, some of the main decision makers of the firm usually include the president, the vice-president for sales, the vice-president for manufacturing, the chief financial officer, the controller, and the board of directors. (The *controller* is the head accountant for the firm and is responsible for the collection of data regarding the firm's costs and revenues and for setting up its budgets, thereby performing a crucial role in the firm's decision-making process.) The aforementioned managers usually take joint responsibility for decision making. Thus, their fortunes or careers may rise or fall depending on the skill with which they interpret economic problems and the data and advice they receive from staff economists or economic consultants, financial analysts, and market researchers. We shall see that the managers' responsibilities, though centered around achievement of the firm's profit goal, have been expanded to include both liability for criminal offenses and damages that result from the activities of the corporations that the managers oversee. In the important area of antitrust liability, managers must blend their knowledge of economic decision making with that of law, in order to avoid decision errors that could prove disastrous for themselves and their firms.

In this book, it is not our objective to teach you to become a chief financial officer, a controller, the head of a marketing department, or a corporate economist. What we shall attempt to do is to help you learn the economic principles that are relevant to decision making in all areas of firm management. An understanding of these principles will help the future firm manager know *which* questions to ask and thus *what data* are needed, as well as *what decision* to make once the data are obtained, in order to assist the firm in maximizing profits. If you do not eventually become a managerial economist, we hope that at least you will be able to communicate with economists and recognize when help from them can prove useful for problem solving.

OUR APPROACH TO PROBLEM SOLVING

Our emphasis here is on solving economic problems faced by managers. In general, once managerial objectives are known, we take the following steps in analyzing a problem and making a decision:

1. An *identification* of the problem or decision to be made.
2. A statement of *alternative solutions* to the problem.
3. A *determination of what data are relevant* to the decision and an analysis of those data relative to the alternative solutions.
4. The choice of the *best solution* consistent with our firm's or agency's objectives.

The time period under consideration will often be an important factor in our decision analysis. When decisions concern current operations and objectives are predetermined, alternatives may be very limited. In such cases, step 2 may reduce to a simple statement of the conditions under which the objective will be met. For example, if management wishes to determine what rate of output per quarter will maximize profit from sales of a given product in a single market, there may be no alternative but to determine the output level that is consistent with this objective. However, if management wishes to decide which of a given set of investment projects will add the most to the value of the firm, a large number of alternatives may have to be analyzed. In general, the longer the time period in question, the greater the number of alternatives available to management.

The analyzing and choosing done in steps 3 and 4 rely heavily on standard and broadly accepted tools and criteria of economic analysis. As we progress through the definition of these tools and criteria and their application to specific economic problems of the firm, we will develop decision rules that will be applied time and time again. In general, these rules have their foundation in the *marginal* or *incremental* approach described earlier. Thus, you should keep in mind that we will be looking closely at both the costs and benefits that result from a decision in order to make the best managerial choice. Marginal analysis focuses on *changes* in economic variables and the results that occur directly from them. In a business, the underlying principle of the marginal or incremental approach is that changes in economic variables controlled by the firm (output, price, resource use, investment) should be undertaken any time the result is to add more to the firm's revenues than to its costs—in other words, any time they add to profit. For public sector management, we extend this concept to the effect of changes in public output on *social benefits* and *social costs.* These concepts take into account benefits and costs that accrue to or affect individuals or firms who are not directly involved in the transaction that yields them, called *external costs* and *benefits.* An example of such an additional item would be benefits to the community as a whole of a program to provide vaccinations free of charge to low-income individuals. Another would be the costs of congestion borne by a neighborhood when a domed stadium is constructed there.

ORGANIZATION OF THIS BOOK

This book is organized in a way that we hope will help you quickly master some key economic concepts and recognize relevant data for decision making in business firms or other organizations. In fact, once Parts 1 and 2, dealing with revenue, estimation and forecasting, production, cost, and profit analysis, are completed, virtually all of the tools and decision criteria necessary for the analysis of specific decision problems in the subsequent parts of the book will have been presented.

Once the tool-oriented chapters are completed, we undertake in Part 3 of the book to examine the behavior of firms in different types of markets. This includes not only variations in the structure of product markets but also strategic analysis and the role of gaming approaches and information in decision making. These materials will be especially useful when we consider situations where a given firm's best decision may depend on what decision a rival firm chooses.

Turning to long-run investment decisions, Part 4 considers capital project analysis. The criteria for project acceptability are examined in Chapter 13, and Chapter 14 addresses both risk and issues related to what are sometimes unanticipated or overlooked costs and benefits associated with an investment project.

The focus of the last part of the book, Part 5, is twofold. First, capital project analysis is extended to public sector undertakings in Chapter 15. Not surprisingly, such public investments present some analytical issues that are different from those found in private sector projects. (What is the value of a whooping crane?) Our final chapter, Chapter 16, addresses how laws and regulations affect the business firm. The emphasis there is on knowing what kinds of legal constraints managers are likely to encounter and making strategic decisions to deal with them.

Other Tools for Decision Making

Besides the basic economic concepts and tools outlined in this chapter, other technical tools can greatly assist the manager in making decisions that will maximize firm profits. These tools include the calculus techniques of optimization (with or without a constraint), linear regression analysis, and linear programming.

A review of mathematical functions and graphs and an introduction to calculus are provided in the Mathematical Appendix at the end of the book. Optimization with calculus is covered in the appendix to Chapter 5 and in Chapter 7. Linear regression analysis, a statistical tool that assists the manager in estimating firm revenue and cost functions, is presented in Chapter 3 and its appendix. The appendix to Chapter 7 discusses linear programming, a useful technique when a firm's relevant revenue and cost functions are linear and are subject to linear constraints that can be expressed in the form of inequalities. Throughout the book are many numerical examples showing how to apply various analytical techniques. Be sure to work through these step by step as you read along; and remember, they can be used for review as well.

If mathematics is not your cup of tea, there is no reason to be discouraged. It is not necessary for you to master all of the quantitative tools we have mentioned before you can understand the basic economic principles involved in profit maximization or before you can find this book useful. Of course, various instructors will choose to place different emphases on the expertise you achieve in such methods. We believe, however, that a working knowledge of these tools will be very helpful to the business or public sector manager in economic decision making.

REVIEW OF BASIC DEMAND AND SUPPLY ANALYSIS

The materials to follow in Part 1 and Part 2 of the book assume that students have some familiarity with basic demand and supply concepts. Since this is not always the case, and since managerial economics students come from a wide variety of backgrounds, the final pages of this chapter will provide a demand and supply review.

Demand and Demand Curve

In economic analysis, the term *demand* is used to refer to the various amounts of a good or service someone (a single consumer or a group of buyers) is both willing and able to buy at various possible prices. It is a functional relationship between a good's price and the quantity the buyer or buyers will take. When we are talking about the demand for a firm's product, we therefore mean the amounts of it that buyers will take at various possible prices. This kind of information is shown by either a *demand schedule* or a *demand curve* for the good. The amount that consumers will buy at any given price is usually called the "quantity demanded" of the good.

To further our analysis of demand and the demand curve, we will use the example of the demand for broccoli. Broccoli received some notoriety when George Herbert Walker Bush, the forty-first president of the United States, remarked in 1990, "I am president of the United States, and I am *not* going to eat any more broccoli." Broccoli growers responded by shipping him several tons of it! Today, they are proud to point out that broccoli consumption in the United States has increased from 3.3 pounds per person per year in 1990 to more than 5 pounds per person per year. They are also happy to report that George W. Bush, the former president's son and forty-third president, is not "broccoli challenged."[10]

We will begin with a demand schedule. Table 1-1 shows the amounts of broccoli consumers will purchase per month at various possible prices per bunch. (Broccoli is sold in bunches with an average weight of about one

---

[10] Another good reason to use broccoli as an example is that its market is a competitive one where price actually is determined by supply and demand. In fact, in 1999, a U.S. Department of Agriculture economist reported to one of the authors that "if it were not, we would not have seen prices below cost of production for so much of this past spring and summer." (E-mail from Gary S. Lucier, U.S. Department of Agriculture, September 7, 1999.)

Table 1-1 *Demand for Broccoli*

Price of Broccoli per Bunch (P_b)	Quantity Demanded of Broccoli per Month (Q_b)
$1.20	100,000
1.10	125,000
1.00	150,000
.90	175,000
.80	200,000
.70	225,000
.60	250,000
.50	275,000

pound.) The amount people are willing and able to buy at any given price appears in the quantity demanded column, labeled Q_b. In Figure 1-2, the same data are presented as a demand curve. The demand curve, D_b, is just a plot of the price and quantity-demanded data from the table, with price shown on the vertical axis and quantity demanded on the horizontal axis.

FIGURE 1-2

Demand Curve for Broccoli

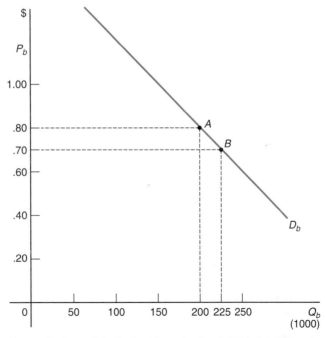

The demand curve for broccoli is obtained from the data in Table 1-1. Points A and B show, as does the table, that purchasers are willing and able to buy 200,000 bunches of broccoli per month at a price of $.80 per bunch and 225,000 at a price of $.70 per bunch. The demand curve slopes downward to the right, consistent with the law of demand.

Note that the demand curve slopes downward to the right (has a *negative* slope). For most goods, we expect this to be the case, since at lower prices people will tend to buy larger amounts per time period. This inverse relation between a good's own price and the quantity demanded of it is a reflection of the **law of demand.** The law of demand simply states that both individuals and groups of consumers will generally increase their purchases of a good when its price falls and decrease their purchases when its price rises. It holds for most goods but cannot be proven to hold for all goods in all circumstances. For example, we know that snob appeal sometimes causes people to buy *more* of a good when its price rises (designer clothes, luxury cars). However, these cases are relatively rare.

Since the law of demand holds in Figure 1-2, we can see that a fall in the price of broccoli will lead to increased purchases of broccoli by consumers. If the price falls from $0.80 per bunch to $0.70 per bunch, consumers will increase their purchases from 200,000 bunches per month to 225,000 bunches. Such a change (from point *A* to *B* in Figure 1-2), which takes place when the good's own price changes and there is a movement *along* a given demand curve, is called **change in quantity demanded.**

Behind the demand curve is a broader concept, the **demand function,** which explicitly recognizes that consumers' purchases of a given item depend on other things besides its price. For example, how much broccoli consumers will buy probably depends not only on the price of broccoli, but also on the prices of other green veggies such as brussels sprouts or green beans. It may also depend on consumer incomes, since cheaper vegetables might be bought instead if consumers were closely watching their budgets. We can represent all this as a demand function with the notational form $Q_b = f(P_b, P_v, I)$, where Q_b is the number of bunches of broccoli sold per month, P_b is the price of broccoli per bunch, P_v is the average price per unit of competing veggies, and I is a measure of consumers' monthly income. The variables other than P_b on the right-hand side of the equation are called **determinants of demand.**

In order to plot the demand curve as we did in Figure 1-2, it is necessary that as we change the price of broccoli, other demand function variables such as the price of competing veggies and consumers' income remain constant. Why? Because the demand curve in the figure will *shift* if one of the other variables changes. Take income, for example. If income rises, some consumers who thought broccoli was too expensive for their dinner tables will decide to buy it. Thus, at all possible prices there will be a greater demand for broccoli. In Table 1-1 we would see a new column of data for quantity demanded, and in Figure 1-2, the demand curve would shift to the right. Such a shift is illustrated in Figure 1-3. This type of change is usually called a "change in demand." Thus, **change in demand** is used to denote a shift in the demand curve, while change in quantity demanded refers to a movement along it. The latter would occur if the price of broccoli changed

The law of demand is the proposition that price and quantity demanded can be expected to be inversely related, so that consumers will be willing and able to buy more of a good at lower prices than they are at higher prices.

A **change in quantity demanded** is a movement along a given good's demand curve when the price of that good changes but other variables do not.

A **demand function** relates the amounts of a good that consumers are willing and able to buy to its own price *and* other relevant variables such as income or the prices of other goods.

The **determinants of demand** are variables other than a good's own price that are in its demand function. A change in one of them will shift the demand curve for a good.

A **change in demand** is a shift in the demand curve that occurs when a variable other than the good's own price changes.

FIGURE 1-3

*A Change in
Demand for
Broccoli*

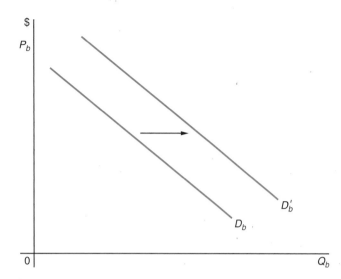

This figure shows an *increase* in the demand for broccoli, meaning that buyers will purchase more broccoli per time period at every possible broccoli price. An increase in income could cause such a change. There are other possible causes, such as an increase in the price of broccoli substitutes which, other things unchanging, would make broccoli a more attractive choice.

while income and the price of other green veggies remained constant. This was implicitly assumed earlier when we changed the price of broccoli from $0.80 to $0.70 per bunch and noted the movement from A to B along the demand curve in Figure 1-2. When we hold other variables constant while we change only one key variable, the phrase "other things equal" is often invoked to indicate that only *one* of the variables is being altered.

Since an increase in income—other things being equal—will shift the demand curve to the right, a decrease in income will shift it to the left. This will be the case for most goods. (Exceptions will be discussed in Chapter 2.) If we consider the effect on demand for broccoli of a change in the price of other green vegetables (*substitutes* for broccoli) it is easy to see that the change in the price of a substitute will also shift the demand curve. In our example, if the prices of other green vegetables fall while consumer incomes remain constant, we can expect the demand for broccoli to decrease (demand curve for broccoli to shift to the left). Why? Because some consumers will substitute the other, now relatively cheaper, vegetables for broccoli. A change in the price of a substitute good will always shift the demand curve in the same fashion: to the right for an increase in the substitute's price and to the left for a decrease in the substitute's price. If a related good is a complement (something used *with* the good in question rather than instead of it), the shift relation reverses. More will be said about this in Chapter 2.

The basics of demand analysis can be summarized as follows:

1. *Demand* is a functional relationship between the price of a good and the quantity demanded of it per time period.

2. The demand curve for a good normally slopes downward to the right, reflecting the law of demand.

3. A demand function states the relation between the quantity of a good consumers will buy and the values of several independent variables, including its own price, prices of related goods, income, and other relevant determinants of demand.

4. When a good's own price changes but other demand function variables remain constant, there is a *change in quantity demanded* (movement along the demand curve).

5. If one of the determinants of demand changes, the demand curve will shift (there will be a *change in demand*). The direction of that shift will depend on whether there is a direct or an inverse relation between that independent variable and consumers' purchases of the good in question.

Supply and the Supply Curve

The **quantity supplied** of a good or service is the amount that producers will make available for purchase at a particular price along a supply curve.

In economic analysis, the term *supply*, like demand, refers to a functional relationship. It is the relation between the various possible prices of a good and the **quantity supplied** by sellers of it per time period. Supply can also be represented as a schedule or a curve. For example, we might say that at a price of $0.60 per bunch sellers of broccoli will be willing and able to bring to market a quantity supplied of 100,000 bunches per month. That would describe *one point* on their supply curve of broccoli. If they will bring to market 300,000 bunches at a price of $1.00 per bunch, we have another point on their supply curve. Table 1-2 is a supply schedule for broccoli, and Figure 1-4 shows the broccoli supply curve. That curve has a positive slope (upward

Table 1-2 *Supply of Broccoli*

Price of Broccoli per Bunch (P_b)	Quantity Supplied of Broccoli per Month (Q_s)
$1.20	400,000
1.10	350,000
1.00	300,000
.90	250,000
.80	200,000
.70	150,000
.60	100,000
.50	50,000

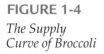

FIGURE 1-4

*The Supply
Curve of Broccoli*

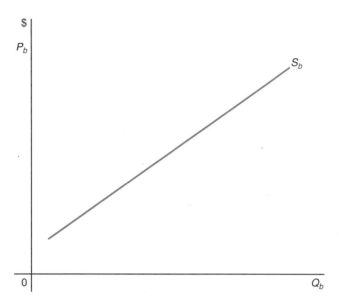

The supply curve for broccoli shows the quantities that producers will make available for sale per time period at various possible broccoli prices. We can expect it to slope upward to the right because production costs for additional units of output are likely to rise as broccoli producers bring more land into cultivation.

to the right), indicating that sellers will offer a larger quantity supplied at higher broccoli prices. We will often use upward-sloping supply curves in subsequent analyses, but occasionally we will consider circumstances where the supply curve does not slope upward. In the case of broccoli, it would be easy to justify an upward-sloping supply curve, since production costs would be likely to go up as broccoli production increased and less suitable land was brought into cultivation of broccoli.

Just as we noted the existence of a demand function behind the demand curve, there is a supply function behind the supply curve. That function relates the amount of a good that sellers are willing and able to offer for sale to both its own price and other relevant independent variables known as the "determinants of supply." For broccoli, the supply function might be of the form $Q_s = f(P_b, P_v, IN_p)$, where Q_s is the number of bunches of broccoli sellers will bring to market per month, P_b is the price of broccoli per bunch, P_v is the price of an alternative product (something the producers might wish to supply instead of broccoli), and IN_p is an index of input prices. If one of the determinants of supply changes, the supply curve will shift. For example, a fall in the price of fertilizer might lead suppliers to be willing to grow and bring to market more broccoli per month at every possible broccoli price. Thus, the supply curve of broccoli would shift to the right. Clearly, rising input prices would do the reverse.

Determination of Market Price

We are now ready to discuss the way supply and demand interact to determine market price. However, one caution is necessary. We will be assuming in what follows that the market in question (the broccoli market) is characterized by large numbers of sellers and buyers and that no individual firm or buyer in the market is powerful enough to affect the market price that is established. In other words, the going market price that tends to hold for broccoli comes about as a result of the actions of the thousands of participants (buyers and sellers) in the market but not because any one of them is so large that he or she directly impacts the result. This is the condition known in economic theory as **perfect competition.** In a market characterized by perfect competition, the seller sees no need to offer a price lower than the going price, since a large number of buyers are willing to pay the market price. Similarly, the seller is aware that trying to charge a price *above* the going level would result in zero sales, as the buyers know that a large number of sellers are willing and able to sell at the market price. For example, if broccoli is selling everywhere for $0.80 a bunch, and seller Jilly Johnson decides she wants to charge $0.85 per bunch, a higher price will not result because buyers will simply purchase 80-cent broccoli from the other sellers.

Perfect competition is the name for a market type that is characterized by many buyers and sellers, where each one believes it is not possible to affect market price by their own individual actions.

The equilibrium price is the prevailing market price when quantity demanded equals quantity supplied.

The "going price" we have mentioned is an **equilibrium price** toward which the actions of the multitude of sellers and buyers in the market will cause price to move. This can be explained easily if we combine the demand and supply curve diagrams introduced in the earlier figures into one graph, as in Figure 1-5. Now, the upward-sloping supply curve of sellers intersects the demand curve of consumers at point E. Point E identifies the equilibrium values of both price and quantity demanded or supplied, since if price is either greater or less than P_e, market forces will cause price to return to that level. Note, of course, that P_e is the only price that will equate the quantity demanded by buyers with the quantity supplied by sellers. This quantity, the equilibrium quantity, is labeled Q_e and conforms to 200,000, if the supply and demand curves are plotted from Tables 1-1 and 1-2.

We can also algebraically solve for the equilibrium price and quantity in Figure 1-5 as follows. The equation for the demand curve depicted in Figure 1-2, corresponding to the data in Table 1-1, is

$$Q_{d_b} = 400 - 250P_b,$$

where Q_{d_b} is the quantity demanded of broccoli in thousands of bunches per month and P_b is the price per bunch of broccoli in dollars. Similarly, the equation for the supply curve depicted in Figure 1-4, corresponding to the data in Table 1-2, is

$$Q_{s_b} = -200 + 500P_b,$$

where Q_{s_b} is the quantity supplied of broccoli in thousands of bunches and P_b is the price per bunch of broccoli in dollars.

FIGURE 1-5

Equilibrium in the Broccoli Market

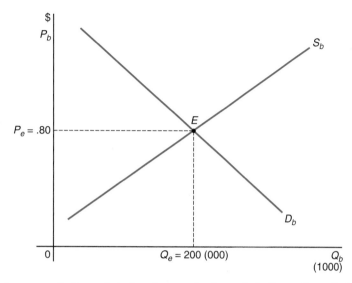

Equilibrium occurs in the market when the quantity demanded of broccoli equals the quantity supplied. For the data we have in Tables 1-1 and 1-2, those quantities are equal when price is $.80 per bunch.

When the broccoli market is in equilibrium, $Q_{d_b} = Q_{s_b}$ at the going market price for broccoli. Thus, we can solve for the equilibrium price by setting $Q_{d_b} = Q_{s_b}$ and solving for price. Therefore, at equilibrium,

$$Q_{d_b} = Q_{s_b}.$$

Substituting for Q_{d_b} and Q_{s_b} from the equations for the demand curve and the supply curve, respectively, we have

$$400 - 250P_b = -200 + 500P_b,$$

$$750P_b = 600, \text{ and}$$

$$P_b = \$0.80.$$

We can find the equilibrium value for Q_b by substituting $0.80 for P_b in either the equation for the demand curve or the equation for the supply curve:

$$Q_{s_b} = -200 + 500P_b,$$

$$Q_{s_b} = -200 + 500 \,(0.80),$$

$$Q_{s_b} = -200 + 400 = 200 \text{ (in thousands)},$$

or

$$Q_{d_b} = 400 - 250P_b,$$

$$Q_{d_b} = 400 - 250\ (0.80),$$

$$Q_{d_b} = 400 - 200 = 200\ \text{(in thousands)}.$$

As we found from Tables 1-1 and 1-2 and Figure 1-5, the equilibrium price of broccoli is $0.80 per bunch and the equilibrium quantity is 200,000 bunches.

The nature of the equilibrium at point E can be examined by asking what would happen if price were temporarily at some value other than P_e. In panel (a) of Figure 1-6, suppose price is temporarily at P_H. This price is above the equilibrium price at E and results in a quantity supplied (Q_s) that exceeds quantity demanded (Q_d). As the diagram shows, there will be a surplus of broccoli in the market because sellers will want to sell more at price P_H than buyers will be willing and able to buy. Sellers will build up inventories of the stuff, and they will have to reduce price in order to get rid of it. Note that this will be true for any price above P_e.

If, on the other hand, price is temporarily below P_e (as at price P_L in panel (b) of the figure), there will be a shortage of broccoli in the market, since quantity demanded (Q_d) will exceed quantity supplied (Q_s). Sellers will see their inventory levels drawn down. Also, some consumers who, as the demand curve indicates for quantities less than Q_e, would be willing and able to pay higher prices for broccoli will not be able to get the amounts they want. Sellers will be happy to accommodate them at a higher price that will

FIGURE 1-6

Market Adjustment to Equilibrium

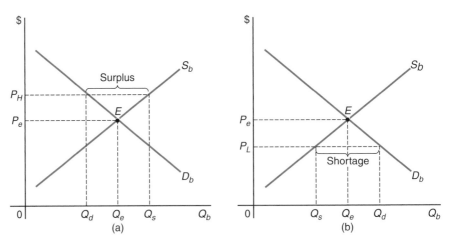

In the left-hand panel, if price is P_H, quantity supplied exceeds quantity demanded, and the resulting surplus causes price to fall. In the right-hand panel, a price of P_L results in a quantity demanded that exceeds quantity supplied, and the resulting shortage causes price to rise.

make additional production profitable. As quantity supplied increases and price rises, some consumers reduce their quantity demanded. The price of broccoli will rise until P_e is reached, where quantity supplied equals quantity demanded. Thus, any price other than P_e is a disequilibrium price, which will bring on forces that will return the price to P_e and the quantity traded to an equilibrium volume of Q_e per month.

CARRYOVER TO ANALYSIS OF OTHER MARKETS

Perfect competition is an idealized market structure that is only approximated by markets in the real world. Nonetheless, many markets, like that for broccoli, tend to adjust in ways *similar* to those described in the perfectly competitive case. Because of this, it is frequently useful to think of the frictionless, self-regulating market of perfect competition as the point of departure for examining markets where, perhaps, sellers are not so numerous and adjustments are not so smooth or automatic. Even in those situations, we will have to ask what we think sellers will do in terms of quantity supplied at various prices and what the demand of consumers for their product looks like. The notions about demand and supply that have been reviewed here will enter the picture time and time again, and we will have to consider whether and how to modify them on a case-by-case basis.

SUMMARY

An Introduction to Managerial Economics

The purpose of this chapter has been to provide an introduction to what managerial economics is about and to set the stage for the more deeply analytical chapters to follow. We saw that managerial economics has three major themes:

1. Identifying problems and opportunities.
2. Analyzing alternatives from which choices can be made.
3. Making choices that are best (optimal) from the standpoint of the firm or organization.

Corollary to these themes, we identified 10 economic principles for managers:

1. The role of managers is to make decisions.
2. Decisions are always among alternatives.
3. Decision alternatives always have costs and benefits.
4. The anticipated objective of management is to increase the firm's value.
5. The firm's value is measured by its expected profits.
6. The firm's sales revenue depends on demand for its product.

7. To maximize profit the firm must minimize cost, *given* the quantity and quality of output it wishes to produce.

8. The firm must develop a strategy consistent with its market.

9. The firm's growth depends on rational investment decisions.

10. Successful firms deal rationally and ethically with laws and regulations.

As other chapters of the book unfold new analyses, it will become clear that the principles above apply time and time again.

The chapter also discussed the approach to problem solving used in managerial economics. It involves four steps:

1. An identification of the problem or decision to be made.

2. A statement of alternative solutions to the problem.

3. A determination of what data are relevant to the decision and an analysis of those data relative to the alternative solutions.

4. The choice of the best solution consistent with our firm's or agency's objectives.

Following these steps should lead a decision maker to the best solution in a wide variety of managerial decision problems.

The final sections of this chapter provided a review of basic demand and supply analysis. Emphasized here were the *Law of Demand,* the distinction between a change in *quantity demanded* and a *change in demand,* and also, similar concepts for supply and the supply curve. Supply and demand curves were used to discuss the determination of market price and the adjustments that would occur if price were temporarily above or below the one that would equate quantity demanded with quantity supplied and result in market equilibrium.

QUESTIONS

1. What are the central themes of managerial economics, and how do they relate to managerial decision making in both business and the public sector?

2. What is the relationship between the globalization of economic activity and the decisions managers must make in today's economy?

3. Ten principles of managerial economics are discussed in this chapter. Can you see how they are interrelated?

4. What is the principal-agent problem, and how is it related to managerial behavior?

5. What are some of the alternative hypotheses to profit maximization as the goal of the business firm?

6. What kinds of devices have been used to provide incentives for managers to maximize profit?

7. What four steps are usually taken in solving a managerial economics problem?

8. What is the Law of Demand, and what does it imply about the slope of a demand curve?

9. How does a change in quantity demanded differ from a change in demand?

10. What is the usually expected slope of a short-run supply curve? Why?

11. In a competitive market, if the price of a product is too high for equilibrium, what will happen?

PROBLEMS

1. Employ a demand curve to explain what would happen to the demand for:

   a. new cars, if consumer income increased.

   b. cream, if coffee prices increased 400 percent.

   c. mopeds, if the price of gasoline tripled.

   d. DVD players, if the price of video discs fell 50 percent.

2. Given:

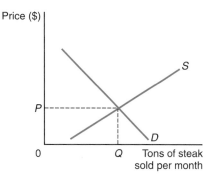

Suppose consumers' incomes increase. Explain what will happen in the diagram, assuming no change in the supply of steak.

Price of Apples (per Bushel)	Quantity Demanded (Bushels per Week)	Quantity Supplied (Bushels per Week)
$50	1,000	7,000
45	2,000	6,000
40	3,000	5,000
35	4,000	4,000
30	5,000	3,000
25	6,000	2,000
20	7,000	1,000
15	8,000	0

3. Suppose the following data describe the demand and supply for apples in a given competitive market:

   a. What is the equilibrium price of apples? How do you know?

   b. Sketch the demand and supply curves for apples in a single quadrant, and indicate the equilibrium price and quantity.

   c. Why would it be impossible for a price of $25 to be maintained in this apple market?

4. Suppose the demand and supply curves for a given product have the following equations.

$$\text{Demand: } Q = 1000 - 10P$$

$$\text{Supply: } Q = -100 + 10P$$

   a. At what price will quantity demanded equal zero?

   b. At what price will quantity demanded equal 200?

   c. Write the demand equation with price as a function of quantity demanded.

   d. Use the two given equations to determine the market equilibrium price and quantity traded by buyers and sellers.

5. Given the following table:

Price	Quantity Supplied (Q_s)	Quantity Demanded (Q_d)	$(Q_s - Q_d)$
0	0	600	____
20	100	500	____
40	200	____	-200
60	300	300	____
80	400	200	200
100	500	____	400

   a. Fill in the blanks in the table.

   b. Identify the equilibrium price and quantity traded.

   c. When $(Q_s - Q_d)$ is negative it measures _____, but when positive, it measures _____. (Fill in.)

Revenue of the Firm

Consumer sovereignty is the economic proposition or hypothesis that people who have both the desire and the ability to purchase *determine* what is produced and how resources are allocated.

The year 2002 saw both the investigation of the Enron debacle and the release of the *Star Wars Episode II* "prequel." Many U.S. firms were doing a brisk business in toys, computer games, and all sorts of paraphernalia related to *Star Wars*, but scarcely an Enron toy or memento was produced. (One wag did try to sell framed shares of virtually worthless Enron stock for $35 apiece.) It could be argued that this difference was a manifestation of **consumer sovereignty,** the economic proposition or hypothesis that people who have both the desire and the ability to purchase *determine*, in a capitalist market economy, what is produced and how resources are allocated. People with the wherewithal to buy wanted *Star Wars* products, and that was what firms produced. They did not want Enron mementos, so very few were produced.

Of course, anyone who has viewed the slapstick comedy, *Spaceballs*, the brainchild of Hollywood writer-producer-director-actor-comedian (did we leave anything out?) Mel Brooks, could easily predict what a *Star Wars* prequel would bring with it. In *Spaceballs*, Brooks, playing the great teacher "Yogurt," sets out to reveal the secret of The Force:[1] "Moichandising!" he declares to his young protege in an accent betraying the urban East Coast, and goes on to reveal how high-powered marketing of toys, T-shirts, posters, and other products related to the movie will be a source of great wealth and power.

---

[1] In his own inimitable fashion, Brooks had renamed it "The Schwartz."

The *Star Wars* prequel and its related goods were introduced with a great deal of marketing fanfare, and, certainly, marketing is important. Billions are spent on it each year, and broadcasters remind us annually how much it costs to buy an advertising minute during such spectacles as the Super Bowl. It seems that ads are popping up everywhere—not just on shopping carts and city buses but in church bulletins, on cash-register receipts, and most recently—whether by popular request or not—in some spots you cannot help but notice in washrooms at restaurants and other public establishments. Ads are so important to the Internet that numerous firms have gone into electronic commerce to sell goods at or near cost, getting their profits mainly from handling charges and selling ad space.[2]

What does the consumer want? Do firms introduce new products only if they respond to consumer wants? Can businesses manipulate the wants of consumers? Many years ago it was frequently argued that businesses could and did manipulate consumer wants. An oft-cited example is the tailfins that appeared on certain automobiles—styling that served no purpose but was touted to consumers as the wave of the future. It was argued that such frills did not cater to any preexisting want, but that the desire for tailfins was created in the consumer's mind by the producer. The producer was characterized as not caring much about what the consumer wanted and being interested only in what resulted in the greatest profit for the firm. Today's equivalent might be the sport-utility vehicle (SUV), which keeps getting larger and brawnier, despite the fact that most consumers just drive the vehicle to work or to other everyday destinations. This has led to concerns over both safety (SUVs are said to be four times as likely to roll over as are passenger cars, and many small cars are no match for them in an accident) and fuel economy.[3]

In this new century, while the emphasis on the bottom line remains very much alive, many businesses are coming around to the view that the bottom line will not look good if consumers' wants are not carefully attended to. Gordon Bethune, chief executive officer of Continental Airlines, analyzed substantial losses in previous years at Continental this way: "We had a crappy product, and we were trying to discount ourselves into profitability. Nobody wants to eat a crummy pizza, no matter if it's 99¢."[4]

---

[2] Buy.Com and onsale.com's atcost service both were pursuing this strategy in 1999. Sales were skyrocketing, but profits were another story. In 2002, buy.com was still in operation, but onsale.com, which had merged with Egghead, was not. Egghead subsequently filed for bankruptcy protection, and its assets were bought by Frye's Electronics.

[3] For more on SUVs and their problems, see "Rollover: The Hidden History of the SUV," PBS, *Frontline* (Program no. 2013, original airdate: February 21, 2002), and "Sport-Utility Vehicles Road Test," *Consumer Reports*, July 1999, especially pp 52, 58.

[4] "The Right Place, The Right Time," *Business Week*, May 27, 1996, p. 74. See also Gordon Bethune and Scott Huler, *From Worst to First: Behind the Scenes of Continental's Remarkable Comeback* (New York: John Wiley & Sons, 1998).

Former Ford Motor Company chairman Donald E. Petersen is reported to have said, "If we aren't customer-driven, our cars won't be either." Thus, Ford and many other companies have solicited consumer input, not only regarding how satisfied customers are with the products and services they have chosen to buy, but also about what new products and product improvements they want to see. Ford, for example, has a program called the "Consumer Insight Experience" which involves customer participation in efforts to unravel design problems and to anticipate consumer preferences.[5] Many firms have availed themselves of consumer satisfaction consultants such as J. D. Power, Inc., HayGroup, and Vickie Henry's Feedback Plus (see Managerial Perspective: "Can't Get No Satisfaction?").

Despite the new attention businesses are paying to consumer wants, there is evidence that consumers are far from satisfied with what they are getting. Many have taken to the World Wide Web to express their dissatisfaction. In 2002, one website complained about IBM's Mwave card, an allegedly faulty combined sound card/modem installed in IBM Aptiva computers that resulted in a costly class action suit against the company. Others were dedicated to complaints about companies like American Express, Best Buy, Dell Computer, GTE, Packard Bell, UUNET, and Wells Fargo bank. The snowballing of consumer complaint sites on the Internet has also led to the development of sites, such as www.consumeraffairs.com and www.complaints.com dedicated to consumer awareness and dispute resolution.

Some years ago, a 32-year-old professional in the computer industry summed up his views on being a consumer in the United States this way: "I live in the best country on the face of the earth, so I guess I'll put up with high prices, mediocre quality, and poor service.[6] There is little evidence that things have improved. In 2002, a *Newsweek* writer described customer service as "Kafka country" and recounted numerous stories of consumers trying to work their way through the maze of Merlinesque devices designed to fend off customers with problems.[7] Such consumer/business encounters present managers with both a challenge and an opportunity. Clearly, satisfied customers benefit managers and their firms. Likewise, customer satisfaction is one of the ingredients that can make for a healthy bottom line.

After going through years of restructuring by means of cost cutting termed *re-engineering, downsizing, rightsizing,* or sometimes *dumbsizing,* two new buzz phrases for firm managers have emerged: *yield management* and *economic value added.* Both of these concepts have a long history in economic analysis. Yield management (also known as *revenue management*) has been

---

[5] See www.ford.com for more on Ford and customer satisfaction.

[6] Alix M. Friedman, "Most Consumers Shun Luxuries, Seek Fewer Frills But Better Service," *Wall Street Journal,* September 19, 1989, p. B1.

[7] Jonathan Alter, "Press 1 to Cut Short Your Life," *Newsweek* (May 20, 2002), p. 45.

Can't Get No Satisfaction?

Consumers are getting very used to media reports on the product surveys done by J. D. Power and Associates. J. D. Power specializes in research on consumers' satisfaction with the products they buy, and the most visible J. D. Power reports deal with the automobile industry. In fact, an incident in that industry gave the firm a very big boost and a great deal of attention from the media over 30 years ago. It seems Mr. Power and his wife noticed in press reports that consumers were having trouble with a new engine that had been installed in just one brand of motor vehicle marketed in the United States—the Mazda. Mazda produced several vehicles that were equipped with a rotary engine, known as a Wankel engine. The Mazda rotary engine was held together by some very long bolts that went through sections of the block and were sealed against leakage by many o-rings. (O-rings are rubber rings that fit around bolts or in pipe connectors to provide a seal against leakage of liquids or gasses.)

The Powers realized that virtually all of the complaints appearing in the news about the Mazda rotary had to do with failure of the engine's o-rings. The Powers' firm surveyed Mazda buyers to verify this and came out with a report that was widely cited in the news. The name J. D. Power became synonymous with quality assessment and satisfaction research, and, today, the firm is a leader in that field.

Another interesting firm that measures customer satisfaction is Feedback Plus. The brainchild of entrepreneur Vicki Henry, Feedback Plus sends its field representatives, who often are ordinary consumers with other jobs, to sample service and products as "Mystery Shoppers" at a wide variety of firms. Feedback Plus is hired by the subject firms themselves to supply reports on consumers' assessments of their products and services. For example, Feedback Plus may be asked to send someone to a restaurant to report on the quality of its food or service. It may even ask them to report on how a specific employee or manager treats customers.

Satisfaction consulting, like that done by J. D. Power and Feedback Plus, has become an important industry. In their attempts to assess demand, increase firm value, and retain customers, many businesses have found the information provided by satisfaction consultants to be extremely valuable, and it is likely that this type of consulting will continue to grow.

References: On the Internet, sites of satisfaction consultants include www.jdpower.com/, www.gallup.com, haygroup.com, and www.gofeedback.com. Also see Steven Levy, "The Customer Is Always Wrong," *Newsweek* (March 11, 2002), p. 54; Keith Naughton, "Tired of Smile-Free Service?" *Newsweek*, March 6, 2000, pp. 44–45; and Andrea Adelson, "People Buy the Cars He Says They Like," *New York Times*, October 16, 1997, p. 27.

described as "a way for business to maximize revenue, and thereby profits, by selling their products to the right customer at the right price at the right time."[8] This, essentially, is *price discrimination*, something that has been

---

[8] Robert Oberwetter, "Revenue Management," www.abovetheweather.com.

described and analyzed by economists for over 130 years and a topic that we will address later in much detail.[9]

There is no doubt that skillful revenue management can add to the value of the firm. In fact, that second buzz phrase, economic value added, has to do exactly with what managers must do to maximize the value of the firm. The notion of economic value added refers to a return to the firm that is greater than what it would receive if its assets were put to their next best use. In finance, one would say that an undertaking is an acceptable one if its rate of return exceeds a specific target, usually a risk-adjusted cost of capital (the rate at which the firm can raise funds *plus* an appropriate risk premium). In economics, this has been known for over a century as a "greater than normal profit." (Normal profit is that profit necessary to keep the firm in business over a time period sufficiently long to make investment and reinvestment decisions.) Many firms have formally adopted economic value added policies in recent years. One example is Siemens, the giant German manufacturer of electrical and electronic equipment. Siemens announced in its 1998 Annual Report that it had "introduced a new value-based measure of economic activity called Economic Value Added, which became the obligatory performance measure within the entire Siemens organization on October 1, 1998."[10] Siemens has continued to use the Economic Value Added (EVA) approach, as have many other companies worldwide. Even in South Africa, over 700 firms now use EVA to measure their performance. Over long periods of time, it can be expected that firms that are exceptionally successful in creating economic value added will see that success reflected in rising prices of their shares in stock markets.

Although revenue management is important, businesses cannot afford blind pursuit of revenue enhancement, whether through price discrimination, better marketing, or improved customer satisfaction strategies, to the exclusion of other considerations. In the final analysis, it is the difference between revenue and *cost* that determines a firm's profits; therefore, economic value added will depend on the decisions that affect *both* of these factors. It is no surprise, then, that firms exert so much effort and expense trying to increase revenue while attempting to keep costs at as low a level as possible, *given a particular quality of output and output volume.* Still, it is clear that without a market for its product, a firm will not be successful—no matter how low its costs. Accordingly, we emphasize the importance of managerial decisions relating to demand for a firm's product by discussing first how the firm manager should cope with both external and internal factors that affect dollar sales and, ultimately, the firm's success or failure. As we shall see early

---

[9] A very interesting article by a former airline CEO who employed the approach regularly is Robert L. Crandall, "How Airline Pricing Works," *American Way* (May 1998), p. 8. Also see "Launching the Revenue Rocket: How Revenue Management Can Work for Business," *Cornell Hotel and Restaurant Administration Quarterly* (April 1997): 32.
[10] Siemens reports can be viewed at www.siemens.com/.

in this chapter, the term for total dollar sales is *total revenue* in the language of economists, and it will be our main focus for the present. Later, in Chapters 5 and 6, we will address the issue of cost, examining both the nature of the production process and its relation to the expenses the firm incurs in supplying output to its customers.

ADVERTISING, CONSUMER DEMAND, AND BUSINESS RESEARCH

The fact that U.S. corporations spend $45 to $50 billion per year on television advertising certainly suggests that they believe consumer demand for their products will be significantly affected as a result.[11] However, it should also be clear that advertising is not the only factor affecting the quantity that consumers demand of a particular product. In spite of advertising, consumers preferred "old" Coca-Cola to "new" Coke, and the DIVX videodisc was a flop.[12] Other products that failed shortly after introduction include the Fresh and Lite line of low-fat frozen Chinese entrees, the Apple Newton computer, Zima beverages, and the Lincoln Blackwood pickup truck (produced for only nine months starting in November 2001).

Much to its dismay, top management in the U.S. automobile industry discovered during the 1980s and 1990s that many consumers preferred Japanese cars to those produced by U.S. firms. The Japanese producers, through various strategies including investment in U.S. production facilities, obtained about a one-third share of the U.S. car and light truck market. The largest U.S. producer is General Motors (GM). At GM's 1980s peak, it had about 42 percent of that market, but in recent years its best performances have brought it to the neighborhood of just 30 percent. In fact, GM is so concerned about what factors influence the demand for its automobiles that it invests money in a statistical analysis department, whose task, among other things, is to estimate the impact of various factors such as advertising, price, individual preferences, and personal income on the quantity of GM cars that potential consumers will purchase. Ford, too, has engaged in expensive research programs to determine both what consumers want to see in new cars and what they dislike about existing products. Close attention to changing consumer attitudes and tastes has allowed the U.S. auto producers to regain some of the ground they lost in the 1980s and early 1990s. Much of

---

[11] Data from *Advertising Age,* a leading trade journal. You can visit its website at www.adage.com/ for more information.

[12] "Circuit City Pulls the Plug on Its Divx Videodisk Venture," *Wall Street Journal,* June 17, 1999, p. B10. For more flops, see Bill Adler, Julie Houghton, and Loel Baer, *America's Stupidest Business Decisions: 101 Blunders, Flops, and Screwups* (New York: William Morrow & Co., 1997), and "Flops," *Business Week* (August 16, 1993), pp. 88–94.

this recovery was accomplished by developing new car and truck models and improving product quality.

The revamping of the U.S. auto industry was accompanied by massive expenditures on advertising. However, firm managers cannot be successful by simply assuming that advertising expenditures will solve all revenue problems; they must recognize that diverse factors affect product sales. In fact, survey research has suggested that advertising has little influence on consumer purchasing decisions. One survey found that only 25 percent of those questioned stated that a television ad would convince them to try a new product or brand; the comparable figures for newspaper and magazine ads were 15 percent and 13 percent, respectively.[13]

Moreover, while consumers sometimes are entertained by whimsical and amusing ads, there is growing evidence that advertising that is offensive or out of place can create quite a backlash. One of the most invasive and detested recent ad strategies is that of "spamming" on the Internet. Spamming, the practice of sending consumers unsolicited commercial e-mail, had its precursor in junk faxes. It took a federal Telephone Consumer Protection Act (1991) to rein in the junk fax advertisers. Spamming is headed down the same path, with several states having passed antispamming laws in recent years and the U.S. Congress considering a "Can Spam Act."[14]

In the face of various forms of consumer backlash, firms are becoming more and more interested in marketing in a much broader sense—the entire process of moving goods from the producer to consumers. This far more inclusive view of marketing stresses the importance of determining consumer attitudes and wants and then analyzing the profitability aspect of proposed goods and services. Thus, businesses are finding that competition for consumers makes information regarding their tastes, preferences, and buying decisions critical to profitability. For example, Fingerhut has built a database that contains more than 500 bits of information on more than 50 million actual or potential customers. Using information technology to *micromarket,* Target adjusts its inventory to the particular tastes of customers in each location, so that stores within 15 minutes driving time of each other may contain different merchandise.[15]

Market research is becoming particularly important as companies attempt to successfully enter international markets, where customer tastes may differ dramatically from those of domestic customers. For example, Frito-Lay found that the favorite flavor of potential Thai customers was shrimp, but that these potential customers also thought an American snack

---

[13] "Study Finds Ads Induce Few People to Buy," *Wall Street Journal,* October 17, 1995, p. B10.
[14] In 2002, more about the spamming issue could be found at www.cauce.org, the website of the Coalition Against Unsolicited Commercial Email.
[15] "Data Is Power. Just Ask Fingerhut," *Business Week* (June 3, 1996), p. 69; "Where to Buy," *Consumer Reports* (July 2002), pp. 11–15; and "High-Tech Inventory System Coordinates Retailers' Clothes with Customers' Taste," *Wall Street Journal,* June 12, 1996, pp. B1, B6.

with that flavor would be inappropriate. As a result, Frito-Lay cautiously decided to stick with their traditional flavors in the Thai market.[16]

A widely recognized development in consumer market research is called "VALS"—the consumer Values and Lifestyles program of SRI International (formerly Stanford Research Institute). This methodology divides consumers into categories based on their self-images, goals, and the products they use.[17] It looks at who consumers are, how they live, what they buy— and more important, why they buy it. It was expanded (VALS[2]) to include specific relationships between consumer attitudes and purchase behavior. This approach to consumer research (known also as *psychographic analysis* of consumers) is more comprehensive than the old one of looking only at demographic characteristics of consumers—age, education, income, and number of children, for example. Researchers are finding that consumers who used to have similar buying patterns now are parts of many different groups with diverse wants and interests. While the preceding steps are still important, a new wave in businesses' efforts to attract the consumer directs attention to service and customer satisfaction. Naturally, this strategy will require continuing emphasis on the wants and preferences of consumers as well as a great deal of research on how to attract—and keep—customers.[18]

Understanding what economists are saying about issues relating to consumer choices requires that you comprehend their special terminology and the precise definitions they attach to everyday expressions such as "changes in demand." Therefore, we shall first define *demand* and other revenue terms as economists use them. Later in this chapter, we provide some insights into what things influence the demand for a firm's product and how to deal with them, so that with proper management of these factors and their costs, the firm can achieve maximum profits. Most important, we hope that when you finish this chapter you will have gained a great respect for the power that consumers have in determining the success of an enterprise.

DEMAND AND REVENUE CONCEPTS

The demand function for a firm's product (or service) relates the quantities of a product that consumers would like to purchase during some specific period to the variables that influence a consumer's decision to buy or not to buy the good. Such variables often include the price of the product, the prices of other related goods, consumers' incomes, the season of the year,

---

[16] "Major U.S. Companies Expand Efforts to Sell to Consumers Abroad," *Wall Street Journal,* June 13, 1996, pp. A1, A6.

[17] For more on VALS, see John C. Mowen and Michael Minor, *Consumer Behavior,* 6th ed. (Upper Saddle River, NJ: Prentice-Hall, 2000), Chapters 6, 7.

[18] It may be possible for you to participate in SRI's Internet VALS survey at www.sric-bi.com.

and dollars spent on advertising. For example, the quantity of a particular brand (Brand X) of up-market, built-in stainless steel and ceramic-interior microwave oven purchased by consumers during a year may be a function of the price of the oven, the price of a competing brand of oven, the number of households with two working partners, consumer annual disposable income, and dollars spent yearly on advertising. We could represent this relationship in functional notation as

$$Q_X = f(P_X, P_Y, H, I, A),$$

where

Q_X = quantity demanded per year of Brand X,

P_X = the price of Brand X,

P_Y = the price of Brand Y,

H = the number of two-income households,

I = the average annual per capita disposable income, and

A = the dollars spent per year on advertising.

When the firm plans its operations, it would be useful for it to know the exact functional relationship between the quantity demanded of its product (Q_X) and the independent variables (P_X, P_Y, H, I, and A) that affect that quantity. We should note, however, that some of the independent variables in the demand function are completely beyond the control of the firm. The firm cannot significantly affect average household annual income or the number of two-income households, even though its managers certainly should recognize how changes in these variables affect the quantity it can sell of its product. The firm may also not be able to affect the price of a competing good. Advertising and the price set for the firm's product, on the other hand, are variables controlled by management.

The price that the firm charges for its product is one of the variables that the firm can usually control. Therefore, the firm often finds it particularly useful to give special attention to the relationship between quantity demanded over some specific time period and possible prices that the firm might charge during that period. As noted in Chapter 1, the graphical representation of this relationship between price and quantity demanded is called the *demand curve*.

The firm can perform a statistical analysis to determine the behavior of its demand function and then use that function to define its demand curve. For example, assume our hypothetical demand function for Brand X microwave ovens purchased was statistically determined to be the following:

$$Q_X = 26,500 - 100P_X + 25P_Y + 0.0001H + 1.3I + 0.02A$$

and that $P_X = \$400$, $P_Y = \$500$, $H = 40,000,000$, $I = \$20,000$, and $A = \$50,000$. Solving for Q_X (the number of Brand X microwave ovens purchased per year), by letting the independent variables take on these values, we find that

$$Q_X = 26,500 - 40,000 + 12,500 + 4,000 + 26,000 + 1,000$$

$$= 30,000 \text{ ovens per year.}$$

If all of the independent variables remain at the values just stated, the firm will sell 30,000 microwave ovens per year.

If we hold all the variables except Q_X and P_X constant, we can graph the demand curve for Brand X ovens as shown in Figure 2-1. With all variables other than P_X and Q_X held constant, the demand function becomes

$$Q_X = 70,000 - 100P_X,$$

which is the equation for the straight-line demand *curve* plotted in the figure. The equation for the demand curve is found by substituting the given values for all of the variables except Q_X and P_X in the demand function above.

Changes in Demand and Quantity Demanded

If one of the variables held constant when we drew the demand curve should change, the demand curve shifts. We call this event a *change in*

FIGURE 2-1

Demand Curve for Brand X Microwave Ovens

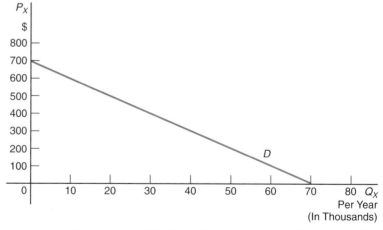

This graph depicts the demand curve, D, for Brand X microwave ovens. P_x represents the price of an oven, and Q_x is quantity demanded of ovens (in thousands) per year. At a price of $700 apiece, no ovens would be purchased. If the ovens were given away, 70,000 would be demanded per year.

Chapter Two

Revenue of the Firm

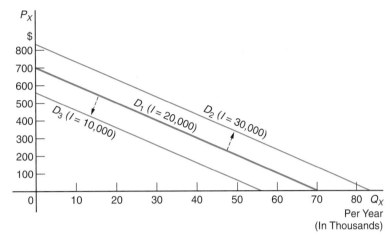

FIGURE 2-2

Changes in Demand

A change in income will cause the demand curve for Brand X microwave ovens to shift. If income increases from $20,000 to $30,000, demand will increase. If income decreases from $20,000 to $10,000, demand will decrease.

demand. For example, if average per capita income falls to $10,000 or rises to $30,000, the demand curve drawn in Figure 2-1 will shift, as shown in Figure 2-2. A change in demand, therefore, refers to a shift in the demand curve—as contrasted with a *change in quantity demanded,* which refers simply to a change in the amount of a good or service that consumers are willing to purchase over some time period *because of a change in the price of the good.* The behavior of consumers in the latter situation is represented by a *different point on the same demand curve.* A change in quantity demanded as P_X changes from $500 to $400 is illustrated in Figure 2-3.

Note that consumers purchase a larger quantity per time period at the lower price because the demand curve slopes downward to the right. This is consistent with the law of demand, a concept introduced in Chapter 1. Also, the negative coefficient of P_X (that is, −100) in both the demand curve equation and the equation for the demand function indicates that there is an inverse relation between the price of Brand X microwave ovens and the quantity purchased.

Total Revenue and Average Revenue

Total revenue is the total dollar sales of a firm during some particular time period. It is equal to the price of the product multiplied by the quantity sold.

The **total revenue** (total dollar sales) of a firm is directly related to the demand for the firm's product. In fact, if we know the demand curve equation for a firm's product and the price set by the firm, we can determine the firm's total revenue, which is price *multiplied by* quantity demanded. To find total revenue, we would first substitute the value for the product's price in the demand curve equation and solve for quantity demanded. Total revenue

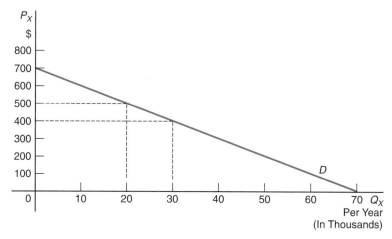

FIGURE 2-3

*Change in
Quantity
Demanded*

A change in the quantity demanded of microwave ovens occurs if there is a change in the price of the ovens. For example, if the price falls from $500 to $400, the quantity demanded will increase by 10,000 ovens per year.

is then found by multiplying price by quantity demanded (the number of units sold). Total revenue, therefore, is a function of price and quantity demanded, or $TR = g(P, Q)$. Since price can also be considered a function of the quantity demanded or sold, we can write price in terms of quantity and then write total revenue as a function only of quantity sold. Thus, for our microwave oven manufacturer,

$$Q_X = 70{,}000 - 100P_X,$$

and

$$100P_X = 70{,}000 - Q_X$$

Therefore

$$P_X = 700 - 0.01Q_X,$$

and

$$TR = P_X \cdot Q_X = (700 - 0.01Q_X)\,(Q_X) = 700Q_X - 0.01Q_X^2.$$

Average revenue is total revenue divided by quantity demanded. *When all units of the product are sold at the same price, average revenue is equal to the product's price.*

$$AR = \frac{TR}{Q} = \left(\frac{P \times Q}{Q} \right) = P,$$

where AR is average revenue, TR is total revenue, Q is quantity demanded, and P is price. The result that average revenue is equal to price requires all buyers to be charged the same price for the product, which we shall assume is the case throughout most of this text. The special case of multiple prices for a single product will be discussed in Chapter 11. For the microwave oven demand curve, the AR formula is the same as the price equation we employed to get total revenue. In other words,

$$AR = P_X = 700 - 0.01Q_X.$$

From Average and Total Revenue to Marginal Revenue

For a deeper understanding of a price (or AR) equation such as the one for our microwave ovens, it is useful to consider the general mathematical equation for a straight line. This equation can be written as $Y = a + bX$ and graphed as in Figure 2-4. In the figure, a is the point where the demand curve hits the Y axis, called the Y-axis *intercept* of the line, and b is the *slope* of the line, which can be defined as either the ratio $\Delta Y/\Delta X$ or rise/run for the movement along the line from R to T. The line slopes upward to the

FIGURE 2-4

Slope of a Straight Line

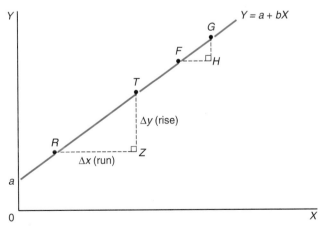

For the straight-line $Y = a + bX$, the slope is $\Delta Y/\Delta X$, which is the ratio of the length of the vertical side to the horizontal one (rise over run) for any right triangle formed under the line. Thus, this ratio is the same for either triangle RZT or triangle FHG. Since Y increases when X does, this line has a positive or upward-to-the-right slope.

FIGURE 2-5

A Downward or Negative-Sloping Straight-Line Demand Curve

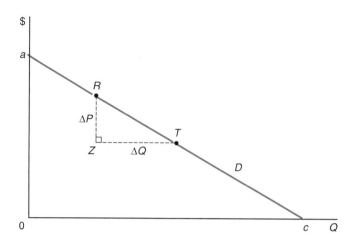

The straight-line demand curve in this figure has a slope equal to $\Delta P/\Delta Q$. Its slope is negative, since an increase in Q occurs with a *fall* in P. As in Figure 2-4, a is the vertical axis intercept of the straight line, and we can write the demand curve's equation as $P = a - bQ$, where b is the ratio of distance $0a$ to distance $0c$. The minus sign in front of b indicates negative slope.

right because if ΔX is positive, ΔY will also be positive. (If we go from T to R, both ΔX and ΔY are negative, so the ratio is still positive.) For a straight line, the ratio $\Delta Y/\Delta X$ will be the same between any two points on the line, so the rise/run for the small triangle *FHG* is the same as it is for the large one, *RZT*.

A straight-line demand curve behaves similarly to the line in Figure 2-4, except that it has a negative (downward to the right) slope equal to $\Delta P/\Delta Q$. (See Figure 2-5.) In Figure 2-5, if we move from point R to point T, ΔQ is positive, but P falls, so ΔP is negative. Following the same form of equation we used for the line $Y = a + bX$, we can say that for a straight-line demand curve, it will be true that $P = a - bQ$, where the negative sign indicates negative slope. We can also say that b = distance $0a$/distance $0c$, since triangle aOc has the same ratio of rise to run as triangle RZT. The negative of this ratio is $\Delta P/\Delta Q$. So, we can think of *all* downward-sloping, straight-line demand curves as having the formula $P = a - bQ$, where a is the price axis intercept and b is the ratio of the height of the triangle the demand curve forms with the P and Q axes to the base of that same triangle, or $0a/0c$. We can then say:

$$AR = P = a - bQ, \text{ and, multiplying through by } Q,$$

$$\text{Total Revenue} = TR = Q(AR) = Q(P) = aQ - bQ^2.$$

This is the same result we obtained earlier when we wrote the *TR* equation for our microwave ovens.

Marginal Revenue is the rate of change of total revenue with respect to quantity sold, or $\Delta TR/\Delta Q$. It indicates how total revenue will change when there is a change in the quantity sold of a firm's product. For a downward-sloping, straight-line demand curve, marginal revenue will be another straight line having the same vertical axis ($ axis) intercept as the demand curve but intercepting the *Q* axis at exactly half the value of *Q* that occurs where the demand curve crosses that axis. It will take a graph and a little bit of algebra to see why this is so.

Take a look at the demand or AR curve in Figure 2-6. Let's start with price *P* and quantity *Q* that correspond to point *A* on the demand curve. Since total revenue is just price times quantity, it is equal to the area of the rectangle *OPAQ*. (Any rectangle's area is its length times its width.) Rectangle *OPAQ* is composed of the shaded area plus area I. If price is lowered to *P′*, quantity will be *Q′*, and total revenue will equal the area of rectangle *OP′BQ′*. This *TR* is equal to the shaded area plus rectangle II. Thus, TR is greater at *Q′* than at *Q*, since rectangle II is larger than rectangle I.

Now let's consider the *change* in total revenue, *ΔTR*. That must be equal to the difference between the area of rectangle II and that of rectangle I, since

FIGURE 2-6

A Total Revenue Change Caused by a Price Change

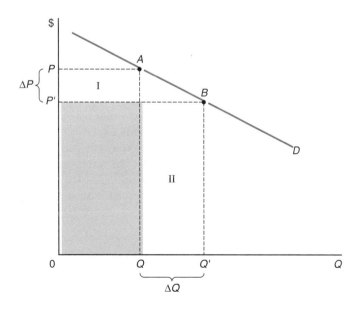

If price falls from *P* to *P′*, total revenue, which is *P(Q)*, changes from the area of rectangle *OPAQ* to that of rectangle *OP′BQ′*. The two total revenues differ by the amount that the area of rectangle II exceeds that of rectangle I, since the shaded rectangle is common to both of them.

both *TR* values include the shaded area. Keeping in mind that ΔP is negative, we can write this difference as follows.

$$\Delta TR = \Delta Q(P') + \Delta P(Q)$$

Dividing by ΔQ, we get

$$\frac{\Delta TR}{\Delta Q} = P' + \frac{\Delta P}{\Delta Q}(Q)$$

Now, the slope of the demand curve is $\Delta P / \Delta Q$, and for a straight-line demand curve, it is the same at every point or between any two points like *A* and *B* in the figure. We have also found earlier that if we write the equation of the demand curve as $P = a - bQ$, the slope is equal to $-b$. So, we can rewrite the expression immediately above as

$$\Delta TR / \Delta Q = P' - bQ$$

Suppose we let the change in *Q* be very small so that Point *B* approaches Point *A*. The limit to this is when there is no space between *A* and *B*, which means there is no difference between *P'* and *P*. However, we know $P = a - bQ$. Therefore, we can now do one more rewrite of our equation, substituting $a - bQ$ for *P'*, and say

$$MR = \Delta TR / \Delta Q = (a - bQ) - bQ = a - 2bQ$$

Now recall again that our formula for price or average revenue was

$$P = a - bQ$$

and note that *MR* is of the same form, except that *Q* is multiplied by $-2b$ instead of by $-b$. This proves the proposition made earlier: **A straight-line, downward-sloping demand curve has a marginal revenue curve that is another straight line with the same vertical axis intercept and twice the negative slope.** This relation holds for *every* straight-line, downward-sloping demand curve, and it means also that the *Q* axis intercept of the *MR* curve will occur at exactly one-half the *Q* value where the *D* or *AR* curve intercepts the *Q* axis.

Returning to our demand curve for microwave ovens, we can summarize the average, total, and marginal revenue equations as follows.

$$AR = P = a - bQ = 700 - 0.01Q_x$$
$$TR = Q(P) = aQ - bQ^2 = 700Q_x - 0.01Q_x^2$$
$$MR = \Delta TR / \Delta Q = a - 2bQ = 700 - 0.02Q_x$$

Arc marginal revenue gives the average rate of change of total revenue with respect to quantity sold over some range of output.

Arc marginal revenue is an approximation of marginal revenue that is employed when tabular or discrete data are used to describe the demand curve instead of an equation. In a table, it is the discrete change in total revenue divided by the discrete change in quantity sold, or

$$\text{Arc } MR = \frac{\Delta TR}{\Delta Q} = \frac{TR_2 - TR_1}{Q_2 - Q_1},$$

where TR_1 and Q_1 are the original total revenue and level of output, and TR_2 and Q_2 are the new total revenue and level of output, respectively. As you can see, arc MR is still $\Delta TR/\Delta Q$, but now we are assuming that ΔQ is *not* small or approaching zero. Arc marginal revenue is only an approximation of marginal revenue because it measures the *average* rate of change of total revenue with respect to quantity sold over the range of ΔQ under consideration. This average rate of change will not be exactly equal to the rate of change of total revenue with respect to quantity at *some particular output level* if this rate of change is different for different levels of output. For example, if Q changes from 100 to 200 and for this change, ΔTR is \$8,000, then $\Delta TR/\Delta Q$ = \$8,000/100 or \$80. This is saying that *each* of the 100 units of output from Q = 100 to Q = 200 added approximately \$80 to TR.[19] There may have been one that added \$86 and another that added \$74, but, on average, they added \$80 apiece.

The relationships among the total revenue, average revenue, and marginal revenue functions for the manufacturer of Brand X microwave ovens are illustrated in Table 2-1 and Figure 2-7. Table 2-1 has two marginal revenue columns, one showing the point value of MR obtained from our equation $MR = 700 - 0.02Q$ and the other showing arc MR as calculated by $(TR_2 - TR_1)/(Q_2 - Q_1)$. In fact, the arc MR is in each case the same as the point MR at the midpoint of the ΔQ range for which it was calculated. That is, for the range from $Q = 0$ to $Q = 10,000$, arc MR is 600, and this is also what we would get for the point MR equation if we let $Q = 5,000$, which is the midpoint of the range 0 to 10,000. ($MR = 700 - 0.02(5,000) = 600$.) By the same approach,

---

[19] Technically, marginal revenue at a particular output level is the value of the derivative of the total revenue function with respect to quantity, dTR/dQ, at that point. Thus, for the manufacturer of Brand X microwave ovens discussed above,

$$TR = 700Q_X - 0.01Q_X^2, \text{ and}$$
$$MR = (dTR/dQ_X) = 700 - 0.02Q_X.$$

At an output level of 30,000 units, marginal revenue is \$100. However, between $Q_X = 20,000$ and $Q_X = 30,000$, arc marginal revenue is \$200, since $\Delta TR = \$2,000,000$ and $\Delta Q_X = 10,000$ (as shown in Table 2-1).

FIGURE 2-7

Geometrical Relationships among Average Revenue, Marginal Revenue, and Total Revenue for Brand X Microwave Ovens

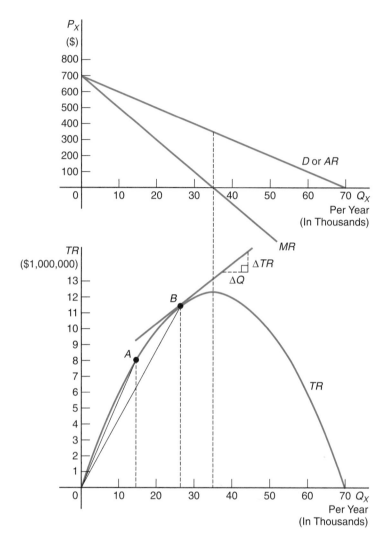

This graph depicts the geometrical relationships among average revenue (*AR*), marginal revenue (*MR*), and total revenue (*TR*) for Brand *X* microwave ovens. Marginal revenue is zero at a quantity of 35,000 ovens per month—the same point where total revenue is at a maximum. With a linear, downward-sloping demand curve, *MR* reaches zero at a quantity level (35,000 units) one-half as large as that where average revenue is zero.

you should verify for yourself that the point value of *MR* is 500 when *Q* = 15,000 and 300 when *Q* = 25,000.

In Figure 2-7, total revenue is depicted in the lower graph, while marginal revenue and average revenue are depicted in the upper graph. Geometrically, average revenue at some quantity is the slope of a line drawn

Table 2-1 *Relationship among Price, Total Revenue, and Marginal Revenue for Brand X Microwave Ovens*

Price of X (Average Revenue)	Total Quantity of X Demanded	Total Revenue	Exact Value of Marginal Revenue $MR = 700 - 0.2Q$	Arc Marginal Revenue $= \Delta TR/\Delta Q$
$700	0	0	$700	
				$600
600	10,000	$6,000,000	500	
				400
500	20,000	10,000,000	300	
				200
400	30,000	12,000,000	100	
				0
300	40,000	12,000,000	−100	
				−200
200	50,000	10,000,000	−300	
				−400
100	60,000	6,000,000	−500	

from the origin to the point on the *TR* curve corresponding to that level of output. This is true because the slope of that line is $TR/Q = AR$. The average revenue in Figure 2-7 is always decreasing, as can be seen from a comparison of the slopes of line segments *OA* and *OB* in the lower graph. We should emphasize that since the *AR* curve gives the relationship between price and quantity demanded for a firm, the *average revenue curve is also the firm's demand curve.*

Marginal revenue at a specific quantity is the slope of the *TR* curve at that quantity demanded. In Figure 2-7, marginal revenue is also always decreasing and is equal to zero when total revenue reaches a maximum, at $Q_X = 35,000$.[20] At any point on the *TR* curve, *MR* can be represented by the

---

[20] For *TR* to be at a maximum (or minimum) at a specific level of quantity demanded, dTR/dQ must be equal to zero. Thus,

$$\frac{dTR}{dQ_X} = MR = 700 - 0.02Q_X = 0,$$

$$-0.02Q_X = -700, \ or$$

$$Q_X = 35,000.$$

The second derivative

$$\frac{d^2TR}{dQ_X^2} = \frac{dMR}{dQ_X} = -0.02,$$

which is less than zero so that the second-order condition for a maximum is satisfied.

slope of a line tangent to the curve. Such a line has been drawn tangent to point *B*, and a slope triangle has been constructed under it to show that its slope is $\Delta TR/\Delta Q$, or *MR*. You should verify for yourself that the tangent will have a zero, or horizontal, slope at the *TR* maximum and a negative slope at any point beyond $Q = 35,000$.

As was proved earlier, when the *AR* curve is a straight line, the *MR* curve will be a straight line with a slope twice as steep as the *AR* curve and will thus intersect the quantity axis at a level of output half as large as that at the point where the demand *(AR)* curve intersects the same axis.[21]

Both Figure 2-7 and Table 2-1 illustrate that *as long as price must decrease in order for the firm to increase the quantity demanded of its product, marginal revenue is less than price.* Marginal revenue is less than price because we are assuming that to sell a larger quantity, the firm must lower its price on *all* units sold. Hence, if the firm in Table 2-1 wishes to sell 30,000 units rather than 20,000, it must lower the price—from $500 to $400—on *all 30,000* of the units. Therefore, the firm gives up the opportunity to sell the first 20,000 units at a price $100 higher.

We can show the effect of this price decrease on the revenue from the first 20,000 units sold as follows:

Gain in revenue from sale of an additional	
10,000 units = 10,000 × $400	= $4,000,000
Loss in revenue from sale of first 20,000 units	
at $400 rather than $500 = 20,000 × (–$100)	= $2,000,000
Net increase in total revenue	$2,000,000

$$Arc\ Marginal\ Revenue = \frac{\Delta TR}{\Delta Q} = \frac{\$2,000,000}{10,000} = \$200$$

---

[21] If $TR = 700Q_X - 0.01Q_X^2$, then $AR = TR/Q_X = 700 - 0.01Q_X$ and, as stated above, $MR = 700 - 0.02Q_X$. The slope of the marginal revenue curve is –0.02, which is twice as steep as the slope (–0.01) of the average revenue curve. In more general terms, if

$$AR = a - bQ,\ \text{then}$$
$$TR = aQ - bQ^2,\ \text{and}$$
$$MR = a - 2bQ.$$

The slope of the marginal revenue curve is –2*b*, which is exactly twice the slope of the average revenue curve.

FIGURE 2-8

*Horizontal
Demand Curve
(P = MR)*

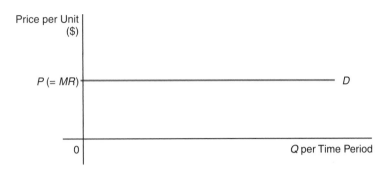

D is a horizontal demand curve. A firm can sell as many units of its product as it wishes to at the going market price. Price and marginal revenue are equal.

If the firm did not have to lower price to sell a larger quantity, the demand curve would be a horizontal line and price would equal marginal revenue, as shown in Figure 2-8.[22]

The relationships among demand and total marginal revenue will be discussed further below. Moreover, in Chapter 7 we shall see that marginal revenue plays a very important role in helping the firm locate its profit-maximizing level of output.

Firm Demand Versus Industry Demand

The demand function that we have been discussing relates the quantity purchased of a particular brand of microwave oven (Brand X) to other variables. Since more than one brand of microwave oven is available, we could also talk about the factors that determine the total number of microwave ovens (all brands) purchased during a year. This relationship is the *industry demand function*—as contrasted with the demand function for Brand X microwave ovens, the demand function for a firm. Many of the same variables will appear in the industry demand function as in the demand function of the firm, although their coefficients will usually be different in size and sometimes in sign. For example, the price of Brand Y will affect the industry quan-

---

[22] If $TR = P \times Q$, then

$$MR = \frac{dTR}{dQ} = P + Q\left(\frac{dP}{dQ}\right)$$

using the product rule for differentiation. If price does not change as quantity sold changes, $(dP/dQ) = 0$, and $MR = P$.

NUMERICAL EXAMPLE

The Demand for Draperies

Alicia Gartiz has estimated the following demand function for economical draperies sold by her firm, Pleats, Inc.:

$$Q_d = 1,200 - 20P_d + .1I + .08A,$$

where

$$Q_d = \text{quantity demanded of pairs of drapes}$$

$$P_d = \text{price per pair of drapes}$$

$$I = \text{per capita income in the market area, and}$$

$$A = \text{her firm's advertising expenditure.}$$

All data are on a monthly basis. The current values of the income and advertising variables are, respectively, $1,200 per month and $4,000 per month.

1. Assuming the above values for I and A remain constant, what is the equation of the demand curve for Pleats, Inc.'s drapes?

2. If Alicia wished to obtain the maximum monthly sales revenue, given the data above, what price would she charge and what would the revenue be?

Answer

1. Substituting the stated values into the demand function, we have $Q_d = 1,200 - 20P_d + .1(1,200) + .08(4,000)$, or $Q_d = 1,640 - 20P_d$.

2. The maximum total revenue will occur at the midpoint of the demand curve, where MR is zero and $Q_d = 820$. There, P_d will be $41. Total revenue will be $41(820) = $33,620. From the stated demand curve, $P_d = 82 - .05Q_d$, and, since MR will have the same intercept as AR on the vertical axis but be zero at the quantity corresponding to the midpoint of AR, $MR = 82 - .1Q_d$. This relationship holds because the MR curve's slope is twice as steep as that of the AR curve. Setting MR equal to zero locates maximum TR, or $82 - .1Q_d = 0$, so $Q_d = 820$. By substitution, $P_d = 82 - .05(820) = $41.

tity demanded of microwave ovens (as well as the quantity demanded of Brand X and of Brand Y ovens). However, its coefficient will probably be *negative* in the industry demand function, indicating that an increase in P_Y will *decrease* the total quantity of microwave ovens demanded. In the demand function for Brand X ovens, the coefficient of P_Y had a *positive* sign, indicating that an increase in P_Y would increase the quantity demanded of Brand X ovens. In the example above, we would expect that the coefficients of (1) the number of women employed variable and (2) the average household annual income variable will be larger in the industry demand function than in the firm demand function, which indicates that a change in either one of these variables will have a greater effect on the *total quantity demanded* of microwave ovens than on the quantity demanded of Brand X. The size of the coefficient of the advertising dollars variable will depend on the extent that firm advertising serves to increase overall quantity demanded of microwave ovens—as opposed to merely increasing the quantity demanded of the microwave ovens of one firm at the expense of the sales of another firm.

Although most of the demand functions presented in this chapter are demand functions for the product of a *firm,* the concepts discussed can generally be applied to either industry or firm demand functions.

DETERMINANTS OF DEMAND

The **determinants of demand** for a given good or service are demand function variables other then its own price.

Any demand function variable that will cause a demand curve to shift is usually called a **determinant of demand.** In other words, for Brand X microwave ovens, all of the variables on the right-hand side of the demand function equation except P_X are determinants of demand.

The determinants of demand are what cause consumers to change their view of how much they will buy of a given good or service at all possible prices that could be charged for it. Exactly what they are will depend on the good in question. For example, how many ice-cold drinks you want to buy at various possible prices is likely to depend on how hot the weather is. It would therefore be reasonable to include some measure of this (degrees Fahrenheit or Celsius) in the demand function for ice-cold drinks. But the weather is not likely to have a significant effect on your demand for ham sandwiches or pizza, and one would not likely include a weather variable in the demand functions for them.

If we tried to list all possible determinants of demand for goods and services, we would probably have a very long list. The following factors, however, are some of the most widely applicable:

1. Consumer incomes
2. Prices of related goods and services
3. Consumer tastes
4. Number of consumers in the market
5. Credit terms on loans
6. Advertising

We will consider each of these in turn, starting with two that are almost universally important, *income and prices of related goods.* Normally, as consumers' incomes increase, they tend to purchase more goods and services.

A **normal good** displays a positive relation between consumer purchases and income.

If an individual consumer purchases more of a good when his or her income increases, that good is said to be a **normal good** with respect to income. If the reverse occurs, the good is an **inferior good.** It is often argued that hamburger is an inferior good for many people, since they will consume less hamburger and more of other meats (steaks, roast beef) if their incomes increase. In a demand function, a negative sign on the coefficient of the income variable indicates an inferior good, while the coefficient of the income term for a normal good will be positive. For a normal good, an increase in income will shift the demand curve to the right, while a decrease in income will shift it to the left. The reverse occurs for an inferior good.

An **inferior good** displays a negative relation between consumer purchases and income.

The relation of the quantity purchased of a given good to the price of a related good depends, in a very basic sense, on whether the two are substitutes or complements. In the case of **substitute goods,** one can be used in place of the other and will, in fact, be substituted if one becomes relatively cheaper than the other. For example, frozen yogurt and ice cream are substitutes, and if the price of frozen yogurt drops while that of ice cream does not, some people will purchase yogurt instead of ice cream. In the demand function for ice cream, the coefficient of the price of the related good, frozen yogurt, will have a positive sign, indicating that a rise in the yogurt price would lead to a greater quantity sold of ice cream, while a fall in the yogurt price would do the reverse. Likewise, one would expect a demand function for frozen yogurt to include the price of ice cream as an independent variable, with the coefficient taking a positive sign to indicate the substitute nature of the relation between the two goods. An increase in the price of a substitute, then, will shift the demand curve for a given good to the right, while a decrease in the price of a substitute will do the reverse.

A **substitute good** is a good that can be used in place of some other good.

Complementary goods are generally used with one another.

For **complementary goods,** goods that are used together, the coefficient of the related good's price will be negative. For example, lettuce and salad dressing are complementary goods. If lettuce prices rise dramatically (as they have when freezing weather in California, Florida, and Texas has spoiled winter crops), people will buy less lettuce *and* less salad dressing. Thus, the price of lettuce is a determinant of the demand for salad dressing. Lettuce price would appear in a demand function for salad dressing with a negative coefficient in front of it, since an increase in that price would lead to a reduction in purchases of salad dressing (demand curve for salad dressing shifts to the left).

Clearly, consumer tastes can also serve as a determinant of demand, but they are not always easy to measure. Sometimes a proxy variable for them can be used, for example, percent of consumers in a given age group or ethnic group. If a given good appeals to the particular preferences of teenagers, the percentage of teenagers in the market area might serve as a good proxy for taste in the demand function. The number of consumers in the market is also an important determinant of demand. Clearly, the demand curve for any good or service will shift to the right if more consumers enter the market for it. A good example would be the demand for housing in Florida, which has increased dramatically as older people from all parts of the United States have decided to retire there.

The remaining items on our determinants-of-demand list are credit terms and advertising. Credit terms (availability of loans as well as the interest rate on them) are especially important demand function variables for *durable goods*—goods that last a long time and for which purchases can be postponed for some length of time. Examples are houses, cars, and large home appliances like washers and dryers. The housing market reacts greatly to changes in availability of home mortgages and changes in mortgage interest rates. If interest rates increase or loans simply become difficult to qualify for, the demand for both new and used homes will fall. Likewise, people will postpone new car purchases if credit terms are unfavorable, and automobile manufacturers are well aware that sales can be stimulated by offering buyer incentives in the form of easy credit terms. Advertising, too, can shift the demand curve, and firms spend huge sums on it in attempts to do so. Normally, we expect increases in advertising expenditure by an individual firm to lead to a rightward shift of the demand curve for its product. However, in the face of competing advertising by rival firms, it is possible for this impact to be canceled out.

A NOTE ON DETERMINANTS OF SUPPLY

A supply function relates the amount that sellers will offer of a good to the independent variables that determine it. For example, a supply function for frozen yogurt might include as independent variables the price of frozen yogurt, the prices of the inputs used to make the yogurt, the prices of alternative products, and the number of suppliers in the market. The **determinants of supply** are those variables other than a good's own price that will increase or decrease the quantity of the good sellers are willing and able to sell. Besides the variables already mentioned, these might include government tax or subsidy policies, technology, and producer expectations about future market conditions.

Determinants of supply are those variables other than a good's own price that change the quantity of the good sellers are willing and able to sell.

If all of the determinants of supply remain constant, we can identify the supply curve of a given good as the curve or line showing the quantity of it that sellers will place on the market at various possible prices. The supply curve of a seller may slope upward to the right, indicating that the quantity supplied is a rising function of price. It probably does slope upward in many cases. (Figure 1-3, in Chapter 1, shows an example of an upward-sloping supply curve.) Later, when we examine market structures, more will be said about supply. However, the focus of the present chapter is demand, not supply, and it will be sufficient at this point to note that movements along a supply curve for a given good (changes in quantity supplied) take place when, other things equal, the price of the good itself changes. The entire supply curve will shift, however, when one of the determinants of supply changes.

ELASTICITY OF DEMAND

The managers of a firm must pay close attention to the responsiveness of the quantity demanded of its product to various factors, for only by understanding these relationships can they hope to make reliable predictions of sales. As we stated previously, the quantity demanded of a firm's product is determined both by factors outside the firm's control and by factors such as price and advertising, which are often within its control. The ability to predict revenue is crucial, for without an adequate level of sales relative to costs, the firm cannot be successful.

One measure of such responsiveness that is feasible if the demand function for the firm's product is known is merely to substitute different values for the independent variables in that function and then solve for the resulting quantity demanded and total revenue. However, it is also often useful for a firm to know the *relative responsiveness* of quantity demanded of its product to changes in the values of the variables that it knows affect that demand. Roughly speaking, the relative responsiveness of quantity demanded of Brand X to a change in some variable Z is defined as the percentage change in Q_X divided by the percentage change in Z, or

$$E_Z = \frac{percentage\ change\ in\ Q_X}{percentage\ change\ in\ Z}$$

This responsiveness is called the *elasticity of demand* for Product X with respect to variable Z.

Arc versus Point Elasticity

Point elasticity of demand (for X) with respect to Z refers to the elasticity of demand *given* (or at) some specific value for Q_X and Z. Since the point elasticity of demand formula usually involves the use of partial derivatives, we shall place our discussion of such elasticities in footnotes and concentrate on arc elasticity in the text. The *arc elasticity of demand* for product X with respect to variable Z refers to the average responsiveness of Q_X to a change in Z

between two different values of Z, Z_1, and Z_2. The formula for arc elasticity of demand with respect to Z is given by[23]

$$E_Z = \frac{\Delta Q_X}{\dfrac{Q_{X_2} + Q_{X_1}}{2}} \div \frac{\Delta Z}{\dfrac{Z_2 + Z_1}{2}}, \text{ or}$$

$$E_Z = \frac{\Delta Q_X}{\Delta Z} \cdot \frac{Z_2 + Z_1}{Q_{X_2} + Q_{X_1}} = \frac{Q_{X_2} - Q_{X_1}}{Z_2 - Z_1} \cdot \frac{Z_2 + Z_1}{Q_{X_2} + Q_{X_1}}.$$

Since with arc elasticity we are trying to measure the *average responsiveness* of Q_X to changes in Z *over some range of* Z, we use an average of the first and second values of both Q_X and Z.

For example, let us examine the elasticity of demand of Brand X microwave ovens with respect to P_X. The demand function given earlier in this chapter was

$$Q_X = 26,500 - 100P_X + 25P_Y + 0.0001H + 1.3I + 0.02A,$$

and we said that if $P_X = \$400$, $P_Y = \$500$, $H = 40,000,000$, $I = \$20,000$, and $A = \$50,000$, then $Q_X = 30,000$.[24] By substituting $P_X = \$500$ in the demand function above, we find that at a price of $500 the quantity demanded falls to

---

[23] The general formula for point elasticity of demand for good X with respect to variable Z is

$$E_Z = \left(\frac{\partial Q_X}{\partial Z}\right)\left(\frac{Z}{Q_X}\right), \text{ or}$$

$$E_Z = \left(\frac{dQ_X}{dZ}\right)\left(\frac{Z}{Q_X}\right),$$

if Q_X is a function solely of Z.

[24] At that point, the price elasticity of demand for Q_X is given by

$$E_P = \left(\frac{\partial Q_X}{\partial P_X}\right)\left(\frac{P_X}{Q_X}\right)$$

$$= -100\left(\frac{400}{30,000}\right) = -1.33.$$

20,000 microwave ovens per year. Thus, the arc price elasticity of demand between $P_X = \$400$ and $P_X = \$500$ is given by

$$E_p = \frac{\Delta Q_X}{\Delta P_X} \cdot \frac{P_{X2} + P_{X1}}{Q_{X2} + Q_{X1}} = \frac{Q_{X2} - Q_{X1}}{P_{X2} - P_{X1}} \cdot \frac{P_{X2} + P_{X1}}{Q_{X2} + Q_{X1}}$$

$$= \frac{-10,000}{100} \cdot \frac{900}{50,000} = -1.8.$$

The preceding equation assumes that $P_{X_2} = \$500$ and $P_{X_1} = \$400$, or that a price *increase* has occurred. However, a price decrease over this same range would also result in an elasticity coefficient of –1.8. This result holds because if price falls from \$500 to \$400, then the change in price will be –\$100 and the change in quantity demanded will be +10,000. Therefore, the only change in the elasticity calculation occurs in the signs of the numerator and denominator of $\Delta Q_X / \Delta P_X$.

We can illustrate why it is necessary to use both sets of prices and quantities in the arc elasticity formula with the following example. Suppose that we used only $P_{X_1} = \$400$ and $Q_{X_1} = 30,000$. Then

$$E_p = \frac{\Delta Q_X}{\Delta P_X} \cdot \frac{P_{X1}}{Q_{X1}} = \frac{-10,000}{100} \cdot \frac{400}{30,000} = -1.33.$$

On the other hand, if we were to use only P_{X_2} and Q_{X_2},

$$E_p = \frac{\Delta Q_X}{\Delta P_X} \cdot \frac{P_{X2}}{Q_{X2}} = \frac{-10,000}{100} \cdot \frac{500}{20,000} = -2.5.$$

Neither of these values (–1.33 or –2.5) adequately represents the price elasticity of demand over the entire price range from \$500 to \$400. Therefore, *the use of both prices* and *both quantities in the arc price elasticity formula appears to be one reasonable way of approximating the price elasticity of demand over this region of the demand curve.* As we found above, this approach gives us an intermediate value for E_p of –1.8. We shall examine the concept of price elasticity of demand further in the next section.

Price Elasticity of Demand

Price elasticity of demand measures the degree of responsiveness of quantity demanded to a change in the price of a good or service. It is the ratio of the percentage change in quantity demanded to the percentage change in price.

The **price elasticity of demand** measures the relative responsiveness of quantity demanded of a product to a change in its price. As indicated in the previous section, the arc price elasticity of demand is given by

$$E_P = \frac{\Delta Q_X}{\Delta P_X} \cdot \frac{P_{X_2} + P_{X_1}}{Q_{X_2} + Q_{X_1}}.$$

We also found that E_p for microwave ovens was equal to −1.8 between $P_X =$ $400 and $P_X =$ $500. This arc elasticity value means that over the interval between $P_X =$ $400 and $P_X =$ $500, a *1.0 percent increase* in P_X will result, on the average, in a *1.8 percent decrease* in quantity demanded.

As has been stated repeatedly, since the price of a firm's product is normally at least one of the variables in the demand function for its product over which the firm has some control, the price elasticity of demand is of far more than casual interest to the firm. Moreover, once the firm knows the price elasticity of demand for its product at some point (or over some price range), it also knows something about the behavior of its total revenue at that point (or over that price range). This fact is important because total revenue is one of the two factors (cost is the other) that determine a firm's total profit.

Since price and quantity demanded usually move in opposite directions, the sign of E_p is usually negative, as we found above. Therefore, we shall classify E_p according to its *absolute* value (or absolute size, disregarding the negative sign). We denote the absolute value of something by two vertical lines, | |. We say, then, that if $|E_p|$ is less than one, the quantity demanded is *inelastic* with respect to price. If $|E_p|$ is greater than one, the quantity demanded is *elastic* with respect to price. If $|E_p|$ is equal to one, the quantity demanded is *unitary elastic* with respect to price. These classifications seem reasonable if we reflect that when $|E_p|$ is greater than one, or elastic, it means that quantity demanded changes by a greater percentage than the percentage change in price. This occurrence means that quantity demanded is very responsive to a change in price; that is, it is elastic. On the other hand, if $|E_p|$ is less than one, it means that quantity demanded changes by a smaller percentage than the percentage change in price and therefore is relatively unresponsive or inelastic.

We use the same terminology in everyday life. If the waistband of a pair of slacks stretches (that is, if it is responsive to a pull), the waistband is said to be elastic. However, a cold iron rod is not very responsive if someone tries to stretch it. Thus, the rod is said to be inelastic.

In the case where $|E_p|$ is greater than one, we saw that quantity demanded would change by a large percentage relative to the percentage change in price. In other words, a change in price would result in a more than proportional change in quantity demanded. In this case we would expect that the firm might be inclined toward price decreases. However, *both cost and revenue* changes must be considered, as we shall see in the next two sections of the chapter.

Note that *quantity demanded usually falls when price is increased, regardless of whether demand is elastic or inelastic.* Accordingly, quantity demanded rises when price is decreased—for either elastic or inelastic demand. It is the relative, or *proportional*, changes in quantity demanded and price that are important in determining the elasticity of demand.

Two special cases occur when $E_p = 0$ and $E_p = -\infty$. If $E_p = 0$, then the price elasticity of demand is completely inelastic and a change in price will not affect quantity demanded. The demand curve in this case is a vertical line, as in Figure 2-9, panel (a). If $E_p = -\infty$, then the price elasticity of demand is infinitely elastic, which means that if a firm raises price above the going market price, it will lose *all* of its sales. In this case the demand curve is a horizontal line (see Figure 2-9, panel (b)). These cases (where demand is either totally inelastic or infinitely elastic) are rarely found in the real world. For example, there is a price at which most people could not even afford necessities, such as medical treatment. Still, we do associate the

FIGURE 2-9

Two Special Cases of Elasticity

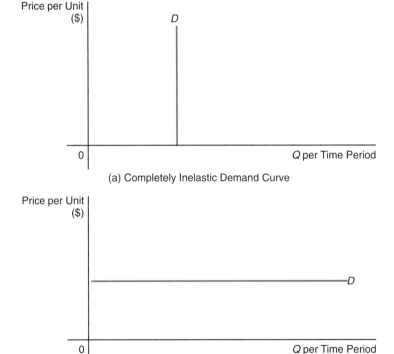

(a) Completely Inelastic Demand Curve

(b) Infinitely Elastic Demand Curve

A completely inelastic demand curve is depicted in panel (a). The quantity demanded will not change in response to a change in price. Panel (b) shows an infinitely elastic demand curve. In this case, a firm can sell as many units of its product as it wishes to at the going market price, but it will sell zero units at a higher price.

FIGURE 2-10

*A Unitary
Elastic Demand
Curve*

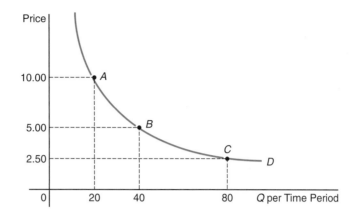

D is a unitary elastic ($|E_p| = 1$) demand curve. Unitary elastic demand curves have the property that total revenue ($P \times Q$) is the same for all prices.

horizontal demand curve with the perfectly competitive firm; and the demand for some products, such as table salt, over at least some price ranges is highly inelastic.

Of course, demand curves are not necessarily straight lines. For example, the demand curve shown in Figure 2-10 has the property that the elasticity of demand (in absolute value) is equal to 1.0 at all points on the curve. In this case, quantity demanded will change by an exactly offsetting proportion as a result of a price change, and total revenue will be the same at all prices and quantities on the demand curve. For example, at point A in Figure 2-10, total revenue is equal to $\$10 \times 20 = \$200$. At point B, total revenue is equal to $\$5 \times 40 = \$200$, and at point C, total revenue is equal to $\$2.50 \times 80 = \$200$. Few, if any, demand curves in the real world are unitary elastic at *all* prices. However, a curve such as that shown in Figure 2-10 could represent the quantity of money demanded for transactions purposes (such as paying bills and buying goods) at various prices. Many economists have argued that this relationship is unitary elastic with respect to changes in the general level of prices. Other types of *nonlinear* (curved) demand curves would also be possible.

Determinants of Price Elasticity of Demand

The same factors that determine the size of changes in quantity demanded in response to a price change also affect the price elasticity of demand. For example, the *greater the number of substitute goods* that are available, the higher the price elasticity of demand. If the price of one of the products increases while the prices of goods that are substitutes for it remain the same, we would expect consumers to switch some of their spending on the first product to purchases of the substitute goods. The greater the number of alternative goods available, the greater the opportunities for substituting spending on a product whose price has risen to purchases of a similar item whose price has remained the same.

Second, the greater the *proportion* of spending on an item to *consumers' total income,* the higher will be the price elasticity of demand. Consumers usually do not spend a large fraction of their incomes on table salt or lead pencils. Consequently, even a substantial percentage increase in the price of table salt or the price of lead pencils is unlikely to have a major effect on their budgets if they continue purchasing the same amounts of these products as before. Third, the price elasticity of demand at a given point in time will depend on *consumer expectations* regarding future price changes. If a grocery store has soda pop on sale for a week, consumers will likely purchase more of it during that week if they believe that the price will return to its original level at the end of the week than if they believe that the price cut is a new "permanently" low price.

Finally, the price elasticity of demand will be greater the longer the time period allowed consumers to adjust their spending habits. During longer time periods, consumers gain more information about the availability of alternative products, and additional substitute products are often developed. Purchases of smaller cars in response to gasoline price increases in the early 1970s are one example. In addition, consumers learned to develop new habits, such as car pooling or using mass transit, in response to an increase in gasoline prices.

Price Elasticity of Demand and Total Revenue

As we have already stated, the firm can know immediately whether its total revenue, or total sales dollars, will change in a positive or negative direction as a result of a proposed price change if it knows whether the price elasticity of demand for its product over the relevant range is inelastic, elastic, or unitary elastic. If demand is *inelastic* with respect to price, and price is lowered, total revenue will *decrease.* That is because quantity demanded will *not* increase *by a large enough proportion* to counteract the effect of a lower price received from each unit sold. The opposite effect occurs (for the same reason) when price is raised; that is, total revenue increases.

For example, the price elasticity of demand for basic household telephone service is probably inelastic. Unless the basic rate would increase drastically (such as a 100 percent increase), probably few people would have their phones removed. We might consider the frequent requests of Southwestern Bell for higher basic rates in Texas as evidence that Bell may believe that the demand for such service is inelastic. In contrast, there has been a tendency for interstate long-distance rates to fall by much more than local rates.[25] AT&T and other long-distance carriers seem interested in keeping rates on interstate long-distance phone calls relatively low, indicating that they may believe the demand for such service is significantly more elastic than that for basic local telephone service. (Note also that there are many substitutes for one carrier's long-distance service but none for that of a one-and-only local phone company.)

If demand is price *elastic* and price is lowered, total revenue will *increase*—an effect opposite to that obtained when demand is price inelastic. This result occurs because quantity demanded will increase by a sufficiently large percentage to more than make up for the lower price received on each unit sold. An example of this phenomenon is the special price reductions offered periodically by restaurants. Another example is the reduced prices of airline tickets when advance purchase requirements are met. Correspondingly, if demand is elastic and price is increased, total revenue will decrease. Finally, if demand is unitary elastic, a change in price will not affect total revenue, since price and quantity will change in equal proportions and therefore have exactly offsetting effects. These results are summarized in Table 2-2.

This information regarding price changes and total revenue can be very significant for the firm. For example, suppose that an ice-skating rink finds that quantity demanded by skaters is such that the rink is not being used close to its capacity level and that the (absolute value of the) price elasticity of demand is greater than one. In such cases the rink should strongly consider lowering its price, since a large portion of its costs (like interest on money borrowed to finance the rink purchase and electricity to cool the ice) won't

Table 2-2 *Summary of Relationship Between Price Elasticity of Demand and Total Revenue*

E_p	Classification	Effect of Price Change on Total Revenue
$|E_p| > 1$	Elastic	Increase in price lowers *TR*. Decrease in price raises *TR*.
$|E_p| < 1$	Inelastic	Increase in price raises *TR*. Decrease in price lowers *TR*.
$|E_p| = 1$	Unitary Elastic	Price change does not affect *TR*.

---

[25] See, for example, "All Those Long-Distance Discounts Are Sweet, But…," *Business Week* (September 19, 1994), p. 67, and U.S. Federal Communications Commission, "FCC to Ensure That All Consumers Benefit from Long Distance Competition," Report No. CC-925, July 9, 1999. The FCC report promises to look into flat charges and fees that long-distance carriers load onto the bills of low-volume users. Like flat fees for local basic service, these charges are characterized by inelastic demand, so increases in them enhance phone company revenues. The choice is between paying them and going without long-distance service.

change very much. A similar situation could occur for a movie-theater owner, which may help to explain the practice by theaters of offering matinee showings at bargain prices. A smart firm attempts to estimate the price elasticity of demand at different times of the day and for different movies. Movie theaters do, then, attempt to take advantage of such differences to some extent with special afternoon rates and different rates for different movies.

Even government policymakers have reason to be concerned about the price elasticity of demand. The U.S. government raised gasoline taxes by 4.3 cents a gallon (about 4.3 percent) in 1993, with the twin—but opposing—goals of increasing federal revenues (reducing the federal budget deficit) and reducing oil imports. An early estimate indicated that the demand for gasoline was inelastic—that the quantity demanded would fall by only 1.9 percent. As a result, the impact of the gasoline tax was likely to be greater on the federal budget than on the quantity of oil imports. Likewise, an increased tax on cigarettes was touted as a way to both raise funds for a federal health care plan and encourage people to stop smoking, which would lead to better health. Estimates of the price elasticity of demand for cigarettes ranged from –0.4 in the short run to –0.75 in the long run. Since these estimates were also in the inelastic range, they indicated that the effect of the higher taxes would likely be greater on government revenue than on quantity demanded.[26] In Sweden the government found out that its workers apparently became healthier when a new law was passed that cut back on sick-leave benefits. The new law specified that workers would receive only 75 percent, rather than 100 percent, of their pay for the first three days of illness. As a result, employee claims for sick-leave days fell by almost 20 percent.[27]

Price Elasticity of Demand, Average Revenue, and Marginal Revenue

Now that we know the relationships among E_p, price changes, and the effect on total revenue, we can discern the relationships among E_p, price changes, average revenue, and marginal revenue. Figure 2-7, showing the relationships among the latter three variables, is reproduced in Figure 2-11. In addition, the relationships among E_p and average revenue and marginal revenue are indicated. Where $|E_p| > 1$, marginal revenue is *positive*, since a decrease in price increases total revenue. Where $|E_p| = 1$, marginal revenue is *zero*, since

---

[26] "Why There Won't Be Too Much Pain at the Pumps," *Business Week* (August 23, 1993), p. 14; "Taxes Curb Smoking," *Wall Street Journal,* September 1, 1993, p. A1; and "Still Hooked on the Evil Weed," *Business Week* (July 5, 1999), p. 18.

[27] "Sick Pay Cuts Gives Swedes Healthier Lives," *San Antonio Express-News,* March 23, 1991, p. 4-A.

a decrease in price will not change total revenue. Finally, if $|E_p| < 1$, marginal revenue is *negative,* since a decrease in price will decrease total revenue.[28] As shown in Figure 2-11, with a linear demand curve, the price elasticity of demand will be equal to one in absolute value at the midpoint of the demand curve, the point where marginal revenue is equal to zero.

FIGURE 2-11

Relationships Among Total Revenue; Marginal Revenue; Average Revenue; and Price Elasticity of Demand

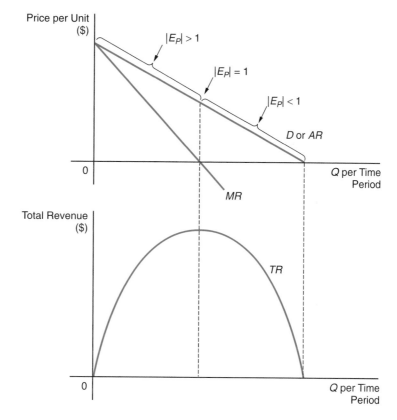

These graphs depict the relationships among total revenue (*TR*), marginal revenue (*MR*), average revenue (*AR*), and price elasticity of demand. When *MR* is positive, *TR* is rising and $|E_p|$ is greater than one. When *MR* = 0, *TR* is at a maximum and $|E_p| = 1$. When *MR* is negative, *TR* is falling and $|E_p|$ is less than one.

---

[28] We can also derive another relationship between E_p, marginal revenue, and price. If

$$TR = P \cdot Q,$$

$$MR = \frac{dTR}{dQ} = P + Q\frac{dP}{dQ}, \, or$$

$$MR = P\left(1 + \frac{Q}{P} \cdot \frac{dP}{dQ}\right).$$

(Footnote continues on p. 68)

Nevertheless, a firm should not base its pricing decisions solely on the manner in which price affects total revenue; its costs must also be considered. When the price elasticity of demand is *inelastic,* the decision rule is straightforward: *raise price.* In this case, total revenue will increase, and since quantity sold will decrease, total costs should at worst remain the same, resulting in an increase in total profit.

In the case of *elastic* demand, the situation is more complicated. A *decrease* in price will *increase* total revenue, but the resulting increase in sales will likely increase total costs to some extent. *If* the lower price causes output to increase sufficiently so that total revenue *increases by a greater amount than total cost,* then the price cut will result in greater total profit. But if a price cut results in a greater increase in total cost than in total revenue, total profit will fall. A similar analysis would hold for a price *increase,* except in this case the effect on total profit would depend on whether the *decrease* in total revenue were greater or less than the *decrease* in total cost. We shall reserve further discussion of the costs of the firm, however, for a later chapter.

NUMERICAL EXAMPLE

Elasticity and the Straight-Line Demand Curve

Where is the range of elastic demand on the demand curve having the equation $Q_d = 8,000 - 50P$?

Answer

Demand is elastic from $Q_d = 0$ up to the midpoint quantity (where $MR = 0$) on the straight-line demand curve. Thus, it will be elastic in the range $Q_d = 0$ up to $Q_d = 4,000$. From the equation, we can determine that $50P = 8,000 - Q_d$, and $P = 160 - .02Q_d$. Thus the elastic range can be stated in terms of price as that from $P = 160$ to $P = 80$. Of course, right at the midpoint, where $P = 80$ and $Q_d = 4,000$, there will be unitary elasticity.

(Footnote continued from previous page)

However, $\dfrac{Q}{P} \cdot \dfrac{dP}{dQ}$ is equal to $(1/E_p)$, so $MR = P(1 + 1/E_p)$.

As noted in a previous section of this chapter, if the demand curve is a horizontal line, price is equal to marginal revenue. We can now prove this statement with the use of the relationship developed above. Since we know that $E_p = -\infty$ if the demand curve is horizontal, then in this case

$$MR = P(1 + 1/-\infty) = P(1 + 0) = P.$$

If $-\infty < E_p < 0$,

$$MR = P[1 + \text{some negative number}],$$

so $MR < P$, as already discussed in this chapter.

Finally, if $E_p = 0$,

$$MR = P(1 + 1/0) = \infty.$$

Firms are now becoming far more concerned about pricing policies than they have been in the past. At the retail level this has become readily apparent as three major new pricing approaches have become popular. These are *yield management, price matching,* and *everyday low pricing.* The first strategy, *yield management,* uses computer software to track sales volume and market conditions so that the firm can raise prices when demand increases and lower them when it slacks off or quickly respond in other ways such as product adjustments when the market changes. The airlines and large hotel chains have used this strategy extensively. Basically, successful yield management depends on ascertaining how consumer demand differs over time as well as among consumers.

Price matching also involves a careful analysis of consumer behavior. Stores employing it have found that few consumers actually take advantage of the offer to match competitors' prices. In addition, a number of economists have analyzed price matching, and most conclude that it results in generally higher, rather than lower, prices. This may seem strange, but remember, the consumer group that does not take advantage of price matching constitutes a segment of the market willing to pay higher prices—so they do.[29] As we will see in a later chapter, both yield management and price matching are special cases of market segmentation—basically, dividing up markets into segments with different elasticities of demand.

The third approach, *everyday low pricing,* has both a demand and a cost element. Both Sears and its former rival Montgomery Ward (Wards) attempted in the past to move toward everyday low pricing. Some of the savings involved in this strategy come from reductions in advertising expenditures for publicizing special sales events. However, neither Sears nor Wards eliminated sales and frequent newspaper insert ads. The strategy certainly did not work for Wards, which went out of business and liquidated all its assets in 2001. In general merchandise stores, Wal-Mart has become the leader in everyday low pricing. It has worked for Wal-Mart because the company has also been extremely efficient in controlling costs. It introduced checkout scanners years before its competitors installed them, and it put together a highly efficient distribution system that kept both shipping and inventory costs down. Combining these cost savings with a focus on customer satisfaction, Wal-Mart was able to generate 35 percent more sales revenue per square foot of floor space than was its competition.[30]

---

[29] Aaron S. Edlin and Eric R. Emch, "The Welfare Losses from Price Matching Policies," *Journal of Industrial Economics* 47, No. 2 (June 1999): 145–167.

[30] Two interesting books that analyze Wal-Mart's success are Sandra Stringer Vance and Roy V. Scott (Contributor), *Wal-Mart: A History of Sam Walton's Retail Phenomenon* (New York: Twayne Publishers, 1997) and Sam Walton and John Huey (Contributor), *Sam Walton: Made in America* (New York: Bantam Books, 1995). Not everyone is pleased with Wal-Mart's effects on U.S. retailing. For example, see Bob Ortega, *In Sam We Trust: The Untold Story of Sam Walton and How Wal-Mart Is Devouring America* (New York: Times Books, 1998).

Building a Business on E_P: The Saga of Southwest Airlines

Look out Yankees, a Texas airline has invaded Hartford! Actually, the only folks who need be concerned are Southwest's competitors. For more than 30 years, Southwest has expanded its markets, providing low-cost fares and only one class of service to consumers all across the country. It is now the nation's fourth largest carrier.

Southwest entered the market when airlines were not very profitable but succeeded by following some very simple strategies. Herb Kelleher, the (now retired) CEO of Southwest Airlines, tells the story more or less this way. Long about 1972, the founders of Southwest Airlines believed something that industry leaders, as well as the CAB (the Civil Aeronautics Board, which then was in charge of regulating U.S. air transportation), scoffed at. It had to do with how low- and middle-income consumers felt about air travel. According to Kelleher, the CAB and the major airlines' managers believed that air travel was largely reserved for people who had the ability to pay high fares—the rich and those flying on business budgets—while the average American would choose car travel over air travel for most needs. Ordinary people, they argued, viewed air travel as a luxury good and would not increase their purchases of it very much if prices were reduced any feasible amount from those then prevailing. Kelleher and his associates believed the opposite—that lower fares would result in large increases in the quantity of air travel purchased by the general public. As Kelleher has put it, "We were certain that demand was much more elastic than any of them believed it to be." In fact, at the time of the elasticity debate, the CAB regulated all interstate fares in the United States, and it did not permit price competition. Kelleher says that the only way his group could test their proposition was to establish an *intrastate* airline in a market area large enough to make bargain air travel attractive to the consumer. That, he says, had to

be either California or Texas. They chose Texas. Southwest began by flying routes between the three large Texas cities, Dallas, Houston, and San Antonio. They offered "no frills" service (food never got fancier than peanuts and a drink), and there was only one class of seating, with no reserved seats. Ticket counters issued simple cash register receipts along with a plastic, reusable boarding pass. In short, service was unpretentious, but the airline got the passengers to their destinations efficiently and *very* cheaply.

Consumer response to Southwest's low fares was tremendous. For a brief period, there was intense competition from Braniff (then a very large airline) on the intrastate routes, but Southwest persevered and kept to its game plan. The price competition that was begun by Southwest and other upstarts in the industry led eventually to a new era in air transportation, with more discount fares, huge increases in traffic, and the eventual phaseout of the CAB. Not only did Southwest change the way firms perceived passenger demand, but it also taught the industry a lot about operating at low costs through innovations in scheduling, reservations, ticketing, and employee and customer relations. Following the Southwest model, but with larger, more luxurious aircraft, a new airline, JetBlue, was launched in February 2000. By mid-2002, it had 27 Airbus A320 aircraft and served 19 cities. JetBlue also had 123 new A320s on order from Airbus and was the only U.S. airline other than Southwest to post a profit in 2001.

References: For additional material on Southwest, see "Southwest Airlines Turns More Agressive," *Wall Street Journal*, July 15, 2002, p. B6, and "Airline Adds Flights from New England," *San Antonio Express-News*, July 14, 1999, p. 8E. The quotation about elasticity is from a speech Mr. Kelleher gave to business and economics students and faculty at the University of Texas at San Antonio. For information on JetBlue, see www.jetblue.com/learnmore.

Income Elasticity of Demand

Income elasticity of demand is measured by the ratio of the percentage change in quantity taken of a product to the percentage change in income.

Income elasticity of demand measures the relative responsiveness of the quantity purchased of a product to changes in income. The arc formula for income elasticity of demand of Q_X is

$$E_I = \frac{\Delta Q_X}{\left(\frac{Q_{X2}+Q_{X1}}{2}\right)} \div \frac{\Delta I}{\left(\frac{I_2+I_1}{2}\right)} = \frac{\Delta Q_X}{\Delta I} \cdot \frac{I_2+I_1}{Q_{X2}+Q_{X1}}$$

$$= \frac{Q_{X2}-Q_{X1}}{I_2-I_1} \cdot \frac{I_2+I_1}{Q_{X2}+Q_{X1}}.$$

As stated earlier, in our microwave oven example, when $P_X = \$400$, $P_Y = \$500$, $H = 40,000,000$, $I = \$20,000$, and $A = \$50,000$, then Q_X is equal to 30,000. When all of the above independent variables except income (I) remain constant, and I increases to $\$24,000$, then Q_X increases to 35,200. Thus, E_I between $I = \$20,000$ and $I = \$24,000$ is given by[31]

$$E_I = \frac{5,200}{4,000} \cdot \frac{44,000}{65,200} = 0.88.$$

Since the above income elasticity of demand is greater than zero, we can say that Brand X microwave ovens are *normal goods*. In our previous discussion of the determinants of demand, normal goods are defined as products for which the quantity demanded increases as income increases (and vice versa). If $E_I > 1$, then the product is a normal good that is also a *superior good*. Such a value for E_I means that the quantity demanded of superior goods increases more than proportionally to the percentage increase in income. Such goods are also often called *cyclical normal goods*, since the quantity purchased of them varies proportionally more than income does over the business cycle. If the income elasticity of demand is negative, it means that the quantity demanded of a good *decreases* as income *increases*. We call these products *inferior* goods.

---

[31] The point formula for income elasticity of demand is

$$E_I = \frac{\partial Q_X}{\partial I} \cdot \frac{I}{Q_X}.$$

In our microwave oven example, the point income elasticity of demand where $P_X = \$400$, $P_Y = \$500$, $H = 40,000,000$, $I = \$20,000$, $A = \$50,000$, and $Q_X = 30,000$ is given by

$$E_I = 1.3 \times \frac{20,000}{30,000} = 0.87.$$

Knowing the approximate income elasticity of demand for its product over the relevant region, a firm can estimate how a change in income will affect the quantity demanded of that good or service and can plan its production accordingly. This information is crucial to firms such as those in the automobile or appliance industries, where the demand for their products is very much affected by changes in the level of income. For example, consider the drastic production cutbacks in the automobile industry during 1991 and the early 1980s, when national income in *real terms* (that is, adjusted for price increases) was falling. The recessions also similarly affected the home appliance and furniture industries.[32] The United States also fell into recession in 2001, even prior to the terrorist attacks of September 11. Consumer spending, except on air travel and related tourism, remained quite robust, partly because Baby Boomers were the fastest-growing segment of American households, enjoying both accumulated wealth and high incomes.[33]

The income elasticity of demand has also been a useful concept in describing one of the problems of firms in the agriculture industry in the United States during at least part of the twentieth century. The problem arises because the income elasticity of demand for agricultural products is less than one—a fact that means the quantity demanded of agricultural products does not increase by as great a percentage as the percentage increase in income.

Cross Price Elasticity of Demand

> **Cross price elasticity of demand** is measured by the ratio of the percentage change in quantity demanded of a product to the percentage change in price of a related product.

The **cross price elasticity of demand** for Product X with respect to the price of Product Y is a measure of the relative responsiveness of quantity demanded of Product X to changes in P_Y. The arc cross price elasticity of demand formula is

$$E_{XY} = \frac{\dfrac{\Delta Q_X}{Q_{X2} + Q_{X1}}}{\dfrac{\Delta P_Y}{P_{Y2} + P_{Y1}}} = \frac{\Delta Q_X}{\Delta P_Y} \cdot \frac{P_{Y2} + P_{Y1}}{Q_{X2} + Q_{X1}}$$

$$= \frac{Q_{X2} - Q_{X1}}{P_{Y2} - P_{Y1}} \cdot \frac{P_{Y2} + P_{Y1}}{Q_{X2} + Q_{X1}}$$

---

[32] See, for example, "Tough Economic Times Are Knocking Stuffing Out of Many Furniture Stores," *Wall Street Journal,* January 20, 1992, pp. B1, B2; "Big Three U.S. Car Output to Sink to a 33-year Low," *Wall Street Journal,* April 11, 1991, p. A2; and "Recession Hits Major-Appliance Makers, Causing Layoffs; Recovery Isn't in Sight," *Wall Street Journal,* June 23, 1980, p. 12. The boom in single-family housing in 1986 also favorably affected the appliance industry. See "Consumers May Be Ready to Put on Their Shopping Shoes," *Business Week* (May 19, 1986), p. 34.

[33] "Bless the Baby Boomers," *Business Week* (June 10, 2002), p. 30.

For our microwave oven demand function, when P_X = $400, P_Y = $500, H = 40,000,000, I = $20,000, and A = $50,000, then Q_X is equal to 30,000. If P_Y decreases to $400, then Q_X decreases to 27,500 units. Therefore, between P_Y = $500 and P_Y = $400,[34]

$$E_{XY} = \frac{-2,500}{-100} \cdot \frac{900}{57,500} = 0.39.$$

If, as in the preceding situation, the cross price elasticity of demand is positive, we say that the two goods are *substitute goods*. A positive value for E_{XY} means that an increase in P_Y will result in an increase in Q_X (and vice versa), which indicates that an increase in P_Y causes some customers to purchase Brand X instead of Brand Y (and vice versa). If E_{XY} were negative, it would indicate that an increase in the price of Good Y would decrease the quantity purchased of Good X. In this case, Good X and Good Y are said to be *complementary goods*. As stated previously in our discussion of the determinants of demand, complementary goods are, generally speaking, goods such that having more of one (at least to a point) increases the enjoyment a consumer obtains from the second. Examples of complementary goods are CDs and CD players, hamburger and hamburger buns, and gasoline and automobiles. If E_{XY} = 0, we say that the goods are *not* related.

Cross price elasticity information can be useful to the firm in several ways. If the firm produces two related goods or services, it is beneficial for it to be able to estimate how a change in the price of one will affect the quantity demanded of the other. For example, Procter & Gamble would like to know the effect of a price decrease for Crest toothpaste on the quantity demanded of the other brands of toothpaste that the company sells. A second situation in which cross price elasticity information is helpful occurs when another firm selling a related product has changed, or is expected to change, the price of that good or service. Thus, Ford would like to know the impact of General Motors' rebates on the quantity sold of Ford vehicles. In the market for used cars, low prices on used rental cars sold by the automakers affected the

---

[34] The formula for point cross price elasticity of demand is

$$E_{XY} = \left(\frac{\partial Q_X}{\partial P_Y} \right) \left(\frac{P_Y}{Q_X} \right)$$

At the point where P_X = $400, P_Y = $500, H = 40,000,000, I = $20,000, A = $50,000, and Q_X = 30,000,

$$E_{XY} = 25 \left(\frac{500}{30,000} \right) = 0.42.$$

MANAGERIAL PERSPECTIVE

Some Dimensions of the Demand for Automobiles

Automobiles are a fixture of the American way of life, and it seems Americans are always interested in the attributes and prices of new cars. Economic studies of their demand for automobiles have produced some interesting results. First, there is a marked difference between demand for new cars in the aggregate and demand for a given model of car. Second, consumers can always purchase a used car instead of a new one, so there is a substitute relationship not only between different makes of new cars but also between new and used.

The market demand for new automobiles has been estimated in a number of well-known studies. At different points in time and with different sets of data, these seem always to show the same result—that the price elasticity of demand for new cars is relatively low, usually around –1.1 to about –1.4. What this means is that when automobile manufacturers use rebates (a form of price cut) to help dealers entice customers to buy new cars, they realize very little, if any, increased revenue from those sales. However, the law of demand still works, so they do increase quantity sold and, therefore, reduce inventories.

While the elasticity of the aggregate demand for new cars is low, that for a specific model is much higher. This results from the fact that all cars are substitutes for one

another, and some models of certain cars are very close substitutes for specific models of others. For example, a study published in 1983 found that the own price elasticity for a Chevrolet Impala was –14.79 and that for a Ford Mustang was –8.42. The same study also found a cross elasticity of +19.30 for a Chevrolet Impala with respect to the price of a Pontiac Catalina, a close "cousin" of the Impala. Another study published in 1995 reported own price elasticities in the range of –5 to –6.7 for low- to medium-priced cars and –3 to –4 for high-priced cars. Thus, manufacturers (and dealers) can get buyers to switch purchases from one make of car to another by lowering price. Of course, other variables, such as style changes, safety features, or government fuel economy standards, can also cause switching from one make of car to another or even from cars to light trucks or sport-utility vehicles.

References: Paul E. Godek, "The Regulation of Fuel Economy and the Demand for Light Trucks," *The Journal of Law and Economics* 40, No. 2 (October 1997): 495–507; Steven Berry, James Levinsohn, and Ariel Pakes, "Automobile Prices in Market Equilibrium," *Econometrica* 63, no. 4 (July 1995): 841–890; and F. Owen Irvine, Jr., "Demand Equations for Individual New Car Models Estimated Using Transaction Prices with Implications for Regulatory Issues," *Southern Economic Journal* 49 (January 1983): 764–782.

quantity demanded of other used cars.[35] In the mid-1990s, cereal makers lowered the prices on many of their brands to allegedly counter a threefold increase in the demand for bagels as a breakfast food.[36]

Finally, a third situation in which cross price elasticity information could be of critical importance is if the firm were defending itself in an antitrust

---

[35] Neal Templin, "Sales of Used Rental Cars by Big Three Depress Other Second-Hand Auto Prices," *Wall Street Journal,* January 6, 1992, pp. B1, B2.

[36] "Cereal Makers Fight Bagels with Price Cuts," *Wall Street Journal,* June 20, 1996, pp. B1, B8.

case by demonstrating (1) that its product has a positive cross price elasticity relationship with other products, therefore (2) that there are recognized substitutes for the product, and (3) that it accordingly does *not* have a monopoly. This type of approach was quite helpful to du Pont in defending itself in a famous antitrust case.[37] Du Pont had nearly 75 percent of the market for cellophane wrapping materials. However, the company successfully argued that the relevant market was the entire market for flexible packaging materials, including waxed paper and aluminum foil; it supported its position by showing that there were positive cross price elasticities between cellophane and these products and that therefore the products were substitutes. When the total market for flexible packaging materials was considered, du Pont had a much smaller market share.

Other Elasticity of Demand Concepts

As we stated when the concept of elasticity (of demand) was introduced, we can use an elasticity coefficient to indicate the relative responsiveness of the quantity demanded of a product to a change in any variable that may affect it. In our microwave oven example, we could also talk of the advertising elasticity of demand and the elasticity with respect to two-income households. For some products, population growth and, hence, the population elasticity of demand might be significant. The wise firm will try to discover the values of those elasticities that it believes are important factors affecting its revenue.

Much of the information needed for demand studies can be obtained from Bureau of the Census data on population, income, and already existing businesses. Such reports can frequently be found in local libraries. Local planning authorities and trade associations are other important sources of information. In addition, consulting firms in the area of market research will be happy to supply and/or analyze data, for a fee. A more thorough discussion of demand estimation and forecasting techniques will appear in Chapters 3 and 4.

SUMMARY

Demand, Elasticity, Revenue, and the Firm

In this chapter we have emphasized one of the most critical factors for the success of a firm: *the demand for its product*. We have defined the *demand function* as the mathematical relationship that indicates how the quantity

---

[37] See *United States v. E. I. du Pont de Nemours and Co.*, 351 U.S. 377, 100 L. Ed. 1264, 76 S. Ct. 994 (1956).

demanded of a firm's product over some time period is affected by variables such as the price of the good (or service), prices of other goods, income of consumers, and advertising expenditures. The *demand curve* gives the relationship between the quantity demanded of a good and its price. The demand curve is obtained from the demand function by holding all variables (except price and quantity demanded) constant at some level. Those variables held constant when the demand curve is obtained are called *determinants of demand*. We noted that a change in a good's own price will cause a movement along its demand curve but that a change in one of the determinants of demand (income, prices of related goods, and tastes, for example), will shift the entire curve.

We also related the demand curve to the total revenue, average revenue, and marginal revenue functions. *Total revenue* relates total sales dollars received by the firm to quantity sold. Total revenue is equal to price times quantity purchased and can be derived from the equation for the demand curve. *Average revenue* is obtained by dividing total revenue by quantity sold and is equal to price. The average revenue curve, therefore, is the demand curve. *Marginal revenue* is the rate of change of total revenue with respect to quantity sold and is, consequently, the slope of the total revenue function. We found that for a straight-line, downward-sloping demand curve, marginal revenue is also a straight line with the same vertical axis intercept as the demand curve and *twice* the negative slope. *Arc marginal revenue* is a measure of marginal revenue with discrete or tabular data and is the average rate of change of *total revenue* with respect to a particular change in quantity sold, or

$$\text{Arc } MR = \frac{\Delta TR}{\Delta Q}.$$

We have emphasized that the profit-maximizing firm is concerned about the responsiveness of the quantity demanded of its product to changes in other variables—such as the price of the good or service, the prices of related goods, and the income of consumers. The measure of responsiveness that we have utilized here is *elasticity* of demand, which is given by

$$\frac{\text{percent change in quantity demanded}}{\text{percent change in a specific related variable}}$$

In this chapter, we discussed three types of elasticity of demand—*price, income,* and *cross price.* We classified price elasticity of demand according to whether it was *elastic, inelastic,* or *unitary elastic;* and in each case we related price changes to total revenue and marginal revenue. Given the income elasticity of demand, we classified a product as being either a *normal* (including superior) *good* or an *inferior good.* Using the cross price elasticity of demand between one product and another product, we can classify the two goods as *substitutes* or *complements.* We also demonstrated in each case the various ways in which such information can be useful to the manager.

Before a firm commits much time and money to a given line of product or type of service, it should gather enough information to substantiate its belief that a sufficient market exists for the item it wants to sell. Once it has established that the market does exist for its product and therefore has gone into business, the wise firm will use its knowledge of the concepts we have discussed in this chapter to gather and analyze the information that will enable it to predict and increase its revenue. Thereby it will be well on its way toward maximizing profit.

In the next two chapters, we will summarize some techniques of demand estimation and forecasting. Then, in the following chapters we consider production and the cost of production—another major factor determining the degree of success or failure of an enterprise.

QUESTIONS

1. Define total revenue, marginal revenue, and average revenue. Why is knowledge of each of these elements important for the firm?

2. Define price elasticity of demand. How is E_p related to total revenue for a firm?

3. Explain what is meant by the *determinants of demand.*

4. Discuss two situations in which knowledge of the income elasticity of demand is helpful.

5. What factors do you think affect the price elasticity of demand?

6. Which demand curve do you think would generally be less price elastic—that for a firm's product or that for an industry's product? Why?

7. What is the relationship between goods that are substitutes? between goods that are complements? How is the classification of goods in this manner related to the cross price elasticity of demand?

8. What is the value of marginal revenue when total revenue is maximized?

9. Without using calculus, explain why the marginal revenue curve for a downward-sloping, linear demand curve is a straight line that falls twice as fast as does the demand curve.

PROBLEMS

1. The table that follows gives price and corresponding quantity demanded data for a firm.

   a. Complete the table by finding total revenue and arc marginal revenue.

b. Plot the demand curve, the total revenue curve, and the arc marginal revenue curve. Note that the *arc marginal revenue between two levels of output should be plotted midway between the two levels.*

c. Find the price elasticity of demand between $P = \$35$ and $P = \$30$ and between $P = \$15$ and $P = \$10$. In which price range is it more elastic?

P	Q	TR	ARC MR
$40	0		
35	5		____
30	10		____
25	15		____
20	20		____
15	25		____
10	30		____
5	35		____
0	40		____

2. Barker Cement Company is considering lowering the price on an 80-pound bag of cement from $3 to $2. Presently, Barker sells 10,000 bags of cement per week, and its market analysts believe the price elasticity of demand to be –2 over this price range.

a. If Barker Cement Company lowers the price, will its total revenue increase, decrease, or remain unchanged? Why?

b. What will be the new level of quantity demanded? of total revenue?

3. a. Complete the following table by finding total revenue and price.

P	Q	TR	ARC MR
120	0	0	
			105
	10		
			75
	20		
			45
	30		
			15
	40		
			–15
	50		

   b. How would marginal revenue and price be related if price were constant? How are they related when price must decrease for quantity demanded to increase?

4. Jennie's Healthfoods now sells 2,000 lbs. of passion fruit per week at a price of $1.40 per lb. An economist has reported to management that the arc elasticity of demand for the fruit over the price range $1.40 to $1.20 per lb. is –2.0. Given that Jennie lowers her passion fruit price to $1.20 per lb., determine the following:

   a. How many pounds of passion fruit will she sell per week?

   b. How much will her total revenue (*TR*) from passion fruit sales change?

5. Zeerok Shoe Company has hired a consultant to estimate the elasticity of demand for its most awesome basketball shoe. At present, Zeerok is charging $90 for a pair of the shoes. The consultant estimates that the arc price elasticity of demand for them is –1.40 for a price cut of $10.

   Currently, Zeerok is selling 20,000 pairs of the shoes per week at its $90 price. If the consultant is correct and the company cuts its price from $90 to $80 per pair,

   a. What will be the new sales quantity per week of Zeerok's awesome shoe?

   b. Calculate the change in Zeerok's total revenue from sales of the shoe that follows from the change in part a.

6. International Video Machines, Inc., is a manufacturer of a commercial video-recording device. The firm is considering lowering the price of its product from $800 to $600. The company's market analysts have estimated the price elasticity of demand to be –2 over this price range. Presently, this firm sells 1,000 video recorders per month.

   a. What will be the new quantity sold if the price is lowered to $600?

   b. What will be the new level of total revenue in part a?

   c. What additional information does International Video Machines, Inc., need to know before it can determine whether or not a price decrease will increase the firm's profit?

   d. Suppose that after International Video Machines lowers its price, its competitor, Videoview, lowers the price of its machine from $900 to $800. The cross price elasticity of demand between the quantity sold of International Video Machines' video recorders and the price of Videoview's machine is 0.5. What will be the effect of Videoview's price decrease on the quantity sold by International Video Machines? (Use the quantity you found in part a as Q_1. Round your answer to the nearest whole number.)

7. A manufacturer of stuffed animals, Texas Teddy Bear, Inc., is trying to determine the price of its stuffed animals (all sell at the same price) during the upcoming Christmas season. In the past, the price of its stuffed animals has been $10, but the firm is getting worried because of the popularity of space toys. The firm has produced some new stuffed animals in an effort to increase its share in the toy market, but it is also considering a price decrease to $8. Texas Teddy Bear's market research department has estimated the price elasticity of demand for the

firm's stuffed animals to be –1.5. The estimated quantity that would be sold this Christmas season (October–December) at a price of $10 is 40,000.

a. How many stuffed animals would be sold at a price of $8 if E_p were –1.5?

b. What would be the effect on the firm's total revenue if the price were lowered to $8?

8. Dirt Cheap Videos, Inc., estimates its price elasticity of demand for used movies to be –4. Currently, DCVI sells 1,000 videos per week at a price of $5 each. If DCVI lowers its price to $4,

a. What will happen to total revenue? How do you know?

b. What will be the new quantity sold?

9. Brand X auto manufacturer has just lowered the price of its new car by $2,000 (from $12,000 to $10,000), and Brand Y is concerned about the effect this action will have on the quantity demanded of its cars. At the old price, Brand Y sold 10,000 cars per month. If the cross elasticity of demand of Y's cars relative to X's prices is 1.5, what will be Y's new quantity sold?

10. Charles Sr., an East Coast fast-food chain, has been considering a price cut in its 1/4 lb. hamburger, the Astroburger. Currently, Astroburgers sell for $1.89, and Charles is selling 220,000 of the burgers per week. Charles's research department has suggested reducing the price of the Astroburger to $1.65 and estimates that the arc elasticity of demand for the product is –1.80 over the range of the proposed price change.

a. If the research department is correct, what will be the weekly quantity sold of the Astroburgers after the price cut occurs?

b. What will be Charles's new total revenue from Astroburger sales?

Charles's major competitor, Mindy's, sells the Superburger, which is a close substitute for the Astroburger. Mindy's Superburger sells for $1.79, and, before Charles's price cut, 160,000 were sold per week. If the arc cross price elasticity of demand between the Superburger and the Astroburger is +2.20 over the range of the Charles price change:

c. Calculate the change in the quantity sold of Mindy's Superburger that occurs when Charles cuts the price of the Astroburger.

d. Calculate the dollar amount of change in Mindy's total revenue following the price cut by Charles.

11. The Hotel Madrileña, a small Spanish hotel, is considering lowering its room rates to increase occupancy during the low season. At the present time, the price of its rooms in U.S. currency is $100 per night, and it rents an average of 25 rooms each night.

a. Find the new quantity of rooms rented per night if the Hotel Madrileña lowers its price to $80 and its price elasticity of demand is –1.5.

b. *After* the Hotel Madrileña lowers its price, a little pensión across the street lowers its room rate from $35 to $30 per night. Find the new quantity of rooms rented per night for the Hotel Madrileña after the pensión lowers its price if the cross price elasticity between the price of the pensión's rooms and the quantity demanded of the Madrileña's rooms is 1.0. (*Hint:* Use the number you found in part (a) as Q_1 in this problem.)

c. What will be the final effect of the price decreases in parts (a) and (b) on Hotel Madrileña's total revenue?

12. A firm has estimated the following demand function for its product:

$$Q = 2{,}000 - 50P + 40P_Y + 0.01I$$

a. P_Y is the price of a related good, and I is household income. If these are, respectively, $P_Y = \$30$ and $I = 40{,}000$, what is the Q equation for the firm's demand *curve?*

b. Given the information above, what is the firm's average revenue or price equation for the demand curve? In this form, is the demand or AR curve a straight line? Explain.

c. What is the firm's total revenue equation?

d. What is the firm's marginal revenue equation? (*Note: Given the discussion of marginal revenue in the chapter, you do not need calculus to answer this question.*) *Hint:* How is the slope of the *MR* curve related to that of the price or *AR* curve when the latter is a straight line?

e. At what quantity sold will *MR* equal zero?

f. What will be the maximum total revenue the firm can obtain? At what combination of price and quantity will this occur? Explain.

13. Answer (c) and (d) from problem 12 for the following two straight-line demand curves.

a. $Q = 2{,}400 - 10P$

b. $Q = 1{,}800 - 5P$

The following problems require calculus:

C1. If $P = 120 - 1.5Q$ is the equation for the demand curve, find the corresponding total revenue function, marginal revenue function, and average revenue function.

C2. The statistics department of an appliance manufacturer has estimated that the demand function (number purchased annually) for their (Brand X) automatic washer is as follows:

$$Q_X = 197{,}000 - 100P_X + 50P_Y + 0.025I + 0.02A + 10{,}000P_L,$$

where

Q_X = quantity purchased,

P_X = the price of the company's washer,

P_Y = the price of a major competitor's washer,

I = the average household income,

A = the annual dollars spent on advertising, and

P_L = cost of doing one load of wash in a self-service laundry.

a. If $P_Y = \$300$, $I = \$40,000$, $A = \$200,000$, and $P_L = \$.30$, find the price elasticity of demand between $P_X = \$350$ and $P_X = \$400$. (When $P_X = \$400$, with the values of the other variables as given above, then $Q_X = 180,000$.)

b. Is E_pX elastic, inelastic, or unitary elastic? Why? If the price is cut, does total revenue increase, decrease, or not change?

c. Find the income elasticity of demand for Q_X, given $P_X = \$400$. The other variables are as given in part (a). Interpret your answer—that is, what does it say, if anything, about the demand for Brand X washers?

C3. Alpha Company has estimated that the demand curve for its product is represented by the equation $Q = 2,840 - 20P$, where Q is the quantity sold per week and P is the price per unit.

a. Based on the estimated demand curve, write the equations for Alpha's

(i) Average revenue,

(ii) Total revenue, and

(iii) Marginal revenue.

b. What will be the maximum total revenue per week that Alpha can obtain from sales of its product? (Give the exact dollar amount and explain how you determine it.)

c. Calculate the point price elasticity of demand for Alpha's product when $Q = 1,600$. Is demand elastic or inelastic at this quantity? How do you know?

d. Calculate the *arc* price elasticity of demand for Alpha's product between $Q = 1,000$ and $Q = 1,100$. Interpret your result and relate it to what will happen to total revenue if Alpha is initially at $Q = 1,000$ and decides to cut price to increase its sales from 1,000 to 1,100 units.

C4. A mathematical demand function for new Toyotas sold per year for a dealer is as follows:

$$Q_T = 200 - 0.01P_T + 0.005P_M - 10P_G + 0.01I + 0.003A,$$

where

Q_T = quantity purchased,

P_T = the average price of Toyotas,

P_M = the average price of Mazdas,

P_G = the price of gasoline,

I = per capita income, and

A = dollars spent annually on advertising.

a. Find the point price elasticity of demand for the Toyotas if $P_T = \$25,000$, $P_M = \$20,000$, $P_G = \$1.00$, $I = \$15,000$, and $A = \$10,000$.

b. Is the price elasticity of demand elastic, unitary elastic, or inelastic? Why?

c. Find the arc cross elasticity of demand for Toyotas and Mazdas between $P_M =$ $20,000 and $P_M =$ $22,000. (All other figures except P_T remain the same as in part (a).)

d. Are Toyotas and Mazdas substitutes or complements? Why?

C5. Paradise Lake, Inc., is a developer of mobile-home lots. Through statistical research, Paradise Lake has estimated the annual demand function for its lots to be as follows:

$$Q_L = 3{,}536 - 0.5P_L + 0.2P_C + 0.008I + 0.0001A,$$

where

Q_L = the number of Paradise Lake's lots purchased per year,

P_L = the price of a Paradise Lake lot,

P_C = the price of a competing land company's lots,

I = average annual household income, and

A = the annual amount spent by Paradise Lake on advertising.

a. Find the income elasticity of demand for Paradise Lake's lots where $P_L =$ $10,000, $P_C =$ $8,000, $I =$ $45,000, and $A =$ $4,000.

b. Are these lots a normal good or an inferior good? Why?

c. What does your answer in part a tell Paradise Lake about the demand for its lots?

d. Find the price elasticity of demand for Paradise Lake's properties at the same point as in part (a).

e. Is the price elasticity of demand for Paradise Lake's properties elastic, inelastic, or unitary elastic? How do you know?

C6. Smooth Sailing, Inc., has estimated the demand function for its sailboats (quantity purchased annually) as follows:

$$Q_S = 89{,}830 - 40P_S + 20P_X + 15P_Y + 2I + 0.001A + 10W,$$

where

Q_S = quantity purchased,

P_S = the price of Smooth Sailing sailboats,

P_X = the price of Company X's sailboat,

P_Y = the price of Company Y's motorboat,

I = per capita income in dollars,

A = dollars spent on advertising, and

W = number of favorable days of weather in the southern region of the United States.

a. Suppose that P_S = $9,000, P_X = $9,500, P_Y = $10,000, I = $15,000, A = $170,000, and W = 160. Find the price elasticity of demand at that point.

b. Is E_P elastic, inelastic, or unitary elastic in part (a)? Why?

c. What information does your answer in part (a) give Smooth Sailing that would be useful if the company were considering changing its price?

d. Find the cross price elasticity of demand for Smooth Sailing sailboats relative to Brand X sailboats between P_X = $9,500 and P_X = $10,000. Are the two boats substitutes or complements?

e. Find the income elasticity of demand for Smooth Sailing sailboats at the point given in part (a). Are the boats a normal good or an inferior good? Why?

C7. A firm's demand function for product X has the following equation:

$$Q_X = 1,420 - 20P_X - 10P_Y + 0.02I + 0.04A,$$

where

$$Q_X = \text{the number of units of } X \text{ sold per week,}$$

$$P_X = \text{the price charged per unit of } X,$$

$$P_Y = \text{the price charged for a related good, } Y,$$

$$I = \text{per capita income in the market area,}$$

$$A = \text{the amount spent per week on advertising.}$$

Suppose the firm spends $1,200 per week on advertising, that P_Y is $40, and that income in the market area is $8,000 per capita.

a. Write the equation of the demand curve for product X.

b. Briefly explain how product X is related to product Y, given the equation for the demand function. (Is Y a substitute or a complement, and how can you tell?)

c. Given the stated values of the other independent variables in this problem, calculate the point price elasticity of demand for X at P_X = $50.

d. Given the stated values of P_Y, I, and A, at what price and quantity demanded will total revenue from sales of X be maximized? What will the maximum revenue be?

C8. Advanced Consumer Electronics manufactures high-resolution digital cameras, and its marketing department has estimated the following monthly demand function for the cameras:

$$Q_{ACE} = 270 - 0.8P_{ACE} - 3P_M + 0.4P_C + 0.006I + 0.03A,$$

where

Q_{ACE} = the quantity of Advanced Consumer Electronics cameras demanded per month,

P_{ACE} = the price of an Advanced Consumer Electronics camera,

P_M = the price of a memory card,

P_C = the price of a competing camera,

I = annual average household income, and

A = monthly advertising expenditures.

a. Find the price elasticity of demand for ACE digital cameras if P_{ACE} = $600, P_M = $40, P_C = $500, I = $50,000, and A = $1,000.

b. Is the price elasticity of demand for ACE digital cameras elastic, unitary elastic, or inelastic at the point specified in part (a)? What does the value you found in part (a) tell you about the quantity demanded of ACE digital cameras?

c. What is the cross price elasticity of demand between the quantity demanded of ACE digital cameras and the price of the memory cards? Are these two items substitutes or complements? What does the value of this cross price elasticity tell you about the demand for ACE digital cameras?

d. What is the cross price elasticity of demand between the quantity demanded of ACE digital cameras and the price of the competing brand of camera at the point given in part (a)? Are the two brands of cameras substitutes or complements?

e. Find the income elasticity of demand for ACE digital cameras at the point specified in part (a). Are the cameras normal goods or inferior goods? Are they cyclical normal goods? Explain. What does this income elasticity of demand value tell you about the quantity demanded of ACE digital cameras?

f. What is the equation of the *demand curve* for ACE digital cameras given the values for P_M, P_C, I, and A specified in part (a)?

g. What are the total revenue and marginal revenue functions that correspond to the demand function in part (f)?

SELECTED REFERENCES

Houthakker, H. S., and L. D. Taylor. *Consumer Demand in the United States: Analyses and Projections.* Cambridge, MA: Harvard University Press, 1970.

Kagel, John H., Raymond C. Battalio, Howard Rachlin, and Leonard Green. "Demand Curves for Animal Consumers." *Quarterly Journal of Economics* 96, No. 1 (February 1981): 1–18.

Landsberg, Steven E. *Price Theory and Applications,* 5th ed. Cincinnati: South-Western College Publishing, 2001, Chapters 1–4.

Mansfield, Edwin, and Gray W. Yohe. *Microeconomics: Theory and Applications,* 10th ed. New York: W. W. Norton, 2000, Chapters 3–5.

McGuigan, James R., and R. Charles Moyer. *Managerial Economics,* 9th ed. Cincinnati: South-Western College Publishing, 2002, Chapter 3.

Nicholson, Walter. *Microeconomic Theory: Basic Principles and Extensions,* 8th ed. Cincinnati: South-Western College Publishing, 2002, Chapters 3–7.

Sheppard, Stephen. "Estimating the Demand for Housing, Land, and Neighbourhood Characteristics." *Oxford Bulletin of Economics and Statistics* 60, No. 3 (August 1998): 357–369.

Economics of Consumer Behavior

In *Chapter 2* we looked at the relationships among price, quantity demanded, and total revenue. We also examined the concept of elasticity, and saw how it could be used to depict the effects of changes in variables such as income and the prices of related goods on the quantity demanded of a product.

It is also often useful to be aware of the notions about consumer behavior that lie in the background of the demand curve. In order to grasp the theory of consumer behavior put forth by economists, we must first recognize that the primary goal of consumers is assumed to be the maximization of their *utility* or *satisfaction.* In other words, consumers wish to achieve the greatest satisfaction possible within the bounds of their budget constraints.

CARDINAL UTILITY APPROACH

Early theories of consumer behavior implicitly assumed that personal utility or satisfaction could be measured in exact units of measurement, called *utils,* just as we measure length, temperature, and volume in inches, degrees, and liters. John and Sue Brown could say, for example, that they received 200 utils of satisfaction from an Anthony's super deluxe pizza and 50 utils of satisfaction from a bag of buttered microwave popcorn. With this type of measurement system, called a *cardinal measurement system,* we could say that John and Sue received four times as much satisfaction from a super deluxe pizza as from a bag of popcorn.

The *total utility* associated with a good or service is the total amount of satisfaction that the consumer obtains from the good or service. We can calculate marginal utility in the same way that we calculate other marginal values. *Arc marginal utility* is the addition to total utility provided by another unit of a good or service. For example, suppose your total utility is 1,500 utils. Someone gives you two bags of popcorn, and as a result, your total utility jumps to 1,600 utils. The marginal utility of a bag of popcorn in this case is equal to

$$\frac{\text{change in total utility}}{\text{change in bags of popcorn}} = \frac{100}{2} = 50 \text{ utils.}$$

In general, the *arc marginal utility of a good,* Good X, is given by

$$MU_X = \frac{\Delta TU_X}{\Delta X},$$

where *MU* is marginal utility and *TU* is total utility.

Economists have shown, and we can easily see, that given a cardinal utility function, consumers will maximize their satisfaction by dividing their budget among goods and services so that the marginal utility per additional dollar cost of another unit of each of these products is equal. For example, if you are dividing your monthly entertainment budget between pizza and compact discs, you will maximize your utility only if the

$$\frac{MU_{pizza}}{P_{pizza}} = \frac{MU_{CD}}{P_{CD}}$$

where

$$MU_{pizza} = \text{the marginal utility of a pizza,}$$

$$MU_{CD} = \text{the marginal utility of a compact disc,}$$

$$P_{pizza} = \text{the price of a pizza, and}$$

$$P_{CD} = \text{the price of a compact disc.}$$

Let us suppose that the price of a pizza is $5.00, the price of a compact disc is $10.00, the marginal utility of a pizza is 300 utils, and the marginal utility of a compact disc is 500 utils. In this case,

$$\frac{MU_{pizza}}{P_{pizza}} = \frac{300 \text{ utils}}{\$5.00} = 60 \text{ utils per additional dollar.}$$

while

$$\frac{MU_{CD}}{P_{CD}} = \frac{500 \text{ utils}}{\$10.00} = 50 \text{ utils per additional dollar.}$$

Here,

$$\frac{MU_{pizza}}{P_{pizza}} \text{ is greater than } \frac{MU_{CD}}{P_{CD}},$$

(60 is greater than 50).

Thus, to maximize your utility, you must reallocate your spending so that more pizza and fewer compact discs are purchased. For example, suppose you buy one less compact disc and two more pizzas. As a result, you will have a net gain of 100 utils for the same amount of money, as shown below.

Buy one less compact disc:

$$\text{Change in utility} = -500 \text{ utils}$$

$$\text{Change in spending} = -\$10.00$$

Buy two more pizzas:

$$\text{Change in utility} = (2 \times 300) = 600 \text{ utils}$$

$$\text{Change in spending} = (2 \times \$5.00) = \$10.00$$

Net effect of budget reallocation:

$$\text{Net change in utility} = -500 \text{ utils} + 600 \text{ utils} = +100 \text{ utils}$$

$$\text{Net change in spending} = -\$10.00 + \$10.00 = \$0$$

Do these results mean that you should buy all pizzas and no compact discs? Certainly not! As you begin to purchase more pizzas and fewer CDs per month, you will probably find that the marginal utility of another pizza will fall, while that of another CD will rise. This phenomenon results from the *principle of diminishing marginal utility*, which states that as more and more units of a good or service are consumed, total utility may increase, but after some point the marginal utility of another unit will begin to fall.

Thus, as you begin to reallocate your monthly budget so that you are purchasing more pizzas and fewer compact discs, we would expect the marginal utility of another pizza to fall and that of another CD to rise. As a result, you would eventually reach a combination of pizzas and compact discs where your utility would be at a maximum, given your budget. This point might occur, for example, where the MU_{pizza} = 275 utils and the MU_{CD} = 550 utils, so that

$$\frac{MU_{pizza}}{P_{pizza}} = \frac{275}{\$5} = \frac{MU_{CD}}{P_{CD}} = \frac{550}{\$10} = 55 \text{ utils per } \$1.00.$$

At this point there is no way that you can reallocate your spending between these two goods and increase your total utility.

ORDINAL UTILITY THEORY

In recent years economists have placed increasing emphasis on the fact that the amount of utility a consumer receives from a particular combination of goods and services is a subjective phenomenon. Moreover, it may be quite difficult for the consumer to develop a utility function with cardinal measurements of utility even for himself or herself. Furthermore, twentieth century economists have found that the important conclusions of their theory of consumer behavior could be derived from an *ordinal* utility function, which has the benefit of being much easier to construct.

An ordinal utility function does not require precise measurements of the actual utility received from a good or service; it requires only that consumers be able to state whether they prefer one combination of goods to another or are indifferent between them. A consumer who is *indifferent* between two sets of goods likes them both equally well; they both yield the same amount of satisfaction. Two additional assumptions that economists make in the ordinal utility approach are (1) that consumers are consistent in their rankings and (2) that a consumer also prefers more to less of a good in the *relevant range* of choice. The first assumption means that if you prefer three hamburgers to four tacos but you prefer four tacos to two hot dogs, then you must also prefer three hamburgers to two hot dogs. The second assumption means that if someone offered you a choice between two hamburgers and three hamburgers for free, you would always choose three hamburgers.

Given these assumptions, we can construct an ordinal utility function for a consumer. All that is required is that the consumer tell us how he or she would rank combinations of goods and services in order of preference. We then can assign utility numbers to these combinations, following the rule that if one combination of goods and services is preferred to a second, then the first combination must have a higher utility number than the second. If a consumer is indifferent between two combinations of goods and services, they must have *the same* utility number assigned to them.

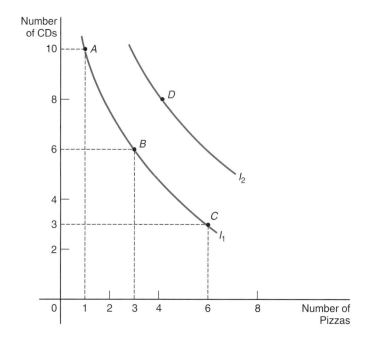

After the consumer's utility function has been constructed, we can draw indifference curves based on that data. An *indifference curve* shows various combinations of two goods and services about which a consumer is indifferent. Of course, each combination of goods and services on an indifference curve must have the same utility number assigned to it.

For example, Figure 2A-1 shows two indifference curves for combinations of compact discs and pizzas. The number of compact discs purchased per month is shown on the vertical axis and the number of pizzas on the horizontal axis. Each indifference curve represents a different level of utility. Points *A*, *B*, and *C* in the diagram indicate that this consumer is indifferent between ten compact discs and one pizza, six compact discs and three pizzas, and three compact discs and six pizzas.

We should pause here for a few moments to note some properties of indifference curves. First, indifference curves must have a *negative* slope— that is, they must slope downward to the right. This characteristic is the direct result of our assumption that a consumer always prefers more to less of a good. If some of one good is given up, more of the second good must be obtained for the consumer to remain at the same level of satisfaction and vice versa. Second, indifference curves cannot intersect. If they did intersect, that would mean that the combination of goods and services at the point of intersection gave a consumer two different levels of utility, which is impossible!

Third, higher (farther to the right) indifference curves must represent higher levels of utility. We can see why this relationship must hold by comparing points B on I_1 and D on I_2 in Figure 2A-1. Point D represents a combination of pizzas and compact discs that contains more of both goods than does B. Since a consumer prefers more to less of a good, I_2 must represent a higher level of satisfaction than does I_1.

MARGINAL RATE OF SUBSTITUTION

Points A, B, and C in Figure 2A-1 can be used to illustrate the marginal rate of substitution, a term that plays an important role in modern consumer theory. The *marginal rate of substitution (MRS)* indicates the rate at which a consumer is willing to substitute one good for another. In other words, it is the rate at which the consumer can substitute one good for another while remaining at the same level of satisfaction (on the same indifference curve). It is also equal to (–1) multiplied by the slope of the indifference curve at the relevant point. In general, we can write the marginal rate of substitution of Good X for Good Y as $MRS = (-1)(\Delta Y / \Delta X)$, where Good Y is on the vertical axis and Good X is on the horizontal axis.

In Figure 2A-1, the marginal rate of substitution between points A and B is equal to

$$(-1) \frac{\text{change in number of compact discs}}{\text{change in number of pizzas}} = (-1) \frac{(-4)}{2} = 2$$

In other words, between points A and B the consumer will maintain the same level of utility by giving up two CDs in exchange for another pizza. Between points B and C, the MRS is equal to

$$(-1) \frac{\text{change in number of compact discs}}{\text{change in number of pizzas}} = (-1) \frac{(-3)}{3} = 1$$

Between points B and C the consumer is willing to trade only one compact disc for one pizza.

The change in the MRS between points A and B and points B and C illustrates the principle of diminishing marginal rate of substitution. A *diminishing marginal rate of substitution* of Good X for Good Y means that as consumers obtain more of Good X relative to Good Y, they are willing to give up less of Good Y to get one more unit of Good X. This principle is related to the notion of diminishing marginal utility, as we shall see shortly.

When we move from one point to another on an indifference curve, the amount of utility that we lose by giving up some of one good must be exactly offset by the utility we gain from getting more of the second good. Thus for two goods, X and Y, along an indifference curve,

(2A-1)
$$\left(\Delta Y \cdot \frac{\Delta TU}{\Delta Y}\right) + \left(\Delta X \cdot \frac{\Delta TU}{\Delta X}\right) = 0.$$

By subtracting $\Delta X(\Delta TU/\Delta X)$ from both sides of equation (2A-1), we obtain

(2A-2)
$$\Delta Y \cdot \frac{\Delta TU}{\Delta Y} = -\Delta X \cdot \frac{\Delta TU}{\Delta X}.$$

Dividing both sides of equation (2A-2) by $\Delta TU/\Delta Y$, we get

(2A-3)
$$\Delta Y = -\Delta X \cdot \frac{\left(\dfrac{\Delta TU}{\Delta X}\right)}{\left(\dfrac{\Delta TU}{\Delta Y}\right)}.$$

Finally, dividing both sides of equation (2A-3) by $-\Delta X$, we find

(2A-4)
$$-\frac{\Delta X}{\Delta Y} = \frac{\left(\dfrac{\Delta TU}{\Delta X}\right)}{\left(\dfrac{\Delta TU}{\Delta Y}\right)}.$$

The left-hand side of equation (2A-4) is equal to the *MRS* of Good X for Good Y. The right-hand side is equal to MU_X/MU_Y. Thus we have shown that

(2A-5)
$$MRS = -\frac{\Delta Y}{\Delta X} = \frac{MU_X}{MU_Y}.$$

If we think for a minute, equation (2A-5) makes a lot of sense. It states that the rate at which a consumer is just willing to trade Good Y for Good X is equal to the ratio of the marginal utility of Good X to that of Good Y. If the MU_X is 50 units and the MU_Y is 100, then the consumer would be willing to trade one unit of Y for two of X, or

$$MRS = \frac{1}{2} = \frac{MU_X}{MU_Y}.$$

Note that the consumer will give up less of the good with the higher marginal utility in exchange for the good with the lower marginal utility. In other words, the rate at which the consumer will trade Good Y for Good X *varies inversely* with the ratio of the marginal utility of Y to the marginal utility of X. Thus,

$$MRS = (-1)\frac{\Delta Y}{\Delta X} = \frac{MU_X}{MU_Y}, \; not \; \frac{MU_Y}{MU_X}.$$

CONSUMER EQUILIBRIUM

A consumer will maximize his or her satisfaction by allocating purchases in order to be on the highest indifference curve possible given the budget available. In Figure 2A-2 we see three indifference curves: I_1, I_2, and I_3. A consumer's budget line, denoted by $Y'X'$, is also drawn.

We can derive the equation for the consumer's budget line as follows. First assume that our consumer has B_0 dollars to spend on goods X and Y. Then the maximum amount that the consumer can spend on each good is given by

(2A-6)
$$P_Y \cdot Y + P_X \cdot X = B_0,$$

where

$$P_Y = \text{the price of Good } Y,$$
$$Y = \text{the quantity purchased of Good } Y,$$
$$P_X = \text{the price of Good } X, \text{ and}$$
$$X = \text{the quantity purchased of Good } X.$$

Equation (2A-6) states that the price of Good Y multiplied by the quantity purchased of Good Y plus the price of Good X multiplied by the quantity purchased of Good X is equal to B_0.

FIGURE 2A-2

Consumer Equilibrium

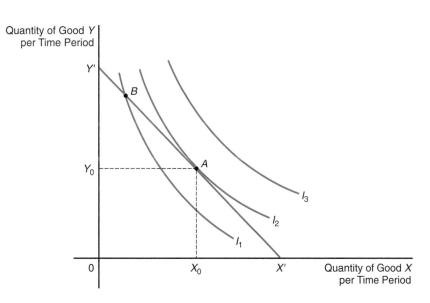

To get equation (2A-6) in a form where it can be graphed easily, as in Figure 2A-2, we first subtract $P_X \cdot X$ from both sides of the equation, obtaining

(2A-7)
$$P_Y \cdot Y = B_0 - P_X \cdot X.$$

Now, dividing both sides of this equation by P_Y, we get

(2A-8)
$$Y = \frac{B_0}{P_Y} - \frac{P_X}{P_Y} \cdot X.$$

Equation (2A-8) is in the familiar linear form of $Y = a + bX$. The Y-axis intercept, Y' in Figure 2A-2, is equal to B_0/P_Y. That is the number of units of Y that can be purchased if the consumer's entire budget is spent on Good Y. Similarly, the X-axis intercept, X' in Figure 2A-2, is given by B_0/P_X.

The slope of the consumer's budget line is equal to $-P_X/P_Y$. In other words, the rate at which a consumer can trade off spending on one good for spending on another is given by the ratio of their prices. More specifically, $\Delta Y/\Delta X$ along the budget line is equal to $-P_X/P_Y$.

As we can see from Figure 2A-2, the consumer will maximize his or her satisfaction at point A, on indifference curve I_2, by purchasing Y_0 units of Y and X_0 units of X. At this point, indifference curve I_2 is just tangent to the consumer's budget line.

Our consumer could, of course, manage to spend the entire budget by purchasing the quantities of Goods X and Y denoted by point B on indifference curve I_1. However, I_1 represents a lower level of utility than does I_2, so the consumer could do better than this point. On the other hand, no points on indifference curves higher than I_2 can be achieved with this budget. Consequently, this consumer will find that utility is maximized at point A, given the budget line.

Since the consumer's budget line must be tangent to the relevant indifference curve at the utility-maximizing point, the slope of the budget line and the slope of the indifference curve must be equal at that point. We just found the slope of the budget line to be $-P_X/P_Y$. The slope of the indifference curve is equal to $(-1) MRS = -MU_X/MU_Y$. Thus the consumer will maximize his or her satisfaction only if

(2A-9)
$$-\frac{P_X}{P_Y} = -\frac{MU_X}{MU_Y}.$$

We can easily show that equation (2A-9) is equivalent to the utility-maximizing rule developed with the cardinal utility approach. First, we multiply both sides of equation (2A-9) by $-MU_Y$ to find

(2A-10)
$$\frac{MU_Y}{P_Y} \cdot P_X = MU_X.$$

If we now divide both sides of equation (2A-10) by P_X we obtain our earlier utility-maximizing condition:

$$\frac{MU_Y}{P_Y} = \frac{MU_X}{P_X}.$$

DERIVING A DEMAND CURVE

We now need go only one short step further to derive a consumer's demand curve for a product. This process is illustrated in Figure 2A-3, which shows two budget lines for Jim Bob, who is dividing his lunch money budget between fajita tacos and slices of pizza. He can get either one a la carte at a shopping mall where he works. Initially, the price of a taco is $1, the price of a slice of thick Sicilian pizza is $2, and Jim Bob has $20 a week to spend on lunches. (He drinks water for free.) This relationship is depicted by budget line $Y'X'$. With these prices and a budget of $20, Jim Bob will maximize his satisfaction at point A by purchasing 10 tacos and 5 slices of pizza.

Suppose that the price of pizza falls to $1. The new budget will now be given by $Y'X''$. At the new price Jim Bob can now buy 20 rather than 10 slices of pizza if he spends all of his money on pizza. However, if he spends all of his budget on tacos, he can buy only the same number as before (20). With

FIGURE 2A-3

Effect of a Price Change

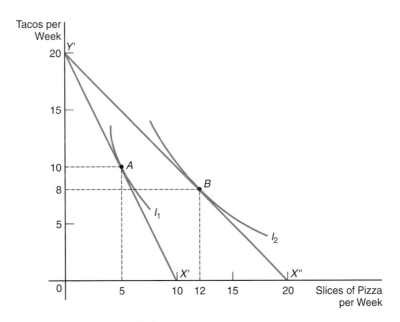

FIGURE 2A-4

*Demand Curve
for Pizzas*

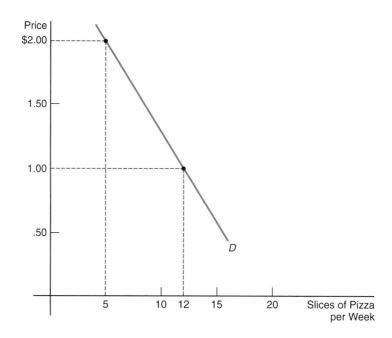

the new, lower price for pizza, Jim Bob will maximize his satisfaction by purchasing 8 tacos and 12 slices of pizza, as shown in Figure 2A-3 at point *B*. As depicted in Figure 2A-4, we now have two points on Jim Bob's demand curve for pizza, given that the prices of other products and his budget in dollar terms remain the same. At a price of $2 Jim Bob will purchase 5 slices of pizza per week, whereas at a price of $1 he will purchase 12 slices of pizza per week.

We can separate the effect of the price change on the quantity purchased of pizzas into two parts: the (real) income effect and the substitution effect. The *income effect* occurs because if the price of a good or service purchased by a consumer changes, it has an effect on the consumer's *real* budget or income—what that dollar budget can purchase. In Jim Bob's case, when the price of a slice of pizza falls, his real income rises (by $1 times the 5 slices of pizza he previously purchased). He can now buy 10 slices of pizza for the same amount of money as he paid for 5 slices at a price of $2. The *substitution effect* occurs because the price of a slice of pizza is cheaper relative to the price of a taco than it was before.

Figure 2A-5 shows how the price effect can be separated graphically into the two parts. Lines *Y′X′* and *Y′X″* are the two budget lines from Figure 2A-3. Initially, Jim Bob purchases 10 tacos and 5 slices of pizza per week, as shown at point *A*. After the decrease in the price of pizza, Jim Bob purchases 8 tacos and 12 slices of pizza per week, at point *B*. Line *RS* is drawn parallel to the new budget line, *Y′X″*, but tangent to the original indifference curve,

FIGURE 2A-5

Income and Substitution Effects

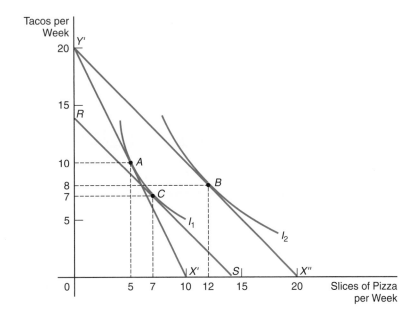

I_1. Consequently, line *RS* has the same price ratio (its slope) as the new budget line, but it allows the consumer to achieve only the same level of satisfaction as before the price decline. In this sense, budget line *RS* keeps the consumer's real income constant.

With budget line *RS*, Jim Bob will maximize his satisfaction by purchasing 7 tacos and 7 slices of pizza per week, at point *C*. The decrease by three units in the number of tacos purchased and the two-slice increase in the quantity of pizza purchased between points *A* and *C* show the substitution effect at work. The price ratio of the two goods has changed, but real income has remained constant.

The movement from point *C* to point *B* shows the income effect at work. The increase in real income Jim Bob experiences as a result of the fall in the price of pizza results in his purchasing 5 additional slices of pizza and 1 additional taco over what his position would be allowing for the substitution effect alone.

The substitution effect is always negative. That is, an increase in the price of a good or service relative to the prices of other products will always have a negative impact on our purchases of it. The opposite effect happens for a price decrease. The income effect may be either positive or negative, depending on whether a product is a normal or inferior good. In the preceding case, both tacos and pizza are normal goods.

CHAPTER THREE

Demand Analysis and Estimation

The primary objective of this chapter is to deal with the question of how the firm's managers can obtain information sufficient to put into operation the demand concepts we will repeatedly use in our discussions of revenue, profit maximization, and product markets. Obviously, *the more closely the firm can estimate demand conditions for its product, the more likely it is to determine correctly its profit-maximizing rate of output and price, or whether to produce a particular product at all.* The importance of accurate demand estimation is underscored by the results of a study that examined sales forecasts for 63 start-up computer software firms. The survey found that 43 percent of the companies' estimates of first-year sales were off by at least 30 percent; 77 percent of the companies' estimates were incorrect by at least 10 percent. On the average, the companies *overestimated* their first-year sales by 28 percent.

Although the companies spent an average of $38,000 on demand estimation, the amount that they spent on these estimates had little relationship with the accuracy of the forecast. However, the accuracy of the forecasts did have a close relationship with how important firm owners *thought* it was to have accurate sales forecasts.[1] Ironically, an otherwise unnecessary business

---

[1] "Sales Projections: Facts or Wishful Thinking?" *Wall Street Journal,* July 2, 1989, p. B3.

failure is likely to be the result of this lack of concern on the part of new firm owners.

Even well-established businesses have problems estimating the demand for their product or products. For example, in late 1998, Circuit City and a related firm launched the DIVX video disc and its special player. The demand for this format, in which a purchased video disc would self-destruct within 48 hours of first viewing unless renewal fees were paid, was totally overestimated. Although consumers did not have to return rented material to a video store, the format was much more expensive than renting a VHS tape, especially when one considers that a DIVX player would have to be purchased to use it at all. DIVX was withdrawn from the market after only nine months, and Circuit City offered anyone who had purchased a player before June 16, 1999, a $100 cash rebate.[2]

The DIVX failure definitely had a historical predecessor, the RCA SelectaVision videodisc (CED) player, produced from 1981 to 1984. This machine had absorbed 15 years and $150 million in development costs. In 1984, RCA stopped production of the CED player after losses of $580 million. The company overestimated the demand for its players in the first few years after they were introduced because it did not foresee how rapidly the prices of videocassette recorders would fall during that period and the extent of consumer loyalty to the VCRs. Ironically, RCA finally abandoned the players just as their sales were rapidly increasing.[3]

Further examples of incorrect market analysis are afforded by Ford Motor Company. Already mentioned in Chapter 2 is the Lincoln Blackwood pickup truck, which, like DIVX, had a very short run in the market. Ford has never revealed what kind of demand analysis led its management to believe an annual market for 10,000 such vehicles existed, but, according to one source, the sad fact is that between its introduction in November 2001 and April 2002, when it was announced production would end in 2003, only 550 of the trucks had been sold.[4] In July 2002, it was also reported that Ford planned to discontinue production of its largest sport-utility vehicle (SUV), the Excursion. The company blamed the 2001 recession for sluggish sales, but, again, the company seemed to have overestimated demand—this time for an SUV of gargantuan size. One

[2] Rob Landley (TMF Oak), "DIVX Post Mortem," *The Motley Fool,* online, June 21, 1999 www.fool.com/portfolios/rulemaker/1999/rulemaker990621.htm October 14, 2002.

[3] See "Pioneer Electronics Videodisk Business Grows in Consumer Area That RCA Quit," *Wall Street Journal,* January 9, 1985, p. 6; "CBS Will End Its Production of Videodisks," *Wall Street Journal,* July 10, 1984, p. 8; "Slipped Disc," *Time* (April 16, 1984), p. 47; and "RCA's Rivals Still See Life in Videodiscs," *Business Week* (April 23, 1984), pp. 88–90.

[4] Kathleen Kerwin, "Sport-Ute Trucks Still Have Miles to Go," *Business Week Online,* April 22, 2002 www.businessweek.com:/print/magazine/content/02_16/b3779601.htm?mainwindow, September 18, 2002; and "Blackwood Becomes Deadwood," CNWbyWEB.com, online, May 2002 www.nvo.com/cnwbyweb/blackwoodbecomesdeadwood/, September 18, 2002.

British writer noted that not only was the Excursion "one of the grandest examples of American excess," clumsy, and a gas guzzler, but it also would not fit in the garage of a typical U.S. home and would not fit in a normal parallel parking space.[5]

The extent to which demand is *actually analyzed* varies greatly from firm to firm. One reason for this is market structure. (Firms that are perfectly competitive are unlikely to view demand estimation as a very significant activity since they do not have a sufficient market share to significantly affect the market price of their product.) Another reason is that expertise and/or resources to obtain and analyze product demand differ greatly from one firm to another. Thus, demand estimation by firms runs the gamut from rough, rule-of-thumb decision making and "educated guesses" to the development of complicated econometric models relating a large number of variables to the quantity demanded of a given product. Nevertheless, more and more companies are investing substantial amounts of money as they move to "database marketing"—an approach to demand management that involves the use of computers to construct and analyze extensive data sets regarding customer characteristics.[6] We will begin with a discussion of market surveys and then consider statistical estimation of demand functions and techniques for the generation of market data.

MARKET SURVEYS

Many larger firms are able to allocate a substantial portion of resources and managerial effort to the task of demand analysis. More complicated demand functions involving variables other than price can be estimated from market data, and surveys or experiments can be undertaken to obtain a profile of consumer preferences. Generally, management can place a good deal more confidence in the results of a well-designed market experiment than in the results of a survey (that is, a questionnaire either filled out by respondents or administered by an interviewer), since the market experiment provides information on how consumers *actually* react to certain changes, while the survey tells only how consumers *think* they will react *if* certain changes take place.

Surveys *can* be quite useful when questionnaires do not call for very fine discrimination by the respondents. For example, one might successfully survey consumer preferences regarding small cars versus large cars, since consumers may be able to differentiate easily between the two. However, it

---

[5] David Schepp, "Ford Expected to Axe Mammoth SUV," *BBC Online*, July 31, 2002 http://news.bbc.com.uk/1/hi/business/2164966.htm, September 20, 2002.
[6] "Database Management," *Business Week* (September 5, 1994), pp. 56–62.

might be much more difficult for a consumer to determine whether a reduction in price of, say, 3 percent would be a sufficient incentive to buy a car this year instead of waiting until next year.

One method frequently used by firms to do market surveys is to append a survey questionnaire to a product registration form. The buyer is urged to return the form in case the company might need to notify her or him about a product recall or some safety issue. Occasionally, a sweepstakes entry is promised in exchange for return of the form. The questionnaires often ask for a great deal of information, some of it not at all related to the product in question. A form that came with a recently purchased Black & Decker home appliance (an electric iron) asked for all of the following data and more:

1. Price paid for the product
2. The three factors (from a list) that most influenced purchaser's decision to buy the product
3. What other home appliances the purchaser owns
4. Whether any of the aforementioned are Black & Decker products
5. Purchaser's age
6. Whether or not purchaser has a home office
7. Purchaser's income
8. Purchaser's occupation
9. Which credit cards purchaser uses regularly
10. Make, model, and year of purchaser's two newest motor vehicles

Obviously, this type of information is relevant to more than the question of what motivated the purchaser to buy a particular iron. In fact, not only can the company that gathers such information use it in its own research on consumer demand, but some companies actually *sell* the results obtained to other firms, thereby making a profit center out of their survey research department. More often than not, they even ask you to buy the stamp to pay the postage for returning the questionnaire!

For small businesses, direct survey research such as that done by Black & Decker may be too costly (in terms of the in-house allocation of time and resources or the fees that might be paid to a subcontract research firm) to be a practical strategy for assessing market demand. There are other alternatives. Historical market data or data from smaller-scale market surveys or experiments can be used. Employing the statistical programs that are now a part of popular spreadsheet software, small businesses can examine data from trade sources or data obtained from simple, and not very expensive, customer surveys. A primary statistical tool for this task is *linear regression analysis,* to which we now turn.

DEMAND ESTIMATION WITH REGRESSION ANALYSIS

Regression analysis is a statistical technique used to "fit" an equation to empirical data in order to estimate the relationship between a dependent variable and one or more independent variables. In demand estimation, when regression analysis is employed, the dependent variable is the quantity of some product purchased or sold per unit of time, and the independent variables usually include such items as price of the product, prices of related goods (substitutes or complements), consumer income, advertising expenditure, and credit terms. The regression equation is usually linear or log-linear (a form in which the natural logarithm of the dependent variable is a linear function of the logs of the independent variables).[7] If there is more than one independent variable, the equation-fitting technique is called *multiple regression.*

Figure 3-1 provides a simple vehicle for explaining what regression analysis does. Suppose the quantity of frozen bagels sold is envisioned to be affected solely by the price of the bagels. In order to estimate monthly demand, we obtain data from a group of supermarkets (of about the same size and located in similar neighborhoods) over a period of time short enough so that any other factors that might affect bagel purchases will remain constant.

The points labeled Y_1, Y_2, and so on, in panel (a) of Figure 3-1 represent the price–quantity observations we obtained from the data on supermarket sales of bagels (each Y_i is a price–quantity sold combination that existed at some point in time in *one* of the supermarkets). Thus, panel (a) of Figure 3-1 constitutes a scatter diagram of the relationship of the quantity of bagels sold to price per package of bagels. We can see that the set of points forms a kind of band that slopes downward to the right.

Using a linear regression model, a statistician can estimate a straight-line demand function, given a set of data points such as those in Figure 3-1, in a way that will ensure a statistical "best fit" to the scatter diagram. In panel (b) of Figure 3-1, the line drawn through the scatter diagram is a *regression line* representing the best linear approximation of the relationship of quantity sold of bagels to bagel prices. It is a best fit in the sense that the sum of the squares of the horizontal distances between the observed data points and estimated points lying on the regression line has been minimized.[8]

---

[7] We discuss natural logarithms in the appendix to this chapter.

[8] The *horizontal* distances are minimized because we are placing the *dependent* variable, Q_b, on the horizontal axis, as is customarily done for demand functions in economics.

FIGURE 3-1

*Price and
Quantity-Sold
Observations and
Corresponding
Regression Line*

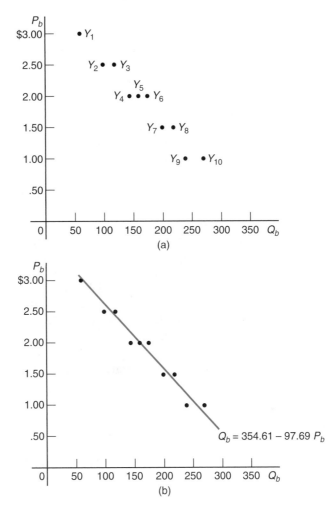

In panel (a), data are plotted showing different prices charged for bagels and corresponding quantities sold by a firm. In panel (b), a regression equation, $Q_b = 354.61 - 97.69P_b$, has been estimated. This equation represents the best linear approximation of the relationship of quantity sold of bagels to bagel prices.

Many computer programs are available that perform the task of calculating the regression line when raw data on observed points are fed into the computer. The multiple linear regression demand function estimated by the computer will be of the form

$$Q_d = \alpha + \beta_1 X_1 + \beta_2 X_2 + \ldots + \beta_n X_n + \varepsilon,$$

where Q_d is the dependent variable, the X_i are the independent variables, and ε is an error term. For our scatter diagram in panel (b) of Figure 3-1, the regression equation turns out to be $Q_b = 354.61 - 97.69P_b$, which, given the current set of data, is the best linear approximation of the demand curve for bagels. (Here, Q_b is the number of 16-ounce packages of bagels sold per week in a supermarket of given size and characteristics, and P_b is the price of a package in dollars.)

The closer the observed data points lie to the regression line, the more confidence we can have in the predictive accuracy of the regression model. A measure of how closely the estimated relationship reflects or accounts for the variation in the observed data is R^2, the *coefficient of determination*. Briefly, R^2 measures the proportion of the total variation in the dependent variable that is *explained* by the variation of the independent variable(s). For our bagel model, the R^2 of 0.97 indicates that 97 percent of the variation in bagel quantity sold is *explained* by the variation of bagel prices.

The word *explained* is italicized because a large (close to 1.00) R^2 does not necessarily mean that variation in the independent variable(s) *caused* the variation in the dependent variable. Large R^2s are merely indications that the independent variables are *correlated* with the dependent variable; that is, the independent variables *vary together* with the dependent variable.

The values of R^2s that are obtained in regression analysis vary widely (theoretically, from 0.00 to 1.00). When an estimate of a demand function using linear regression analysis has been obtained, it is then important to analyze the statistical significance of both the corresponding R^2 and the estimated coefficients of the independent variables and, perhaps, the constant term.

The statistical significance of the estimated coefficients as well as the estimated constant term is tested by calculating a t statistic. The t statistic to test whether an estimated coefficient, b, is statistically significantly different from some hypothesized value for the true coefficient, β, is calculated with the following formula:

$$t = \frac{b - \beta}{\sigma_b}.$$

The statistical significance of the calculated value for t is then checked by using a table showing the probabilities associated with different values of t. These topics are discussed more carefully in the appendix to this chapter.

One needs a course in advanced statistics to understand thoroughly the regression model and to learn how to interpret the obtained results. Nevertheless, the manager of a firm is often able to hire the expertise necessary to perform a statistical demand analysis and to establish a degree of confidence in its predictions. The cost of such a study can be quite small if the manager has kept accurate records of the relevant data. Furthermore, without too much effort, the manager can learn enough about statistics to be able to communicate with such experts and to use effectively the results of their analyses in making pricing and output decisions. We turn now to some actual cases of demand estimation using regression analysis.

Examples of Regression Studies

It is difficult to obtain regression studies of demand that have been prepared by private firms because firms generally avoid making public any information that might prove useful to competitors. Moreover, it is only on rare occasions that small firms will engage the expertise necessary to execute a soundly constructed regression analysis of demand. Because of such limitations, available studies tend to deal with product demand at fairly high levels of aggregation. In addition, many current studies employ techniques that are far more advanced than ordinary least-squares (OLS) multiple regression analysis. For clarity, therefore, we defer to some older, but still interesting, analyses. We review three of these next.

Chow: The Demand for Automobiles The demand for automobiles in the United States has been examined numerous times. A classic regression analysis is that done by Gregory Chow (1960).[9] Chow's estimated automobile demand function is

$$X_t = -0.7247 - 0.048802P_t + 0.025487I_{e_t},$$

where

$\quad X_t$ = The per capita stock of automobiles at the end of time period t, given in hundredths of a unit,

$\quad P_t$ = an automobile price index, and

$\quad I_{e_t}$ = expected per capita income.

The R^2 for Chow's equation is 0.895.

Since the coefficient of P_t is negative while that of I_{e_t} is positive, the equation indicates that an increase in automobile prices will reduce X_t, whereas an increase in expected income will increase X_t—which is as we would expect. As we learned in Chapter 2, it is possible from Chow's equation to calculate price and income elasticities of demand for *car ownership*

---

[9] See G. C. Chow, "Statistical Demand Functions for Automobiles and Their Use for Forecasting," *The Demand for Durable Goods,* edited by A. C. Harberger (Chicago: University of Chicago Press, 1960), p. 158.

when P_t and I_{e_t} are specified.[10] For the year 1960, Chow computed these elasticities to be about –0.6 and +1.5, respectively. Thus, Chow's study supports the hypothesis that auto sales are much more likely to respond to increases in expected consumer income than to price reductions. Subsequent studies, some a good deal more complicated than Chow's, tend to support his results.[11] The generally low price elasticities may explain automakers' past reluctance to reduce list prices, even though they have been known to offer sizable rebates when caught with large inventories in periods of declining expected real consumer incomes. (The rebates and other incentives offered consumers during the 1980s, the early 1990s, and 2002–2003 are a case in point.)[12]

In a 1980 study involving the automobile industry, Carlson and Umble estimated the following demand function:

$$D_t^i = \beta_0 + \beta_1 Y_t^D + \beta_2 P_t^i + \beta_3 G_t + \beta_4 Z_t^E + \beta_5 Z_t + \varepsilon_t,$$

where

D^i = the demand for cars of size i;

Y^D = real (adjusted for inflation or deflation in the economy) disposable income, seasonally adjusted and adjusted for population size;

P^i = the average car price (adjusted for general inflation or deflation in the economy) for size i;

G = gasoline price (not adjusted for general price changes);

Z^E = a dummy variable to indicate periods of gasoline shortages;

---

[10] For example, if $P_t = 120.0$ and I_{e_t} is $600, then

$$X_t = -0.7247 - 0.048802(120.0) + 0.025487(600) = 8.71126.$$

Thus

$$E_p = (\partial X_t / \partial P_t) \times (P_t / X_t) = -0.048802 \,(120.0/8.71126) = -0.672261,$$

or approximately –0.67.
Also,

$$E_I = (\partial X_t / \partial I_{e_t}) \times (I_{e_t} / X_t) = 0.025487 \,(600/8.71126) = 1.755452,$$

or approximately +1.76. Chow estimates that the price and income elasticities of demand for *new cars* are –1.2 and +3.0, respectively.

[11] For example, see H. F. Gallasch, Jr., "Elasticities of Demand for New Automobiles," Societal Analysis Department, Research Laboratories, General Motors Corporation, Warren, Michigan (May 21, 1976). However, Gallasch obtained estimates of price elasticity of demand between –1.6 and –1.3 and of income elasticity of demand of 1.0.

[12] See: Earle Eldridge, "Financing Deals, Rebates Drive August Auto Sales Higher," *USA Today*, online, September 6, 2002 www.usatoday.com/money/autos/2002-09-04-aug-auto-sales_x.htm October 14, 2002; Joseph B. White, "Stumbling Auto Makers Face Tough '91," *Wall Street Journal*, January 7, 1991, p. B1; "Motor City Madness," *Business Week* (March 6, 1989), pp. 22–23; and "Detroit's Sad New Year," *Newsweek* (February 15, 1982), p. 68.

Z = a dummy variable to indicate United Auto Worker strikes; and

ε = an error term.[13]

Carlson and Umble found that of the independent variables, disposable income appeared to have the greatest impact on the demand for automobiles. The coefficient of the automobile price variable was also statistically significantly different from zero, with the expected negative sign. The coefficient of the gasoline price variable was statistically significant and positive in the estimated demand equations for subcompact and compact cars, significant and negative in the equation for standard full-size cars, and not significantly different from zero in the equation for luxury cars. The coefficient of the variable for gasoline shortages was statistically significant and positive in the estimated equation for subcompact cars, not significantly different from zero in the equation for compact cars, and significant and negative in the equations for the other models.

Harp and Miller: The Demand for a New Convenience Food Regression analysis can also be applied to the estimation of demand for a *new* product. The easiest way to approach this problem is to examine data for goods that are close substitutes for the new product in question. Since only about 10 percent of new products introduced survive one year, it is important for firms to have an estimate of the potential demand for a new product.[14] In research done under the auspices of the U.S. Department of Agriculture, H. H. Harp and M. Miller provide a regression equation that is an estimate of the demand function for a new convenience food.[15] The Harp and Miller equation is in log form and relates annual sales in 100 million serving units of product to nine independent variables. The equation is

$$
\begin{aligned}
\log Y = &-0.6 - 0.60\,(\log X_1)^2 - 0.85 \log X_2 \\
&+ 0.28\,(\log X_3)^2 + 0.31 \log X_4 \\
&+ 0.65 \log X_5 - 0.16\,(\log X_5)^2 \\
&+ 0.44 \log X_6 + 0.23 \log X_7 \\
&- 0.58 X_8 + 0.33 X_9,
\end{aligned}
$$

where the variables are defined in the following manner:

Y = sales in units of 100 million servings,

X_1 = cents per serving of convenience foods,

---

[13] See Rodney L. Carlson and M. Michael Umble, "Statistical Demand Functions for Automobiles and Their Use in Forecasting in an Energy Crisis," *Journal of Business* 53 (April 1980): 193–204.

[14] See H. H. Harp and M. Miller, "Convenience Foods: The Relationship Between Sales Volume and Factors Influencing Demand," *Agricultural Economic Report No. 81*, Economic Research Service, U.S. Department of Agriculture, revised October 1965.

[15] Ibid.

X_2 = percentage market share of convenience foods that are close substitutes for the new one,

X_3 = cents per serving of fresh or home-prepared foods,

X_4 = cents per serving of highest volume near-substitute convenience food,

X_5 = importance of convenience food group in question in the consumer purchase pattern,

X_6 = index of availability in supermarkets,

X_7 = sales of highest volume competing good, and

X_8, X_9 = dummy variables to adjust for unusually high or low predicted sales.

In the Harp and Miller equation, the *coefficients* of the independent variables (such as X_2, X_4, X_6, and X_7), which are expressed in log form and are not squared, give estimates of their respective elasticities of demand. In other words, when the dependent variable and the independent variables are in log form, a *constant* elasticity of demand is estimated for each of the independent variables.[16] Since variables X_3 and X_4 refer to the cost of substi-

---

[16] For example, suppose we have a hypothesized demand function,

$$Q_d = \alpha_1^{\beta_1} X_2^{\beta_2},$$

which in natural log form is

$$\log Q_d = \log \alpha + \beta_1 \log X_1 + \beta_2 \log X_2.$$

The estimated β_i values give us estimates of the elasticity of demand with respect to X_1 and X_2, respectively.

To see why this is so, recall that the elasticity of demand with respect to variable Z is given by

$$E_Z = \frac{\partial Q_d}{\partial Z} \cdot \frac{Z}{Q_d}.$$

If we examine the elasticity of demand with respect to X_1, we find

$$\frac{\partial Q_d}{\partial X_1} = a\beta_1 X_1^{\beta_1-1} X_2^{\beta_2}, \text{ and}$$

$$E_{X_1} = a\beta_1 X_1^{\beta_1-1} X_2^{\beta_2} \cdot \frac{X_1}{Q_d}$$

$$= a\beta_1 X_1^{\beta_1-1} X_2^{\beta_2} \cdot \frac{X_1}{aX_1^{\beta_1} X_2^{\beta_2}}$$

$$= \beta_1, \text{ since } X_1^{\beta_1-1} \text{ times } X_1 = X_1^{\beta_1}.$$

A similar result holds for X_2.

tutes for the new convenience food, the positive values of the estimated coefficients of the terms involving those variables support our expectations that they would have positive cross price elasticities of demand. Variables X_1 and X_2, respectively, relate to the cost of the new convenience food and the market share of competing foods. As we would expect, we find that the estimated coefficients of the terms involving those variables are negative, indicating negative elasticities of demand with respect to X_1 and X_2.

Regression analysis is a powerful tool on which a large proportion of market research studies are based. If sufficient data can be obtained without unreasonable expense, a firm's management might be wise to undertake demand estimation using the regression approach whenever it is uncertain about the demand and revenue situation it faces. However, the regression model and its results must be carefully examined to ensure that the functional relationship specified is one that constitutes a reasonable depiction of the actual demand situation.

Since, as was stated earlier, variables that are related statistically do not necessarily have a cause-effect relationship to one another, management must always be careful in its use of statistically estimated demand functions. Moreover, important variables may have been excluded. In the Harp and Miller study, for example, an R^2 of 0.87 was obtained for the regression equation stated previously. However, the authors cautioned that their model is limited by the exclusion of three variables—product quality, brand promotion (advertising), and product life cycle.

Wilson: The Demand for Electricity An example of an estimated demand function that has an unclear interpretation is the following:

$$Q = 21{,}737 - 1{,}178P + 144G - 1.370Y + 47.9R + 0.069C,$$

where

Q = quantity of electricity demanded by households,

P = Federal Power Commission's computed typical bill for 500 kilowatt-hours in the corresponding (to the household) city,

G = price of natural gas in cents per therm,

Y = median annual family income,

R = average number of rooms per housing unit, and

C = number of degree days.[17]

---

[17] John W. Wilson, "Residential Demand for Electricity," *Quarterly Review of Economics and Business* 11 (Spring 1971): 7–22.

As we would expect, the coefficient of the price variable is negative, which indicates negative price elasticity of demand. The coefficient of the gas price variable is positive, which indicates both a positive cross price elasticity of demand and the fact that gas and electricity are substitutes, which is also as we would expect.

The sign of the income variable coefficient is *negative,* however, which indicates a negative income elasticity of demand and implies that as incomes rise, people use *less* electricity. Although it seems realistic to hypothesize that the income elasticity of demand is quite small (at least at high-income levels), it is difficult to think of a reason why it should be negative. The problem may be the way in which the study was set up—it covered a cross section of 77 cities during one time period. It is possible that the negative income elasticity coefficient resulted because many of the higher income households were in areas where a large percentage of homes were heated by natural gas rather than by electricity.

Also, the coefficient of the house size variable was not significantly different from zero at the 10 percent level of statistical significance (those of the other variables were significant). The R^2 was only 0.52. Thus, the researcher in this case should perhaps have tried to change the estimated demand function to see if a regression relationship could be obtained without the problems mentioned previously. For example, a variable could be added that would indicate whether or not most homes in a particular area were heated with gas or electricity. Such matters are discussed in greater detail in the appendix to this chapter.

MARKET EXPERIMENTS

Where there is uncertainty about product demand and the data required to perform a regression analysis are not available, it may be possible or desirable to conduct a market experiment that will generate such data. In a market experiment, those variables that are anticipated to be determinants of the quantity sold of a product are changed by the seller. For example, if management believes the quantity of its product that can be sold is primarily a function of price and advertising, it can adjust (change) these two variables over a certain period of time or across different markets and study the relationship of these variables to quantity sold.

Market experiments, though useful, are inherently risky and expensive. For example, an experiment in which price is increased could lead to both a temporary reduction in revenues and a permanent loss of customers to rival firms. If the experiment includes increases in advertising, additional costs will be incurred. Another problem is that there are almost always some relevant variables that the experimenters cannot control (income, tastes, and prices of related goods). Finally, because of their expense, the size and duration of market experiments are usually limited. Therefore, such experiments may not generate a sufficiently large number of observations to allow much confidence in their results.

The airline industry provides an interesting historical example of market experimentation that helps to define the complex milieu of airfares passengers are confronted with today. Until 1984, airfares in the United States were regulated by a federal agency, the Civil Aeronautics Board (CAB). In 1975 National Airlines, a carrier that no longer exists, convinced the CAB to permit a 10-week pricing experiment. The airline and its rivals (who were opposed to the experiment) would be allowed to lower fares by as much as 35 percent. After the experiment ended, National claimed that its revenue increased by $4 million over the trial period and that 56 percent of the passengers it carried at the low fares were people who otherwise would not have flown. However, rival firms, including Delta Airlines, argued that their revenues had fallen and that many customers had just switched to National because National had put on a vigorous advertising campaign for its new fares.[18]

National's pricing experiment was inconclusive, but Southwest Airlines, with a then modest route structure, had shown that consumers would respond significantly to low fares. So, the CAB allowed the airlines to try additional pricing experiments, and, eventually, more competition was allowed in airfares. On December 31, 1984, with airfares no longer regulated, the CAB was phased out completely.[19]

Deregulation resulted in a great deal of competition among the airlines with respect to fares as well as other promotional items, including frequent-flyer bonuses and discounts on hotels and car rentals. New airlines entered the industry, but a significant number of companies have either filed for bankruptcy protection/reorganization, merged with former competitors, or gone out of business. Some of the remaining airlines have often had trouble making a profit.[20] Following the 9/11 terrorist attacks of 2001, most airlines were in deep trouble and received significant financial aid from the government. Decisions on pricing and the management of such perquisites as frequent-flyer programs became even more complex.

---

[18] "National Says 'No Frills' Air Fare Helps, But Eastern Counters That Loss Resulted," *Wall Street Journal,* July 8, 1975, p. 7.

[19] See "The CAB Flies into the Sunset Today," *Wall Street Journal,* December 31, 1984, p. 8; and "CAB Flies into the Sunset, 'Closed Forever,'" *San Antonio Express News,* January 1, 1985, p. 1–C.

[20] See, for example, David Koenig, "Southwest Plans Expansion," *San Antonio Express-News,* February 19, 2002, pp. 1A, 5A; "Fast Growth Lands Low-Cost Airline in Trouble," *Wall Street Journal,* September 10, 1996, pp. B1, B4; "Piloted by Bethune, Continental Air Lifts Its Workers' Morale," *Wall Street Journal,* May 15, 1996, pp. A1, A8; and "Takeoff Is Bumpy for Start-Up Airlines As They Try to Grab a Piece of the Sky," *Wall Street Journal,* July 1, 1993, pp. B1, B11.

Peter Rabbit, Fatal Attraction, and Market Experiments

Waldenbooks, one of the largest booksellers in the United States, some years ago conducted a market experiment with selected books. Waldenbooks negotiated an agreement that in exchange for not returning certain unsold books to the publisher, it could initially purchase these books at cheaper-than-usual prices. To be included were some children's books such as *Peter Rabbit* and *The Wind in the Willows*, some former bestsellers such as *Eat to Succeed*, and some art books.

Waldenbooks planned to keep track of the time each of these books spent on the shelf in its stores. If a book was not sold within 60 days, its price would be lowered. If it remained unsold for 90 days, the price would be lowered again. After 120 days, the price might be lowered for a third time, depending on the original price of the book. The in-store location of a book would change as each price reduction was made; presumably it would be displayed more prominently as a sale or bargain book. Dara Tyson, senior manager for public relations and promotions at Waldenbooks, described the program as "very revolutionary. It represents value and spontaneous buying."

Although Waldenbooks recognized that the new policy might reduce profit margins on these books, it anticipated that volume—and, correspondingly, inventory turnover—would increase sufficiently so that there would be a net positive effect on total profit. Some competing bookstore owners predicted that the new plan would not work and offered such comments as "I don't think the public can be fooled," and "if they don't want to buy a book, they won't, regardless of the price."

The authors have not seen a report on the results of this particular experiment; however, they have noted the presence of bargain books at a number of bookstores in recent years.

Waldenbooks was not the only company engaged in market experiments. Movie studios such as Paramount were conducting market experiments with home videos. Although Paramount was pricing videotapes of some hit movies, such as *Fatal Attraction*, at $89.95, it listed others—*Top Gun*, for example—at $26.95. Disney took a similar approach when it set the list prices of *Lady and the Tramp* and *Good Morning Vietnam* at $29.95. While Paramount sold 500,000 copies of *Fatal Attraction* the first three months after its release, Disney sold 2 million copies of *Good Morning Vietnam* in the *first month* after its release. Disney figured that it had to sell 1.6 million copies of the movie at the lower price for it to make a greater profit than at a price of $89.95. (However, the expected sales volume at a price of $89.95 was not specified.) By September 1988, customers had purchased 3 million copies of *Top Gun* and 3.2 million of *Lady and the Tramp*. *E.T.* was expected to be a sure winner at $24.95.

Still, deciding which movies or other products will have a sufficiently high price elasticity of demand for the cheaper prices to be profitable is not always easy. Help in making this decision can come from companies such as Talus Solutions Inc., which developed yield-management software for airlines and hotels and is now teaching these strategies to firms in other industries.

References: "The Power of Smart Pricing," *Business Week* (April 10, 2000), pp. 160–164; "Waldenbooks to Cut Some Book Prices in Stages in Test of New Selling Tactics," *Wall Street Journal*, March 29, 1988, p. 32; "Sales Can Soar, If the Price Is Right," *Wall Street Journal*, September 23, 1988, p. 19. Also see "Movie Studies Produce Uneven Picture with Efforts to Win More Video Buyers," *Wall Street Journal*, June 6, 1990, pp. B1, B4.

SUMMARY

Techniques of Demand Estimation

This chapter has examined several techniques of demand analysis and demand estimation. At the beginning of the chapter, we discussed *market surveys,* devices through which firms question customers about their preferences or their probable reaction to certain changes, such as changes in the price of a good. Although a market survey is certainly one method of obtaining information about consumer tastes and spending, we pointed out that consumer surveys do not guarantee sufficiently detailed or reliable data to present a firm with a precise estimate of its demand function.

Linear regression analysis, one of the main statistical techniques that a firm can use to estimate its demand function, was also examined. We discussed the interpretation of the estimates of the coefficients of the independent variables in the demand function as well as that of the coefficient of determination, R^2. We pointed out that even though a given firm's management may not have the expertise to carry out a statistical demand estimation procedure, it is possible to hire someone to perform such an analysis. We noted that without a great deal of study, one can gain enough knowledge of statistics to interpret and use the results of such an investigation.

Finally, we pointed out that if the firm does not have sufficient data available for statistical demand analysis, it may wish to conduct market experiments by changing price and/or the amount of advertising and recording the corresponding quantity sold. However, we also cautioned that market experiments may be costly, especially in terms of lost sales.

We have emphasized both in this chapter and in Chapter 2 the importance of a firm's knowing the demand function for its product. Without such insight, the firm's profit maximization would be the result of sheer luck. However, the firm must decide *how much* data it will obtain and in what ways that data will be gathered, taking into consideration both the cost and accuracy of the information. The firm should always be aware of the value of keeping records of prices charged, advertising expenditures, and corresponding quantities sold; these statistics comprise one source of information regarding its demand.

In Chapter 4 we examine different types of forecasting techniques that business firms and government policymakers can use to predict future values of economic variables. As you might expect, some of these techniques employ the statistical tool of regression analysis, which was discussed in this chapter and is explained in greater detail in the appendix.

Then, in Chapters 5 and 6, we turn our attention to production and cost. As we will see later, two elements are essential if a business firm is to maximize its profit: an accurate analysis of the demand for the product and efficient production of that good or service.

QUESTIONS

1. What is a market survey? What are some of the problems associated with the use of market surveys to estimate the demand for a firm's product?

2. What information is obtained through the use of linear regression analysis?

3. Discuss market experiments: what they are, how they may be used, and any drawbacks they might have.

4. Explain how a hotel in Miami Beach might estimate the demand for its rooms. Be specific, including a description of what variables you would consider and why, as well as any other relevant information as to how you would conduct the experiment.

5. Using linear regression analysis, Estate Lighting Company estimated its demand function for a particular chandelier with the following results:

$$Q_E = 995 - 2.51P_E + 1.78P_C + 0.05I,$$

where

Q_E = quantity sold per year of the Estate Lighting chandeliers,

P_E = price of the Estate Lighting chandelier,

P_C = price of a competing firm's chandelier, and

I = average annual household income.

a. How can Estate Lighting use this information to find its price, income, and cross price elasticities of demand?

b. What would an R^2 of 0.84 indicate?

c. Can you think of a potentially important variable that Estate Lighting has ignored in its demand analysis?

6. In the Wilson article cited in footnote 17 of this chapter, a log (base 10) form of the demand function for electricity was also estimated with the following results:

$$\log_{10} Q = 10.25 - 1.33 \log_{10} P + 0.31 \log_{10} G - 0.46 \log_{10} Y$$
$$+ 0.49 \log_{10} R - 0.04 \log_{10} C, (R^2 = 0.566),$$

where

Q = quantity demanded (kilowatts) of electricity,

P = cost of the Federal Power Commission's typical bill for 500 kilowatt-hours per month,

G = average price of natural gas (cents per therm),

Y = median annual family income,

R = average size of housing units, and

C = degree days.

a. What does each of the estimated coefficients represent in the preceding demand function? Interpret the economic significance of each of them.

b. What does a value of $R^2 = 0.566$ mean?

SELECTED REFERENCES

Anderson, David R., Dennis J. Sweeney, and Thomas A. Williams. *Statistics for Business and Economics,* 8th ed. Cincinnati: South-Western College Publishing, 2001.

Doti, James L., and Esmael Adibi. *The Practice of Econometrics with EViews.* Irvine, CA: Quantitative Micro Software, 1998.

Greene, William H. *Econometric Analysis,* 4th ed. Upper Saddle River, NJ: Prentice Hall, 2000.

Griffiths, William E., R. Carter Hill, and George G. Judge. *Undergraduate Econometrics.* New York: John Wiley & Sons, 2001.

Gujarati, Damodar. *Basic Econometrics,* 4th ed. Boston: McGraw-Hill/Irwin, 2002.

Johnston, J. *Econometric Methods,* 3d ed. New York: McGraw-Hill, 1984.

Kennedy, Peter. *A Guide to Econometrics,* 4th ed. Cambridge, MA: MIT Press, 1998.

Maddala, G. S. *Introduction to Econometrics,* 2d ed. New York: Macmillan Publishing Co., 1992.

Verleger, Philip K., Jr. "Models of the Demand for Air Transportation." *The Bell Journal of Economics and Management Science* 3 (Autumn 1972): 437–457.

Linear Regression Analysis

In this appendix we seek to help the interested student achieve a better understanding of how a linear regression model is constructed and how it can be interpreted.

THE LINEAR REGRESSION MODEL AND UNDERLYING ASSUMPTIONS

If a researcher uses linear regression analysis, the assumption is made that two variables, Y and X, are related in the following manner:

(3-1)
$$Y_i = \alpha + \beta X_i + \varepsilon_i$$

which states that Y is a linear function of X plus an error term.[1] Researchers usually include an error term in a regression model because they believe that while *on the average*, $Y = \alpha + \beta X$, there may also be other variables representing less important factors affecting Y that are left out of the regression model.

---

[1] We first discuss the case of one independent variable and one dependent variable. The case of more than one independent variable (multiple linear regression) is conceptually quite similar and will be explained briefly at the end of this appendix.

Also, measurement errors may be present. Another way to state what we have just said is that

(3-2)

$$\mu_{YX} = \alpha + \beta X,$$

where μ_{YX} is the *mean or average* value of Y given a particular value for X, α is the Y-axis intercept, and β is the slope of the function.

For example, suppose a supermarket has sold milk at a price of $0.80 per half gallon for only four weeks and that during week 1, week 2, week 3, and week 4, it sold 100, 80, 90, and 110 cartons of milk, respectively. The average value of Y or Q_d, given X, or P = $0.80, is

$$\frac{100 + 80 + 90 + 110}{4} = \frac{380}{4} = 95.$$

Thus, the mean, μ_{YX}, of Y *given* X is found by adding up all of the Y values corresponding to that particular X value and dividing by the number of observations. Thus

$$\mu_{YX} = \frac{\sum\limits_{i=1}^{n} Y_i | X}{n}$$

where *n* is the number of observations of Y associated with that particular value of X.

In order to compute some of the statistics and to interpret the statistical significance of the results obtained in most linear regression analyses done in the area of economics, the following additional assumptions must usually be made:

1. The error term, ε_i, is a random variable with a normal (bell-shaped curve) distribution.

2. The mean or expected value of ε is zero. We write this as E(ε) = 0. This assumption means that, while some values of ε may be positive, some negative, and others zero, the *average* value of ε is zero.

3. The *variance* of the ε_i terms *given each X value* is assumed to be the same and equal to σ_{YX}^2. We find the variance, σ_{YX}^2, by finding

$$\sum\limits_{i=1}^{n} \frac{(Y_i - \mu_{YX})^2}{n}$$

Thus, we sum the squared differences or deviations of each Y value from its mean, μ_{YX}, given a particular X. For our milk example,

$$\sigma_{YX}^2 = \frac{(100-95)^2 + (80-95)^2 + (90-95)^2 + (110-95)^2}{4}$$

$$= \frac{25+225+25+225}{4} = \frac{500}{4} = 125.$$

The *standard deviation* is given by

$$\sqrt{\sigma_{YX}^2} = \sqrt{125},$$

which is approximately equal to 11.18 in the milk carton example. We also assume that $E(\varepsilon_i\,\varepsilon_j) = 0$, *where i does not equal j*, which means that ε_i and ε_j are not related.

4. In economic research, we usually assume that X is a random variable with a normal distribution. (In a controlled experiment, the X values could be fixed.)

Estimators of the Slope and Intercept Terms

If we could observe all of the combinations of X and Y that have occurred in the past or would occur in the future for all possible values of X, our task of finding α and β or "fitting" the relationship hypothesized in equation 3-1 would be made much easier. All of these observations of X and Y are called the *population*. Unfortunately, in economics we usually cannot observe the entire population because obtaining all of the data is either impossible or too expensive. Thus, we must make do with a *sample* (which we assume is randomly drawn) from the population data. This situation is one in which we must rely a great deal on the laws of statistics.

In the real world, therefore, our task is to find an estimate of α and β in equation 3-1 from a sample of data. Thus, we want to find

(3-3)
$$\hat{Y} = a + bX,$$

where a and b are estimates of α and β, respectively, and $\hat{Y}$ is the computed value of Y given a particular value of X and our estimated relationship. Then

$$Y_i = a + bX_i + e_i,$$

where e_i is the error term for our estimated relationship and is an estimate of ε_i, the population error term. Thus

$$Y_i - \hat{Y}_i = e_i.$$

We would like our estimates of α and β to have at least two characteristics. First, if we took repeated samples and estimated α and β for each sample, we would like the mean or expected value of a to be equal to α and the mean or expected value of b to be equal to β. In other words, we want $E(a) = \alpha$ and $E(b) = \beta$. In this case, we say a and b are *unbiased estimators*. Second, we would like the values of a and b, which are found from each sample, to vary as little as possible among the samples. Thus, we want σ_a^2 and σ_b^2 to be minimized.

Furthermore, we want our regression equation to be such that the sum of the squared error terms, $\sum_{i=1}^{n} e_i^2$ *(where n is the number of sample observations),* is minimized. We want to minimize the sum of the *squared* error terms because if our assumptions are correct, the sum of the error terms themselves should equal zero. It turns out that if we use a mathematical method to find a and b that minimizes $\sum_{i=1}^{n} e_i^2$, these estimators of α and β will also have the other two desirable properties (unbiasedness and minimum variance) mentioned previously. These estimators are

(3-4)
$$a = \overline{Y} - b\overline{X}$$

and

(3-5)
$$b = \frac{\sum_{i=1}^{n}(X_i - \overline{X})(Y_i - \overline{Y})}{\sum_{i=1}^{n}(X_i - \overline{X})^2},$$

where $\overline{Y}$ is the average or mean value of Y for the *whole sample* and $\overline{X}$ is the average or mean value of X for the sample.[2]

---

[2] We can derive a and b in the following manner. Recall that

$$e_i = Y_i - \hat{Y}_i = Y_i - a - bX_i.$$

Then

(3-6)
$$\sum_{i=1}^{n} e_i^2 = \sum_{i=1}^{n}(Y_i - a - bX_i)^2.$$

We wish to find the values of a and b such that $\sum_{i=1}^{n} e_i^2$ is minimized. To minimize $\sum_{i=1}^{n} e_i^2$, we take the first (partial) derivatives of equation 3-6 with respect to a and b and set them equal to zero to satisfy the first order conditions:

(3-7)
$$\frac{\partial \sum e_i^2}{\partial a} = -2\sum_{i=1}^{n}(Y_i - a - bX_i) = 0$$

and

(3-8)
$$\frac{\partial \sum e_i^2}{\partial b} = -2\sum_{i=1}^{n} X_i(Y_i - a - bX_i) = 0. \qquad \text{(footnote continues)}$$

The term $\overline{Y}$ is somewhat different from μ_{YX} discussed earlier, which is the *population mean of Y given a specific X value.* It is also different from μ_Y, which is the *population mean of all the Y values.* We usually cannot observe the population means, so we must therefore "make do" with the sample means. We call the estimators *a and b for* α and β, respectively, which can be found from equations 3-4 and 3-5, given previously, the *least-squares estimators* because they minimized $\sum\limits_{i=1}^{n} e_i^2$.

We can also say that *a* and *b* are the *best linear unbiased estimators (BLUE)* because they have the additional two desired properties of minimum variance and unbiasedness. If the sample we take has *n* observations (values of *X* and *Y*), we can easily use an electronic calculator to compute *a* and *b*:

(3-4′)
$$a = \frac{\sum Y}{n} - b\frac{\sum X}{n},$$

and

(3-5′)
$$b = \frac{n\sum XY - \sum X \sum Y}{n\sum X^2 - \left(\sum X\right)^2},$$

where the sums are taken over the *n* sample observations.

(footnote continued from previous page)

Simplifying equations 3-7 and 3-8, we obtain the *normal equations*

(3-9)
$$\sum_{i=1}^{n} Y_i = na + b\sum_{i=1}^{n} X_i$$

and

(3-10)
$$\sum_{i=1}^{n} X_i Y_i = a\sum_{i=1}^{n} X_i + b\sum_{i=1}^{n} X_i^2.$$

When equations 3-9 and 3-10 are solved simultaneously, we obtain

$$a = \overline{Y} - b\overline{X}$$

and

$$b = \frac{\sum\limits_{i=1}^{n}(X_i - \overline{X})(Y_i - \overline{Y})}{\sum\limits_{i=1}^{n}(X_i - \overline{X})^2}.$$

Table 3A-1 gives an example of a sample of milk prices and quantity sold data collected by our supermarket. Notice that there are *six* observations, so $n = 6$. Given the information in Table 3A-1, we find

$$b = \frac{n\sum XY - \sum X \sum Y}{n\sum X^2 - \left(\sum X\right)^2}$$

$$= \frac{6(480) - 700(4.30)}{6(3.19) - (4.30)^2}$$

$$= \frac{2880 - 3010}{19.14 - 18.49}$$

$$= \frac{-130}{0.65}$$

$$= -200,$$

and

$$a = \frac{\sum Y}{n} - b\frac{\sum X}{n}$$

$$= 116.67 - (-200)(0.72)$$

$$= 260.67.$$

Thus our estimated demand function is $\hat{Y} = 260.67 - 200X$. In order to check casually to see how closely our estimate of the demand function reflects the actual sample points, we compute $\hat{Y}$ at $X = \$0.70$ and find $\hat{Y} = 120.67$. In this

Table 3A-1 *Data for Milk Demand Problem*

Quantity Demanded Y	Price of Milk X	XY	X²
160	$.50	80	.25
140	.60	84	.36
120	.70	84	.49
110	.80	88	.64
90	.80	72	.64
80	.90	72	.81
$\Sigma Y = 700$	$\Sigma X = \$4.30$	$\Sigma XY = 480$	$\Sigma X^2 = 3.19$

$$\frac{\Sigma Y}{n} = 116.67 \qquad \frac{\Sigma X}{n} = .72 \qquad (\Sigma X)^2 = 18.49$$

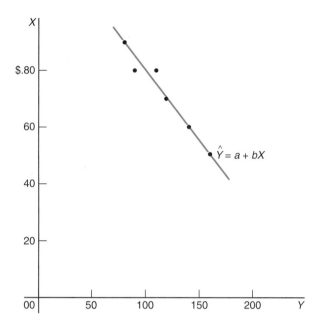

The sample points indicating the quantity demanded of milk and corresponding prices and the estimated demand function are shown here.

case the error, e_i, which is equal to $Y - \hat{Y} = 120 - 120.67 = -0.67$. Similarly, at $X = \$0.90$, we find $\hat{Y} = 80.67$ and $e_i = 80 - 80.67 = -0.67$. The sample points and the estimated demand function are shown in Figure 3A-1.

Interpretation of the Regression Statistics

Our casual observation indicated that our estimated regression equation fairly closely approximated the actual Y_i values in the sample. However, we usually wish to determine, using standard statistical measures, how closely an estimated function fits the sample data and what inferences we can draw from the estimate, which is based on the *sample,* regarding the *population* (quantities that would be demanded at *all possible prices*). Thus, we will discuss statistics that give us an indication of the statistical significance of the coefficient estimates and of the coefficient of determination, R^2. Finally, we will discuss a statistic that will allow us to find a confidence interval for Y, given X.

Statistical Significance of Estimates of α and β

First, let us examine the statistical significance of an estimate, b, of a coefficient, β, of the independent variable, X. Frequently in regression analysis, one of the prime concerns of the statistician is to determine whether or not the *actual* coefficient is different from zero (and sometimes whether it is positive or negative). This information is very important because it indicates the relationship between the independent variable and the dependent variable, which is the relationship of primary interest to the researcher in that type of situation. It turns out that we can use a statistical test to tell us whether or not we can reject the hypothesis (called the *null hypothesis*) that the coefficient in question is equal to zero (or some other number), *given a particular level of probability or chance that we are rejecting the hypothesis when it is true.*

To set up this test, we must calculate a *t statistic*. The *t statistic* has a distribution similar to the normal (bell-shaped) distribution when the sample size is large, and either the *t* distribution or the normal distribution could be used to analyze the statistical significance of the coefficients in this case. However, when the sample size is small, perhaps less than 40 observations, the *t* statistic should be used.

The *t* statistic that we need to calculate is given by

(3-11)
$$t = \frac{b - \beta}{\hat{\sigma}_b},$$

where b is the estimate of β and $\hat{\sigma}_b$ is the estimate of the standard deviation (square root of the variance) of b. We already know for our example that $b = 200$. The formula for $\hat{\sigma}_b$ is

$$\hat{\sigma}_b = \sqrt{\hat{\sigma}_b^2} = \sqrt{\frac{\hat{\sigma}_{yx}^2}{\sum (X - \bar{X})^2}}$$

The square root of the term $\hat{\sigma}^2_{YX}$ is called the estimated standard deviation of the regression or the estimated standard error of the estimate. We can find $\hat{\sigma}^2_{YX}$ from the following relationship:

(3-12)
$$\hat{\sigma}_{YX}^2 = \frac{1}{n - 2} \sum (Y - \hat{Y})^2$$

Since $Y - \hat{Y}$ represents the "error," or difference between the *actual* value of Y and our *estimate* of Y or $\hat{Y}$, it is easy to see how $\hat{\sigma}^2_{YX}$ got its name. The YX subscript indicates that we estimated the functional relationship between Y and X, or $Y = f(X)$. The term $n - 2$ represents *degrees of freedom*, which, briefly, indicate the number of elements or values that can vary freely in computing t. We get six degrees of freedom from the sample observations ($n = 6$) for computing $Y - \hat{Y}$, but we lose two degrees of freedom because a and b—which we use to find $\hat{Y}$—are already determined by the regression equation. Thus, for our example the degrees of freedom equal 4.

Table 3A-2 *Calculations for* $\hat{\sigma}^2_{YX}$

Quantity Demanded Y	Price of Milk X	$X - \bar{X}^a$	$(X - \bar{X})^2$	$\hat{Y}$	$Y - \hat{Y}$	$(Y - \hat{Y})^2$
160	$.50	−.22	.048	160.67	−.67	.449
140	.60	−.12	.014	140.67	−.67	.449
120	.70	−.02	.000	120.67	−.67	.449
110	.80	.08	.006	100.67	9.33	87.049
90	.80	.08	.006	100.67	−10.67	113.849
80	.90	.18	.032	80.67	−.67	.449
			$\Sigma(X - \bar{X})^2 = .106$			$\Sigma(Y - \hat{Y})^2 =$ 202.694

$$\hat{\sigma}^2_{YX} = \frac{\Sigma(Y - \hat{Y})^2}{n - 2} = 50.674$$

[a]Recall from Table 3A-1 that $\bar{X} = \dfrac{\Sigma X}{n} = .72$

In Table 3A-2 we give the original sample values of X and Y and the computed values for $(X - \bar{X})$, $(X - \bar{X})^2$, $\hat{Y}$, $(Y - \hat{Y})$, and $(Y - \hat{Y})^2$. Thus, we can find

$$\hat{\sigma}^2_{YX} = \frac{1}{n - 2} \Sigma(Y - \hat{Y})^2$$

$$= \frac{1}{4}(202.694) = 50.674.$$

Now we can find

$$\hat{\sigma}_b = \sqrt{\frac{\hat{\sigma}^2_{YX}}{\Sigma(X - \bar{X})^2}} = \sqrt{\frac{50.674}{0.106}}$$

$$= \sqrt{478.057} = 21.86.$$

The calculated value for t now becomes

$$t = \frac{b - \beta}{\hat{\sigma}_b} = \frac{-200 - \beta}{\hat{\sigma}_b}$$

(3-13)

$$= \frac{-200 - \beta}{21.86}.$$

If we wish to test the hypothesis that $\beta = 0$, we substitute $\beta = 0$ into equation 3-13 and obtain

$$t = \frac{-200}{21.86} = -9.15.$$

Table 3A-3 *The t Distribution*

ϕ *Degrees of Freedom*	γ *5 Percent*	γ *1 Percent*
1	6.314	31.821
2	2.920	6.965
3	2.353	4.541
4	2.132	3.747
5	2.015	3.365
6	1.943	3.143
7	1.895	2.998
8	1.860	2.896
9	1.833	2.821
10	1.812	2.764

Source: R. A. Fisher, *Statistical Methods for Research Workers,* 14th ed. (New York: Hafner Press, 1972), abridged from Table IV.

To interpret this value for t, we must look at a table for the t distribution. A partial t table is given in Table 3A-3. Each value of t given in the table indicates the probability for ϕ degrees of freedom that t would be greater than the value given, assuming that the hypothesis used to calculate t is true. A corresponding interpretation holds for t being less than (minus one) times the value given in the table. Thus, from Table 3A-3 we see that for $n = 4$ degrees of freedom, the $P(t > 2.132) = 0.05$ or 5 percent. Also, the $P(t < -2.132) = 0.05$ or 5 percent, where P stands for the probability or chance of some event occurring. The statement $P(t > 2.132) = 0.05$ means that in only 5 out of 100 times (on the average) would we calculate a t value greater than 2.132 *if the null hypothesis were true.* A similar interpretation holds for the figures in the 1 percent column.

The kind of probability statements just given are called *one-tailed tests* because they indicate the probability of t being *greater than* some number, or the probability of t being *less than* some number if we consider $P(t < -2.132)$. If we wish to find the probability that t lies outside the interval given by plus or minus the t value given in the table, we must multiply the stated probability percentage by two (there is a $0.05 + 0.05$ probability that t will be in either one or the other "tail"). Thus

$$P(t > 2.132 \text{ or } t < -2.132) = 0.10$$

for four degrees of freedom. We call this probability statement a *two-tailed test.* We could also state that the

$$P(-2.132 < t < 2.132) = 0.90,$$

since the probability of t being *outside* an interval plus the probability of t being inside the interval must equal 1.00.[3]

Now let us examine the t statistic that we computed for b, based on the null hypothesis that $\beta = 0$. In this case, our computed value for $t = -9.15$. We see from Table 3A-3 that for four degrees of freedom,

$$P(t < -3.747) = 0.01, \text{ and}$$

since our computed value for t is *smaller* than -3.747, we can say that the chances are less than 1 in 100 that we would obtain a t value of -9.15 if the null hypothesis were true. Therefore, we can reasonably reject the null hypothesis and accept the hypothesis that β is less than zero. Another way of stating our conclusion is to say that b is significantly less than zero at the 1 percent level of significance.

We can also compute a t statistic for a, the estimate of the Y-axis intercept. The computed value of t for a is given by

(3-14)
$$t = \frac{a - \alpha}{\hat{\sigma}_a}$$

where

(3-15)
$$\hat{\sigma}_a = \sqrt{\hat{\sigma}_a^2} = \sqrt{\frac{\hat{\sigma}_{XY}^2 \sum X^2}{n \sum (X - \bar{X})^2}}$$

From Tables 3A-1 and 3A-2, we can find

$$\hat{\sigma}_a = \sqrt{\frac{50.674(3.19)}{6(0.106)}}$$

$$= \sqrt{254.167}$$

$$= 15.94.$$

If our null hypothesis is $\alpha = 0$ and our alternative hypothesis is $\alpha > 0$, then

$$t = \frac{260.67 - 0}{15.94}$$

$$= 16.35.$$

---

[3] The probability of a *certain* event occurring is 1.00; the probability of an *impossible* event occurring is 0; and the sum of the probabilities of individual events occurring, one and only one of which must and can occur (but is not predetermined to occur), must be 1.00.

From Table 3A-3, it is obvious that we can reject the null hypothesis that $\alpha = 0$ and can accept the alternative hypothesis that $\alpha > 0$; we can say that a is significantly greater than zero at the 1 percent level of significance.

The Coefficient of Determination: R^2

Another measure of the statistical significance of the regression line that we have found from the sample points is the coefficient of determination, or R^2. To understand what R^2 represents, note first that we may separate the deviation of the actual Y values from the *sample mean* into two parts in the following manner:

(3-16)
$$
\underset{\text{(Total Deviation)}}{(Y - \bar{Y})} \quad = \quad \underset{\text{(Unexplained Deviation)}}{(Y - \hat{Y})} \quad + \quad \underset{\text{(Explained Deviation)}}{(\hat{Y} - \bar{Y})}
$$

The term $(\hat{Y} - \bar{Y})$ represents the portion of the deviation of the Y values that is *explained* by the regression equation that was obtained from the sample points. You should recall that $Y - \hat{Y} = e_i$. It is also true, given our assumptions at the beginning of this appendix, that

(3-17)
$$
\Sigma(Y - \bar{Y})^2 = \Sigma(Y - \hat{Y})^2 + \Sigma(\hat{Y} - \bar{Y})^2.
$$

$\Sigma(Y - \bar{Y})^2$ is called the *total* sum of squares, $\Sigma(Y - \hat{Y})^2 = \Sigma e_i^2$ is the *unexplained* sum of squares, and $\Sigma(\hat{Y} - \bar{Y})^2$ is the *explained* sum of squares. If we divide equation 3-17 by $\Sigma(Y - \bar{Y})^2$, we obtain

(3-18)
$$
1 = \frac{\Sigma(Y - \hat{Y})^2}{\Sigma(Y - \bar{Y})^2} + \frac{\Sigma(\hat{Y} - \bar{Y})^2}{\Sigma(Y - \bar{Y})^2}.
$$

R^2 is defined as

(3-19)
$$
R^2 = \frac{\Sigma(\hat{Y} - \bar{Y})^2}{\Sigma(Y - \bar{Y})^2},
$$

or the ratio of the explained sum of squares to the total sum of squares. When the *unexplained* deviation equals zero, $Y = \hat{Y}$ and

$$
R^2 = \frac{\Sigma(\hat{Y} - \bar{Y})^2}{\Sigma(Y - \bar{Y})^2} = \frac{\Sigma(Y - \bar{Y})^2}{\Sigma(Y - \bar{Y})^2} = 1.
$$

When the *explained* deviation equals zero, $\hat{Y} = \bar{Y}$ and

$$
R^2 = \frac{\Sigma(\hat{Y} - \bar{Y})^2}{\Sigma(Y - \bar{Y})^2} = 0.
$$

Table 3A-4 *Analysis of Variance*

Y	$Y - \bar{Y}$ *	$(Y - \bar{Y})^2$	$\hat{Y}$	$Y - \hat{Y}$	$(Y - \hat{Y})^2$	$\hat{Y} - \bar{Y}$ *	$(\hat{Y} - \bar{Y})^2$
160	43.33	1,877.489	160.67	−.67	.449	44	1,936
140	23.33	544.289	140.67	−.67	.449	24	576
120	3.33	11.089	120.67	−.67	.449	4	16
110	−6.67	44.489	100.67	9.33	87.049	−16	256
90	−26.67	711.289	100.67	−10.67	113.849	−16	256
80	−36.67	1,344.689	80.67	−.67	.449	−36	1,296
		$\Sigma(Y - \bar{Y})^2 = 4{,}533.334$			$\Sigma(Y - \hat{Y})^2 = 202.694$		$\Sigma(\hat{Y} - \bar{Y})^2 = 4{,}336$

* Recall from Table 3A-1 that $\bar{Y} = \dfrac{\Sigma Y}{n} = 116.67$.

Consequently, the *maximum* value that R^2 can be is one, and the minimum value that R^2 can be is zero.

In Table 3A-4 we have computed the values for the total sum of squares, the unexplained sum of squares, and the explained sum of squares for our example. Thus, we can find

$$R^2 = \frac{\Sigma(\hat{Y} - \bar{Y})^2}{\Sigma(Y - \bar{Y})^2} = \frac{4{,}336}{4{,}5333.334} = 0.956.$$

Therefore, the regression line we estimated from sample points can account for almost 96 percent of the variation in the observed values of Y.[4] In the case where X and Y can both vary (as we have assumed here is true), the correlation coefficient, R, which is the square root of R^2, also can be interpreted as a

---

[4] An R^2 value adjusted for degrees of freedom is often computed as

$$R'^2 = 1 - \frac{\dfrac{\Sigma(Y - \hat{Y})^2}{n-2}}{\dfrac{\Sigma(Y - \bar{Y})^2}{n-1}}$$

$$= 1 - \frac{\Sigma(Y - \hat{Y})^2}{\Sigma(Y - \bar{Y})^2} \times \frac{n-1}{n-2},$$

where $n - 2$ is the degrees of freedom of $\sigma_{YX}^2 = \left[\dfrac{\Sigma(Y - \hat{Y})^2}{n-2}\right]$ and $n - 1$ is the degrees of free-

dom of $\sigma_Y^2 = \left[\dfrac{\Sigma(Y - \bar{Y})^2}{n-1}\right]$. This latter term loses one degree of freedom because $\bar{Y}$ is fixed.

measure of the degree of *covariability* of X and Y (of the extent to which X and Y vary together).[5]

Confidence Interval for Y

Suppose we wish to make a prediction regarding an individual Y value—such as a prediction about the quantity demanded of milk when the price of milk = \$1.00. Usually, we would like to have some objective measure of the confidence we can place in our prediction, and one such measure is a *confidence interval* constructed for Y.

A confidence interval for a predicted Y, given a value for X, can be constructed in the following manner. We first find the value of a t statistic for Y where

(3-20)
$$t = \frac{Y - \hat{Y}}{\hat{\sigma}_{XY}\sqrt{1 + \dfrac{1}{n} + \dfrac{(X - \overline{X})^2}{\sum (X - \overline{X})^2}}}$$

with $n - 2$ degrees of freedom. We also know that

$$P\,(-t_{0.05} < t < t_{0.05}) = 0.90,$$

which means that

(3-21)
$$P\left[-t_{0.05} < \frac{Y - \hat{Y}}{\hat{\sigma}_{XY}\sqrt{1 + \dfrac{1}{n} + \dfrac{(X - \overline{X})^2}{\sum (X - \overline{X})^2}}} < -t_{0.05}\right] = 0.90$$

For our example,
$$R'^2 = 1 - \frac{202.694}{4,533.334} \times \frac{5}{4}$$
$$= 1 - 0.054$$
$$= 0.946.$$

In our case R'^2 is quite close to R^2; and, in general, they will be very close when the degrees of freedom are large.

[5] This matter is discussed extensively in Taro Yamane, *Statistics: An Introductory Analysis*, 3d ed. (New York: Harper & Row, 1973), Chapter 15.

Multiplying both sides of the inequality by $\hat{\sigma}_{YX}$ times

$$\sqrt{1+\frac{1}{n}+\frac{(X-\overline{X})^2}{\Sigma(X-\overline{X})^2}}$$

we obtain

$$P\left[-t_{0.05}\,\hat{\sigma}_{YX}\sqrt{1+\frac{1}{n}+\frac{(X-\overline{X})^2}{\Sigma(X-\overline{X})^2}} < Y-\hat{Y}\right.$$

$$\left. < t_{0.05}\,\hat{\sigma}_{YX}\sqrt{1+\frac{1}{n}+\frac{(X-\overline{X})^2}{\Sigma(X-\overline{X})^2}}\right] = 0.90,$$

or

$$P\left[\hat{Y}-t_{0.05}\,\hat{\sigma}_{YX}\sqrt{1+\frac{1}{n}+\frac{(X-\overline{X})^2}{\Sigma(X-\overline{X})^2}} < Y\right.$$

$$\left. < \hat{Y}+t_{0.05}\,\hat{\sigma}_{YX}\sqrt{1+\frac{1}{n}+\frac{(X-\overline{X})^2}{\Sigma(X-\overline{X})^2}}\right] = 0.90.$$

If we wish to find the 90 percent confidence interval for quantity demanded (or Y) at a price of \$1.00 (or $X = \$1.00$) for our preceding example, we first compute

$$\hat{Y} = 260.67 - 200\,(1.00) = 60.67.$$

From Table 3A-3, we find $t_{0.05}$ for four degrees of freedom = 2.132. We know $\hat{\sigma}_{YX} = \sqrt{50.674} = 7.119$. Finally, we compute

$$\sqrt{1+\frac{1}{n}+\frac{(X-\overline{X})^2}{\Sigma(X-\overline{X})^2}}$$

$$= \sqrt{1+\frac{1}{4}+\frac{(1.00-0.72)^2}{0.106}}$$

$$= \sqrt{1.25+\frac{0.078}{0.106}}$$

$$= \sqrt{1.986} = 1.409.$$

Consequently, the 90 percent confidence interval for Y, given $X = \$1.00$, is given by

$$P\,[60.67 - 2.132(7.119)\,(1.409) < Y < 60.67 + 2.132(7.119)\,(1.409)]$$

$$= P\,(60.67 - 21.38 < Y < 60.67 + 21.38) = 0.90,$$

or

(3-22)
$$P\,(39.29 < Y < 82.05) = 0.90.$$

We can interpret our confidence interval (3-22) as follows: If we were to select 100 samples and construct 100 corresponding confidence intervals for $X = \$1.00$, we should expect that 90 out of 100 of those confidence intervals will contain the actual value of Y corresponding to $X = \$1.00$.

Notice that the term

$$\sqrt{1 + \frac{1}{n} + \frac{(X - \bar{X})^2}{\sum (X - \bar{X})^2}}$$

gets larger as the given X value [in the numerator of $\dfrac{(X - \bar{X})^2}{\sum (X - \bar{X})^2}$ gets farther and farther away from the sample mean, $\bar{X}$. Consequently, the farther the given X for which we wish to predict Y is from $\bar{X}$, the wider the confidence interval for Y for a given probability level, and our prediction of Y is less reliable. This last statement is particularly relevant if the given X value is outside the range of the sample observations.

Multiple Linear Regression

Our discussion until now has focused on simple linear regression, analyses that involve one dependent variable and one independent variable. In many cases in economics, however, the value of a dependent variable is determined by more than one independent variable. Chapter 2 noted that the quantity demanded of a product is typically affected not only by its own price but also by the prices of related goods and the incomes of consumers. Other variables such as advertising expenditures, credit terms, and the climate may also be important factors affecting the quantity demanded of certain products. Wilson's estimated demand function for electricity, for example, included the price of electricity, the price of natural gas, median annual family income, the average number of rooms per housing unit, and the number of degree days as independent variables. We can examine the relationship between a dependent variable and a *group* of independent variables through the use of *multiple* regression analysis.

Let us assume, for example, that we have a regression model where Y is related to X_1, X_2, and X_3 in the following manner:

$$Y_i = \alpha + \beta_1 X_{1i} + \beta_2 X_{2i} + \beta_3 X_{3i} + \varepsilon_i.$$

In multiple regression analysis, we make the same basic assumptions regarding the error terms, ε_i, that were made earlier in the chapter in the case of simple linear regression analysis. In addition, we assume that no one of the X variables is determined by any linear combination of the other two. If this latter assumption does not hold, then the independent variables are not really free to vary independently of one another, and we have the problem of *multicollinearity*, discussed in the next section. The value of R^2 for multiple regression that is analogous to the R^2 in simple regression is called the *coefficient of multiple determination*, and its positive square root, R, is called the *multiple correlation coefficient*. Tests of the significance of the estimates of α and the coefficients of the X variables can be done using the t statistic in the same manner as in the case of simple linear regression. The degrees of freedom will be equal to $n - k - 1$, where n is the number of observations and k is the number of independent variables.

For example, suppose we wish to investigate the nature of a demand function for a video game, "Fantastic Frieda." Table 3A-5 gives data on the quantity demanded per year of the games, Q_F, the price of the games, P_F, the price of competing games, P_C, median annual family income, Y, and monthly advertising expenditures, A. In this case, our regression model is given by

$$Q_{F_i} = \alpha + \beta_1 P_{F_i} + \beta_2 P_{C_i} + \beta_3 Y_i + \beta_4 A_i + \varepsilon_i.$$

A wide variety of computer software packages are available that will make the calculations necessary for the estimates of α, the coefficients of P_F, P_C, Y, and A, the coefficient of multiple determination (R^2), and the values of the t statistic for α and each estimated coefficient. Using any of the standard multiple regression computer packages and the data in Table 3A-5, you should be able to obtain the following estimated demand function for "Fantastic Frieda" video games:

Table 3A-5 *Demand for Video Games Data*

Year	Q_F	P_F ($)	P_C ($)	Y^a ($)	A ($)
1983	50,000	18	20	24,580	7,500
1984	60,000	16	20	26,433	10,500
1985	55,000	16	18	27,735	10,500
1986	61,000	17	20	29,458	11,500
1987	63,000	17	21	30,970	12,000
1988	65,000	18	22	32,191	12,400
1989	75,000	16	21	34,213	13,000
1990	70,000	20	24	35,353	12,500
1991	75,000	20	24	35,939	14,000

[a]*Source: Statistical Abstract of the United States,* Washington, DC: U.S. Government Printing Office, 1992, p. 449; and *Economic Report of the President,* Washington, DC: U.S. Government Printing Office, 1993, p. 380.

$$Q_{F_i} = 10{,}749.360 - 2{,}979.179P_{F_i} + 2{,}785.712P_{C_i} + 1.337Y_i + 0.467\,A_i.$$

$$(9{,}986.243) \quad (1{,}344.300) \qquad (1{,}397.794) \quad (0.825) \quad (1.488)$$

The standard error of each coefficient is given in parentheses under the respective coefficient. The R^2 is equal to .96, and R'^2 (the adjusted coefficient of multiple determination) = .94. The t values can be calculated for each estimated coefficient by dividing it by its respective standard error. Thus, the t values for α, β_1, β_2, β_3, and β_4, respectively, are 1.076, –2.216, 1.993, 1.621, and 0.314. The degrees of freedom are equal to $n - k - 1 = 9 - 4 - 1 = 4$. Therefore, the estimated value of β_1 is significantly less than zero at the 5 percent level of significance, and the estimated values of β_2 and β_3 are significantly greater than zero at the 10 percent level of significance. However, the estimated values of α and β_4 are not significantly greater than zero at the 10 percent level of significance.

Possible Problems in Linear Regression

Several problems may occur in linear regression analysis. If there is more than one independent variable, two of these variables may be so closely related that estimation of the relationship between these variables and Y is made very difficult. This is the problem of *multicollinearity*.

Another problem may occur when the ε_i terms are not statistically independent. In this case $E(\varepsilon_i\,\varepsilon_j) \neq 0$, for $i \neq j$, σ_b may be *underestimated* and, as a result, the statistical significance of b *overestimated*. This problem is called *autocorrelation*.[6] Although the least-squares estimators of the coefficients will still be unbiased, they will not satisfy the minimum variance property; that is, the least-squares estimators are no longer the *best* linear unbiased estimators.

---

[6] One common statistic that can be used to test for the presence of autocorrelation is the Durbin-Watson statistic, computed as follows:

$$d = \frac{\sum\limits_{t=2}^{n} (e_t - e_{t-1})^2}{\sum\limits_{t=1}^{n} e_t^2}$$

where the subscript t refers to time period. Durbin and Watson computed values for d_L and d_U such that:

if $d < d_L$,   reject the hypothesis that there is no autocorrelation and accept the alternative hypothesis of *positive* autocorrelation;

if $d > 4 - d_L$,   reject the hypothesis of no autocorrelation and accept the alternative hypothesis of *negative* autocorrelation;

if $d_U < d < 4 - d_U$, do not reject the hypothesis of no autocorrelation;

otherwise, the test is inconclusive.

See J. Durbin and G. S. Watson, "Testing for Serial Correlation in Least-Squares Regression," *Biometrika* 37 (1950): 409–428, and 38 (1951): 159–178.

A third problem may occur if the variance of ε_i is not the same for each value of X. In this situation we have the problem of *heteroscedasticity*. Again, least-squares estimates of the coefficients will be unbiased, but they will no longer be the estimates that have the minimum variance. Also, the estimated standard errors calculated for the least-squares estimators will in general no longer be correct, so that confidence intervals and hypothesis tests may give misleading results.

Finally, a fourth problem is that of *identification*. The identification problem occurs because the data points that we observe, and therefore use in our statistical analyses, are various *equilibrium* values for price and quantity. Thus, to observe more than one data point (one value for P and Q), either the demand curve or the supply curve (or both) must shift. If *only* the supply curve shifts, the price and quantity equilibrium points will trace out the demand curve. However, if the demand curve shifts or if *both* the demand curve and the supply curve shift, the equilibrium price and quantity pairs will not be on a single demand curve. Figure 3A-2 illustrates the results we could get if the demand curve were shifting or if both the demand and the supply curves were shifting while the sample observations were gathered. Thus, if we attempt to estimate a demand function for a good with its price as the only independent variable, we must assume that all variables other than price that affect quantity demanded are held constant, so that the demand function is stable over that period.

We shall leave a discussion of possible solutions to these problems to more advanced statistics texts.[7] At this point, we merely wish to warn our readers that such problems might occur.

LOGARITHMIC TRANSFORMATIONS

In this last section, we will discuss logarithms. Since *linear* regression analysis can be used only for the direct estimate of linear relationships between two (or more) variables, logarithmic transformations are often a useful means of changing a nonlinear function, which we cannot directly estimate, into an equivalent linear relationship, which we can.

Before we discuss this procedure, we will first briefly explain what a logarithm is. The *logarithm* of a number is the power to which *another* number, called the base, must be raised in order for the whole term to be equal to the original number in question. Thus, since $3^2 = 9$, we can say that $\log_3 9 = 2$, where 3 represents the base. We can also say that $\log_2 16 = 4$, since $2^4 = 16$. In this case, 2 is the base. In general, we can say that $\log_a N = x$, which means that $a^x = N$. Two bases that are commonly used are the base 10 and the base e.

---

[7] See J. Johnston, *Econometric Methods*, 3d ed. (New York: McGraw-Hill, 1984), Chapters 6–12, for a more detailed discussion of these problems and possible solutions. Also see Yamane (note 5), Chapter 23.

FIGURE 3A-2

Effect of a Shifting Demand Curve

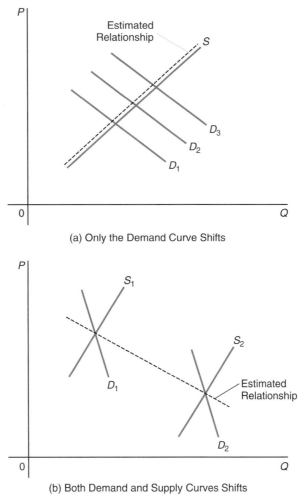

(a) Only the Demand Curve Shifts

(b) Both Demand and Supply Curves Shifts

If the demand curve shifts over the period for which the demand function is being estimated, identification of the relationship becomes a problem. If only the demand curve shifts, as in panel (a), the supply curve may be estimated. If both the demand and the supply curves shift, as in panel (b), identification of which relationship (if any) is being estimated becomes more difficult.

Logs taken to the base 10 are called *common* logarithms and are often used in computations. Logs taken to the base e are called *natural* logarithms, where e is approximately equal to 2.718. The base e is often used in studies involving growth or decay over time, since an amount A_0 growing constantly at rate r for t time periods is equal to A_t, where

$$A_t = A_0 e^{rt}.$$

The following rules hold for logarithms to *any base*, although we shall state them in terms of logs to base *e*.

1. Log of a Product

$$\log_e (XY) = \log_e X + \log_e Y.$$

The log of the product of two numbers is equal to the sum of the logs of each number.

2. Log of a Quotient

$$\log_e (X/Y) = \log_e X - \log_e Y.$$

The log of the quotient of two numbers is equal to the log of the denominator of the original fraction subtracted from the log of the numerator.

3. Log of a Number Raised to an Exponent

$$\log_e (X)^n = n \log_e X.$$

The log of a number raised to an exponent is the exponent multiplied by the log of the number.

4. $\log_e e = 1$, since $e^1 = e$.

As previously indicated, logarithms, especially natural logarithms, are frequently used to transform nonlinear relationships into equivalent linear relationships, which can then be estimated using linear regression analysis. For example, suppose we wish to estimate α, β_1, and β_2 in the following hypothetical demand function:

$$Q_d = \alpha P^{\beta_1} Y^{\beta_2} e^{\varepsilon},$$

where

Q_d is quantity demanded per time period of a product,

P is price per unit of this product,

Y is income, and

ε is an error term.

We can transform this expression into a linear function by taking the logs of both sides of the equation as follows:

$$\log Q_d = \log \alpha + \beta_1 \log P + \beta_2 \log Y + \varepsilon.$$

As we stated and proved earlier in Chapter 3, β_1 and β_2 represent the price and income elasticities of demand, respectively. Thus, this type of demand function has constant elasticities of demand.

SUMMARY

The Linear Regression Model

In this section, we will summarize our assumptions regarding the linear regression model and the statistics that we have discussed.

A. Assumptions
   1. The two variables Y and X are related in the following manner:

$$Y_i = \alpha + \beta X_i + \varepsilon_i,$$

   where ε_i is the population error term.

   2. The error term ε_i is a random variable with a normal distribution.

   3. The mean or expected value of ε is zero.

   4. The variance of ε *for each* X value is the same. Also, $E(\varepsilon_i \varepsilon_j) = 0$, where i *does not equal j*, which means that ε_i and ε_j are not related.

   5. X and Y can both vary.

B. The Regression Model

   From a sample of values for X and Y, we wish to estimate a and b such that

$$\hat{Y} = a + bX,$$

   where the expected value of a equals α [$E(a) = \alpha$], and $E(b) = \beta$. The best linear unbiased estimators of a and b are given by

$$a = \bar{Y} - b\bar{X},$$

   and

$$b = \frac{\sum (X - \bar{X})(Y - \bar{Y})}{\sum (X - \bar{X})^2} = \frac{n \sum XY - \sum X \sum Y}{n \sum X^2 - (\sum X)^2},$$

   where $\bar{Y}$ is the mean value of Y ($= \Sigma Y_i / n$) for the sample, $\bar{X}$ is the mean value of X ($= \Sigma X_i / n$) for the sample, and n is the number of observations in the sample. Each sum is to be taken over the sample observations.

C. Tests of Statistical Significance
   1. Test for b.

   Compute $t = \dfrac{b - \beta}{\hat{\sigma}_b},$

where $\hat{\sigma}_b = \sqrt{\dfrac{\hat{\sigma}_{YX}^2}{\sum(X - \overline{X})^2}}$

and $\hat{\sigma}_{YX}^2 = \dfrac{\sum(Y - \hat{Y})^2}{n - 2}$.

The degrees of freedom are given by $n - 2$. We can use a table for the t distribution to decide whether or not to reject a null hypothesis regarding β.

2. Test for a.

Compute $t = \dfrac{a - \alpha}{\hat{\sigma}_a}$,

where $\sigma_a = \dfrac{\sqrt{\hat{\sigma}_{YX}^2 \left(\sum X^2\right)}}{n \sum(X - \overline{X})^2}$,

and then use a t table to test a null hypothesis regarding α.

3. The Coefficient of Determination: R^2.

$$R^2 = \frac{\text{explained sum of squared deviations}}{\text{total sum of squared deviations}}$$

$$= \frac{\sum(\hat{Y} - \overline{Y})^2}{\sum(Y - \overline{Y})^2},$$

Briefly, R^2 gives a measure of how much of the variation in Y can be accounted for by the variation in X, according to the estimate of the relationship between the two variables. A large R^2, however, does not mean that a change in X *caused* a change in Y but merely that the two variables vary together.

4. Confidence Interval for Y given X.
   The 90 percent confidence interval for Y given X can be found by computing

$$P\left[\hat{Y} - t_{0.05}\hat{\sigma}_{YX} = \sqrt{1 + \frac{1}{n} + \frac{(X - \overline{X})^2}{\sum(X - \overline{X})^2}} < Y\right.$$

$$\left. < \hat{Y} + t_{0.05}\hat{\sigma}_{YX}\sqrt{1 + \frac{1}{n} + \frac{(X - \overline{X})^2}{\sum(X - \overline{X})^2}}\,\right] = 0.90,$$

   for $n - 2$ degrees of freedom.

PROBLEMS

1. Given the following sample points for sales of milk and corresponding prices for the supermarket mentioned in the appendix:

Quantity Demanded (Y)	Price of Milk (X)
240	$.20
230	.30
200	.40
160	.50
150	.50
140	.60
120	.70
110	.80
90	.80
80	.90

a. Find the least-squares estimators a and b of α and β, where

$$Y_i = \alpha + \beta X_i + \varepsilon_i,$$

and

$$\hat{Y} = a + bX.$$

b. Compute the R^2 for the regression line that you found above.

c. Test the hypotheses that $\alpha = 0$ and that $\beta = 0$.

d. Compute the 90 percent confidence interval for Y, given $X = \$0.50$.

e. Would you expect the estimates of α and β to be more reliable for a small sample or a large sample? Why?

These problems can be solved with Microsoft Excel using the regression tool provided in the data analysis package.

2. Eastern Electric produces a 25-inch thin-walled television. The company wants to get a better grasp on the sensitivity of the quantity demanded of its product to the various factors that affect it.

   You have been hired as a consultant to estimate the following demand function:

$$Q_E = \beta_0 + \beta_1 P_E + \beta_2 P_G + \beta_3 I,$$

where

Q_E = the average monthly quantity demanded of Eastern Electric's televisions during a given calendar year,

P_E = the price of Eastern Electric's television,

P_G = the price of a television set made by a competing company, Generally Excellent, and

I = average annual household income.

Quantity of Televisions	Price of Eastern Electric Televisions	Price of Generally Excellent Televisions	Average Annual Household Income
250	$900	$1,400	$30,000
400	800	1,500	30,000
330	800	1,200	30,000
360	800	1,200	32,000
445	700	1,200	32,000
380	700	1,000	31,000
440	675	1,000	32,000
400	675	900	32,000
450	630	900	32,000
500	630	950	38,000
440	630	800	38,000
500	595	800	38,000
470	595	750	38,000
520	595	750	42,000
480	595	700	42,000
440	625	700	42,000
410	625	700	39,000
460	625	750	39,000

a. Find the estimated values for β_0, β_1, β_2, and β_3.

b. Which of the estimated values that you found in part (a) are significantly different from zero (one-tailed tests) at the 5 percent level of significance? Why?

c. What is the value of R^2?

3. Connie Jefferson is the primary flower retailer in her hometown of San Flores. Connie has watched the sales volume of her favorite flower, the yellow rose, change over the past 10 weeks. The changes are due to an experiment that Connie is conducting. She has been told she could sell more roses by reducing the price, and Connie tends to agree. In her experiment, Connie has set out to determine the relationship between the price charged for yellow roses and the quantity demanded. Over the last 10 weeks, Connie has carefully tracked the selling price of her roses and the quantity sold. Her data are as follows:

Week	Price	Quantity Sold
1	$30	50
2	8	270
3	10	240
4	27	90
5	25	110
6	21	130
7	12	200
8	15	190
9	19	160
10	20	150

a. Use linear regression to assist Connie in the following:

   (i) Determining the relationship between price and quantity demanded using regression analysis. (Determine the demand function.)

   (ii) Graphing the relationship between price and quantity demanded.

   (iii) Determining R^2. What does this answer mean? How reliable is your estimate of the demand function?

b. (Requires completion of Chapter 2 in the textbook.) Using the demand function you helped Connie determine in part (a), assist her in the following:

   (i) Determining the total, average, and marginal revenue functions for the demand function of yellow roses.

   (ii) Obtaining graphic representation of those three functions.

   (iii) Determining the revenue-maximizing quantity and price. What total revenue will be generated given this price?

SELECTED REFERENCES

Brightman, Harvey, and Howard Schneider. *Statistics for Business Problem Solving.* Cincinnati: South-Western, 1992.

Griffiths, William E., R. Carter Hill, and George G. Judge. *Learning and Practicing Econometrics.* New York: John Wiley and Sons, 1993.

Johnston, J. *Econometric Methods,* 3d ed. New York: McGraw-Hill, 1984.

Maddala, G. S. *Introduction to Econometrics,* 2d ed. New York: Macmillan, 1992.

Mansfield, Edwin. *Statistics for Business and Economics.* New York: W. W. Norton, 1980.

Yamane, Taro. *Statistics: An Introductory Analysis,* 3d ed. New York: Harper & Row, 1973.

CHAPTER FOUR

Economic Forecasting

In Chapters 2 and 3, the importance of accurate revenue data to a profit-maximizing firm was stressed; in Chapter 6, the corresponding importance of accurate cost data will be highlighted. In Chapter 3 and its appendix, various procedures for estimating a firm's demand function were examined; and in Chapter 6, several techniques for estimating a firm's cost function will be described.

In this chapter we turn specifically to the issue of forecasting. **Forecasting** refers to the process of analyzing available information regarding economic variables and relationships and then predicting the future values of certain variables of interest to the firm or economic policymakers. As we will see later, economic forecasting has been one of the fastest growing industries in the United States.

Forecasting is the process of analyzing available data on economic variables and relationships and predicting future values of certain economic variables.

TYPES OF ECONOMIC FORECASTS

Forecasts are made regarding a great variety of economic variables. For example, on an *aggregate* (national economy or macroeconomic) level, forecasts are made regarding future levels of the gross national product or gross domestic product, investment spending, consumption spending, government expenditures, and net exports.

Gross national product for a country is the market value of all final goods and services produced with factors of production owned by residents of the country during some particular time period, usually one year.

Gross domestic product is the market value of all final output produced within the geographical area of a country during a given time period (generally one year).

Investment spending includes all purchases of capital goods, including buildings, equipment, and inventories by private businesses and nonprofit institutions. It also includes all expenditures for residential housing.

Consumption spending is the market value of purchases of newly produced goods and services by individuals and nonprofit organizations and the value of goods and services received by them as income in kind. It includes the value of owner-occupied houses but does not include the purchases of dwellings, which are considered to be capital goods.

Gross national product (GNP) is the final market value of goods and services produced with factors of production owned by the residents of a country during some time period. In the United States, the time period under consideration is usually one year. The gross national product is measured by the *final* market value of newly produced goods and services in order to avoid double counting. For example, a ton of iron ore may pass through several stages and forms (such as sheet metal) before it finally becomes part of an automobile. Nevertheless, the value of all of the work that takes place on the iron ore and steel will eventually be reflected in the price of the automobile when it is sold to a consumer.

It is also important to note that GNP refers to the value of goods and services *produced* during the time period in question. For example, if you sold your old car to a friend, the price of your car to your friend would not be included in GNP, since the car was not newly produced. (However, the *profits* of used-car dealers are included because the dealers do perform a productive service.)

In 1991, the U.S. Department of Commerce began emphasizing gross *domestic* product rather than gross *national* product. Many other countries have traditionally emphasized GDP as a measure of the economic activity occurring within the country, and the change in emphasis by the Commerce Department reflects the integration of the United States into the global economy. The difference between the gross national product and the gross domestic product is that gross national product measures the market value of final output produced annually by all labor and other assets supplied by U.S. residents, *regardless of where the labor and property are located*, whereas **gross domestic product** (GDP) measures the market value of final output produced annually *within the United States, regardless of the ownership of the productive factors.* Although GDP is believed to be a more accurate index of economic activity within a nation, GNP more accurately reflects the income of a nation's citizens and permanent residents. Since many other countries report GDP statistics, reporting GDP as part of U.S. national income and product accounts makes U.S. data more easily compared with data of other nations.[1]

Investment spending refers to the purchases of new plant, equipment, and inventories by businesses. It also includes purchases of new residential housing by individuals. Inventory investment varies to a greater degree than the other two types of investment spending when the level of GNP changes.

Consumption spending refers to expenditures by individuals and nonprofit organizations on newly produced goods and services (except for housing). Consumption spending is frequently broken down into three

---

[1] Currently, the difference between GNP and GDP for the United States is very small. In 1996, GNP was reported to be greater than GDP by about 0.02 percent. See *Economic Report of the President* (Washington, DC: U.S. Government Printing Office, 1998), p. 310.

categories: nondurable goods, durable goods, and services. *Nondurable goods* are consumption goods with an expected useful life of less than three years.[2] Accordingly, *durable goods* have an expected useful life of at least three years. By contrast, *services* cannot be stored but must be consumed at the point of production. Consumer expenditures on durable goods are most affected by changes in GNP.

Government expenditures are expenditures for goods and services by state and local governments and the federal government. These expenditures include such items as national defense goods and wages for firefighters and teachers. Government expenditures do not include such things as welfare payments. These are considered to be transfers of income, not payment for goods and services.

Finally, **net exports** is the term denoting the value of newly produced U.S. goods and services purchased by foreigners (exports) less the value of newly produced foreign goods purchased by the United States (imports). Net exports make an allowance for the excess of goods produced in the United States but purchased by foreigners over the value of goods produced abroad but purchased by U.S. citizens.

In addition to the aggregate levels of gross national product, investment spending, consumption spending, government expenditures, and net exports, forecasts are made regarding the regional (such as southwestern United States or northern Florida) or local (such as Kansas City, Missouri) values of these variables. Forecasts are also made for individual components of each type of production and spending—for example, federal government spending on defense equipment, business expenditures on new plants, and consumer expenditures on durable goods. Forecasts are also made at the industry, firm, and individual product level—for example, the annual sales of the automobile industry, of General Motors Corporation, and of Chevrolet Impalas, respectively.

Forecasts can be short run or long run. In many cases, a business needs to forecast its quarterly, monthly, or even weekly sales. A bakery will try to predict accurately its *daily* sales. However, when a firm makes decisions regarding long-term investment projects, it is important for the firm to obtain accurate forecasts of sales and costs perhaps 5, 10, or even 20 years in the future. In practice, some inputs are *not* variable in the short run. Consequently, a firm manager finds making decisions about investment in plant and equipment to be a hopeless task without forecasts. The recent difficulties of some firms in the automobile, airline, and steel industries are just a few examples of the need for accurate forecasting.

Government expenditures are expenditures for newly produced goods and services, including government investment expenditures, by all levels of government.

Net exports are equal to the purchases of new goods and services produced in the home country by foreigners *(exports)*, less the purchases of new foreign-produced goods and services by the residents of the home country *(imports)*.

---

[2] See U.S. Department of Commerce, Bureau of the Census, *Historical Statistics of the United States, Colonial Times to 1970*, Bicentennial Edition, Part 1, p. 218.

TWO MAJOR KINDS OF DATA

Time series data are observations of a particular variable over a number of time periods.

Cross-section data are observations of a variable at a specific point in time.

The two general types of data that are used by forecasters are time series data and cross-sectional data. **Time series data** are observations regarding a specific variable over a number of time periods. For example, data giving the sales of Ford Motor Company over the last 10 years would be time series data. **Cross-sectional data** are observations regarding a particular variable at a single point in time. For example, the sales of each U.S. automobile manufacturer in 2001 would be cross-sectional data.

FACTORS AFFECTING ECONOMIC VARIABLES

The types of factors that affect the values of economic variables are often classified into four general categories: trend, seasonal, cyclical, and other.

Trend Factors

Trend factors are related to movements in economic variables over time.

Trend factors are those that reflect movements in economic variables over time. One example of a trend factor that would affect the demand for automobiles is the average annual rate of growth of real GNP over several years. (*Real GNP* is the value of gross national product adjusted for inflation so that it better reflects changes in the production of goods and services that have occurred over the period in question.) Another relevant trend factor would be the population growth rate. A third trend factor would be a change in consumer tastes that occurs progressively over time.

Seasonal Factors

Seasonal factors are connected with a specific season of the year.

Seasonal factors are those related to a specific season of the year (spring, summer, fall, or winter) that affect the economic variable or variables in question. For example, more bathing suits are generally sold during the spring than during the fall. More construction activity is usually carried on during the summer than during the winter. More snowmobiles and sleds are sold during the winter than during the summer.

Cyclical Factors

Cyclical factors are related to fluctuations in the general level of economic activity.

Cyclical factors are those related to fluctuations in the general level of economic activity. Economists often use the term *business cycle* to refer to these fluctuations.

A business cycle consists of four parts—a peak, a contraction, a trough, and an expansion, as shown in Figure 4-1. At the peak, economic activity has reached its greatest positive deviation from the long-term trend index of business activity. During a contractionary period, real GNP is falling and

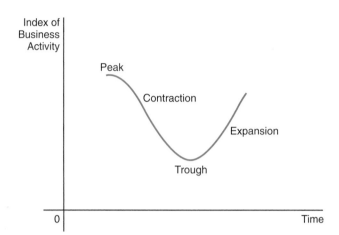

FIGURE 4-1

A Business Cycle

A business cycle consists of four parts—a peak, a contraction, a trough, and an expansion. At the peak, economic activity has reached its greatest positive deviation from the long-term trend index of business activity. At the trough, economic activity has reached its greatest (in absolute value) negative deviation from the trend.

unemployment is rising. At the trough, economic activity has reached its greatest (in absolute value) negative deviation from the trend. During an expansionary period, aggregate real GNP is rising and unemployment is falling.

Other Factors

This category includes all other factors that affect the values of an economic variable. Changes in consumer tastes or preferences not specifically related to the passage of time would be one example of an *other* factor. The level of advertising by a firm's competitors could also be an *other* factor.

It is frequently rather difficult in practice to separate the effects of trend, seasonal, cyclical, and other factors. Linear regression analysis, discussed in the appendix to Chapter 3, is one means of breaking down the effects of various factors. Other techniques for dealing with this problem involve less sophisticated and less formal procedures.

Some of the general types of forecasting techniques will be discussed in the next section.

FORECASTING METHODS

Five different types of forecasting techniques are discussed in this chapter: trend analysis, ARIMA models, barometric forecasting, surveys, and econometric models. Each procedure has its advantages and its disadvantages;

thus, in a given situation, a firm may find it worthwhile to use more than one of the procedures.

Trend Analysis

Trend analysis is a forecasting technique that relies primarily on historical data to predict the future.

Trend analysis relies primarily on historical data to predict the future. The more naive models emphasize the manipulation of historical data in order to discern a long-run trend (rate of change over time) and treat as less important the understanding of the underlying causal relationships.

Probably the simplest form of forecasting using trend analysis is the projection into the future of the current value of an economic variable. For example, we might forecast that $Y_{t+1} = Y_t$, where Y_{t+1} is the dollar value of a firm's sales during the coming year and Y_t is the dollar value of sales for the year just completed.

A slightly more sophisticated model would predict that next year's dollar sales would be a function of this year's sales and the change in dollar sales between this year and last year. For example, a marketing department might predict that $Y_{t+1} = Y_t + \gamma(Y_t - Y_{t-1})$, where $(Y_t - Y_{t-1})$ is the increase in dollar sales this year over last year. The forecasters might estimate a value for γ based on casual observation or through linear regression analysis (discussed in Chapter 3) using time series data.

A forecaster using trend analysis might also predict the dollar value of future sales by sketching a line that appears to "best fit" the historical data, plotted with Y (dollar sales) on the vertical axis and time *(t)* on the horizontal axis, as shown in Figure 4-2. Finally, linear regression analysis could be

FIGURE 4-2

Forecasting by Sketching a Best Fit Line

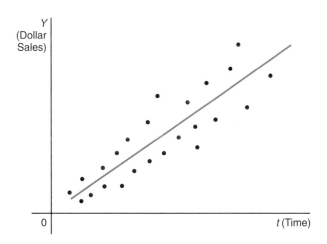

Using this method, a forecaster predicts the dollar value of future sales by sketching a line that appears to *best fit* the historical data.

used to determine the straight line that would best represent the historical data. In this case, the forecaster would use those techniques to estimate α and β in an equation of the form $Y_{t+1} = \alpha + \beta t$, where t represents the number of time periods that have passed since some base period.

Far more sophisticated models than those discussed here may be used in trend analysis, and they may be quite useful in making long-run forecasts. However, regardless of their sophistication, models that consider *only* trend factors will probably not be as useful, at least for short-run forecasts, as will models that attempt to incorporate causal relationships that include adjustments for seasonal, cyclical, and other factors. Seasonal factors will be quite important when forecasting the monthly sales of items such as bathing suits, boats, snowblowers, snow and water skis, air conditioners, and coats, for example. Cyclical factors will be important in forecasting the sales of products such as automobiles, new houses, and automatic dishwashers, since the level of consumer income is an important determinant of consumer spending on such items.

ARIMA Models[3]

Autoregressive integrated moving average (ARIMA) models are a general class of models used often in forecasting time series. These models are based on the hypothesis that adequate forecasts of future values of a time series can be obtained from past values of the series. In general, ARIMA models are linear functions of the sample data, and the sample data must generally constitute a stationary series.[4] The assumption of stationarity is important because the ARIMA models by their nature, based solely on past observations of the series to be forecasted, assert that there is some regularity to the process that is generating the series. Such a situation will not occur, for example, if the value of a series is constantly growing over time. In addition, these models

---

[3] This section may be omitted without loss of continuity. It will be helpful to students to be familiar with the appendix to Chapter 3 on linear regression analysis before they read this section.

[4] A *stationary* time series is one that has both a constant mean and a constant variance over time. We state these conditions more formally as follows.

A time series, X_t, is weakly stationary if the following three conditions are satisfied:

1. The mean, μ, is constant at all points in time:

$$E(X_t) = \mu \text{ for all } t.$$

2. The variance, σ^2_X, of the series is the same over time:

$$\text{Var } (X_t) = E[(X_t - \mu)^2] = \sigma^2_t = \sigma^2_X \text{ for all } t.$$

3. The covariance between any two values of the series depends only on the number of time periods between them, not on their absolute location in time:

$$\text{Cov } (X_t, X_{t-k}) = E[(X_t - \mu)(X_{t-k} - \mu)] = \gamma_k$$

for all t, where γ_k is the covariance between any two values separated by k time periods.

are most useful for nonseasonal data or data from which the seasonality aspect has been removed.[5] ARIMA models are frequently utilized by forecasters because they yield adequate representation of the time series under investigation with relatively few parameters. This attempt to find efficiently parameterized models is known as the *principle of parsimony*. Some of the special subclasses of the general ARIMA models are discussed next.

Autoregressive Models   Autoregressive models are based on the assumption that future values of a series are a function of the past values of the series. For example, a first-order autoregressive model is of the form

$$X_t = A + \phi_1 X_{t-1} + \varepsilon_t,$$

where A is a constant, ϕ is the autoregressive parameter, and ε_t is an error term. The assumptions regarding ε are similar to those involving the error term in linear regression analysis discussed in the appendix to Chapter 3: it is assumed that (1) ε is a random variable with zero mean and constant variance over all time periods, and (2) the ε_t are not autocorrelated, so there is no correlation between ε_t and the error in any other time period.[6] A more general form of the autoregressive model of order ρ, denoted by $AR(\rho)$, is given by

$$X_t = A + \phi_1 X_{t-1} + \phi_2 X_{t-2} + \ldots + \phi_\rho X_{t-\rho} + \varepsilon_t.$$

Some statistical programs estimate this model in a slightly different form where the constant term, A, is omitted and the mean, μ, of the series is subtracted from each value of X:

$$\dot{X}_t = \phi_1 \dot{X}_{t-1} + \phi_2 \dot{X}_{t-2} + \ldots + \phi_\rho \dot{X}_{t-\rho} + \varepsilon_t$$

where $\dot{X}_t = X_t - \mu$.

Moving Average Models   Moving average models express a time series as a function of past and present values of the ε terms, where the ε_t series exhibits all of the properties discussed above and is said to be generated by a white noise process. A first-order moving average model is of the form

$$X_t - \mu = \dot{X}_t = \varepsilon_t + \theta_1 \varepsilon_{t-1},$$

---

[5] More advanced ARIMA models can be constructed to deal with seasonal data. See Paul Newbold and Theodore Bos, *Introductory Business & Economic Forecasting*, 2d ed. (Cincinnati: South-Western Publishing Co., 1994), pp. 319–356.

[6] A series formed by $X_t = \varepsilon_t$, where ε_t has a zero mean, constant variance, and the correlation $(\varepsilon_t, \varepsilon_S) = 0$, where $t \neq S$, is often said to be generated by a *white noise* process.

where θ is a fixed parameter and ε_t is white noise. A more general moving average model of order q, denoted by $MA(q)$, has the following form:

$$X_t - \mu = \dot{X}_t = \varepsilon_t + \theta_1 \varepsilon_{t-1} + \theta_2 \varepsilon_{t-2} + \ldots + \theta_q \varepsilon_{t-q},$$

where $\theta_1, \theta_2, \ldots \theta_q$ are moving average parameters.

Autoregressive Moving Average Models   Autoregressive moving average (ARMA) models are a combination of autoregressive and moving average models. An autoregressive moving average model of order (ρ, q), denoted by ARMA (ρ, q), is of the form

$$\dot{X}_t = \phi_1 \dot{X}_{t-1} + \ldots + \phi_\rho \dot{X}_{t-\rho} + \varepsilon_t + \theta_1 \varepsilon_{t-1} + \ldots + \theta_q \varepsilon_{t-q},$$

where $\dot{X}_t = X_t - \mu$ and ε_t is white noise. For example, a first-order autoregressive moving average ARMA (1,1) model is

$$\dot{X}_t = \phi_1 \dot{X}_{t-1} + \varepsilon_t + \theta_1 \varepsilon_{t-1}.$$

Pure autoregressive models and pure moving average models are special subclasses of the more general ARMA models. The advantage of this more general model is that it can at times provide an acceptable representation of the behavior of a series using fewer parameters than would be necessary using only a pure autoregressive model or a pure moving average model.

Integrated Moving Average Models   We stated earlier that the models discussed previously could be used when a series is stationary. However, many times business and economic data cannot be represented by a stationary series. Such would be the case, for example, when the series grows over time. Series of GDP data, consumption, and investment spending for the United States over time would be nonstationary series. A nonstationary series can frequently be transformed into a stationary series by taking the *first differences* of the series. The first differences of the series X_t are given by $X_t - X_{t-1}$. An autoregressive moving average model is then fitted to the series of first differences. In some cases *second differencing,* or differencing of the first differences, may be necessary to achieve stationarity. A process for which differencing is necessary to achieve stationarity is called an *integrated process,* and autoregressive moving average models applied to such data are called *autoregressive integrated moving average (ARIMA)* models. General autoregressive integrated moving average models are denoted by ARIMA (ρ, d, q), where ρ is the order of the autoregressive process, d is the degree of differencing, and q is the number of moving average terms in the model. Two simple models that are special cases of ARIMA models are the random walk model and a simple exponential smoothing model.

The *random walk* model is of the form

$$X_t - X_{t-1} = \varepsilon_t$$

and is denoted by ARIMA (0,1,0). It states that the change in the series from one period to the next is generated by a random process. Some investigators have found such a model to provide an adequate description of the behavior of prices in speculative markets, such as the stock market and foreign currency markets.

A simple *exponential smoothing* model is of the form

$$X_t - X_{t-1} = \varepsilon_t - (1 - \alpha)\,\varepsilon_{t-1},$$

where α is a smoothing parameter. Such a process is an ARIMA (0,1,1) model, which means that the first differences of the series follow a first-order moving average process.

Simple exponential smoothing models like the preceding one are relatively easy to estimate and are frequently used when forecasts of a large number of time series are required on a regular basis. For example, such models can be used by a firm with a number of mature product lines when the firm wishes to estimate the monthly sales of each one.

An alternative specification of an exponential smoothing model that can be used for forecasting nonseasonal time series with a constant mean is

$$X_t = \alpha X_{t-1} + \alpha(1 - \alpha)\,X_{t-2} + \alpha(1 - \alpha)^2\,X_{t-3} + \ldots + \varepsilon_t,$$

where α is the smoothing constant. This is in the form of an autoregressive equation with $\phi_j = \alpha(1 - \alpha)^{j-1}, j = 1, 2, 3. \ldots$ However, for small values of α, a large number of the autoregressive terms may be needed to obtain adequate forecasts. In this case, the preceding model can be easily transformed into the ARIMA (0,1,1) exponential smoothing model discussed earlier.

Such exponential smoothing models use a weighted average of past values of a series to forecast a future value. It would be possible to use a simple arithmetic average of the past values of the series to forecast the future. Such a procedure results in each past value of the series being given equal weight in the forecasted value, although in many cases it may seem appropriate to give greater weight to values in the more recent past. The other extreme would be to consider only the value in the most recent past to forecast the future. Exponential smoothing models are a compromise between these two positions in that they consider data over a number of periods, but the weights attached to each value decrease as the values fall further in the past.

Box and Jenkins have developed a procedure for estimating ARIMA models. Basically, this methodology involves an iterative procedure with three steps. The first task is to select a specific model from the general class of ARIMA models. This means that the autoregressive order p, the degree of differencing parameter d, and the moving average order q must be specified. These decisions are made based on statistics calculated from the sample data. The second step is to estimate the parameters of the chosen model, and the third step is to check the estimated model to see if it adequately represents the series. A number of computer programs written for personal as well as mainframe computers are available for the Box-Jenkins procedure.[7]

Barometric Forecasting

Barometric forecasting involves the use of current values of certain economic variables called *indicators* to predict the future values of other economic variables.

The philosophy behind barometric forecasting is that if researchers can find a set of economic variables whose fluctuations in value consistently *precede* similar fluctuations in other economic variables, then the first set of variables—called *leading indicators*—can be used to predict future values of the second set of variables. Much of the current barometric forecasting, at least on a macroeconomic level, is based on work done at the National Bureau of Economic Research by Arthur Burns, Geoffrey Moore, Julius Shiskin, and Wesley C. Mitchell.[8]

As we have stated, variables whose current changes give an indication of future changes in other variables are called leading indicators. Variables whose changes roughly coincide with changes in other economic variables are called *coincident indicators*. Finally, variables whose changes typically follow changes in other economic variables are called *lagging indicators*.[9]

The Conference Board publishes a monthly report on the indicator variables entitled *Business Cycle Indicators*.[10] These indicators are subdivided according to the aspect of the economy being described and their timing at business cycle peaks and troughs. The general classification headings of these variables include labor force, employment, and unemployment; output, production, and capacity utilization; sales, orders, and deliveries; fixed capital investment; profits and cash flow, inventories, and inventory investment; prices; wages, labor costs, and productivity; personal income, consumption expenditures, and consumer attitudes; saving; money, credit, interest rates, and stock prices; national defense; and exports and imports.

The Conference Board also publishes a shorter list of indicator variables, shown in Table 4-1. These variables were selected on the basis of six characteristics—economic significance, statistical adequacy, consistency of

---

[7] See G.E.P. Box and G. M. Jenkins, *Time-Series Analysis, Forecasting and Control* (San Francisco: Holden-Day, 1970).

[8] See, for example, A. F. Burns and W. C. Mitchell, *Measuring Business Cycles* (New York: National Bureau of Economic Research, 1946); W. C. Mitchell and A. F. Burns, *Statistical Indicators of Cyclical Revivals*, Occasional Paper 69 (New York: National Bureau of Economic Research, 1938); and G. H. Moore and J. Shiskin, *Indicators of Business Expansions and Contractions* (New York: National Bureau of Economic Research, 1967).

[9] The values of coincident and lagging indicators may be used to confirm short-run trends in the economy previously indicated by the leading indicators.

[10] Prior to 1996, the Department of Commerce published data on more than 100 leading, coincident, lagging, and unclassified indicators in the *Survey of Current Business*, also a monthly publication.

Table 4-1 *Index of Cyclical Indicators and Rate of Growth of Real GDP*

	1980	1990	1994	1995	1996	1997
Rate of Growth of Real GDP	−0.3	1.2	3.5	2.0	2.8	3.8
LEADING INDICATORS						
Composite Index, 1992 = 100	89.3	99.2	101.3	100.8	102.0	103.8
Indexes:						
Stock prices, 500 common stocks (1941–43 = 100)	118.8	334.6	460.3	541.6	670.8	872.7
Index of consumer expectations, (percent)	56.8	70.2	83.8	83.2	85.7	97.7
Percent:						
Interest rate spread, 10-year treasury bonds less federal funds	−1.9	0.5	2.9	0.7	1.1	0.9
Vendor performance, slower deliveries diffusion index	40.6	47.9	60.1	52.8	50.5	53.9
Average weekly initial claims for unemployment insurance (1,000)	488.9	385.8	341.9	358.2	351.7	319.3
Average weekly hours, manufacturing	39.7	40.7	41.9	41.6	41.5	42.0
Building permits, new private housing units (1,000)	1,246.4	1,155.1	1,366.9	1,335.8	1,418.2	1,437.2
Manufacturers' new orders, consumer goods and materials (1992 dols.) (bil. dol.)	96.2	118.0	136.3	139.2	144.1	153.5
Manufacturers' new orders, nondefense capital goods (1992 dols.) (bil. dol.)	27.1	34.6	34.6	38.8	42.0	45.6
Money supply (M2) (1992 dols.) (bil. dol.)	2,635.5	3,475.6	3,328.1	3,310.8	3,391.5	3,486.4
COINCIDENT INDICATORS						
Composite Index, 1992 = 100	80.1	100.2	106.1	109.6	112.6	116.4
Employees on nonagricultural payrolls (bil.)	90.4	109.4	114.1	117.2	119.5	122.3
Personal income less transfer payments (1992 dols.) (bil. dol.)	3,358.2	4,390.4	4,612.8	4,772.5	4,913.8	5,105.4
Industrial production index, 1992 = 100	79.7	98.9	109.2	114.5	118.5	124.4
Manufacturing and trade sales (1992 dols.) (tril. dol.)	434.3	563.0	628.0	651.9	678.4	716.1
LAGGING INDICATORS						
Composite Index, 1992 = 100	103.7	106.8	100.2	103.5	104.4	104.7
Percent:						
Labor cost per unit of output, manufacturing	11.1	0.8	−1.8	−1.7	−0.9	−1.1
Average prime rate	15.3	10.0	7.1	8.8	8.3	8.4
Consumer price index for services	14.6	5.8	3.2	3.5	3.3	2.9
Average duration of unemployment (weeks)	11.9	12.0	18.8	16.6	16.7	15.8
Inventories to sales ratio, mfg., and trade	1.5	1.4	1.4	1.4	1.4	1.4
Commercial and industrial loans outstanding (1992 dols.) (tril. dol.)	345.3	454.7	460.1	512.4	528.1	548.0
Consumer installment credit to personal income, ratio	14.4	14.7	15.6	16.9	17.8	17.7

Source: The Conference Board, New York, NY, *Business Cycle Indicators,* monthly (copyright); *Economic Report of the President, 1998;* and U.S. Department of Commerce, *Statistical Abstract of the United States, 1998.*

MANAGERIAL PERSPECTIVE

The Economic Indicators: Astronomy, Astrology, or Gambling?

In the spring of 1990, Alan Greenspan, chairman of the Federal Reserve Board, told Congress that there was only a 20 percent chance of a recession in 1990, compared with a 30 percent chance predicted a year earlier. He went on to say, moreover, that the National Bureau of Economic Research's monthly Experimental Recession Index indicated that the risk of an economic slowdown was even lower—only a 10 percent chance. Of course, that prediction was made before Iraq invaded Kuwait in August of that year and oil prices skyrocketed.

Although we cannot expect Mr. Greenspan to have been able to predict the actions of Iraqi president Saddam Hussein, the predictions of the Federal Reserve Board and other economic soothsayers have not always been accurate in the past, even in the absence of unanticipated international crises. Among other things, the Federal Reserve's predictions are based on an analysis of the Conference Board's leading economic indicators. Unfortunately, these indicators have had only a 64 percent accuracy record for predicting recessions over the last 40 years.

Recently, however, the Federal Reserve has been using a new model of the U.S. economy that takes the expectations of financial

markets, businesses, and consumers into account. The Fed hopes that this computerized model will enable the central bank to better predict the impact of its policy actions on expectations and, consequently, their eventual effects on the economy.

Some economic forecasting skeptics assert that Greenspan's predictions would be as nearly accurate (or no more inaccurate) if he used the "Hemline Index" or the "Super Bowl Index." During the 1940s, 1950s, and 1960s, it appeared that there was a relationship between the length of women's dresses and the economy: when hemlines rose, the economy tended to grow; when hemlines fell, the economy declined. The Japanese equivalent to the hemline index is the bikini index. Some fund managers argue than an increase in bikini sales at Tokyo department stores is an indicator of confidence in the economy.

Another interesting predictor variable is the winner of the Super Bowl, which so far has a 87.5 percent accuracy rate. In 28 of the 32 years since Super Bowl I, a National Football Conference team winning the Super Bowl was followed by rising stock prices and a booming economy, while an American Conference team winner was followed by falling

timing at business peaks and troughs, conformity to business expansions and contractions, smoothness, and prompt availability. Of these superior indicators, 10 are leading indicators, 4 are coincident indicators, and 7 are lagging indicators.

Each group of indicators (leading, coincident, or lagging) is then used to calculate a *composite*, or overall, indicator for the group.[11] Since they give

---

[11] See George R. Green and Barry A. Beckman, "Business Cycle Indicators: Upcoming Revision of the Composite Indexes," *Survey of Current Business* 73, No. 10 (October 1993): 44–51; and Geoffrey H. Moore (ed.), for the National Bureau of Economic Research, *Business Cycle Indicators,* Volume 1: *Contributions to the Analysis of Current Business Conditions* (Princeton, NJ: Princeton University Press, 1961), Chapter 3, especially p. 72.

stock prices. Although an NFC team won the 1990 and 1991 Super Bowls, the economy grew only slightly in real (inflation-adjusted) terms in 1990, and real GDP decreased in 1991. Nevertheless, while the relationship between an NFC team win and a growing economy did hold from 1992 to 1997, economic growth did not vanish when an AFC team won the Super Bowl in 1998. In 2001, both Super Bowl teams had ties to the old NFL, so some observers said the market and economy would do well no matter who won. However that did not come to pass. (The Japanese equivalent of the Super Bowl index is the performance of the Tokyo Giants baseball team—a winning season for the Giants bodes well for the economy.)

Some economists contend that forecasts based on the leading indicator series sometimes do not pan out because some of the variables that make up this series are no longer as relevant as they should be. For example, Professor Paul Samuelson has stated that the indicators do not properly consider inflation. Others argue that there was a problem with how the Commerce Department constructed its series on contracts and orders for plant and equipment because it did not reflect orders placed with foreign firms. In addition, it has been suggested that the service sector is not adequately represented by the indicator series. Other recommended additions to the series include a Dow Jones price index for 20 corporate bonds, a measure of the number of operating businesses, the rate of worker layoffs, and the rate at which workers quit their jobs. Recognizing the difficulties facing economic forecasters, David Hale, chief economist for Kemper Financial Services, stated: "I have more in common with seismologists than with meteorologists." However, Mr. Hale probably had less in common with Mr. Greenspan, since a study released in 2000 showed that the Fed's forecasting record was significantly better than the consensus of private economic forecasts.

References: Amy Baldwin, "Win-Win Seen on the Gridiron," *San Antonio Express-News,* January 26, 2001, pp. 1E, 8E; "The Infallible Mr. Greenspan," *Business Week,* August 4, 2000, p. 28; "Playing What-If at the Fed," *Business Week* (November 25, 1996), pp. 124–128; "The Real Truth about the Economy," *Business Week* (November 7, 1994), pp. 110–118; "If the Poky Truck Driver Wears a Bikini, Good Times Are Here," *Wall Street Journal,* June 20, 1994, p. B1; "Laying Odds on a Recession: How the Game Is Played," *Newsweek* (February 12, 1990), p. 43; "A Mess of Misleading Indicators," *Time* (June 13, 1988), p. 49; and "Shaky Statistics Pose Peril for Forecasters," *Wall Street Journal,* May 9, 1988, p. 1.

diversified economic coverage based on a superior set of indicators, the composite indexes tend to give more reliable signals than do the individual indicators. The relationship of the values of these variables to the growth rate of gross domestic product from 1980 to 1997 is also shown in Table 4-1.

Ideally, to be good predictors, changes in leading indicators would consistently precede changes in the values of other variables that the researchers are trying to predict. Moreover, these changes should not only always precede changes in the other variables, but also consistently precede them by a certain length of time, such as one month or six months.

Unfortunately, the leading indicator variables are not always that reliable. As a result, the notion of a diffusion index has been developed. A *diffu-*

sion index indicates what percentages of values of the leading indicators are rising (with half of the unchanged components considered rising). Thus, if the values of all of the leading indicators are rising, the diffusion index is equal to 100. If all of the values are falling, the diffusion index is equal to zero. Moore found that the diffusion index is usually above 50 percent during business cycle expansions and below 50 percent during business cycle contractions.[12]

Barometric techniques are frequently used to forecast turning points in the level of general economic activity in a country. They may also be useful in forecasting the *direction of change* in the values of other economic variables. However, these forecasting methods are not as useful in predicting the *magnitude* (size) of such changes.

Surveys

The use of surveys by firms in estimating the demand for their products was discussed in Chapter 3. However, surveys are also used to predict future levels of general economic activity.

Surveys can be quite useful in indicating the plans of businesses to purchase new plants and equipment. Such investment spending can have a relatively large impact on the economy-wide demand for goods and services.

Several agencies regularly conduct surveys of business investment in plant and equipment. For example, McGraw-Hill conducts a survey of such plans twice a year and publishes the results in *Business Week* in November and April. The McGraw-Hill survey covers all large corporations and a great number of medium-sized firms. A joint quarterly survey is conducted by the Department of Commerce and the Securities and Exchange Commission and published in the third month of each quarter in the *Survey of Current Business*. The National Industrial Conference Board surveys capital expenditures commitments made by the boards of directors of 1,000 manufacturing firms. The results of these surveys are also published in the *Survey of Current Business*.

Consumer spending has an important effect on the aggregate level of income (GNP) through its impact on aggregate demand. Both the Bureau of the Census and the Survey Research Center at the University of Michigan conduct surveys regarding consumer intentions to purchase specific products. The information gathered by the Census Bureau is published quarterly in "Consumer Buying Indicators," *Current Population Reports* (Series P-65). The Survey Research Center surveys consumer attitudes and buying plans, and an index of general attitudes is calculated. The results of these surveys are reported annually in the *Survey of Consumer Finances*, published by the

---

[12] Ibid.

Survey Research Center. The Conference Board also publishes a Consumer Confidence Index, based on five survey questions that relate to consumers' current perceptions of local business conditions and job availability and their expectations for the next six months.[13]

Surveys regarding business expectations of future sales and business plans for inventories are also conducted by the Department of Commerce and the Securities and Exchange Commission. These results are published quarterly in the *Survey of Current Business*.

Econometric Models

Econometric models are a fifth way of forecasting in the field of economics. These models range from simple linear demand functions for the product of a firm to very large models containing hundreds of equations, designed to describe many of the economic relationships in an entire nation, including its global environment. Both models describing firm- or industry-level relationships and models describing relationships involving economic aggregate variables (covering large sectors of or an entire national economy) can be quite useful to firm managers.

For example, we have already explained how important it is for a firm to know the nature of the demand function for its product. Given estimates of consumer incomes, competitors' prices, advertising expenditures, and the price it plans to charge, a firm can make a prediction about the future sales of its product. However, the larger econometric models can be quite valuable to a firm in developing forecasts of general business conditions in the economy and, consequently, what consumer incomes and competitors' prices will be in the future. This information, in turn, is necessary in making forecasts regarding the sales of the individual firm. The procedure for estimating the demand function for an individual firm was discussed at length in the appendix to Chapter 3. In this chapter, therefore, we will concentrate on explaining the nature of larger econometric models.

One of the first mathematical models describing the workings of an entire economy was developed in 1939 by the Nobel Prize-winning Dutch economist, Jan Tinbergen. However, this model was not sufficiently well specified to be very useful for forecasting. Since that time, however, many advances have been made in the areas of mathematical economics, statistics, and the development of computers and computer programs. Three of the largest current econometric models are those of Wharton Econometric Fore-

---

[13] See "Forecasting Consumer Spending: Should Economists Pay Attention to Consumer Confidence Surveys?" Federal Reserve Bank of Kansas City *Economic Review* (May/June 1991): 57–71; and Dawn M. Spinozza, "Two Indexes Track Consumer Confidence" Federal Reserve Bank of Richmond *Cross Sections* (Summer 1991): 8–9.

casting Associates (headed by Nobel Prize winner Lawrence Klein); Data Resources, Incorporated; and Chase Econometrics.

All econometric models have two types of equations—behavioral equations and identities. *Behavioral equations* describe how the values of one or more economic variables are related to the behavior of economic units and, therefore, the value of another economic variable. *Identities* are equations that must be true by definition—for example, $(4/2) \equiv 2$. The sign $\equiv$ means "identically equal to."

The workings of a macroeconomic econometric model can be illustrated by the following simple one. Suppose that aggregate consumption spending, C, is a function of aggregate income or GNP last period, Y_{t-1}, plus the change in income during this time period, ΔY_t. We can write one version of this relationship as follows:

$$C_t = \alpha + \beta_1 Y_{t-1} + \beta_2 \Delta Y_t + \varepsilon_t.$$

The subscript t refers to values for the current period, and $t-1$ refers to values for the last period. As discussed earlier in this chapter and in the appendix to Chapter 3, the term ε_t is a term reflecting random errors, with an expected value of zero. Furthermore, let us hypothesize that aggregate investment spending (new plant and equipment, residential housing, and inventories) will be a value determined by factors outside our model. Thus, $I_t = I_t^*$.

Finally, if there were no government expenditures or foreign trade, as we will assume is true in our simple model, the aggregate level of income in an economy must, by definition, be equal to the sum of consumption and investment spending. Therefore

$$Y_t \equiv C_t + I_t.$$

In other words, everything that is produced in an economy during period t must be demanded by some economic unit—consumers or businesses. (However, businesses might find that some of their investment spending has gone for inventories in excess of desired levels.)

Our simple model, therefore, consists of the following three relationships:

(4-1)
$$C_t = \alpha + \beta_1 Y_{t-1} + \beta_2 (Y_t - Y_{t-1}) + \varepsilon_t,$$

(4-2)
$$I_t = I_t^*$$

and

(4-3)
$$Y_t \equiv C_t + I_t.$$

Equations 4-1 and 4-2 are behavioral relationships because they indicate something about the behavior of consumption and investment spending, respectively. Equation 4-3 is an identity. The variables C_t and Y_t are called *endogenous* variables because their values will be determined within the framework of our model.

Investment, I_t^*, is an *exogenous* variable because its value is determined by factors outside this model. In this case Y_{t-1} is a *predetermined* variable—its value has already been determined by the time we are ready to try to predict C_t and Y_t. The remaining terms—α, β_1, and β_2—are called *parameters*. Although their values may change from time to time, they represent numerical constants that describe the behavior of economic units (consumers, in this case). They are not thought to vary as much as the values of the endogenous variables.

If we substitute equations 4-1 and 4-2 into 4-3 for C_t and I_t, respectively, we can obtain the following equation for Y_t, which involves only predetermined or exogenous variables and parameters, except for Y_t itself:

$$Y_t = \alpha + \beta_1 Y_{t-1} + \beta_2 (Y_t - Y_{t-1}) + I_t^* + \varepsilon_t.$$

Subtracting $\beta_2 Y_t$ from both sides, we obtain

$$Y_t - \beta_2 Y_t = \alpha + \beta_1 Y_{t-1} - \beta_2 Y_{t-1} + I_t^* + \varepsilon_t.$$

Factoring out $(1 - \beta_2)$ on the left-hand side, we get

$$Y_t (1 - \beta_2) = \alpha + \beta_1 Y_{t-1} - \beta_2 Y_{t-1} + I_t^* + \varepsilon_t.$$

Finally, dividing by $1 - \beta_2$, we obtain

$$Y_t = \frac{\alpha}{1-\beta_2} + \left(\frac{\beta_1}{1-\beta_2}\right) Y_{t-1} - \left(\frac{\beta_2}{1-\beta_2}\right) Y_{t-1} + \left(\frac{1}{1-\beta_2}\right) I_t^* + \left(\frac{1}{1-\beta_2}\right) \varepsilon_t,$$

or

(4-4)
$$Y_t = \frac{\alpha}{1-\beta_2} + \left(\frac{\beta_1 - \beta_2}{1-\beta_2}\right) Y_{t-1} + \left(\frac{1}{1-\beta_2}\right) I_t^* + \left(\frac{1}{1-\beta_2}\right) \varepsilon_t.$$

Now, substituting for Y_t from equation 4-4 into equation 4-1, we find

$$C_t = \alpha + \beta_1 Y_{t-1}$$
$$+ \beta_2 \left[\left(\frac{\alpha}{1-\beta_2}\right) + \left(\frac{\beta_1 - \beta_2}{1-\beta_2}\right) Y_{t-1} + \left(\frac{1}{1-\beta_2}\right) I_t^* + \left(\frac{1}{1-\beta_2}\right) \varepsilon_t - Y_{t-1} \right] + \varepsilon_t,$$

or

$$C_t = \alpha + \beta_1 Y_{t-1}$$

$$+ \beta_2 \left[\left(\frac{\alpha}{1-\beta_2} \right) + \left(\frac{\beta_1 - \beta_2}{1-\beta_2} - 1 \right) Y_{t-1} + \left(\frac{1}{1-\beta_2} \right) I_t^* + \left(\frac{1}{1-\beta_2} \right) \varepsilon_t \right] + \varepsilon_t,$$

Simplifying, we get

$$C_t = \alpha + \left(\frac{\alpha \beta_2}{1-\beta_2} \right)$$

$$+ \left[\frac{\beta_2(\beta_1 - \beta_2)}{1-\beta_2} - \beta_2 + \beta_1 \right] Y_{t-1} + \left(\frac{\beta_2}{1-\beta_2} \right) I_t^* + \left(\frac{\beta_2}{1-\beta_2} \right) \varepsilon_t + \varepsilon_t,$$

$$C_t = \left(\frac{\alpha - \alpha\beta_2 + \alpha\beta_2}{1-\beta_2} \right) + \left[\frac{\beta_2\beta_1 - \beta_2^2 - \beta_2 + \beta_2^2 + \beta_1 - \beta_2\beta_1}{1-\beta_2} \right] Y_{t-1}$$

$$+ \left[\frac{\beta_2}{1-\beta_2} \right] I_t^* + \left[\frac{\beta_2 + 1 - \beta_2}{1-\beta_2} \right] \varepsilon_t,$$

and

(4-5)

$$C_t = \left(\frac{\alpha}{1-\beta_2} \right) + \left(\frac{\beta_1 - \beta_2}{1-\beta_2} \right) Y_{t-1} + \left(\frac{\beta_2}{1-\beta_2} \right) I_t^* + \left(\frac{1}{1-\beta_2} \right) \varepsilon_t.$$

Equations 4-4 and 4-5 are said to be in *reduced form* because they express the relationships for Y_t and C_t, respectively, in terms of only exogenous and predetermined variables and the parameters.

Using historical data and regression analysis techniques, an econometrician could now statistically estimate the values for $[\alpha/(1-\beta_2)]$, $[(\beta_1 - \beta_2)/(1-\beta_2)]$, and $[1/(1-\beta_2)]$ in equation 4-4. The same procedure could also be used to estimate the constant term and the coefficients of Y_{t-1} and I_t^* in equation 4-5. Once these relationships are statistically estimated, the current value of Y_t and the expected value of I_{t+1}^* could be used to forecast Y_{t+1} and C_{t+1}.[14]

In recent years, econometric models have been developed for use on personal computers. At least one of these programs, the FAIRMODEL, has performed quite favorably compared with the larger models. The personal computer versions of the models are much cheaper to use than the big mod-

---

[14] Other methods of statistically estimating relationships involving simultaneous equations may be desirable. See J. Johnston, *Econometric Methods,* 3d ed. (New York: McGraw-Hill, 1984), Chapter 11.

els, and economists anticipate that these smaller models will be quite helpful to businesspeople in forecasting the future path of economic activity.[15]

ACCURACY OF FORECASTS

As we have indicated, forecasts may be either long run or short run. Businesses use short-run forecasts, for example, to plan short-run production schedules and inventory holdings. Long-term forecasts are essential for decisions regarding investment in plant and equipment. Many of the best-known macroeconomic forecasts are short run (that is, they cover not more than two years in the future); we will discuss their reliability next.

Short-Run Forecasts

The American Statistical Association and the National Bureau of Economic Research have collected the short-run forecasting records of over 50 separate forecasting operations since 1968. These organizations then put together a *median* (middle value) forecast based on the figures.[16] Several studies have now been made of these forecasts.

According to an investigation by Su and Su, the root-mean-square errors in terms of 1958 dollars of the median forecasts for the period from late 1968 to mid-1973 were $3.0 billion and $6.1 billion for quarterly and annual nominal (current dollar) predictions of GNP and $3.4 billion and $7.0 billion for forecasts of real GNP.[17] There is also evidence to indicate that the forecasting errors were larger during the first half of the 1970s than during the earlier (but partly overlapping) period.[18] The errors usually amounted to approximately one-

---

[15] "How Personal Computers Are Changing the Forecaster's Job," *Business Week* (October 1, 1984), pp. 123–124.

[16] The American Statistical Association and the National Bureau of Economic Research (NBER) publish the median (middle value) forecasts in the *American Statistician* and *Explorations in Economic Research,* published by the NBER.

[17] See Vincent Su and Josephine Su, "An Evaluation of ASA/NBER Business Outlook Survey Forecasts," *Explorations in Economic Research* 2 (Fall 1975): 588–618, especially p. 600. The root-mean-square error is equal to

$$\left[\frac{\sum_{t=1}^{n} (GNP_t - G\hat{N}P_t)^2}{n} \right]^{1/2}$$

where GNP_t is the actual value of GNP, $G\hat{N}P_t$ is the predicted value of GNP, and n is the number of time periods.

[18] See Stephen K. McNees, "How Accurate Are Economic Forecasts?" *New England Economic Review* (November/December 1974): 2–19; and Stephen K. McNees, "An Evaluation of Economic Forecasts," *New England Economic Review* (November/December 1975): 3–39.

fourth of the *change* for nominal quarterly forecasts but only about one-eighth of the change for nominal annual forecasts. The corresponding figures for forecasts of real GNP are one-half and one-third, respectively.[19] Annual forecasts tend to be more nearly accurate than quarterly forecasts because the impact of short-run events (such as strikes, production bottlenecks, and inventory adjustments) is less significant over an entire year.

Approximately 60 percent of the forecasts whose predictions are compiled by the American Statistical Association and the National Bureau of Economic Research used a judgmental approach, basing forecasts on the forecaster's judgment and exogenous variables. About 20 percent used primarily econometric models, whereas 10 percent used a leading indicators approach. According to one source, the differences between the forecasting errors resulting from the use of judgmental methods and those resulting from the use of econometric models have been relatively small—with the judgmental forecasts tending to be more nearly accurate. However, the accuracy of the econometric models was improved when their use was combined with a judgmental approach with respect to such things as the future values of exogenous variables. The record of those forecasters using the indicators approach reflected greater errors than did the other two approaches with respect to nominal GNP and greater errors than did the judgmental approach with respect to real GNP.[20]

In another study, Professor Geoffrey Moore found that since the 1950s business executives have generally outperformed economists in forecasting inflation rates for the coming year. There was hardly any relationship between the previous year's inflation rate and the businesspeople's predictions. However, economists' forecasts were highly correlated with past inflation rates.[21] Thus, these results further reinforce the conclusion that the performance of forecasters using econometric techniques could be improved if they would also use a judgmental approach in analyzing the results from the models.

Stephen McNees, of the Boston Federal Reserve Bank, compared the record of seven forecasters using econometric models with a naive prediction that the future growth rate of GNP would be equal to the latest observed growth rate. These forecasts were also compared to those from a simple forecasting rule espoused by economist Milton Friedman that GNP in one quarter would be proportional to the average level of the money supply two quarters *earlier.* McNees summarizes his findings this way:

> Clearly, the naive same-change rule is far inferior to the monetarist [Friedman's] forecasting procedure. All of the economic [econometric

[19] William Ascher, *Forecasting: An Appraisal for Policy-Makers and Planners* (Baltimore: Johns Hopkins University Press, 1978), p. 74.

[20] Ibid., pp. 75–76, 81.

[21] See "Executives Make the Best Inflation Forecasters," *Business Week* (June 9, 1986), p. 24.

model] forecasters, on the other hand, were more successful than the monetarist rule. The margin of superiority varies widely: the Fair model's forecasting errors were, on average, about 10 percent smaller than the monetarist technique while the most successful GNP forecasters' errors are only a little more than half as large as the monetarist formula.[22]

In another recent study, McNees compared the accuracy of the official forecasts generated by the Council of Economic Advisors (CEA), the Congressional Budget Office (CBO), and the Federal Open Market Committee (FOMC) Humphrey-Hawkins forecasts with a number of private sector forecasts. His results were consistent with the hypothesis that the one-year-ahead forecasts of the CEA, the CBO, and the private sector are about equally accurate and more accurate than simple rules of thumb. However, his findings were also consistent with the hypothesis that the multiyear real GNP forecasts of prominent private forecasters and the CBO were more accurate than those of the CEA. The FOMC's July forecasts for the coming year had somewhat greater accuracy than a standard private sector forecast.[23]

In another study, Howrey compared annual forecasts of real GNP growth, the rate of inflation, the civilian unemployment rate, and the Treasury Bill rate generated by the Research Seminar in Quantitative Economics (RSQE), based on the Michigan Quarterly Econometric Model, with those of a four-variable vector autoregressive (VAR) model. His findings were that the RSQE forecasts of the rate of inflation, the unemployment rate, and the interest rate were more nearly accurate than those of the VAR forecasts. However, the VAR forecasts of the annual rate of growth of real GNP were slightly better than those of the RSQE.[24]

Another recent article presented an overview of studies of forecasting practice and performance, particularly among business firms. These studies generally found that forecasts of larger firms were more nearly accurate than those of small firms and that a longer time horizon usually resulted in decreased forecast accuracy. Moreover, a greater level of accuracy was generally attained by preparing forecasts at higher levels within the firm, utilizing a greater number of forecasting techniques, forecasters with more formal training, and seasonally adjusted data. In several studies, wholesale and

---

[22] Stephen K. McNees, "How Accurate Are Economic Forecasts?" *New England Economic Review* (November/December 1974): 19. The FAIRMODEL is relatively judgment free.

[23] See Stephen K. McNees, "An Assessment of the 'Official' Economic Forecasts," *New England Economic Review* (July/August 1995): 13–23.

[24] E. Philip Howrey, "An Analysis of RSQE Forecasts: 1971–1992," *Atlantic Economic Journal* 23, No. 3 (September 1995): 203–219. Forecasters in the United Kingdom and the other countries in the Group of 7 (Canada, France, Germany, Italy, and Japan) besides the United States also have difficulty with the accuracy of their forecasts. See "Dismal Science: Dismal Record," *Barclays Economic Review* (November 1992): 19–34; and David Poulizac, Martin Weale, and Garry Young, "The Performance of National Institute Economic Forecasts," *National Institute Economic Review*, No. 156 (May 1, 1996): 55–62.

retail industries had more nearly accurate forecasts than did manufacturing industries.[25]

Long-Run Forecasts

Five well-known organizations that make long-term economic forecasts are the National Planning Association, the Joint Economic Committee of the U.S. Congress, McGraw-Hill, the Committee for Economic Development, and the Organization for Economic Cooperation and Development. Short-term factors, such as temporarily high interest rates or a temporary change in government spending, have a less significant effect on long-run forecasts than on short-run forecasts. Still, since many of these forecasts rely on estimates of the long-run productive capacity of the economy and give less consideration to demand factors, they tend to be overly optimistic with regard to their projections of GNP growth.[26]

The Current Prognosis

Economic forecasters continue to have problems with the accuracy of their forecasts. Many forecasters did not predict the recession that began in the summer of 1990. In May 1990, only 19 percent of the forecasters surveyed by the *Blue Chip Economic Indicators* predicted a recession to begin in that year.[27] Moreover, once it began, the recession lasted longer than was expected. A 1980 *Business Week* article argued:

> Not only have the economists missed the intensity and timing of each of the seven postwar recessions, but their forecasts seem to be getting worse, even as their acceptance by policymakers and businessmen rises.[28]

The difficulties of the forecasters, especially those using econometric models, can be explained at least partly by changes in the structure of the economy since the 1960s. For example, during the 1970s and early 1980s, inflation was a far more important factor than it had been in the 1950s and 1960s. Supply shortages of some basic materials developed, and the structure of the international oil market changed. Furthermore, the impact of international product and money markets on the domestic economy has expanded, and there

---

[25] See Heidi Winklhofer, Adamantios Diamantopoulos, and Stephen F. Witt, "Forecasting Practice: A Review of the Empirical Literature and an Agenda for Future Research," *International Journal of Forecasting* 12, No. 2 (1996): 193–221, especially p. 215.

[26] William Ascher, *Forecasting: An Appraisal for Policy-Makers and Planners* (Baltimore: Johns Hopkins University Press, 1978), p. 92.

[27] Mark W. Watson, "Using Econometric Models to Predict Recessions," Federal Reserve Bank of Chicago *Economic Perspectives* 15, No. 6 (November/December 1991): 22.

[28] "1980: The Year the Forecasters Really Blew It," *Business Week* (July 14, 1980), p. 88.

have been some significant shifts in consumer behavior. The fact that the Gulf War and its preceding hostilities were not predicted probably had a significant impact on consumer confidence and, as a result, on household purchasing decisions. Finally, economic forecasters have not always correctly anticipated the monetary and fiscal policies that were implemented over the last two decades.

When structural factors in the economy change, the parameters in large econometric models estimated using historical data may no longer be valid. Robert Solow, an economist at the Massachusetts Institute of Technology, summarized the problem this way:

> One advantage the physicist has over the economist is that the velocity of light has not changed over the past thousands of years, while what was in the 1950s and 1960s a good wage and price equation is no longer so.[29]

Another problem forecasters face is inadequate data. Government spending on data gathering in real terms has increased little since the 1970s, although the economy is much larger and more complex. A recent *Fortune* article quoted Harvard University economist Zvi Griliches:

> Our data are weakest in precisely those areas where economic change has been most dynamic, such as technological innovation, the service sector, and trade.[30]

It is argued that measurement errors regarding inflation cause the greatest distortions because these affect wage and productivity data as well as growth of GDP. Also, U.S. data regarding exports of products and services probably significantly underestimate their true values.[31]

Nevertheless, econometrics has been one of the fastest growing industries in the United States. Its annual revenues were estimated to be over $100 million in the early 1980s; its customers included most major corporations as well as large governmental departments.[32] McNees concludes:

> When revisions often change actual outcomes by several tenths of a percentage point even well after the fact, it would be naive to expect forecast errors of essentially zero. From this perspective, it is comforting to see that multiple-percentage-point errors are rare. Far more often than not, macroeconomic forecasts have anticipated the level of the inflation and unemployment rates a year or more into the future within 1 percentage point. Simple rules of thumb have been far less reliable.[33]

---

[29] "Theory Deserts the Forecasters," *Business Week* (June 29, 1974), p. 53.

[30] Louis S. Richman, "Why the Economic Data Mislead Us," *Fortune* (March 8, 1993), p. 108.

[31] Ibid., pp. 108–113; "The Real Truth about the Economy," *Business Week* (November 7, 1994), pp. 110–118; and "Silver Lining in a Flawed CPI," *Business Week* (October 9, 1995), p. 30.

[32] "Where the Big Econometric Models Go Wrong," *Business Week* (March 30, 1981), p. 70.

[33] Stephen K. McNees, "An Assessment of the 'Official' Economic Forecasts," *New England Economic Review* (July/August 1995): 22.

More and more corporations are beginning to use *consensus forecasting*, a technique that involves making a composite forecast based on the predictions of many other forecasters. Chrysler Corporation maintains that this technique has worked successfully with forecasts of GNP and inflation, though not so well for interest rates.[34] Another study of the *Blue Chip Economic Indicators* consensus forecast computed from those of 50 leading economists found that the consensus forecasts performed best with respect to October forecasts of the growth of real GNP for the next year. The forecasts of inflation for the next year were not quite as accurate as those for real GNP. However, forecasts of quarterly growth rates had average errors more than twice those of the other predictions.[35] Finally, a recent study examined the track record of individual participants in the semiannual survey of economic predictions reported by *The Wall Street Journal.* It suggested that combining the forecasts of a few individuals with superior records in the past would result in a forecast with greater accuracy than combining the forecasts of all participants into one consensus forecast.[36]

John Mahaffie has argued that forecasts are the best guess among many plausible alternatives, and those who wish to make forecasting a predictive science will probably be disappointed. He states that even with improvements in predictive tools, forecasting is likely to remain an art. He lists eight common errors of forecasters: failure to examine assumptions, going beyond one's expertise, being too conservative in considering possibilities for the future, neglecting real-world constraints, excessive optimism, reliance on mechanical extrapolation, making forecasts before all factors are considered, and being overly specific. Mahaffie believes that it is important for forecasters to blend quantitative statistical data and qualitative information in making their predictions. Moreover, forecasts will be most helpful if the purpose of a forecast is clearly stated, several possible future outcomes are presented and analyzed, the assumptions used in making the forecast are stated, and social and technological forces are accounted for.[37]

In any event, it seems apparent that despite the problems associated with economic forecasting, corporate managers still believe that an attempt must be made to predict the economic future. After all, it is on the basis of such projections that many managers must bet the life—or at least the good health—of their firms.

---

[34] John Koten, "They Say No Two Economists Ever Agree, So Chrysler Tries Averaging Their Opinions," *Wall Street Journal,* November 3, 1981, p. 29.

[35] See Jim Eggert, "Consensus Forecasting—A Ten-Year Report Card," *Challenge* (July–August 1987): 59–62.

[36] See Dong W. Cho, "Forecast Accuracy: Are Some Business Economists Consistently Better Than Others?" *Business Economics* 31, No.4 (October 1996): 45–49.

[37] John B. Mahaffie, "Why Forecasts Fail," *American Demographics* (March 1995): 34–40.

SUMMARY

Economic Forecasting and the Firm

Economic forecasts can be made regarding a great variety of economic variables. On an aggregate level, for example, forecasts are made regarding future levels of the gross national product, investment spending, consumption spending, government expenditures, and net exports. On a microeconomic level, forecasts are made regarding such variables as sales of a firm and its competitors and the level of input prices. Forecasts may be either long run or short run.

Forecasters use two major types of data in studying the nature of economic relationships—time series data and cross-sectional data. *Time series data* are observations of a specific variable over a number of time periods. *Cross-sectional data* are observations of a particular variable at a single point in time.

The types of factors that affect the values of economic variables are often classified into four general categories: trend, seasonal, cyclical, and other. *Trend factors* are those that reflect long-term movements in economic variables. *Seasonal factors* are related to a specific season of the year. *Cyclical factors* are related to fluctuations in the general level of economic activity. Other factors include such things as changes in consumer tastes not specifically related to the passage of time.

We discussed five forecasting methods—trend analysis, ARIMA models, barometric techniques, surveys, and econometric models. *Trend analysis* relies primarily on historical data to predict the future. These techniques range from rather simple projections of past data to more sophisticated methods.

Autoregressive integrated moving average (ARIMA) models are a general class of models used in forecasting time series based on the hypothesis that adequate forecasts of future values of a time series can be obtained based solely on past information of the series. In general, ARIMA models are linear functions of the sample data, and the sample data must generally constitute a nonseasonal, stationary series. Autoregressive models and moving average models are subsets of the more general ARIMA model class. The random walk model and an exponential smoothing model are two relatively simple ARIMA models that are sometimes used in economic forecasting.

Barometric forecasting involves the use of current values of certain economic variables called *indicators* to predict the future value of other economic variables. The indicator variables are divided into three categories: leading, coincident, and lagging. *Leading indicators* are variables whose current changes give an indication of future changes in other economic variables. *Coincident indicators* are variables whose changes roughly coincide with changes in other economic variables. *Lagging indicators* are variables whose changes typically follow changes in other economic variables.

The use of *surveys* by firms in estimating the demand for their products was discussed in Chapter 3. Surveys are also conducted by various governmental agencies and private firms regarding business investment and consumer spending plans and expected sales and inventory changes.

Econometric models are a fifth method of economic forecasting. These models range from simple, linear demand functions for the product of a firm to very large models containing hundreds of equations, designed to describe many of the economic relationships in an entire nation and its global environment. Econometric models have two types of equations—behavioral equations and identities. *Behavioral equations* describe how the changes in certain economic variables are related to changes in another economic variable. *Identities* give relationships that are true by definition.

Unfortunately, none of the forecasting methods discussed in this chapter yields completely accurate forecasts. Nevertheless, economic forecasting, particularly econometrics, has been one of the fastest-growing industries in the United States. Its customers include major corporations as well as large governmental departments.

QUESTIONS

1. What is the difference between time series data and cross-sectional data?

2. Explain how barometric forecasting is done. What are indicator variables?

3. What is trend analysis? How does it work?

4. What is an econometric model? Can you construct a simple one?

5. List and explain four general categories of factors that may affect the quantity demanded of a product. Give an example.

6. Explain how forecasts involving aggregate economic (macroeconomic) variables can be useful to a businessperson. Give some examples.

7. What are two sources of survey information regarding planned business investment and planned consumer spending?

8. Discuss the accuracy of economic forecasts in recent years. What factors have led to problems in making forecasts? How might forecasters improve their accuracy?

SELECTED REFERENCES

Burns, Arthur F. *The Business Cycle in a Changing World.* New York: National Bureau of Economic Research, 1969. Distributed by Columbia University Press, New York.

Granger, C.W.J. *Forecasting in Business and Economics,* 2d ed. Boston: Academic Press, 1989.

Henry, William R., and W. Warren Haynes. *Managerial Economics: Analysis and Cases,* 4th ed. Dallas: Business Publications, 1978, Chapters 4 and 5.

Johnston, J. *Econometric Methods,* 3d ed. New York: McGraw-Hill, 1984.

Lansing, John B., and James N. Morgan. *Economic Survey Methods.* Ann Arbor: Institute for Social Research, University of Michigan, 1971.

McGuigan, James R., R. Charles Moyer, and Frederick H. deB. Harris. *Managerial Economics,* 9th ed. Cincinnati: South-Western, 2002, Chapter 5.

Newbold, Paul, and Theodore Bos. *Introductory Business & Economic Forecasting,* 2d ed. Cincinnati: South-Western, 1994, especially Chapter 7.

Robertson, John C., and Ellis W. Tallman. "Data Vintages and Measuring Forecast Performance." Federal Reserve Bank of Atlanta, *Economic Review* 83, No. 4 (Fourth Quarter 1998): 4–20.

Robertson, John C., and Ellis W. Tallman. "Vector Autoregressions: Forecasting and Reality." Federal Reserve Bank of Atlanta, *Economic Review* 84, No. 1 (First Quarter 1999): 4–18.

Rogers, P. Mark. "A Primer on Short-Term Linkages between Key Economic Data Series." Federal Reserve Bank of Atlanta, *Economic Review* 83, No. 2 (Second Quarter 1998): 40–54.

Simon, Julian L. "Great and Almost-Great Magnitudes in Economics," *Journal of Economic Perspectives* 4 (Winter 1990): 149–156.

Are There Two Markets for HCM Ovens?

Cuisine Tech, Inc. (CTI), manufactures a new type of oven, the HCM oven (halogen/convection/microwave), and is trying to determine its optimal pricing strategy. (The HCM oven was first unveiled by General Electric in 1999–2000.)[1] In the past CTI has been manufacturing a deluxe model of oven for people in the upper-middle-income bracket. The demand function of people (in this category) for the deluxe model is given by

$$Q_H = 60,000 - 40P_H + 20P_C + 5H + .10I_H + .0001A_H,$$

where

Q_H = annual sales (number of units) of the deluxe model,

P_H = price of the deluxe model,

P_C = price of a competing-brand oven,

H = number of two-income households (in millions) in this income bracket,

---

[1] For more on the this type of convection oven, which uses halogen light tubes to brown foods as they cook but also can be operated as a microwave, see: "G. E. Advantium Oven: General Electric's New Technology-A Lightwave Oven," *Kitchen Quest.com.* online, February 6, 2000 www.kitchenquest.com/critique/advantium, September 7, 2002.

I_H = average annual income of households in this bracket, and

A_H = annual dollar expenditures on advertising for the high-priced model.

Currently, $P_H = \$750$, $P_C = \$625$, H = 10, $I_H = \$56,000$, $A_H = \$500,000$, and Q_H = 48,200.

For several years after the deluxe model oven was introduced, demand grew rapidly. Now, however, CTI believes that the market for this model is fairly well saturated and that prospects for future growth in sales are limited. (Note the small size of the coefficients of I_H and A_H.)

Consequently, CTI is trying to determine if its profits would be greater if it added a second model—less elaborate, but cheaper—to its product line. Some researchers in the marketing department have argued that there exists a large potential market among middle- and lower-middle-income consumers if CTI were to develop a substantially cheaper model that performed the basic function of fast cooking and browning foods like chicken and beef. In fact, the researchers were so convinced such a market existed that they mailed a questionnaire to 10,000 families living in the suburbs of several large U.S. cities. They selected residents of neighborhoods populated primarily by people in the target income bracket.

From the 5,000 questionnaires that were returned and from U.S. government statistics indicating the number of households in the target income range, the market researchers estimate that the demand function for the cheaper HCM oven is

$$Q_L = 20,900 - 100P_L + .5H + .7I_L,$$

where

Q_L = annual sales (number of units) of the lower priced model,

P_L = price of lower priced model,

H = number of two-earner households (in 1,000s) that are in these income brackets, and

I_L = average annual income of households in the target income range.

Currently, H = 15,000 and $I_L = \$28,000$.

QUESTIONS

1. If management is prepared to design a microwave oven specifically for the moderate-income market, how can it use the estimated demand curve for the lower

priced product to assess the relationship of its pricing decision to quantity sold and to the behavior of sales revenue? Suppose the managers were particularly interested in the following possible sales prices:

$$P_L = \$480, \$450, \$425, \$400, \$375, \$350, \$325, \$300, \$275,$$
$$\$250, \$225, \$200, \text{ and } \$175.$$

What would be the estimated quantity sold at each price, and how would total revenue and arc marginal revenue vary from price to price?

2. Over what price range is the estimated demand for the low-priced oven *elastic*? Is it *inelastic* at any price or prices? If so, which?

3. What is the income elasticity of demand for this product between $I_L = \$28,000$ and $I_L = \$30,000$? (Assume $P_L = \$350$ and $H = 15,000$.) What do you think the prospects are for future sales growth as income rises? Why?

4. What is the effect of changes in the number of households in this income bracket on the quantity demanded of this product? Be sure that your answer is complete and precise.

5. What other variables (not in the estimated demand function for the cheaper model given above) might affect the demand for this product? How might the firm obtain information on their effects on demand after the new model is introduced?

6. Suppose that the cost *per unit* incurred by CTI to produce additional units of the cheaper model is $125 over its feasible range of output. Can you determine from the table you constructed in Question 1 the optimal quantity of this oven for CTI to produce? Why? (We shall discuss this issue carefully in Chapters 5, 6, and 7.)

Omega Distributing Company I

Omega Distributing Company specializes in supplying laundry and cleaning products to chain grocery stores. One of the products it sells is a fabric softener marketed under the brand name Blast. Although the product has generated substantial net revenues for Omega, management is unsure of its pricing and advertising strategies and has undertaken, with the cooperation of some retail stores, to conduct a statistical analysis of demand for the product in its market area.

Omega's analysts believe that the principal determinants of consumer purchases of Blast are (1) the price charged for Blast, (2) the price of Cloud (a competing brand of softener sold by a rival firm), and (3) advertising expenditures on Blast. The following data were collected from a group of representative stores.

Q = Weekly Quantity of Blast Sold (hundreds)	P_b = Price of Blast (dollars)	P_c = Price of Cloud (dollars)	A = Advertising $ (ten thousands)
1027	1.45	1.42	3.97
1204	1.29	1.45	4.54
974	1.47	1.39	3.77
1111	1.33	1.43	3.29
1042	1.44	1.40	3.49
1304	1.32	1.47	4.27
1054	1.33	1.38	4.11
997	1.35	1.37	3.50
1223	1.31	1.43	3.97
1247	1.30	1.44	3.88
1049	1.46	1.43	3.99
1250	1.27	1.47	4.54
972	1.47	1.38	3.75
1184	1.32	1.46	3.31
1054	1.43	1.41	3.49

In the table, the price of Cloud is the retail price charged consumers, while the price of Blast is the price Omega charges its customers. However, since the retailers use markup pricing, the price charged by Omega does determine what consumers pay for Blast.

Omega's analysts hypothesized that a linear demand function of the following form would describe the relation between quantity sold and the set of independent variables shown in the table:

$$Q = B_0 + B_1 (P_b) + B_2 (P_c) + B_3 (A).$$

Using multiple regression analysis and the data in the table, they estimated the values of the coefficients B_0 through B_3 to be the following:

$B_0 = -820$

$B_1 = -689$

$B_2 = 1,972$

$B_3 = 18$ (all rounded to the nearest whole number).

QUESTIONS

1. Assume that Omega's analysts found no statistical reason to reject the regression results or any of the estimates of the coefficients of the demand function. Management asks what the demand function indicates about how the sales volume of Blast is related to its price, the price of Cloud, and advertising expenditures on Blast. Duncan Haynes, a member of the team that carried out the study states that a number of important conclusions can be drawn by setting each of the variables in the table equal to its mean value and determining the quantity sold that the demand model estimates. He says that the signs of the estimated coefficients and the elasticity of the sales quantity with respect to each of the independent variables will indicate that Omega should consider some alterations in its current pricing and advertising strategies. Using the mean values of the independent variables in the table with the estimated regression equation, determine what strategy changes Duncan would be likely to suggest.

The following part of this exercise should be carried out only by students who have access to a computer and a multiple regression program and have the statistical background to interpret the results.

2. Using the data obtained by Omega and the form of regression equation given above, estimate a linear regression equation for Omega's sales volume of Blast. Check to see whether your results agree with the linear function estimated by Omega's analysts. Interpret the results of the equation with regard to (a) overall goodness of fit and (b) significance of the estimated coefficients of the independent variables.

CHAPTER FIVE

Production Analysis

The basic function of a firm is to ready and present a commodity or service for sale—presumably at a profit. When the firm's activities center around a tangible product rather than a service, the firm may merely obtain the item from another enterprise and sell it to a third party, or it may also undertake the partial or complete (from raw materials) manufacture of that item. We will use the term production in a broad sense so that it refers to all of the procedures that a firm may go through to present its good or service for sale.

One of the latest developments in corporate structure is the *virtual corporation.* The virtual corporation consists of a partnership of firms, wherein each one contributes some specific competency at which it excels in a cooperative effort to produce a good or service. These virtual corporations may consist of companies at many different locations—even different countries—linked by informational networks. Such organizations may be temporary, depending on the nature of the market that is being met.[1] A very interesting virtual corporation in the baking business is majority owned by former Pitts-

---

[1] Sidney Hill, "The 'Virtual' Corporation," *Manufacturing Systems* 14, No. 3 (January/February 1996): 32–40; and "The Virtual Corporation," *Business Week* (February 8, 1993), pp. 98–103.

burgh Steelers running back Franco Harris.[2] Harris's company subcontracts the major responsibilities of manufacturing, selling, and shipping to other firms. Its in-house activities consist of managing, contracting, quality control, and product development. In fact, Franco Harris retained a master baker to develop improved product formulations for the subcontracted baking companies.

British Airways (BA), during the past decade, has focused on becoming a "virtual airline." In an effort to cut costs and increase flexibility in its operations, BA wants to lease most of its planes, including leasing their engines by the hour. The airline also wants the suppliers of the planes and engines to furnish spare parts, routine maintenance, and flight training. Airbus and Boeing have even considered the possibility of providing British Air with flight crews.[3]

When making product decisions, a firm's management must consider both *what* is to be produced and *how* to produce it. Companies that are successful over long periods of time usually have performed outstandingly well in both of these areas. General Motors is a firm that in the past achieved long-run success attributable at least in part to careful product design and efficient organization of production. However, in the 1980s and early 1990s the automaker's attempts to more fully automate its plants with robots ran into difficulties. GM's Japanese competitors, with less automation, high productivity, and their just-in-time inventory system, were able to achieve lower costs in both their U.S. and Japanese plants. In fact, much of the automation in GM's old Cadillac plant in Hamtramck, Michigan, caused so many problems that it was removed.[4] More recently, GM has built some new plants in Brazil and in the United States where robotization and modular assembly are expected to produce better results. (See the Managerial Perspective near the end of this chapter for more details.)

It is clear that international trade and investment are having more and more impact on the productive process. The *Financial Times* reported that a significant share of recent increases in British productivity was due to the missionary effect. The *missionary effect* refers to new production ideas and methods introduced by foreign investors and suppliers.[5] Today's business publications are full of stories about trends toward "smart factories," "work

---

[2] Brad Edmonds, "Character Sketch: A Capitalist Role Model," lewrockwell.com, online, March 2001, www.lewrockwell.com/orig/edmonds6.html, June 20, 2002; and Tim R. Davis and Bruce R. Darling, "How Virtual Corporations Manage the Performance of Contractors: The Super Bakery Case," *Organizational Dynamics* 24, No. 1 (Summer 1995): 70–75.

[3] "British Airways Moves Closer to Being 'Virtual Airline,'" *Wall Street Journal*, June 25, 1998, p. B4.

[4] Some Manufacturers Drop Efforts to Adopt Japanese Techniques," *Wall Street Journal*, May 7, 1993, pp. A1, A12; and "Auto Makers Discover 'Factory of the Future' Is Headache Just Now," *Wall Street Journal*, May 13, 1986, pp. 1, 12.

[5] "An International Blend of Ideas," *Financial Times*, July 21, 1997, p. 8.

teams," "concurrent engineering," "flexible manufacturing," and the "quest for quality" in U.S. industry.[6] Computer-integrated manufacturing (CIM) and computer-aided design (CAD) are two tools that have helped firms to be more efficient and respond quickly to market changes. However, as the examples just cited have shown us, no mechanical or electronic device will substitute for careful, efficient, on-the-ball management. Making the right choices at the right time, simplifying and reorganizing production for greater efficiency, and producing products that are qualitatively equal to or better than imported alternatives depend on people skills, not just automation or robotics.

Another aspect of the globalization of production is coordination of offshore plants with home-country management and markets. Fruit of the Loom, whose market share of men's and boy's underwear in the United States is about 32 percent, provides a glaring example of this difficulty. After decades of successful operation, its fortunes waned in the late 1990s as, following many other garment manufacturers, it cut back its U.S. operations and began to produce offshore. It had production problems in its non-U.S. plants and could not keep its supply flow in tune with the demands of customers. In response to weakening demand, it cut back offshore production but then had trouble getting it back to the appropriate level when demand rebounded. Fruit of the Loom was forced to file for bankruptcy protection in December 1999. In 2001–2002 a deal was concluded whereby Fruit of the Loom was acquired by Berkshire Hathaway. Its CEO was confident that the acquisition would "pave the way for emergence from Chapter 11."[7]

Perhaps the most dramatic adjustments in production take place when a new technology causes fundamental changes in the way the production process is carried out. A very recent example is the Italian tiremaker, Pirelli. Pirelli has developed a new tiremaking process that is completely different from older technologies and has great promise for the new, more integrated role that input suppliers are playing in the world automobile industry. With the new process, called the Modular Integrated Robotized System (MIRS), a tire that used to take six days to get from raw material to final product now takes 72 minutes. A tire can come off the MIRS line every three minutes. In addition, MIRS plants are so compact that they can be set up in an area of

---

[6] See Rick Roff, "Boeing's Factory of the Future Will Be Highly Visual in Its Operation," *Boeing Frontiers*, online, Vol. 1, No. 2, June 2002, www.boeing.com/news/frontiers/i_cal.html, July 16, 2002; Brian McWilliams, "Re-engineering the Small Factory," *Inc.* (January 1, 1996), pp. 44–47; Gary S. Vasilash, "Lean—and Beyond," *Automotive Production* 108, No. 1 (January 1996): 60–63; "Small, Flexible Plants May Play Crucial Role in U.S. Manufacturing," *Wall Street Journal*," January 13, 1993, pp. A1, A2.

[7] "Berkshire Hathaway Gets Green Light for Fruit of the Loom Purchase," and "Berkshire Hathaway to Acquire Fruit of the Loom for $835m," *Fashion United*, online, January 8, 2002 and November 1, 2001, www.fashionunited.co.uk/business/media/fruit.htm July 18, 2002; and James P. Miller, "Fruit of the Loom Bottoms Out on Production Troubles," *Wall Street Journal*, September 20, 1999, p. B4.

about 400 square yards right within an automobile plant. The first such installation was teamed with a BMW plant in Germany that produces the Mini-Cooper.[8]

As the above discussion illustrates, there are many dimensions to a firm's production of its chosen output. In Chapter 2, we discussed the necessity of producing a product for which a sufficient market could be obtained, and in Chapters 3 and 4 we considered ways to estimate and forecast the size of that market. In the next two chapters, we will discuss how managers can use economic principles to ensure that the firm's product is obtained at the lowest possible cost, *given a certain desired level of output.*

In the **long run** all inputs are variable, whereas in the **short run** some inputs are fixed.

As we discuss production, it will be helpful to distinguish between two general categories of time periods—the long run and the short run. The **long run** is distinguished from the short run by being a period of time long enough for all inputs, or factors of production, to be variable as far as an individual firm is concerned. The **short run,** on the other hand, is a period so brief that the amount of *at least* one input is fixed. Certainly the length of time necessary for all inputs to be variable may differ according to the nature of the industry and the structure of the firm. For example, the long run for General Motors would likely be a greater length of time than that for a firm specializing in temporary office help. In a practical sense, economists think of the long run as a planning period involving decisions regarding investment in new plant and equipment, while the short run involves operations from existing plant and equipment.

THE PRODUCTION FUNCTION AND THE LONG RUN

The economic analysis of production can be undertaken by either first considering the long run and then the short run, or vice versa. Here we have chosen to begin with the long run for the following reason: *The condition for obtaining the cost-minimizing combination of inputs for a given level of output in the long run also applies in the short run to all variable inputs.* Thus, the long-run case provides a rule with general applicability to the question of choosing the proper combination of what may be very numerous available combinations of variable inputs. After developing our picture of the long run, it will be easy to turn to the short run, which has the added restriction that some inputs are fixed in amount.

---

[8] "Pirelli busca rentabilidad a traves de la tecnologia," elmundomotor.com, online, June 20, 2002, www.elmundomotor.elmundo.es, June 30, 2002; "Re-Inventing the Wheel," *The Economist* (April 22, 2000), pp. 57–58; and "Pirelli Launches Eufori@: The First MIRS Tyre," Automotriz. net, October 29, 2001, www.automotriz.net, July 12, 2002.

The **production function** is a statement of how inputs can be combined to get various quantities of output of some given product.

We will begin our discussion of the long run by concentrating on the nature of the production function itself. Briefly, a **production function** is a mathematical statement of the way that the quantity of output of a particular product depends on the use of specific inputs or resources. In the long run, it is possible to vary the amount of each input that is included in the function and therefore to use virtually any combination of the inputs to obtain output. For each possible combination of inputs, the production function indicates the *maximum quantity of output that can be produced*. For example, one production function might be $Q = L^2 + 2KL$, where Q equals quantity of output, K is quantity of capital, and L is quantity of labor. Another production function might be $Q = 10K^{1/2}L^{1/2}$. Table 5-1 gives some approximate quantities of output for the latter production function corresponding to different amounts of capital and labor. We say that the production function indicates *maximum* quantities that can be produced with each combination of inputs because we assume *all* inputs are being used efficiently; that is, none are idle or wasted. In other words, no workers are playing cards when they are supposed to be tightening bolts on an assembly line.

Marginal Product of an Input

A fuller understanding of the meaning of a production function can be gained by examining what happens to output if the amount of just one input is changed. If we select some combination of inputs from Table 5-1 and assume a firm is operating with it, there will be specific changes in output that occur from changing one or the other of the two inputs. For example, if the firm is using three units of K with two of L, output will be 24.49. If K is increased by one unit, output will expand to 28.28. The change in output that occurs, 28.28 minus 24.49 or 3.79, is called the **marginal product** of input K. It tells us the impact on output (Q) of a one-unit change in K; it can also be written

The **marginal product** of a variable input is the rate of change of total product with respect to the input, all other inputs are kept fixed.

$$MP_K = \frac{\Delta Q}{\Delta K}.$$

Similarly, the marginal product of a unit of L is $\Delta Q / \Delta L$, and if the firm is currently using 3 of units of K with 2 units of L, the marginal product of a *third unit of L* will be 30 minus 24.49 or 5.51. You should examine Table 5-1 enough to see that at other combinations of K and L, the marginal products of the two inputs are not the same as they are at $K = 3$ and $L = 2$. The reason for this is that while inputs may be partial substitutes for one another, they also generally complement one another in some way, so that the marginal product of one of them will be greater the more of another it has to work with. Thus, in the table, when $L = 2$ but $K = 4$ rather than 3, the marginal product of L will be 34.64 minus 28.28 or 6.36—higher than it is when K is only 3. That is because when $K = 4$ instead of 3, labor has more capital to work with; therefore, an additional unit of labor can add more to total output.

Table 5-1 *Values of Q, K, and L for the Production Function* $Q = 10K^{1/2}L^{1/2}$

K	Output Quantity (Q)				
5	22.36	31.62	38.73	44.72	50.00
4	20.00	28.28	34.64	40.00	44.72
3	17.32	24.49	30.00	34.64	38.73
2	14.14	20.00	24.49	28.28	31.62
1	10.00	14.14	17.32	20.00	22.36
	1	2	3	4	5	L

Marginal product is usually written as *MP* with a subscript for the name of the input. Thus, MP_K indicates the marginal product of K and MP_L the marginal product of L. In this book, we will also adopt the convention that calculation of marginal product from tabular data (also called discrete data) will be called *arc marginal product*. This is the same convention we used in Chapter 2 when arc marginal revenue was defined. There we were interested in how much total revenue changed per unit of output as output *(Q)* changed by one or more units. Here we focus on how much *output* changes per unit of *input,* as some input such as capital or labor changes by one or more units. Thus, if a firm employs four more workers and its daily output rises by 20, we will say that the arc marginal product of a worker is 5 units of output per day (assuming no other inputs are changed). When combined with knowledge of *how much the firm must pay* to obtain an additional unit of a given input, the marginal product of an input provides extremely useful information on choosing the best input combination, as will be shown later in this chapter.

Isoquants and the Production Function

In general, we can represent the production function for a firm as

$$Q = f(K,L,M, \ldots, Z),$$

where $K, L, M, \ldots, Z$ are amounts of various inputs and Q is the level of output for a firm. Although a firm usually has more than two types of inputs and a more general case can be handled mathematically without too much difficulty, we will restrict our discussion to a situation in which there are only two inputs. Thus, we will use a production function of the form

$$Q = f(K,L),$$

where K and L are inputs (also called *factors of production*) and Q is quantity of output. We are limiting our discussion to the two-input case because it can be illustrated easily and because all of the economic principles that we

FIGURE 5-1

*The Production
Function*

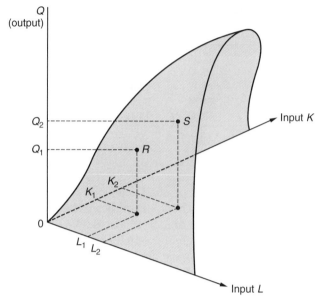

Figure 5-1 depicts a production function—the relationship between the quantities used of two inputs, K and L, and the quantity produced of output, Q. For example, at R with L_1 of input L and K_1 of input K, quantity Q_1 of output can be produced. A similar explanation holds for L_2, K_2 and Q_2 at point S.

derive from this case apply to a more general case as well. The production function relationship $Q = f(K,L)$ can be graphed as a surface in three-dimensional space so that the surface generally reaches higher altitudes as the quantities used of inputs K and L increase (see Figure 5-1). Such a function indicates that a greater level of output can be achieved with greater amounts of the inputs—an assumption that seems realistic.

As we will see later, the economic way of looking at the most efficient (that is, the cheapest) combination of two inputs that will produce a particular level of output is most easily understood if we first visualize the production surface in Figure 5-1 as consisting of a series of isoelevation contours (lines of equal height above the K,L plane), each of which corresponds to a particular level of output (see Figure 5-2).

Now imagine that these contours have been projected down into the K, L (input) plane (see Figure 5-3). These contours, which are called **isoquants** (meaning, literally, *equal quantity*), give the various combinations of inputs K and L that would enable a firm to produce a particular level of output. Thus, each isoquant corresponds to a specific level of output and shows different ways, all technologically efficient, of producing that quantity of output. As we proceed northeastward from the origin, the output level corresponding to each successive isoquant increases because, as we stated earlier, a higher level of output usually requires greater amounts of the two inputs.

An **isoquant** is a contour line that shows the various combinations of two inputs that will produce a given level of output.

FIGURE 5-2

Iso-Quantity Contours on the Production Surface

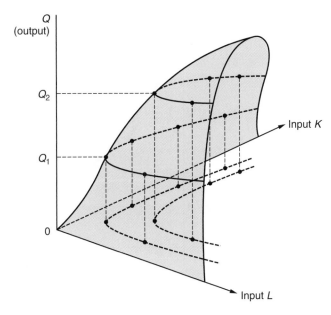

The iso-quantity contours depict various combinations of inputs L and K that can be used to produce levels of output equal to Q_1 and Q_2, respectively.

Slope of an Isoquant (Marginal Rate of Substitution)

The slope of an isoquant is significant because it indicates the rate at which factors K and L can be substituted for each other while a constant level of production is maintained. Specifically, the slope of an isoquant in Figure 5-3, or

FIGURE 5-3

Isoquant Curves

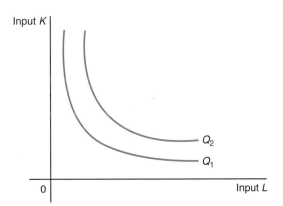

The iso-quantity contours depicted in Figure 5-2 are projected onto the input (L,K) plane in Figure 5-3. Here, they are called *isoquants*.

FIGURE 5-4

Diminishing Marginal Rate of Substitution

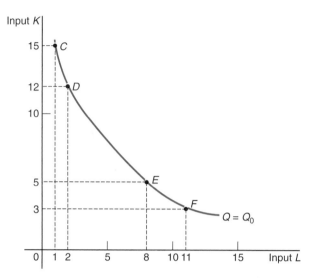

In Figure 5-4, the marginal rate of substitution of input L for input K decreases as the amount of input L used relative to input K increases. Between points C and D, MRS = $-(\Delta K/\Delta L)$ = $-(-3/1)$ = 3. Between points E and F, MRS = $-(-2/3)$ = 2/3.

The **marginal rate of (technical) substitution (MRS)** is the negative of the slope of an isoquant and shows how much of one input can be substituted for another, output constant.

$\Delta K/\Delta L$, can be obtained by finding the amount of input K that can be given up if one more unit of input L is added while the level of output is held constant. Economists call the negative of this term $(-\Delta K/\Delta L)$ the **marginal rate of (technical) substitution (MRS)** of input L for input K:

$$MRS = -\left(\frac{\Delta K}{\Delta L}\right)_{Q\,\text{constant}} = (-1) \times \text{isoquant slope.}$$

In Figure 5-4 the marginal rate of substitution between points C and D is $(-\Delta K/\Delta L) = - [(12-15)/(2-1)] = - (-3/1) = 3$. In this range of the isoquant, one unit of input L can be used in place of *three* units of input K. However, between points E and F the MRS is only $- [(3-5)/(11-8)] = - (-2/3) = 2/3$. In this region of the isoquant, it takes *three* units of input L to replace *two* units of input K and keep output at the same level. The MRS has decreased because inputs L and K are *not* perfect substitutes for each other. Therefore, as more of input L is added, less of input K can be given up in exchange for another unit of input L while keeping the level of output unchanged.

In Figure 5-5 we find an isoquant corresponding to an output level of 20 units for the production function illustrated in Table 5-1. That table indicated that 20 units of output could be produced in the ways shown here:

Input Combination	Level of Output (Q)	Amount of Capital (K)	Amount of Labor (L)
A	20	4	1
B	20	2	2
C	20	1	4

The two inputs involved are capital, measured on the vertical axis, and labor, measured on the horizontal axis. The marginal rate of substitution of labor for capital between points A and B is equal to $-(\Delta K/\Delta L) = -(-2/1) = 2$. Between points B and C, the marginal rate of substitution is equal to $-(\Delta K/\Delta L) = -(-1/2) = 1/2$. In this case also, the marginal rate of substitution is decreasing, and the inputs (capital and labor) are imperfect substitutes.

Relation of MRS to Marginal Product of Inputs

The marginal rate of substitution $-(\Delta K/\Delta L)$ is equal to the ratio of the *arc* marginal product of input L to the *arc* marginal product of input K. As we explained earlier in the chapter, the arc marginal product of an input is the average change in output resulting from a one-unit increase in that input, holding the other input(s) constant. Thus, $MP_L = \Delta Q/\Delta L$ and $MP_K = \Delta Q/\Delta K$. Along an isoquant, the *increase* in output resulting from the addition of input L must be exactly offset by the *decrease* in quantity from a reduction in input

FIGURE 5-5

An Isoquant for 20 Units of Output

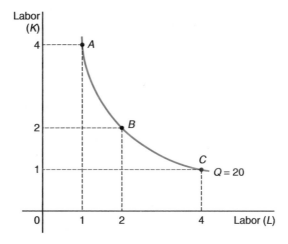

Figure 5-5 depicts an isoquant for 20 units of output. That level of output can be produced using 4 units of capital and 1 of labor, 2 units of capital and 2 of labor, or 1 unit of capital and 4 of labor.

K, or $\Delta Q = 0 = MP_L(\Delta L) + MP_K(\Delta K)$. Thus, $MP_L(\Delta L) = -MP_K(\Delta K)$, and dividing both sides by $\Delta L(MP_K)$, we obtain the following equation:[9]

$$\frac{MP_L}{MP_K} = -\frac{\Delta K}{\Delta L}, Q \text{ constant}.$$

If we think about it, it must be the case that the rate at which one input can be substituted for another, while maintaining the same level of output, is inversely related to their relative productivities. For example, if 1 unit of capital will add 20 units of output per hour and 1 unit of labor will add 10 units of output per hour, then we can substitute 2 units of *labor* for 1 unit of *capital.* This relationship holds, since in this case one unit of labor is only *half* as productive as one unit of capital [$MP_L = 10 = (1/2)MP_K$]. Thus

$$MRS = -\left(\frac{\Delta K}{\Delta L}\right)_{Q \text{ constant}} = -\left(\frac{-1}{2}\right) = \frac{1}{2} = \frac{10}{20} = \frac{MP_L}{MP_K}.$$

Substitutability of Inputs

Three general types of shapes that an isoquant might have are shown in Figure 5-6. In Figure 5-6, panel (a), the isoquants are right angles, indicating that inputs K and L must be used in fixed proportions and therefore are *not substitutable.* An example of this type of situation would be yeast and flour for a specific type of bread. Tires and a battery for an automobile would be another example. In any such case of nonsubstitutable inputs, the *MRS* will be zero along the horizontal portion of the isoquant, since when an additional unit of L is used, there is no amount of K that can be given up if output is to remain constant. (The *MRS* is undefined along the vertical portion of the isoquant, since no amount of input L can be given up in exchange for a greater amount of input K.)

The other extreme case—where inputs L and K are *perfect substitutes*—is shown in Figure 5-6, panel (b). In this case, input L can be substituted for input K at a fixed rate, as indicated by the straight-line isoquants (which have a constant slope and *MRS*). In the area of baking, honey and brown sugar are often nearly perfect substitutes. Natural gas and fuel oil are close substitutes in energy production.

---

[9] Precisely, in calculus terms, the slope of an isoquant is dK/dL, with quantity constant. We can find the slope of the isoquant by first finding the total differential of the production function. If $Q = f(K,L)$, then the total differential is

$$dQ = \left(\frac{\partial Q}{\partial L}\right)dL + \left(\frac{\partial Q}{\partial K}\right)dK.$$

Along an isoquant, $dQ = 0$, since quantity of output does not change and so $(\partial Q/\partial L)dL + (\partial Q/\partial K)dK = 0$. Solving for dK/dL, we find $dK/dL = -(\partial Q/\partial L)/(\partial Q/\partial K)$, the slope of the isoquant. Finally, $\partial Q/\partial L$ is the marginal product of input L, and $\partial Q/\partial K$ is the marginal product of input K; so $dK/dL = -MP_L/MP_K$.

FIGURE 5-6

Substitutability of Inputs

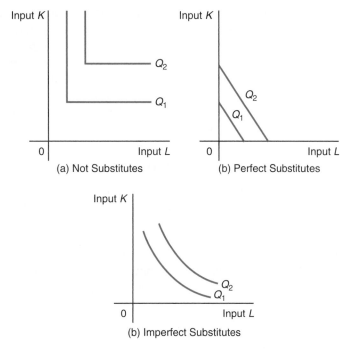

(a) Not Substitutes

(b) Perfect Substitutes

(b) Imperfect Substitutes

Panel (a) depicts the case of two inputs that are not substitutable. In this case, one particular combination of inputs is required to produce a specific level of output. Output cannot increase without increased quantities of both inputs. Panel (b) depicts the case of two inputs that are perfect substitutes. They can be substituted for each other at a constant rates while the firm maintains the same level of output. Panel (c) depicts the case of inputs that are imperfect substitutes. They can be substituted for each other at changing rates, while the firm maintains the same level of output.

The most common situation is depicted in Figure 5-6, panel (c) (and was discussed previously). In this situation, the inputs are *imperfect substitutes,* and the rate at which input K can be given up in return for one more unit of input L while maintaining the same level of output (the MRS) diminishes as the amount of input L being used increases (observe points $C, D, E,$ and F in Figure 5-4). In farming, combines and labor for harvesting grain provide an example of a diminishing MRS; in general, capital and labor are imperfect substitutes.

The choice of which input combination to use is easy in the cases of inputs that are not substitutable and inputs that are perfect substitutes. In the first situation, there is no decision to be made. An automobile requires one engine, one transmission, and four wheels; no other combination of these inputs will do.

In the case of perfectly substitutable inputs, it is easy to calculate which, if either, of the two inputs is cheaper relative to its productive ability. For example, suppose 10,000 cubic feet of natural gas can produce the same amount of energy as one barrel of oil. Furthermore, suppose that 1,000 cubic feet of natural gas costs $3.30 and that one barrel of oil costs $36.00. In this case (all other factors being equal), a firm would use natural gas to produce its energy, since $10 \times \$3.30 = \$33.00$ (the cost of 10,000 cubic feet of natural gas) and $\$33.00$ is less than $\$36.00$ (the cost of one barrel of oil).

Since the decision-making process is relatively simple in cases where inputs are not substitutable or are perfect substitutes, we will concentrate most of our attention on the case of inputs that are *imperfect substitutes*. Determining the cheapest combination of inputs that will enable a firm to produce a given level of output is somewhat more complicated in the last case, as we will see shortly.

Least Cost Combination of Inputs

Once we have established the *technical* (physical) tradeoff possibilities between inputs L and K in production, in order to make an *economic* (profit-maximizing) decision on their employment we still need to consider the rate at which they can be exchanged in the firm's budget. To aid our thinking in this regard, economists have developed the concept of the **isocost** (equal cost) **line,** which shows all combinations of inputs L and K that can be employed for a given dollar cost. Therefore, the equation for an isocost line is of the form

The **isocost line** shows the various combinations of two inputs that can be bought for a given dollar cost.

$$C_0 = P_K(K) + P_L(L),$$

where C_0 is the firm's total cost of inputs for some specific time period, P_K and P_L are the prices of input K and input L, respectively, and K and L represent the physical quantities of the two inputs. Verbally, the isocost equation states that when the firm's total cost is C_0, the price of input K times the *amount* of input K purchased (used) plus the price of input L times the *amount* of input L purchased (used) must equal C_0.

In Figure 5-7 we have drawn isocost lines for $C_1 = \$50$, $C_2 = \$80$, and $C_3 = \$100$, where $P_L = \$5$ and $P_K = \$10$. Note that these three isocost lines are *parallel*. They must be parallel because the slope of each line is equal to $-P_L/P_K$, or $-5/10 = -1/2$.[10] Note that the slope of an isocost line must be equal to $-P_L/P_K$, since that represents the rate at which input L can be substituted for input K while maintaining the same level of cost. In the preceding example, if $P_L = \$5$ and $P_K = \$10$, then we can substitute two units of L for every one unit of K while maintaining the same cost level. Thus

$$\left(\frac{\Delta K}{\Delta L} \right)_{\text{cost constant}} = -\frac{P_L}{P_K} = -\frac{\$5}{\$10} = -\frac{1}{2}.$$

---

[10] If the equation for an isocost line is $P_K(K) + P_L(L) = C_0$, then the slope of the isocost curve (when K is on the vertical axis) can be found by solving for K and observing the resulting coefficient of L. Thus, $P_K(K) = -P_L(L) + C_0$, and $K = -(P_L/P_K)L + C_0/P_K$. Therefore, as long as P_L/P_K remains constant, the slopes of the isocost curves will remain the same.

FIGURE 5-7

Isocost Curves

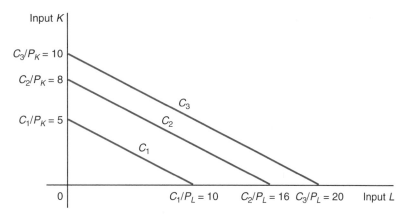

Figure 5-7 shows three isocost lines for inputs L and K. C_1, C_2, and C_3 represent cost levels of $50, $80, and $100, respectively. The price of input L, P_L, is assumed to be $5, and the price of input K, P_K, is assumed to be $10. For a cost level of C_1 = $50, the firm can buy $50/$5 = 10 units of input L or $50/$10 = 5 units of input K. For an expenditure of $50 it can also purchase other combinations of L and K lying on isocost line C_1.

The K-axis intercept for each isocost line is equal to C_i/P_K, since dividing the total amount of expenditure by the price of an input will give the maximum amount of the input that can be purchased if no other input is purchased. Thus, for C_1, the K-axis intercept is C_1/P_K = $50/$10 = 5. For C_2 it is C_2/P_K = $80/$10 = 8. Similarly, the L-axis intercept is C_1/P_L = 10 in the case of isocost line C_1, and it is C_2/P_L = 16 for isocost line C_2.

To obtain the combination of inputs L and K that will enable a firm to produce the *greatest output* for a *given cost* (or what is the same thing, to produce a *given* output at the lowest possible cost), the firm owner must employ the two inputs in such a manner that the isocost line corresponding to the given level of expenditure (cost) touches the highest isoquant possible. Such a point will occur where the isocost line is just *tangent* to an isoquant, and the point of tangency will identify the input combination that is most economical (see Figure 5-8). This result requires that the slopes of the isoquant curve and the isocost line be equal at that point, or $-P_L/P_K = (\Delta K/\Delta L)$ when output is held constant.[11] We call this combination of inputs the **least cost combination of inputs.** (We should note here that this formula for the least cost combination of inputs is valid only if the firm can assume that P_L and P_K are constant. We will discuss this matter further in Chapter 12.)

In Figure 5-8 if P_L = $5 and P_K = $10, then –5/10 (or –1/2) must be equal to $\Delta K/\Delta L$ at point X, where 6 units of input L and 2 units of input K are

A **least cost combination of inputs** requires that the marginal product per additional dollar spent on each input be equal. This condition will hold at the point of tangency between an isocost line and an isoquant.

---

[11] A least cost combination of inputs requires that $-P_L/P_K = (dK/dL)$ when Q is held constant, using calculus terms.

FIGURE 5-8

A Least Cost Combination of Inputs

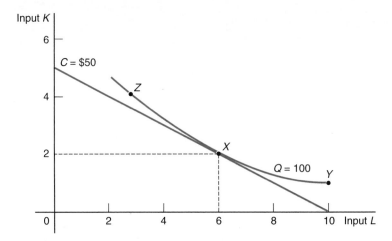

A least-cost combination of inputs will be found where an isocost line ($C = 50$) is tangent to an isoquant curve ($Q = 100$). In this case, the cheapest way to produce 100 units of output is with 6 units of input L and 2 units of input K. This combination of inputs will also yield the greatest output (Q) for a cost of $50.

employed at a total cost outlay of $50 to produce 100 units of output. The same quantity of output could be produced using other combinations of L and K; for example, $L = 10$ units and $K = 1$ unit (point Y) or $L = 3$ units and $K = 4$ units (point Z), but they would cost more ($60 and $55, respectively). Moreover, there is no way to produce a quantity greater than 100 units with a cost limitation of $50. Thus, at point X the firm is producing 100 units of output in the cheapest manner possible or, alternatively, producing the greatest level of output possible for $50 cost.

Since $-\Delta K / \Delta L$ (the *MRS*) along the isoquant is equal to MP_L / MP_K, it must also be true that for the firm to be using the least cost combination of inputs for a given output,

$$\frac{P_L}{P_K} = \frac{MP_L}{MP_K}.$$

Rearranging terms, we can see that this condition also requires that[12]

$$\frac{MP_L}{P_L} = \frac{MP_K}{P_K}.$$

_____

[12] Given $(P_L / P_K) = (MP_L / MP_K)$, we can multiply both sides of the equation by (MP_K) and obtain $MP_K \cdot (P_L / P_K) = MP_L$. Dividing both sides of the equation by P_L, we obtain $MP_K / P_K = MP_L / P_L$.

This equation states that for the firm to be employing a *least cost* combination of inputs L and K, the *additional output obtainable from spending another dollar on input L must equal the additional output obtainable from spending another dollar on input K*. If this relationship did not hold, the firm would be better off purchasing either less of the input with a lower additional output per additional dollar expenditure or more of the input with a greater additional output per additional dollar expenditure, or both. For example, if the firm has two inputs—capital and labor—and if $MP_L = 10$, $P_L = \$10$, $MP_K = 80$, and $P_K = \$50$ (all in per-hour terms), then

$$\frac{MP_L}{P_L} = \frac{10 \text{ units}}{\$10} < \frac{MP_K}{P_K} = \frac{80 \text{ units}}{\$50},$$

or 1 unit per \$1 is less than 1.6 units per \$1. In this situation, the firm would be better off using less labor and more capital.

For example, suppose that the firm used 5 fewer units of labor and 1 more unit of capital. Assuming that each of the 5 units of labor removed had the same marginal product, the results that follow would be obtained. From using 5 fewer units of labor:

$$\text{Change in cost} = -5 \times \$10 = -\$50 \text{ per hour}$$

$$\text{Change in output} = -5 \times 10 \text{ units} = -50 \text{ units per hour}$$

From using 1 more unit of capital:

$$\text{Change in cost} = 1 \times \$50 = \$50 \text{ per hour}$$

$$\text{Change in output} = 1 \times 80 \text{ units} = 80 \text{ units per hour}$$

$$\text{Net change in cost} = \$0$$

$$\text{Net change in output} = +30 \text{ units per hour}$$

Thus, by substituting 1 unit of capital for 5 units of labor, the firm would obtain an additional 30 units of output per hour without incurring any additional cost.

The firm would probably not, however, find it in its best interest to fire all its workers and use *only* capital. Why not? As more and more capital is substituted for labor, the marginal product of capital will most likely fall and the marginal product of labor will rise. This phenomenon occurs because the inputs are not perfect substitutes, and, as stated previously, in this case the marginal rate of substitution will vary as more of one input is used relative to another input.

This point is easy to understand if we visualize a plumbing contractor who has the job of digging a trench for a water line. The use of some capital equipment, such as trenching machines and jackhammers, may be less costly than using all labor. Nevertheless, at the extreme it is hard to imagine trenching machines and jackhammers running themselves in a very productive fashion—some amount of labor will be required for a least cost combination of inputs.

Example of a Production Problem

Now let us consider a more realistic situation that a manager might face. Alert Concrete Company is considering modernization of its concrete-batching plant. Presently, it takes two workers to operate the plant at a rate of 30 yards of concrete batched per hour. If a third worker is employed in batching, output will increase to 50 yards per hour.

The result that can be obtained by modernizing the plant and retaining only two workers is an output rate of 60 yards per hour. The wage rate of the workers is $12.80 per hour, and management estimates that the additional costs associated with the modernization of the plant (depreciation, fuel, opportunity cost of funds, etc.) will be $28,832 per year, based on 265 working days of 8 hours each. Should the company hire an additional worker or should it modernize the plant?

To answer this question, the firm must get all of the figures on the same *per-unit basis,* such as per hour or per year. All of the figures given in the preceding two paragraphs are on a *per-hour* basis except for the cost of modernizing the plant. Therefore, we will transform the latter figure. If plant modernization will result in costs of $28,832 per year, based on 265 working days of 8 hours each, the *per-hour* cost of plant modernization is $28,832 divided by 2,120, or $13.60. (The figure 2,120 is 265 times 8, the total number of hours the plant is in operation per year.)

Now, to determine whether Alert Concrete should hire another worker or modernize its plant, we must compare marginal product per hour relative to cost per hour for a third worker versus modernizing the plant. For a third worker, $MP_L/P_L = 20/\$12.80 =$ approximately 1.6 units of output per additional dollar spent. For modernizing the plant, $MP_K/P_K = 30/\$13.60 =$ about 2.2 units per additional dollar spent. Thus, the firm would get the most additional output per additional dollar spent by modernizing the plant.

We should point out, however, that the firm might want to go beyond our simple least cost rule and consider over what period of time it would desire to produce a higher level of output and how much higher that output should be. That is because modernizing the plant would give the firm less flexibility with regard to level of cost relative to level of output than would hiring another worker. In addition, the firm would need to consider how wage rates might rise in the future relative to unit costs for modernizing the plant.

NUMERICAL EXAMPLE

The Least Cost Input Combination

Perfectmat, Inc. is now providing mat-cutting services to its customers, who are local professional photographers, using ABM 400 mat cutters. It leases the computerized cutters from ABM for $100 per month each and can lease more for this same amount. Perfectmat's business has increased, and it is planning to lease an additional cutter. Although the ABM 400 machine is still available, the ABM representative has told management that if it leases a new PS600 cutter, mat-cutting output on that machine should be about 54 standard mats per day—a high figure for their type of business. The PS600 cutter leases for $140 per month.

If Perfectmat's past experience indicates that an additional ABM 400 model yields 40 standard mats per day, should management lease the PS600 cutter or another 400 model? Explain, relating your answer to the least cost input rule. (Assume 20 workdays per month.)

Answer

Relate mats per additional machine (marginal product) to the respective machine's price. On a monthly basis, this would be 800 mats for the ABM 400 and 1,080 mats for the PS600. So,

$$\frac{MP_{ABM}}{P_{ABM}} = \frac{800}{100}; \quad \frac{MP_{PS}}{P_{PS}} = \frac{1080}{140}$$

$$8 > 7.71$$

Since the *MP* of $1 worth of the ABM 400 model exceeds the *MP* of $1 worth of the PS600 model, there is no reason to choose the newer model cutter. The old model, though less productive per unit, provides more bang for the buck!

Economic Region of Production

Finally, we should emphasize that the firm should not use certain combinations of inputs in the long run *no matter how cheap they are* (unless the firm is being *paid* to use them). These input combinations are represented by the portion of an isoquant curve that has a positive slope. A positively sloped isoquant means that merely to maintain the *same level* of production, the firm must use more of *both* inputs if it increases its use of one of the inputs. What is happening in this situation is that the marginal product of one input is negative; using more of that input would actually cause output to *fall* unless more of the other input were also employed.

This situation is illustrated in Figure 5-9. Point C on I_0 marks the spot where $MP_K = 0$. Beyond that point (greater amounts of K) on I_0, the MP_K is negative. We can see that beyond point C, if we use more of input K, we must also

---

MANAGERIAL PERSPECTIVE

Input Substitution At New Balance

When the price of a unit of labor is high relative to that of a unit of capital equipment, economic analysis argues that the rational producer will substitute capital for labor to attain production at least cost. An interesting case in point is New Balance, a producer of athletic footwear. New Balance produces its shoes both in the United States and in Asia. Many other firms that sell similar shoes in the U.S. market have no U.S. production at all. Most rival firms' production takes place overseas, and some of these firms have been accused of subcontracting their production to operators of sweatshops.

Certainly, Asian production has everything to do with the cheap labor found in that part of the world, especially now in China. But shoes do not have to be produced the way they are in Chinese factories, and that is not the way they are produced by New Balance in its U.S. plants in Lawrence, Massachusetts, and four other locations. In the United States New Balance uses small numbers of well-trained, highly skilled workers to operate sophisticated machines, some of which are computerized and can control numerous sewing heads at once. The U.S. employees are trained in a variety of skills, change tasks frequently, and work in teams. In contrast, at Asian subcontractor plants also used by New Balance, the labor force is much larger, low-skilled, constrained

to simple, monotonous tasks, and equipped with machinery that is totally obsolete by U.S. or European standards.

Of course, the difference between New Balance's U.S. operations and those in Asia make economic sense, since Asian labor is a great deal cheaper than that in the United States. In fact, the company's U.S. workers get about $14 per hour, while some Asian workers receive 40 cents per hour or less. A *Business Week* writer reports that the U.S. plants can turn out a pair of shoes in less than one-sixth the time it takes in China. If you do the math, this labor productivity differential does not make up for the difference in wages. Nonetheless, New Balance states that U.S. production is profitable. The U.S. labor cost per pair of shoes is $4, as compared to $1.30 in China. However, shipping costs and advantages of producing in the United States (ability to change styles more quickly and fill store orders faster than rivals) offset the $2.70 per pair differential between the U.S. and foreign labor costs.

References: Aaron Bernstein, "Low-Skilled Jobs: Do They Have to Move?" *Business Week,* February 26, 2001, pp. 94–95; and John Pike, "New Balance Employs 475 in Lawrence," *Massachusetts News* (online edition: www.massnews.com), October 1, 2001.

Ridge lines: The lines connecting the points where the marginal product of an input is equal to zero (one line for each input) in the isoquant map and forming the boundary for the economic region of production.

use more of input L to maintain the same level of output. At point D, the MP_L is 0, and if a greater quantity of input L is used, its marginal product becomes negative. At point E on I_1, the MP_K is zero, and at point F, the MP_L is zero. Lines such as $0X$ and $0Y$, which connect the points on the isoquants where the marginal product of each respective input becomes zero (MP_K for $0X$, MP_L for $0Y$), are called **ridge lines.**[13] They bound the **economic region of production,** since the marginal product of one input is negative outside the ridge lines.

---

[13] Ridge line $0X$ connects points where the isoquants are vertical ($MP_L/MP_K = MP_L/0 = \infty$), and ridge line $0Y$ connects points where the isoquants have a zero slope ($MP_L/MP_K = 0/MP_K = 0$).

FIGURE 5-9

The Economic Region of Production

The **economic region of production** is the range in an isoquant diagram where both inputs have a positive marginal product. It lies inside the ridge lines.

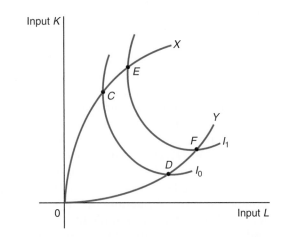

Ridge line $0X$ connects the points where the MP_K is zero. Ridge line $0Y$ connects the points where the MP_L is zero. A profit-maximizing firm will try never to produce using input combinations outside the ridge lines.

Expansion Path of the Firm

The **expansion path** is the path of least cost input combinations in the isoquant diagram that occurs as the firm expands its long-run output at given input prices.

Given fixed input prices and our assumption about the slope of the isoquants (diminishing marginal rate of substitution), and if we assume the isoquant is a *smooth* curve, there will be one least cost combination of inputs for each level of output. The line connecting all such points is called the **expansion path** of the firm (see Figure 5-10). As we will see later, the point that the firm finally chooses when it maximizes profit will depend on revenue considerations as well as on cost.

FIGURE 5-10

The Expansion Path

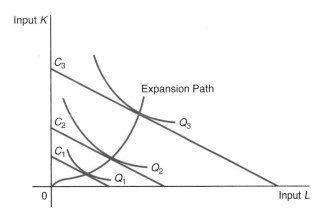

The expansion path connects least cost combinations of inputs for different levels of output. It is assumed that the input price ratio is constant.

Returns to Scale

Returns to scale measures the effect on output of increasing all the inputs in a production function by the same proportion (e.g., doubling all inputs).

Returns to scale is a term that refers to how output changes when *all* inputs are increased by the same multiple (for example, doubled or tripled). If output increases by a greater multiple than that by which the inputs are increased, then *increasing* returns to scale are present. If output increases by the same multiple, *constant* returns to scale are present. Finally, if output increases by a smaller multiple, *decreasing* returns to scale are present.

For example, suppose a firm's production function is given by $Q = 2K^2 + LK + L^2$, where K is the quantity of capital and L is the quantity of labor. If the firm uses 5 units of labor and 5 units of capital, output equals 100. If labor and capital are both doubled to 10 units each, $Q = 400$, which is more than double the original quantity. In this case the firm has increasing returns to scale. On the other hand, if the firm's production function is $Q = 10K^{1/2}L^{1/2}$, and $L = 2$ and $K = 2$, then $Q = 20$. If capital and labor are doubled (to 4 units each), $Q = 40$, which is exactly double the original level of output. In this case the firm has constant returns to scale. Finally, if the firm's production function is $Q = 100 + 5K + 10L$, and $L = 5$ and $K = 5$, then $Q = 175$. If labor and capital are doubled to 10, $Q = 250$, which is less than double the original output level. In this case the firm faces decreasing returns to scale.

As we will see in Chapter 6, with fixed input prices, if a firm has increasing returns to scale, its cost per unit of output will decline as output increases. On the other hand, if a firm has decreasing returns to scale, its cost per unit of output will increase as output increases. Finally, if a firm has constant returns to scale, its cost per unit of output will remain constant.

The nature of its returns to scale is very important to a firm, not only because of the way returns to scale affect its own costs, but also because of the way in which such returns affect the firm's ability to compete with other firms of various sizes in the same industry. It's likely that three firms among those most aware of this principle are General Motors, Ford, and Daimler-Chrysler, since it has long been argued that increasing returns to scale is an important phenomenon in the automobile industry.[14] However, the nature of returns to scale in this industry may be changing somewhat as production shifts to smaller cars and is assisted by computer-integrated manufacturing and computer-aided design.[15]

---

[14] See "The Global Six," *Business Week* (January 25, 1999), pp. 68–72; and *Administered Prices: Automobiles*, Report of the Subcommittee on Antitrust and Monopoly of the Committee of the Judiciary, United States Senate, Eighty-Fifth Congress, Second Session, November 1, 1958, especially pp. 13–16.

[15] See "Two Sides of a Giant: GM Can Learn a Few Lessons from Its Dynamic European Offshoot," *Time* (February 19, 1990), pp. 68–70; "Is Your Company Too Big?" *Business Week* (March 27, 1989), pp. 84–94; John Koten, "Ford Decides Bigness Isn't a Better Idea," *Wall Street Journal*, September 16, 1981, p. 25; and "Small Is Beautiful Now in Manufacturing," *Business Week* (October 22, 1984), pp. 152–156.

Relation of Long-Run Least Cost Condition to the Short Run

The short run was defined earlier as a period of time when one or more inputs in a multi-input production function is fixed in amount. It is usually viewed as corresponding to a situation wherein the firm has determined its plant size or production capacity and is able to vary only the use of other inputs (labor, materials, fuel, equipment that would not require a major investment, etc.). In the short run, substitution of the latter type of variable inputs may be possible. Thus, if a firm had 5 short-run fixed inputs and 20 short-run variable inputs, the MP_i/P_i condition would still apply to any of the variable inputs that were substitutable for one another. For example, a firm that produces kitchen cabinets might have to decide on the optimal combination of electric staple drivers and air-driven staple drivers to use in applying trim to its wood cabinets. The prices of these two types of tools will probably not be equal, and neither will their marginal products. The optimal combination of the two to employ will be the one that comes closest to yielding the same marginal product per dollar spent on each type of tool. Again, the point we are making is that the condition for a least cost combination of variable inputs in the short run is the same as that for *all* inputs in the long run. This is why we chose to discuss the long run first in our examination of production.

Note that making a decision like the one facing our cabinet manufacturer, while it involves some outlay for tools or equipment, is not the same as determining what size plant to build. In other words, a given cabinetmaker in the short run definitely might have some flexibility regarding the purchase or lease of certain types of equipment, but this decision is very different from one about establishing a completely new manufacturing facility or substantially expanding an old one. The latter are long-run decisions. However, there is more to say about the firm's production in the short run, as the next section will show.

PRODUCT CURVES AND THE SHORT RUN

Although all inputs are variable in the long run for a firm, they usually are *not* all variable in the short run. In this section we will return to the two-input production function $Q = f(K,L)$ and assume that input K is a fixed input.

Because we are treating input K as being fixed, we will make use of a function that relates total output to levels of input L only. Accordingly, we will define the **total product function** of input L, TP_L, as the function that indicates the maximum level of output possible with various amounts of input L and a fixed amount, K_0, of input K, so that $TP_L = f(K_0, L)$. We can also define the **average product** of input L as the total product of L divided by the quantity of L in use, or

The **total product function** of a variable input indicates the maximum output that can be obtained from different amounts of the input, while all other inputs are kept fixed.

The **average product** of a variable input is equal to total product divided by the number of units of the input in use.

$$AP_L = \frac{TP_L}{L}.$$

Finally, the marginal product of input L gives the rate of change of total output with respect to changes in input L. As has already been indicated, arc marginal product of input L is defined as the average addition to output or total product obtained by adding one more unit of input L, or

$$MP_L = \frac{\Delta TP_L}{\Delta L}.$$

As arc marginal revenue was an approximation to marginal revenue, so is **arc marginal product** of input L an *approximation* to the marginal product of input L. That is because arc marginal product of input L measures the average rate of change of total output with respect to input L over *some* range of values for input L, rather than measuring the rate of change at a *single* value for input L.[16] Thus the *short-run product functions* of the firm are

> **Arc marginal product** is an approximation to marginal product over some range of output and is equal to the change in total product divided by the change in the variable input.

Total product = total output per time period related to different amounts of a variable input;

Average product = output per unit of variable input; and

Marginal product = rate of change of output as the variable input increases.

As we have already seen, managers of the profit-oriented firm are deeply interested in how its output will vary with respect to the quantity used of an input. The reason, of course, is that such information is essential for determining the profit-maximizing level of output.

Law of Diminishing Returns

Figure 5-11 demonstrates the relationships among total product, average product, and marginal product. At point A, marginal product (which is the slope of the total product curve) reaches a maximum, and beyond that point, diminishing returns to input L set in. The portion of the marginal product curve after point A illustrates the economic **law of diminishing returns** (or diminishing marginal productivity). This law asserts that if equal increments of one variable input are added while keeping the amounts of all other inputs fixed, total product may increase; but *after some point, the additions to total product (the marginal product) will decrease.* This

> The **law of diminishing returns** states that in the short run the marginal product of a variable input will eventually fall as output is increased.

---

[16] Technically, the marginal product of input L is given by $dTP_L/dL = \partial Q/\partial L$, where input K is held constant at some level, K_0.

Changing Production Functions in U.S. Manufacturing

In a world of global competition, many American firms have come around to the view that the best defense is a good offense. Recent examples of firms that have taken the offensive in manufacturing include one small firm in the steel industry and one very large firm that makes automobiles. Nucor Corporation, of Darlington, South Carolina, has become a leading innovator in the steel industry. Its thin-slab process created a revolution in the steel industry during the 1990s. Nucor revised the production function for making flat-rolled steel sheets. Its process, which creates a much thinner piece of steel for the rolling mill than any previous technology, reduced the number of worker hours required per ton of sheet steel by 75 percent.

Nucor has continued to be an innovator. In the late 1990s, it built a plant, jointly with U.S. Steel, to make iron from iron carbide in Trinidad. This proved too costly. So in 2002, Nucor joined a group including Rio Tinto, Mitsubishi, and a Chinese steelmaking enterprise to build a new plant in Western Australia that converts iron ore to liquid metal using a completely new process, HIsmelt, that is expected to be both cleaner and more economical than other technologies.

In the automobile industry, production functions have also changed. General Motors has been moving toward leaner and more flexible plants that eliminate many of the bottlenecks in traditional automobile manufacturing by having outside suppliers deliver modules directly to the assembly line. This modularization reduces the number of suppliers by 60 percent and the number of parts GM must deal with by 50 percent. New robots also help to make these plants very efficient. GM's first

such plant was inaugurated at Gravataí, in Brazil, in 2000. It produced its first Chevrolet Celta, a car designed for the Brazilian market, in 2001. At Gravataí, GM was joined by 16 supplier firms that built their plants right across the highway from the GM facility. The suppliers are partners in the design and engineering of subassemblies, which further streamlines car production.

In 2001, GM inaugurated another new plant, this time in Lansing, Michigan, to build its redesigned Cadillac line. Production began in 2002 with the new CTS, a Cadillac aimed at younger buyers. The Lansing Grand River plant is building very different vehicles than the plant in Gravataí, but some of the same new approaches are found there. At least five supplier firms have set up manufacturing facilities adjacent to the plant, and modular, robotized assembly is also used there. Ford and DaimlerChrysler have followed suit, farming out many subassemblies to outside suppliers. These changes have made U.S. production more like Japanese production, but with allowances for differences in U.S. input and product markets. Overall, they should make auto plants in the United States more competitive with their international counterparts.

References: "Nucor Signs Ironmaking Technology Agreement," www.steelnews.org, April 4, 2002; "Big Steel Is Facing David vs. Goliath Test," *Wall Street Journal*, October 17, 1989; "Why Detroit Is Going to Pieces," *Business Week Online*, September 3, 2001; Andy Henion, "For GM in Lansing the Future Is Now," *Lansing State Journal* (online edition, www.lsj.com), November 11, 2001; and "GM do Brasil Inaugurates a New Industrial Model: The Gravataí Automotive Complex," *Automotive Intelligence* (www.autointell.com), July 25, 2000.

FIGURE 5-11

*Total Product,
Average Product,
and Marginal
Product Curves*

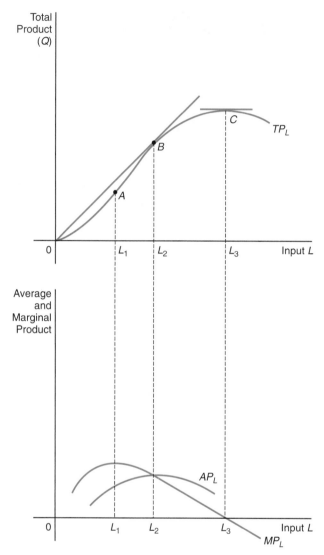

Figure 5-11 depicts the relationships among the total product (TP_L), average product (AP_L), and marginal product (MP_L) of input L. The TP_L is at a maximum when $MP_L = 0$. Also, $MP_L = AP_L$ when AP_L is at a maximum.

law merely recognizes the fact that inputs are usually not perfect substitutes. For example, in farming, the first unit of labor, when combined with some machinery and a field of wheat, might increase total product significantly. After some point, however, the next unit of labor will surely increase the total bushels of wheat produced by a smaller amount than did the previous unit of labor employed.

Table 5-2 *Total, Average, and Marginal Product of Input L, Given K = 1*

L	TP_L	AP_L	Arc MP_L
0	0	—	
			10.00
1	10.00	10.00	
			4.14
2	14.14	7.07	
			3.18
3	17.32	5.77	
			2.68
4	20.00	5.00	
			2.36
5	22.36	4.47	

Examples of the law of diminishing returns are shown in Tables 5-2 and 5-3, which are derived from Table 5-1. In Table 5-2, diminishing returns to factor L set in after the first unit of L is added (input K is fixed at 1 unit). Diminishing returns to K also set in after the first unit of K is added in Table 5-3.

The average product for a particular amount of input L, AP_L, is given by the slope of a line segment extending from the origin to the point on the total product curve corresponding to that quantity of the input. We know that the AP_L must be given by the slope of the line segment from the origin to the corresponding point on the TP_L curve, because the slope of that segment is equal to

$$\frac{\text{change in vertical distance}}{\text{change in horizontal distance}} = \frac{TP_L}{L},$$

with the origin as the starting point. The AP_L reaches a maximum at point B in Figure 5-11, where line segment OB is tangent to TP_L. At this point, $MP_L = AP_L$, since MP_L for some amount of input a is given by the slope of the line tangent to TP_L at the corresponding output level.

Total product attains its maximum at point C, where the total product curve reaches its peak. Since the slope of the total product curve is zero at

Table 5-3 *Total, Average, and Marginal Product of Input K, Given L = 4*

K	TP_K	AP_K	ArcMP_K
0	0	—	
			20.00
1	20.00	20.00	
			8.28
2	28.28	14.14	
			6.36
3	34.64	11.55	
			5.36
4	40.00	10.00	
			4.72
5	44.72	8.94	

NUMERICAL EXAMPLE

Relation of Average and Marginal Product to Total Product

Complete the table below, assuming that the firm is in the short run and that L is the only variable input.

Units of L	TP_L	AP_L	Arc MP_L
0	0	—	
2		80	
4	340		
			70
6			

Answer

a. The first missing TP_L is 160, which is AP_L (L), or 80(2). The second missing TP_L is 480, which is obtained by multiplying the given MP_L of 70 times the change in L of 2, and adding on to the previous TP_L of 340, or 70(2) + 340 = 480. This follows from the definition $MP_L = \Delta TP_L / \Delta L$. So, $MP_L(\Delta L) = \Delta TP_L$.

b. The missing AP_L values are 340/4 = 85 and 480/6 = 80, since $AP_L = TP_L/L$.

c. Since $MP_L = \Delta TP_L / \Delta L$, the missing MP_L values are 160/2 = 80 for the change from $L = 0$ to $L = 2$ and 180/2 = 90 for the change from $L = 2$ to $L = 4$.

this point, MP_L must also be zero. This relationship becomes obvious if we recognize that if TP_L is at a maximum, then at that point the addition of another unit of input L will not change the level of total output produced. By definition, however, this fact means that MP_L is zero.

Average-Marginal Relationship

Figure 5-11 shows an important quantitative relationship between the average and marginal product curves for the variable input L. Note that when MP_L falls, it passes through the maximum point of the AP_L curve. When an average curve has a maximum point, the corresponding marginal curve will pass through that point. This is because of a mathematical property known as the **average-marginal relationship.** The AP_L is rising to the left of its maximum because the amount added to total product by the next unit of input is greater than the average product of previous units. This *causes* the average to rise. To the right of the maximum of AP_L, an additional unit of input L adds less to total product than the average amount added by previous units, thereby lowering the average. In short, any time a marginal curve is *above* its correspon-

Because of the **average-marginal relationship,** an average curve cannot rise unless the related marginal curve is above it; the average cannot fall unless the marginal is below it.

Table 5-4 *Total, Average, and Marginal Product of Input L for a Case Where* AP_L *Has a Maximum*

Units of L (L)	TP_L (Q)	AP_L (Q/L)	MP_L ($\Delta Q/\Delta L$)
1	100	100	
			200
2	300	150	
			300
3	600	200	
			140
4	740	185	
			100
5	840	168	
			60
6	900	150	

ding average curve, the average curve will be *rising*; any time the marginal is *below* the average, the average will be *falling*. You can verify this numerically by looking at Table 5-4, where data on TP_L, AP_L, and MP_L are shown.

In Table 5-4, when the second and third units of input L are added to the production process, the average product of L rises, since the marginal product of the additional unit is greater than the previous average in both instances (200 > 100, and 300 > 150). However, beyond $L = 3$, average product declines. This is because the marginal product of each additional unit is lower than the average of all the previous units (140 < 200, 100 < 185, and 60 < 168).

The average-marginal relationship holds even if the average curve does not have an extreme value (maximum or minimum). For example, if you review Tables 5-2 and 5-3, you will see that the average product of the variable input always falls in those tables. This is because the marginal product (shown in the rightmost column) is always less than the average. If you go back to Chapter 2, you can verify that this relationship also holds for marginal revenue and average revenue.

In fact, the average-marginal relationship is not restricted to economics. You may note that if you have a "B" overall grade average (3.0 on a 4-point system) but only manage to turn in a "C" performance for this term, your average will fall. On the other hand, if this turns out to be an "A" term for you, your average will rise. The average-marginal relationship will turn up again in the next chapter, which is on cost.

Production in the Short Run Versus the Long Run

We can contrast a short-run situation of one fixed input and one variable input with the long-run situation (all inputs are variable) by utilizing the isoquant map in Figure 5-12. Points *A, B, C,* and *D* represent *least cost* combina-

FIGURE 5-12

Effect of a Fixed Input on Cost of Production

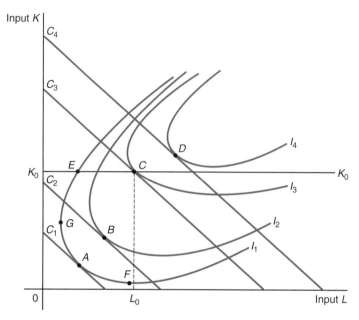

The input combination L_0, K_0 is the least-cost combination of inputs for the output level represented by I_3. However, if input K is fixed at K_0 in the short run, the costs of the firm will be higher at any other level of output than they would be with a least-cost combination of inputs.

tions of inputs L and K required to produce the levels of output represented by I_1, I_2, I_3, and I_4, respectively. Assume the firm has been operating at point C (with K_0 units of K and L_0 units of L) and that K is fixed in the short run. In the short run, therefore, the firm must operate along the line $K_0 K_0$, and its costs for producing any output level different from that of I_3 will be greater than would be necessary with the optimal combination of inputs.

As we discussed earlier in this chapter, point E on I_1 illustrates a point at which the combination of L and K is especially undesirable—where the marginal product of one input (K) is negative. This result is clear if we observe that I_1 has a positive slope at E—which indicates that if more of input K is used in production, more of input L must also be used to maintain the *same* level of output. Similarly, the marginal product of input L is negative beyond point F on I_1. The profit-maximizing firm would not plan to be in a position where the marginal product of an input is negative unless the firm were paid for using the input.

In Figure 5-12, if input K was fixed as far as expenditure was concerned but *not fixed in its utilization,* and if the firm desired to produce the quantity represented by I_1, the *short-run* best combination of inputs would be achieved by using input K only to the point where its marginal product became zero. That is because decreases or increases in the *use* of this input will have no effect on expenditures for it in the short run. This position is represented by point *G*. One example of such a reduction in utilization of an input that is relatively fixed in expenditure is the closing off of dining areas in a restaurant during less busy periods when they are not needed for seating. A smaller number of servers are able to give good service to a given number of people if the people are seated in an area that is not so large. Another example is shutting down one assembly line in a factory or shutting down one plant of a firm with multiple plants.[17]

Optimal Use of Variable Inputs in the Short Run

We will leave a thorough discussion of the optimal use of variable inputs for a later chapter. Here we will merely state that such optimal use requires that a variable input be employed up to the point where the additional revenue brought into the firm by the last (or next) unit of that input is just equal to its marginal cost, or the cost of that additional unit. We call this additional revenue the **marginal revenue product of an input;** it is equal to the marginal (physical) product of the input times the additional net marginal revenue (marginal revenue net of raw materials or components cost) that the firm can obtain from output produced. If we state this principle for input *L*, the firm would employ input *L* until

Marginal revenue product of an input is the rate of change of total revenue with respect to a change in the variable input.

$$MRP_L \equiv (MP_L \cdot NMR) = MC_L,$$

where MRP_L is the marginal revenue product of input *L*, MP_L is the marginal (physical) product of input *L*, *NMR* is the net marginal revenue obtained from each additional unit of output, and MC_L is the marginal cost of input *L*, or $\Delta TC/\Delta L$. While the condition that $MRP_L = MC_L$ is relevant to the optimal use of input *L*, it is really a profit-maximizing condition rather than just a production decision rule. Thus, further discussion of it will be deferred to Chapter 12, where the relationship between employment of inputs and profit is examined.

SUMMARY

Production and the Firm's Profit

We have repeatedly emphasized that only two main factors are of concern to the profit-maximizing firm: *revenue* and *cost*. In this chapter we have shown that if its profit is to be at the maximum level, the firm must be using a com-

---

[17] General Motors has begun working with its suppliers to use plants and workers that it has idled. In some cases, GM may even pay part of the workers' wages, since after GM employees are laid off for 36 weeks, they receive full pay whether or not they work from a GM-funded Jobs Bank. See "Smart Step for a Wobbly Giant," *Business Week* (December 7, 1992), p. 38.

bination of inputs that will minimize cost at the *optimal level of output*. Production at the lowest possible cost *for a given level of output* requires that the additional output that would be obtained per additional dollar spent for another unit of one input is equal to that obtained per additional dollar spent for every other input. We called this a *least cost combination of inputs*.

While deriving the condition for achieving the least cost combination of inputs, we developed the concepts of the production function, isoquant and isocost curves, and the marginal rate of substitution of one input for another. The *production function* indicates the maximum quantities of output a firm can produce using various combinations of inputs. An *isoquant* curve shows different combinations of two inputs that can be used to produce a specific level of *output*, whereas an *isocost* curve indicates different combinations of two inputs that can be used for a given dollar cost. The *marginal rate of substitution* is the negative of the slope of an isoquant curve, and it indicates the rate at which one input may be substituted for another while the same level of output is maintained. The least cost combination of inputs for a particular level of output is located where an isocost curve is tangent to the isoquant curve corresponding to that level of output. At this point, the marginal rate of substitution equals the ratio of the input prices, or

$$\frac{MP_L}{MP_K} = \frac{P_L}{P_K}.$$

The set of all least cost input combinations makes up the *expansion path* of the firm.

It is also important for a firm to be aware of the *returns to scale* of its operations so that the firm can estimate how its unit costs will be affected as it expands or contracts its scale of operations. If the firm has *increasing returns* to scale, an increase in its scale of operations will more than proportionally increase its output and thereby lower unit costs. If the firm has *constant returns* to scale, an increase in its scale of operations will increase output by the same proportion, and unit costs will remain constant. Finally, with *decreasing returns* to scale, an increase in the scale of the operations of a firm will increase its output by a smaller proportion, so that unit costs will increase.

We also pointed out that in the short run, some inputs a firm employs are fixed (at least with regard to cost outlay), so the firm may not be able to achieve the least cost combination of inputs at its optimal level of output at all times. This latter possibility emphasizes the importance to the firm of predicting accurately what its profit-maximizing level of output will be in the future. Fulfillment of the desire of the profit-oriented firm to produce at least cost (*given* the level of output) requires that it be able to at least estimate parts of its production function and future input prices.

In the short run, the profit-oriented firm should be aware of how its output varies with respect to changes in the amount of its variable input or inputs. In this connection we introduced the following terms: total product, average product, and marginal product. The *total product* of a variable input indicates the maximum output that can be obtained from different amounts of one variable input, keeping all other inputs fixed. The *average product* of a variable input is obtained by dividing total output by the number of units of the input in use. The *marginal product* of an input is the rate of change of total product with respect to changes in the amount of the input. The *law of diminishing returns* states that the marginal product of an input will decrease after some point.

To *maximize profit* in the short run, the firm should employ a variable input (say, input L) up to the point where the additional revenue that another unit of input will bring in is just equal to its cost, or where the marginal revenue product of input L equals its marginal cost ($MRP_L = MC_L$). Even though the *cost* associated with the fixed inputs of a firm may be fixed in the short run, their *utilization* may not be fixed. In this case, the firm should avoid using so much of a fixed input that its marginal product becomes negative.

In the next chapter, we relate level of cost directly to level of output for a firm. We will also discuss several cost concepts that the profit-maximizing firm must understand and be able to use.

QUESTIONS

1. What is a production function? How does it differ from a total product function?

2. What condition(s) must be satisfied for a firm to achieve a least cost combination of its inputs? Why can't the firm always attain a least cost combination of inputs in the short run?

3. Does obtaining a least cost combination of inputs ensure that a firm is maximizing profit? Why or why not?

4. Compare the concepts of diminishing marginal productivity and decreasing returns to scale.

5. Define isoquant and isocost curves. Why would information given by these two curves be useful to the firm?

6. What are ridge lines? What is their significance to a firm?

7. Explain the meaning of the expansion path for a firm. What might cause it to change?

PROBLEMS

1. Yolanda Von Sweeny owns an art factory in Palermo, Italy. She is thinking of expanding her exports of large-size paintings of picturesque Italian cityscapes. She has had little difficulty recruiting new artists to Palermo to work a 40-hour

week in the factory. The weekly wage is now up to 500 euros, which translates to $480 in U.S. currency, and she thinks she can hire as many artists as she needs for that rate. An additional artist normally adds 96 paintings per week to the output of the factory. However, Yolanda has been approached by a Hong Kong dealer who is selling remarkable computerized robots that can closely duplicate the work of some of her current artists. A robot can paint 210 pictures per week and has a daily operating and financing cost of $168 (U.S. currency) per operating day. Regardless of whether she uses the robots or additional artists, Yolanda plans to operate the factory only five days per week.

a. Employ the least cost input rule to determine whether Yolanda should consider buying the robots. (It will be easier if you use dollars rather than euros.)

b. Given the current daily cost of robots, what artist wage would make Yolanda indifferent between employing the robots and hiring more artists?

c. What other considerations might influence Yolanda's decision?

2. Suppose a firm has the following total product curve, assuming that input L is its only variable input and that Q = output per time period.

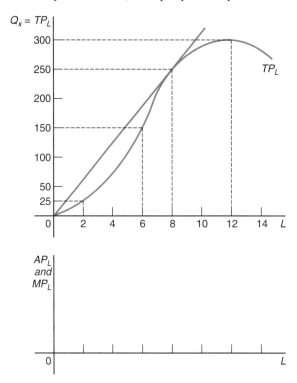

(*Note:* Plot MP_L values at the midpoint of each ΔL that you use to determine them.)

a. In the quadrant below the given diagram, sketch the curves of marginal product and average product of input L. (Provide an appropriate scale on the vertical axis.)

b. What is the maximum value of AP_L?

c. Can you employ geometry to determine the value of MP_L when it is at a maximum? (*Hint:* Draw a tangent to TP_L at its inflection point and evaluate its slope.)

3. Diamond Brewery is reevaluating its optimal combination of inputs as a result of recent union-negotiated wage rate increases. At the present time, the MP of labor on the production line is 5 cases of beer per hour and the wage rate is $6. The MP of capital is 10 cases of beer per hour, and the price of a unit of capital's services for one hour is $10. Is the combination of inputs at Diamond optimal? Why or why not?

4. Determine whether each of the following production functions exhibits increasing, constant, or decreasing returns to scale.

a. $Q = 100{,}000 + 500L + 100K$

b. $Q = 0.01K^3 + 4K^2L + L^2K + 0.0001L^3$

c. $Q = 50K^{1/2}L^{1/2}$

d. $Q = 0.001M + 50{,}000$

e. $Q = 15K + 0.5KL + 30L$

f. $Q = AK^{1-\alpha}L^{2\alpha}, \alpha > 0$

5. Shiny Apple Company can use either labor or a combination of labor and machines to pick apples. Labor can be obtained very cheaply—the going rate is $7 per hour, while the cost (depreciation, gasoline, maintenance, etc.) of using a machine for one hour is $30. The firm is currently using only labor to pick apples, reasoning that labor is cheaper in dollars per day than the machine. In the present situation, the marginal product of an additional unit of labor is 4 bushels of apples per hour, while the additional product contributed by an apple-picking machine is 40 bushels per hour. You are hired by the firm managers as a consultant to advise them on whether or not to purchase such a machine. What recommendation do you make? What additional data might you also want to take into consideration?

6. Use the following table to complete this problem.

MP_L	L	Q	AP_L
	0	0	—
8.0	5	20	
	10		
	15	90	
	20	110	
	25		5.0
2.0	30		
	35	140	

a. Complete the table, given that L is labor units, Q is units of output per day, and L is the only variable input.

b. Suppose the firm is producing between 90 and 110 units of output per day and that the price of a unit of input L is $40. If at that level of production the marginal product of its only fixed input, capital, is 24 units of output per day, should it consider adding to its capital equipment if the price of a unit of capital is $120? Explain.

7. The following table gives the quantities of output that can be produced with different amounts of capital and labor used by a firm.

Units of K	Units of Output						
6	122	174	213	244	274	300	
5	112	158	194	224	250	274	
4	100	142	173	200	224	244	
3	87	122	150	173	194	213	
2	71	100	122	142	158	174	
1	50	71	87	100	112	122	
0	1	2	3	4	5	6	Units of L

a. What are the returns to scale for this firm over the range of capital and labor shown in the table? Why?

b. Compute the marginal product and average product of capital for $L = 3$ units as K varies from 1 unit to 6 units

c. Compute the marginal product and average product of labor for $K = 1$ unit as L varies from 1 unit to 6 units.

d. Suppose the firm is producing 87 units of output using 1 unit of capital and 3 units of labor. The cost of a unit of labor is $10, and the cost of a unit of capital is $20. Is the firm using a *least cost* combination of inputs? Why or why not?

8. A small local plumbing contractor is trying to decide whether to rent a backhoe or to hire more labor for an especially large plumbing job. The contractor estimates that 600 tons of dirt and rocks must be dug and moved. It is believed that a backhoe could move 10 tons of dirt per hour and would cost $30 per hour to rent (including the operator). On the average a worker can move 2 tons of dirt per hour, and the wage rate is $9 per hour.

a. Should the contractor rent a backhoe or hire enough workers to do the job? Why?

b. Suppose the backhoe could be rented on a full eight-hour-day basis only (a full day would be charged for any partial days). Would this change your answer in part (a)? Why or why not?

9. A total product curve for input a is drawn in the following diagram:

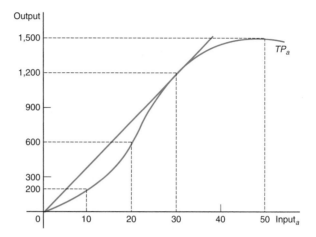

a. Find the average product of input *a* at amounts of *a* equal to 10, 20, 30, and 50 units.

b. Find the marginal product of *a* between 0 and 10 units, 10 and 20 units, 20 and 30 units, and 30 and 50 units.

c. Sketch the average and marginal product curves for *a*, and label the axes appropriately.

d. Where is AP_a at its maximum? Where is MP_a at its maximum?

e. At what point do diminishing returns to input *a* set in?

10. Use the isoquant diagram that follows to fill in the blank spaces in statements a through e.

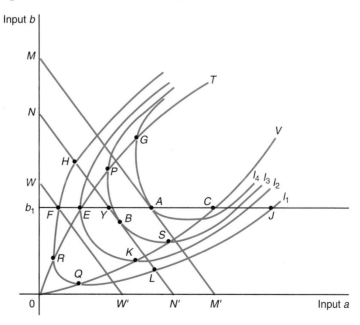

a. At point ____ the total product of input a will reach its maximum when input b is fixed at b_1.

b. Point ____ and point ____ represent least cost combinations of inputs, given the isocost curves drawn in the diagram.

c. With expenditures limited to the level represented by isocost curve NN', a firm would produce at point ____ in the short run where $b = b_1$. In the long run, with the same budget, it would produce the level of output represented by isoquant ____.

d. On I_1, the marginal product of b equals zero at point ____; at point ____ on the same isoquant, the marginal product of a equals zero.

e. In the short run, with plant size b_1 (and fixed in utilization at b_1), output level I_1 could be produced at point ____ or at point ____. However, the cost-minimizing firm with plant size b_1 (but not fixed in utilization) would choose to produce I_1 at point ____.

11. An automobile manufacturer is considering buying a robot to paint automobiles. One robot can paint 40 cars an hour and costs $12,000 a year (based on 240 working days of eight hours each). A person can paint 60 cars an hour and costs $11.50 per hour. Should the firm purchase the robot or hire a person if it wishes to maximize profit? Why?

12. The following table gives corresponding values for amounts of labor and capital used by a firm and the corresponding maximum quantities of output that can be produced.

Units of K	Units of Output						
7	70	140	210	280	350	420	490
6	60	120	180	240	300	360	420
5	50	100	150	200	250	300	350
4	40	80	120	160	200	240	280
3	30	60	90	120	150	180	210
2	20	40	60	80	100	120	140
1	10	20	30	40	50	60	70
0	1	2	3	4	5	6	7	Units of L

a. Complete the following table when capital is fixed at 4 units.

Units of L	TP_L	AP_L	Arc MP_L
1			
2			
3			
4			
5			
6			

b. If the cost of a unit of capital's services (P_K) is $30 and the cost of a unit of labor's services is $10, is $K = 4$ and $L = 3$ a least cost combination of inputs? Why or why not?

c. Given the information in part b and in the table, what is the cheapest way this firm can produce 120 units of output?

d. Does the production function depicted in the table have constant, increasing, or decreasing returns to scale? Why?

e. What happens to the marginal product of labor as the amount of capital used by the firm increases? Why?

13. Suppose a firm operates in a *perfectly competitive market* (for definition, see Chapter 1) where it can sell any amount of its product for $8 per unit. This means that its marginal revenue will be $8. Now let's suppose that it has two variable inputs, labor and materials. The materials cost per unit of output is $3, and the firm must pay $12 per unit of labor that it hires, or $MC_L = 12$. If L is the number of units of labor hired and the firm's marginal product of labor in the short run is $MP_L = 20 - 0.2L$, answer the following:

a. How much labor would be employed if the firm operated its plant at capacity (maximum output)?

b. Given the $12 price of labor, how many units of labor should the firm hire in order to maximize profit (minimize loss)?

The following problems require calculus:

C1. A production function for a firm has the following relationship between the level of output (Q) and the levels of capital (K) and labor (L).

$$Q = 4KL + 3L^2 - (1/3)L^3$$

a. Find the isoquant equation for $Q = 100$.

b. Derive the expression, or function, that gives the slope of the isoquant (in terms of quantities of K and L).

c. Derive the marginal product of labor function from the preceding production function if K is fixed at 5 units.

d. If K is fixed at 5 units, where do diminishing returns to labor set in?

C2. A given firm has the following simple short-run total product function:

$$Q = 400L - 0.5L^2$$

where

Q = output per month, and

L = units of labor.

a. What is the equation for the firm's average product?

b. What is the equation for its marginal product?

c. At what level of labor use is marginal product zero?

d. What is the firm's maximum output per month?

C3. Suppose a firm has the following production function:

$$Q = 12KL + KL^2 - (1/12)KL^3$$

If the firm is operating in the short run and capital (K) is fixed at $K = 4$, determine the following:

a. The maximum output that the firm can produce when $K = 4$;

b. The level of use of input L where AP_L is at a maximum;

c. The output level where diminishing marginal returns to input L occurs.

C4. Toadhall Company has the following total product function with input Z as its only short-run variable input:

$$Q = 160Z + 18Z^2 - (1/3)Z^3$$

a. At what Z value will the MP_Z for this firm equal zero?

b. What will be the maximum short-run output the firm can produce?

c. What is the numerical value of the marginal product of Z, MP_Z, when MP_Z is at its maximum?

d. At what Z value will the average product of Z be maximized?

C5. Suppose Zeta Company has the following total product function, where Q is output per time period and L is the number of units of labor hired.

$$Q = 44L + 10L^2 - \frac{1}{3}L^3$$

(Show all calculations.)

a. What will be the maximum short-run output the firm can produce?

b. At what L value will the MP_L for this firm be maximum?

c. At what level of output will the firm reach the point of diminishing marginal returns to L?

d. What will be the numerical value of AP_L when it is at its maximum?

C6. Excellence Company has the following total product function with labor (L) as its only short-run variable input:

$$Q = 84L + 11L^2 - \frac{2}{3}L^3$$

a. At what L value will the MP_L for this firm equal zero?

b. What will be the maximum short-run output the firm can produce?

c. What L value corresponds to the maximum point of AP_L?

d. What will be the numerical value of MP_L when it is at its maximum?

C7. Where L is the only variable input, suppose that on a daily basis the short-run total product curve for a firm is $TP_L = Q = 50L - 0.1L^2$. The firm must pay a fixed price of $130 a unit (one worker day) for labor, so that $MC_L = 130$. It sells in a perfectly competitive market (see definition in Chapter 1) and can sell all of the product it wants to for $20 per unit. It uses only labor and materials to produce output, and the materials cost per output unit is $7. Determine:

a. The maximum short-run output the firm can produce.

b. The output that is consistent with optimal use of the variable input L.

C8. Consider the following total product function for input Z.

$$Q = 84Z - 0.01Z^2$$

a. What is the equation for the marginal product of Z?

b. What can you say about diminishing returns for this total product function?

c. What is the equation for the average product of Z?

d. Suppose you solve the average product equation for $AP_Z = 0$. What do you get, and what is it telling you about the total product curve?

SELECTED REFERENCES

Besanko, David A., and Ronald R. Braeutigam. *Microeconomics: An Integrated Approach.* New York: John Wiley and Sons, 2002, Chapter 6.

Bilas, Richard A. *Microeconomic Theory,* 2d ed. New York: McGraw-Hill, 1971, Chapter 6.

Hyman, David N. *Microeconomics,* 4th ed. Chicago, IL: Richard D. Irwin, 1997, Chapter 9.

Lyons, Ivory L., and Manuel Zymelman. *Economic Analysis of the Firm.* New York: Pitman, 1966, Chapter 15.

McGuigan, James R., R. Charles Moyer, and Frederick H. deB. Harris. *Managerial Economics,* 9th ed. Cincinnati, Ohio: South-Western, 2002, Chapter 7.

Miller, Roger LeRoy, and Raymond P.H. Fishe. *Microeconomics: Price Theory in Practice.* New York: HarperCollins, 1995, Chapter 8.

Perloff, Jeffrey M. *Microeconomics,* 2d ed. Boston: Addison Wesley Longman, 2001, Chapter 6.

Pindyck, Robert S., and Daniel L. Rubinfeld. *Microeconomics,* 5th ed. Upper Saddle River, NJ: Prentice Hall, 2001, Chapter 6.

Wibe, Sören. "Engineering Production Functions: A Survey." *Economica* 51 (November 1984): 401–411.

Mathematics of Determining the Least Cost Combination of Inputs

We can mathematically solve for the least cost combination of inputs to produce a given level of output or (what is essentially the same type of problem) to find the combination of inputs that will maximize output, subject to the condition that only a particular level of cost be incurred by the firm. Mathematical methods often have the advantage of being simpler and more precise than graphical techniques.

The simplest mathematical technique, *if* the cost and production functions are mathematically simple, is that of substitution. For example, assume that our production function is

(5-1)
$$Q = L^2 + 5LK + 4K^2,$$

that the price of a unit of labor services and a unit of capital services is $5 and $10, respectively, and that our cost limitation is equal to $1,000 per time period. Our goal, then, is to find the quantities of K and L that will maximize output (Q) subject to the condition that

(5-2)
$$5L + 10K = 1,000.$$

If we solve Equation (5-2) for L in terms of K and substitute in Equation (5-1), we obtain

(5-3)
$$L = 200 - 2K,$$

$$Q = (200 - 2K)^2 + 5(200 - 2K)K + 4K^2,$$

$$Q = 40{,}000 - 800K + 4K^2 + 1{,}000K - 10K^2 + 4K^2,$$

and

(5-4)

$$Q = 40{,}000 + 200K - 2K^2.$$

Using the first order condition for an extremum, we find dQ/dK and set it equal to zero, as shown in Equation (5-5):

(5-5)

$$dQ/dK = 200 - 4K = 0.$$

Solving Equation (5-5) for K, we find $K = 50$, and substituting in Equation (5-3), we find $L = 100$. The second order condition for a maximum is also satisfied.

   If the functions are such that the substitution method is difficult, the Lagrangian multiplier method is useful. The Lagrangian multiplier method essentially involves adding the constraint (in a form in which it will equal zero when it is satisfied) to the original function to be maximized or minimized. Then, through creation of a new independent variable (the Lagrangian multiplier), the satisfaction of the constraint becomes a first order condition for a new function.

   Using our production function in Equation (5-1), we obtain a new, augmented function to be maximized:

(5-6)

$$Z = L^2 + 5LK + 4K^2 + \lambda(1{,}000 - 5L - 10K).$$

Here, the Greek λ is the Lagrangian multiplier. In this form, λ is readily interpretable as the marginal effect on the production function (on output) of relaxing the cost constraint.

   Now, applying the optimizing conditions for a function of more than one independent variable, we find the following first order conditions:

$$\frac{\partial Z}{\partial L} = 2L + 5K - 5\lambda = 0,$$

$$\frac{\partial Z}{\partial K} = 5L + 8K - 10\lambda = 0,$$

and

$$\frac{\partial Z}{\partial \lambda} = -5L - 10K + 1{,}000 = 0.$$

Note that we are treating λ the same way as any regular independent variable. Solving Equations (5-7) through (5-9) simultaneously, we find $L = 100$, $K = 50$, and $\lambda = 90$.

PROBLEM

1. A firm's production function is given by $Q = L^2 + 10LK + K^2$, and its cost function is given by $TC = 5L + 20K$. What is the maximum quantity the firm can produce for a cost of \$1,150? What quantities of capital and labor should it use?

2. Miller Company uses two inputs, X and Y, in its production function. The production function is:

$$Q = 40X^{.5}Y^{.5},$$

where inputs and output are in units per week.

    The market price of input X is \$100 per unit and that of input Y is \$20 per unit. Miller has a budget constraint of \$16,000 per week. Find its best input combination and the maximum weekly output it can produce.

Cost of Production

Cost, as we have repeatedly emphasized, is one of the two major factors with which profit-maximizing firms *must* deal wisely. Successful managers are certainly aware that it is the *level of cost relative to revenue* that determines the firm's overall profitability. In the last two decades, as the force of global competition has impacted firms, the motto across all sectors of business has seemed to be "Cut costs or else!" Big manufacturers such as General Motors and General Electric have pressured their suppliers to cut costs or lose their business, and, as the last chapter discussed, have introduced new technologies and reorganized production to reduce costs. The same is true in the retail sector, where Wal-Mart has been a model of efficiency, especially in the management of its supply chains. Wal-Mart has developed its own Internet-based software system, called *Retail Link*, which tracks inventories and keeps in constant touch with suppliers around the globe to make sure its shelves are stocked. Kmart instituted something similar, but it still had serious inventory problems that probably contributed to its filing of Chapter 11 bankruptcy in January 2002.[1]

---

[1] "Kmart Files Chapter 11," *CNNmoney*, online, January 22, 2002, www.money.cnn.com, March 12, 2002; and Don Steinberg, "Wal-Mart," *Smart Business*, online, September 1, 2001, www.smartbusiness.com, March 14, 2002.

Service enterprises, such as hospitals and hotels, have also trimmed their budgets. To cut costs, some hospitals have changed "housekeepers" into "service partners" whose job descriptions include wielding mops, feeding patients, and even performing CPR.[2] The Chicago Hyatt Regency found some years ago that it could save $220,000 a year simply by eliminating the nightly ritual of turning down the beds.[3]

The 9/11 terrorist attacks on the United States made the airline industry take a close look at costs. In the face of falling demand for air travel, most airlines did what seemed the obvious and instituted many cutbacks in schedules and workforce. They also sought other ways to reduce their total cost of operations and/or enhance revenues. For example, in 2002 American Airlines announced it would cut out all food service on domestic flights. However, Southwest Airlines, historically known for maintaining a low-cost and efficient operation, consistently made an operating profit while all of the other major U.S. airlines were plagued with losses.[4]

The entertainment industry affords us another example of how important attention to cost is to a firm's success. Michael Eisner, who has served as CEO of both Paramount and Disney, has been known for careful cost management. Movies, especially those with special effects or virtual characters, have been becoming more and more costly. (*Stuart Little II,* a 2002 Columbia release, was said to have cost $120 million, and its star was 100 percent computer-generated.)[5] When Disney's *Pearl Harbor* (2001) was initially proposed, potential budgets ranging from $145 million to $208 million were considered. Eisner finally agreed to $135 million, with possible increases of an additional $10 million. In the 1980s, the highly successful *Raiders of the Lost Ark* was made for less than $20 million, though Eisner, then head of Paramount, was at first told by George Lucas and Steven Spielberg that the opening scene alone would probably cost about $25 million. Cost control, like that practiced by Eisner, is very important to a studio, since it allows for the production of a greater number of films per year and, therefore, better chances of producing a hit.[6]

Interestingly enough, with new digital technology, low-budget filmmakers have become a significant force in the movie industry. They typically produce movies for a fraction of the average cost of a major-studio film, yet they

---

[2] "Daily Grind," *Wall Street Journal,* June 25, 1996, p. A1.
[3] "Why Hyatt Is Toning Down the Glitz," *Business Week* (February 27, 1995), p. 92.
[4] Melanie Trottman, "Southwest Airlines Turns More Aggressive: Moves Follow the Successful Outcome of Gamble on Continued Growth After Sept. 11," *Wall Street Journal,* July 15, 2002, p. B6.
[5] Tom King, "The Mouse That Soared," *Wall Street Journal,* July 12, 2002, p. W9.
[6] "Newsweek Features Pearl Harbor," movieheadlines.net (press release), May 7, 2001, www.movieheadlines.net, May 17, 2002; "Thrift Becomes Paramount in Hollywood As Big-Budget Films and Economy Falter," *Wall Street Journal,* January 17, 1991, pp. B1, B5; and "A Slasher Is Loose on Paramount's Lot," *Business Week* (January 28, 1991), pp. 52–53.

have achieved some spectacular successes.[7] Cost also plays a critical role in the financial success of Broadway plays. When the musical *Rent* opened, its weekly costs were estimated at $250,000 compared with *Beauty and the Beast*'s $400,000. As a result, *Rent* was expected to begin making a profit within six months. It took *Beauty and the Beast* at least a year to reach that point.[8]

Cost has also been in the forefront of efforts to change the design process in many industries. Using computer-aided design software and related developments, auto manufacturers have been able to bring new products through the design stage much more quickly and at much lower costs than they faced when many steps in the process were done by hand. A related noteworthy example is the development of the V-Rod motorcycle by Harley Davidson. A radical departure from Harleys of the past, the V-Rod "relied only on computer engineering, instead of actual prototypes, until just before production."[9] Although the V-Rod marked a milestone in Harley's cost picture, the company had already taken many steps to reduce its operating costs in its traditional motorcycle line. *Forbes* Magazine reported that Harley had reduced its supplier base from 4,000 firms to 80 from 1995 to 2002.[10]

It is clear that careful cost management can be critical to a firm's survival. In addition to the preceding examples, many other industries, including core manufacturing, have been remaking themselves in ways that will markedly reduce costs. According to *Business Week*:

> For the erstwhile Rust Belt of the 1980s, it has been a Cinderella transformation. And it's by no means over. The Fairy Godmother of technology is still sprinkling factories with new, magic-dust acronyms like CME, for collaborative manufacturing environment, and XML, for extensible markup language, the new scheme for tagging data on Web sites. (XML) … may enable entire supply chains, and maybe even whole industries, to function as a unified, well-oiled machine.[11]

Changes like those above make the connection between production and cost all the more evident. Of course, if a firm can reduce its unit costs over those of comparable firms in its industry, it has a head start in making a profit— either by selling its product at the same price as its rivals and reaping the benefits of a greater price-cost differential or by being able to lower price and successfully capture a larger market share.

---

[7] See David Germain, "Low Budget Films Turn into Big Summer Hits," *The Cincinnati Enquirer*, August 6, 2001, online www.enquirer.com, May 12, 2002; and "A Down-Home Movie Mogul," *Newsweek* (January 12, 1987), p. 41.

[8] "Putting on a Musical for a Song," *Business Week* (May 6, 1996), p. 44.

[9] Gail Kachadourian, "Harley Takes Page from Auto Manual," *Automotive News*, online, August 8, 2001, www.autonews.com, June 10, 2002.

[10] "High-Octane Hog," *Forbes.com*, online, September 10, 2001, www.forbes.com, July 10, 2002.

[11] "Brave New Factory," *Business Week* (July 23, 2001), pp. 75–76.

Nevertheless, cost cutting must be done carefully, or it can reduce a company's profitability. Some of the downsizing and restructuring that occurred in the 1990s as companies attempted to become more competitive has been dubbed "dumbsizing" for its negative impact on consumer satisfaction and firm profits. For example, Delta Airlines embarked on an aggressive cost-cutting mission in the mid-1990s. However, the airline also fell to last place among the 10 largest airlines in on-time performance, and consumer satisfaction declined. As management consultant Eileen Shapiro stated, "What you want to be is *low-cost relative to the benefits* you offer customers" (emphasis added).[12]

TYPES OF COSTS

Historical costs or **explicit costs** are those costs of production that involve a specific payment by the firm to some person, group, or organization outside the firm.

There are many different types of costs that a firm may consider relevant under various circumstances. Such costs include historical costs, opportunity costs, fixed costs, variable costs, incremental costs, private costs, and social costs. **Historical costs** or **explicit costs** are costs of the firm for which *explicit payment* has been made sometime in the past or for which the firm is committed in the future. These are the costs that a financial accountant attempts to record as data and are gathered for the firm's income statement.[13] Examples of explicit costs include wages and salaries, rent, materials costs, depreciation (related to the amount paid for a machine), and interest payments. The obvious advantage of restricting cost figures to those based on historical costs is that of objectivity—records of transactions should exist from which the figures can be verified.

Implicit costs are the costs of using firm-owned resources. They are opportunity costs that cannot be accounted for by payments to outsiders. These costs represent opportunities that a firm gives up by using a resource in one way rather than another.

Most economists consider the concept of explicit or historical costs to be too narrow, however, when estimating the total costs of the firm, and they would include *implicit opportunity costs* that the firm incurs as well as explicit costs in the firm's cost figures. **Implicit costs** are those that do not involve actual payment by a firm to factors of production but nevertheless represent costs to the firm in the sense that in order to use certain inputs in

[12] "Call It Dumbsizing: Why Some Companies Regret Cost-Cutting," *Wall Street Journal*, May 14, 1996, p. A6. Also see "Oops, That's Too Much Downsizing," *Business Week* (June 8, 1998), p. 38; and "Reengineering Revisited," *Executive Report*, Financial Executives Research Foundation, Inc. (Vol. 6, No. 3, June 1999). Cost cutting at Delta did raise the stock price, however. See "Cost Cutting at Delta Raises the Stock Price But Lowers the Service," *Wall Street Journal*, June 20, 1996, pp. A1, A8; and "A Slimmer Delta Still Loves to Fly But Does It Show?" *Wall Street Journal*, January 26, 1996.

[13] The Securities Exchange Commission in the past required that some firms adjust their cost figures to reflect the current value of assets used in the production process. See Fredrich Andrews, "Replacing Cost Accounting Plan Adopted by SEC," *Wall Street Journal*, March 25, 1976, p. 6. The Financial Accounting Standards Board in late 1986 issued a statement that relieved these companies of this requirement. They still are encouraged to provide this information on a voluntary basis. See *Management Accounting* (January 1987): 9, and FASB No. 82.

the production process, the firm has had to abandon opportunities to use them elsewhere.

For example, let us suppose that John and Ruth Brown (1) have opened a delicatessen in a building that they own in a shopping mall; (2) have invested $60,000 of their own financial capital in it; and (3) consider its management to be their full-time jobs. A monthly income statement such as might be prepared by an economist is shown in Table 6-1. Notice that both explicit and implicit costs are included.

The first part of the income statement is straightforward, resulting in an income figure consistent with that found by using currently accepted accounting principles. From that amount, however, we have subtracted amounts for the firm owners' implicit opportunity costs—estimated rental income that the firm's owners could have earned on the building by leasing it to another business, the monthly salary that John and Ruth could expect to make if they worked for someone else, and an expected return on the $60,000 capital if invested elsewhere (with equal risk). Note the presence of the words *expected* or *estimated* in the list of opportunity costs. Such words reflect the fact that the firm must estimate what revenue its resources listed above would bring in if they were employed according to the *next best* opportunity. This nonobjectivity of the implicit cost figures bothers some accountants and is the main reason that such figures are not generally acceptable in financial statements for use by stockholders or investors. Still, if implicit costs are positive, actual economic costs for a firm will be larger than accounting costs; therefore, economic profit generally will be smaller than accounting profit. Thus, the inclusion of implicit costs is important for managerial decision making by a firm's owner(s) because it helps the owner(s) to better understand the economic implications of the demands that the firm is placing on *all* resources.

We will now briefly consider the other cost items listed at the beginning of the chapter. **Fixed costs** are those costs that are fixed in the short run and

Fixed costs are costs that do not vary with the level of output in the short run.

Table 6-1 *John and Ruth's Deli Statement of Economic Profit for Month Ended July 31, 2000*

Total Revenue (Sales)		$140,000
Less Cost of Goods Sold		60,000
Gross Profit		$ 80,000
Less Operating Expenses		50,000
Operating (Accounting) Net Income		$ 30,000
Less		
Implicit Rental Income	$ 5,400	
Implicit Salary Income	12,000	
Implicit Interest Income	600	18,000
Economic Profit		$ 12,000

Variable costs are costs that increase of decrease as a firm's output increases or decreases.

Semivariable costs are costs that are fixed over some ranges of output and variable over others.

Incremental cost is the additional cost that a firm will incur if it undertakes one more activity or if it takes one course of action rather than another.

The private costs of a firm include all of the costs of resource use, both explicit and implicit, the firm must bear to produce its output.

The social costs of a firm are the private costs of the resources that the firm uses plus any additional costs imposed on society by the firm's operation.

therefore do not vary with the level of output produced by the firm during that time period. **Variable costs** are those costs that do vary with the level of production of the firm. Note that *in the long run, all costs of the firm are variable.* It is possible to distinguish a third category, **semivariable costs,** which are fixed over some ranges of output and variable over others. Two examples might be a firm's water bill and the wages paid to supervisors. For simplicity we will assume that all short-run costs fall into one of two categories—fixed or variable—and that *all* cost items are variable in the long run.

Incremental costs associated with some decisions by the firm are the additional costs that a firm would incur if it took one course of action rather than another. In many instances, the profit-maximizing firm owner makes decisions based on a comparison of incremental revenue and incremental costs. We will discuss this topic further in Chapter 7.

Finally, the **private costs** of a firm are the sum of the explicit and implicit costs that it incurs, as we have already discussed. The **social costs** of a firm are those that society in general bears because of the firm's activities. Social costs would include the private costs of a firm, since presumably all of the firm's resources could be used elsewhere in producing goods of value to (at least some members of) society. However, social costs would also include costs paid for by society but not by the firm, even though such costs were a result of production by the firm. Examples might include air, water, and noise pollution. A firm could, in addition, generate *negative* social costs (social benefits) such as the beauty of a well-kept golf course and the resultant increase in the values of surrounding properties. Most people would be pleased that an exclusive country club had decided to locate near their property—even if they wanted only to sell that property for a profit. Social costs are important considerations in economic decision making (and law making) by society in general. However, since the part of social cost that is not included in private cost is not usually considered by the *profit-maximizing* firm in its decision-making process, it will generally be ignored in our discussion of the firm. We will now turn to a more detailed discussion of the firm's private costs.

COSTS IN THE LONG RUN

Once we know the production function and the prices and quantities of its inputs, we can then easily discover how total costs vary with the level of output. As in Chapter 5, we will continue to use $Q = f(K,L)$ for a firm's production function, where Q is the quantity of output and K and L are inputs. In Figure 6-1, panel (a), we have shown a series of optimal input combinations (at points A, B, C, D, and E) corresponding to different levels of production derived using the rules for least cost production discussed in Chapter 5. In

MANAGERIAL PERSPECTIVE

The Cost of Being "Your Own Boss"

Many people dream of owning their own business—being their own boss, gathering the respect of the community as a successful businessperson, and, certainly, making a lot of money. However, turning those dreams into reality may involve considerable opportunity costs in the form of *sweat equity*. Sweat equity is the value that people build in a business (or home) by investing their time and, usually, plenty of hard work and brain power as well. Many small-business owners give up huge amounts of time and effort that could have been allocated to alternative pursuits.

A three-year study by the National Federation of Independent business found that 53 percent of the owners of firms that had been in business for 18 months spent 60 or more hours a week in that endeavor. For some, the time commitment was even more substantial: 11 percent of those who started their own company and 14 percent of those who bought companies reported spending 80 or more hours a week in managerial duties. However, recent studies indicated that less than 20 percent of executives in big corporations spent that much time on the job. Moreover, almost 20 percent of new business owners claimed to be working additional part- or full-time jobs as well.

While owning a small business is sometimes thought of as an "American dream," both the dream and the reality are quite common in other countries, too. A European Community study found that almost 50 percent of self-employed persons work over 50 hours per week, and a British study found that shopkeepers were working as many as 70 hours per week and that 25 percent of those surveyed had not had a holiday in four years.

When one considers these data regarding the expenditure of managerial blood, sweat, and tears, along with the fact that only 20 percent of all new businesses survive for five years, it is clear that owning your own business is not an easy road to riches. Although we do not wish to discourage any budding entrepreneurs, they cannot make an economic decision regarding a new enterprise without counting the considerable opportunity cost in their own time and energy.

References: "Open All Hours of the Day," *Huddersfield Daily Examiner* (online edition: ichuddersfield.icnetwork.co.uk), June 20, 2002; *Self-Employment: Choice or Necessity* (Dublin: European Foundation for the Improvement of Living and Working Conditions, 2000); "Like 60-Hour Weeks? Try Your Own Business," *Business Week* (August 10, 1987), p. 75.

Long-run total cost is the minimum economic cost of producing each possible level of output when the time period is sufficiently long to change all inputs of the firm's production function.

Figure 6-1, panel (b), we have graphed corresponding output levels and **long-run total cost (LTC)**. Note that we are still assuming that both inputs, K and L, are variable so that LTC in Figure 6-1, panel (b), is applicable only when the firm can achieve the lowest cost input combination for its desired level of output. In other words, the firm must be operating on its expansion path [line OX in Figure 6-1, panel (a)]. Thus, LTC in Figure 6-1, panel (b), must be the long-run total cost curve of the firm. As stated in Chapter 5, the least cost combination of inputs for each level of output requires that

$$\frac{MP_L}{P_L} = \frac{MP_K}{P_K} = ... = \frac{MP_n}{P_n},$$

FIGURE 6–1

Variation of Long-Run Total Cost

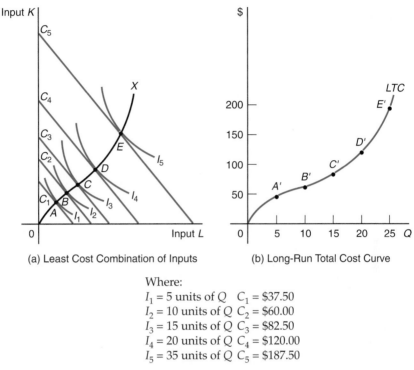

(a) Least Cost Combination of Inputs

(b) Long-Run Total Cost Curve

Where:

$I_1 = 5$ units of Q $C_1 = \$37.50$
$I_2 = 10$ units of Q $C_2 = \$60.00$
$I_3 = 15$ units of Q $C_3 = \$82.50$
$I_4 = 20$ units of Q $C_4 = \$120.00$
$I_5 = 35$ units of Q $C_5 = \$187.50$

Least cost combinations of inputs for levels of output corresponding to I_1, I_2, I_3, I_4, and I_5 are given by points A, B, C, D, and E, respectively, in panel (a). These points then determine corresponding points (A', B', C', D', and E', respectively) on the long-run total cost curve (*LTC*), in panel (b).

for all inputs of the firm, where MP_i is the marginal product of input i and P_i is the price of input i (and assumed to be constant).

Long-run average cost is equal to long-run total cost divided by the level of output. It measures cost per unit of output when all inputs are variable.

Long-run average cost (LAC), or per-unit cost, at some output level Q can be found by dividing *long-run total cost (LTC)* by output *(Q):*

$$LAC = \frac{LTC}{Q}.$$

Since *long-run average cost* gives the cost per unit of output in the long run when all costs are variable, it follows that *LAC* for a particular output level is calculated by dividing *LTC* at that level of output by the number of units of output. We would find the average value of anything else in the same manner: divide the total value by the number of cases involved. For example, the average weight of the students in your classroom would be obtained by adding up the weight of each student in the room and dividing by the number of students.

Geometrically, *LAC* for a particular level of output is equal to the *slope* of the line segment drawn from the origin to *LTC* at that same level of output.

FIGURE 6–2

*Deriving
Average Cost
from the Total
Cost Curve*

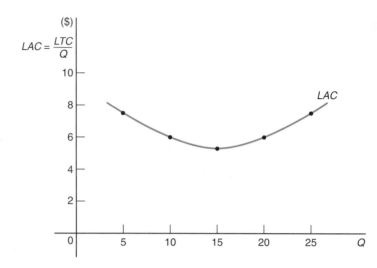

The long-run average cost curve can be derived from the long-run total cost curve by dividing each *LTC* figure by the corresponding quantity of output.

The slope of this line must be equal to *LAC* because its slope is equal to the change in the vertical distance divided by the change in the horizontal distance between any two points on the line. Between the origin and any other point on the long-run total cost curve, the vertical change is equal to the value of *LTC* at that point, and the horizontal change is equal to the value of *Q* at that point. Thus, the slope of the line is equal to *LTC/Q*, which is the definition of long-run average cost. The long-run average cost curve corresponding to *LTC* in Figure 6-1, panel (b), is drawn in Figure 6-2.

**Long-run marginal
cost** is the rate of
change of long-run
total cost as the
level of output
changes.

> **Long-run marginal cost,** or the rate of change of long-run total cost with respect to output, at a particular quantity of output is given by the slope of the total cost curve at that output level.[14] In discrete terms, *arc marginal cost* is an approximation to marginal cost and is the *average rate of change* of total cost with respect to the quantity of output *between two levels of output.* Thus, *marginal cost answers the question, "How much will production of one more unit of output cost the firm?" Arc long-run marginal cost (LMC)* can be found by dividing the change in total cost by the change in the quantity of output, or

$$\text{Arc } LMC = \frac{\Delta LTC}{\Delta Q}.$$

---

[14] For example, at Q_1 this slope is equal to the slope of a line tangent to *LTC* at LTC_1; and, mathematically,

$$LMC_1 = \frac{dLTC}{dQ} \text{ at } Q_1.$$

The long-run total cost curve *(LTC)* drawn in Figure 6-1, panel (b), has first decreasing, then increasing, marginal cost.

The relationships among long-run total, average, and marginal costs for the long-run total cost curve in Figure 6-1, panel (b), are further demonstrated in Figure 6-3. We observe that long-run marginal cost *(LMC)* is decreasing until $Q_1 = 10$, at which point the *LTC* curve has its smallest slope. Minimum long-run average cost *(LAC)* is reached at $Q_2 = 15$, where a line drawn from the origin to point LTC_2 is just tangent to *LTC*, since this is the least steeply sloped line that can be drawn from the origin to a point on the long-run total cost curve. At Q_2 also, marginal cost equals average cost = $5.50, since long-run marginal cost is by definition the slope of a line tangent to *LTC* at the point under consideration. We also know that marginal cost must be equal to average cost when average cost is at a minimum because of

FIGURE 6–3

The Relationships among Total Cost, Average Cost, and Marginal Cost

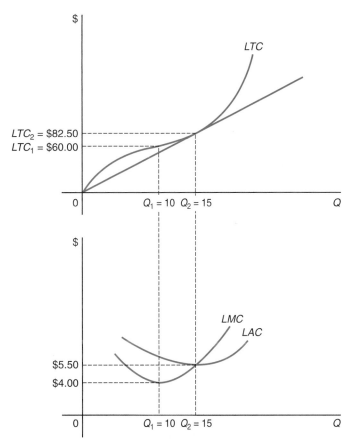

Figure 6–3 depicts the relationships among long-run total cost *(LTC)*, average cost *(LAC)*, and marginal cost *(LMC)*. *LMC* reaches its minimum where the slope of *LTC* reaches its smallest value. *LMC* is equal to *LAC* when *LAC* is at a minimum.

Table 6-2 *Summary of Numerical Values for LTC, LAC, LMC, and Arc LMC[a]*

Q	LTC	LAC	LMC	Arc LMC
0	$ —	Undefined	$10.00	
5	37.50	7.50	5.50	$ 7.50
10	60.00	6.00	4.00	4.50
15	82.50	5.50	5.50	4.50
20	120.00	6.00	10.00	7.50
25	187.50	7.50	17.50	13.50

[a] These relationships are easily derived mathematically. The total cost function drawn in Figure 6-1, panel b, is given by $LTC = 10Q - 0.6Q^2 + 0.02Q^3$. The long-run average cost function is given by $LAC = LTC/Q = 10 - 0.6Q + 0.02Q^2$. The long-run marginal cost function is obtained by taking the derivative of LTC with respect to Q, $LMC = dLTC/dQ = 10 - 1.2Q + 0.06Q^2$. LMC reaches its minimum when $dLMC/dQ = -1.2 + 0.12Q = 0$, or $Q = 10$. At this point, $LMC = 10 - 1.2(10) + 0.06(100) = \$4.00$. LAC reaches its minimum where $dLAC/dQ = -0.6 + 0.04Q = 0$, or where $Q = 15$. At this point, $LAC = 10 - 0.6(15) + 0.02(15)^2 = \$5.50$.

the marginal-average relationship. When marginal cost is greater than average cost, average cost must be rising; and when marginal cost is less than average cost, average cost must be falling. Only when marginal cost is equal to average cost does average cost not change, and this happens only when average cost is at a minimum.

The numerical relationships among long-run total cost, long-run average cost, long-run marginal cost, and arc long-run marginal cost are also summarized in Table 6-2. Note that both the data in this table and the per-unit curves in the lower panel of Figure 6-3 are consistent with the average-marginal relationship. Thus, the *LMC* curve passes through the minimum of the *LAC* curve.

It should be emphasized, however, that the cost curves discussed previously give the firm information on costs when the *lowest possible* cost for a particular level of output can be achieved, *given current input prices*. These cost curves assume that the firm can vary all inputs and thus achieve a least cost combination of inputs for every possible level of output. It follows that they are relevant *only* for long-range planning by the firm regarding level of production, size of plant, and other similar decisions. In the next section, we will discuss the short-run cost situation of the firm.

COSTS IN THE SHORT RUN

In the short run, *at least one* input is fixed, so a firm may not be able to achieve the best combination of inputs for its desired level of output. In Figure 6-4, panel (a), input K is fixed at K_0. Thus, in the short run, the least cost combination of inputs can only be achieved for the level of output associated with I_3, since this is the only point on K_0 that is also on the expansion path for the firm, given current input prices. If the firm should desire to produce any

NUMERICAL EXAMPLE

Isoquants and Long-run Cost

Given the following diagram:

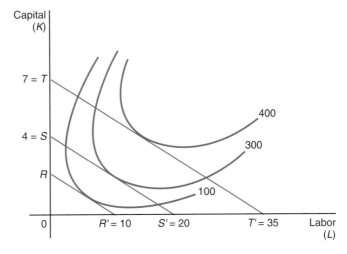

If the price of a unit of labor, P_L = $50, complete the following.

a. At an output of 400, TC = _____.
b. The price of a unit of capital, P_K = _____.
c. The maximum number of units of capital that could be purchased with a budget represented by line RR' is _____.
d. From the three outputs shown, the lowest average cost obtainable is _____.

Answer

a. TC = $1,750, which is the value of the budget on line TT', or the same as $L(P_L)$ = 35($50).
b. P_K = $250. Anywhere along TT', for example, $1,750 is spent. This includes point T, where K = 7. Thus P_K = $1,750/7 = $250.
c. At point, R, K = 2. Anywhere along RR', TC = $500 = $L(P_L)$ = 10($50). Since P_K = $250, only two units of K can be bought with the budget represented by RR'.
d. Minimum AC for these outputs occurs when Q = 300 and AC = $1,000/300 = $3.33. The other two ACs are $500/100 = $5.00 and $1,750/400 = $4.38, respectively, for the 100 and 400 output levels.

other level of output in the short run, it must do so at a greater cost than it could achieve with an optimal combination of inputs. In Figure 6-4, panel (b), the *STC* curve associated with input K fixed at K_0 is higher than the long-run total cost curve *(LTC)* at all output levels except Q_3. Moreover, in general, short-run costs will be greater than long-run costs except for those output

FIGURE 6–4

*Short Run Cost
and Production*

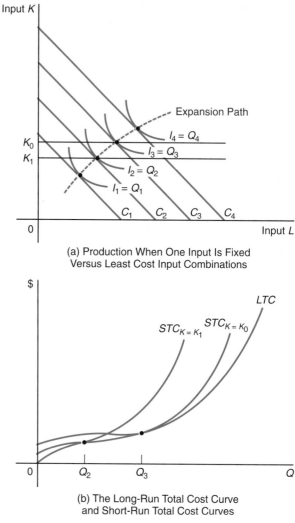

(a) Production When One Input Is Fixed
Versus Least Cost Input Combinations

(b) The Long-Run Total Cost Curve
and Short-Run Total Cost Curves

The expansion path of the firm determines the long-run total cost curve (*LTC*). However, in the short run the firm may not be able to achieve a least cost combination of inputs. For exmple, if input K is fixed at K_0 in the short run, the total cost curve appropriate for various levels of output will be $STC_{K=K_0}$. It will represent a least cost combination of inputs at Q_3 only. At other levels of output, $STC_{K=K_0}$ is greater than *LTC*. A similar explanation holds if input K is fixed at K_1.

levels for which the fixed inputs are at their optimal levels. In Figure 6-4, panel *(a)*, if input K were fixed at K_1 units, short-run total cost would be greater than the lowest possible cost for every output level except Q_2 [see Figure 6-4, panel *(b)*].

Because of the presence of both fixed and variable costs in the short run, we can identify seven different types of short-run cost curves: total fixed

Total fixed cost is the private economic cost of the firm's fixed inputs in the short run. The TFC curve is a horizontal line since these costs do not vary with the level of output in the short run.

cost, total variable cost, total cost, average fixed cost, average variable cost, average total cost, and marginal cost. Although these short-run cost terms represent seven different cost concepts, the facts that (1) their names tell us what they are and (2) the relationships among the total, average, and marginal cost functions in the short run are in many ways similar to the relationships among total, average, and marginal cost in the long run make it relatively easy to remember them. The relationships among the short-run cost curves are illustrated in Figure 6-5. **Total fixed cost (TFC)** is a horizontal

FIGURE 6–5

Graphical Relationships among the Short-Run Cost Curves

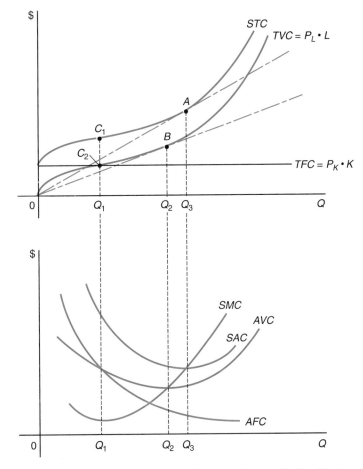

In Figure 6-5, it is assumed that input K is fixed and that input L is variable. Total fixed cost (TFC) is equal to the price (P_K) of input K multiplied by the quantity of input K. Total variable cost (TVC) is equal to $P_L \cdot L$. Short-run total cost (STC) is equal to $TVC + TFC$. Average fixed cost (AFC) is equal to TFC/Q. Average variable cost $(AVC) = TVC/Q$. Short-run average cost (SAC) is equal to $STC/Q = AVC + AFC$. Short-run marginal cost is equal to the slope of the STC curve or the slope of the TVC curve. SMC passes through AVC and SAC at their respective minimum points.

Short-run total variable cost is the sum of all private economic costs of the firm that vary with its level of output in the short run.

Short-run total cost includes all of the private economic costs of the firm in the short run. Short-run total cost is equal to total fixed cost plus short-run total variable cost.

Average fixed cost is fixed cost per unit of output in the short run. Average fixed cost is equal to total fixed cost divided by the level of output.

Short-run average variable cost is the variable cost per unit of output produced in the short run. It is equal to short-run total variable cost divided by the level of output.

Short-run average total cost is the cost per unit of output in the short run. It is equal to short-run total cost divided by the level of output. It is also equal to average fixed cost plus short-run average variable cost for each level of output.

Short-run marginal cost is the rate of change of *either* short-run total cost or short-run total variable cost as the level of output changes in the short run.

straight line at an amount equal to $P_K \cdot K$ if input K is fixed. **Short-run total variable cost *(TVC)*** is given by $P_L \cdot L$, where L is the variable input. **Short-run total cost *(STC)*** is the summation (vertical) of *TFC* and TVC, or

$$STC = TFC + TVC.$$

Directing our attention to unit costs, we observe that **average fixed cost *(AFC)***, or fixed cost per unit of output, is found by dividing a given dollar amount of fixed cost by larger and larger levels of output:

$$AFC = \frac{TFC}{Q}.$$

Thus, *AFC* approaches, but does not reach, zero (the quantity axis) and is the shape of a rectangular hyperbola.[15] **Short-run average variable cost *(AVC)***, variable cost per unit of output, is found by dividing short-run total variable cost by the corresponding level of output:

$$AVC = \frac{TVC}{Q}.$$

Short-run average total cost *(SAC)*, average total cost per unit of output, can be found by dividing short-run total cost by the level of output or by adding *AFC* and *AVC*:

$$SAC = AFC + AVC = \frac{STC}{Q}.$$

As explained in our discussion of long-run costs, per-unit (average) costs for a particular level of output can be obtained geometrically by finding the slope of a line segment extending from the origin to the point on the total cost curve corresponding to that quantity of production. The same procedure can also be used to find *SAC* and *AVC* from the *STC* and *TVC* curves, respectively. Thus, in Figure 6-5 short-run average cost at Q_3 is the slope of line segment *OA*.

Short-run marginal cost is defined in the same manner as marginal cost is defined in the long run: the rate of change of short-run total cost with respect to the level of output. *Arc short-run marginal cost (SMC)* between two levels of output can be found by dividing either the change in short-run *total cost* or the change in short-run *total variable cost* by the change in quantity:

$$arc\ SMC = \frac{\Delta TVC}{\Delta Q} = \frac{\Delta STC}{\Delta Q}.$$

---

[15] A rectangular hyperbola is given by the functional form $XY = a$ where a is a constant.

Table 6-3 *A Numerical Example of the Relationships among Short-Run Cost Curves*

Q	TFC	TVC	STC	AFC	AVC	SAC	SMC	Arc SMC
0	$1,000	$ 0	$1,000	$ —	$ —	$ —	$80	
5	1,000	275	1,275	200.00	55.00	255.00	35	$55.00
10	1,000	400	1,400	100.00	40.00	140.00	20	25.00
15	1,000	525	1,525	66.67	35.00	101.67	35	25.00
20	1,000	800	1,800	50.00	40.00	90.00	80	55.00
25	1,000	1,375	2,375	40.00	55.00	95.00	155	115.00
30	1,000	2,400	3,400	33.33	80.00	113.33	260	205.00

Since fixed cost does not change in the short run, the changes in *STC* and *TVC* must be equal. Therefore, arc short-run marginal cost measures the average rate of change in either total variable cost or total cost with respect to changes in the level of output in the short run.[16] Table 6-3 gives a numerical illustration of all of the short-run cost functions.

Finally, we observe in Figure 6-5 that *SMC* reaches its minimum where *STC* and *TVC* reach their respective flattest points—that is, where their slopes are least (at C_1 and C_2). Also, *AVC* reaches its minimum where the slope of a line segment from the origin to a point on the *TVC* curve is at its minimum (at point *B* in Figure 6-5). At this point, *AVC* = *SMC*, since both are equal to the slope of *OB*, which is tangent to *TVC* at quantity Q_2. For the same reasons, *SAC* reaches its minimum at Q_3, and *SMC* = *SAC* at that point. Again, we know that marginal cost must be equal to average variable cost

---

[16] Instantaneous short-run marginal cost (or short-run marginal cost *at some level of output*) is obtained by finding *dTVC/dQ* or *dSTC/dQ* and is the slope of both the short-run total cost and the short-run total variable cost curves:

$$SMC = \frac{dTVC}{dQ} = \frac{dSTC}{dQ}.$$

For example, if

$$STC = 1,000 + 80Q - 6Q^2 + 0.2Q^3,$$

then

$$TVC = 80Q - 6Q^2 + 0.2Q^3,$$

and

$$SMC = \frac{dSTC}{dQ} = \frac{dTVC}{dQ} = 80 - 12Q + 0.6Q^2.$$

Table 6-3 gives a numerical illustration of all the short-run cost functions.

and to short-run average total cost at their respective minimum points because of the average-marginal relationship. When marginal cost is greater than average variable cost, *AVC* must be rising, and when marginal cost is less than average variable cost, *AVC* must be falling. Only when marginal cost is equal to *AVC* does *AVC* not change, and this is true only at its minimum point. The same relationship must also hold for short-run average total cost and marginal cost. Notice that *SAC* reaches its minimum later (at a larger quantity) than *AVC* because of the presence of fixed costs. As explained earlier, the *SMC passes through the respective minima of AVC and SAC,* in keeping with the average-marginal relationship.

It should be readily apparent that costs need not always vary with output according to the relationships hypothesized in Figure 6-5. In fact, it is often assumed in managerial accounting, at least in the relevant range of production in the short run, that average variable cost (and therefore marginal cost) is constant. Appropriate cost curves, given the assumption of constant unit variable costs, are shown in Figure 6-6. This assumption greatly simplifies analysis of the costs and, consequently, of the corresponding profit-maximizing position of the firm. Moreover, for many firms in the short run and over relatively small ranges of production, such an assumption is probably a fair approximation of reality.

RELATIONSHIP OF SHORT-RUN COST CURVES TO SHORT-RUN PRODUCT CURVES

The total product, average product, and marginal product curves discussed in Chapter 5 are closely related to total variable cost, average variable cost, and marginal cost in the short run. We can demonstrate the reason this statement is true in the following manner. First, assume we have a general production function of the type used in Chapter 5.

$$Q = f(K, L),$$

where K and L are inputs, Q is output, and input K is *fixed* in the short run at 4 units. We will assume that the corresponding total product of L, average product of L, and marginal product of L are as given in Table 6-4.

Turning to the cost curves, we recall from Figure 6-5 that short-run total cost is composed of total fixed cost plus total variable cost, or

$$STC = TFC + TVC.$$

Also, total fixed cost is equal to $P_K \cdot K$, and total variable cost is equal to $P_L \cdot L$, where P_K and P_L are the prices of inputs K and L, respectively, and K and L are the quantities of the inputs. Suppose that K is fixed at 4 units and that P_K is

FIGURE 6-6

Short-Run Cost Curves with Constant Average Variable Cost

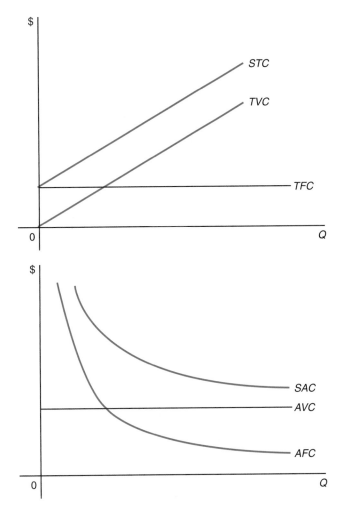

Average variable cost (*AVC*) is constant, *STC* and *TVC* are straight lines. *AVC* = *SMC* in this case.

Table 6-4 *Relationships Between Productivity of Variable Input and Short-Run Cost Curves[a]*

Input L (Units)	Input K (Units)	Output (Q) (Units)	Arc AP_L	Arc MP_L	SMC	AVC	AFC	SAC	TVC	TFC	STC
0	4	0	—			—	—	—	0	$200	$200.00
				5	$ 7.20						
2	4	10	5			$ 7.20	$20.00	$27.20	$ 72.00	200	272.00
				15	2.40						
4	4	40	10			3.60	5.00	8.60	144.00	200	344.00
				10	3.60						
5	4	50	10			3.60	4.00	7.60	180.00	200	380.00
				4	9.00						
6	4	54	9			4.00	3.70	7.70	216.00	200	416.00
				2	18.00						
7	4	56	8			4.50	3.57	8.07	252.00	200	452.00

[a] P_L is $36, and P_K is $50.

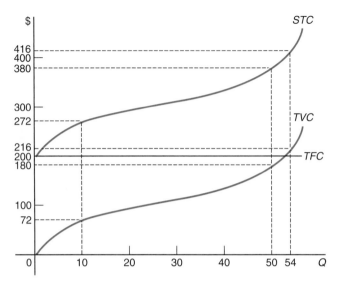

FIGURE 6–7

*Short-Run Total
Cost, Total
Variable Cost,
and Total Fixed
Cost*

Since input K is fixed at 4 units and P_K = \$50, $TFC = P_K \cdot K$ = \$200. $STC = TVC + TFC$.

equal to \$50. Thus, since both P_K and K are fixed, total fixed cost is a horizontal line at $P_K \cdot K$ = \$50 × 4 = \$200, as shown in Figure 6-7.

Total variable cost (= $P_L \cdot L$) is derived from the TP_L curve by multiplying each amount of input L by P_L and plotting the obtained TVC value against its respective level of output or Q value (Q on the horizontal axis), as shown in Figure 6-8. (In Figure 6-8 we have assumed that P_L is \$36.) For example, at Q = 50 units, L is equal to 5 units, and TVC is equal to \$36 × 5 = \$180. At Q = 54 units, L is equal to 6 units, and TVC is equal to \$36 × 6 = \$216.

Important relationships exist among the AP_L curve and the MP_L curve and the average variable cost, short-run average total cost, and short-run marginal cost curves. We know that

$$SAC = \frac{STC}{Q} = \frac{TFC}{Q} + \frac{TVC}{Q} = AFC + AVC.$$

If

$$TFC = P_K \cdot K \text{ and } TVC = P_L \cdot L,$$

then

$$AFC = \frac{P_K \cdot K}{Q} \text{ and } AVC = \frac{P_L \cdot L}{Q},$$

FIGURE 6–8

Relationship Between Total Product of Input L and Total Variable Cost

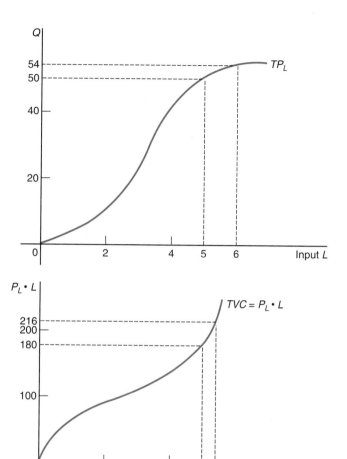

The productivity of a variable input and short-run costs vary inversely. If input L is the only variable input, $TVC = L \cdot P_L$. Note that the more steeply sloped the TP_L curve, the less steeply sloped the TVC curve (or, the greater the MP_L, the smaller the SMC).

and

$$SAC = \frac{P_K \cdot K}{Q} + \frac{P_L \cdot L}{Q}.$$

Since $AVC = (P_L \cdot L)/Q$, we can write

$$AVC = \left(\frac{L}{Q}\right) \cdot P_L = \frac{1}{\left(\frac{Q}{L}\right)} \cdot P_L = \frac{1}{AP_L} \cdot P_L = \frac{P_L}{AP_L}.$$

FIGURE 6–9

Relationship Between Average Product of L and Average Variable Cost

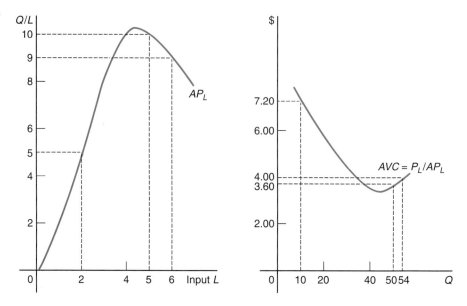

The greater the average product of the variable input (input L), the smaller is AVC. For example, when the amount of input L is 2 units, $AP_L = 5$ units. $AVC = P_L/AP_L = \$36/5 = \$7.20$. When 5 units of input L are used, then $AP_L = 10$ units, and $AVC = \$3.60$.

Therefore, AVC is equal to P_L/AP_L where AP_L is the average product of input L. In other words, AVC is the reciprocal of AP_L, multiplied by P_L (see Figure 6-9). This relationship makes sense because it must be true that *if the average productivity of the variable input increases, there will be a corresponding fall in average variable cost.* The new value of average variable cost, however, will also be determined by the price of the input. If we think about it, it would seem obvious that AVC must be equal to the *average amount of the variable input required per unit of output, $L/Q = 1/AP_L$,* multiplied by the price of the input, P_L. For example, at $Q = 10$ units, AP_L is equal to 5 units and $AVC = P_L/AP_L = \$36/5 = \$7.20$. At $Q = 50$, AP_L is equal to 10 units and $P_L/AP_L = \$36/10 = \$3.60$. Again, we have assumed $P_L = \$36$.

As shown in Figure 6-5, the average fixed cost curve is a rectangular hyperbola, since $P_K \cdot K$ is constant. Some points on the AFC curve for $TFC = \$200$ are shown in Figure 6-10. The SAC curve is shown in Figure 6-10 as the vertical summation of AFC and AVC.

Finally, we will consider the relationship between the marginal product of input L and short-run marginal cost. In Chapter 5 we said that

$$\text{arc } MP_L = \frac{\Delta Q}{\Delta L} = \frac{\Delta TP_L}{\Delta L},$$

FIGURE 6–10

*Short-Run
Average Cost,
Average Variable
Cost, and
Average Fixed
Cost*

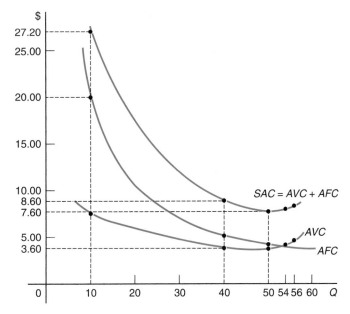

Short-run average cost (*SAC*) is equal to *AVC* + *AFC*. For example, at 10 units of output, *AVC* =
$7.20, *AFC* = $20.00, and *SAC* = $7.20 + $20.00 = $27.20.

and in this chapter we have said that

$$\text{arc } SMC = \frac{\Delta STC}{\Delta Q} = \frac{\Delta TVC}{\Delta Q}.$$

We know that $TVC = P_L \cdot L$ (as long as P_L remains constant). Then

$$\text{arc } SMC = \left(\frac{\Delta L}{\Delta Q} \right) P_L = \left[\frac{1}{\left(\frac{\Delta Q}{\Delta L} \right)} \right] \cdot P_L$$

$$= \left(\frac{1}{\text{arc } MP_L} \right) \cdot P_L,$$

where MP_L is the marginal product of input *L*. Thus, *SMC* is the reciprocal
of the marginal product of *L* multiplied by P_L, or P_L / MP_L, as shown in

FIGURE 6–11

Relationship Between Marginal Product of L and Short-Run Marginal Cost

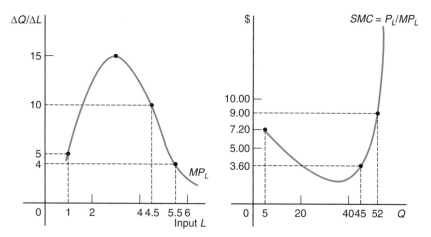

The greater the marginal product of the variable input (input L), the smaller the short-run marginal cost (SMC). For example, the marginal product of the first unit of input L is 5 units of output. The marginal cost of those first 5 units of output is equal to $P_L/MP_L = \$36/5 = \$7.20$. The marginal product of the fifth unit of L is 10 units of output, so SMC at this point (between 40 and 50 units of output) is $3.60.

Figure 6-11.[17] Again, it makes sense that if the *marginal product* of a variable input *rises*, there will be a corresponding *fall* in *short-run marginal cost*, and if the *marginal product* of a variable input *falls*, *short-run marginal cost* must *rise*. Moreover, how much a change in the marginal product of an input changes marginal cost must depend on the price of the input.

These relationships seem reasonable if one thinks about them for a moment. Suppose the average worker on a soda pop assembly line turns out 6 cases of soda an hour and the hourly cost of one worker (one unit of L) is $9.00. The *average variable cost* per case of soda must be $P_L/AP_L = \$9.00/6$ cases = $1.50 per case. If the *marginal product* of an additional worker is 3 cases per hour, then the *marginal cost* of another case of soda will be $P_L/MP_L = \$9.00/3$ cases = $3.00 per case.[18]

---

[17] In calculus terms,

$$MP_L = \frac{\partial Q}{\partial L} \quad \text{and} \quad SMC = \left(\frac{\partial L}{\partial Q}\right) \cdot P_L,$$

so

$$SMC = \left(\frac{1}{MP_L}\right) \cdot P_L.$$

[18] We are temporarily ignoring the cost of additional containers and other materials. In reality, the per-case amounts of these items would be added onto the AVC and SMC figures. We discuss the matter of component costs more thoroughly in Chapter 12.

NUMERICAL EXAMPLE

Relation of Short-Run Product to Cost

The following data pertain to Dynamo Corporation, a small firm that employs college students to do fast-food delivery using bicycles. Each employee must furnish his or her own bicycle. Naturally, there is no allowance for fuel. Complete the last column of the table, assuming that each additional worker is paid $6 per hour and that marginal product is measured in deliveries per hour.

Number of Workers	Arc Marginal Product of a Worker	Marginal Cost
0		
1	5	
2	8	
3	6	
4	4	
5	2	

Answer

The easiest way to obtain marginal cost from these data is to use the relation $SMC = (P_L)/MP_L$, where L is the variable input. Thus, for the first worker, we have $SMC = (\$6/5) = \$1.20$, and for the second, $SMC = (\$6/8) = \$0.75$. For the third, fourth, and fifth workers, the respective SMCs are $1.00, $1.50, and $3.00. If you use $SMC = \Delta TVC/\Delta Q$, you will obtain the same results.

By examining Figures 6-7, 6-9, and 6-11, we can observe that the productivity of an input and costs vary inversely. Other things being equal, the greater the productivity of a variable input, the lower the short-run costs of a firm. The lower the productivity of an input, the higher the short-run costs of a firm. For example, in Figure 6-9, when the AP_L is equal to 5 units, average variable cost is equal to $7.20. When AP_L is doubled to 10 units, AVC is cut in half. In Figure 6-11, when the MP_L is 5 units, SMC is equal to $7.20. When MP_L decreases to 4 units, SMC rises to $9.00. Certainly these relationships mesh with what our common sense would lead us to conclude.

Figure 6-12 shows the relationship between the short-run marginal cost curve and the AVC and SAC curves. Note that the rising SMC curve passes through the minimum point of the AVC curve as well as the minimum point of the SAC. This is in keeping with the *average-marginal relationship*, which was discussed in the preceding chapter and mentioned again earlier in this chapter. The AVC is falling to the left of its minimum because the amount added to total cost by the next unit of output is less than the average variable cost of previous units. In the case of a single variable input, we can say this

FIGURE 6–12

*Relation of SMC
to AVC and SAC*

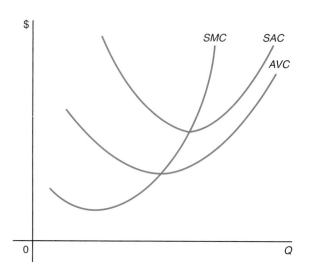

A marginal curve will always pass through the extreme value of the corresponding average curve. Thus, as it rises, *SMC* passes through the minimum of *AVC* and through the minimum of *SAC*.

occurs because the marginal product of additional units of that input exceeds its average product, causing *AP* to rise. Rising average product yields falling average variable cost. Once the marginal product of the input falls below its average product, *AP* will fall and *AVC* will rise. This happens to the right of minimum *AVC*, where an additional unit of output adds more to total cost than the average variable cost of previous units. If input *L* is the only variable input, it will follow that the output level where *SMC* = *AVC* is the *same* output where $MP_L = AP_L$, or that *minimum AVC* corresponds to maximum AP_L.

RELATION OF SHORT-RUN TO LONG-RUN AVERAGE COSTS

Once again we emphasize that for any given output, short-run total cost (and therefore short-run average cost) is unlikely to be as low as the level achievable when *all* inputs are variable. Typically, *only one* of all possible output levels attainable in a short-run setting will be characterized by cost data equal to long-run least possible cost for that level of output. Accordingly, short-run total cost will exceed long-run total cost for all other possible short-run outputs. (An exception, discussed at the end of this section, is the case in which not all inputs are divisible.)

In Figure 6-4, we indicated the relationship between short-run total cost curves and the long-run total cost curve. Figure 6-13 demonstrates the rela-

FIGURE 6–13

Relationship Between Short-Run Average Cost Curves and the Long-Run Average Cost Curve

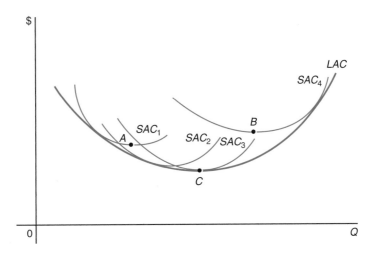

Each point on the long-run average cost curve (*LAC*) represents a least cost combination of inputs and a point on one short-run average cost curve.

tionship between short-run average cost curves and the long-run average cost curve. Notice that the long-run average cost curve is an *envelope* curve for the short-run average cost curves. In other words, it is made up of points that indicate the lowest unit costs obtainable for each level of output. We further observe that such points are not necessarily the minimum points of the short-run average cost curves. In fact, for outputs smaller than that corresponding to the minimum point of the long-run average cost curve, the short-run average cost curves are tangent to the long-run curve to the *left* of their respective minimum points. This occurs because of the existence of **economies of scale,** which means that smaller unit costs can be obtained by producing with a larger size plant than by producing at the minimum short-run average cost corresponding to a smaller plant size. (See point *A* in Figure 6-13.) The opposite result occurs if **diseconomies of scale** are present, so that it is cheaper to produce beyond the point of minimum short-run average cost corresponding to a smaller plant than by producing at the minimum short-run average cost point corresponding to a larger plant. (See point *B* in Figure 6-13.) Only at the minimum point of the long-run average cost curve, where constant returns to scale are obtained, can the firm produce a given level of output most cheaply by producing at the minimum point of a short-run average cost curve. (See point *C* in Figure 6-13.) The regions of economies of scale, diseconomies of scale, and constant returns to scale are summarized in Figure 6-14. These economies and diseconomies of scale occur because of the nature of the firm's production function and are *not* caused by changes in external data such as input prices. Thus, they are sometimes called *internal* economies and diseconomies.

Economies of scale are technological and organizational advantages that accrue to the firm as it increases output in the long run. Economies of scale reduce long-run average costs.

Diseconomies of scale are technological and organizational disadvantages that the firm encounters as it increases output in the long run. Diseconomies of scale increase long-run average costs.

FIGURE 6–14

*Long-Run
Average Cost and
Returns to Scale*

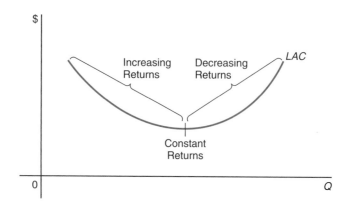

When the firm experiences increasing returns to scale, *LAC* declines. When the firm has constant returns to scale, *LAC* is constant. When the firm has decreasing returns to scale, *LAC* is increasing.

Cost elasticity is the percentage change in long-run total cost from a 1 percent change in output.

The cost elasticity reflects the presence of either economies or diseconomies of scale. **Cost elasticity,** E_C, is defined as the percentage change in long-run total cost from a 1 percent change in output:

$$E_C = \frac{\text{percentage change in } LTC}{\text{percentage change in } Q}.$$

It measures the relative responsiveness of long-run total cost to changes in the level of output. The formula for *arc cost elasticity* is given by[19]

$$E_C = \frac{\Delta LTC}{\Delta Q} \cdot \frac{Q_2 + Q_1}{LTC_2 + LTC_1}.$$

If the cost elasticity is less than one, then a given percentage increase in output will result in a smaller percentage increase in long-run total cost, and economies of scale will be present. On the other hand, if the cost elasticity is greater than one, then *LTC* will increase by a greater percentage than the percentage change in output, and diseconomies of scale will occur. If *LTC* and

---

[19] The formula for point cost elasticity is

$$E_C = \frac{\partial LTC}{\partial Q} \cdot \frac{Q}{LTC}.$$

output change by exactly the same percentage, then constant returns to scale will be present. These relationships are summarized as follows:

$E_C < 1$	*LTC* increases by a smaller percentage than the percentage increase in output.	economies of scale
$E_C = 1$	*LTC* changes by the same percentage as the percentage change in output.	constant returns to scale
$E_C > 1$	*LTC* increases by a larger percentage than the percentage increase in output.	diseconomies of of scale

Economies of scale, or the absence of them, can play an important role in the structure of firms, industries, and markets. For example, Kraft General Foods, Inc., found that its salespeople from Kraft, General Foods, Oscar Mayer Foods, and Maxwell House would frequently all appear at a

MANAGERIAL PERSPECTIVE

Technological Change and Economies of Scale

In 1984, a desktop computer that one would classify as nearly useless by today's standards cost over $2,000. Such a computer would contain something like two 5 1/4" floppy drives, no hard drive, and about 64 KB of RAM. A 14-inch monochrome monitor might also be included. By 1997, a computer with 16 MB of RAM, a Pentium 120 MHZ processor, a 2 GB hard drive, a color monitor, and a modem cost less than $1,000. By 2002, models far better equipped than these were selling for under $400. How could this happen?

For one thing, competition in the computer industry was a factor in lowering prices. However, technological developments and economies of scale in the manufacture of components for computers were also critical elements enabling computer manufacturers to lower prices on their machines.

A similar progression has occurred with regard to other consumer electronics. For

example, in the early 1970s, a 19-inch color television cost approximately $400. Now, a technically superior color television with a 27-inch screen can be purchased for less than $200. Similar, or even more dramatic, stories could be told with respect to VCRs and camcorders. Now, many consumers are eagerly awaiting the benefits of advancing technological development and mass production that will further reduce the production costs and prices of all types of electronic products.

References: Jonathan Sidener, "2002 Likely to Be Big Year for HDTV," *The Arizona Republic*, January 1, 2002 (reprinted at www.hd.net/clipping.html); David Hendricks, "Inexpensive Electronics Buck Marketplace Trend," *San Antonio Express-News*, January 30, 1999, pp. 1E, 2E; "Breaking the $1,000 Barrier," *Business Week* (February 17, 1997), p. 75; and "Now PC Buyers Are Getting More for Even Less," *Wall Street Journal*, June 18, 1996, pp. B1, B6.

particular grocery store at the same time, all of them wanting to talk to the manager simultaneously. To avoid this pandemonium and to lower costs as well, the four divisions were combined into Kraft Foods, Inc., with a single sales force organized around marketing teams, and each team was assigned to one chain of stores. In the steel industry, economies of scale were thought to be very important. However, in recent years, technological changes have made it possible for smaller minimills to achieve the same or even lower unit costs than the large steel mills. A similar phenomenon has occurred in computer chip factories, where "minifabs"— smaller, more automated, and more flexible versions of wafer fabrication plants—became competitive with respect to costs or even more efficient than the traditional, larger plants.[20] Other things remaining equal, when technology enables small firms to achieve the same or lower per unit costs as large firms, the probability of greater competition in that industry and market is increased.

We should point out that drawing the *LAC* curve as a smooth, U-shaped curve implies that all inputs are perfectly divisible. In reality, all inputs are not necessarily infinitely divisible. For example, only a limited number of sizes of steelmaking furnaces are readily available. When inputs are indivisible, the firm's long-run average cost curve merely consists of those points on the short-run average cost curves corresponding to the sizes of plant that are available that represent the lowest unit cost possible for each level of output. This situation produces a scalloped long-run average cost curve, such as that shown in Figure 6-15.

THE LEARNING EFFECT

Some authorities in the area of production and cost have observed that average costs of production for a given level of output decline as a firm's *cumulative* output of a product (total output produced to date) increases. In this situation, the firm's production of additional units of output causes its long-run average cost curve to shift downward. This phenomenon is attributed to a *learning effect* of increased production on the part of both management and labor. Costs are reduced as both management and labor become more familiar with the production processes required to manufacture the item and, as a result, become more efficient in its production.

---

[20] "Will So Many Ingredients Work Together?" *Business Week* (March 27, 1995), pp. 188, 191; and "Huh? Chipmakers Copying Steelmakers?" *Business Week* (August 15, 1994), pp. 97–98.

FIGURE 6–15

*Long-Run
Average Cost
Curve When
Four Plant Sizes
Are Available*

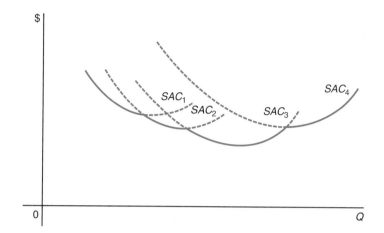

If only four plant sizes are available, the *LAC* curve will be determined by finding the plant size with the lowest per-unit costs for each level of output. SAC_1, SAC_2, SAC_3, SAC_4 are short-run average cost curves corresponding to the four plant sizes. The long-run aveage cost curve is the heavy line.

ECONOMIES OF SCOPE

Economies of scope occur when the average cost of undertaking two or more activities together is less than the sum of the costs of each activity separately.

Economies of scope occur when it is cheaper for a firm to undertake two or more activities together than the sum of the costs that the firm would incur to pursue each activity separately. For example, the average cost of selling an insurance policy per dollar of premium received may be lower for a firm that sells life insurance together with home and automobile insurance than for a firm that sells only life insurance *or* home insurance *or* automobile insurance. The lower cost per premium dollar could be achieved because one customer could be sold all three types of premiums during the same visit.

CHOOSING THE OPTIMAL
PLANT SIZE: AN EXAMPLE

To get an idea of the type of analysis a firm must go through in trying to determine its optimal plant size, consider once more the case of John and Ruth Brown and their delicatessen, discussed at the beginning of this chapter. In Table 6-5 the income statement presented in Table 6-1 is reproduced with some additional information. Suppose that the deli, by selling 20,000 meals per month, is operating near its capacity level and that the Browns are contemplating expanding their restaurant.

In fact, assume that John and Ruth are considering two possibilities for expansion. The first possibility would involve building an addition onto the

Table 6-5 *John and Ruth's Deli Statement of Economic Profit for Month Ended July 31, 2000*

Total Revenue (20,000 meals @ average price of $7.00)		$ 140,000
Less Cost of Goods Sold (food and beverages—20,000 meals @ $3.00)		60,000
Gross Profit		$ 80,000
Less Operating Expenses		
Fixed	$20,000	
Variable (20,000 meals @ $1.50)	30,000	50,000
Operating (Accounting) Net Income		$ 30,000
Less		
Implicit Rental Income	$ 5,400	
Implicit Salary Income	12,000	
Implicit Interest Income	600	18,000
Economic Profit		$ 12,000

original deli, so that the back wall would extend further into the mall parking area. This plan would increase the deli's capacity by 50 percent to 30,000 meals per month and would involve an initial outlay of $100,000 for construction and equipment. John and Ruth have $60,000 additional money of their own that they could invest, and they know where they can borrow the remaining $40,000. *If* the expanded restaurant were to operate at capacity, its income statement (with additional information) would be like that presented in Table 6-6. Note that the Browns do expect to achieve some internal economies of scale through lower per unit variable operating expenses.

Table 6-6 *John and Ruth's Deli Statement of Economic Profit for Month Ended _____ (at Capacity under Expansion Plan 1)*

Total Revenue (30,000 meals @ average price of $7.00)		$ 210,000
Less Cost of Goods Sold (food and beverages—30,000 meals @ $3.00)		90,000
Gross Profit		$ 120,000
Less Operating Expenses		
Fixed	$30,000	
Variable (30,000 meals @ $1.40)	42,000	72,000
Operating (Accounting) Net Income		$ 48,000
Less		
Implicit Rental Income (existing building)	$ 5,400	
Implicit Salary Income	12,000	
Implicit Interest Income	1,200	18,600
Economic Profit		$ 29,400

The second expansion possibility involves buying the small vacant building adjoining the deli in the mall. This additional area would double the deli's capacity to 40,000 meals per month, and the Browns could get a good deal on the building, so that the initial outlay necessary for the building, remodeling, and equipment would be only $140,000. Again, the Browns could put up an additional $60,000 of their own money and borrow the remaining $80,000. If the restaurant were to follow this expansion plan *and were to operate at capacity,* John and Ruth expect that their monthly economic profit statement would be similar to that presented in Table 6-7. Note that if the Browns expand the restaurant to double the capacity, they *do* expect to be able to take advantage of some external and greater internal economies of scale, such as discounts for greater volume buying of both food and other operating supplies and more efficient equipment.

If John and Ruth think they have a high probability of being able to sell 40,000 meals per month, then obviously they should decide in favor of the larger expansion plan. However, suppose that they expect to be able to sell only 29,000 meals per month for the next few years. Then, assuming they cannot take advantage of volume food buying at that level of business under either plan, they expect monthly results under each expansion plan to be similar to those computed in Tables 6-8 and 6-9. In this case, without additional factors to consider, it appears that John and Ruth should select the smaller expansion plan.

Nevertheless, the Browns may well wish to consider some additional factors before they make their final decision. For example, they would perhaps wish to consider a longer time horizon than three or four years, especially if they expect sales to continue expanding. As they expand the time

Table 6-7 *John and Ruth's Deli Statement of Economic Profit for Month Ended _____ (At Capacity Under Expansion Plan 2)*

Total Revenue (40,000 meals @ average price of $7.00)		$ 280,000
Less Cost of Goods Sold (food and beverages—40,000 meals @ $2.75)		110,000
Gross Profit		$ 170,000
Less Operating Expenses		
Fixed	$50,000	
Variable (40,000 meals @ $1.20)	48,000	98,000
Operating (Accounting) Net Income		$ 72,000
Less		
Implicit Rental Income (existing building)	$ 5,400	
Implicit Salary Income	12,000	
Implicit Interest Income	1,200	18,600
Economic Profit		$ 53,400

Table 6-8 *John and Ruth's Deli Statement of Economic Profit for Month Ended _____ (At 29,000 Meals Under Expansion Plan 1)*

Total Revenue (29,000 meals @ average price of $7.00)		$ 203,000
Less Cost of Goods Sold (food and beverages—29,000 meals @ $3.00)		87,000
Gross Profit		$ 116,000
Less Operating Expenses		
Fixed	$30,000	
Variable (29,000 meals @ $1.40)	40,600	70,600
Operating (Accounting) Net Income		$ 45,400
Less		
Implicit Rental Income (existing building)	$ 5,400	
Implicit Salary Income	12,000	
Implicit Interest Income	1,200	18,600
Economic Profit		$ 26,800

Table 6-9 *John and Ruth's Deli Statement of Economic Profit for Month Ended _____ (At 29,000 Meals Under Expansion Plan 2)*

Total Revenue (29,000 meals @ average price of $7.00)		$203,000
Less Cost of Goods Sold (food and beverages—29,000 meals @ $3.00)		87,000
Gross Profit		$116,000
Less Operating Expenses		
Fixed	$50,000	
Variable (29,000 meals @ $1.20)	34,800	84,800
Operating (Accounting) Net Income		$ 31,200
Less		
Implicit Rental Income (existing building)	$ 5,400	
Implicit Salary Income	12,000	
Implicit Interest Income	1,200	18,600
Economic Profit		$ 12,600

period under consideration, the second plan may look more and more desirable. The Browns would also want to consider the risks associated with each expansion plan in the event that their projected levels of sales are incorrect. They should also consider the possibilities for expanding their restaurant *after* they have already used the first expansion plan. We will discuss further the techniques John and Ruth should use in this type of analysis in Chapters 13 and 14. They would also be wise to consider the results after changing their price structure and probably should do some investigation of the

Lean, Mean, and Green

It hardly seemed worth bothering. The blades on the saws in Georgia Pacific sawmills could be made half as thick as they were before, thanks to a new, stronger metal alloy used to make the blades. Yet, that smaller blade will result in 800 additional railcars of Georgia Pacific products each year rather than sawdust on the mill floor.

Georgia Pacific is not alone in its effort to reduce waste. Companies all over the United States are finding that they must become more efficient if they are to survive in the international market environment in which they find themselves. Through automating its refineries, weeding out unprofitable service stations, and modernizing high-volume stations, Exxon has been able to increase the volume sold through the stations by one-third. A supplier company recently supplied Ford Motor Company with 1.6 million oil pump parts without a single defect. According to its president, the company found that quality control that once was believed to be impossible is now necessary for survival. Xerox found that quality improvements could save as much as $2 billion on sales of $10 billion, certainly a significant figure. The CEO of Xerox stated, "Over the years, you grow up thinking that the greater quality you give a customer, the higher the price. We now know that's not true. Quality drives costs down." The cost saving comes because doing it right the first time is often cheaper than repairing manufacturing defects and working to regain loyalty from dissatisfied customers.

Companies are finding that being "green" is profitable as well. Measures to improve the environmental impact of their products help companies to avoid obvious costs like fines and lawsuits. However, environmentally responsible policies can result in lower production and marketing costs as well. ARCO Chemical found that it could reduce its energy costs by 35 percent by using a new, more efficient plant. By getting workers on the shop floor to buy into the notion of reducing hazardous wastes, General Electric was able to trim waste oil accumulation at an aircraft engine plant by 20 percent. Hewlett-Packard and Xerox have both gotten into the business of recycling toner cartridges for personal computer laser printers, a practice that not only kept millions of pounds of materials out of landfills but also kept the cartridges from falling into the hands of rival recyclers.

Clearly, careful cost management has become imperative for successful companies in the twenty-first century, and environmentally sound policies with respect to resource use and disposal are a part of this mandate as well.

References: Myles White, "Recharge It," *Your Office Online*, July 15, 2002, www.youroffice.ca, August 11, 2002); "It's Empty, Not Broken," TonerRefillKits.com, online, July 15, 2002, www.tonerrefillkits.com/its_empty_not_broken.htm, July 15, 2002; "Don't Waste Your Wood Advantage," *The Wood World Monitor* 3, no. 3 (3rd Quarter 1999): 1; "The Greening of Corporate America," *Business Week* (April 23, 1990), p. 100; and "America's Leanest and Meanest," *Business Week* (August 10, 1987), p. 110.

demand function of their deli's product. Demand analysis, demand estimation, and forecasting were discussed at length in Chapters 2, 3, and 4. Profit analysis is explained in Chapter 7, and alternative pricing strategies are considered in much greater depth in Chapter 11.

ESTIMATION OF COST

One of the tasks with which a profit-maximizing firm manager must contend is that of estimating what the costs of the firm will or should be for different levels of output. For example, strong financial controls and cost estimation have contributed significantly to the profitability of the General Electric Company. In order to compete with it, rival firm Siemens has had to pay "ruthless attention to costs."[21] In Detroit, Ford and General Motors make cost calculations to fractions of a cent.[22]

There are two general methods of estimating costs: through utilization of historical cost data and through utilization of estimates by engineers. Managers who choose the historical cost method try to estimate future costs from data about actual costs incurred by the firm in the past. These historical cost figures must be adjusted to include opportunity costs and to take into consideration any changes in input prices or technology that will affect a firm's costs. An attempt should be made to separate short-run cost data from long-run cost data. Such an analysis will necessitate a study of those cost-output combinations that were obtained with a least cost combination of inputs and those that were not. Moreover, an attempt must be made to match historical costs with the appropriate level of output. Some costs, such as certain maintenance and repair expenses, may not always be incurred by the firm at the same time that the responsible level of output was produced. Finally, historical cost figures must also be adjusted for inflation if they are to be useful in estimating future costs.

Once the historical cost figures have been adjusted, firm managers can use various methods to estimate a firm's cost function or functions. We will briefly discuss three of them here—the high-low method, the visual-fit method, and the regression method. To use the high-low method, one merely draws a straight line connecting the highest and lowest cost figures on a scatter diagram showing the adjusted historical cost data, as demonstrated in Figure 6-16. Employing the visual-fit method, one draws a line through points on a scatter diagram that appears to be most representative of (or "best fits") the underlying cost data. This method is illustrated in Figure 6-17. The third method, regression analysis, requires the use of more sophisticated statistical techniques to estimate the cost function and the correlation of cost with the level of output. This method, though more precise, is also more difficult to use. It was discussed in Chapter 3 and its appendix in connection with demand estimation.

---

[21] Jack Ewing, "Siemens Climbs Back," *Business Week Online*, June 5, 2000, www.business-week.com/2000/00-23/b3684011.htm, January 9, 2003.

[22] "GM and Ford Cut Costs to Realize Q2 Profit Targets," *Taipei Times*, July 8, 2002, reprinted online at www.chinacars.com, January 9, 2003.

FIGURE 6–16

*High-Low
Method of Cost
Estimation*

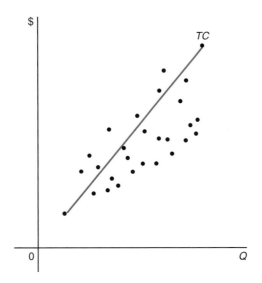

The high-low method of cost estimation involves drawing a total cost curve by connecting the lowest level of cost witht he highest level of cost.

FIGURE 6–17

*Visual-Fit
Method of Cost
Estimation*

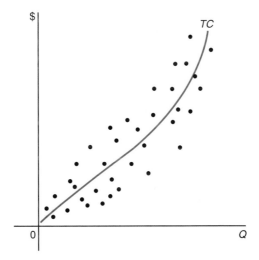

The visual fit method of cost estimation involves sketching that total cost curve which appears to "best fit" the historical cost data.

A firm might estimate several different forms of the long-run total cost function through regression analysis. The simplest one is a linear cost function of the form

$$LTC = \alpha Q + \sum_{i=1}^{n} \beta_i X_i + \varepsilon,$$

where

LTC = long-run total cost,

Q = quantity of output, and

X_i = other factors that affect long-run total cost, such as input prices.

In this case, if input prices did not change, marginal cost would be constant and equal to α.[23]

Nonlinear forms of the long-run total cost function are also estimated. One type is a function that is quadratic with respect to the quantity of output:

$$LTC = \alpha_1 Q + \alpha_2 Q^2 + \sum_{i=1}^{n} \beta_i X_i + \varepsilon,$$

where LTC, Q, and X_i are defined as before. In this case, marginal cost would be a straight line given by the equation $\alpha_1 + 2\alpha_2 Q$.[24]

A second type of nonlinear function that can yield the typical marginal cost curve frequently found in economics textbooks is a cubic cost function:

$$LTC = \alpha_1 Q + \alpha_2 Q^2 + \alpha_3 Q^3 + \sum_{i=1}^{n} \beta_i X_i + \varepsilon,$$

where LTC, Q, and X_i are defined as before. In this case, marginal cost is equal to $\alpha_1 + 2\alpha_2 Q + 3\alpha_3 Q^2$.[25] With appropriate values for α_1, α_2, and α_3, marginal cost will first decrease, reach a minimum, and then increase.

---

[23] In this case,

$$LMC = \frac{\partial LTC}{\partial Q} = \alpha.$$

[24] Again, marginal cost is given by

$$LMC = \frac{\partial LTC}{\partial Q} = \alpha_1 + 2\alpha_2 Q.$$

[25] As before, marginal cost is found as

$$LMC = \frac{\partial LTC}{\partial Q} = \alpha_1 + 2\alpha_2 Q + 3\alpha_3 Q^2$$

A third type of nonlinear cost function that is estimated is a *multiplicative* cost function. The following is one example of this type of function:

$$LTC = Q^\alpha X_i^{\beta_i} \varepsilon,$$

where the variables are still defined as before. In this form, α would be equal to the cost elasticity with respect to output, E_c. The β_i terms would represent the elasticity of LTC relative to each respective X_i variable. In this case, marginal cost depends on the values of the X variables.[26] As we discussed in Chapter 3 and its appendix, multiplicative functions can be transformed into linear equations by taking the logarithms of the variables:

$$\log LTC = \alpha \log Q + \sum_{i=1}^{n} \beta_i \log X_i + \log \varepsilon.$$

In recent years, other types of cost functions involving flexible functional forms have been developed.[27]

Engineering cost estimates are another technique of cost estimation. This method of cost estimation utilizes engineering and other manufacturing experts in the firm to develop the cost function. Engineering cost estimates have an advantage in that the cost figures obtained in this manner should already be based on current technology and current prices. Also, there should not be the problem of separating long-run and short-run cost figures or the problem of matching costs incurred with the relevant levels of production. However, engineering cost estimates are still only that—*estimates*. The better the engineers understand the nature of a firm's production relationships and the more closely they can estimate future prices, the more nearly accurate their cost estimates will be. Even these figures, however, must still be adjusted to reflect implicit or opportunity costs.

Thus, it is evident that the estimation of a firm's costs is rarely a simple task. Still, the difficulty of estimating a firm's costs does not diminish the importance of that information to the managers of a business. Managers face the job of finding a proper (profit-maximizing) balance between more precise information regarding the firm's costs and the corresponding cost of obtaining it and less reliable, but cheaper, information.

---

[26] Marginal cost is now equal to

$$LMC = \frac{\partial LTC}{\partial Q} = \alpha Q^{\alpha-1} X_i^{\beta_i} \varepsilon.$$

[27] One example of this type of cost function and a discussion of its features can be found in Lila J. Truett and Dale B. Truett, "Economies of Scale in the Mexican Automotive Sector," *Journal of Productivity Analysis* 7, No. 4 (October 1996): 429–446.

SUMMARY

Costs and the Firm

We have repeatedly emphasized the crucial role that costs play in determining the profitability of the firm. The profit-oriented firm manager must consider both opportunity costs and explicit costs in order to use time, money, and physical resources economically. Obviously, a firm does not always have totally accurate information about its costs; but it is very important that it have reliable *estimates* of its fixed costs, of how its costs vary with respect to output over the relevant range of production, and of whether or not its costs would be lower (and if so, how much) with a different size plant.

We have discussed three general types of cost classifications in this chapter: (1) *explicit*, or *historical*, costs and *implicit*, or *opportunity*, costs; (2) *fixed* and *variable* costs; and (3) *private* and *social* costs. Explicit costs are costs for which the firm has made direct payment or will make direct payment in the future and are the basis for most accounting cost figures. Opportunity costs are costs that the firm incurs by utilizing its resources in one activity when such resources could also be used in another manner, even though the firm is making no explicit payment for their use. Examples of such resources are the owner-manager's time and money. The manager's consideration of both the explicit and implicit costs of a firm is necessary to ensure that *all* of the firm's resources are being used to maximize profits. Thus, *economic costs* include both explicit and implicit costs. Fixed costs are costs that do not vary with the level of a firm's output in the short run, whereas variable costs do vary with the level of output. By classifying costs in this manner, a firm manager can separate opportunities and decisions relevant to the short run from opportunities and decisions that are relevant to long-run planning. Private costs are costs that a firm incurs, whereas social costs are those borne by society as a whole. A classification of costs as to which are private and which are social is most useful for decisions involving social policy.

Next, we discussed the firm's long-run costs, all of which are assumed to be variable and are derived by finding a series of least cost combinations of inputs. The long-run costs were discussed in terms of *total cost, average cost,* and *marginal cost*. Long-run total cost is all of the costs that a firm incurs, given that the firm is producing with the optimal input mix. Average cost is the average cost per unit of output, or LTC/Q. Marginal cost is the rate of change of total cost with respect to the level of output.

Because of the existence of fixed costs in the short run, short-run costs must be discussed in terms of *total cost, total fixed cost, total variable cost, average total cost, average fixed cost, average variable cost,* and *marginal cost*. The definition of each of these terms is similar to that for corresponding long-run terms (total, average, or marginal). Of course, *total fixed cost* and *average fixed cost* have no long-run counterparts, since all costs are variable in the long run. We also demonstrated the close relationships between short-run product curves and cost curves.

Moreover, we discussed the relationships among short-run average cost, long-run average cost, and returns to scale. We also gave a simple example of some of the analysis that a profit-maximizing firm manager should undertake when determining the optimal plant size for the firm.

Finally, we ended this chapter with a brief discussion of cost estimation techniques. The two general types of methods used are the historical cost method and the engineering cost method, and data used in both methods usually require some adjustments. Obtaining information about a firm's costs can be an expensive project for a manager, who must determine when (and how much of) that expense is in the best interests of the firm.

As those who operate successful businesses understand, in order to be profitable, a firm must produce a good or service that people desire, market it well, and price it correctly, *in addition to* keeping its unit costs low relative to those of other firms in the same industry. In the next chapter we will discuss how the profit-maximizing firm determines its optimal level of output (and price), given its cost and revenue data.

QUESTIONS

1. Define and compare historical costs, accounting costs, opportunity costs, economic costs, private costs, and social costs.

2. Why is it important that a firm owner consider opportunity costs when making economic decisions regarding the firm? Give some examples of opportunity costs.

3. What is a least cost combination of inputs? How do such input combinations relate to the long-run total cost curve for a firm?

4. What is the difference between the long run and the short run for a firm? How do the firm's costs differ in the two time periods?

5. How are the short-run average cost curves and the long-run average cost curve related?

6. Why can arc short-run marginal cost be found by finding either $(\Delta STC/\Delta Q)$ or $(\Delta TVC/\Delta Q)$?

7. How do returns to scale affect the shape of the long-run average cost curve?

PROBLEMS

1. a. Complete the following table, which gives short-run cost data for a firm.

Q	STC	TFC	TVC	SAC	AFC	AVC	Arc SMC
0	10,800		0	—	—	—	
1,000			1,000				
2,000			1,600				
3,000			2,400				
4,000			3,600				
5,000			5,000				
6,000			7,200				

   b. Sketch the cost curves, given the data that you have computed in the preceding table.
2. a. In the following table, complete the cost data for a firm.
   b. Sketch the cost curves, given the data in part a.

Q	STC	TFC	TVC	SAC	AFC	AVC	Arc SMC
0			0	—	—	—	
							20
1					120		
							16
2							
							12
3							
							16
4							
							21
5							
							29
6							

3. Given that $Q = f(a,b)$, as shown in the following diagram, and that $P_a = \$1$ and $P_b = \$2$, answer the questions in parts a through e.

   a. If $b_3 = 450$ units of input b, what is the total cost of producing 300 units of output?

   b. What is the long-run *average* cost of producing 300 units of output? Is this consistent with point H' in the lower diagram?

   c. Assuming the curve in the lower diagram *is* long-run average cost, how many units of a is a_1 equal to in the upper diagram?

   d. What is the dollar amount of TC_2?

   e. If $a_4 = 1{,}400$ units and $Q_4 = 400$ units, find average cost at point J in the upper diagram.

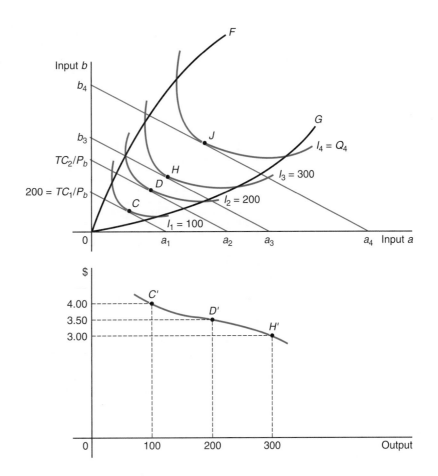

4. Complete the following table, given that the price of input *a* is constant and that *a* is the only variable input. (*Hint:* The price of input *a* and total fixed cost can be determined from the information given in the table.)

Input a (Units)	Q (Output in Units)	Arc MP$_a$	Arc SMC	AVC	SAC
0	0			Unde-fined	Unde-fined
			$10.00		
1	5			$10.00	$30.00
2	20				
3	40				
4	55				
5	65				

5. Exclusive Excavating Corporation digs holes. Its only variable input is labor, and each worker must bring his or her own shovel. Each worker costs $100 per day, and Exclusive's total fixed cost per day is $300. The following table contains some of the company's daily production and cost data.

a. Complete the table.

b. Where is SMC at a minimum? Where is MP_L at a maximum?

SMC	MP_L	Q	L	TVC	SAC
		0	0	0	—
		40	2		12.50
		100	4		
4.00		150	6		
		190	8		
5.88		224	10		
		254	12		5.91
		274	14		
		284	16		

6. Given the following diagram and the information that input *a* is the only variable input, answer the questions in parts *a* through *d*.

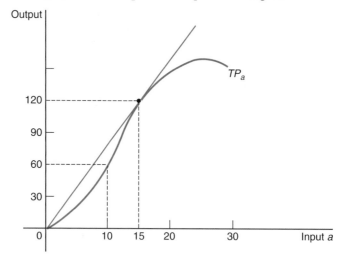

a. What is the maximum value of AP_a?

b. At approximately what quantity of input *a* will MP_a be at a maximum?

c. If P_a is $96, what is the minimum AVC?

d. If P_a is $96 and *TFC* is $4,800, find *STC* and *SAC* at an output level of 60 units.

7. Complete the following table, assuming that the firm is in the short run, that input *a* is the only variable input, and that P_a, the price of input *a*, is fixed.

Input a (Units)	Output (Units)	AP$_a$	Arc MP$_a$	Arc SMC	AVC	AFC	STC
0	0	—			$ —	$ —	
			5.0	$ 40.00			
2	10				40.00		
				22.22			
4		7			28.57		
			10.0				
6	48					14.00	
				50.00			
8	56	7			28.57		
10		6					
			1.5	133.33			
12	63				38.10		

[a] Take note in your calculation of marginal product that Δa is 2 units of *a* between output values.

8. Complete the following table, assuming that *L* is the only variable input and that its price, P_L, is fixed.

SMC (Marginal Cost)	MP$_L$ (Marginal Product)	L (Input)	TP$_L = Q_X$ (Output)	TVC (Total Variable Cost)	STC (Total Cost)
		5	100	200	600
		10	200		
		15	450		
		20	550		
4.00	10				
		25	600	1,000	
		30	625		
10.00	4				
		35	645		
		40	660		2,000

a. Now calculate the following:

   i. Average fixed cost at an output of $Q = 200$.

   ii. Average product of *L* at an output of $Q = 600$.

b. Suppose total fixed cost is increased by 25 percent. Which of the numbers in the table would change? Why?

9. The following data represent the quantities of product *X* that can be obtained from various combination of two inputs, *Y* and *Z*.

Units of Input Y	Output of Product X						
6	122	205	277	345	408	468	
5	112	190	256	317	374	429	
4	100	168	228	283	334	383	
3	86	145	197	245	289	331	
2	70	119	160	200	236	270	
1	50	84	114	142	167	191	
0	1	2	3	4	5	6	**Units of Input Z**

a. How will the long-run average cost curve for the production of X behave? Explain how you know from the given data.

b. Suppose the price of a unit of Y is $14 and that of a unit of Z is $12. Do one unit of Y and two units of Z constitute a least cost combination of inputs for an output of 84 units of Product X? Explain why or why not.

c. Suppose input Z is fixed at Z = 4. Complete the following table, assuming the same production function and input prices. (Assume also that no output can be obtained if Y = 0.)

SMC	MP_Y	Output of X	Input of Y	AP_Y	AVC	STC
		0	0	—	—	

10. In the following table, assume that L is the only variable input and that P_L, the price of a unit of labor, is fixed.

a. Given that L is labor units and Q is units of output per time period, complete the table.

MP_L	L	Q	STC	AFC	AVC	TVC	MC
	0	0	120	—	—	0	
___	2	20		6		160	___
___	4	60					___
___	6	90				480	___
___	8	110					___
___	10	125					___

b. Explain what a 25 percent increase in total fixed cost would do to the concepts listed in the table.

11. Suppose a firm has two inputs, *a* and *b*, and that *b* is fixed in the short run. Its short-run total product is described by the following table.

a	Q = Output
0	0
2	50
4	120
6	180
8	230
10	270
12	300

a. Fill in the table below, assuming that the price of a unit of input *a* is $40.

SMC	MP_a	Output (Q)	Input of a	AP_a	AVC	STC
			0			
___	___					
___	___					
___	___					744
___	___					
___	___					
___	___					

    b. What will be the value of average fixed cost when output is at a level of $Q = 180$? How do you know?

    c. Suppose the price of a unit of b is fixed and that the amount employed of b is constant at $b = 12$. How much is the firm paying per unit of b? (What is b's price?) Explain how you know.

12. Suppose a firm determines that its average variable cost can be represented by the equation $AVC = 10 + 4Q$, where Q is its daily output. Suppose also that its total fixed cost is $TFC = 100$. Do the following:

    a. Plot the firm's AVC curve for the range $Q = 1$ to $Q = 15$ units of output per day.

    b. Plot its AFC over the same range of output.

    c. Add the two curves to develop the short-run average cost SAC curve. Does SAC appear to have a minimum point? If so, at what output? If not, explain why not.

13. In the preceding problem, $AVC = 10 + 4Q$. Continuing with that information do the following.

    a. Write an equation for total variable cost or TVC.

    b. Calculate TVC for $Q = 2, 4, 6, 8,$ and 10.

    c. Plot your TVC data in a graph, and draw a curve through the plot points.

    d. Given your graph of TVC, say what you can conclude about marginal cost for this data set.

    e. The AVC equation in this problem is a straight line, $AVC = a + bQ$. Furthermore, the TVC equation you wrote for this problem should be of the form $TVC = aQ + bQ^2$. Using a delta operator (Δ) approach similar to that employed in Chapter 2 to relate the straight-line demand curve to its MR curve, can you determine the equation of SMC from this problem's TVC equation? (*Hint:* Consider $(TVC_2 - TVC_1)$, where $TVC_2 = a(Q + \Delta Q) + b(Q + \Delta Q)^2$, which will give you ΔTVC. Then divide by ΔQ, and determine for the resulting expression what occurs when any remaining ΔQ approaches zero.)

The following problems require calculus.

C1. A firm has the following short-run total cost function:

$$STC = \$1{,}000 + 240Q - 4Q^2 + (1/3)\,Q^3.$$

    a. Write equations for the firm's SMC, AVC, and SAC.

    b. Determine the output level at which SMC will be minimized.

    c. Determine the output level at which AVC will be minimized.

C2. Suppose a firm has the following total cost function:

$$STC = 300 + 40Q - 8Q^2 + (2/3)\,Q^3$$

    a. Write equations for

      i. Average fixed cost

      ii. Average variable cost

b. What will be the value of short-run average cost when $Q = 60$?

c. Write the marginal cost equation for this firm.

d. What will marginal cost be when $Q = 20$?

e. For this firm, what will be the dollar value of *AVC* at its minimum?

C3. Juno Corporation has the short-run total cost function

$$STC = TFC + TVC = 800 + 60Q - 4.5Q^2 + 0.15Q^3,$$

where Q is output. Answer the following:

a. What is the dollar value of average fixed cost at an output of 20 units?

b. At what level of output will marginal cost be at its minimum?

c. What will be the value of average variable cost when it is at its minimum?

C4. A firm has the following long-run total cost function:

$$LTC = 180Q - 3Q^2 + 0.02Q^3$$

a. Write expressions for long-run marginal cost and long-run average cost.

b. Does the *LAC* curve have a minimum? If so, at what quantity? If not, explain why.

c. What does your answer to part b suggest about returns to scale in this firm's production function?

C5. IMOVISION, a maker of liquid crystal display screens for scientific plotting calculators, is considering production of a new model screen in a foreign location. It plans to make 400 of the screens per day whether it produces them at its home plant or at the foreign location. Estimated daily U.S. dollar costs, including all fixed costs are as follows:

$$\text{Home plant: } STC = 5,000 + 10Q + 0.02Q^2$$
$$\text{Foreign plant: } STC_F = 6,400 + 9Q + 0.01Q^2$$

a. In which plant will the firm attain the lowest *minimum* average cost for the projected 400-unit-per-day output?

b. In which plant will the firm attain the lowest *minimum* average cost per screen?

c. Suppose that $1,800 of the daily fixed cost in the home plant consists of allocated fixed costs that would exist whether or not production of the screen in question occurs there, but that all of the fixed costs in the foreign plant are directly associated with the production of the new screens. What advice would you give to management regarding the choice between home and foreign production?

C6. Consider the following short-run total cost function.

$$STC = 400 + 6Q + 0.01Q^2$$

a. Briefly describe what this total cost function will look like when plotted as a diagram.

b. Will short-run marginal cost have a minimum point? Explain.

c. What kind of line or curve would represent the average variable cost curve related to this *STC*?

d. Will *SAC* have a minimum point? If so, explain, and give the minimum value of *SAC*.

C7. Suppose the total cost function is $550 + 9Q - 0.15Q^2 + 0.005Q^3$.

a. Find the marginal cost, average variable cost, average cost, and the average fixed cost functions.

b. Sketch the functions that you derived in part a.

c. At what level of output does the *SMC* reach its minimum? *AVC*? *AFC*?

d. Find *SMC* and *AVC* when *AVC* is at its minimum.

SELECTED REFERENCES

Bailey, Elizabeth E., and Ann F. Friedlander. "Market Structure and Multiproduct Industries." *Journal of Economic Literature* 20, No. 3 (September 1982): 1024–1048.

Besanko, David A., and Ronald R. Braeutigam. *Microeconomics: An Integrated Approach* (New York: John Wiley & Sons, 2002), Chapters 7, 8.

Cookenboo, Leslie, Jr. "Production Functions and Cost Functions: A Case Study." *Crude Oil Pipe Lines and Competition in the Oil Industry.* Cambridge, MA.: Harvard University Press, 1955.

Mansfield, Edwin. *Microeconomics: Theory and Applications,* 9th ed. New York: W. W. Norton, 1997, Chapter 8.

McGuigan, James R., R. Charles Moyer, and Frederick H. deB. Harris. *Managerial Economics,* 9th ed. Cincinnati: South-Western, 2002, Chapters 8, 9.

Moore, Frederick T. "Economies of Scale: Some Statistical Evidence." *Quarterly Journal of Economics* 78, No. 2 (May 1959): 232–236.

Moroney, John R. "Cobb-Douglas Production Functions and Returns to Scale in U.S. Manufacturing Industry." *Western Economic Journal* 6, No. 1 (December 1967): 39–51.

Nicholson, Walter. *Microeconomic Theory: Basic Principles and Extensions,* 5th ed. Chicago: South-Western, 2002, Chapter 12.

Willig, Robert D. "Multiproduct Technology and Market Structure." *The American Economic Review Papers and Proceedings* 69, No. 2 (May 1979): 346–351.

INTERNATIONAL CAPSULE I

Some International Dimensions of Demand, Production, and Cost

As a business firm develops its strategy regarding product lines, organization of production, and efficiency in the use of its resources, its managers frequently perceive that there are opportunities to sell in markets other than those of its home country. In addition, foreign sales of a product are often followed by a managerial decision to produce that product at a foreign location or, in some cases, to *purchase* certain component parts from foreign suppliers. Although these options are available to firms of all sizes, those that have been most successful in pursuing them are large multinational corporations, many of which are headquartered in the United States. Some examples are General Motors, Ford, and General Electric, large drug manufacturers such as Eli Lilly, and chemical companies such as Celanese.

THE BASIS FOR INTERNATIONAL TRADE

In order to understand why firms enter international markets, we must first look at the economic rationale underlying foreign trade. Economic theory argues that international trade occurs because of country-to-country differences in relative prices. More precisely, it is argued that a country will export goods that are relatively cheap in its home market and import those that are relatively expensive. A simple example will help to illustrate this point.

Suppose we consider two countries, the United States and Mexico, both of which produce two goods: red wine and beer. Assume at first that there is no trade between the two countries. Each will be willing to give up some of one of the two goods only if it gets a suitable amount of the other in return. Thus we are examining a basis for two-way trade, where each country both exports to and imports from the other.

Of course, in this example and in international trade generally, each country's internal prices will be stated in its own currency. This will not deter us from identifying goods that are relatively cheap or relatively expensive, since the relative value of any good can be measured in terms of how much of some other good must be given up in order to obtain it. Let us suppose that in Mexico a bottle of wine sells for 40 pesos, while a bottle of beer sells for 8 pesos. In other words, a bottle of wine is worth 5 bottles of beer. Now suppose that in the United States bottle of wine is priced at $3, and a beer is priced at $1. In the U.S., then, a bottle of wine is worth only 3 bottles of beer. In relative terms, then, wine is expensive in Mexico, while beer is expensive in the United

States. (Beer costs one-third of a bottle of wine in the U.S. but only one-fifth of a bottle of wine in Mexico.)

Table I-1 summarizes the price information. How can we determine whether two-way trade will occur? The answer is that we must know the *exchange rate* between pesos and dollars in order to analyze this situation. For example, suppose that in the market for currencies, a dollar can be obtained for 10 pesos. The exchange rate is thus 10 pesos per dollar, or $0.10 per peso (the peso is 1/10th of a dollar).

As Table I-2 shows, the Mexican internal prices of wine and beer (40 pesos and 8 pesos, respectively) translate into $4.00 per bottle for wine and $0.80 per bottle for beer. On the other hand, the U.S. internal prices ($3.00 for wine and $1 for beer) translate into 30 pesos for wine and 10 pesos for beer. Mexican consumers will find U.S. wine attractive at 30 pesos per bottle, since equivalent Mexican wine costs 40 pesos. Likewise, U.S. consumers will be attracted by the price of Mexican beer—$.80 per bottle—since equivalent U.S. beer costs them $1.00 per bottle. Thus we do have a basis for two-way trade at the exchange rate of 10 pesos per dollar. Mexico will export beer, and the U.S. will export wine.

The importance of the exchange rate cannot be overstressed. If, in the example just cited, the exchange rate had been 7 pesos per U.S. dollar, the dollar price of Mexican beer would be 8/7 or $1.14 per bottle, while Mexican wine would be priced at 40/7 or $5.71 per bottle. Thus U.S. consumers would not wish to buy either product from Mexico, since the U.S. equivalent products would be cheaper ($3.00 per bottle for wine and $1 per bottle for beer). However, Mexican consumers would find *both* U.S. products attractive. (U.S. wine would cost 21 pesos and U.S. beer, 7 pesos.) There would be a basis for one-way trade, but not for two-way trade.[1]

Why Relative Prices Differ

Until about the 1960s, the most widely accepted explanation for international differences in relative prices was variation in production costs from country to country. Thus, in our example, it would be argued that production costs for beer were lower in Mexico than in the United States, while for wine the reverse was true. The supposed reason for the lower production costs was said to be relative abundance or scarcity of resources. The

Table I-1 *Local Currency Prices of Wine and Beer in Mexico and the United States*

	Price of:	
	Wine in Local Currency	Beer in Local Currency
Mexico	40 pesos	8 pesos
United States	$3.00	$1.00

Table I-2 *Translation of Internal Prices to Foreign Currency*

	Money Price of Product in:			
	Pesos		Dollars	
	Wine	Beer	Wine	Beer
Mexico	40	8	4	0.8
United States	30	10	3	1

---

[1] One-way trade is not feasible for very long. In this example, the desire of Mexico to buy both wine and beer from the United States would flood the currency markets with pesos and cause the price of the peso to fall until some Mexican goods became attractive to American buyers.

relative production cost explanation (called the Heckscher-Ohlin theorem after the two Swedish economists who developed it) was widely accepted, since it seemed to do a good job of explaining why countries with an abundance of unskilled labor (Latin American countries, India, and some Asian countries) tended to export products that required relatively large doses of labor to produce. Of course, it also seemed to explain why industrialized countries such as the United States, Japan, and Germany tended to export goods that required relatively large amounts of capital goods to produce. However, the production cost approach did not seem to explain why most of world trade occurs *among* the industrialized countries, all of which are relatively capital abundant. One answer was put forth by Staffan Linder, who argued that different relative prices might well depend as much on demand as on cost of production.

Linder looked at modern trade patterns and observed that the lion's share of world trade is carried out by the industrialized countries (United States, Japan, Western Europe) trading among themselves. These countries both import and export large amounts of manufactured goods, and all of them have an abundance of capital equipment, skilled labor, and advanced technology. Since all of them can supply manufactured goods at relatively low costs of production, why do they trade so much with one another? Linder reasoned that the explanation could be found in overlapping patterns of demand. The industrialized countries in general have large internal markets and relatively affluent consumers. Thus products that can be sold in one of them can probably be sold in all of them. If a company introduces a battery-powered electric face scrubber in the United States, it probably will find a market for that product in Germany and France. However, it is unlikely to find much of a market for it in Peru. Many other U.S. products might be successfully marketed in a country like Peru, but the *range* of products Peruvians will buy is much smaller than the range of products that can be sold in Western Europe.

Different intensities of demand certainly can account for different relative prices, even if production costs are the same in the United States as in Europe. For example, if Germans become absolutely wild about designer sweatsocks, the relative price of these garments may become much higher in Germany than it is in the United States, opening up an opportunity for U.S. manufacturers to sell them in Germany.

PAYMENT FOR EXPORTS

What we have said about the importance of exchange rates in determining trade leads to a further question. That is, if a firm exports merchandise to a foreign buyer, what can the seller do to make sure that payment for the merchandise is received? There are three types of risk involved, *default risk, inconvertibility risk,* and *foreign exchange risk.* Default risk is basically the same kind of risk that sellers face in domestic trade. Thus, a seller firm must evaluate the ability of the buyer to make payment. If goods are received by the buyer before payment is made, even if the seller and buyer are both in the same country, the seller is assuming some risk regarding the creditworthiness of the buyer. However, default risk is more of a problem in international trade since legal action against debtors may be more costly and less likely to succeed when they are located in a foreign country.

Inconvertibility risk is the risk that the government of a given country will place controls on its currency that make it impossible to exchange it for some other currency. There are several ways an exporter can avoid default and inconvertibility risk. One option is, of course to demand payment in your own currency in advance. However, this generally only occurs in international trade when the buyer has extremely poor credit or the buyer's currency is very weak. Somewhat more common is the confirmed, irrevocable letter of credit. This is a document issued by the buyer's bank. When it is *confirmed* by a bank in the seller's home country, that bank agrees to allow the exporter (seller) to draw the funds from the bank when proof is presented that the merchandise has been shipped. Aside from payment in advance, the confirmed, irrevocable letter of credit is the least risky payment instrument for exporters. However, this method is burdensome to importers, and they, therefore, tend to seek sellers who will accept simpler terms of payment. As a result, most exports are paid for by *commercial drafts* drawn by the exporter on the importer, with commercial banks in both countries serving as intermediaries. However, this method depends on the importer alone for payment and is, therefore, more risky than cash in advance or a letter of credit. Commercial drafts are also subject to inconvertibility risk.

Foreign exchange risk is the risk that the exchange rate between the currency of the seller and that of the buyer will change before payment for merchandise occurs. For example, suppose the exchange rate between British pounds and U.S. dollars is £1 = $1.50. If you export a piece of equipment to England and the buyer agrees to pay you £10,000 for it, that will translate into a payment of $15,000. However, if, by the time payment is made, the pound depreciates to £1 = $1.35, you will only receive $13,500. There are two methods for dealing with foreign exchange

risk. The easiest is, of course, to make a contract that calls for payment in your own currency. Note, however, if you are an exporter, what this does is to transfer the foreign exchange risk to the importer in the other country. No matter how the contract is drawn, one or the other party will face a foreign exchange risk. Since exporters and importers seldom wish to become speculators in foreign exchange, when they face foreign exchange risk they normally use a method called *hedging* to offset it.

Hedging is the process of buying or selling an asset (like foreign currency) for the purpose of offsetting the risk of a change in its value. For example, if you are a U.S. exporter who wants to receive a payment equal to $15,000 for a piece of equipment sold to someone in England who agrees to pay in pounds sixty days in the future, you can hedge against the possibility that the number of dollars in a pound may fall by selling to someone a contract to deliver pounds on that date. There is a futures market in foreign exchange known as the forward market. What you will have to do is to calculate the number of pounds equal to $15,000 at the forward rate. Let's assume that today's exchange rate (known as the spot rate) is £1 = $1.50 but that the 60-day forward rate is £1 = $1.40. Thus, the number of pounds you will need to obtain $15,000 by selling them forward is $15,000/1.4 = £10,714. You will quote this pound price to the English buyer instead of the £10,000 that would be equivalent to $15,000 at the spot rate. As soon as the contract for purchase of the equipment is signed, you will sell in the forward market a forward exchange contract to deliver £10,714 in 60 days. You will immediately receive £10,714(1.4) = $15,000 from whoever purchases the forward contract. In effect, the export has been paid for in dollars. In 60 days, when the pound payment is made by the English buyer of the equipment, the pounds are simply delivered to the buyer of the forward contract. Naturally, there are some transactions costs associated with hedging, but they are generally regarded as small relative to the benefit produced by virtually eliminating foreign exchange risk.

THE PROBLEM OF TRADE BARRIERS

Today's world is full of pitfalls to international trade that make it imperative for a company entering a foreign market to proceed with caution. One commonly encountered problem is trade barriers. These take two forms: tariffs and nontariff barriers. Import tariffs are taxes levied on imported goods. They are frequently used to protect home industries from foreign competition. Sellers of an imported good simply view the import tariff as an additional cost of production, and they are willing to supply the imported good only at a price that will cover the costs of production *including* the tariff.[2] Thus the tariff raises the price of the imported good and may actually make it impossible for the imported good to compete with equivalent locally produced goods. In many developing countries, local manufacturing is protected by very high import tariff rates—perhaps 100 percent or more of the invoice price of the imported article. In effect, these tariffs totally prohibit the importation of many kinds of goods (automobiles and television sets, for example).

Nontariff barriers may actually prohibit imports in a more decisive fashion than do import tariffs. Two examples of these devices are the *import quota* and the *import license*. An import quota is a limitation on the physical amount of a particular good that will be allowed to enter the country. For example, if Pulistonia decides to establish an annual import quota of 200 motorcycles, then no more than 200 motorcycles will be allowed to enter the country each year. This has a more certain effect than a tariff, since a tariff pushes price up but does not specifically limit quantity. Presumably, anyone wishing to pay the tariff can still import the good. Quotas are usually accompanied by a licensing system, since the government must keep track of the quantity of imports and determine who gets to do the importing. Thus, Pulistonia would require a license to import motorcycles and devise some means for dividing the quota among the licensees (auctioning off the licenses, for example, or giving them only to in-laws of government officials).

Licensing often occurs even when there is no quota. In other words, under a system that appears to rely mainly on import tariffs for protection, a license may also be required to import a particular item and thereby enjoy the privilege of *paying* the tariff. Mexico has employed such a system in the past; the government simply refused to give out licenses whenever it wished to prohibit the importation of some particular good. For decades, Mexico had an elaborate system of tariffs on automobiles; the rates were meaningless, however, since almost no one could get a license to import a car anyway.

These are not the only kinds of trade barriers firms encounter when they attempt to enter a foreign market. Frequent restrictions are placed on size and labeling. (Example: "Do not send product in quart

---

[2] Economic theory shows that the price paid by consumers in the importing country will rise by less than the amount of the tariff if foreign supply is not infinitely elastic.

bottles, we allow only liters," or "Do not label product on the side, only on the bottom.") A firm may also find that government agencies are allowed to purchase its product only if locally produced output is nonexistent, regardless of price differentials between the two. In fact, something like the latter restriction is used by many state governments in the United States ("Buy American" laws). The moral is that no firm should seriously consider entering a foreign market without first determining the nature and extent of trade barriers found in that market. This may require considerable research at significant expense, but it is *absolutely necessary.* If insurmountable trade barriers are present, a firm may have to choose between giving up a specific foreign market or entering it by investing in production facilities located there.

Analyzing Foreign Demand

Whether a firm is considering export or foreign production, an important step in its decision process will be the assessment of potential foreign demand for its product. For a product that has been successful in the home market, the firm might simply choose to look for foreign markets where consumer preferences are likely to be similar to those in its own country. If its product is not unique, there are likely to be other firms already selling in the chosen foreign market. Statistical data on production, consumption, and imports in that market may make it possible for the firm to estimate a market demand function for the product or at least estimate the rate of growth of demand. (Statistical procedures for demand estimation were discussed in Chapter 3.)

Rapid growth of demand is one indicator that a foreign market is ripe for entry. However, even if data on a firm's product are not available, an assessment of potential demand can be made from other information on the characteristics of the foreign market. For example, for many countries, data on population, per capita income, and income distribution are easily obtained. As Staffan Linder suggested, for certain manufactured goods it would be important to identify sizable markets where the middle class is large and per capita income is relatively high. Although this set of circumstances seems to describe the industrialized countries only, it also applies to the urban middle-class consumers found in many of today's developing countries (Brazil and Mexico, for example). Moreover, a firm might find that a smaller country constitutes a feasible export market simply because there is no local production of its product.

Data Sources

To make an evaluation of foreign demand requires knowledge of basic sources of secondary data (data not directly gathered by the firm). The U.S. Department of Commerce produces many publications that contain data on foreign markets, including not only data on U.S. exports by commodity and country but also an international marketing information series. The latter provides (1) global market surveys covering 15 or more countries for certain target industries or products; (2) foreign country market surveys covering leading industrial sectors in a single country; (3) "Overseas Business Reports" including background data and economic conditions for both industrialized and developing countries; and (4) a variety of other valuable information on foreign economic trends and new developments in world trade. There is also a great deal of basic data available from international agencies such as the United Nations, the Organization of

American States, and the Organization for Economic Cooperation and Development (for industrialized countries).

The governments of most industrialized countries and many of the developing countries provide data on their own production, consumption, and foreign trade. In fact, these are the basic sources of much of the statistical data published by the international agencies. Statistics vary widely in terms of both availability and accuracy. For some countries, there is a great deal of lag in data publication, so that the latest available information may pertain to the economy of five years ago rather than that of the present. Other countries do not even gather economic and demographic data on a regular basis.

Where secondary data are not available, a firm may have to either collect its own information or rely on expert opinion regarding a foreign market opportunity. It may be relatively easy to have survey research done on a potential market in an industrialized country, although pitfalls related to cultural and language differences must be avoided. (Do not ask about the size of a car "trunk" in a country where the luggage compartment is called a "boot.") In a developing country, the obstacles to market research may be substantial, since many consumers will not have telephones or even access to reliable mail service. The best sources of information in such cases may be local experts such as consultants, industry colleagues, or economic officers assigned to embassies or consulates.

Product Adaptation

Analysis of the need for product adaptation often goes hand in hand with analysis of foreign demand. Product adaptation means changing the product to fit the characteristics of the foreign market environment. It may involve production costs. For example, electrical appliances presently manufactured for 110-volt current in the home market may have to be redesigned for 220-volt current in the foreign market. Sometimes product adaptation has more to do with how the product is *presented* to potential buyers in the foreign market than with its physical characteristics. A case in point is the Chevrolet Nova, a car that was produced and sold by General Motors in a number of countries. The name of the car presented a problem in the Spanish-speaking world, since *no va* in Spanish means "it won't run." There are other cases in which cultural norms make product adaptation imperative. For example, one U.S. candy manufacturer reportedly planned to introduce a chocolate candy with peanuts into the Japanese market. Fortunately, the firm found out in time that an old Japanese belief held that eating peanuts with chocolate would cause nosebleeds.[3] In a case like this, it would probably be advisable to develop a new product aimed at local tastes and preferences rather than attempt to change the perception of the existing product.

It is clear that the product adaptation question has at least three dimensions: (1) change in the physical attributes of the product; (2) change in buyer perception of the product; and (3) development of an entirely new product for foreign consumers. While the second item has mainly to do with marketing, the economics of production is of substantial importance for the other two. Production can take place, in whole or in part, either at home or in a foreign location.

---

[3] Philip R. Cateora, *International Marketing* (Homewood, Ill.: Irwin, 1983), p. 270.

Producing in a Foreign Country

Having examined various dimensions of identifying a foreign market for a product, the time has come to consider what it means to produce a product in a foreign location. There are numerous advantages to such a strategy, but it is an arena into which a firm should enter only after a good deal of careful study.

The decision to produce abroad is usually made either for reasons of cost or for political reasons. When a firm produces in its home market and exports to a foreign market, its production costs are determined by resource prices in its home country. To sell abroad, it must also pay transportation costs and any other costs incurred in getting the good to the foreign market. In the foreign location, the firm may find that certain resources are lower priced than at home. This could be reason enough to consider producing all or part of the good in the foreign country rather than at home. However, political factors may also determine the location of production.

Many developing countries provide incentives for firms to invest in production facilities. These range from tax breaks and loan guarantees for foreign investors to provision of plant space in government-sponsored industrial parks. Often such incentives are coupled with barriers against importation of finished products, so that the only access to the country's market is through local production or assembly of the final product. To some extent, firms in industrialized countries are pushed into establishment of foreign production facilities when they realize that their only hope for gaining a foothold in a potentially large foreign market is through such investments.

The Product Cycle

Where costs rather than government policies determine foreign investment, the develop-ment of foreign production facilities often follows the pattern described by the *product cycle* theory of international trade. This theory, popularized by Raymond Vernon of Harvard University, argues that new product development takes place in advanced, industrialized nations. The firm that develops such a product is likely to be its first producer, and the product is aimed first at consumers in the home market. Once the product is successful, the firm may look to foreign markets for increased sales. It may also try to reduce costs by seeking foreign sources of certain parts, even though final production still occurs at home. Finally, it may decide to set up a foreign subsidiary to manufacture the good. If foreign production proves cheaper than home country production, the firm may choose to shut down its home country facilities. The result is that the home country then becomes an *importer* of the very product that it first exported.

The product cycle theory seems to provide a reasonable approximation of how U.S.-based multinational corporations have expanded into overseas production, especially in Europe and parts of Asia. Here, costs rather than government policies attracted the firms' investments. In situations like these, deciding whether or not to set up foreign plants is based rather straightforwardly on the kinds of cost analyses firms are familiar with from their operations at home. If long-run production costs are minimized by producing in the foreign location, and if investing there does not appear to be overly risky, then foreign production may well be the strategy to choose.

Analysis of Foreign Costs

In comparing foreign costs with those at home, it is important to be aware of political or environmental differences that may make the total cost of inputs higher than their nominal price. For example, seemingly lower labor costs often make foreign production appear to be attractive, but firms have learned that low wage rates may be offset by both lagging worker productivity and government requirements for such benefits as social security, medical services, paid holidays, and severance pay. In terms of the production analysis presented in Chapter 5, this means that the marginal product of labor is lower in the foreign location than at home and that the price of foreign labor is actually much higher than its wage rate implies. Further, the cost of foreign labor may escalate rapidly if a politically powerful union can make unwarranted demands on foreign-owned firms.

Other dimensions of foreign cost analysis include the availability of raw materials and intermediate goods, added costs related to communications and transportation, the costs of training and workforce development, and the cost implications of such government policies as restrictions on employment of non-native personnel. Costs for the firm can be substantially increased if it must purchase inputs from local suppliers who are either inefficient or corrupt. Tariffs against imported inputs may have been put in place to forward the interests of such producers at the expense of both consumers and foreign investors. The costs of transporting inputs within the foreign country may not be comparable with those at home, and communications may not measure up to those in the home country (in some countries telephone service is unreliable). Nationalistic fervor often leads to the passage of labor laws that discriminate against the employment of foreign technicians and managers and cause firms to employ less-experienced or less-qualified local personnel.

The foregoing are just a few of the issues a firm must investigate before taking as bold a step as investing in foreign production facilities. Thus analysis of foreign production costs requires perhaps even more scrutiny than analysis of foreign demand.

QUESTIONS AND PROBLEMS

1. How are relative prices related to the basis for international trade?

2. Given the table below:

Units of Labor Required to Produce One:

	Tablecloth	Barrel of Wine
France	10	5
England	4	4

a. Explain why the data *do* provide a basis for two-way trade between France and England. (Assume labor costs reflect relative prices in each country.)

b. Which good will be exported by France? Why?

c. Assume that the numbers in the table represent domestic prices (in euros for France and pounds for England) instead of labor costs. If one euro = one pound is the exchange rate, will two-way trade occur? (If *yes*, explain why. If *no*, tell what would have to take place in order for two-way trade to occur.)

SELECTED REFERENCES

Caves, Richard E., Jeffrey A. Frankel, and Ronald W. Jones. *World Trade and Payments.* New York: Harper Collins, 1993.

Cundiff, Edward W., and Marye Tharp Hilger. *Marketing in the International Environment.* Englewood Cliffs, N.J.: Prentice-Hall, 1984.

Keegan, Warren J. "Multinational Product Planning: Strategic Alternatives," *Journal of Marketing* 33 (January 1969), pp. 58–62.

Linder, Staffan B. *An Essay on Trade and Transformation.* New York: Wiley, 1961.

Vernon, Raymond. "International Investment and International Trade in the Product Cycle," *Quarterly Journal of Economics* 80, no. 2 (May 1966), pp. 190–207.

Yarbrough, Beth V. and Robert M. Yarbrough. *The World Economy: Trade and Finance,* 6th ed. Mason, OH: South-Western, 2003.

CHAPTER SEVEN

Profit Analysis of the Firm

Throughout this book, we are assuming that the primary concern of the firm is its level of *profit*. To have profit, of course, a firm needs to have income, normally from sales of its product or service. In Chapter 2 we focused our attention on demand and revenue, and we subsequently examined demand estimation and forecasting. Next, we analyzed production and cost. Now we are ready to put the materials from these earlier chapters together and examine the difference between revenue and cost (profit), with particular attention to maximizing that difference. We recognize that some firms may have subsidiary goals, such as a large volume of sales or a good company image. In what follows, however, any such concerns are assumed to be *definitely secondary* to the concern for generating profits, and we recognize that often the attention paid to such secondary goals merely reflects the impact company officials believe such variables may have on future company profits. With this in mind, we will direct our attention to decision rules for determining the profit-maximizing level of output and price for the individual firm.

Profit maximization: Making the greatest economic profit possible.

Although **profit maximization** is the primary goal of a firm, we do not mean to suggest that the firm should maximize profit with no regard for legal or ethical considerations. The firm that wishes to remain a successful and responsible part of our society in the long run must consider the ethical ramifications of its actions. Henry Ford II once remarked:

On Profit Maximization and Business Ethics

There is no doubt that the profit strategies of certain businesses have raised ethical questions. For example, the late 1990s saw a rash of charges leveled at U.S firms that subcontracted to domestic producers who ran sweatshops or to foreign sweatshop operators who employed child labor. Such well-known names as Liz Claiborne, the Gap, Nike, Wal-Mart, and Kathie Lee Gifford were involved in the controversies that flared when the situation was publicized. The sweatshop incidents were followed in the early 2000s by several cases of alleged fraudulent accounting and scandalous insider trading related to some of the biggest corporate bankrupcies in U.S. history (Enron, Worldcom). Naturally, these discoveries raised questions regarding ethics and profit-maximizing behavior.

Two business ethics scholars, Patrick Primeaux and John Stieber, produced an interesting article that addressed the connection between profit maximization and the laws, ethics, and mores of society. Primeaux, a Marist Father and theology professor at St. John's University (in New York), and Stieber, a professor in finance and economics at Southern Methodist University (Dallas), argued that profit-maximizing managerial decisions are inherently quite consistent with ethical behavior. Primeaux and Stieber began their analysis with the proposition that in business, as in football or baseball, there are rules of the game. Those rules are related to the role of the manager in the social system as a whole,

where business managers serve the function of allocating scarce resources.

Primeaux and Stieber explained that managers are driven to be efficient in the use of resources because, if they are not, their businesses will not be profitable, or, at least, will not be as profitable as they *could be*. Thus, there is an ethical dimension to profit maximization, since failure to produce the "right" amount of output (failure to operate where $MR = MC$) misallocates resources, resulting in the supply of either too little or too much of the firm's product. When resources are misallocated, society as a whole pays the bill, so that consumers, shareholders, managers, and employees will eventually be worse off. The authors stated:

> From a behavioral perspective, profit maximization is defined as *the act of producing the right kind and the right amount of goods and services the consumer wants at the lowest possible cost (within the legal and ethical mores of the community).*

They added that the phrase, "within the legal and ethical mores of the community," was placed in parentheses because community standards are already contained within the costs of the firm.

The idea that the legal and ethical mores of society are contained within the costs of the firm deserves some explanation. What Primeaux and Stieber had in mind is the concept of opportunity cost. They argued that

There is no such thing as planning for a minimal return less than the best you can imagine—not if you want to survive in a competitive market. It's like asking a professional football team to win by only one point—a sure fire formula for losing. There's only one way to compete successfully—all

managers "are aware (and if not, should be aware) that opportunity costs can be significant for any decision." Legal and ethical considerations are a part of such opportunity costs. Thus, businesses face the prospects of losing customers or being saddled with litigation expenses, payments for damages, and fines if their managers make decisions that violate community standards. A real-world example that Primeaux and Stieber offered was the case of General Motors (GM) having chosen to install Chevrolet engines in Oldsmobiles produced in 1977. To GM, this seemed a reasonable efficiency move, but the company clearly miscalculated the cost of public indignation, bad publicity, customer compensation, and legal expenses that, when all was said and done, proved to be some of the opportunity costs of its decision. (GM offered a cash settlement to the affected car buyers and, of course, had to bear substantial legal expenses and suffer a monumental loss of customer good-will.)

A more startling case not discussed by Primeaux and Stieber was that of the Ford Pinto gas tank shield. In that instance, Ford managers actually were aware that deletion of a shield from the gas tank area of the subcompact Pinto would lead to horrible injuries and numerous deaths from fiery explosions that would occur if the car were to be struck from behind. However, they calculated that the costs to the firm in litigation and damages expenses would be outweighed by the savings in the production costs of the cars. It would be easy to argue that this was a calculation so terrible that it should never have been made. But other cases are less clear cut. For example, should all cars have *side impact* air bags and antilock

brakes? Or should automakers have installed passenger-side air bags when they apparently did have some knowledge that the bags could injure or kill children placed, with or without infant safety seats, in the front passenger area?

While managers who are behaving properly when they make profit-maximizing decisions certainly should *try* to take into account the ethics-related opportunity costs of those decisions, it is likely that in many cases imperfect information will lead to miscalculations. In addition, there will always be some managers who see opportunities to profit from decisions that wrongfully harm some members of society but are not likely to affect the firm's bottom line because of the inability of the parties who are negatively affected to obtain redress. However, none of this is reason to condemn profit-maximizing behavior in general. As Primeaux and Stieber stressed, when properly carried out, profit maximization demands that the ethics and mores of the community become integral to the decision-making process.*

References: Jenny Strasburg, "Gap Resists Settlement of Saipan Sweatshop Suit," *San Francisco Chronicle,* March 2, 2002, p. B-1; "The Shame of Sweatshops," *Consumer Reports* (August 1999), pp. 18–20; Marilyn M. Helms and Betty A. Hutchins, "Poor Quality Products: Is Their Production Unethical?" *Management Decision* 30, No. 5 (1992): 35–46; and Patrick Primeaux and John Stieber, "Profit Maximization: The Ethical Mandate," *Journal of Business Ethics* 13, No. 4 (April 1994): 287–294.

---

* Primeaux and Stieber do not carefully consider the impact of market structure or possible divergences between private and social costs and benefits in their analysis. More will be said about these issues in Chapter 15.

out. If believing this makes you a greedy capitalist lusting after bloated profits, then I plead guilty. The worst sin I can commit as a businessman is to fail to seek maximum long-term profitability *by all decent and lawful means* [emphasis added]. To do so is to subvert economic reason.

More recently, a member of another generation of the Ford family restated this same philosophy:

> We have an obligation to shareholders to give them the best return they can possibly get. We have an obligation to customers to give them what they want. And we have an obligation to the environment to make whatever we make as clean as it can possibly be.[1]

Maximizing profit is an obligation that corporate managers have to the company's shareholders, but it is also an obligation to society. If the firm is not maximizing profits, scarce resources are typically being wasted. Yet, as Mr. Ford intimated, both the business enterprise and society are benefited in the long run only when the goal of maximum profit is achieved by "decent and lawful means."

To understand the importance of the profit-maximizing guidelines presented in this chapter, we must first recognize the fact that things can go sour—even for a firm that has apparently established itself. A classic example is NordicTrac. The company, which manufactured a variety of physical fitness machines, was started in a basement in 1976. In 1986, when it was sold to CML for $22 million, the demand for its product was booming. By 1993, annual sales of its cross-country-ski machines were approaching $500 million, but by December 1998 NordicTrac was in Chapter 11 bankruptcy. Was this bankruptcy filing the result of calamitous factors external to the firm? *Only partly.* Many new competing fitness machines with significantly lower prices *had* entered the market since the NordicTrac was developed. Nevertheless, an important factor in NordicTrac's downfall was a movement from direct marketing to traditional retail stores in high-rent shopping malls. As a result, its costs rose substantially, affording it little opportunity to lower prices to match the competition. Moreover, the retail stores had little room for customers to try out the equipment, nor did they have sufficient stock to allow buyers to immediately take a machine home. Thus, the new stores did little to stimulate additional sales.[2]

More recent examples of poor managerial decision making leading to losses, bankruptcy filings, and even a complete business failure include Kmart (2001), Montgomery Ward (2001), Sunbeam Corporation (2001), and General Cinema (2000). Analysts attributed Kmart's problems to its inefficiencies, particularly in its supply chain and in poor management of stocking at individual stores. To be profitable in a market with rivals like Wal-Mart and Target requires a much tighter ship than Kmart was running.[3] Another big retailer, Montgomery Ward, has simply been shuttered and is out of business—this after 128 years of being a major firm in its market.

---

[1] "Latest Ford in Charge Drives for Legacy," *USA Today,* May 13, 1999, p. 6B.
[2] See "How NordicTrack Lost Its Footing," *Business Week* (December 14, 1998), p. 138.
[3] "Kmart's Woes Casting a Pall," *San Antonio Express-News,* January 24, 2002, pp. 1E, 4E.

Wards did not meet the combined challenges posed by big discount chains, on the one hand, and arch-rival, Sears, on the other. In addition, Ward's management made a disastrous decision to allocate a significant portion of sales effort and store space to consumer electronics, where it "got clobbered by newfangled category-killers such as Circuit City Stores, Inc."[4]

The tribulations of Sunbeam and General Cinema can also be tied to specific management decisions. According to one analyst, Sunbeam, producer of home appliances like Mr. Coffee, Oster blenders, and Sunbeam mixers, was in need of "reconstruction of its brands." Although Sunbeam had a long history of producing good-quality small appliances, it simply had not developed new product lines, so its sales stagnated. General Cinema, with 1,070 screens nationwide, "succumbed to declining patronage and intensifying competition from newer and fancier theater complexes." General, along with four other theater chains that filed for bankruptcy protection in 2000, had too many obsolete "multiplex" theaters in a market that was changing to "*mega*plexes." Observers noted, however, that a Chapter 11 bankruptcy filing might constitute *ex post* rational management, since it would likely allow the firms to terminate leases on money-losing multiplex properties.[5]

While the early 2000s have provided ample illustrations of flawed managerial decisions leading to losses and bankruptcies, they have also supplied many cases of good management decisions contributing either to profitable operation or cutting losses. In retail trade, for example, J.C. Penney Company achieved a turnaround in 2001–2002 by remodeling stores and focusing on new and popular fashions in its clothing line. On the cost side, Penney's centralized its purchasing, which allowed it to get better prices from suppliers.[6]

A case where losses were minimized in a bad market is provided by Continental Airlines. Although plagued, like other carriers, by the travel downturn after the 9/11 terrorist attacks, Continental's management decided to continue with previously planned upgrades of customer service. So, while other major airlines were cutting back on meal service and perquisites for business travelers, Continental was moving in the opposite direction. When four of the six big, full-service carriers turned in losses of over $1 billion in 2001, Continental held its losses to only $95 million, and its decrease in passenger traffic was the smallest in the group. Thus, Continental at least had a temporary success, but it still faced problems similar to those of other major airlines.[7] These would call for many more careful

---

[4] Kevin Helliker, "Montgomery Ward Files for Chapter 11 Protection," *Wall Street Journal,* December 29, 2000, p. A3.

[5] "Sunbeam's Sole Ray of Hope," *Business Week* (February 19, 2001), p. 62, and Joseph Pereira and Nikhil Deogun, "Parent of General Cinema Chain Files for Chapter 11, as 2 Executives Resign," *Wall Street Journal,* November 12, 2000, p. A4.

[6] Stephanie Anderson Forest, "A Speedy Makeover at Penney's," *Business Week* (April 29, 2002), pp. 92, 93.

[7] Scott McCartney, "Continental Airlines Takes Risk in Wooing Travelers," *San Antonio Express-News,* February 17, 2002, p. 5K.

management decisions in the future, decisions of the type we are about to examine.

PROFIT MAXIMIZATION

The decision rule for profit maximization can be explained by using either total or marginal curves, and we will do both in this chapter. In the simplest terms, total profit is equal to total revenue minus total cost. In Chapter 2, total revenue was defined as the total sales of a firm, equal to the price multiplied by the quantity sold of each product. Chapter 6 explained that the total cost of a firm includes both explicit and implicit, or opportunity, costs. Thus, we can define **total profit** as the "pure" or "economic" profit remaining after all explicit and implicit costs—including a normal or average return for the funds invested in this business—have been subtracted from total revenue.

> **Total profit** or **economic profit** for a firm is equal to total revenue minus total cost, where total cost includes all opportunity costs associated with the firm's activities.

In Figure 7-1 we have drawn a total revenue curve, a total cost curve, and a total profit curve. Since we are assuming that the goal of the firm is to maximize profit, we wish to establish a decision rule that will enable the firm to find that output level and price which will make total profit (that is, total sales revenue less total cost) the greatest amount possible. In Figure 7-1 the profit-maximizing output is Q_3.

Notice that at Q_3, the slopes of the total revenue and total cost curves are equal, and the slope of the total profit curve is zero. In Chapter 2 we pointed out that the slope of the total revenue curve at a particular output level is marginal revenue at that level of output; correspondingly, we stated in Chapter 6 that the slope of the total cost curve is marginal cost. In the same manner, the slope of the total profit curve is **marginal profit,** or the rate of change in the total profit of the firm with respect to output.[8] Marginal profit can be approximated by the change in total profit divided by the change in quantity produced between two levels of output:

> **Marginal profit** is the rate of change of total profit with respect to changes in the level of output.

$$M\pi = \frac{\Delta T\pi}{\Delta Q} = \frac{T\pi_2 - T\pi_1}{Q_2 - Q_1}$$

This latter value we call *arc marginal profit,* as it gives the average rate of change of total profit with respect to output *between two levels of output* Marginal profit can also be found by subtracting marginal cost from marginal revenue:

$$M\pi = MR - MC.$$

---

[8] Mathematically speaking, instantaneous or point marginal profit is the derivative of the total profit function with respect to quantity:

$$M\pi = \frac{dT\pi}{dQ}$$

FIGURE 7–1

*Total Revenue,
Total Cost, and
Total Profit*

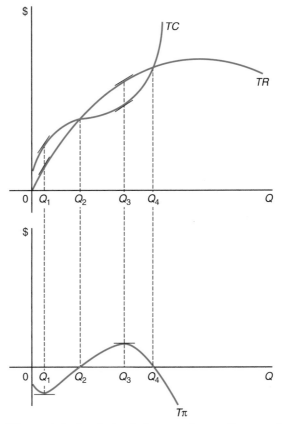

Total profit ($T\pi$) will be maximized at the level of output where total revenue (TR) minus total cost (TC) is at its greatest positive level. At this point, the slope of the TR curve (marginal revenue) will equal the slope of the TC curve (marginal cost).

Thus, for profit maximization, the profit to be gained by producing another unit of output, marginal profit, must be zero, or $M\pi = 0$. Moreover, $M\pi = 0$ implies $MR - MC = 0$, so that $MR = MC$. In other words, at the profit-maximizing level of output, the additional revenue to be gained from another unit of output must be equal to the additional cost the firm incurs by producing it.

Therefore, at Q_3 in Figure 7-1, marginal revenue equals marginal cost, marginal profit is zero, and total profit is at a maximum. In Figure 7-2 we have sketched the marginal revenue, marginal cost, and marginal profit curves corresponding to the total revenue, total cost, and total profit curves in Figure 7-1.

To emphasize what we have shown so far, we reiterate that it is not a coincidence that marginal revenue and marginal cost are equal where profit

FIGURE 7–2

*Marginal
Revenue,
Marginal Cost,
and Marginal
Profit*

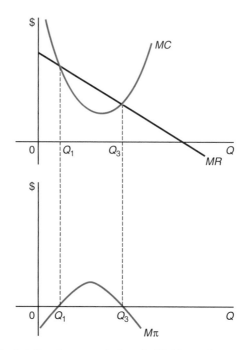

Total profit is maximized at Q_3, where marginal profit ($M\pi$) is equal to zero, and MC is greater than MR at higher levels of output. At Q_1, $M\pi$ is equal to zero, but MC is less than MR at higher levels of output. In this case the firm will increase profit by expanding output.

is maximized. The fact that marginal profit ($M\pi$) is zero at the profit-maximizing level of output means that marginal revenue minus marginal cost equals zero ($MR - MC = 0$). By adding MC to both sides of this equation, we see that it must be true that $MR = MC$ at the profit-maximizing level of output. Again, recall that marginal revenue is the additional revenue the firm receives from selling another unit of output. Marginal cost is the cost of producing another unit of output. As long as the additional revenue from producing another unit is greater than the cost of the unit (that is, if marginal profit is positive), the firm will find it profitable to expand its output.

For example, if the marginal revenue from producing another television set is $200 and the set's marginal cost is $100, the firm will add $100 to profit by producing the TV. Even if the marginal revenue of a television set were $175 and the set's marginal cost were $174, the firm would still add $1 to profit by producing the TV. On the other hand, if the marginal revenue from producing another TV is $160 and the TV's marginal cost is $180, the firm's profit will decrease by $20 if it produces another TV. Only when the additional revenue from producing another unit of output is equal to its cost will profit be maximized.

However, we need to add a condition to our decision rule that the profit-maximizing level of output occurs where $M\pi = 0$. If marginal profit is zero at a particular level of output (such as Q_3 in Figure 7-2), that fact *may* be an indication to the firm that at larger output levels, *marginal profit* will be *negative* and total profit will consequently decline. However, we can also observe that $MR = MC$ and $M\pi = 0$ at Q_1 in Figure 7-2. At this point, total profit reaches a relative *minimum* and will increase if the level of output is increased. Thus, the decision rule that the firm should follow to maximize total profit is the following one:

> Produce at the level of output where $MR = MC$ ($M\pi = 0$) and *MR is below* MC at higher output levels.[9]

The firm can find its corresponding profit-maximizing price by substituting that level of output for quantity demanded in its demand function or by dividing the corresponding total revenue by that quantity.

In Figure 7-3 we demonstrate both the relationships among *average* revenue, *average* cost, and *average* profit and the relationships among *marginal* revenue, *marginal* cost, and *marginal* profit. *Marginal profit* is maximized at Q_1, where the difference between MR and MC is the greatest positive amount. **Average profit** is maximized at Q_2, where the difference between AR (price) and AC is the greatest positive amount. However, *total profit* for the firm is maximized at a level of output (Q_3) that is *greater than* either Q_1 or Q_2. In other words, total profit is usually maximized *not* where average or unit profit is maximized, but rather at a higher level of output. We can find total profit at Q_3 by multiplying average profit at Q_3 by Q_3 (multiply $A\pi_3$ by Q_3). Total profit is also equal to (price minus average cost) or ($P_3 - AC_3$) multiplied by Q_3, since P_3 (or AR_3) minus AC_3 must equal $A\pi_3$. Total

Average profit is the profit per unit sold. It is equal to total profit divided by quantity of output. It is also equal to price minus average cost.

---

[9] The condition that MR be below MC at higher levels of output is merely a statement in economic terms of the mathematical second-order condition for a maximum, given in the Mathematical Appendix to this book. The first-order condition for maximum total profit is that the first derivative of the total profit function be equal to zero. Since

$$T\pi = TR - TC,$$

then the first-order condition is that

$$M\pi = \frac{dT\pi}{dQ} = \frac{dTR}{dQ} - \frac{dTC}{dQ} = MR - MC = 0,$$

or

$$MR = MC.$$

The second-order condition is that

$$\frac{d^2T\pi}{dQ^2} = \frac{dMR}{dQ} - \frac{dMC}{dQ} < 0,$$

which requires that marginal revenue be less than marginal cost at higher levels of output.

FIGURE 7–3

*Relationships
among Marginal
Revenue,
Marginal Cost,
and Marginal
Profit and
Average
Revenue,
Average Cost,
and Average
Profit*

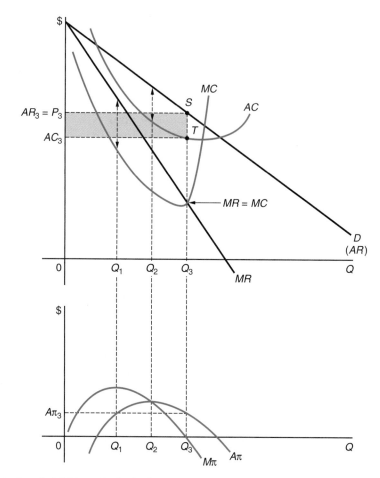

Marginal profit ($M\pi$) is maximized where $MR - MC$ is at its greatest positive level, at Q_1. Average profit ($A\pi$) is maximized at Q_2, where $AR - AC$ is greatest. However, total profit is maximized at Q_3, where $MR = MC$, $M\pi = 0$, and $MR < MC$ at higher levels of output.

profit is, therefore, identical in value to the area of rectangle P_3STAC_3; and, given the curves drawn in Figure 7-3, this area will be greatest at Q_3. Remember:

> The greatest profit per unit is *not* the goal of the firm; rather, the firm's goal is the greatest *total* profit.

An understanding of these relationships will be quite helpful in Part 3 of this text.

In Table 7-1 we can see once again how our $MR = MC$ decision rule can be utilized by the firm to maximize profit. Between 5 and 10 units of output, marginal profit is zero. However, marginal cost is falling below marginal revenue, so marginal profit is positive at higher levels of output. Profit is

Table 7-1 *Revenue, Cost, and Profit Maximization*

Q	P	TR	TC	Tπ	Arc MR	Arc MC	Arc Mπ
0	200	0	200	−200			
					190	200	−10
5	190	950	1,200	−250			
					170	170	0
10	180	1,800	2,050	−250			
					120	80	40
15	160	2,400	2,450	−50			
					80	50	30
20	140	2,800	2,700	100			
					40	30	10
25	120	3,000	2,850	150			
					30	20	10
30	105	3,150	2,950	200			
					21	21	0
35	93	3,255	3,055	200			
					−11	25	−36
40	80	3,200	3,180	20			

maximized between 30 and 35 units of output, where marginal revenue and marginal cost are again equal and marginal profit is zero. Beyond 35 units of output, marginal revenue falls below marginal cost, and marginal profit becomes negative. Thus, to summarize what we have been saying, the firm should expand its output up to the point where the production of additional units would *add more to the firm's costs than to its revenues.*[10]

---

[10] Using calculus, a firm manager can find the precise level of output that would maximize total profit if the firm's total revenue and total cost functions are known. For example, suppose the firm's total revenue function is

$$TR = 100Q - 2Q^2,$$

and the total cost function is

$$TC = 30 + 120Q - 5Q^2 + (1/12)\,Q^3.$$

The total profit function would then be given by total revenue minus total cost or

$$T\pi = -(1/12)\,Q^3 + 3Q^2 - 20Q - 30.$$

To find the level of output that would maximize total profit, we find the marginal profit function, set it equal to zero, and solve for the quantity of output. Therefore

$$M\pi = \frac{dT\pi}{dQ} = -(1/4)Q^2 + 6Q - 20 = 0.$$

To solve this equation, we first multiply both sides by −4 and then factor:

$$Q^2 - 24Q + 80 = 0$$

and

$$(Q - 20)\,(Q - 4) = 0.$$

Thus, at $Q = 20$ and at $Q = 4$, marginal profit is zero. *(footnote continues)*

NUMERICAL EXAMPLE

Algebra of Profit Maximization

A firm has the following total and marginal cost functions, where Q is output per week:

$$STC = 500 + 20Q + 0.05Q^2$$
$$SMC = 20 + 0.1Q$$

What will be its profit-maximizing output, assuming it faces a fixed market price of $40 for its product? How much will the maximum profit be?

Answer:

To find the profit-maximizing quantity, set marginal profit or $(MR - MC)$ equal to zero.

$$40 - 20 - 0.1Q = 0$$

Thus

$$20 = 0.1Q,$$

and

$$Q = 200.$$

Profit equals

$$TR - STC = \$40(200) - 500 - 20(200) - 0.05(40,000)$$
$$= 8,000 - 500 - 4,000 - 2,000$$
$$= \$1,500$$

We can tell that a profit maximum occurs at $Q = 200$ since at higher levels of output MR is less than MC.

(*footnote continued from previous page*)

Nevertheless, we must still check the second-order condition for a maximum to see if profit is maximized at either $Q = 4$ or $Q = 20$. The second derivative of $T\pi$ is

$$\frac{dM\pi}{dQ},$$

and

$$\frac{d^2T\pi}{dQ^2} = \frac{dM\pi}{dQ} = -.5Q + 6.$$

At $Q = 4$ the second derivative is positive, so $T\pi$ is minimized at that level of output. At $Q = 20$ the second derivative is negative, so profit is maximized at that level of output.

SHUTDOWN POINT

There is *one more qualification* to our profit-maximization decision rule. The firm maximizes profits by producing where $MR = MC$ (with marginal revenue thereafter *below* marginal cost) *as long as price is greater than or equal to average variable cost.* If price is less than average variable cost, the firm should not produce at all—even in the short run.

For example, suppose a restaurant has fixed costs of $4,000 per month, an average price of $4.00, and an average variable cost of $4.50 for each meal served. If the restaurant operates for a month selling 10,000 meals, its total sales revenue will be $40,000 and its total variable cost will be $45,000. In this case, the firm's revenues will not cover $5,000 of its variable costs or *any* of the $4,000 fixed costs, so the firm will be losing $9,000 per month (see Table 7-2). If the firm did not produce at all, the most it could lose would be the $4,000 per month fixed cost. Therefore, the firm will minimize its loss by temporarily shutting down. Firms frequently make this choice during recessionary periods, when demand falls but is expected to increase in the future. Of course, a firm would go out of business permanently if it were not able to increase revenue or reduce costs enough so that it could eventually make a normal return or a profit.

On the other hand, if the average price of a meal were $4.60, the average variable cost were $4.40, and the firm were to sell 9,000 meals, then the firm's total revenue would be $41,400, its total variable cost would be $39,600, and its total loss would be $2,200 (see Table 7-3). This last example illustrates the principle that in the short run, it is in the firm's best interests to continue to operate as long as it can cover its variable costs and make something toward covering its fixed costs.

In the long run, the firm presumably would require that *all* of its economic costs be covered if it were to stay in business. An exception to this principle would be owner-managed enterprises where an opportunity-cost loss of the owner's time and/or money is accepted in return for the pleasure of owning the business and being one's own boss. However, this type of owner violates our profit-maximization assumption; therefore, we will disregard this

Table 7-2 *Total Loss for a Restaurant When Price Is Less Than Average Variable Cost*

Total Sales (10,000 meals @ $4.00 each)	$40,000
Less:	
Total Variable Cost	
(10,000 meals @ $4.50 each)	45,000
	($5,000)
Less:	
Total Fixed Cost	4,000
Net Income (loss)	($9,000)

Table 7-3 *Total Loss for a Restaurant When Price Is Greater Than Average Variable Cost But Less Than Average Total Cost*

Total Sales (9,000 meals @ $4.60 each)	$41,400
Less:	
Total Variable Cost	
(9,000 meals @ $4.40 each)	39,600
	$ 1,800
Less:	
Total Fixed Cost	4,000
Net Income (loss)	($2,200)

The **profit-maximizing rule** (or **loss-minimizing rule**) is to produce up to the point where marginal revenue is equal to marginal cost and at higher output levels marginal revenue is less than marginal cost, as long as price is greater than or equal to average variable cost in the short run or long-run average cost in the long run.

possibility throughout the remainder of the book. The **profit-maximizing rule** (or **loss-minimizing rule**) is that a firm produce up to the point where marginal profit is zero, as long as price is at least as great as average variable cost in the short run or as great as long-run average cost in the long run. This point will be where marginal revenue is equal to marginal cost.

NUMERICAL EXAMPLE

Profit Maximization, Tabular Data

Complete the following table and find the profit-maximizing output, assuming total fixed cost is $400.

Arc MR	Q	P	TR	TVC	Arc MC
	0	100	0	0	
95					60
	10	95	950	600	
	20	90	1,800	1,000	
75					60
	30	85	2,550		
65					70
	40	80	3,200		
	50	75	3,750	3,150	

Answer:

The missing *MR* values are 85 and 55, each obtained by calculating $\Delta TR/\Delta Q$. The missing *MC* values are 40 and 85, each obtained by calculating $\Delta TVC/\Delta Q$. Finally, the missing *TVC* values are 1,600 and 2,300, each obtained by multiplying the relevant *MC* by ΔQ and adding on the ΔTVC to the preceding *TVC* value.

Profit is maximized where, for an increase in Q, *MC* > *MR*. This occurs at *Q* = *30*, since increasing Q to 40 would result in *MC* = 70, but *MR* = 65. Profit is *TR* – *TC* = *2,550 – 1,600 – 400 = 550.*

The Remaking of PepsiCo

PepsiCo's major activity: selling a substitute for Coke. Right? *WRONG!* Actually, Pepsi's soft-drink sales now account for only about 25 percent of its total revenue. Its biggest winner is Frito Lay, acquired through merger many years ago. In a given quarter, Frito Lay might contribute as much as 71 percent of PepsiCo's total profit. While there is much synergy between soft drinks and snacks, PepsiCo's bottom line suffered for many years because it had also gotten into the fast-food business, acquiring Pizza Hut, Taco Bell, and KFC. Net margins on these businesses were typically much lower than on Pepsi's sales of goods to supermarkets.

PepsiCo began its remake in 1996 under the leadership of CEO Roger Enrico, when it spun off the restaurant operations. Its next big move was to acquire Tropicana orange juice for $3.3 billion. Still searching for operations that would enhance its supermarket sales, it purchased the Quaker Oats Company in 2001 (Aunt Jemima, Cap'n Crunch, Gatorade). Another important acquisition was Sobe beverages. PepsiCo also sells Aquafina bottled water, Dole juices, Lipton ready-to-drink tea, and Rold Gold Pretzels. With this array of products, it now ranks second only to Kraft Foods (now part of Phillip Morris) as a source of U.S. supermarket sales.

By tightly focusing its efforts on sales through supermarkets and spinning off its sluggish restaurant business, PepsiCo succeeded in increasing both its margin on sales and its bottom-line profit. (The bottom-line was also enhanced by the new restaurant company relieving the old PepsiCo of significant debt.) PepsiCo maintained both its growth and its earnings during the 2001 recession and weathered the stock market decline of mid-2002 quite well. Interestingly enough, the restaurant spinoff also did well, perhaps because the management there could concentrate its efforts on just that sector of the business. In 2002, the spinoff changed its name from Tricon Global to YUM Brands, and acquired both the Long John Silver's and A&W fast food chains.

References: "PepsiCo Announces Double-Digit Growth for First Quarter of 2002," *TinyTalksVending.com,* online, April 26, 2002, www.tinytalksvending.com/news/pepsi2.htm, July 17, 2002 "PepsiCo," *Vending Times* online, April 25, 2002-May 24, 2002, vendingtimes.com/ws/2002_04_vic_pepsi.htm, Vol. 42, No. 4), July 17, 2002; "The Top 25 Managers," *Business Week Online,* January 8, 2001, www.businessweek.com, July 17, 2002; and John A. Byrne, "How Roger Enrico Is Remaking the Company … PEPSICO," *Business Week* (April 10, 2000), pp. 172–180.

BREAKEVEN ANALYSIS

Breakeven analysis is in some respects a simplification of profit-maximization analysis. In a typical breakeven problem, a constant price, a constant average variable cost, and a specific level of fixed costs are assumed; and the resulting level of output (or sales) necessary for the firm to cover its total costs (to break even) is then calculated. Alternatively, the firm may wish to determine the level of output required to cover its total costs and achieve a target level of income. With these assumptions we can derive the formula for breakeven output quite easily.

To break even, a firm's revenue must equal its costs, or

(7-1)
$$TR = TC = TVC + TFC.$$

We can write total revenue as price times quantity $(P \times Q)$ and total variable cost as average variable cost times quantity $(AVC \times Q)$, so that equation 7-1 becomes

(7-2)
$$P(Q) = AVC(Q) + TFC.$$

If we subtract $AVC \times Q$ from both sides of equation 7-2, we obtain

(7-3)
$$P(Q) - (AVC)(Q) = (P - AVC)(Q) = TFC.$$

Dividing both sides of equation 7-3 by $(P - AVC)$, we get the formula for breakeven point quantity, which is

(7-4)
$$Q_{BEP} = \frac{TFC}{P - AVC}.$$

The term $(P - AVC)$ is called the *unit contribution margin* because it indicates the contribution that each unit sold will make toward covering fixed cost and, eventually, generating profit.

To see how breakeven analysis is used, assume that the Magic S (for "magic sandwich") is a fast-food restaurant that specializes in submarine sandwiches. The Magic S has fixed costs per month of $60,000. Most of the revenue for this firm is derived from its featured meal: a hot submarine sandwich, small drink, and french fries for $6.00. The average variable cost of the meal is approximately constant at $3.60 over the relevant range of production. To find out how many of the specials the Magic S must sell per month to break even, we substitute these figures into equation 7-4 and obtain

$$Q_{BEP} = \frac{\$60,000}{\$6.00 - \$3.60} = 25,000 \text{ specials.}$$

Moreover, we could find out how many specials the Magic S would have to sell to make a target income of, say, $24,000 per month by substituting fixed costs plus $24,000 in place of only fixed costs and obtain

$$Q = \frac{\$84,000}{\$2.40} = 35,000 \text{ specials.}$$

The assumptions of a constant price and constant unit variable cost enable us to graph the total revenue and total variable cost curves for the Magic S as straight lines, and we obtain a graphical solution for the

FIGURE 7–4

Breakeven Quantity for the Magic S

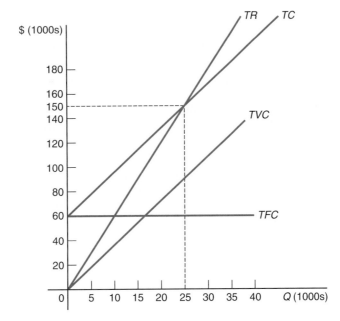

Total cost (*TC*) is equal to *TVC* + *TFC*. The breakeven level of output occurs where total revenue (*TR*) = *TC*, at an output level of 25,000 specials per month.

breakeven quantity for the Magic S, as shown in Figure 7-4. The breakeven point is, of course, where the total revenue curve cuts and rises above the total cost curve. We can translate breakeven quantity to breakeven dollar sales merely by multiplying breakeven point quantity by price. For the Magic S, breakeven point dollar sales are 25,000 × $6.00 = $150,000.

Moreover, if we multiply both sides of our breakeven point quantity formula (equation 7-4) by price, we can derive the breakeven dollar sales formula, which is

$$P(Q_{BEP}) = \frac{P(TFC)}{(P - AVC)} = \frac{TFC}{[1 - (AVC / P)]} = \frac{TFC}{\text{contribution margin ratio}}.$$

Note that [1 − (*AVC/P*)] is called the *contribution margin ratio*, since this term is the ratio of the unit contribution margin to price. The contribution margin ratio indicates the fraction of the price of each unit sold that contributes to covering fixed cost and, eventually, generating a profit. Breakeven dollar sales could thus be found graphically by using dollar sales, rather than units sold, along the horizontal axis.

Firms often use breakeven analysis to determine expected profits under several different, but presumably feasible, alternatives being considered—with various prices, for instance, or different unit variable costs, different fixed costs, or some combination of those possibilities. For example, suppose a company that manufactures small electric motors has current plant capacity of 1 million motors per year. Unit variable costs associated with this plant are $10, and fixed costs are $1 million. The current capacity number of motors can be sold for $20 each. The firm is considering expanding and modernizing its plant facilities so that the current capacity will be doubled. Under this proposal, unit variable costs would be expected to decrease to $5, and fixed costs would be expected to increase to $2 million. The firm estimates that it could sell 1.5 million motors at a price of $15.

Two things in which the motor company would be vitally interested are the quantities required to break even for both the present plant and the proposed plant and the expected profits from each plant. Breakeven points for the two plants are found as follows:

$$\text{Present plant: } Q_{BEP} = \frac{\$1,000,000}{10} = 100,000 \text{ motors;}$$

$$\text{Proposed plant: } Q_{BEP} = \frac{\$2,000,000}{10} = 200,000 \text{ motors.}$$

The expected profits from each plant would be the following:

Present Plant

Quantity Sold:	1,000,000	
Price: $20		
Total Revenue:		$20,000,000
Less:		
Total Variable Costs:		10,000,000
		$10,000,000
Less Fixed Costs		1,000,000
Net Income Before Taxes		9,000,000

Proposed Plant

Expected Quantity Sold:	1,500,000	
Price: $15		
Total Revenue:		$22,500,000
Less:		
Total Variable Costs:		7,500,000
		$15,000,000
Less Fixed Costs		2,000,000
Expected Net Income Before Taxes		$13,000,000

Thus, our data indicate that the expected profits would be greater with the larger plant. Nevertheless, before it makes a final decision on so significant a matter, the firm might want to consider expected profits with an intermediate-sized plant. It might also want to consider expected profits from using different prices with each sized plant. Furthermore, the risk associated with each plant should be taken into account (see Chapter 14).

A person considering starting a new enterprise could also find breakeven analysis a useful tool in obtaining a rough estimate as to whether or not the business could reasonably be expected to be successful under any of several proposed plans.[11] For example, suppose that our Magic S sandwich place has not yet been built and that the prospective owners believe that they cannot expect to sell 25,000 submarine specials per month. The prospective owners could, among other things, consider the feasibility of lowering fixed costs by building a smaller establishment or of increasing demand by offering a greater variety of sandwiches. They could also consider increasing quantity demanded by lowering price.

PROFIT MAXIMIZATION VERSUS BREAKEVEN ANALYSIS

Breakeven analysis in its most sophisticated usage is a simplified approximation to profit maximization. In traditional profit-maximization analysis, the firm presumably knows its revenue and cost functions and chooses to produce at the level of output and charge the price that will maximize profits (where marginal revenue equals marginal cost). Price and average variable cost are *not* required to be constant.

On the other hand, when it uses breakeven analysis, a firm *usually assumes* a constant price and a constant average variable cost in the relevant range of production and recognizes explicitly or implicitly a capacity limitation. The firm then solves for the quantity of sales necessary to break even or to achieve some target level of income.[12]

The firm may use breakeven-type analysis to reach a fairly close approximation to profit maximization by considering expected profits under a variety of alternatives. Such alternatives would include various prices, different-sized plants, and different levels of advertising expenditures. However, if the firm has enough information regarding the preceding variables to approximate the results achieved using profit-maximization analysis, it

---

[11] For example, see "Tigers, A Volcano, Dolphins, and Steve Wynn," *Business Week* (November 20, 1989), pp. 70–71; and "Vacancy Signs Are Lit, But More New Hotels Are on the Way," *Business Week* (March 17, 1986), pp. 78–79.

[12] It is possible to use nonlinear total revenue and cost functions (price and average variable cost are not constant) in breakeven analysis. However, this approach is not used frequently.

would most likely be easier for the firm to construct total revenue and total cost functions corresponding to its best information and to produce where marginal revenue equals marginal cost (and marginal revenue is falling below marginal cost).

Breakeven analysis offers some advantage over traditional profit-maximization analysis when the information available to the firm regarding its future costs and revenues is seriously limited, and a rough approximation to profit maximization is the best that the firm owner may reasonably expect to accomplish. If more detailed information is available, then profit maximization is more efficient.

INCREMENTAL PROFIT ANALYSIS

Incremental profit is equal to incremental revenue less incremental cost resulting from a specific change in the activity of a firm.

Incremental profit analysis is simply a variation of traditional profit maximization and represents a quite useful way of thinking about a current or prospective sales order, change in equipment, or other activity of the firm. All that is required for incremental profit analysis is that the firm ask itself whether the sales order, equipment change, or other activity contributes (or will contribute) more to total revenue than to total cost—that is, whether its contribution to the total profit of the firm will be *positive*. When the firm considers whether or not the incremental profit is positive, it should ignore all revenue that will be obtained and all costs that will be incurred by the firm regardless of the decision it makes on the matter under consideration. In other words, it merely considers the **incremental revenue** and *incremental cost* pertaining to the activity being considered.

Incremental revenue is the additional revenue that a firm will receive by undertaking a particular project.

When examining the incremental costs associated with a particular undertaking, a firm usually must distinguish between direct and indirect costs. *Direct costs* associated with a particular product or activity are costs that can be obviously and physically identified with that product or activity. *Indirect costs*, while they may be associated with a product or activity, generally must be allocated on some basis, since the precise amount required for (or associated with) each line of endeavor is less clear. For example, the cost of materials or intermediate products that physically make up a final product is a direct cost. The cost of the labor required to process and/or assemble these materials is also a direct cost. On the other hand, the cost of warehouse storage space that is shared by several products is an indirect cost. Direct costs associated with an activity will be incremental costs, while indirect costs frequently will not.

The use of incremental profit analysis can be illustrated with the example of a retail firm that sells three brands of appliances—Brand *X*, Brand *Y*, and Brand *Z*. Table 7-4 shows total revenue, total direct costs, and total indirect costs attributed to each product line. In this case, indirect costs are assigned to each product line according to the proportion that total revenue from each line's sale is of the total revenue of the firm.

Table 7-4 *Revenue and Costs for an Appliance Store*

	Brand X	Brand Y	Brand Z
Total Revenue	$150,000	$100,000	$50,000
Total Direct Costs	60,000	50,000	35,000
Total Indirect Costs	60,000	40,000	20,000
Net Income (loss)	$ 30,000	$ 10,000	$(5,000)

After a quick glance at Table 7-4, it appears that Brand Z is subtracting from the total profits of the firm by the amount of the net loss attributed to it ($5,000). However, a more in-depth analysis is required before that conclusion can be justified. This analysis should include answers to such questions as how much, if any, will indirect costs be lowered if the firm no longer carries Brand Z? Is there another, more profitable, brand of merchandise that the firm could carry rather than Brand Z? For example, if the indirect costs will be unchanged if the firm no longer carries Brand Z (or a third product line) and if the firm has no more profitable brands that it can sell in place of Brand Z, then total profits of the firm would actually be *reduced* by $15,000 if the firm were to drop Brand Z! Let's see why this is so. If the $20,000 of indirect costs assigned to Brand Z would be incurred even if the firm did not

NUMERICAL EXAMPLE

Incremental Profit Analysis

Ventana Corporation makes upmarket 3-D accelerated video cards for personal computers. The cards are sold to computer assemblers and wholesale vendors who buy 50 to 100 cards at a time. Currently, the cards are priced at $150 each, and sales are 4,000 cards per month. Ventana has been approached by a midsized personal computer manufacturer located in Mexico to supply 1,500 cards per month for a two-year period. The price this buyer is willing to pay is 1,400 Mexican pesos per card. The peso has been relatively stable at 10 pesos per U.S. dollar. Because it has some old, high-interest debt it wishes to pay off, Ventana's management does not wish to expand capacity beyond the current 4,000 cards per month. Savings that would accrue to Ventana by taking the proposed deal are related to packaging, distribution, and advertising costs. Specifically, it is estimated that the company's advertising budget could be reduced by $15,000 per year if the deal is accepted. In addition, packaging and distribution costs would fall by $2.50 per unit on the cards sold to the computer manufacturer. Ventana could also lay off two sales representatives who now receive $24,000 per year plus 10 percent commission on the cards they sell.

(continues)

NUMERICAL EXAMPLE *(continued)*

Using incremental profit analysis, determine:

1. The incremental changes in total revenue and total cost that would occur if Ventana accepts the deal.
2. The price of cards that would be acceptable to Ventana, assuming management would only commit 1,500 units of output to a single buyer for an incremental profit of at least $270,000 per year, which is $22,500 per month.

Also identify specific factors related to the international nature of the transaction that Ventana's management would have to take into consideration in making its decision.

Solution

1. In U.S. dollars, the Mexican firm is offering only $1,400/10 = \$140$ for the cards. Therefore, total monthly revenue will change by $\Delta TR = \Delta P \times 1,500 = -10\,(1,500) = -\$15,000$. Total monthly cost will change in a number of ways. First, monthly advertising cost will change by $-\$15,000/12 = -\$1,250$. There will be a change in monthly packaging and distribution cost of $-\$2.50(1,500)$, and the reduction in sales force will result in a cost change of $-\$48,000/12$ in salaries and $-0.10\,(1,500)\,(150)$ in commissions. Thus,

$$\Delta TC = -1,250 - 2.5(1,500) - 4,000 - 0.1(1,500)\,(150) = -\$31,500$$

and

$$\Delta T\pi = \Delta TR - \Delta TC = -15,000 - (-31,500) = \underline{\$16,500}.$$

The incremental profit is positive and equals $16,500 per month.

2. The difference between the required incremental profit of $22,500 per month and the estimated amount of $16,500 per month tells how much monthly TR would have to increase. Since $TR/Q = P$, it follows that $\Delta TR/Q = \Delta P$. Thus,

$$\Delta P = (22,500 - 16,500)/Q = 6,000/1,500 = \$4.00.$$

Therefore, the price would have to be $140 + \$4.00 = \underline{\$144.00}$.

Given that the buyer quoted the price in Mexican pesos, Ventana would need to assess its foreign exchange risk. If the peso depreciates, 1,400 pesos will no longer equal $140 (nor will the required price of $144 in part 2 be 144 (10) = 1,440 pesos). It would be advisable for Ventana to insist on payment in dollars and require a letter of credit from a U.S. bank (generally, an irrevocable document backed by the issuing bank) for each shipment. Also, the overall solvency of the foreign buyer will be important, since any contract with it will have international legal ramifications and may be difficult to enforce.

MANAGERIAL PERSPECTIVE

Earnings, Cash Flow, EVA, and "Creative Accounting"

Although in this chapter profit has been treated as a number simply obtained by subtracting total cost from total revenue, in the world of corporate accounting, earnings and other performance measures are much more complex. With the Enron and Worldcom debacles of 2001 and 2002, and myriad other scandals related to whether one or another firm really, really had earnings, investors and government regulators searched for concepts to insure that firms' reports reflected their actual financial condition. One accounting firm, Arthur Andersen, was tried and convicted of fraudulent practices for engaging in accounting creativity that pumped up Enron's earnings and artificially inflated its share value. "Earnings, Schmernings—Look at the Cash," a *Business Week* writer said many years ago. Accounting net income reflects total sales less total accounting costs. However, the cash flow to the firm may be something entirely different in any accounting period.

The cash flow of a firm is its net cash receipts over the period. The cash flow of a firm will be *affected* by the net income of a firm, but the two figures are typically not equal to one another. For one thing, most firms allow some customers to purchase their goods on credit. As a result, the total dollar sales of the firm for a particular period, say a month, and the cash collected by the firm from those sales may be quite different. The credit sales may merely be reflected by an increase in accounts receivable. On the other hand, the firm may have some cash receipts from collections of accounts receivable from sales in prior months. The firm, in turn, may purchase some inputs on credit; thus, the variable input costs for the period may not always be immediately reflected in cash outflows. Alternatively, the firm may have to pay the entire purchase price for a new machine at the time it is acquired,

and a cash outflow equal to the entire amount spent for the machine will be incurred immediately. The entire amount paid for the machine will not be reflected as a cost in the firm's income statement for the period, however; it will be written off as depreciation over a period of time that reflects the expected life of the machine. Thus, in those later periods depreciation will be a cost item that does not represent a cash outflow. On the other hand, debt payments (not including interest payments) represent outflows of cash that are not costs, although they may very well be related to costs incurred in the past.

One category of cash flow is perhaps most important for the firm's viability: the *free* cash flow is what remains after essential capital expenditures have been made and dividends have been paid. A firm with free cash flow can decide to pay additional dividends, pay off debt, make new investments, or buy back shares, among other things. Because a firm with free cash flow can develop a cushion of cash assets as a reserve against a temporary decline in sales, it is less vulnerable to the movements of the business cycle. Firms that have no free cash flow may not be able to make principal and interest payments on their debt during periods of temporary declines in sales; thus, they may find their very existence in jeopardy.

Now comes economic value added (EVA), one of the newest indicators of a firm's progress. Simply put, EVA is net operating income minus an appropriate capital charge for the opportunity cost of all assets used to produce that profit. A positive EVA adds to the value of the firm. However, since EVA is related to net operating income, over-

(continues)

statement of the latter will also overstate EVA. Looking at both cash flow and EVA, in addition to a firm's stated net income, certainly gives investors more information about the firm's operations and its value. However, many of the same accounting concepts that are behind the income statement also affect both cash flow and EVA. Thus, creative accounting can also apply to them. In July 2002, Federal Reserve chairman Alan Greenspan went before Congress to speak about the economy and the crisis of confidence attributed to the Enron and Worldcom cases. "I don't think you can legislate morality," he said. But he did hold out hope that some changes in accounting standards could

make it more difficult to manipulate earnings reports. When asked whether he thought that other U.S. corporations would revise their earnings, he answered yes, and added "and I agree with you that the number that are going to be restated *up* won't take very long to read."

References: Jeanne Aversa, "Greenspan Opposes CEOs Having to Verify Statements," *San Antonio Express-News,* July 16, 2002, p. 3E; Anne Tergesen, "Cash Flow Hocus Pocus," *Business Week* (July 15, 2002), pp. 130, 132; "This Economy Has Fuel Injection," *Business Week* (August 2, 1999), pp. 28–29; "What Do Shareholders Want?" *Accountancy* 115, No. 2 (May 1995), p. 44; and "Earnings, Schmernings—Look at the Cash," *Business Week* (July 24, 1989), pp. 56, 57.

carry a third brand of appliance, then the sale of Brand Z *does contribute* $15,000 toward covering those costs.

Nevertheless, the firm should be careful to consider its alternatives in both the long run and the short run. In the long run, it may be possible for the firm to eliminate the $20,000 of indirect costs if the firm does not sell a third brand of appliance. It may also be possible to become a dealer in a more profitable third brand. Moreover, dropping Brand Z may increase the revenue from sales of Brand X and Brand Y. Thus, the firm must consider how its decision about Brand Z will affect both long-run and short-run revenue and cost. Still, all of these deliberations are merely utilizing a version of the profit-maximization rule, which states that the firm should continue to produce as long as marginal revenue is greater than marginal cost and should not produce when marginal revenue is less than marginal cost.

Continental Airlines made explicit use of incremental profit analysis in adjusting certain parts of its fare structure in 1982.[13] There is also evidence that restaurants use incremental profit analysis when determining their price structure.[14]

---

[13] "Most Big Airlines Cut Intercontinental Fares," *San Antonio Express,* February 10, 1982, p. 1B.
[14] See "With Liquor Sales Slipping, Restaurants Try Fancier Desserts and Higher Prices," *Wall Street Journal,* June 14, 1985, p. 23.

SUMMARY

Profit Maximization and the Real World

We have assumed that the goal of the firm is to maximize its profits. Accordingly, in this chapter we have developed a decision criterion that, when followed, will ensure profit maximization. That criterion is to *produce up to the point where marginal revenue equals marginal cost, subject to the conditions that marginal revenue is less than marginal cost at higher levels of output and that price is at least as great as average variable cost.* If price is less than average variable cost, the firm should at least temporarily shut down.

In reality, a firm manager does not always have precise information regarding the firm's costs and revenue, and obtaining such information may be costly. In this situation, a firm manager often uses breakeven analysis to determine what level of output is necessary for the firm to break even or to achieve a target level of income. When using this type of analysis, the firm manager assumes that price and average variable cost are constant, a simplification that is *not* necessary with traditional profit maximization techniques. In these circumstances, the formula for breakeven output is

$$Q_{BEP} = \frac{TFC}{P - AVC}.$$

The manager may use breakeven analysis to determine the approximate profit-maximizing price and level of output by considering expected profits under a variety of alternatives (such as various prices, different plant sizes, and different levels of advertising expenditures).

Breakeven analysis offers some advantages over traditional profit maximization analysis only when the information available to the firm manager regarding the firm's costs and revenues is quite limited and a rough approximation to profit maximization is the best that can be expected. Still, the firm manager may find that the firm falls far short of profit maximization unless some reliable estimates of its revenue and costs relative to the level of output can be obtained. The wise firm manager, therefore, must attempt to gain such information about its costs and the demand for its product up to the point where the expected cost of obtaining additional information is greater than the expected benefits of such information. (Some techniques of demand estimation were discussed in Chapter 3, and cost estimation techniques were briefly summarized in Chapter 6.)

Finally, we discussed *incremental profit analysis*—a variation of traditional profit maximization analysis that is useful to the firm manager when he or she is analyzing such problems as accepting an additional sales order, trading in a piece of equipment, adding or dropping a product line, or similar alternatives. We stated that the profit-oriented manager should undertake an activity as long as its *incremental revenue less incremental cost* (its *incremental profit*) is greater than zero.

In the appendix, we will discuss linear programming—a profit-maximization technique the firm can use when its revenue and cost functions and any other constraining functions are linear.

QUESTIONS

1. What do we mean when we say that the goal of a firm is profit maximization?
2. Is the assumption of profit maximization a realistic goal? Why or why not?
3. Compare breakeven analysis and (the more traditional) profit maximization. How are they alike? How are they different?
4. What is incremental profit analysis? Give several examples of situations in which it would be useful.

PROBLEMS

1. Complete the following cost and revenue table and indicate the profit-maximizing output and price.

Q	Arc MR	TR	P	Arc MC	AFC	AVC	SAC	TC
0			21		—	—	—	
	20			25				
1					28			
	18			15				
2								
	16			11				
3								
	14			5				
4								
	12			4				
5								
	8			6				
6								
	6			11				
7								
	4			19				
8								

2. Penny Car Rental has fixed costs per month of $300,000 and variable costs per car rented per day of $6. If Penny charges $30 per day to rent a car, how many car-rental days (the number of cars rented times the number of days each is rented) must Penny have each month to break even? to make $60,000 before taxes?

3. Complete the following cost and revenue data and find the profit-maximizing price and output.

Q	P	TR	Arc MR	Arc MC	TFC	AVC	Arc Mπ
0	$5.00	0				—	
			$4.90	$3.00			$1.90
10		49					
				1.00			
20		96			60		
				1.00			
30		135					
				.50			
40		160					
				1.00			
50		175					
				1.50			
60		180					
				2.00			
70		175					
				3.00			
80		144					
				4.50			
90		90					
				7.00			
100		10					

4. A firm making sofas has the following income data for one week:

Sales (50 sofas at $1,000)		$50,000
Less cost of goods sold:		
Variable manufacturing costs	$20,000	
Fixed manufacturing costs	5,000	25,000
Gross margin		$25,000
Less selling and administrative expenses:		
Variable	$10,000	
Fixed	5,000	15,000
Net income		$10,000

a. Find the firm's breakeven quantity.

b. Find the firm's new breakeven output if it builds a new plant that will raise fixed manufacturing costs to $10,000 but decreases variable manufacturing cost to $300 per unit. Assume average variable selling expenses, fixed selling expenses, and selling price remain the same.

5. In the following table, complete the cost and revenue data for a particular model of side-by-side refrigerator-freezer sold in a department store. What is the profit-maximizing price and output?

P	Q	TR	Arc MR	Arc MC	AFC	TVC	TC	Arc Mπ
900	0				—			
				500				
875	10							
				400				
850	20							
				350				
800	30							
				300				
750	40				150			
				250				
675	50							
				200				
600	60							
				180				
500	70							
				200				
400	80							
				300				
200	90							

6. For the month of October, the Crossroads Diner had the income situation shown in the table.

Crossroads Diner
Income Statement for Month Ended October 1991

Gross sales (10,000 meals @ average price of $6.00)		$60,000
Less cost of goods sold:		
Cooks	$ 9,000	
Servers, etc.	9,500	
Food	21,000	
Utilities (prorated—food service)	900	
Depreciation (prorated—kitchen, dining area, and equipment)	4,500	44,900
Gross margin		$15,100
Less administrative and selling expenses:		
Monthly advertising expense	$ 6,900	
Transportation expense	1,500	
Office salaries and supplies	3,000	
Utilities (prorated—office)	600	
Depreciation (prorated—office)	600	12,600
Operating income		$ 2,500
Less interest expense		6,000
Net income (loss)		($ 3,500)

a. Compute the number of meals that the diner would have to sell monthly to break even. You may assume in this part that average variable costs and average revenue per meal are constant. *Do state whether and why you classify each cost item (or some portion thereof) as variable or fixed.*

  b. What implicit costs do you think would have been incurred by the owners of the Crossroads Diner but are not presented in the (accounting) income statement?

  c. As the economic consultant for the Crossroads' owners, what suggestions can you make to help them improve their income from the diner? *Tell why you* think each of your suggestions will be helpful.

7. The next table gives monthly sales and cost data for a bicycle manufacturer.

  a. Complete the table.

  b. What is the profit-maximizing price and level of output for the firm? Why?

Price	Quantity	Total Revenue	Marginal Revenue	Marginal Cost	TVC	AFC	Marginal Profit
$200	0				$0	—	
190	1,000				150,000		
	2,000	360,000			290,000	6.00	
170	3,000				420,000		
160	4,000				540,000		
150	5,000			100			
140	6,000			80			
130	7,000			75			
120	8,000			80			
	9,000		30	100			
	10,000		10		1,095,000		
90	11,000				1,235,000		

8. The following annual income statement is for Alamo Chemical Company, which produces slug and snail bait. Of the $300,000 advertising expense, $250,000 is variable, and all but $100,000 of the travel expense is variable. Alamo considers $50,000 of the office salaries to be variable.

Sales (1,000,000 two-pound bags @ $5)		$5,000,000
Less cost of goods sold:		
Direct labor	$700,000	
Direct materials	350,000	
Variable overhead	150,000	
Fixed overhead	600,000	1,800,000
Gross margin		$3,200,000
Less administrative and selling expenses:		
Sales commissions (@ $.50 per bag)	$500,000	
Travel expenses	600,000	
Advertising expense	300,000	
Office supplies	10,000	
Office salaries	90,000	1,500,000
Net operating income		$1,700,000
Less interest expense		500,000
Net income before taxes		$1,200,000

a. Find the breakeven quantity for Alamo Chemical.

b. Alamo is considering installing some new machinery that would raise its fixed manufacturing costs to $1,000,000. This machinery would lower the direct labor cost to $0.15 per bag and double the firm's capacity to 2,000,000 bags. (Presently, the firm is operating at capacity.) Interest expense would also increase to $1,000,000. *The firm believes it can sell to the new capacity level if it lowers price to $4.50 per bag.* Other average variable costs and fixed costs would not change.

   Do you recommend that Alamo install the new machinery? Why or why not? What will be its expected new level of net income before taxes if the machinery is installed and the price is lowered to $4.50?

9. Mueller Brewery manufactures a full-flavored, dark German beer. Shown in this problem is Mueller's income statement for a month earlier this year.

Sales (100,000 cases @ $7 per case)		$700,000
Less cost of goods sold:		
Direct materials (nonreturn bottles)	$195,000	
Direct labor	210,000	
Fixed manufacturing expenses	50,000	455,000
Gross margin		$245,000
Less administrative and selling expenses:		
Delivery expenses	$ 30,000	
Sales commissions	50,000	
Advertising expenses	10,000	
Travel expenses	5,000	
Fixed administrative and selling expenses	10,000	105,000
Net income before taxes		$140,000

a. Find the number of cases of beer Mueller's must sell per month to break even.

b. Mueller expects to sell, on the average, 100,000 cases per month for the rest of the year. Its capacity is 120,000 cases per month. Because of a strike by brewery workers in a foreign country that usually does not import Mueller's beer, a major hotel chain in that country has made an all-or-nothing offer to import 40,000 cases per month for the next three months at a price of $5.75 per case. Mueller's can supply from inventory only 30,000 of the total additional cases required for the three-month period because it did not anticipate receiving such an order. There will be no delivery expense, sales commissions, travel expense, or advertising expense connected with this order. Should Mueller agree to supply the hotel chain with the beer? *Why* or *why not?*

10. Kokkakola Company, a firm located in Algeria, produces a popular soft drink normally sold in single-serving cans. Because of government price controls, it knows that the wholesale price it can charge for the drink is 80 dinars per can. Its market studies show there is nothing to be gained by charging less. If Kokkakola's total cost function per month in dinars is

$$TC = 8{,}000{,}000 + 20Q + 0.0001Q^2,$$

and its marginal cost therefore is

$$MC = 20 + 0.0002Q,$$

determine

a. how many cans of the drink it should sell and

b. how much its total monthly profit will be.

11. A firm estimates the following demand information for daily sales of its product, where Q is the quantity sold and P is the price:

$$Q = 136 - 0.4P$$
$$P = 340 - 2.5Q$$
$$MR = 340 - 5Q$$

a. If its marginal cost is described by the function

$$MC = 40 - 10Q + Q^2,$$

what will be its profit-maximizing output and price?

b. Suppose the total cost function from which the above marginal cost was derived is

$$TC = 3{,}000 + 40Q - 5Q^2 + (1/3)\,Q^3,$$

and determine how much profit the firm will have per day.

12. Squiggly Wiggly Corporation sells fishing worms in the wholesale market. The company has monthly fixed costs of $1,960, and it sells worms for $5.00 per gallon.

   a. If its *AVC* is constant at $2.20 per gallon of worms, how many gallons will it have to sell in order to break even?

   b. Suppose Squiggly Wiggly desires to have an economic profit of $12,000. If the preceding costs are the total economic costs of the firm, what monthly quantity of worm sales will yield the desired profit? (Round to nearest gallon.)

13. Omygosh Corporation has estimated the following average and marginal revenue equations for its product:

$$AR = 370 - Q$$

$$MR = 370 - 2Q.$$

The company's cost analysts say that total cost can be approximated by the equation $STC = 10,500 + 10Q + Q^2$ and that, therefore, its short-run marginal cost is $SMC = 10 + 2Q$. Determine the firm's profit-maximizing output, the price it should charge, and the amount of its total profit.

The following problems require calculus.

C1. A firm has the following total revenue and total cost functions:

$$TR = 21Q - Q^2$$

$$TC = (1/3)Q^3 - 3Q^2 + 9Q + 6$$

   a. At what level of output does the firm maximize *total revenue?*

   b. At what level of output does the firm maximize *total profit?*

   c. How much is the firm's total profit at its maximum?

C2. Find the maximum profit for a firm if its total revenue function is $TR = 50Q - Q^2$ and its total cost function is $TC = 100 - 4Q + 2Q^2$.

C3. Suppose a firm's estimated demand curve has the equation

$$Q = 220 - P,$$

and its total cost function is

$$TC = 1,000 + 80Q - 3Q^2 + (1/3)Q^3.$$

   a. Write an equation for the firm's total revenue function.

   b. Determine the *output* level and *price* that will maximize profit (or minimize short-run loss) for the firm.

   c. Calculate the firm's economic profit or loss at the optimum point.

C4. Suppose a firm has the following short-run total cost function:

$$STC = 4{,}850 + 40Q - 1.5Q^2 + 0.04Q^3,$$

where Q is output, and the constant in the equation represents total fixed cost. Answer the following:

a. What is the dollar value of average fixed cost at an output of 25 units?

b. At what level of output will marginal cost be at a minimum?

c. At what level of output will AVC be at a minimum?

d. If the firm has a fixed product price of $190 per unit, at what level of output will it choose to operate, and what will be its economic profit or loss?

C5. Traumco sells a specialized medical monitoring device. It estimates the monthly quantity demanded to be represented by the equation

$$Q = 350 - 0.25P, \text{ where } P \text{ is price.}$$

Its monthly cost function is

$$STC = 20{,}000 + 200Q - 9Q^2 + (1/3)\,Q^3.$$

Determine the profit-maximizing quantity sold and price for the monitor. How much will the maximum monthly profit be?

C6. Suppose that for a given time period a firm faces the following demand curve:

$$Q = 75 - 0.5P$$

If its total cost function for the same period is:

$$STC = 500 + 30Q - 3Q^2 + 1/3Q^3$$

a. Write the MR equation for the firm.

b. Find:

   i. The sales quantity that will maximize its profit.

   ii. The price it should charge if profit is maximized.

   iii. The dollar value of its total profit at the maximum.

C7. Maurice's makes and sells dog collars studded with genuine semiprecious stones. Based on data collected over a 36-week period, Maurice has estimated that in his area the demand function for such collars is given by the equation

$$Q_c = 50 - 2P_c + 0.1F + 0.002I - 0.01K,$$

where Q_c = number of collars sold per week

      P_c = price per collar

      F = number of resident french poodles in area = 2,000

      I = average annual income of dog owners in area = $90,000

      K = number of resident cats in area = 15,000.

Maurice estimates that his variable cost for the collars is

$$TVC = 20Q_c + 1.5Q_c^2$$

How many collars should maurice plan to sell per week? What price should he charge, and what will be the total profit contribution from the sales of the collars?

Problems C8 and C9 require both partial differentiation and constrained maximization. They should be attempted only if you have covered the material in the appendix that follows Chapter 5.

C8. Lone Star Instruments, Inc. (LSI), makes two deluxe printing models of calculators—a scientific model and a business and financial model. The demand function for the scientific model is

$$Q_S = 20{,}000 - 100P_S,$$

where

Q_S = annual quantity demanded of the scientific model,

and

P_S = price of the scientific model.

The demand function for the business and financial model is

$$Q_B = 50{,}000 - 400P_B,$$

where

Q_B = annual quantity demanded of the business and financial model,

and

P_B = price of the business and financial model.

The total cost function for LSI is given by

$$STC = \$100{,}000 + 25Q,$$

where

$$Q = Q_S + Q_B.$$

LSI also has a capacity limitation of 17,500 calculators per year.

a. Find the profit-maximizing quantity and price for each model of calculator.

b. Solve for the Lagrangian multiplier. What does its value tell you?

C9. Stanislaw's Ping-Pong Emporium sells two types of memberships. One is the individual membership *(I)*, which allows unlimited use of facilities for one person. The second type of membership is the corporate membership *(C)*, which allows the member and his/her family to use the facilities with some restrictions. Stan believes he has 500 units of membership capacity and that an individual membership will use up one unit of capacity, while a corporate membership will use up 1.5 units of capacity because of the added load from family members.

Stan's monthly total profit function is as follows, where *C* is the number of corporate memberships sold and *I* is the number of individual memberships sold.

$$T\pi = 52C - 0.06C^2 + 70I - 0.1I^2 + 0.01CI - 8,000$$

a. Subject to the capacity constraint, what combination of the two types of memberships will maximize Stan's profit? (Solve by the Lagrangian method.)

b. How much will Stan's maximum monthly profit be?

c. Would Stan be wise to consider expanding his capacity? Explain, relating your answer to the Lagrangian multiplier, lambda.

SELECTED REFERENCES

"Airline Takes the Marginal Route." *Business Week* (April 20, 1963), pp. 111–114.

Cyert, R. M., and C. L. Hedrick. "Theory of the Firm: Past, Present, and Future: An Interpretation." *Journal of Economic Literature* 10, No. 2 (June 1972): 389–412.

Dean, Joel. "Measuring Profits for Executive Decisions." *Accounting Review* (April 1951).

Denzau, Arthur. *Microeconomic Analysis: Markets and Dynamics.* Homewood, IL: Richard D. Irwin, 1992, Chapters 17 and 26.

Eaton, B. Curtis, and Diane F. Eaton. *Microeconomics.* Englewood Cliffs, NJ: Prentice-Hall, 1995, Chapters 9 and 10.

Enke, Stephen. "On Maximizing Profits: A Distinction Between Chamberlin and Robinson." *American Economic Review* 41 (September 1951): 566–578.

Landsburg, Stephen E. *Price Theory and Applications,* 4th ed. Cincinnati: South-Western, 1999, Chapter 5.

Nicholson, Walter. *Microeconomic Theory: Basic Principles and Extensions,* 5th ed. Cincinnati: South-Western, 2002, Chapter 13.

Pindyck, Robert S., and Daniel L. Rubinfeld. *Microeconomics,* 5th ed. Upper Saddle River, NJ: Prentice Hall, 2001, Chapter 8.

Perloff, Jeffrey M. *Microeconomics,* 2d ed. Boston: Addison-Wesley Longman, 2001, Chapter 8.

Williamson, O. F. "The Modern Corporation: Origins, Evolution, Attributes." *Journal of Economic Literature* 19 (December 1981): 1537–1538.

Linear Programming and the Firm

In the preceding chapters, we have discussed optimizing decisions made by the firm regarding demand, production, cost, and profit-maximizing output and price, using techniques that depended on the mathematics of calculus. In this appendix we will discuss some of those decisions, using the tools of a different branch of mathematics—that of **linear programming**. Linear programming is a mathematical decision-making tool for optimization problems with a linear objective function and linear constraints that are in the form of inequalities.

Linear programming is a mathematical tool for solving maximization and minimization problems characterized by linear functions and constraints that can be stated as inequalities.

RELATIONSHIP BETWEEN LINEAR PROGRAMMING AND CALCULUS TECHNIQUES

As one should expect, since we are including a discussion of decision making using both tools in this book, calculus and linear programming *each* have areas of applicability where the other cannot be used. For example, linear programming can be used only when the relevant functions or relationships involved are linear.[1] This restriction means the cost, revenue, and total profit functions must all be graphed as straight lines as long as only one independent variable is involved. If there is more than one independent variable, no variable (X_i) must be raised to a power other than 1 or multiplied by any other variable. Thus all functions must be of the form

$$Y = a_0 + a_1X_1 + a_2X_2 + \ldots + a_nX_n,$$

where the a_i are constants. Linear programming techniques require constant returns to scale, constant marginal productivity of a variable input (if we are using short-run cost functions), constant input prices, and constant output prices.

Obviously, such requirements are not necessary for the application of calculus techniques, since many of the functions that we used in the production and cost chapters were *not* linear; and, indeed, over wide variations in levels of output, these relationships are probably nonlinear for most firms. However, as we indicated in our discussion of break-even analysis, over small variations in levels of production the assumption of linearity may be realistic.

On the other hand, linear programming can be used in situations where certain constraints or limitations faced by the firm can be expressed in terms of *inequalities*, whereas the traditional calculus techniques can be used only when these constraints can be expressed as *strict* equalities. Thus, for example, it is easy to see the usefulness of linear programming in a situation in which a firm has certain capacity limitations such that it may use either none of a particular input or various amounts of it up to some maximum amount available. A firm may wish to maximize short-run profit, subject to some minimum requirement on dollar sales. A manufacturing firm may wish to minimize the cost of producing a good, subject to certain minimum safety and/or quality requirements. Later in this appendix, we discuss a marketing problem that involves linear programming, and there are also many uses for linear programming in the area of finance. For example, a firm may wish to maximize the expected return on its investment portfolio, subject to certain minimum constraints on the amounts held of certain types of assets.

The use of linear programming (and calculus) by a firm implies, however, that fractional solution values for the decision variables at the optimal point are acceptable and that, if necessary, the decision maker can round to the profit-maximizing whole number. In cases where such an assumption is unwarranted, a more complex procedure—integer programming—may be necessary. This technique is beyond the scope of this book, but further reading may be done in sources listed at the end of this appendix.

---

1 There is a branch of mathematical programming—nonlinear programming—for which the linearity assumption is not required. However, that topic is too advanced for this book.

THE PRIMAL PROGRAM

Each linear programming problem has two programs: the *primal program* and the *dual program*. The primal program explicitly states the objective of the firm and its constraints and is, therefore, easier to understand. For this reason, we will begin with an example of a primal maximization program, leaving a discussion of the dual program for later.

Profit Maximization with Input Constraints

As we have already stated, frequently a firm wishes to maximize profit, but is constrained because there are maximum amounts available of certain inputs. For example, suppose a winery produces two products—white wine and champagne. In the short run, the firm has three capacity limitations: fermenting capacity, bottling capacity, and champagne purifying capacity. For those who are not familiar with the production processes involved in making champagne, we should explain that champagne requires a double fermentation. This double process is done so that the partially fermented grape juice, along with some grape pulp, is sealed in bottles and allowed to undergo further fermentation to acquire the bubbles and effervescence characteristic of champagne. The champagne mixture is then partially frozen so that the bubbles will not escape when the bottles are unsealed and the sediment is removed. By this means, the champagne is purified and then rebottled.

The maximum amount of initial fermenting capacity becoming available in casks is 600 units each week, the maximum amount of bottling capacity available per week is 500 units, and the maximum amount of champagne purifying capacity available each week is 150 units. Production of one bottle of champagne requires three units of fermenting capacity, two units of bottling capacity, and one unit of champagne purifying capacity. Production of one bottle of white wine requires only one unit of fermenting capacity and one unit of bottling capacity. These relationships are summarized in Table 7A–1.

Table 7A–1 *Input Requirements for Producing White Wine and Champagne*

Input	Units of Input Required per Bottle		Maximum Number of Units of Input Available
	Champagne	*White Wine*	
Fermentation	3	1	600
Bottling	2	1	500
Champagne Purifying	1	0	150

The Graphical Solution

In Figure 7A–1, we have graphed three straight lines indicating the *maximum* amounts of white wine and/or champagne the firm can produce, *given* the three input constraints. These three straight-line relationships were derived in the following manner from the information presented in Table 7A–1. First, consider the constraint on fermentation. If we were to express the information relevant to that constraint presented in the table as a mathematical relationship, we could state that three times the number of bottles of champagne produced plus one times the number of bottles of white wine produced must be less than or equal to 600 units, which is the maximum available amount of inputs required for fermentation. In mathematical notation

$$3Q_C + Q_W \leq 600,$$

where Q_C is the number of bottles of champagne and Q_W is the number of bottles of white wine. Thus, this mathematical relationship summarizes the fermentation constraint because it combines the information that (1) it takes 3 units of fixed fermentation input to produce one bottle of champagne, (2) it takes 1 unit of fixed fermentation input to produce one bottle of white wine, and (3) a maximum of 600 units is available. In a similar manner we can derive mathematical expressions for the other two constraints, which are presented in Table 7A–2.

If we remove the inequality sign from each of these constraints, thus making them strict equalities, we obtain the relationships that indicate the *maximum* quantity of champagne and/or wine that could be produced under each constraint if all available units of the input were used. These equations

Table 7A–2 *Mathematical Expressions of the Fermenting, Bottling, and Champagne Purifying Constraints*

Fermenting	$3Q_c + Q_w \leq 600$
Bottling	$2Q_c + Q_w \leq 500$
Champagne Purifying	$Q_c \leq 150$

Table 7A–3 *Equations Expressing Maximum Quantities of Wine and Champagne that Can Be Produced Under Each Constraint*

Fermenting	$3Q_c + Q_w = 600$
Bottling	$2Q_c + Q_w = 500$
Champagne Purifying	$Q_c = 150$

FIGURE 7A–1

Maximum Quantities of White Wine and Champagne that Can Be Produced, Given Fermenting, Bottling, and Champagne Purifying Constraints

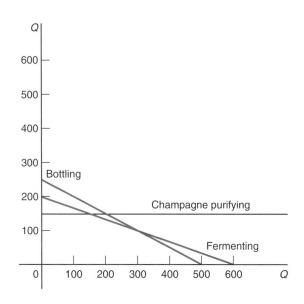

The bottling constraint indicates the maximum quantities of champagne and wine that can be produced with current bottling capacity. The champagne purifying and fermenting constraints have similar interpretations.

are presented in Table 7A–3 and are the equations for the straight-line functions graphed in Figure 7A–1.

Note that when we consider only one constraint, the firm may be able to produce any one of a wide variety of combinations of wine and champagne and still satisfy the constraint. For example, the firm could produce 200 bottles of champagne and no wine *or* 600 bottles of wine and no champagne and still meet the fermenting constraint.

However, the firm must satisfy *all* of the constraints and, consequently, is able to produce only those combinations of champagne and wine that are in (including the boundary) the region of the graph in Figure 7A–1 that is within all three constraints. We have indicated this region in Figure 7A–2 with a heavy black boundary and diagonal lines. The combinations of champagne and wine in this region make up the *feasible region* of production.

Given these constraints, the firm can produce any combination of wine and champagne that is within the feasible region of production. However, we have assumed that the firm wishes to produce that combination of products that will *maximize its profit* (or minimize its loss). To achieve this goal, the firm needs to know the *profit contribution* (price less average variable cost) per unit for each product that it produces. Assume that the profit contribution per bottle of champagne is $2.50, whereas the profit contribution per bottle of white wine is $1.00. With this information, the firm can use *isoprofit*

FIGURE 7A–2

Feasible Region of Production of Wine and Champagne

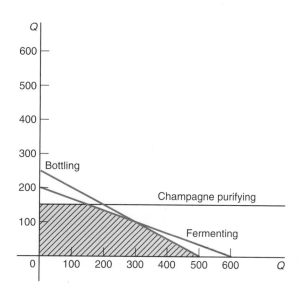

The feasible region of production, indicated by the diagonal lines, represents the quantities of wine and champagne that the firm can produce with its current capacity.

An **isoprofit curve** indicates the different combinations of two products that will result in equal profit for the firm.

curves to graphically find its optimal quantities of wine and champagne. Similar to other economics curves with an *iso-* prefix, an **isoprofit curve** indicates the various combinations of two products that will yield *equal profit* for the firm. (Recall from Chapter 5, for example, that an *isocost curve* indicates the combinations of two inputs that are of *equal cost*.)

In Figure 7A–3, we have graphed three isoprofit curves and the feasible region from Figure 7A–2. We were able to obtain the equation for each isoprofit line by substituting different values for total profit contribution (πC) in the following function:

$$\pi C = \$2.50Q_c + \$1.00Q_w.$$

This function states that the total profit contribution of the firm must be equal to $2.50 times the number of bottles of champagne produced plus $1.00 times the number of bottles of wine produced. By substituting $375 for πC, we can find the equation that indicates the different combinations of wine and champagne that will result in a $375 level of profit contribution. To derive the equations for the other isoprofit curves, we do the same thing for $\pi C = \$550$ and $\pi C = \$650$. (The amounts $375, $550, and $650 were picked because they involved combinations of champagne and wine that were near the boundary of the feasible region.)

FIGURE 7A–3

Isoprofit Lines and the Feasible Region of Production

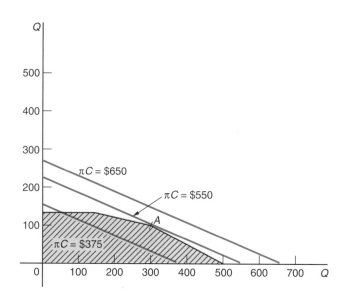

The equation for each isoprofit curve is obtained by substituting each respective level of profit contribution in the equation.

$$\pi C = \$2.50Q_c + \$1.00Q_w,$$

where πC is the total profit contribution, Q_c is the number of bottles of champagne, and Q_w is the number of bottles of wine. The isoprofit curve for $\pi C = \$550$ just touches an outside corner (point A) of the feasible region, and it indicates the profit-maximizing quantities of champagne and wine.

If the firm is to maximize profit, it must be on the highest isoprofit curve possible, given its constraints. In Figure 7A-3 we observe that the isoprofit line for $\pi C = \$550$ just touches an outside corner (point A) of the feasible region; therefore a profit contribution level of $550 is the greatest amount that the firm can achieve, given its capacity constrains. Point A also indicates the profit-maximizing combination of champagne and wine that the firm should produce in this situation—100 bottles of champagne and 300 bottles of wine. Note that although point A is the optimal point, the firm still has some excess champagne purifying capacity.

The Algebraic Solution Method

The graphical method of finding the profit-maximizing combination of products is quite useful for illustration. However, algebraic methods are more precise and more practical when the number of decision variables is greater than two, because graphing is difficult when there are more than two variables. There are a variety of algebraic methods in use, and often these operations would be performed by a computer. Consequently, in this book we will discuss only one of the simplest algebraic procedures.

As indicated in the preceding paragraph, the objective function (or goal) of the firm is to maximize

$$\pi C = \$2.50Q_c + \$1.00Q_w,$$

subject to the following constraints (see Table 8–2):

Fermenting	$3Q_c + Q_w \leq 600,$
Bottling	$2Q_c + Q_w \leq 500,$ and
Champagne purifying	$Q_c \leq 150.$

To solve this problem algebraically, we create three new variables called *slack* variables. Each of these slack variables represents excess capacity in some area, and since there cannot be *negative* excess capacity, the value of each of these variables must be greater than or equal to zero. The values of Q_c and Q_w must likewise be greater than or equal to zero.

Since each slack variable represents excess capacity in some area, we place one slack variable in each of the preceding constraints, which changes it to an equality:

(7A-1)
$$3Q_c + Q_w + S_F = 600,$$

(7A-2)
$$2Q_c + Q_w + S_B = 500,$$

and

(7A-3)
$$Q_c + S_P = 150.$$

In this case, S_F represents excess fermenting capacity, S_B represents excess bottling capacity, and S_P represents excess champagne purifying capacity. The addition of these slack variables transforms these constraints into equalities because the amount of a particular kind of input used in producing champagne and wine, plus the excess capacity left over, must equal the total available amount of the input.

Before proceeding any further, we should note that in this case corners of the boundary (also called *extreme points*) of the feasible region occur (1) where two constraints intersect, (2) where a constraint intersects either the horizontal or vertical axis, or (3) at the origin. Therefore, at any extreme point, at least *two* of the five variables (Q_c, Q_w, S_F, S_B, and S_P in the constraint equations) must be zero. It is also true in the general case with m constraints and n decision variables that the number of *zero-valued* variables must be great enough so that the number of *nonzero-valued* variables is no greater than the number of constraints. Usually, if there are m constraints, there will be m variables that are nonzero.

FIGURE 7A–4

Constraints and the Boundary of the Feasible Region

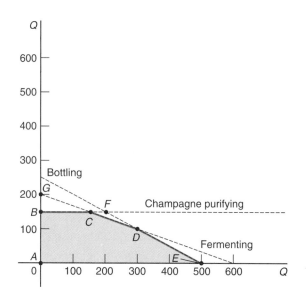

Points *A, B, C, D,* and *E* mark the corners of the boundary of the feasible region of production. Points *G* and *F* lie outside the feasible region.

To draw each constraint line, we assumed that all available capacity of the corresponding input was being utilized. This means that along a capacity constraint line, the value of the corresponding slack variable is zero. Thus, in Figure 7A–4, at point *A*, Q_C and Q_w are zero; at point *B*, Q_w and S_p are zero; at point *C*, S_p and S_F are zero; at point *D*, S_F and S_B are zero; and at point *E*, S_B and Q_c are zero.

Observe that not all points where two of these variables are zero are *necessarily* part of the feasible region. For example, at point *F*, S_p and S_B equal zero, but point *F* is not part of the feasible region because it is outside the fermenting constraint. At point *G*, Q_w and S_F are zero, but point *G* is also outside the feasible region.

Furthermore, *at least one* of the extreme (boundary corner) points of the feasible region will mark a profit-maximizing combination of champagne and wine to be produced. (If a constraint happens to coincide with an isoprofit curve, then two extreme points, both on the constraint, and all points in between, will be equally profitable.) Therefore, by solving the constraint equations for Q_c and Q_w at each extreme point of the feasible region and determining the corresponding πC from the objective function, we can discover the optimal combination of champagne and wine.

As long as the profit contribution per unit of output is positive, we can ignore the origin, since at that point, $Q_c = 0$, $Q_w = 0$, and $\pi C = 0$. At point *B*,

S_P and Q_w are zero, and substituting those values into Equations 7A–1 through 7A–3, we obtain the following equations:

$$3Q_c + S_F = 600,$$
$$2Q_c + S_B = 500,$$

and

$$Q_c = 150.$$

Substituting $Q_c = 150$ in the first and second equations, we obtain $S_F = 150$ and $S_B = 200$. From the objective function, we find that $\pi C = \$2.50(150) + \$1.00(0) = \$375$. The values of the slack variables tell us that there are 150 excess units of fermenting capacity and 200 excess units of bottling capacity.

At point C, S_P and S_F are zero, and substituting these values in Equations 7A–1 through 7A–3, we obtain

$$3Q_c + Q_w = 600,$$
$$2Q_c + Q_w + S_B = 500,$$

and

$$Q_c = 150.$$

Substituting $Q_c = 150$ in the first equation, we find $Q_w = 150$. Substituting $Q_c = 150$ and $Q_w = 150$ in the second equation, we find $S_B = 50$. From the objective function, we find $\pi C = \$2.50(150) + \$1.00(150) = \$525$.

At point D, S_F and S_B are zero, and substituting those values into Equations 7A–1 through 7A–3, we obtain

$$3Q_c + Q_w = 600,$$
$$2Q_c + Q_w = 500,$$

and

$$Q_c + S_P = 150.$$

Subtracting the second equation from the first, we obtain $Q_c = 100$. Substituting $Q_c = 100$ in either of those equations, we find $Q_w = 300$. Substituting $Q_c = 100$ in the last equation, we get $S_P = 50$. From the objective function, we find $\pi C = \$2.50(100) + \$1.00(300) = \$550$.

At point E, Q_c and S_B equal zero, and in a manner similar to that used for the other points, we obtain $Q_w = 500$, $S_F = 100$, $S_P = 150$, and $\pi C = \$500$.

The information that we have obtained by examining each of the boundary corners of the feasible region is summarized as follows:

Point A

$Q_c = 0, Q_w = 0$
$S_F = 600, S_B = 500, S_P = 150$
$\pi C = 0$

Point B

$Q_w = 0, S_P = 0$
$Q_c = 150, S_F = 150, S_B = 200$
$\pi C = \$375$

Point C

$S_F = 0, S_P = 0$
$Q_c = 150, Q_w = 150, S_B = 50$
$\pi C = \$525$

Point D

$S_F = 0, S_B = 0$
$Q_c = 100, Q_w = 300, S_P = 50$
$\pi C = \$550$

Point E

$Q_c = 0, S_B = 0$
$Q_w = 500, S_F = 100, S_P = 150$
$\pi C = \$500$

As we have already found graphically, the optimal combination of champagne and wine is given by point D, where $Q_c = 100$, $Q_w = 300$, and $\pi C = \$550$—the highest profit contribution level obtainable by this firm.

How did we know that points A, B, C, D, and E made up the boundary corners of the feasible region, as opposed to points like F and G? Before we solved for the values of the nonzero slack variables, the only way we could tell was from the graph. *After* we solved for the values of the nonzero slack variables, we could tell because the values of those variables were positive. At points such as F and G, the value of at least one slack variable will be negative, meaning that at least one constraint is being violated. For example, at point G, $S_P = -50$, meaning that the purifying constraint has been violated. However, it is often helpful to use a graph together with the algebraic method of finding the profit-maximizing point in order to locate more easily the corners of the feasible region boundary (as long as the number of decision variables is not too large).

We now turn to an example of the primal program in a cost minimization problem.

Example of a Linear Programming Cost Minimization Problem

Linear programming is quite useful for certain types of cost minimization decision problems, as well as for profit-maximization problems, so long as the linearity requirement is met. For example, suppose that a manufacturer of high quality, and relatively high-priced, speakers for stereo component systems is trying to decide on the optimal combination of advertisements in two magazines. The cost per ad in the first magazine is $500, while the cost per ad in the second magazine is $400. The firm has certain minimum quantities of different types of people whom it wants to reach through these advertisements. Specifically, it wants to reach at least 600,000 people under 50 years of age, at least 180,000 people with annual incomes of $40,000 and over, and at least 260,000 people who already own stereo systems.

The firm believes that no person subscribes to both magazines, as the characteristics of people who read the first magazine differ significantly from the characteristics of those who read the second magazine. Accordingly, the firm believes that each ad placed in the first magazine will reach 20,000 *new* readers who are under 50 years of age, 15,000 new readers who have annual incomes of at least $40,000, and 10,000 new readers who already have stereo systems. The corresponding figures for the second magazine are believed to be 30,000 new readers under 50 years of age, 5,000 with incomes of $40,000 and over, and 10,000 who already own stereo systems.

The objective of the stereo speaker manufacturer is to minimize the cost of the advertisements while fulfilling the minimum goals for reaching each type of audience. Thus our linear programming problem becomes this:

$$\text{Minimize } TC = \$500Q_1 + \$400Q_2,$$

where Q_1 is the number of advertisements placed in the first magazine and Q_2 is the number of advertisements placed in the second magazine, subject to the following constraints:

Age	$20{,}000Q_1 + 30{,}000Q_2 \geq 600{,}000,$
Income	$15{,}000Q_1 + 5{,}000Q_2 \geq 180{,}000,$ and
Stereo ownership	$10{,}000Q_1 + 10{,}000Q_2 \geq 260{,}000,$

where

$$Q_1 \text{ and } Q_2 \text{ are } \geq 0.$$

The first constraint states that 20,000 times the number of ads placed in the first magazine (which will equal the number of people under 50 years old reached by that magazine) plus 30,000 times the number of ads placed in the second magazine (which should equal the number of people under 50 years old reached by the second magazine) must be greater than or equal to 600,000, the *minimum* number of people under 50 years of age that the speaker manufacturer wishes to reach. The second and third constraints have similar interpretations. Note that the constraint inequalities in this minimization problem are in the form of greater-than-or-equal-to constraints, whereas in the maximization problem they were less-than-or-equal-to constraints. This difference

FIGURE 7A–5

Constraints and the Feasible Region for Advertisements in Two Magazines

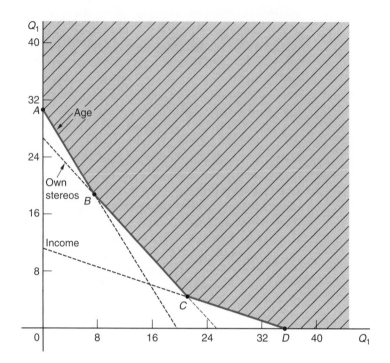

In this case the feasible region, denoted by the diagonal lines, is above *ABCD*.

occurs because in the first case the constraints are placing a limit on making something *larger*, while in the second case they are placing a limit on making something *smaller*. The constraints and the feasible region for the stereo speaker manufacturer are graphed in Figure 7A–5, and the respective extreme points are designated by points *A*, *B*, *C*, and *D*.

Using the algebraic method developed in the previous section, we use slack variables to transform the constraints into strict equalities, as follows:

(7A-4)
$$20{,}000Q_1 + 30{,}000Q_2 - S_A = 600{,}000,$$

(7A-5)
$$15{,}000Q_1 + 5{,}000Q_2 - S_I = 180{,}000,$$

and

(7A-6)
$$10{,}000Q_1 + 10{,}000Q_2 - S_O = 260{,}000.$$

Here, the slack variables represent the *additional* people reached by advertisements in a particular classification above the minimum number required. As before, the values of all variables must be greater than or equal to zero.

We now examine each boundary corner point. At point A, S_A and Q_2 are equal to zero. Substituting these values into the constraint Equations 7A–4 through 7A–6, we obtain:

$$20,000Q_1 \qquad = 600,000,$$

$$15,000Q_1 - S_1 = 180,000,$$

and

$$10,000Q_1 - S_O = 260,000.$$

From the first constraint, we find $Q_1 = 30$, and substituting for Q_1 in the second and third constraints, we find $S_1 = 270,000$ and $S_O = 40,000$. From the objective function, we obtain $TC = \$500(30) + \$400(0) = \$15,000$.

At point B, S_A and S_O are zero, and substituting these values into the constraint equations, we obtain the following:

$$20,000Q_1 + 30,000Q_2 \qquad = 600,000,$$

$$15,000Q_1 + 5,000Q_2 - S_1 = 180,000,$$

and

$$10,000Q_1 + 10,000Q_2 \qquad = 260,000.$$

By subtracting twice the third equation from the first equation, we obtain $10,000Q_2 = 80,000$ or $Q_2 = 8$. Substituting for Q_1 in the third equation, we find $Q_1 = 18$. Substituting for Q_1 and Q_2 in the second equation, we find $S_1 = 130,000$. From the objective function, we can obtain $TC = \$500(18) + \$400(8) = \$12,200$.

In a similar fashion, we can find the values for $Q_1, Q_2, S_A, S_1, S_O,$ and TC at points C and D. Our results are summarized as follows:

Point A

$Q_1 = 30, Q_2 = 0, S_A = 0$
$S_1 = 270,000, S_O = 40,000$
$TC = \$15,000$

Point B

$Q_1 = 18, Q_2 = 8, S_A = 0$
$S_1 = 130,000, S_O = 0$
$TC = \$12,000$

Point C

$Q_1 = 5, Q_2 = 21,$
$S_A = 130,000$
$S_1 = 0, S_O = 0$
$TC = \$10,900$

Point D

$Q_1 = 0, Q_2 = 36,$
$S_A = 480,000$
$S_1 = 0, S_O = 100,000$
$TC = \$14,400$

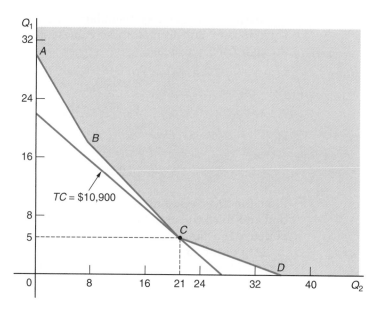

The firm will minimize advertising cost at point C, with 5 advertisements in the first magazine and 21 in the second magazine.

Thus the firm will minimize its advertising cost, given these constraints at point C, where $Q_1 = 5$, $Q_2 = 21$, and $TC = \$10,900$. Therefore the firm should advertise 5 times in the first magazine and 21 times in the second magazine. In Figure 7A–6, we have graphed the boundary of the feasible region and the isocost curve for $TC = \$10,900$, and we have indicated the optimal values of Q_1 and Q_2.

Summary of Primal Program Solution Procedure

The steps that should be followed to obtain the optimal solution to a primal program using a combination of graphical and algebraic methods are summarized as follows:

1. Set up the objective function and the constraints in mathematical notation.

2. Graph the constraints by considering them to be strict equalities and determine the extreme points of the boundary of the feasible region, recalling that the values of all slack variables and the quantities produced of the products must be greater than or equal to zero. Moreover, these corner points must include *the* optimal point or at least *one of a set* of equally optimal points. If the constraints cannot be graphed easily, go to the third step, using the algebraic technique described earlier to examine

each point where the number of nonzero variables is at least no greater than the number of constraints.

3. Using the algebraic technique described earlier, examine each of the extreme points in turn, solving for the quantities of each of the products and the slack variables at each point and the resulting level of profit contribution or cost in order to determine at which point profit will be maximized or cost will be minimized. (It will often be helpful to graph an isoprofit/isocost curve that falls near the outermost/innermost boundary of the feasible region as an aid in eliminating some extreme points from consideration without having to solve the constraint relationships for each point algebraically.)

In the next section, we examine the nature of the dual programs in the two examples of the optimization problems presented previously.

THE DUAL PROGRAM

Every linear programming problem that involves maximizing or minimizing an objective function has a corresponding linear programming problem called the *dual* program. As we have indicated, the original programming problem that directly states the objective of the firm is called the *primal* program. For every primal *maximization* problem, there can be constructed a corresponding dual *minimization* problem; conversely, for every primal minimization problem, there can be constructed a corresponding dual maximization problem. Both the primal and the dual programs will give the same values for the *decision variables* in the *primal* objective function at their respective optimal points. Also, the optimal value for the primal objective function will equal the optimal value for the dual objective function.

The dual program is useful for two reasons. First, it may be easier to find the optimal values of the decision variables in the primal program by solving the dual program. Second, the dual program gives an imputed value of the opportunity cost to the firm of the decision variables in the primal objective function and of the constraints.

Dual Minimization Problem

Consider the primal maximization problem that we discussed earlier in this chapter. The primal objective function that the firm wished to maximize was

$$\pi C = \$2.50 Q_C + \$1.00 Q_W,$$

where Q_C and Q_W were the quantities of champagne and wine, respectively, to be produced by the firm, and \$2.50 and \$1.00 were their respective profit contributions per unit. This objective function was to be maximized subject to the following constraints (see Table 8–2):

Fermenting	$3Q_c + Q_w \leq 600,$
Bottling	$2Q_c + Q_w \leq 500,$ and
Champagne purifying	$Q_c \leq 150,$

where Q_c and Q_w are ≥ 0.

The corresponding dual program is concerned with finding the *minimum* values that can be assigned to the three inputs represented by the capacity constraints and still account for *all* of the unit profit contribution of each product. These minimum values of the fixed inputs represent their marginal value or opportunity cost to the firm in terms of the profit contribution that results from their use by the firm.

Thus the dual objective function that the firm wishes to minimize in this case is

$$TOC = 600V_F + 500V_B + 150V_p,$$

where TOC is the total opportunity cost to the firm of the three resources, V_F is the marginal opportunity cost of the fixed resources used in fermentation, V_B is the marginal opportunity cost of the fixed bottling resources, and V_p is the marginal opportunity cost of the fixed champagne purifying resources. The coefficients 600, 500, and 150 represent the total available amounts of fixed resources used in fermenting, bottling, and champagne purifying, respectively.

As should be expected, the constraints set limits on the values to be assigned to the three resources, and these limits are stated in terms of the unit profit contribution of each product. Accordingly, the constraints are

(7A–7)
$$3V_F + 2V_B + V_p \geq \$2.50,$$

and

(7A–8)
$$V_F + V_B \geq \$1.00.$$

These two constraints state that the sum of the marginal value or opportunity cost of each input times the amount of that input used to produce a unit of a particular product must be greater than or equal to the unit profit contribution for that product. Thus the first constraint applies to champagne and indicates that three units of the fixed fermenting resource, two units of the fixed bottling resource, and one unit of the champagne purifying resource are needed to produce one bottle of champagne with unit profit contribution of $2.50. A similar interpretation can be made of the second constraint, which applies to wine.

Since it is difficult to graph in three-dimensional space (V_F, V_B, and V_P necessitate three dimensions), we shall solve the dual program algebraically. First, as with the primal, the inequalities must be transformed into equalities by adding new variables:

$$3V_F + 2V_B + V_P - L_c = \$2.50,$$

and

$$V_F + V_B - L_w = \$1.00,$$

where L_c and L_w are greater than or equal to zero. In this case L_c represents the *net* opportunity cost to the firm of producing champagne, and L_w represents the *net* opportunity cost of producing wine.[2] If, for example, L_c were positive, it would indicate to the firm that the opportunity cost of the resources used in producing a bottle of champagne was greater than its unit profit contribution. In this case, the profit-maximizing firm would not produce *any* champagne and the optimal Q_c would be zero. A similar interpretation holds for L_w.

Unfortunately, if we do not already know the optimal Q_c and Q_w (and since we cannot easily eliminate any *un*feasible solutions by graphing), we have 10 possible solution points to consider.[3] Recall that at any boundary corner of the feasible region there will be *at least* a sufficient number of zero-valued variables in the constraint equations so that the number of remaining variables is equal to (or possibly less than) the number of constraints. We have listed the results for all 10 possibilities as follows:

Point 1

$V_F = 0, L_c = 0, L_w = 0$
$V_B = \$1.00, V_P = \$.50$
$TOC = 600(0) + 500(\$1.00) + 150(\$.50)$
$= \$575$

Point 2

$V_B = 0, L_c = 0, L_w = 0$
$V_F = \$1.00, V_P = -\$.50$
Not a feasible solution, $V_P < 0$

---

2   The *net* opportunity cost is the cost incurred by the firm from producing a particular product because the opportunity cost of the fixed resources used up is greater than the profit contribution of the product.

3   The number of possible solution points is obtained by finding the number of possible combinations of five things taken three at a time, since there are five variables (three of which must be zero at any solution point). The formula for the number of possible combinations of five things taken three at a time is

$$C_3^5 = \frac{5!}{3!\,2!} = \frac{5 \cdot 4 \cdot 3 \cdot 2 \cdot 1}{3 \cdot 2 \cdot 1 \cdot 2 \cdot 1} = 10.$$

Point 3

$V_P = 0, L_c = 0, L_w = 0$
$V_F = \$.50, V_B = \$.50$
$TOC = 600(\$.50) + 500(\$.50) + 150(0)$
$= \$550$

Point 4

$V_F = 0, V_B = 0, L_c = 0$
$V_P = \$2.50, L_w = -\$1.00$
Also not a feasible solution,
as $L_w < 0$

Point 5

$V_F = 0, V_B = 0, L_w = 0$
Impossible—violates the second
constraint

Point 6

$V_F = 0, V_P = 0, L_c = 0$
$V_B = \$1.25, L_w = \$.25$
$TOC = 600(0) + 500(\$1.25) + 150(0)$
$= \$625$

Point 7

$V_F = 0, V_P = 0, L_w = 0$
$V_B = \$1.00, L_c = -\$.50$
Not a feasible solution, $L_c < 0$

Point 8

$V_B = 0, V_P = 0, L_c = 0$
$V_F = \$.83, L_w = -\$.17$
Not a feasible solution, $L_w < 0$

Point 9

$V_B = 0, V_P = 0, L_w = 0$
$V_F = \$1.00, L_c = \$.50$
$TOC = 600(\$1.00) + 500(0) + 150(0)$
$= \$600$

Point 10

$V_F = 0, V_B = 0, V_P = 0$
$L_c = -\$2.50, L_w = -\$1.00$
Not a feasible solution, as L_c
and L_w are negative

By examining the solution values at the 10 points, we find that the opportunity cost for the firm is minimized at point 3, where $V_F = \$.50$, $V_B = \$.50$, $V_P = 0$, $L_c = 0$, $L_w = 0$, and $TOC = \$550$. Moreover, as we interpret the meaning of these values and relate them to the primal solution, it will become obvious that, given the primal solution, we could have immediately picked point 3 as the optimal solution to the dual program.

First, L_c and L_w being equal to zero means that for both champagne and wine the sum of the opportunity cost valuations placed on the resources necessary to produce one unit of each product is just equal to the respective unit profit contributions of both wine and champagne, and both products will therefore be produced. That V_P is zero indicates that the opportunity cost of using the fixed champagne purifying resources is zero, which means that at the optimal point there is excess or slack champagne purifying capacity. Thus, since we knew from the primal that at the optimal point Q_c and Q_w were positive, we then knew that at the optimal point for the dual program L_c and L_w must be zero. We also knew from the primal program solution that there was excess champagne purifying capacity, so that V_P must be equal to zero.

The value of V_F indicates the marginal effect the fixed fermenting input has on the level of profits for the firm. Thus, another unit of the fixed fermenting resource would add \$.50 to the total profit of the firm. A similar interpretation of V_B holds for the fixed bottling resource. If the market price of a unit of these resources is below \$.50, the firm may wish to make plans to increase its fermenting and/or bottling capacity in the future. It may also wish to reduce its champagne purifying capacity. Note also that the minimum value of *TOC* (equal to \$550) is equal to the maximum πC, which is as it should be, since it states that the opportunity cost valuation of the fixed resources is equal to their contribution to the firm's profit at the optimal point.

In the next section, we construct and solve the dual program for the primal cost minimization problem discussed earlier in the chapter.

Dual Maximization Problem

In this section we shall discuss the dual to the cost minimization problem presented earlier. The original objective was to minimize

$$TC = \$500Q_1 + \$400Q_2,$$

where *TC* was total advertising cost, Q_1 was the number of advertisements in Magazine 1, and Q_2 was the number of advertisements in Magazine 2. The firm wished to minimize *TC* subject to the following constraints:

Age	$20{,}000Q_1 + 30{,}000Q_2 \geq 600{,}000,$
Income	$15{,}000Q_1 + 5{,}000Q_2 \geq 180{,}000,$ and
Stereo ownership	$10{,}000Q_1 + 10{,}000Q_2 \geq 260{,}000.$

These three constraints state that the firm wishes the advertisements to reach at least 600,000 people under 50 years of age, at least 180,000 people with incomes of \$40,000 or greater, and at least 260,000 people who already own stereo systems.

For the dual program, the objective now becomes to maximize

$$Z = 600{,}000V_A + 180{,}000V_I + 260{,}000V_O$$

subject to the constraints that

$$20{,}000V_A + 15{,}000V_I + 10{,}000V_O \leq \$500 \text{ (Magazine 1)},$$

and

$$30{,}000V_A + 5{,}000V_I + 10{,}000V_O \leq \$400 \text{ (Magazine 2)}.$$

In this case, Z represents an imputed value or cost to the firm of the three age, income, and ownership constraints in the primal program, which is obtained by finding an imputed value that is really the *marginal cost* to the firm of changing each individual constraint. The first constraint for the dual program states that the marginal cost to the firm of the age constraint times 20,000 (the number of people under age 50 that an advertisement in Magazine 1 reaches) plus the marginal cost to the firm of the income constraint times 15,000 (the number of people with annual incomes of at least $40,000 that one advertisement in Magazine 1 reaches) plus the marginal cost to the firm of the stereo ownership constraint times 10,000 (the number of people who own stereo systems who are reached by an advertisement in Magazine 1) must be less than or equal to $500 (the cost of placing one advertisement in Magazine 1). A similar interpretation holds for the second constraint. Basically, the constraints state that the imputed value or marginal cost of each of the primal constraints times the number of people in each category reached by an advertisement in a particular magazine must be less than or equal to the cost of such an ad.

If we transform the constraints into equalities, we obtain

$$20{,}000V_A + 15{,}000V_I + 10{,}000V_O + L_1 = 500,$$

and

$$30{,}000V_A + 5{,}000V_I + 10{,}000V_O + L_2 = 400.$$

The two variables L_1 and L_2 represent the net opportunity cost or *relative inefficiency* of using Magazine 1 and Magazine 2, respectively, as advertising media. If neither magazine is relatively inefficient, L_1 and L_2 will both be zero and the firm will advertise in both magazines.

At the optimal primal solution, we found $TC = \$10{,}900$, $Q_1 = 5$, $Q_2 = 21$, $S_A = 130{,}000$, $S_I = 0$, and $S_O = 0$. Since Q_1 and Q_2 are positive, we know that L_1 and L_2 must be zero at the optimal primal solution; that is, both magazines are relatively efficient advertising media. As before, since S_A is positive, there is an excess over the minimum required number of people under age 50 being reached at the optimal point; therefore, the marginal cost of increasing the age constraint, V_A, must be zero at that point. Following a similar line of reasoning, we can also conclude that at the optimal point, V_O and V_I must be positive. Thus we can conclude that the optimal point for the dual program will be found where L_1, L_2, and V_A equal zero.

Substituting these values into the dual constraint equations, we get

$$15{,}000V_I + 10{,}000V_O = \$500,$$

and

$$5{,}000V_I + 10{,}000V_O = \$400.$$

Subtracting the second equation from the first, we obtain $10,000V_I = \$100$, or $V_I = \$.01$. Substituting $V_I = \$.01$ in the second equation, we find that $V_O = \$.035$. We can now find that optimal $Z = 600,000(0) + 180,000(\$.01) + 260,000(\$.035) = \$10,900$, the minimum value we found for TC in the primal program.

To use the values obtained for V_I and V_O, the firm must have a reliable estimate of the actual value or marginal benefit to the firm (in terms of increased profit contribution) obtained by increasing the income and stereo ownership constraints, respectively. For example, if the marginal benefit from increasing the income constraint is greater than $\$.01$, the firm should consider increasing this constraint. On the other hand, if the marginal benefit is less than $\$.01$, the firm should consider reducing the minimum number of people it reaches who have annual incomes of at least $\$40,000$. A similar analysis would apply for the stereo ownership constraint.

Summary of How to Construct the Dual Program

In this section we summarize the steps for setting up the dual program from the primal.

1. The dual objective function will be obtained by assigning a valuation variable to each of the primal constraints and summing the values of these variables multiplied by the numbers that represent the maximum or minimum values of their respective primal constraints. If the primal objective function is to be maximized, the dual objective function should be minimized, and vice versa.

2. The dual constraint inequalities are obtained by finding the sum of each *valuation variable* in the dual objective function multiplied by the *coefficient* of the corresponding *primal objective function* variable in the corresponding primal constraint. There will be one dual program constraint for each primal decision (objective function) variable. Also, the direction of the dual program constraint inequalities will be the reverse of those in the primal program constraints.

We present two general examples of the relationships between the primal and the dual linear programs, as follows:

■ Example 1

Primal

Maximize $\pi = \pi_1 X_1 + \pi_2 X_2$
Subject to $a_1 X_1 + b_1 X_2 \leq Y_1$,
$\qquad\qquad a_2 X_1 + b_2 X_2 \leq Y_2$,
$\qquad\qquad a_3 X_1 + b_3 X_2 \leq Y_3$,
$\qquad\qquad$ and $X_1, X_2 \geq 0$.

Dual

Minimize $TC = Y_1 V_1 + Y_2 V_2 + Y_3 V_3$
Subject to $a_1 V_1 + a_2 V_2 + a_3 V_3 \geq \pi_1$,
$\qquad\qquad b_1 V_1 + b_2 V_2 + b_3 V_3 \geq \pi_2$,
$\qquad\qquad$ and $V_1, V_2, V_3 \geq 0$.

■ Example 2

Primal

Minimize $TOC = C_1X_1 + C_2X_2$

Subject to $a_1X_1 + b_2X_2 \geq Y_1,$

$a_2X_1 + b_2X_2 \geq Y_2,$

$a_3X_1 + b_3X_2 \geq Y_3,$

and $X_1, X_2 \geq 0.$

Dual

Maximize $Z = Y_1V_1 + Y_2V_2 + Y_3V_3$

Subject to $a_1V_1 + a_2V_2 + a_3V_3 \leq C_1,$

$b_1V_1 + b_2V_2 + b_3V_3 \leq C_2,$

and $V_1, V_2, V_3 \geq 0.$

SUMMARY

Linear Programming as an Optimizing Tool

In this appendix we have discussed linear programming, a mathematical decision-making tool particularly useful when a firm faces an optimizing problem that can be specified in terms of a linear objective function and linear constraints in the form of inequalities. The primal program directly specifies the objective of the firm in terms of the decision variables, whereas the dual program gives information regarding various opportunity costs connected with the problem. However, as we demonstrated, it is possible to find the optimal values of the decision variables using either the primal or the dual program.

Here, we have demonstrated only the simplest algebraic and graphical methods of solving linear programs in order to give some examples of how this tool can be used by business without being too complex. In many real-world situations with more variables than those in our examples, decision makers are likely to use more sophisticated algebraic techniques, such as the simplex method, as well as the computer. Moreover, linear programming is only one of a class of mathematical tools called *mathematical programming*. These other techniques, including nonlinear programming and dynamic programming, are beyond the scope of this book, but the interested reader can learn more about them from the sources in the list of references at the end of this appendix.

QUESTIONS

1. Compare the techniques of linear programming and calculus. For what types of decision problems is calculus more useful? For what types of decision problems is linear programming more useful?

2. Give some examples of specific business decisions where linear programming could be useful.

3. Why is maximizing the *total profit contribution* of the firm's inputs equivalent to maximizing its total profit in the short run?

4. What type of information does one get by solving the dual program that one does not obtain by solving the primal program? Give an example.

5. Why may the dual problem be easier to solve than the primal problem? How can the optimal values of the primal problem be found from those of the dual? Give an example.

PROBLEMS

1. Polynesian Pineapple, Inc., is a company that imports raw pineapples. It markets two products, canned pineapple slices and raw pineapples. Polynesian has capacity limitations in three areas: warehouse space, canning facilities, and crating facilities. A raw pineapple requires .6 of a unit of warehouse space before it is shipped, .2 of a unit of crating facilities, and no canning facilities. One can of pineapple slices requires .3 of a unit of warehouse space, .2 of a unit of crating facilities, and .1 of a unit of canning facilities.

   The total available monthly amount of warehouse space is 1,200,000 units; of crating facilities, 600,000 units; and of canning facilities, 250,000 units. The profit contribution is $.20 per raw pineapple and $.25 per can of slices.

   a. Find the monthly profit-maximizing quantities of raw and canned pineapple, respectively, for Polynesian Pineapple.

   b. What is the total monthly profit contribution from pineapples in part a?

2. Holiday on Wheels (HOW) manufactures two types of recreational vehicles. One is a trailer that is towed behind a car or pickup, and the other is a motorized vehicle that moves under its own power. HOW is trying to determine the optimal combination of trailers and motor homes to produce per day, given that three of the inputs (power train assembly, paint and trim line, and body assembly) needed to produce these products are available in limited amounts. Manufacture of one motor home requires 2.0 hours of power train assembly capacity, 2.5 hours of paint and trim capacity, and 3.0 hours of body assembly capacity, whereas the production of one trailer requires only 2.0 hours of paint and trim capacity and 2.0 hours of body assembly capacity.

   HOW has available on a daily basis 300 hours of power train assembly capacity, 500 hours of paint and trim capacity, and 540 hours of body assembly capacity. The profit contribution of a motor home is $4,000, while that of a trailer is $3,000.

a. Using both algebraic and graphical solution methods, find the profit-maximizing combination of motor homes and travel trailers that HOW should produce daily.

b. What is HOW's daily contribution to profit at the optimal point?

3. Set up the dual program for Holiday on Wheels using the data in Problem 2.

a. What useful information would Holiday on Wheels obtain by solving the dual program? Explain.

b. What is the optimal solution to this dual program?

c. State the economic significance of the values of each of the dual variables at the optimal point.

4. A commercial feedlot operation, Best-Fed Beef, Inc. (BFB), is trying to determine the least-cost combination of two types of feed that will meet the nutritional requirements of its cattle. The first kind of feed is a grain mixture, and each ton of grain contains, on the average, 200 pounds of protein, 1,000 pounds of carbohydrates, and 300 pounds of roughage plus 500 pounds of miscellaneous minerals, vitamins, fats, and water. The second feed is a type of silage, and an average ton of silage contains 40 pounds of protein, 400 pounds of carbohydrates, and 600 pounds of roughage, as well as a substantial amount of water and some minerals, fats, and vitamins.

BFB believes that its cattle need a minimum of 1,200 pounds of protein, 8,000 pounds of carbohydrates, and 3,600 pounds of roughage daily. The grain mixture costs $80 per ton, and the silage costs $30 per ton.

a. Find the least-cost combination of grain and silage that will meet the daily nutritional requirements of BFB's cattle.

b. What is the total cost of the optimal combination of feeds found in part a?

c. Set up the dual program, find its optimal solution, and explain the economic significance of the values you found for the dual decision variables.

d. How would the information that you found in part c be useful to BFB? Why?

SELECTED REFERENCES

Chiang, Alpha C. *Fundamental Methods of Mathematical Economics*, 3d ed. (New York: McGraw-Hill, 1984), Chapters 19–21.

Childress, Robert L. *Mathematics for Managerial Decisions*, 2d ed. (Englewood Cliffs, N.J.: Prentice-Hall, 1989), Chapters 5–8.

Dorfman, Robert. "Mathematical, or Linear, Programming," *American Economic Review*, XLIII (December 1953), pp. 797–825.

Garvin, W. W., H. W. Crandall, J. B. John, and R. A. Spellman. "Applications of Linear Programming in the Oil Industry," *Management Science*, III (July 1957), pp. 407–430.

Kamien, Morton I., and Nancy L. Schwartz. *Dynamic Optimization: The Calculus of Variations and Optimal Control in Economics and Management*. (New York: North Holland, 1981).

Silberberg, Eugene. *The Structure of Economic Analysis*, 2d ed. (New York: McGraw-Hill, 1990), Chapter 14.

Takayama, Akira. *Mathematical Economics*, 2d ed. (Hinsdale, Ill.: Dryden Press, 1985), Chapter 1.

Frontier Concrete Products Company[1]

F rontier Concrete Products Company is planning to open a new concrete plant in another city. The owner-manager of the company is currently trying to determine the optimal size plant to build, given the
estimated cost and revenue data presented in Table 1.

The data in Table 1 show that Frontier Concrete Company has determined that there are at least four different combinations of plant size and
labor that would enable the firm to produce a given level of output. Since the
company believes that its optimal level of output will be between 30 and 60
cubic yards of concrete per hour, it is considering only 12 different plant
sizes.

In Table 1 the company has prepared the input figures in terms of standardized units of capital and standardized units of labor. A unit of capital is
estimated to increase the expenses (depreciation, repairs and maintenance,
interest expense, and utilities) of the firm by $18,000 per year, based on a
year consisting of 260 eight-hour working days. The estimated cost to the
firm for one unit of labor is $7.00 per hour. Other costs—for raw materials

---

[1] This case is based on production and cost information from an antitrust case in the readymix
concrete industry.

Table 1 *Various Combinations of Capital and Labor Needed to Produce 30, 45, and 60 Cubic Yards of Concrete per Hour*

Q = 30 Cubic Yards per Hour			
Plant 1	*Plant 2*	*Plant 3*	*Plant 4*
K = 4	K = 3	K = 2	K = 1
L = 1	L = 2	L = 5	L = 10

Q = 45 Cubic Yards per Hour			
Plant 5	*Plant 6*	*Plant 7*	*Plant 8*
K = 6	K = 4.5	K = 3	K = 1.5
L = 1.5	L = 3	L = 7.5	L = 15

Q = 60 Cubic Yards per Hour			
Plant 9	*Plant 10*	*Plant 11*	*Plant 12*
K = 8	K = 6	K = 4	K = 2
L = 2	L = 4	L = 10	L = 20

and delivery, which were not included in Table 1—are estimated to be as follows (*per cubic yard* of concrete produced):

Aggregate (rock)	$3.34
Cement	$7.50
Delivery costs	$4.00

The company has also estimated the demand for its product, and these figures are presented in Table 2.

Table 2 *Estimated Demand for Frontier Concrete Produced by the New Plant*

Cubic Yards per Hour	Price per Cubic Yard
20	$24.00
30	22.34
40	21.26
50	20.40
60	19.66
70	19.00
80	18.38

QUESTIONS

1. How do Frontier's total manufacturing costs (exclusive of raw materials and delivery costs) vary for each of the four capital-labor combinations given as output is increased from 30, to 45, to 60 cubic yards per hour? Does it appear that this production function has increasing, decreasing, or constant returns to scale?

2. What are the total costs, including raw materials and delivery costs, for each of the capital-labor combinations in Question 1?

3. Which capital-labor combination is a least cost combination of inputs for each of the three levels of output?

4. Frontier's owner has plotted a curve showing how the minimum total delivered cost for each output varies when all inputs—including capital, labor, raw materials, and delivery costs—are variable. What should this curve be called? Given the preceding data, what does it look like?

5. What are the long-run average cost figures and the long-run marginal cost figures that correspond to the curve drawn in Question 4?

6. What are the firm's total revenue schedule and marginal revenue schedule, given the information presented in Table 2?

7. Suppose that Frontier had decided to build Plant 10. Suppose also that of the $108,000 annual capital expenses connected with the plant, $96,000 were fixed costs and the remainder were variable. If all labor costs are assumed to be variable and a yard of concrete includes the average variable raw material and delivery costs stated previously, what is the break-even point for this plant, assuming the price of concrete is $20 per cubic yard?

8. Based on the values computed in Question 7, what is the profit-maximizing level of output per hour for Frontier Concrete's new plant?

9. Based on the values computed in Questions 5 and 6, what is the profit-maximizing level of output per hour for Frontier Concrete if all inputs are variable? (Assume $LAC = \$16.17$ for any level of output per hour.)

10. If the cost figures presented here are *accounting costs*, what *types* of adjustments do you think would be needed to transform them into *economic cost* figures?

Shanghai Magnificent Harmony Foundry I

Mr. X. C. Fei is in charge of export sales analysis for a large firm in the People's Republic of China, Shanghai Magnificent Harmony Foundry (SMHF). Most of the foundry's cast-iron output has been destined for the domestic market, principally the locomotive, rail-car, and machinery industries. It has been suggested to Fei that he investigate the overseas market for manhole covers, a product that is simple to manufacture and for which there seems to be endless demand. The target market he has chosen is the United States. Mr. Fei's research assistant has found that India is currently the main source of cast-iron manhole covers that are imported into the United States and that many small Indian foundries make the product. Further, competition is always forthcoming from other less-developed countries, since the United States has a favorable trade policy for such producers.

It is evident to Mr. Fei that SMHF will have to meet the world market price for the covers. In addition, he believes that the amount of output he wishes to sell can be marketed in the United States without cutting price below the world level. Currently, the covers are selling for $0.48 per pound, landed at U.S. West Coast ports. The tariff on such castings is $.02 per lb., but less-developed country producers can qualify for trade preferences that will reduce the tariff to zero. India and certain other producers have successfully qualified for the reduction.

A further consideration that has troubled Mr. Fei is the price of iron ore, which China imports. He expects that while some of his foreign competitors that do not import iron ore will not experience a change in production costs in the near future, his company may have to pay higher ore prices, which could increase the raw materials cost of cast manhole covers by as much as 20 percent.

The central management committee of SMHF has told Mr. Fei that 6,500 short tons per year (one short ton = 2,000 lbs.) of casting capacity can be used for the manhole cover exports but that this type of production will have to carry allocated fixed overhead in the amount of 2,500,000 Renminbi Yuan (RY) annually. The plant must sell all dollar proceeds from its exports to the Chinese government at an official fixed rate of 8 RY to the U.S. dollar. The government is not expected to change this rate for at least three years.

The committee has requested that Mr. Fei prepare a report on the manhole cover exports and has directed that he specifically analyze three cases. First, the best-case scenario, which conforms to (a) obtaining U.S. trade preferences and paying no tariff and (b) not being faced with the 20 percent materials cost increase; second, a case in which the trade preferences are *not* granted, but materials costs remain at their current level; and third, the worst-case scenario, in which the firm does not obtain the trade preferences and also faces a 20 percent increase in raw materials cost.

Fei has been instructed to render the analysis in U.S. dollars, since materials, freight, and the final product are normally priced in dollars in the international market. For the best-case scenario, he has estimated the following unit costs per pound:

Direct materials	$0.10
Fuel	0.11
Direct labor	0.08
Variable selling expenses	0.03

Mr. Fei knows that the average U.S. manhole cover weighs 160 pounds and will use this figure to determine how many he can export. Currently, he believes he will be able to sell all of the covers he can make to U.S. buyers, and he foresees no new investment in plant and equipment to produce the output. He has checked into ocean freight rates and figures the transport cost per pound of finished product will be 10 U.S. cents.

QUESTIONS

1. Complete the best-case scenario for Mr. Fei's report.

2. Explain how the results would change if materials costs were to remain constant but SMHF could not obtain the U.S. trade preference to eliminate the $.02 per lb. tariff. (Assume SMHF absorbs the tariff in its selling price to keep the landed U.S. price at the $0.48 level.)

3. Complete the worst-case scenario, assuming that the tariff must be paid *and* that materials costs rise by 20 percent.

CHAPTER EIGHT

Perfect Competition and Monopoly: The Limiting Cases

To determine its revenue and therefore its profit-maximizing level of output and product price, the individual business firm must develop some notion of the demand for its product. Certain basic demand propositions were reviewed in Chapter 2 and reintroduced in Chapter 7 in connection with our discussion of the conditions for profit maximization. The present chapter deals exclusively with two well-defined market models that represent the opposite ends of a very broad spectrum of possible market situations (called *market structures*) in which a given firm might find itself.

The first limiting case is *perfect competition,* a market structure in which the firm takes market price as given and therefore needs only to determine what cost/output combination maximizes its net revenue or profit. Our second limiting case is *monopoly,* in which there is only one seller of a particular product and the *market* demand curve of consumers is the *firm's* demand curve. Most firms in the real world have to deal with market conditions that lie between the two extremes of perfect competition and monopoly, but we will not discuss these other types of markets until Chapter 9. In this chapter we will concentrate on just the two types of markets, perfect competition and monopoly, that were briefly described earlier. Our emphasis, as in Chapter 7, will be on how firms in these markets maximize profit.

PERFECT COMPETITION AND ITS SETTING

It was noted in Chapter 1 that the perfectly competitive firm is a *price taker* in the sense that it views market price as a given on which it can have no effect. We must now take a closer look, from the viewpoint of the firm, at the market situation that produces such an outcome. Normally, **perfect competition** is described as a product market structure characterized by the following set of conditions:

Under **perfect competition,** there are many small firms, and the individual firm takes the market price as a given.

1. There is a very *large number of buyers and sellers* in the market.

2. The *product* of each seller is identical to that of every other seller *(homogeneous product)*.

3. There are *no artificial interferences* with the activities of the buyers and sellers (for example, government price controls).

4. All buyers and sellers have *perfect knowledge* of market conditions and of any changes in market conditions that occur.

5. Over the long run (the period of time in which it is possible to build or get rid of a plant), there is *freedom of entry* into or *exit* from the industry.

These conditions have some very important implications as far as the operation of the perfectly competitive model is concerned. For example, the existence of a very large number of buyers and sellers in the market (condition 1) and the situation that products of all firms are identical (condition 2) are the basis for the proposition that the individual firm takes market price as given. If a firm knows (condition 4) that there are many other sellers of a product identical to its own and that there is nothing it or anyone else can do to interfere with the activities of such sellers (condition 3), it will conclude that if it raises price, it will lose all its customers to the other firms, since there is no reason to assume that other firms will also raise price. (There are too many firms to be able to get together and effectively agree on restricting quantity supplied and raising price, as many national farm organizations have discovered.) On the other hand, because there are many buyers in the market willing to pay the going price, the firm has no reason to *lower* price either. In a very important sense, the assumption of perfect competition makes the individual firm insignificant with respect to the total market for its product, and that is why it must take price as given.

In a market that is characterized by **free entry,** profit serves the function of drawing new firms into the industry when greater than normal and causing them to leave when less normal.

Our assumptions also ensure one other result: that firms will enter or leave the perfectly competitive industry over the long run depending on the level of profit in that industry. If there are no artificial barriers to entry and there is perfect knowledge of market conditions, there will be incentives for new firms to be established when the industry is more profitable than other industries. When profit is less than in other industries, some firms will leave the industry. We identify the level of profit necessary to keep the number of firms in the industry constant as "normal profit." If there is **free entry** in *any* *market structure*, greater than normal profit will lead to entry, and less than normal profit will cause firms to leave. The result, of course, is that industries characterized by freedom of entry will tend toward only normal profit over the long run, which we can think of as a rate of return on investment similar to that attainable in closely related industries. Finally, as stated in Chapter 7, we will consider normal profit to be a *cost of production*, since over the long run, no output would be produced if the firm's owners did not receive at least a normal return on investment. Thus, all of our cost curves for the firm will include normal profit as an opportunity cost.

What we have said thus far allows us to easily paint a verbal picture of the perfectly competitive model. It is a market structure where individual firms, each of which is insignificant with respect to the total market, go about maximizing profit based on a fixed market price and tend over the long run to attain only normal profit. Most real-world firms do not operate under perfect competition, but its conditions are approximated in some markets. For example, certain agricultural markets, where the government does not operate crop restriction or subsidy programs, come close to being perfectly competitive. Many table vegetables and fruits like apples, cherries, and grapes fall into this group. In addition, some economists argue that the New York stock market approximates the model, since there are many buyers and sellers (both individuals and firms), government interference is minimal, information is abundant, and entry and exit are easy. When these conditions prevail, market demand and that faced by an individual seller are quite different, as we will now show.

Market Demand Versus Firm Demand

The demand curve for the homogeneous product of a perfectly competitive *industry* (i.e., all of the firms that produce the same product) is determined by the preferences of consumers. At any given point in time, if this demand curve is "normal" in the economic sense, it will be characterized by an inverse relationship between the going market price for the product and the quantity consumers are willing to purchase per unit of time (that is, price must be lowered to entice consumers to buy a larger quantity). The demand curve in Figure 8-1, D_i, conforms to such a case. The supply curve of the industry, S_i, shows the amounts that producers are willing to place on the market at various prices. In the short run, we expect such a curve to exhibit a direct relationship between price and the quantity supplied, since production cost per unit (particularly marginal cost, as we saw in Chapter 6) rises as the firms in the industry near their physical capacity per month. An equilibrium price, P_e, is established where the amount of output that producers are willing to put on the market per month is exactly equal to that which consumers are willing to buy. (See Chapter 1 for a mathematical example of determining market equilibrium price.)

FIGURE 8–1

*Industry
Demand and
Supply*

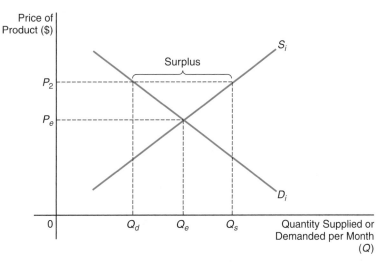

Equilibrium in this market occurs at P_e, Q_e. Any price higher than P_e will result in a surplus and lead to price reductions. Prices below P_e will result in shortages and price increases.

It is obvious in Figure 8-1 that price P_e is the only price at which the quantity that producers are willing to place on the market is equal to that which consumers are willing to buy. Furthermore, we can explain a tendency for this price to be established and to hold as the "going price" by considering what would happen if some other price were temporarily in effect. At P_2, for example, producers would want to put Q_s per month on the market, while consumers would be willing to buy only Q_d. There would be a surplus of $Q_s - Q_d$ units of output in the market, producers' inventories would pile up, and producers would cut price in order to sell more product. This would be the case for any price above P_e. It can easily be verified that for prices *lower* than P_e, the quantity consumers would want to buy in the market would exceed the quantity producers would wish to supply. Consequently, buying activity would reduce producers' inventories and lead to rising prices as consumers bid for the insufficient quantity of output coming into the market. (Use Figure 8-1 to illustrate this situation by drawing a horizontal line over to the S_i and D_i curves for some price lower than P_e. Identify for yourself the shortage in quantity supplied that exists for the lower price.)

In Chapter 1, an **equilibrium price** was defined as a price that equates quantity demanded with quantity supplied. It is clear that P_e is such a price, for it is the only one that can exist for any length of time when market conditions are such as those given by demand curve D_i and supply curve S_i.

It is important to note that D_i, the demand curve of the perfectly competitive industry in Figure 8-1, is *not* the demand curve facing an individual firm in that industry. Remember, we established early in this chapter

An **equilibrium price** is one that equates quantity demanded in the market with quantity supplied so that there is no surplus or shortage of the product being traded.

FIGURE 8–2

Relation of Perfectly Competitive Firm's Demand Curve to the Industry

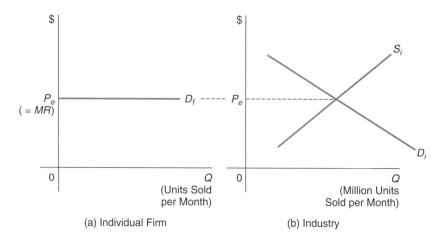

(a) Individual Firm   (b) Industry

The perfectly competitive firm views its demand curve as horizontal at the market price of its product.

that the individual competitive firm takes the market price, P_e, as given and believes it cannot by itself have any effect on this price. Figure 8-2 illustrates the relationship of the market demand curve to that of the individual firm. In panel (b) we see the same market situation that was depicted in Figure 8-1. Panel (a), however, shows the demand curve for the product as it is perceived by the individual perfectly competitive firm. Since the firm takes the market price as given, the horizontal line P_eD_f in panel (a) is its demand curve. Note that the Q axis of panel (a) measures the firm's output in *units* of output per month, whereas the Q axis of panel (b) measures market quantities sold and bought in *millions* of units per month. The point is that movements along P_eD_f in panel (a) are so insignificant that they do not materially affect the equilibrium price and quantity of panel (b). This is a realistic notion as long as the output of the firm is very small with respect to the total market for the product.

From the standpoint of profit maximization, the situation depicted in panel (a) has some further implications for the perfectly competitive firm. First of all, as we know from Chapter 2, the horizontal line P_eD_f is both the marginal and the average revenue curve for the firm, since revenue per unit never changes as output is increased.[1] Finally, since *MR* is the rate of change

---

[1] More formally, we know

$$TR = P \cdot Q, \quad \text{and}$$

$$MR = \frac{dTR}{dQ} = P + Q\frac{dP}{dQ}.$$

of *TR*, the *TR* curve must be a straight line emanating from the origin, as in breakeven analysis.

Profit Maximization under Perfect Competition

If a perfectly competitive firm has short-run cost curves similar to those depicted in Chapter 6 and is incurring greater than normal profit, we can easily illustrate its profit-maximizing output using either marginal and average cost and revenue curves or total cost and total revenue curves. In Figure 8-3, panel (a), we see the firm's total cost and total revenue curves along with a net revenue or profit curve, $T\pi = TR - TC$. The firm maximizes profit at Q_e, where the $T\pi$ curve has its peak and where the slope of the *TR* curve, *MR*, equals that of the *TC* curve, *SMC*, as we learned in Chapter 7. In panel (b) the *Q* axis is identical to that of panel (a), but the $ axis measures per-unit cost and revenue rather than total cost and total revenue. At Q_e in panel (b), *SMC* = *MR* and economic profit per unit is $(P_e - C)$. Total profit may be calculated by taking the per-unit profit $(P_e - C)$ times the number of units sold (OQ_e or CC') and is, therefore, equal to the area of rectangle $CP_eP'C'$. No output greater or less than Q_e will yield a profit as large as the one that exists at Q_e when the market price is P_e.

The firm in Figure 8-3 has profit greater than normal at Q_e, since $T\pi > 0$. This is a feasible result for a perfectly competitive firm in the *short run*, since the number of firms in the industry remains constant and the entry of new producers cannot drive price downward. However, market conditions could easily produce three other possible results for the perfectly competitive firm:

1. normal profit,

2. operating loss, or

3. temporary shutdown.

Panels (a) and (b) of Figure 8-4 provide total and average or per-unit curves for a firm with only normal profit in the short run. Panels (c) and (d) do the same for a firm operating at a loss. Note that in each diagram, the con-

---

Where *P* is constant,

$$\frac{dP}{dQ} = 0,$$

and

$$MR = P.$$

Also,

$$AR = \frac{TR}{Q} = \frac{P(Q)}{Q} = P,$$

the same constant.

FIGURE 8–3

*Perfectly
Competititve
Firm with Profit
Greater than
Normal*

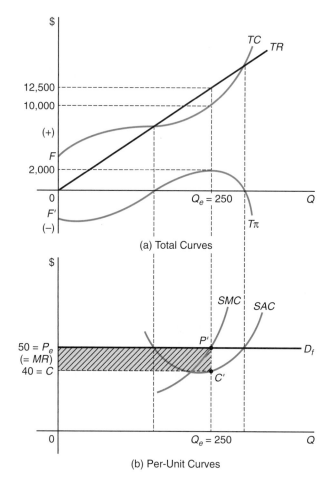

(a) Total Curves

(b) Per-Unit Curves

The firm maximizes profit where $SMC = MR$, which corresponds to the peak of the $T\pi$ curve in panel (a). In panel (b) profit is equal to the area of the shaded rectangle, or $(P - SAC)$ multiplied by Q_e.

dition $SMC = MR$ holds at the equilibrium output, Q_e. In panels (a) and (b), $T\pi = 0$, $C = P_e$, and there is only normal profit. In panels (c) and (d), $T\pi < 0$, $C > P_e$, and there is a loss equal to $0L$ in the upper diagram or to the area $CP_eP'C'$ in the lower diagram.

An important point in this latter case is that the operating loss at output Q_e, $0L$ in panel (c), is less than fixed cost, $0F$. Because fixed cost is $0F$ even when output is zero, the firm should shut down only when $0L$ exceeds $0F$ (or

FIGURE 8–4

Normal Profit and Operating Loss under Perfect Competition

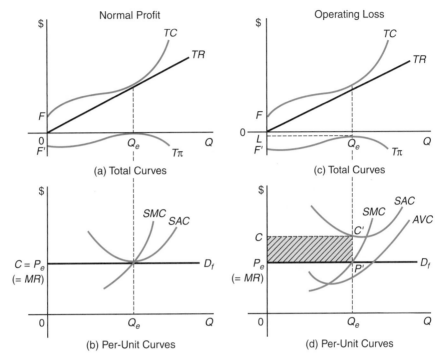

In panels (a) and (b), $T\pi = 0$, since $TC = TR$ and $P = SAC$ at Q_e. In panels (c) and (d), the firm has a loss at Q_e but should operate, since the loss is less than total fixed cost.

$0F'$), as we learned in Chapter 7. You should be able to verify that the firm in Figure 8-5 will minimize its losses by temporarily shutting down.

In the short run, the firm that is a loss minimizer as well as a profit maximizer will not produce when price is below *AVC* but will produce at $SMC = MR = P_e$ when price is above *AVC*. It follows from this profit-maximizing principle that the *short-run supply curve* of a perfectly competitive firm is that portion of its marginal cost curve *(SMC)* that lies above *AVC*. Note in Figure 8-6 that as price (and *MR*) moves upward from P_1 to P_2 to P_3 in response to shifting market demand, the firm's equilibrium output increases from Q_1 to Q_2 to Q_3. Because the firm's *SMC* (above minimum *AVC*) gives the relationship between price and the quantity supplied by the firm, the short-run industry supply curve, S_i in panel (b), which is the sum of the firms' short-run supply curves, is also the sum of the *SMCs* of all firms in the industry. In other words, for each price, we sum the quantities of output supplied by the various firms (sometimes called a "horizontal" sum). It follows that S_i or ΣS_f will shift outward in the long run if firms enter the industry and inward if firms leave the industry.

FIGURE 8–5

*Shutdown
Conditions under
Perfect
Competition*

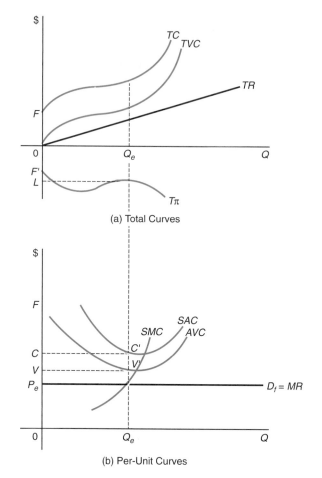

(a) Total Curves

(b) Per-Unit Curves

The firm in these diagrams should temporarily shut down, since its operating loss at Q_e would exceed total fixed cost.

FIGURE 8–6

*Short-Run
Supply under
Perfect
Competition*

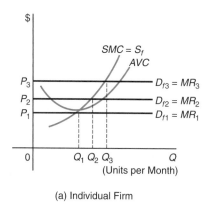

(a) Individual Firm

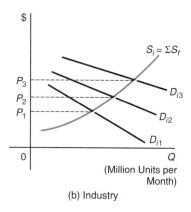

(b) Industry

The perfectly competititve firm's short-run supply curve is its *SMC* curve for the range where *SMC* is above *AVC*. The industry supply curve is the horizontal sum of all the firms' *SMC* curves over the same range.

The Long Run under Perfect Competition

In the long run, the firm will maximize profit by equating long-run marginal cost to the going market price and its constant marginal revenue ($LMC = P_e = MR$). As we indicated in Chapter 7, this involves adjusting plant size to that plant that has a short-run average cost just equal to long-run average cost at the long-run, profit-maximizing output ($LAC = SAC$). This occurs where the SAC curve is tangent to LAC and also where $SMC = LMC = P_e = MR$. Under perfect competition in the long run, there will be only normal profit for the typical firm in the industry. If profit is greater than normal, new firms will enter the industry, thereby increasing industry supply and reducing market price. Entry will continue to take place as long as profit is greater than normal.

In terms of the short- and long-run average cost curves of the individual firm, the long-run equilibrium position is shown in Figure 8-7, panel (a). The industry adjustment to the equilibrium price, P_e, is shown in panel (b). If the short-run industry supply curve is initially at S_i and price is P', the typical firm will have greater than normal profit. (In panel (a), P' would intersect SMC well above the minimum point on the SAC curve.) The entry of new firms attracted by the greater than normal profit shifts the industry supply curve rightward to S_i', where it intersects the market demand curve at a price consistent with attainment of only normal profit by the typical firm. This price must be P_e in Figure 8-7, since minimum long-run average cost is equal to P_e. At any price higher than P_e, the typical firm would still have greater than normal profit, and entry would continue. If S_i were to shift out further than S_i, price would fall below P_e. In this instance, some firms would leave the industry, and S_i would shift leftward until P_e was established.

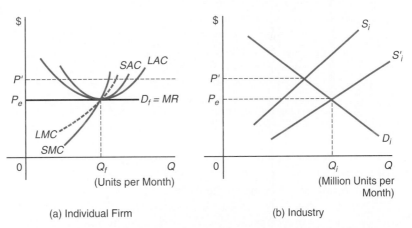

FIGURE 8–7

The Long Run under Perfect Competition

(a) Individual Firm

(b) Industry

In the long run under perfect competition, profit will tend toward normal (zero economic profit), since firms will enter whenever profit exceeds normal and leave whenever profits are below normal.

NUMERICAL EXAMPLE

Perfect Competition and Sunk Costs in Farming

Pansy Witherspoon grows natural cabbage (no chemical fertilizers or pesticides used). She has an 800-acre farm. While her planting and cultivating costs per acre are sunk (have been incurred and cannot be reduced) at $10 per acre, her harvesting costs are still variable. Pansy's land is of uneven quality, and the yield per acre drops as she incorporates less and less productive land into her cabbage production. She has 150 acres that will yield 20 bushels per acre, 150 that will yield 18 bushels per acre, 200 that will yield 16 bushels per acre, 150 that will yield 14 bushels per acre, and another 150 that will yield only 10 bushels per acre.

Pansy figures the harvesting costs for the cabbage are $30 per acre. Assuming she planted the entire acreage, how much of it should she harvest if, when the cabbage is mature, the going market price that she can obtain is $2.75 per bushel?

Answer

Pansy should harvest all but that grown on the lowest-yielding land (the 150 acres that yield only 10 bushels per acre). We have a sunk cost problem here, because the planting and cultivating costs are already expended by harvest time. Thus, the relevant marginal cost for decision making is the marginal cost per bushel for harvesting. For each class of land, this is the acre cost divided by the yield per acre, the figure that appears in the righthand column below:

Acres	Yield	$30/yield = MC per Bu. to Harvest
150	20	1.50
150	18	1.67
200	16	1.88
150	14	2.14
150	10	3.00

Since Pansy's marginal revenue is $2.75 (assume perfect competition), the lowest-yielding land will not be worth harvesting, and the plants should just be left to decay and then ploughed under when ploughing time comes. Pansy will have a profit contribution of $10,750 on the 650 acres she harvests, assuming all variable costs are accounted for in the harvesting costs stated earlier. (At this point, the planting and cultivating costs are sunk costs and must be treated like fixed costs as Pansy makes her decision with regard to how many acres to harvest.)

As long as there are no changes in input prices or technology, the industry long-run equilibrium price will be P_e. This is the long-run equilibrium price because Q_f is the only level of output at which $P (= MR) = LMC$, so the firm's profit-maximization rule is met, and $P = LAC$, so there are no economic profits. Of course, if industry expansion is accompanied by rising input prices, P_e will rise over time. Falling long-run input prices or improvements in technology, on the other hand, could lead to decreases in P_e as the industry expands. Whatever the result in terms of long-run price, firms will tend toward operation at the bottom of the *LAC* curve, with price equal to average cost, and they will tend to settle on the size of plant that has its minimum *SAC* tangent to the lowest point on *LAC*.

Overview of Perfect Competition

We can now summarize the perfectly competitive model and relate it to the behavior of firms in the real world. First, the model assumes that the firm has no market power—in the sense that it can obtain no price higher than the going price for its output and that price cutting is made unnecessary by its ability to sell all it wishes at the going price. In the short run, the firm takes the fixed market price as its marginal revenue curve and maximizes its profit at the output where $SMC = MR = P$. It may operate with normal profit, greater than normal profit, or less than normal profit, but it will temporarily shut down only if market price is less than average variable cost.

In the long run, firms in the perfectly competitive industry will tend to have only normal profit, since entry will occur when profit is greater than normal, whereas less than normal profit will cause some firms to leave. The typical firm will adjust its plant size over the long run to a size that is consistent with minimum long-run average cost, since higher cost plants will not be able to achieve normal profit. Productive efficiency in terms of the least possible cost per unit of output is thus assured in the perfectly competitive industry. This result is one reason perfect competition is frequently used as a norm or standard against which to assess other types of market structures and their consequences.

Many firms, particularly small firms, face some of the conditions of the perfectly competitive model in their everyday operations. However, it is rare that all of the perfectly competitive assumptions prevail. After all, the U.S. economy and industrial economies in general are characterized by the corporate form of business organization, where certain lines of production are dominated by a few very large enterprises. In many of these industries, entry of new firms is extremely difficult, similar products are differentiated from one another by superficial changes and heavy advertising, and the activities of one firm have very substantial effects on others.

It is significant, however, that small firms often cannot block entry into their markets or differentiate their products sufficiently to have much effect on their competitors. In a large city, Hank's Garage may try to develop a reputation for fair prices and good service, but Hank is unlikely to be able to charge prices that are much different from those of other garages, and he can do little or nothing to keep Rosa Alonso from opening a new garage in his market area. If Hank is an efficient operator, however, he will be able to run

The Cocoa Industry and the Competitive Model

It is frequently argued that the model of perfect competition would apply reasonably well to agriculture if there were no government intervention such as price support and acreage restriction programs. It is also argued that certain world commodity markets would conform closely to perfect competition, if there were no international commodity agreements to help stabilize them.

Alas, poor cocoa. After many years of operating with price support from the London-based ICCO, an international organization set up to buy surplus production of cocoa and resell it during periods of shortage, the industry in the 1990s was in a shambles. The price of cocoa had plummeted from a 1977 high of about $5,500 per ton to less than $850 per ton, and, for producers, there seemed to be no relief in sight. At the bottom of the trouble was the shortage of 1977, which not only brought on the $5,000-plus price level and huge industry profits but also prompted many new growers in tropical countries to plant vast tracts of seedling trees. As the trees matured, the cocoa supply curve shifted to the right, and prices fell markedly.

It would be easy to get the idea that cocoa production takes place on a few huge plantations owned by the descendants of foreign adventurers who went to the tropics a century or more ago to exploit the land. However, although there are no doubt some very wealthy third- or fourth-generation planters, there are also many, many smaller growers. In its poverty-stricken Northeast, Brazil alone counts more than 20,000 small cocoa growers,

and small planters are also found in West Africa, Malaysia, and Indonesia.

As noted earlier, the profits reaped by growers in the late 1970s led to entry. As the new cocoa plants matured, prices began their downward trend. There were simply too many new producers bringing too much output to market, and efforts by both the ICCO and the governments of producer nations only had limited impacts on market supply.

In the early 1990s, the ICCO toiled to come up with a new Cocoa Agreement that would regulate supply. A five-year pact was signed in 1994, but many observers believed that it was not likely to have much impact, especially because Indonesia, one of the world's largest producers, would not join the ICCO. By 1998, the ICCO had sold all stocks that it had held for market stabilization purposes, and Indonesia still was not a member. Some suppliers had left the market, and prices had leveled off at about $1,500 per ton. As the millennium approached, prices fell again, to less than $700 in late 2000 and early 2001. It was clear that the ICCO had no way to control the market and that, as the competitive model argues, entry and exit by producers would be the main determinant of cocoa's long-run price.

References: "Cocoa Update," Ganes Consulting, LLC., February 5, 2002; *Market News* (ICCO newsletter), July 14, 1999; "Hot Chocolate," *Economist* (June 11, 1994), p. 62; "Stockpiles and Shortages," *Futures* (December 1993), pp. 52, 54; and "Bitter Times for Cocoa Growers," *Business Week*, April 4, 1988, p. 83.

his business at a normal level of profit. Many other small businesses are in much the same position. In such a setting, they may have greater than normal profit for some short period of time, but this is the exception and not the rule. The small businessperson who "makes a killing" is generally one who was in the right place at the right time and thus was able to cash in on *temporarily* greater than normal profits.

MONOPOLY AND ITS SETTING

Monopoly, in its purest form, is the case of a single seller. The market demand for its product is the only constraint on the firm's pricing policies. Barriers to entry prevent new firms from coming into the industry.

Monopoly is the name applied to the extreme case in which there is only *one* seller of a given product. In a sense, it lies at the opposite end of the product market spectrum from perfect competition, and we will see later that the monopoly model provides the basic analytical framework for virtually all less than perfectly competitive product market structures.

Although, in general, monopoly is relatively rare, there are many monopolies, such as local gas and water companies, in the public utilities business. These firms are monopolies by virtue of franchises granted by government, and, because of that, government usually regulates their operations and pricing. Firms in other types of business may be monopolies because they hold a patent for a good or a production process or control the supply of a scarce resource. For example, it is widely argued that the DeBeers Company controls the supply of large, gem-quality diamonds and constitutes a monopoly in that specific segment of the diamond industry.

The monopoly market structure's key requirement of a single seller with a product that is not duplicated by other firms leads directly to two results:

1. The market demand curve is the firm's demand curve.
2. Entry is blocked over the long run.

Of course, if the firm is a monopolist, it can hardly be unaware that it is the only seller in the market for its product; therefore, it must know that to the extent that it can estimate market demand, it has estimated the demand curve it faces. To remain a monopolist, the firm must be in a setting where entry is effectively blocked. This is possible if the firm controls the sole source of a mineral, for example, or if it has a patent or license that prohibits others from producing its product or selling a similar product within a given geographical area.

We expect the monopolist to have a downward-sloping demand curve that will be elastic over some range. In spite of the fact that a firm is the sole seller, it will be able to raise the price sufficiently to cause a proportionately large reduction in the number of buyers who will want to or be able to purchase its product. Since the monopolistic firm knows it faces such a demand curve, it is aware that the quantity of output it can sell will depend on the price it sets.

Profit Maximization under Monopoly

If the monopoly firm's demand curve is linear, we can expect its profit-maximizing short-run equilibrium to look like Figure 8-8 whenever it is fortunate enough to have greater than normal profit. Note that where $SMC = MR$ and the $T\pi$ curve is at its peak, *both* the *market price* and the *quantity produced* are determined. If one compares Figure 8-8 to Figure 8-3, it is apparent that the differences between the graphical analyses of monopoly and perfect competition stem from their respective assumptions concerning the demand curve of the firm. TR in Figure 8-3 is a straight line from the origin because D_f is a horizontal line, meaning price is constant and equal to marginal revenue. In Figure 8-8, TR is a curve with a maximum because the demand curve, D, is a downward-sloping line. In addition, MR lies below D or AR in the lower panel of Figure 8-8 because price must be lowered on *all* units sold to sell larger levels of output, as was explained in Chapter 2.

FIGURE 8–8

Monopoly in the Short Run with Profit Greater Than Normal

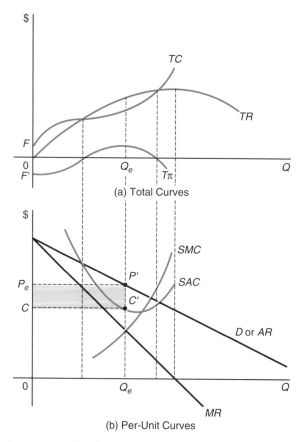

(a) Total Curves

(b) Per-Unit Curves

In panel (a), profit is maximized at Q_e, where the $T\pi$ curve has its peak. In panel (b), $SMC = MR$ at Q_e and profit equals $(P_e - C)$ multiplied by Q_e.

The profit-maximizing monopoly must determine its equilibrium (profit-maximizing) output where $MR = MC$ or where $M\pi = 0$, subject to the usual condition that $M\pi$ is negative for greater output levels. Thereafter, the firm must set its price at the demand curve point that corresponds with its equilibrium output. The firm depicted in Figure 8-8 would first find Q_e, the profit-maximizing output. The corresponding profit-maximizing price, P_e, would then be determined. Suppose, for purposes of illustration, that $Q_e = 200$. *If the firm's demand curve is given by the equation Q = 800 – 2P*, it would follow that at Q_e, $200 = 800 – 2P$. Solving for P, we find:

$$2P = 800 - 200 = 600,$$

and

$$P = 300 = P_e.$$

Thus, to maximize profit, the monopoly would set its price at $300 per unit, where consumers would buy exactly 200 units of output per time period.

Although the monopolist of Figure 8-8 has greater than normal profit, it should be understood that in the short run, the monopoly firm (just like the firm under perfect competition) can also have only normal profit, or operate at a loss, or temporarily choose to cease production, depending on the relationship of demand to the firm's short-run cost structure. In Figure 8-9, panels (a) and (b) show the monopolistic firm operating with only normal profit, while panels (c) and (d) illustrate short-run operation with negative profit. Operation at Q_e in the latter case is rational, since in the upper panel, $0L$ is less than $0F$ (or $0F'$), and in the lower panel, P_e exceeds AVC. If price does not exceed average variable cost at the $SMC = MR$ level of output, the monopolist should temporarily shut down and lose only the fixed costs.

The Long-Run under Monopoly

In the long run, the monopoly firm continues to determine both its profit-maximizing rate of output and its selling price where (long-run) marginal cost is equal to marginal revenue. As in pure competition, if a monopolistic firm has predicted its optimal long-run output correctly, it can produce that output with the optimal combination of inputs; therefore, its long-run cost curves are appropriate for determining its profit-maximizing output. As in the short run, the firm may or may not have greater than normal profit. However, in the event that profit *is* greater than normal, entry will not occur, since other firms are not free to come into the industry. It follows that greater than normal profit can exist indefinitely. Figure 8-10 depicts such a case. Note that Figure 8-10 differs from panel (b) of Figure 8-8 only by the inclusion of the firm's long-run average and marginal cost curves.

FIGURE 8–9

Monopoly in the Short Run: Normal Profit and Operating Loss Cases

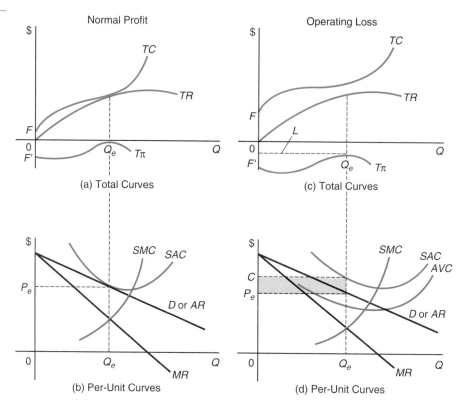

The monopoly in panels (a) and (b) has $T\pi = 0$, since at Q_e, $TC = TR$ and $P = SAC$. In panels (c) and (d), the firm has a loss, since at Q_e, $TR < TC$ and $P > SAC$. However, it should operate, since its operating loss is less than total fixed cost.

If Q_e is a long-run profit-maximizing output, then it must be true that both *SMC* for the appropriate-sized plant and *LMC* are equal to *MR*. The long-run equilibrium of Figure 8-10 differs from that of the perfectly competitive firm in Figure 8-7 not only by the existence of a greater than normal profit but also by the operation of the firm at a level of output where *LAC* is falling, which means that even the least cost plant for producing Q_e produces it at an average cost higher than the long-run optimum plant under perfect competition. (The appropriate plant under perfect competition is the one whose *SAC* is tangent to *LAC* at its minimum point and is both larger and has a lower per-unit cost associated with it than that in a monopoly.) In fact, under monopoly we can draw no special conclusion regarding plant size in the long run when profit is greater than normal, because the long-run equilibrium output for a monopoly in this case may be to the left, right, or at the output level where minimum *LAC* can be achieved.

FIGURE 8–10

*Monopoly in the
Long Run with
Greater Than
Normal Profit*

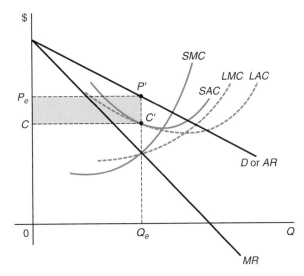

Since there is no entry in the long run under monopoly, the firm can have greater than normal profit indefinitely. In this case, profit is equal to $(P_e - C)$ multiplied by Q_e.

When profit is only normal, however, the monopolist must be producing a level of output where the *LAC* is falling, since normal profit requires that the two appropriate average cost curves (*SAC* and *LAC*) be tangent to the downward-sloping demand curve (*P* must equal *SAC* and *LAC*). Figure 8-11 illustrates the case of a monopolist with only normal profit in the long run.

FIGURE 8-11

*Monopoly in the
Long Run with
only Normal
Profit*

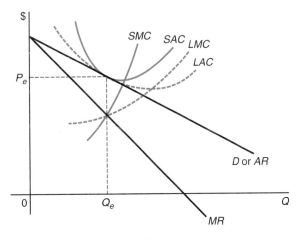

Normal profit is a possibility under monopoly. However, as this diagram shows, the monopoly firm with $P = SAC$ and $T\pi = 0$ will operate in a plant that lies on the falling portion of *LAC*.

NUMERICAL EXAMPLE

The Pricing of Water in a New Housing Development

Artie Fender, a developer in Saugus, California, has opened a new housing tract just outside of town where he also owns the water system. Artie figures that, based on average home size, the demand for water in the development is expressed in the following equation:

$$Q_w = 80,000 - 2000P_w,$$

where Q_w is the number of thousands of gallons of water consumed per month and P_w is the price per 1,000 gallons. If Artie's marginal cost of producing the water is constant at $5 per 1,000 gallons, what price should he charge for the water? If the average home consumes 10,000 gallons per month, what will be the household's water bill? (Assume Artie's company faces no regulation.)

Answer

Since Artie is a pure monopolist, he should just set his marginal cost equal to the marginal revenue from the preceding demand curve. Transposing the demand equation yields

$$P_w = 40 - .0005Q_w$$

$$MR_w = 40 - .001Q_w.$$

Setting $MR = MC$,

$$40 - .001Q_w = 5$$

$$.001Q_w = 35$$

$$Q_w = \underline{35,000.}$$

Substituting,

$$P_w = 40 - .0005(35,000) = \underline{\$22.50}.$$

If the average household uses 10,000 gallons per month, it will pay a water bill of $225 per month.

Since, as we have shown, monopoly firms can indefinitely sustain greater than normal long-run profit, the government has undertaken the regulation of monopoly in many cases. Public agencies utilize two basic tools in the regulation of monopolies: taxes and price regulation. When taxes are used, the monopolist's costs are increased and profit is reduced. If the tax is

MANAGERIAL PERSPECTIVE

Love Your Local Cable TV Monopoly?

In the Orwellian year of 1984, Big Brother decided to deregulate the cable TV industry. At the time, Congress thought such an action would stimulate the growth of the industry and encourage both entry and competition. Well, the industry certainly has grown, and some of the participants in it are extremely profitable firms.

Although there has been some entry into the cable industry at the national level, where a number of large firms are slugging it out, consumers usually deal with only one company at the local level. Some of these companies are quite small when compared to the national cable networks like ESPN, CNN, TBS, or USA. However, the 1984 decision of Congress covered these companies too, thereby approving of deregulated monopoly at the local level. Since there was no entry possible at that level, where a single firm generally had a franchise let by local government, the firms were free to set profit-maximizing prices which move upward as cable demand increases while there is no corresponding increase in supply. Thus, the local cable operators could enjoy returns that are greater than normal with a perfect barrier to entry, the franchise. This, of course, made them ripe for buyouts from large companies such as Time Warner.

In cases where profits are greater than normal, if entry occurred it would lead to lower prices and, therefore, more households served. That is not what happened in local cable markets. Either the local monopolies remained, or they were acquired by larger firms. As the monopoly prices rose, outcries from consumers called for rate regulation. However, Congress, in bills passed in 1993 and 1996, focused mainly on basic and expanded basic cable service, allowing the firms to charge whatever they wanted for higher levels of service. The power it gave the Federal Communications Commission (FCC) to regulate the basic services ended in March 1999. The only option that consumers had left was to appeal to local communities to regulate the basic service tier. However, local governments have often made matters worse by not allowing entry of competing services. (In 2002, Consumers Union reported that 95 percent of U.S. households had only one choice for a cable company.) Even with the FCC in the picture during the 1996–1999 period, the average cable bill increased at four times the rate of inflation. Needless to say, consumer advocates, such as the Consumers Union, have been pessimistic about future rate hikes.

References: Consumer Federation of America/ Consumers Union, "The Telecommunications Act: Consumers Still Waiting for Better Phone & Cable Services on the Sixth Aniversary of National Law," press release, February 6, 2002, www. consumersunion.org/telecom/sixthdc202.htm, June 22, 2002; "Most Cable TV Federal Price Controls to End March 31," *Fox Market Wire*, February 9, 1999, www.foxmarketwire.com April 6, 1999, "Cable TV Rates Soar over Inflation Rate," *Communications Media Center at New York Law School*, January 14, 1998, www.cmcnyls.edu, March 5, 1999, and "Tune in, Turn on, Sort out," *Time*, May 29, 1989, p. 68.

a variable cost, output will also be reduced. When price regulation is used, the regulatory authority must determine whether the firm can cover costs with the price that is set. If it cannot, subsidization will be required to keep the firm from going out of business. We will investigate these topics further in Chapter 16.

Overview of Monopoly

Briefly, we can summarize the monopoly case as that of a firm that is the sole seller of some product and maximizes profit in both the short and long run by equating marginal cost to marginal revenue, having derived marginal revenue from the market demand curve for the product. In determining its equilibrium output, the firm also determines the price of its product, since both price and marginal revenue depend on the amount sold. This can easily be seen from the firm's downward-sloping demand and marginal revenue curves. The monopoly firm may have greater than normal profit, normal profit, or losses in the short run, depending on the relation between its costs and the market demand. If it remains in business over the long run, it can be expected to have at least normal profit.

We should note that the analysis of any firm that perceives or estimates a downward-sloping demand curve is graphically identical to that of monopoly, except that the firm's demand (or *AR*) curve is not the market demand curve for the product when there is more than one seller in the market. In the chapters that follow, therefore, we will see a good deal more of the downward-sloping demand and marginal revenue curves. However, in contrast to monopoly, the market situations to be examined next generally assume that a number of firms are engaged in the production and sale of identical, or at least similar, products.

SUMMARY

Competition, Monopoly, and Analysis of the Firm

In this chapter, we provided a brief review of the two limiting cases in the microeconomic analysis of the firm: perfect competition and monopoly. The discussion was in large part theoretical, since we believe that few real-world firms exactly fit the assumptions of either case. However, the point was made that many real-world firms face situations characterized by such attributes of perfect competition as a market with many buyers and sellers, similar costs from firm to firm, and relatively free entry in the long run. In addition, it was argued that a large number of firms in modern industrial economies depart from the perfectly competitive situation and, in fact, must be viewed in an entirely different light. For such firms, the pure monopoly case holds some analytical keys that will be useful in the chapters that follow.

Our review of perfect competition extended the profit analysis of Chapter 7 to the setting of a firm too small to have any effect on its own price and situated in an industry characterized by long-run freedom of entry. In the short run, the firm acted as a price taker, and management's task was simply to determine the rate of output that would maximize profit or minimize loss. It was seen that the firm could do any of the following in the short run: operate with a greater than normal profit; operate with only normal profit; operate with a loss less than total fixed costs; or temporarily shut down, losing only fixed costs. In the long run, however, it was argued that the firm would have only normal profit because of freedom of entry into the industry. Thus, any occurrence of temporarily greater than normal profits would be followed by the entry of new firms and an increase in industry supply, which would depress the market price and eliminate the abnormal profits of older firms. Below-normal profits would occur only temporarily, since they would provide an incentive to leave the industry in search of higher returns. In this chapter, the long-run equilibrium of the perfectly competitive market was shown to result not only in normal levels of profit but also in economic efficiency, since all firms tended toward operation at the minimum point of the long-run average cost curve.

The discussion of monopoly noted that, although the monopoly firm determines not only its profit-maximizing output, but also the appropriate price to charge for its product, it is still somewhat at the mercy of its demand curve. By this we mean that the monopoly firm's demand curve, which is the market demand curve for the product, might not provide the firm with any opportunities for greater than normal profit. In fact (as we showed previously), in regard to profit, the monopoly firm in the short run has all the same possible outcomes as the perfectly competitive firm, including normal profit, operating loss, and temporary shutdown. In the long run, however, the monopoly firm may reap greater than normal profit indefinitely, since entry into the industry is effectively blocked. The lack of entry that characterizes monopolistic market situations may also lead to inefficiency in production, since there is no assurance that the monopoly firm's profit-maximizing output will occur in an optimum-sized plant. Because of the profit and efficiency problems, monopolies are usually subject to rather strict regulation by government. The nature of such regulation is discussed in Chapter 16.

Many firms that are not monopolies operate under market conditions that approximate monopoly much more closely than they do perfect competition. The giant industrial enterprises of the United States and Europe are cases in point. The issue of government regulation of such firms is controversial and centers around the question of antitrust law. This subject will also be taken up in Chapter 16. Meanwhile, the next few chapters will further extend our analysis of managerial decision making to market situations notably more complex than the two limiting cases that we have reviewed here.

QUESTIONS

1. Under what conditions can we expect to find a perfectly competitive firm with greater than normal profit?

2. What is the profit expectation for a perfectly competitive firm in the long run? Why?

3. How is the short-run supply curve of a perfectly competitive *industry* derived? Is there anything that would ensure that such a curve would slope upward and to the right?

4. What control does the individual perfectly competitive firm have over the price it charges for its product? Explain.

5. The agricultural sector of the U.S. economy is often said to approximate a perfectly competitive market situation. Do you think this characterization is appropriate? What would you predict about the chances for success of farmers' strikes and protest marches (tractor parades), as well as of farm organizations bent on securing higher prices, given what you know about the perfectly competitive model?

6. What kind of market demand situation can we expect a monopolistic firm to face? Why?

7. Must monopoly firms always have greater than normal profits in the short run? Why or why not?

8. Under what conditions would a monopoly firm have only normal profit in the long run? (Assume no regulation.)

9. Why can an unregulated monopoly firm have greater than normal profit indefinitely over the long run?

10. If an unregulated monopoly firm has only normal profit in the long run, will it be operating at the minimum point of its long-run average cost curve? Why or why not?

PROBLEMS

1. Diagram the following situations using both total and per-unit (average, marginal) cost and revenue curves.

   a. A perfectly competitive firm producing output but minimizing its short-run loss.

   b. A monopoly producing its long-run profit-maximizing output with only normal profit.

   c. A perfectly competitive firm in the short run with greater than normal profit.

   d. A monopoly operating but minimizing loss in the short run.

2. Suppose a firm has the following short-run cost data:

SMC	MP_b	Output of X	Input of b	AP_b	AVC	STC
		0	0	—	—	
		100	2		0.40	240
		250	4			
		350	6			
		425	8			
		475	10			
		500	12			

a. Complete the table.

b. Find its best short-run output if it has no choice but to sell its product at the prevailing market price of $0.78.

3. Determine whether the following perfectly competitive firm should produce output in the short run or temporarily shut down. Given

$$P = MR = \$60$$

$$TC = 4{,}000 + 204Q - 3Q^2 + 0.02Q^3$$

$$SMC = 204 - 6Q + 0.06Q^2$$

where

Q is units produced per month.

If the firm does not operate, it will lose its $4,000 of fixed costs. What profit or loss will it have if it operates where $SMC = MR$?

4. Suppose a firm is operating under highly competitive market conditions and the going price for its product is $P_x = \$260$. If the firm's short-run total cost function is

$$TC = 1{,}000 + 80Q_x - 6Q^2_x + 0.2Q^3_x,$$

and therefore marginal cost is

$$MC = 80 - 12Q_x + 0.6Q^2_x,$$

what is the firm's profit-maximizing output? (Show work.) How much profit will the firm have? (Assume all data pertain to monthly operations.)

5. Examine the following diagrams.

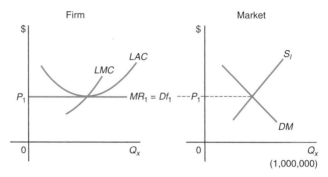

The industry is perfectly competitive. *Explain* and *illustrate* what would happen if market demand increased. That is, what adjustments would occur in the *long run*? (Assume the cost curves do not shift in any way.)

6. The following data pertain to a monopoly firm's demand and costs per quarter.

Q (quantity sold)	P (unit price)	TVC (total variable cost)
0	$20	0
5,000	18	$100,000
10,000	16	120,000
15,000	14	180,000
20,000	12	250,000
25,000	10	330,000
30,000	8	420,000
35,000	6	520,000
40,000	4	640,000

If total fixed costs are $10,000 per quarter, what will be the firm's maximum profit output? How much will profit be at this output level?

7. Complete the following table, assuming that the firm is in the short run and L is the only variable input.

TC	AFC	AVC	AP_L	Input of L	$TP_L =$ Output	MP_L	SMC
	—	—	—	0	0		
						10	
960.00	90.00	6		1	10		
						18	3.33
		4.29		2	28		
		3.75		3	48		
		4.29	14.0	4			
						4	
	15.00			5	60		
						3	20.00
	14.29	5.71	10.5	6			

Assuming the firm operates in a perfectly competitive market and faces a market price of $12 per unit for its product, answer the following:

a. At which of the outputs in the table will it have the greatest profit (lowest loss)?

b. How much will the above profit (loss) be?

8. Complete the revenue and cost data in the following table, assuming that the firm, Calabasa Consolidated Cable, is a monopoly that has been allowed to set its own price for home TV cable service in the very small town of Calabasa, Wisconsin. (Q refers to number of subscribers, and the revenue and cost data are per month.)

MR	P	Q	TR	STC	AVC	TVC	MC
	110		1100			600	
————	100	20		1500	35.00		————
————		30	2700	1700		900	20
————	80	40		2000			30
————	70		3500		32.00		————
————		60	3600				50
————	50	70		3500		2700	————

a. What output and price will Calabasa Cable choose? Explain why, relating your answer to the general condition for a profit maximum.

b. How much total profit will Calabasa have at the maximum?

c. In the table, $300 per month of the cable company's total fixed cost is a franchise fee paid to the city. If no other data change, but the city raises the franchise fee to $500 per month, what will be the effect on the company's output, price, and total profit? *Explain.*

9. Gina Redonda has the only ready-mix concrete company in Hot Pepper, New Mexico. She believes that concrete batching and delivery costs can be viewed as relatively constant at $18 per cubic yard of concrete sold. If she estimates the monthly demand in her market area to be given by the demand curve $Q = 1200 - 10P$, so that $MR = 120 - 0.2Q$:

a. How many yards of concrete should she sell per month?

b. What price should she charge per yard, and how much will her total profit contribution from concrete sales be?

10. Suppose a monopoly firm has a constant marginal cost of $50 per unit of output and that it estimates its demand curve to have the equation $Q = 10,000 - 40P$.

a. At what price and quantity sold will the firm maximize its total *revenue?*

b. At what price and quantity sold will the firm maximize its total *profit?*

c. Compare total profit at the revenue-maximizing output with total profit at the profit-maximizing output. (Assume $TFC = \$300,000$.)

11. A perfectly competitive firm estimates its marginal cost function to be $SMC = 50 + 0.5Q$. The market price of its product is $275.

   a. Find the firm's profit-maximizing output level.

   Suppose the firm has the following average cost function:

   $$SAC = 8,000/Q + 50 + 0.25Q$$

   b. Will this firm have total profit greater than normal in the short run?

   c. If this firm is typical of others in its industry, what do you expect will happen in the long run?

The following problems require calculus.

C1. Suppose the typical firm in a perfectly competitive industry has the following long-run total cost function:

   $$LTC = 240Q_x - 6Q_x^2 + 0.08Q_x^3$$

   If this function remains stable, what will be the long-run going price for Product *x*?

C2. Assume a perfectly competitive firm has the following total cost function for the short run:

   $$STC = 700 + 90Q - 4.5Q^2 + (1/3)Q^3$$

   a. Determine its profit-maximizing or loss-minimizing output for the short run, given that the market price of its product is $180 per unit.

   b. What will be the firm's short-run profit or loss?

C3. A monopoly firm has the following demand curve:

   $$Q = 2,000 - 25P,$$

   where Q is its monthly output. Given that its monthly short-run total cost is described by the function

   $$STC = 500 + 8Q + 0.035Q^2,$$

   answer the following questions.

   a. What will be its profit-maximizing price and output?

   b. How much profit will it have at the preceding output?

C4. The following is a demand curve that has been estimated for a monopoly firm:

   $$Q_x = 4,000 - 20P_x,$$

   where Q_x is the quantity of Product *x* sold per month, and P_x is the price charged by the firm.

If its marginal cost is constant at $20 per unit, at what price and quantity will it maximize profit?

C5. a. Solve problem C4 for a monopoly firm with the same demand curve but the following short-run total cost function:

$$TC = 8{,}750 + 176Q_x - 2.93Q_x^2 + 0.02Q_x^3$$

b. Indicate the dollar amount of profit for the firm at the preceding output per month.

C6. Suppose a monopoly firm has the following demand and short-run total cost curves:

$$Q = 100 - P$$

$$STC = 250 + 180Q - 13Q^2 + (1/3)Q^3$$

a. At what output and price will the firm maximize total *revenue?*

b. At what output and price will the firm maximize total *profit?*

c. Compare the maximum profit obtainable with the profit that the firm would have if it chose a revenue-maximizing strategy. (Show calculations.)

C7. Suppose a perfectly competitive firm has the following total cost function for the short run:

$$STC = 5{,}000 + 150Q - 12Q^2 + (1/3)Q^3$$

a. Determine its profit-maximizing or loss-minimizing output for the short run, given that the market price of its product is $330 per unit.

b. What will be the firm's short-run profit or loss?

c. Now disregard the preceding cost function, and suppose its *long-run* total cost is:

$$LTC = 660Q - 9Q^2 + 0.05Q^3$$

 i. Write an equation for long-run average cost.

 ii. Indicate the firm's long-run price, quantity sold, and profit, assuming the industry is in long-run equilibrium.

C8. Stanley Straing has a soft-drink concession monopoly at the Fort Tippecanoe, Indiana, County Fair. He believes his total cost for supplying the drinks will be

$$STC = 800 + 0.2Q + 0.0001Q^2.$$

If the County Fair Board tells him he must charge $0.80 and demand for the drinks during the fair is given by the demand curve $Q = 5{,}000 - 2{,}500P$, determine the following:

a. The number of drinks sold and Stanley's total profit at the fixed price of $0.80 per drink.

b. Whether the amount Stanley wants to sell is consistent with the amount consumers want to buy at the $0.80 price.

c. Stanley's profit-maximizing output, price, and profit if he were allowed to set his own price instead of having to charge $0.80.

SELECTED REFERENCES

Gegax, Douglas, and Kenneth Nowotny. "Competition and the Electric Utility industry: An Evaluation." *Yale Journal on Regulation* 10, No. 1 (Winter 1993): 63–87.

Landsberg, Stephen E. *Price Theory and Applications,* 4th ed. Cincinnati: South-Western College Publishing, 1999, Chapters 7 and 10.

Mansfield, Edwin, and Gary Yohe. *Microeconomics,* 10th ed. New York: Norton, 2000, Chapters 9, 11.

McConnell, Campbell R., and Stanley L. Brue. *Economics,* 15th ed. New York: McGraw-Hill, 2002, Chapters 23 and 24.

Miller, Roger LeRoy, and Raymond P. H. Fishe. *Microeconomics: Price Theory in Practice.* New York: HarperCollins, 1995, Chapters 10 and 11.

Nicholson, Walter. *Microeconomic Theory: Basic Principles and Extensions,* 8th ed. Cincinnati: South-Western College Publishing, 2002, Chapters 14–18.

Pindyck, Robert S., and Daniel L. Rubinfeld. *Microeconomics,* 5th ed. Upper Saddle River, NJ: Prentice Hall, 2001, Chapter 8.

Schiller, Bradley R. *The Economy Today,* 8th ed. New York: McGraw-Hill, 2000, Chapters 23, 24.

CHAPTER NINE

Monopolistic Competition and Oligopoly

In the preceding chapter, our examinations of perfectly competitive and monopolistic firms demonstrated that such firms had two important points in common: (1) neither type of firm was motivated to differentiate its product from that of other sellers through advertising or other means and (2) neither type of firm needed to be concerned about the effects of rival firms' activities on its own operations or reactions by such firms to its decisions. However, most real-world firms are vitally concerned with one or both of the foregoing considerations. They know that what they do affects firms that are their rivals in the marketplace, and they are aware that they can capture a certain share of the market by convincing buyers that their product or service is superior to that of other sellers. (Thus, Wendy's, Inc., goes to a lot of trouble trying to convince the world that its hamburgers are better than those of McDonald's; and likewise, the amount and kind of advertising done by McDonald's is often a function of the activities of its rivals.) What businesses attempt to do when they whittle away a certain portion of the market for themselves is to create a sort of mini-monopoly position for their individual firm. This is why monopoly analysis, rather than the perfectly competitive model, provides a suitable point of departure for examination of market structures where sellers are few enough in number that they are likely to be aware of the problem of rivalry among themselves.

MANAGERIAL PERSPECTIVE

Oligopoly Advertising and the Pickup Truck Wars

One characteristic frequently found in oligopolistic markets is product differentiation so fierce that it takes the form of negative advertising that literally runs down the product of a rival firm. Some examples are fast-food hamburger chain ads on TV that have attacked the nutritional value of rivals' food and the negative advertising of the few rivalrous "sellers" in political campaigns that reflects the same sort of strategy for gaining "customers" (voters).

A classic oligopolistic advertising battle that heats up from time to time is that between General Motors (GM) and Ford in the pickup truck market. In 1998–1999, Ford became aggressively anti-Chevy when it ran ads stating that "Nobody builds a better full-size truck. Nobody." Ford also said you couldn't find a better truck anywhere, "not even if you look under a rock." This was a direct slam at Chevy's truck ads with Bob Seger singing "Like a Rock." In another ad, Ford asks why anyone would want to drive around in *their* (meaning Chevy's) 3-door extended cab pickup when they could have a Ford F-Series Supercab with 4 doors as standard equipment. Chevy later countered with ads emphasizing that its new models were bigger and more powerful than the rival Fords.

Deja vu. All of this was just a repeat of the negative advertising that occurred in the late 1980s when GM embarked on an all-out effort to bump Ford from its No. 1 position in that market, something Ford had held for over a decade. Chevrolet's marketing gurus whipped up a slate of macho ads that supposedly pit the full-size Chevy pickup against similar Fords and "proved" the Fords to be puny by comparison. In one ad, the 4-wheel drive version of the Ford was left bogged down in the "Ditch of Doom," while a Chevy cruised on by. Ford retaliated with similar comparison ads. Later, Ford announced a new advertising campaign that would emphasize the quality of some of its new and redesigned products. A spokesman for the company stated flatly that their new ads would not mention any other firms' trucks by name but that the program could be restructured to retaliate if the Chevy ad attack resurfaced at a later date. Ford marketing experts said they surveyed consumers to find out what they thought about the ad war. The public, they reported, thought it was "a bunch of baloney" from both the Ford and Chevy sides. In 2000–2002, both Ford and Chevy turned to more positive advertising, emphasizing the qualities of their own product, rather than the shortcomings of their rival's. It remains to be seen whether the negative approach will again surface, but we can be sure that the two firms will continue to spend huge sums on advertising for their pickups, which have been best sellers for both of them.

References: Carol Teegardin, "Ford Gets Agressive," *Auto.com Industry News*, October 1998 (http://auto.com), and "Chevy Turns to Negative Ads in an Effort to Topple Ford as Pickup-Truck Leader," *Wall Street Journal*, December 12, 1988, p. B1.

Oligopoly is a market structure characterized by few sellers and interfirm rivalry.

Economists have settled on the term **oligopoly** to describe product market situations that are characterized by relatively few sellers (few enough so that nothing that approaches perfect competition will exist). More recently, the terms *rivalrous competition* and *rivalrous market structures* have been used to describe a broad range of oligopolistic situations that lie somewhere between the extremes of monopoly and perfect competition. These market structures range from cases in which the number of sellers is very few and the product is homogeneous to cases in which there are relatively large numbers of sellers with products that vary markedly. In fact, efforts to differentiate the firm's product from similar goods produced by rival firms is an important strategy tool in many rivalrous markets. Such **product differentiation** may take the form of actual physical changes in the product or may be limited to advertising that makes people *think* the product is somehow superior to that produced by rivals. Oligopoly analysis is difficult because it tries to deal with some of the most complex interfirm relationships encountered in the real world, and many of these structures are characterized by *uncertainty*. In some cases, therefore, we are able to predict an outcome with respect to price and quantity sold only if certain rather heroic assumptions are allowed to hold. In others, the best we can do is describe a range in which the solution will be found.

> **Product differentiation** refers to a wide variety of activities, such as design changes and advertising, that rival firms employ to attract consumers to their products.

MONOPOLISTIC COMPETITION: A CASE OF MANY FIRMS

> **Monopolistic competition** is the name applied to a market structure with numerous firms that sell slightly differentiated products.

One market structure that is less than perfectly competitive and, as a result, draws on the tools of monopoly analysis is the case called **monopolistic competition.** The theory of monopolistic competition, developed by Harvard economist E. H. Chamberlin in the 1930s, occupies an in-between area in the analysis of market structures because it is not really an explanation of oligopoly or rivalrous competition but does allow for the element of product differentiation. Consequently, individual firms do have some control over price. We can describe monopolistic competition as a situation characterized by a relatively large number of sellers of somewhat differentiated products where each seller firm is not particularly concerned about the relationship between its individual actions and those of other firms in the industry. Each firm attempts to retain or increase its market share by differentiating its product from the output of other firms, by making the product physically different, by advertising, or by combining both methods.

The individual firm thus correctly perceives the relevant portion of its demand curve to be highly elastic (similar to the demand curve under perfect competition) but *not* perfectly so. In this setting, very small price changes cause large changes in quantity demanded; and once the firm locates its profit-maximizing output and price, it tends not to tamper further with price adjustments but rather to focus its attention on product differentiation as a market strategy. Through this choice, it could increase its sales and profit at or near the existing price by attracting customers to the firm.

Short-Run and Long-Run Equilibria under Monopolistic Competition

Although firms do not explicitly recognize the interdependence of their prices under monopolistic competition, the cluster of prices of the differentiated versions of the product do tend to move together whenever something occurs that will affect the pricing decisions of *all* firms (for example, an increase in input prices that increases every firm's marginal cost). This occurs because the market has many buyers and sellers and will tend toward an equilibrium in a manner similar to that described for perfect competition.

Analysis of profit maximization by the individual monopolistically competitive firm requires that we not only consider the highly elastic demand curve (estimated by the firm on the assumption that it can adjust its price independently of other firms), but also a curve that shows what will happen if all firms' prices change together. This latter curve is called the firm's **market share curve.** In Figure 9-1, d is the demand curve perceived by the firm, and M, which looks like a less elastic demand curve, is the individual firm's market share curve. Points on M show the quantities of output the firm can sell at various prices if (1) all firms' prices change together and (2) the firm neither increases nor decreases its share of the total market. However, the normal situation is one where a price change by an individual firm is simply not noticed by others, so each firm focuses on the highly elastic d curve as its demand curve.

It is important to note that the M curve is *not* a market demand curve. As Chamberlin stated, it refers only to the quantities a given firm can sell when all firms change price simultaneously. The individual firm's marginal revenue curve, MR_d, is based on the d curve, since that curve reflects the firm's demand when other firms ignore its price adjustments.[1]

Because firms' prices tend to reach a level consistent with a marketwide equilibrium, the individual firm in equilibrium will always be at the intersection of its d curve with its M curve. In other words, it will be selling the quantity consistent with its current price and market share, and it will believe that it can do just that. If its belief is not consistent with its market share, it will adjust its price or differentiate its product (or both) until it reaches an intersection of d with M that is consistent with the profit-maximizing condition, $SMC = MR_d$.

The **market share curve** describes the amounts the firm can atually sell at various prices as all firms in the industry adjust price together.

---

[1] There is much confusion among economists about the nature of the M curve. Partly, this is attributable to the fact that Chamberlin first labeled the highly elastic individual firm demand curve (our curve d) as DD'. Then when discussing group equilibrium, he changed his labels, designating the firm's *market share* curve DD' (our M curve) and the more elastic individual firm demand curve dd'. See Edward H. Chamberlin, *The Theory of Monopolistic Competition* (Cambridge, MA: Harvard University Press, 1962), p. 90.

FIGURE 9–1

*Demand Curve,
Market Share
Curve, and
Marginal
Revenue Curve of
the Firm under
Monopolistic
Competition*

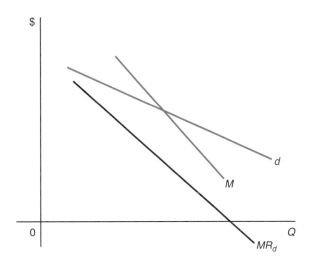

The monopolistically competitive firm ignores its rivals and estimates demand curve *d* and the marginal revenue curve, *MR_d*. The market share curve, *M*, shows how price and this firm's quantity demanded will be related when all firms' prices tend to move together.

The adjustment process could involve *both* revision of its estimate of *d* and the actual shifting of *M* as product differentiation alters its market share. With all firms in the industry practicing product differentiation, it is likely that they will just counteract one another's efforts. In this instance, *M* would hold still, and the path to profit maximization would entail shifting only the *d* curve.

Suppose a monopolistically competitive industry is in a period of falling costs and reductions in price by all firms. As adjustment takes place, an individual firm may find itself in a position such as that shown in panel (a) of Figure 9-2. At price P_a, the firm expected to maximize profit by selling Q_a but finds it can only sell Q_b. Why?—because its market share, shown by the *M* curve, is not sufficient to sell Q_a at price P_a. The firm must therefore adjust its estimate of *d*. It may also adjust its price in order to find the profit maximum. Once it has done so, its solution will look like that in panel (b) of Figure 9-2, where its new estimated demand curve, d_2, and *M* intersect at the output consistent with $MR_{d_2} = SMC$. In this example, the equilibrium price, P_e, is lower than the original one, P_a, and the quantity, Q_e, is higher than Q_b but lower than the previously anticipated quantity, Q_a. We have posited no change in market share, so the *M* curve in panel (b) is the same as the original one in panel (a).

The question arises as to whether, when all is said and done, the firm will regard segment *BE* of the *M* curve as its demand curve. This will not be the case, since the firm continues to believe that other firms will not

FIGURE 9–2

Adjustment to Short-Run Profit-Maximizing Output under Monopolistic Competition

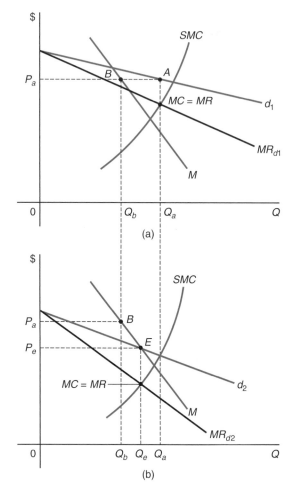

The firm is not in equilibrium in panel (a), since it cannot sell its estimated quantity, Q_a, but only amount Q_b, which is consistent with its market share. In panel (b) equilibrium and profit maximization occur at Q_e and P_e, a combination of output and price that lies on both d_2 and the firm's market share curve, M.

change their prices and that demand will be very elastic, as shown by d_2. Since in panel (b) it has attained a profit maximum relative to d_2 at Q_b, product differentiation (increase in market share) is viewed as the only route to higher profits. Successful product differentiation will move both d and M to the right.

In the long run under monopolistic competition, there is freedom of entry, and therefore firms will tend to have only normal profit. However, the long-run profit-maximizing position of the monopolistically competitive firm differs from that of the perfectly competitive firm because the firm's demand curve, *d*, has some downward slope. The negative slope of *d* ensures that the normal-profit, long-run position of the firm will occur at a level of output where the *LAC* is falling and, therefore, that the firm will utilize a somewhat smaller plant than it would have under perfect competition. In Figure 9-3, the tangency of *d* to *LAC* at Q_e shows that the firm believes it can obtain only normal profit, while the intersection of *d* and *M* at this same point indicates that Q_e, P_e is consistent with the market share of the firm.

Monopolistic Competition and the World of Business

When we look at the real world for examples of the monopolistically competitive market structure, a number of industries stand out as reasonable candidates. Certainly, most of the elements of monopolistic competition are found in independent retail trade in large metropolitan areas. In any given metropolitan market area, businesses such as boutiques, hair-styling salons, bars, and men's furnishings stores abound. Each has a slightly differentiated product in terms of location, brand names handled, atmosphere, or a combination of these characteristics. To the extent that one is more profitable than another, product differentiation will often be the key. However, extraordinary profits are unlikely to persist for any given firm unless it can block entry in the sense of keeping other firms from securing as good a location, array of merchan-

FIGURE 9–3

*Long-Run
Equilibrium
under
Monopolistic
Competition*

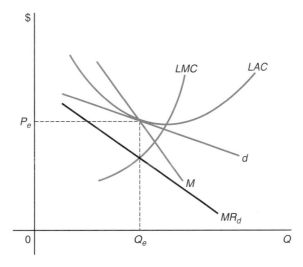

With free entry the long-run result under monopolistic competition is that $T\pi = 0$ and $P_e = LAC$ at Q_e. However, the firm does not produce at minimum LAC.

dise, or atmosphere. Other markets that exhibit most of the characteristics of monopolistic competition are the "no name" clone personal computer market and the mail-order market for cameras and video equipment. Sellers in these markets slightly differentiate their products, and entry or exit is relatively easy. Prices tend to be clustered very closely together.

Obviously, the manager of a firm in this kind of industry will be more successful over the long run to the extent that the firm's operations are adjusted in terms of product differentiation in a way that will provide the firm with at least temporary periods of greater than normal profit. If location or some other factor allows the firm to operate with greater than normal profit on a regular basis, then one would have to conclude that the firm is not monopolistically competitive but rather has succeeded in redefining its own market structure as something closer to differentiated oligopoly (oligopoly with differentiated product) or monopoly.

NUMERICAL EXAMPLE

Monopolistic Competition

Bonnie's Brake Shop is an independent auto repair facility that specializes in quick-service brake jobs. It is one of many similar firms operating in a large metropolitan area. Bonnie currently averages 80 brake jobs per month on American cars at her standard price of $190. Bonnie is about to embark on a new advertising campaign that she believes will increase her market share to the point where she will be able to sell 110 of the brake jobs per month at the same price.

a. If Bonnie's market share curve can be described by the equation $Q_m = 185 - 0.5P$ after the advertising campaign is in place, will she be able to sell 110 brake jobs per month? (Q is monthly output and P is price.)

b. Suppose Bonnie's marginal cost at her new output is $100. If, after determining the result of her advertising campaign, she reestimates her demand curve to be $Q = 280 - P$, will she be maximizing profit? (Assume AVC is covered.)

Answer

a. Bonnie will only be able to sell 90 brake jobs, since her market share at $P = \$190$ is

$$Q_m = 185 - 0.5(190) = 185 - 95 = \underline{90.}$$

b. Bonnie will be maximizing profit if $MC = \$100$, since for her estimated demand curve, $Q = 280 - P$,

$$P = 280 - Q, \text{ and } MR = 280 - 2Q,$$

so, $MR = 280 - 180 = \$100$. Thus $MR = MC$.

DUOPOLY: AN OLIGOPOLY WITH TWO FIRMS

As we noted earlier in this chapter, many conceivable oligopoly situations can be analyzed using tools developed in the monopoly case. Even nineteenth-century economists recognized this relationship, and some tried to extend monopoly by asking what would happen if there were just *two* sellers of a specific product—a case known as *duopoly*. It is important to consider duopoly for two reasons. First, the models show that outcomes in oligopolistic situations will depend on what a given firm believes others will do. Second, study reveals that even in the apparently simple case of only two firms, a wide variety of results can occur.

Cournot's Model

A Frenchman, Augustin Cournot, examined the case of a costless monopolist whose market was entered by a second firm. He argued that if a monopolist selling spring water that was produced at zero cost encountered a rival with a spring yielding the same water at no cost, the two would end up supplying a combined quantity equal to two-thirds of the quantity that would be taken by consumers at a price of zero. Cournot's case is illustrated in Figure 9-4.

Cournot assumed that each of the two firms would profit maximize based on the belief that the other would keep its *output* constant. In panel (a) of Figure 9-4, we see Firm X, the costless monopolist, facing market demand curve D. Q_2 is the amount of spring water consumers would take if it were given away free ($P = 0$). The monopoly firm maximizes profit by selling $Q_1 = \frac{1}{2}Q_2$ and charging P_1. With $MC = 0$, total profit is maximized where total revenue is maximized, or where $MR = 0$. With a straight-line demand curve, $MR = 0$ at Q_1, which is exactly one-half the output level where $P = 0$, or Q_2.

When the rival firm, Firm Z, appears on the scene, it assumes that the first seller will keep output at Q_1 and then profit maximizes on the remaining market Q_1Q_2. Its demand curve is segment AD of the market demand curve, considering Q_1 as the origin, and from this relationship it derives MR'. It will profit maximize by selling quantity Q_1Q' or $\frac{1}{2}Q_1Q_2$, which is $\frac{1}{4}Q_2$. The two firms together are now supplying $\frac{1}{2} + \frac{1}{4} = \frac{3}{4}$ of the zero-price output. However, if Firm X tries to maintain price P_1, it will likely lose some of its customers to Firm Z. If Firm X assumes Firm Z will keep its output constant at $\frac{1}{4}Q_2$, it will readjust to maximize profit based on the remaining $\frac{3}{4}$ of the market. In Figure 9-4, panel *(b)*, we see Firm X profit maximizing at $\frac{3}{8}Q_2$ by allowing $\frac{1}{4}Q_2$ for Firm Z and setting price P_3 based on $\frac{1}{2}$ of the remaining $\frac{3}{4}Q_2$ (in other words $\frac{1}{2} \times \frac{3}{4}Q_2 = \frac{3}{8}Q_2$). Now, the $\frac{3}{8}Q_2$ of Firm X plus $\frac{1}{4}$ or $\frac{2}{8}Q_2$ allowed Firm Z places the total quantity on the market at $\frac{5}{8}Q_2$. However, Firm Z will now react. It will assume that Firm X keeps output constant at $\frac{3}{8}Q_2$ and will maximize profit on the remaining $\frac{5}{8}Q_2$. This means that Firm Z will increase its output to $\frac{5}{16}Q_2$. In Table 9-1 we summarize our results.

FIGURE 9–4

Cournot's Case of the Costless Duopoly

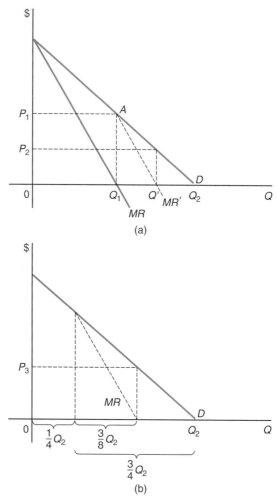

In Panel (a), the second firm, Firm Z, views its demand curve as segment AD, since it believes that Firm X will stay at Q_1. Therefore, Q_1Q' will be the profit-maximizing quantity for Firm Z. In panel (b), Firm X assumes Firm Z will continue to supply $\frac{1}{4}Q_2$ and maximizes profit by selling $\frac{3}{8}Q_2$. Further adjustments lead to an equilibrium where each firm sells $\frac{1}{3}Q_2$.

Note that if Firm X has an output of $\frac{1}{3}Q_2$ and Firm Z maximizes profit on the remaining $\frac{2}{3}Q_2$, Firm Z will sell $\frac{1}{2}$ of $\frac{2}{3}Q_2 = \frac{1}{3}Q_2$, which leaves $\frac{2}{3}Q_2$ not taken by Firm Z. Firm X now will maximize profit by producing $\frac{1}{2}(\frac{2}{3})Q_2$, leaving $\frac{2}{3}Q_2$ for Firm Z. The situation is stable. Each firm finds the other settling on $\frac{1}{3}Q_2$, and together they cover $\frac{2}{3}$ of the zero-price output.

Cournot showed that for costless producers with a straight-line market demand curve, the general production solution is:

$$\frac{n}{n + 1}(Q_2),$$

Table 9–1 *Behavior of Firms Under Cournot Assumptions*

	Round 1	Round 2	Round 3	Final Round
Firm X	$\frac{1}{2}Q_2$	$\frac{3}{8}Q_2$	$\frac{11}{32}Q_2$......	$\frac{1}{3}Q_2$
Firm Z	$\frac{1}{4}Q_2$	$\frac{5}{16}Q_2$	$\frac{21}{64}Q_2$......	$\frac{1}{3}Q_2$
Total Market	$\frac{3}{4}Q_2$	$\frac{11}{16}Q_2$	$\frac{43}{64}Q_2$......	$\frac{2}{3}Q_2$
or,	$(0.750Q_2)$	$(0.688Q_2)$	$(0.672Q_2)$..	$(0.667Q_2)$

where n is the number of firms in the market and Q_2 is the zero-price output. The larger the number of firms, the closer $n/(n + 1)$ approaches 1 and the closer we get to the perfectly competitive solution, which with zero cost would be $P = 0$ and $Q = Q_2$.

It would be hard to justify Cournot's assumption that each firm makes decisions based on the other's keeping its output constant, for there is no particular reason for either firm to believe this. Surely after one complete round of decisions is made, each firm must know the other will indeed adjust its quantity. Furthermore, if there are only two firms, we can ask why they don't get together and set the price and total market quantity back at Q_1, P_1, which, with the given market demand curve, will maximize their joint total revenue and therefore their joint total profit.

Reaction Curves and Cournot Oligopoly

By plotting a line that shows the proportion of the market Firm Z will take *given* the proportion taken by Firm X, one can obtain a **reaction curve** (actually a straight line) for Firm Z. A similar line can be plotted showing Firm X's reactions to Firm Z's choices of market share. This is done in Figure 9-5. Thus, if Firm X were to choose to supply $\frac{1}{2}$ of the zero-price market (the amount consumers would take if the product were given away), Firm Z would supply $\frac{1}{4}$, at point R on its reaction curve. If Firm X were to supply $\frac{1}{4}$ of the market, Firm Z would choose $\frac{1}{2}(\frac{3}{4}) = \frac{3}{8}$ of the market at point T on its reaction curve. Firm X's reaction curve based on Firm Z's choices is derived in the same fashion. Point E represents equilibrium since, there, each firm does the best it can *given* the choice of its rival. This is the same outcome as in Table 9-1, and we can see that there is no other point in Figure 9-5 where a choice by one firm is consistent with what is best for the other.

Bertrand's and Edgeworth's Theories

Cournot was criticized even in his own time for the constant quantity assumption. Joseph Bertrand, a French mathematician and economist who wrote later in the nineteenth century, argued that each of the duopolists would assume that the other's *price* would not change, paying no attention

FIGURE 9–5

*Reaction Curves
for Cournot
Duopoly*

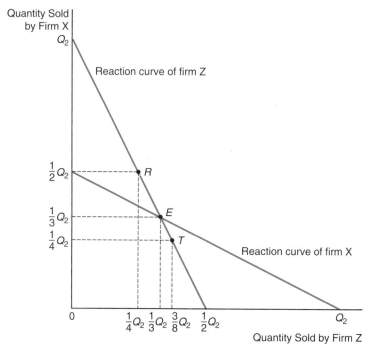

The steeper reaction curve shows the quantity Firm Z will supply, given that chosen by Firm X. The flatter reaction curve shows the quantity Firm X will supply, given that chosen by Z. If Firm X chooses to supply $\frac{1}{2}$ of the zero-price market, as point R indicates, Firm Z will supply $\frac{1}{2}$ of the remaining half, or $\frac{1}{4}$ of Q_2. Like R, points E and T identify reactions of Firm Z to Firm X. However, only E is a point that is also on Firm X's reaction curve. Thus, E, where each firm supplies $\frac{1}{3}$ of the zero-price market, is the Cournot equilibrium.

to the rival's quantity. In Bertrand's analysis, the price simply falls to zero as each duopolist tries to steal the other's customers by cutting price again and again.

At the close of the nineteenth century, British economist F. Y. Edgeworth argued still another solution to the costless duopoly problem. Edgeworth stated that if the duopolists each had limited productive capacity with respect to the quantity consumers would demand at zero price, a lower limit would be established below which price would not fall. However, Edgeworth showed that this price would not be stable, for once it is reached, one firm will assume that the other will stay at the price where it reaches its capacity limit and perceive that under these circumstances (1) the rival firm can sell no more because it is at capacity, and (2) an increase in price will increase profit. Accordingly, one of the firms will now raise price to the level that will give it maximum profit on the remaining market. The other will follow suit but will raise price only to a level slightly *below* the one established by the first. The reaction of the first firm will be to cut price, and, with successive rounds of cutting, the price will fall back to the lower limit. This restores the opportunity for one of the two to gain by raising price, and the price moves back up. This goes on *ad infinitum*, as long as each assumes the other will not follow a price change.

Chamberlin and Duopoly Theory

Of course, the Cournot, Bertrand, and Edgeworth analyses are all based on assumptions of extreme naivete on the part of the two firms. E. H. Chamberlin, who developed the monopolistic competition analysis we surveyed earlier in this chapter, stated in 1933, "When a move by one seller evidently forces the other to make a countermove, he is very stupidly refusing to look further than his nose if he proceeds on the assumption that it will not."[3] Chamberlin argued that the duopolists would recognize their interdependence and settle on a price that conformed to the monopoly price, splitting the profits between them. An agreement was not required, he stated, because the firms would realize quickly that any other strategy would be disastrous over the long run.

Chamberlin's approach to the problem of duopoly and certain of the notions he developed in his study of monopolistic competition represent a clear improvement over the older assumptions of naive behavior on the part of the individual firm or its managers. The key to Chamberlin's approach is what he called the recognition of *mutual interdependence* among oligopolistic firms. By this he meant that a firm in an oligopolistic situation will realize that its decisions affect other firms and that decisions made by other firms affect it. Some ideas about what constitutes rational behavior, from a profit-maximizing standpoint, are bound to emerge from this kind of setting.[4]

The most obvious solution to the management problem of competing or rivalrous oligopolists is to get together (collude) to formulate a strategy that is at least satisfactory to all the parties. The problem with this approach is that in the United States and many other countries, such action would be viewed as a conspiracy in restraint of trade and therefore a violation of antitrust laws. Another possible solution is to merge the firms into a single unit, but such mergers are also prohibited when not clearly in the public interest. What, then, are we left with when oligopolistic firms recognize their mutual interdependence? The answer, of course, is what Chamberlin suggested. The firms' managers will have to analyze their environment carefully and try to adjust their operations in a manner that signals to other

---

[3] Chamberlin, *The Theory of Monopolistic Competition*, p. 46. Chamberlin's book includes an exhaustive bibliography in which the original references for the Cournot, Bertrand, and Edgeworth theories can be found.

[4] For an interesting case of duopoly that apparently did not lead to joint profit maximization, see Ray Rees, "Collusive Equilibrium in the Great Salt Duopoly," *The Economic Journal* 103, No. 419 (July 1993): 833–848.

firms in their group the desire to be profitable without being destructively rivalrous. After all, a price war, even in an industry with a fairly large number of firms, might leave many firms in a position similar to that of Bertrand's poor duopolists—out of business! Moreover, in a setting where one firm is much larger and perhaps more efficient than its rivals, any attempt to crowd out the smaller firms is likely to meet with antitrust action. (The role of government in preventing business behavior that is not

---

MANAGERIAL PERSPECTIVE

Soda Pop Wars and Duopoly Theory

While Coca-Cola Company and Pepsico are not the only players in the soft-drink market, they are certainly the dominant ones for cola beverages. Of course, both companies pump out a tremendous amount of image-oriented marketing hype, and, the two firms battle it out on the price front as well. It is easy to observe this competition at the local grocery store, where one or the other of the two brands is on sale very often.

Coke versus Pepsi has the basic elements of a duopoly case, since neither firm is worried to any great extent about what some third party will do. The pricing pattern of these two soda-pop giants appears to have elements of both the Bertrand and the Edgeworth approaches to duopoly. Certainly, there is price cutting as Bertrand described. However, as in Edgeworth's analysis, a point is reached after which prices begin to rise. Edgeworth attributed the eventual increase in prices to one firm's having run out of production capacity, thereby making it "safe" for the second one to raise price. In the cola market, analysts do not believe that the price oscillations can be traced to such a cause. Rather, they argue that both Coke and Pepsi have focused on enlarging market share as a major corporate goal and have adopted advertising and pricing strategies aimed at getting buyers to switch from one brand of drink to the other. Price increases occur when

both firms believe their profits are suffering from price warring.

The switching strategy reflects the corporate managers' belief that, over the long run, greater market share will be synonymous with a higher value of the firm and, therefore, higher stock prices. However, long and frequent price wars may cost both firms more than either can hope to gain in market share. Industry research shows that about half of all soft-drink consumers are habitual brand switchers and are not likely to stay with a given brand when its price rises relative to that of a substitute. Indeed, PesiCo's strategy in recent years has been to diversify its activities, adding new products and brands so that its fortunes are much less dependent on achieveing fleeting victories in the "Cola Wars." (See Managerial Perspective in Chapter 7.) Nonetheless, the two firms again engaged in price cutting in 2002.

References: Jim Lovell, "Price Cutting Threatens Coke," *Atlanta Business Chronicle*, April 29, 2002, online, July 18, 2002, atlanta.bizjournals.com/atlanta/stories/2002/04/29/story2.html; "Coke's Slower Sales Are Blamed on Price Increases," *Wall Street Journal*, March 31, 1999, pp. A3, A4; "1998 Top-10 Soft Drink Companies and Brands," *Beverage Digest Special Issue*, February 12, 1999, online, May 12, 1999, www.beverage-digest.com; "Coke and Pepsi Step Up Bitter Price War," *Wall Street Journal*, October 10, 1988.

in the public interest or that is unfair to rival firms will be discussed in Chapter 16.) We turn now to several oligopolistic situations in which some standard tools of analysis can be applied to determine the appropriate strategy for managers of an individual firm.

THE QUESTION OF ENTRY

Duopoly analysis, in addition to raising the issues of rival reaction, strategy, and collusion, calls attention to the significance of entry. Usually, as we have seen, industry total profit is lower after entry occurs than monopoly profit was before entry. Even if joint profits are maximized (as Chamberlin argued), the original monopoly firm would logically have to give up some profit to its rival. Thus, in duopoly or other forms of oligopoly, existing firms will benefit in the long run if entry by new firms is somehow restricted. The matter of how entry is deterred or what conditions, known as **barriers to entry,** may keep new firms from coming into an industry is a matter of considerable debate in economics. However, if there are effective barriers to entry, oligopoly firms, like monopolies, can have greater than normal profits in the long run.

Barriers to entry are conditions that make it difficult for new firms to enter an industry or market where existing firms have long-run interests.

Barriers to Entry

A brief survey of the economics literature on barriers to entry turns up several prominent candidates. One is *entry-limit pricing*—the practice of setting a price lower than the one that maximizes profit in order to discourage potential rivals from entering the market. Of course, it is a viable strategy only if existing firms' long-run costs are lower than those possible for new firms. This situation might occur in a mineral industry, for example, where existing firms had bought up the best ore deposits and new firms could enter only by working inferior deposits at higher than existing industry average costs.

Excess capacity and *economies of scale* are also often cited as barriers to entry. Excess capacity in existing firms can serve as a signal to potential entrants that the existing firm will cut price and expand output in the face of any new firm's attempt to gain a share of the market. Furthermore, if there are economies of scale, to be able to price competitively, a new entrant may have to come into the market with substantial sales volume, something that will also depress price and perhaps make entry unattractive.

Capital requirements are another frequently identified barrier to entry. The argument here is that new firms will have to raise tremendous amounts of investment funds to install the plant and equipment needed to enter an industry where existing firms have had many years to build up their facilities. The automobile industry may be a good case in point. It takes a huge investment to establish a new firm in automobile manufacturing, so much that it is difficult to accomplish without support from a government. The Western economies witnessed two attempts to establish new automobile companies during the 1970s and 1980s: Bricklin (Canada) and DeLorean (Northern Ireland). Both had substantial government backing, but neither succeeded. (In Asia, however, Korean producers have managed to enter the industry and even to export to the United States.)

Another way firms can deter entry is through *product differentiation*. If existing companies have managed to establish a preference on the part of consumers for their products, it may be very difficult for new firms to attract customers. Existing preferences, in fact, may have various dimensions, ranging from brand identification based on advertising to consumer experiences with products that provide verification of product quality. Indeed, a long-term study of several hundred U.S. firms found that quality of products and services was very important as a determinant of profitability.[5] Moreover, if existing firms spend large amounts on advertising and promotion, new ones will have to do the same, something that further raises the capital requirements for entry.

Other barriers to entry have been identified: research and development expenditures, government policies, sales networks, economies of scope.[6] In any given industry, more than one barrier may be relevant, and some may be stronger in one industry than in another. Over the long run, barriers are important to managers, who may either employ them to enhance the firm's position or be wary of them when entering new markets or lines of product. In the global marketplace, entry barriers may be even more important: consumer preferences are partly defined by culture, foreign governments may impede entry through regulatory means, and large multinational corporations may present newcomers with tremendous obstacles in terms of economies of scale and scope, capital requirements, and product differentiation.

Contestable Markets

During the 1980s, William J. Baumol and others advanced a new theory of oligopolistic markets that focused on entry.[7] Specifically, they defined what are called **contestable markets** as markets with few sellers but characterized by free entry. The theory, which predicts that oligopolies in such markets will

Contestable markets are oligopolistic markets characterized by free and costless entry and exit by a lack of rival reaction on the part of existing firms.

[5] R. Buzzell and B. Gale, *The PIMS Principles Linking Strategy to Performance* (New York: Free Press, 1987). For more on product quality and profitability, see Stephen Morse, *Successful Product Management* (London: Kogan-Page, 1998), and Donald R. Lehmann and Russell S. Winer, *Product Management* (Chicago: Richard D. Irwin, 1996).

[6] A thorough discussion of barriers to entry is found in Dennis W. Carlton and Jeffrey M. Perloff, *Modern Industrial Organization* (Boston: Addison-Wesley, 1999).

[7] W. J. Baumol, J. C. Panzar, and R. D. Willig, *Contestable Markets and the Theory of Industry Structure* (New York: Harcourt, Brace, Jovanovich, 1982).

price at perfectly competitive levels and have only normal long-run profits, rests on three assumptions:

1. Entry is free and costless.

2. New firms can enter with no price reaction (or other reaction) from existing firms.

3. Exit is also free and costless.

The contestable markets theory was immediately criticized, primarily on the grounds that entry and exit generally are far from costless in an oligopolistic setting and that existing firms will most likely respond to entry (or even a threat of entry) with some price cuts or other types of rivalrous reaction. Some economists have suggested that contestable markets exist only in the minds of the proponents of the theory, while others have stated that the assumption of no reaction from existing firms "stretches credulity to the limit."[8]

Probably the most important aspect of the contestable markets theory is that it points out that because of differences in strength or effectiveness of entry barriers, it is easier to enter some oligopolistic markets than others. However, in virtually all such markets, we can expect that there will be entry and exit costs and that existing firms will in some way react to incursions by new firms. From the standpoint of managerial decision making, then, the important conclusion is that these types of costs and potential rival reactions must be taken into account carefully when planning to enter an existing market.

By their very nature, the issues of entry barriers and contestable markets deal with the long run. However, many short-run situations in oligopoly analysis can be analyzed using the tools we have developed in the contexts of perfect competition, monopoly, and monopolistic competition. We turn now to the kinked oligopoly demand curve, which is a direct descendant of Chamberlin's monopolistic competition model.

THE KINKED OLIGOPOLY DEMAND CURVE: PRICE RIGIDITY WITHOUT COLLUSION

The two demand curves used by Chamberlin in his analysis of monopolistic competition have also been applied to the case of price rigidity in *noncollusive oligopolies* (oligopoly situations where firms do not make any agreement among themselves regarding price, market share, or other conditions).[9] By

---

[8] Donald A. Hay and Derek J. Morris, *Industrial Economics and Organization*, 2d ed. (New York: Oxford University Press, 1991), p. 579.

[9] The kinked demand curve was first used by Paul Sweezy in a 1939 article, "Demand under Conditions of Oligopoly," *Journal of Political Economy* (August 1939): 568–573.

price rigidity we mean the tendency for all firms in an industry to charge approximately the same price for a specific product over long periods of time. Such a phenomenon can be an indication that prices are being administered by collusive agreements in the industry, but it can also mean simply that each firm, acting independently, has determined that it cannot gain by departing from the prevailing price.

In Figure 9-6 we redraw Chamberlin's d and M curves (as in monopolistic competition), but we now use them to describe the situation faced by an oligopolistic firm where mutual interdependence is recognized but firms do not collude. Unlike the monopolistically competitive firm, which always believed that some d curve was its actual demand curve, the oligopolistic firm is aware of the existence of both d and M. It knows that d shows what will happen if it changes price but no one else follows suit and that M shows what will happen if all firms change price together. However, the firm believes that if it raises price, no one else will (quantity will react along d) and customers will be lost to other firms. If it lowers price, everyone will follow suit (there will be a price war, and quantity will react along M) and few new customers will be acquired. In either case, profit is likely to fall because d is highly elastic and M is relatively inelastic. The firm thus takes the view that the demand curve consists of d to the left of Q_e, and M to the right of Q_e. It has a kink in it at Q_e, P_e, and under most circumstances, price will remain at this kink. The reason for the inflexibility of price is that management will usually determine that no other attainable price-quantity combination will yield more profit than the one that exists at Q_e, P_e.

FIGURE 9–6

The Kinked Oligopoly Demand Curve

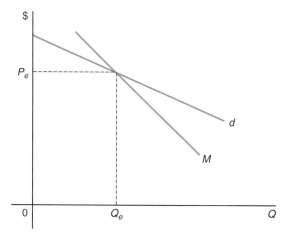

With a kinked demand curve, the firm believes that the d curve will apply for prices higher than P_e, but that the M curve will apply for prices lower than P_e.

FIGURE 9–7

*Kinked Demand
Curve Related to
Marginal
Revenue and
Various
Marginal Cost
Curves*

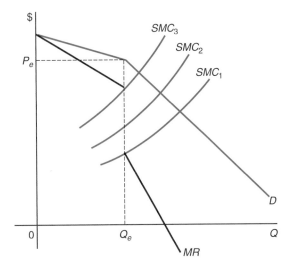

Since the kinked demand curve results in a gap in the MR curve, various marginal cost curves yield an equilibrium at Q_e and P_e.

A **kinked demand curve** consists of an elastic range for price increases and a less elastic (perhaps inelastic) range for price decreases. In oligopoly, a firm facing a kinked demand curve will seldom wish to change price.

The preceding point is examined further in Figure 9-7, where the marginal revenue curve relevant to the **kinked demand curve** is introduced. Note that at Q_e there is a gap in the *MR* curve. To the left of Q_e, the *MR* curve is derived from the elastic portion of the demand curve (a segment of *d*). As the firm's output moves through Q_e, *MR* falls from a relatively high level to a relatively low level and is now derived from the less elastic portion of the demand curve. Finally, SMC_1 represents the lowest short-run marginal cost curve that would result in profit maximization at Q_e. We know profit will be maximized at this quantity, since to the left of Q_e, $MR > SMC_1$ and to the right of Q_e, $MR < SMC_1$. However, notice that this relationship also holds for SMC_2 and SMC_3. Thus, the firm could have a wide range of marginal cost curves, and management still would have to conclude that Q_e and P_e would be the profit-maximizing output and price, respectively. We should also note that shifts in demand and related changes in the quantity sold might not change the profit-maximizing price, since the kink still might occur at price P_e. (Imagine the demand curve in Figure 9-7 shifting outward so that the kink is at a greater Q_e but is at the same P_e—a quite conceivable result.) Returning again to the question of managerial strategy, we note that all of the preceding simply suggests that where the firm expects rivals to match a price cut but ignore a price increase, it is unlikely that profit can be increased by altering price.

Nevertheless, in an inflationary environment such as was characteristic of Western economies some years ago, an oligopoly firm operating under conditions described by the kinked demand curve could easily find itself

FIGURE 9–8

Adjustment of Product Price and Quantity under Kinked Demand Curve Oligopoly after an Increase in Production Cost

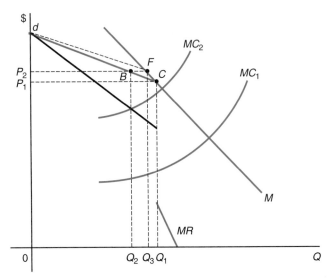

With inflation, this firm's *SMC* curve (*MC$_2$*) intersects the upper segment of *MR*. Thus, it should raise price to *P$_2$*. If all firms' costs rise, a new kink will develop at point *F*.

temporarily in a position where a price increase would make sense whether or not other firms followed suit. In Figure 9-8, the demand curve that management has estimated is *dCM*. The firm initially has marginal cost curve *MC$_1$* and maximizes profit at *Q$_1$*, *P$_1$*. If rising input prices push marginal cost upward to *MC$_2$*, the firm should not wait to see whether other firms raise price, since over the short run it will profit maximize at *Q$_2$*, *P$_2$* (which corresponds to point *B* on the elastic portion of *dCM*). If other firms follow suit (inflation would ensure this result), the first firm will adjust to point *F* on *M*, thereby increasing its quantity sold at price *P$_2$* to *Q$_3$*. Ultimately, management would adjust its view of the market so that the kinked demand curve would be *dFM* and the firm would again be profit maximizing at the kink.

The Kinked Demand Curve Applied

When managers of a firm believe they face a market situation characterized by a kinked demand curve, it will be necessary for them to determine whether or not they can maximize profit at about the same price charged by their rivals. Furthermore, they may wish to look into the prospects for increasing market share (moving the *M* curve to the right) through product differentiation.

It is unlikely that a given firm will be able to maximize profit by pricing to the right of the kink in the demand curve, since this would require either extremely low or even negative marginal cost (an impossibility). However,

FIGURE 9–9

Kinked Demand Curve Analysis for a Firm Selling Electronic Minicalculators

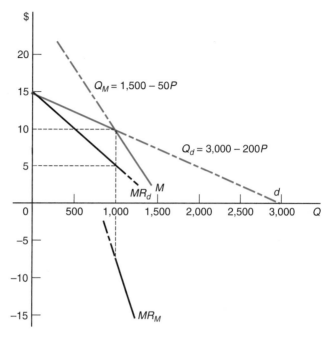

For this firm the gap in *MR* occurs at $Q = 1,000$ where $MR_d = \$5$. As long as *SMC* is less than \$5 at this output, the firm should charge \$10 per unit for its calculators.

when the industry is characterized by high rates of profit, some high-cost firms might well price to the left of the kink in their demand curves.

Suppose a firm selling electronic minicalculators of the type commonly sold in drugstores is operating in a market where management believes that price cutting will lead to retaliation by other firms but that other firms are unlikely to follow a price increase. (Industry profits are high at the going price.) The firm is currently pricing its machine at \$10, but its marketing consultants have just come up with a new estimate of demand. Specifically, they state that if all firms change price equally, the monthly demand curve will be $Q_M = 1,500 - 50P$. However, if the firm can change its price independently of rival reactions, the monthly demand curve will be $Q_d = 3,000 - 200P$. The firm's total cost function is $TC = 1,500 + 3Q + 0.0025Q^2$.

In Figure 9-9 we see the marketing consultant's plot of the two demand curves for the firm's calculators. By solving for the intersection of the two curves ($Q = Q_d = Q_M$ and $P = P_d = P_M$), we obtain the maximum quantity the firm can sell without encountering a precipitous drop in *MR*. (*MR* will not always be negative for outputs greater than that at the intersection of *d* and *M*.) This occurs at $Q = 1,000$, $P = \$10$, or where

$$3,000 - 200P = 1,500 - 50P,$$
$$1,500 = 150P,$$

and

$$P = \$10.$$

Using the d demand function ($Q_d = 3{,}000 - 200P$), we can solve for P and obtain $P = 15 - 0.005Q_d$. In this case

$$TR_d = P \cdot Q_d = 15Q_d - 0.005Q_d^2,$$

and

$$MR_d = \frac{dTR_d}{dQ_d} = 15 - 0.01Q_d$$

Using the market share demand function ($Q_M = 1{,}500 - 50P$), we obtain $P = 30 - 0.02Q_M$. For this demand function,

$$TR_M = P \cdot Q_M = 30Q_M - 0.02Q_M^2$$

and

$$MR_M = 30 - 0.04Q_M$$

If we substitute 750 for Q_M in the MR_M function, we can see that MR_M will be negative for any level of Q_M greater than 750. However, MR_M is not the firm's *actual* marginal revenue function until *after* the kink in the demand curve.

The kink in the demand curve occurs at $P = \$10$, $Q = 1{,}000$, and $MR_d = 5$. However, the firm should only charge $10 per unit if at $Q = 1{,}000$ its marginal cost is $5 per unit or lower. Given management's estimate of the firm's total cost function,

$$TC = 1{,}500 + 3Q + 0.0025Q^2,$$

and

$$SMC = \frac{dTC}{dQ} = 3 + 0.005Q.$$

At $Q = 1{,}000$, $SMC = \$8$ and $TC = \$7{,}000$. Since $TR = 1{,}000\,(\$10)$, the firm would have an economic profit of ($10{,}000 - \$7{,}000) = \$3{,}000$ if it were to continue charging a price of $10.

If the firm's managers are astute, however, they will notice that at $Q = 1{,}000$, $MR < SMC$, since $MR_d = \$5$ and $SMC = \$8$. In Figure 9-10 we show the

FIGURE 9–10

Profit-Maximizing Output and Price for the Minicalculator Firm

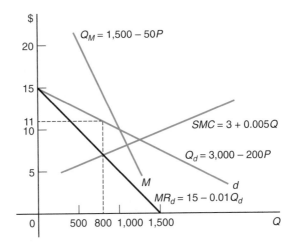

Since the Firm's SMC curve intersects MR_d at $Q = 800$, a price of $11 per calculator should be charged, even though the kink in the demand curve occurs at $P = $10.

marketing consultant's demand curves, along with management's marginal cost curve. Obviously, $MR_d = SMC$ at an output *lower* than 1,000 units per month. Specifically, where $MR_d = SMC$,

$$15 - 0.01Q = 3 + 0.005Q,$$

$$12 = 0.015Q,$$

and

$$Q = 800.$$

Along demand curve d, $P = $11 when $Q_d = 800$. If the firm charges $11 and sells 800 units, TR will be $8,800, TC will be $5,500, and economic profit will be ($8,800 − $5,500) = $3,300 per month. Since this profit is greater than the $3,000 per month economic profit at $P = $10, the price should be adjusted to $11 per unit, even though management does not expect rival firms to follow a price increase.

TACIT COLLUSION AND PRICE LEADERSHIP

It should not be assumed from the analysis of the kinked demand curve that oligopolistic firms always determine their market strategies in the absence of interfirm negotiation or unwritten agreements. At the local level of operation, the existence of trade associations (the local homebuilders' association, for example) provides ample opportunity for exchange of information and tacit live-and-let-live agreements, even for relatively small and numerous firms.

In manufacturing industries characterized by a small number of large firms, the incentive to avoid independent behavior detrimental to the group will be quite strong. However, in the United States, virtually any kind of specific communication agreement that has an effect (even a remote effect) on interstate commerce is subject to prosecution under the antitrust laws. Thus, local firms that engage in price fixing in a given city but do not sell across state lines may still face federal prosecution if they have out-of-state competitors or buy inputs supplied from out of state. In short, it is only under rare circumstances that collusive business practices are immune from the antitrust laws, although some illegal practices do escape detection.

In many instances, consumers are the only ones damaged by unfair business practices, and generally they are able to mount organized local campaigns against oligopolistic lawbreakers only when harm has been widespread and the identity of wrongdoers is obvious. Given the difficulty of prosecution of firms that utilize tacitly collusive business practices, it is not surprising that rather specific pricing patterns have developed in many oligopolistic industries. One of the best known patterns is that of **price leadership.** Usually, when the firm that is the leader changes its price, other members of the group shortly follow suit. In the United States such leadership has prevailed in the steel, automobile, rubber, and petroleum industries, although in any given industry the identity of the leader may have changed from time to time. Two market situations in which there is a clear reason for the price leader's identity are the *efficient firm case* and the *dominant firm case*.

Price leadership occurs when specific firms in an oligopolistic group (perhaps even one firm) set a price that subsequently determines what other members of the group will charge.

Figure 9-11 depicts price leadership by an efficient firm where the market structure is duopoly. Here, Firm A is the efficient firm because of its lower marginal and average costs. The market demand curve is D, and if the two firms agree to split the market equally, each firm faces demand curve D'. (D' shows one-half as much quantity as does D for each price.) Price will be P_a, and quantity Q_a will be sold by each firm. Note that this is the price-quantity combination that maximizes profit for Firm A but that Firm B's managers would rather sell a smaller quantity (Q_b) at a higher price. However, Firm B will have to be content with price P_a, since if it charged P_b, it would at least temporarily lose customers to Firm A. If Firm B persisted in charging P_b, it would get customers only to the extent that they were unaware of Firm A's price or that Firm A's output was depleted. At the latter point, something would have to give, but that something might be that Firm A would expand or duplicate its plant, thereby putting Firm B out of business. The conclusion can be generalized to an oligopoly of many more firms: Inefficient firms will have to follow the pricing decisions of efficient firms in order to survive, even if such action means lower than desired rates of profit for the followers. Of course, if following the price leader still produces normal or greater than

FIGURE 9–11

Price Leadership by an Efficient Firm

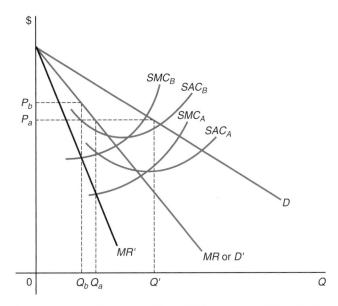

Since Firm A has the lowest *MC* curve, it will establish price P_a and Firm B will be forced to follow.

normal profits for the less efficient firm and if other alternatives are risky, then followership may indeed be management's best strategy.

The dominant firm case of price leadership is usually described as one in which a single large firm is the price leader and smaller firms in the industry simply take its price as the going price, maximizing profit on this assumption. The problem for the dominant firm's management is to determine how much of the market small firms will absorb at each possible price and, based on this information, to choose the specific price that will maximize the profit of the dominant firm. In Figure 9-12 the dominant firm's estimate of market demand and the supply curve of the small firms is shown in the right-hand quadrant. Since the small firms take the leader's price as given, for them $P_e = MR_s$. Each small firm will equate its *MC* to MR_s; therefore, the sum of the small firms' marginal cost curves, ΣMC_s, will be their supply curve, S_s. If the dominant firm were to set price at P_h, the small firms would absorb the entire market, selling the output at which S_s intersects D_M.

In the left-hand quadrant of Figure 9-12, we see the demand, marginal revenue, and marginal cost curves of the dominant firm. The demand curve D_L is derived by determining for each possible price the difference between the total quantity demanded and the quantity that would be supplied by the small firms. Since the small firms would absorb the entire market at price P_h, D_L intersects the vertical axis at this price. At price P_e we see in the right-hand quadrant that small firms will supply quantity Q'_s, the quantity consis-

FIGURE 9–12

*Price Leadership
by a Dominant
Firm*

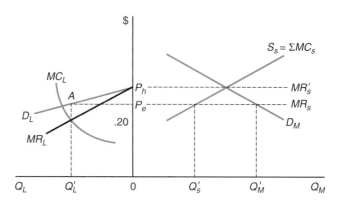

The dominant firm's demand curve, D_L, is obtained by subtracting the quantity supplied by the small firms from the market quantity demanded at each possible price. The dominant firm then sets price P_e at quantity Q_L, which corresponds to the intersection of MC_L with MR_L.

tent with $MR_s = \Sigma MC_s$, leaving $Q'_M - Q'_s$ of the quantity demanded for the dominant firm. Point A on D_L is plotted a distance of $Q'_M - Q'_s = 0Q'_L$ to the left of the vertical axis at price P_e.

If P_e is the profit-maximizing price for the dominant firm, it must be true that at Q'_L, P_e we find $MC_L = MR_L$. This is true in Figure 9-12, so we can conclude that P_e is the price that will be set by the firm's management. The dominant firm would locate P_e by deriving its marginal revenue curve, MR_L, and finding the level of output at which $MR_L = MC_L$.

Of course, the dominant firm may be sufficiently powerful to (1) sustain losses for a period of time, (2) drive the smaller rival firms from the market, and (3) establish a monopoly price based on the market demand curve, D_M. In the United States, the management of such a dominant firm would probably not take this step because of the provision against *predatory price cutting* (cutting price to an unreasonably low level in order to eliminate competition) in the antitrust laws.

U.S. Steel: The Dominant Firm Case Applied

In September 1985, it was reported that domestic steelmaking firms, "following U.S. Steel Corp.'s pricing action," would raise the selling prices of sheet steel products some 3 to 4 percent.[10] At the time, this move amounted to an increase of approximately $18 per ton on cold-rolled sheet steel, the type used in the manufacture of automobile bodies. For many years, United States Steel Corporation (hereafter USS, although today its name is U.S. Steel Group, a unit of USX Corporation) was the dominant firm in its industry.[11] Over the

---

[10] "Big Steelmakers Raising Prices to Fight Slump," *Wall Street Journal,* September 26, 1985, p. 5.
[11] The name of the parent firm was changed to USX Corporation in 1986.

past 20 years, the development of minimills that use scrap as their primary input has led to an increase in the number of small firms selling certain products alongside this giant firm. The new minimills are very efficient, lean on management, and in most cases nonunion. Thus, while the pricing policies of USS are still important in the steel market, the firm does not play the dominant role that it did 10 or 15 years ago.[12]

Things were quite different back when USS was more clearly the dominant firm. A particularly interesting case of price leadership in cold-rolled sheet steel took place in 1976. In April of that year, William Verity, chairman of Armco Steel Corporation, stated at his company's shareholders' meeting that there was a "desperate need for adequate price relief [increases] for the flat-rolled carbon steels, which continue to bear a disproportionate burden in the fight against inflation."[13] However, *The Wall Street Journal* reported that when questioned further, Armco's officers said they would not *initiate* such a price increase.

In mid-August 1976, USS announced that it would increase the base prices of its flat-rolled products an average of 4.5 percent. The price of one of the major items in this category, Class I cold-rolled sheet, would be raised from $296 a ton to $309 a ton.[14]

The Wall Street Journal reported that some of the other firms in the industry were not happy with USS's decision to raise prices by only $13 a ton on cold-rolled sheet. However, it is quite possible that a larger price change would not have been in USS's interest. We can use the dominant firm model to investigate the *type* of situation USS faced, even though we do not have the firm's actual data.

Suppose that USS estimates the supply curve of the smaller firms in the industry over the relevant range to be

$$Q_s = 0.9P + 150,$$

where Q_s is the quantity of cold-rolled sheet that small firms will put on the market (measured in thousands of tons of product per month), P is the market price, and industry demand for the product is (in thousand tons per month)

$$Q_M = 1{,}403 - 2.6P.$$

Figure 9-13 illustrates these two curves in the $200–$400 per ton price range. USS would know that at a price of $358 per ton, $Q_s = Q_M$ and the smaller firms would produce enough cold-rolled sheet to supply the entire market.

---

[12] In fact, in 1994 U.S. Steel Group entered a joint venture with Nucor Corporation, a leading minimill producer, to perfect a new process for making steel from iron carbide. See "The Odd Couple of Steel," *Business Week* (November 7, 1994), p. 106.

[13] "Bethlehem Steel Joins Price Rises on Certain Items," *Wall Street Journal*, April 26, 1976, p. 8.

[14] "U.S. Steel Pricing Likely to Prompt Industry Boosts," *Wall Street Journal*, August 16, 1976, p. 6.

FIGURE 9–13

*Demand Curve
for Cold-Rolled
Sheet and
Solution to U.S.
Steel Price
Leadership
Problem*

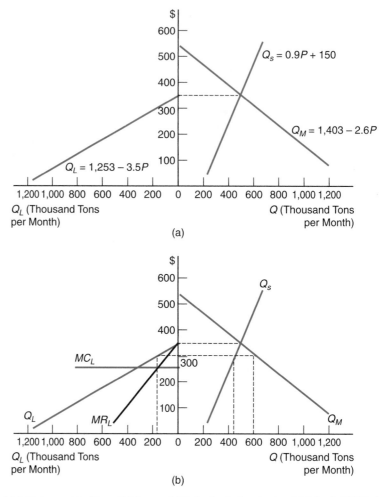

In panel (a), Q_L is equal to $(Q_M - Q_S)$. In panel (b), the leader's price is established at $309, since this price corresponds with the output where $MR_L = MC_L$. The small firms accept the $309 price.

By subtracting the supply curve of the small firms from the market demand curve, the demand curve for USS, Q_L, can be obtained. Thus

$$Q_L = 1{,}403 - 2.6P - (0.9P + 150)$$

$$= 1{,}253 - 3.5P.$$

From the preceding, it follows that

$$P_L = 358 - 0.2857Q_L,$$

$$TR_L = 358Q_L - 0.2857Q_L^2$$

and

$$MR_L = 358 - 0.5714Q_L,$$

where TR_L and MR_L are USS's total and marginal revenue, respectively.

Suppose now that over the relevant range of production for the problem in question, USS estimates its marginal cost for cold-rolled sheet to be constant at $260. At the existing price of $296 per ton, the preceding demand curve shows that Q_L = 1,253 − 3.5 (296) = 217. Accordingly, MR_L = 358 −(0.5714) (217) = $234. Since marginal revenue is less than marginal cost ($234 < $260), a price increase and reduction in quantity sold are warranted. USS should adjust its output to the point where MR_L = $260 = MC_L and charge the corresponding price. We can easily see that the above condition is met where

$$MR_L = 358 - 0.5714Q_L = 260,$$

or where

$$Q_L = 171.5 \text{ thousand tons per month}$$

and

$$P_L = 358 - (0.2857)(171.5) = \$309 \text{ per ton.}$$

In panel (b) of Figure 9-13, we illustrate the outcome of USS's pricing decision. At the $309 price, total quantity demanded will be 599,600 tons per month. USS will supply 171,500 tons per month, and the other firms in the industry will supply 428,100 tons per month. If USS's capacity is such that it can increase output substantially at a constant marginal cost of $260, then other firms cannot successfully charge a price higher than $309, since they will simply lose customers to USS. Of course, USS will be quite happy to take their customers at MR = $309, since this is a great deal more than the firm's $260 marginal cost.

The preceding example has used a combination of actual and hypothetical data to illustrate how a dominant firm might determine a market price it wishes to establish for a single product. Currently, the steel industry is characterized by a more complex pricing system in which other firms sometimes play the role of leader. In addition, the industry has been much transformed by both imports of foreign steel and joint ventures with foreign firms. (USS has joint ventured in California with Posco, the leading

Korean producer.) However, it is clear that rival firms still keep a close eye on USS because it is such a large producer.[15]

PERFECT COLLUSION—THE CARTEL

A **cartel** is a group of firms that have joined together to make agreements on pricing and market strategy.

A **cartel** exists when a number of firms get together and agree on a policy of managing operations in a way that will maximize the joint profits of the group. *Perfect collusion* is simply another label applied to this market situation. In the United States, firms are prohibited from forming cartels for purposes of domestic trade. However, U.S. firms can form cartels for purposes of foreign trade, and a number of such organizations have been important in U.S. industry.

In terms of the conditions for profit maximization, there is absolutely no difference between the optimal managerial strategy of a cartel and that of a monopolistic or oligopolistic firm that has several different plants. Still, the cartel's management does face the additional problem of *distribution of profits* among its members once the profit-maximizing price has been established, and there is no particular rule that must be followed in that distribution. Moreover, the main difference between the cartel and an oligopolistic firm with several plants is that the latter must estimate a demand curve that is something other than the market demand curve. Thus, it should be clear that there are a number of good reasons to examine carefully the case of the multiple-firm cartel.

To maximize profit, managers of a cartel must allocate *production* to the individual member firms based on the "rule of marginal cost." Simply stated, this rule dictates that marginal or incremental output should always be allocated to the firm that has the lowest marginal cost. Thus, if the cartel consists of two firms, Firm A and Firm B, and management is adjusting output in a situation where $MC_B < MC_A$, then additional output should be allocated to Firm B. Presumably, as Firm B's output is increased, its marginal cost will increase. When marginal cost reaches a level equal to that in Firm A, additional output may be allocated to Firm A. In fact, at any time that $MC_A \neq MC_B$, the cartel can gain by switching output from the firm with higher marginal cost to the one with lower marginal cost. Thus, where profit is maximized, it must be true that $MC_A = MC_B = MR$.

This condition can be generalized to a cartel consisting of any number of firms. For example, a graphical solution for a cartel consisting of three firms is shown in Figure 9-14. Management determines the cartel's total output

---

[15] USS is still the largest U.S. producer of steel mill products. They have a very informative website at www.usx.com. For more on current issues relating to the problem of imported steel, see "The Debate over Steel Trade," *Metal Center News Online* (www.metalcenternews.com), June 1999.

FIGURE 9–14   *Allocation of Production by a Centralized Cartel*

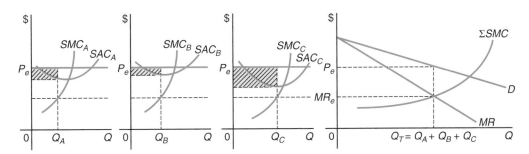

The marginal cost curves of Firms A, B, and C are summed horizontally to obtain the ΣSMC curve. The cartel's price is established in keeping with $\Sigma SMC = MR$, and output is allocated to each firm at the quantity where its $SMC = MR_e$.

and price at Q_T, P_e, in the quadrant to the extreme right. This quantity-price combination corresponds to the intersection of ΣSMC (the horizontal sum of SMC_A, SMC_B, and SMC_C) with MR. MR_e, the level of MR consistent with P_e, is projected to the cost curve diagrams for Firms A, B, and C, and each firm is allocated the output at which its $SMC = MR_e$. The cartel's total profit is the sum of the areas of the profit rectangles for the three firms, or $(P_e - SAC_A) Q_A + (P_B - SAC_B)Q_B + (P_C - SAC_C)Q_C$.

The cartel agreement might prescribe that each firm keep the amount of profit it produces, or it might provide for some other division of the total. For example, some of the profits of high-cost firms might be redistributed to the lower-cost firm (Firm C in Figure 9-14) as an incentive for the lower-cost firm to cooperate with the cartel. Otherwise it might try to break away and increase its market share by lowering price.

Usually the managers of a cartel place high priority on strategies that will keep the cartel from breaking up, since under rivalrous competition both group and individual firm profits are likely to be smaller in the long run. Nonetheless, bickering among cartel members over output and pricing decisions can occur. The oil cartel, the Organization of Petroleum Exporting Countries (OPEC), represents such a case, where failure to agree on economic strategy led in 1990 to the Iraqi invasion of Kuwait and subsequent disasters.

The possibility of cartel breakup explains why managers might depart from the optimal solution of Figure 9-14 to a lower profit (for the short run) strategy that has a higher probability of keeping the organization intact. For example, where the cartel's markets are geographically widespread, the managers might decide only to divide markets, allowing prices to settle around a level so that price differentials are so small that it is not profitable for intermediaries to attempt to buy from one cartel member and sell in

NUMERICAL EXAMPLE

Cartel Output Allocation

Producers in three countries, Irun, Sheran, and Uwaq have formed a cartel to sell highly prized desert oasis water in the world market. Suppose world demand for the water is consistent with the equation $P = 8.30 - .0005Q_T$, where Q_T is the total number of gallons the cartel sells, and the producers have managed to maximize profit at a price of $5.65 per gallon. Suppose also that the countries have the following marginal production costs.

Irun: $MC_i = .25 + .00125Q_i$

Sheran: $MC_s = .60 + .002Q_s$

Uwaq: $MC_u = .15 + .0015Q_u$

How much production should the cartel managers allocate to each country?

Answer:

If the cartel has succeeded in maximizing profit at the $5.65 price with the given world demand curve, then all three of the above marginal cost functions will be equal to MR at that price ($MC_i = MC_s = MC_u = MR$). The marginal revenue function for the given demand curve will have the same dollar axis intercept as the demand curve and twice the negative slope, so it is $MR = 8.30 - .001Q_T$. To determine Q_T, substitute the price of $5.65 into the demand curve equation to obtain $.0005Q_T = 2.65$ and $Q_T = 5,300$. Substituting $Q_T = 5,300$ into the MR function yields $MR = 8.30 - 5.30$, so that $MR = 3$ Setting each of the three MCs equal to 3 will yield the following:

Irun: $MC_i = .25 + .00125Q_i = 3$
$.00125Q_i = 2.75$; $Q_i = \underline{2,200}$.

Sheran: $MC_s = .60 + .002Q_s = 3$
$.002Q_s = 2.40$; $Q_s = \underline{1,200}$.

Uwaq: $MC_u = .15 + .0015Q_u = 3$
$.0015Q_u = 2.85$; $Q_u = \underline{1,900}$.

Of course, the sum of the three quantities (2,200 + 1,200 + 1,900) is 5,300, so that quantiy supplied equals quantity demanded.

another member's territory. This approach might allow a higher cost producer to charge a somewhat higher price, particularly if that producer's territory is somewhat removed from those of other producers. Thus, although the perfect collusion approach to cartel management provides a point of departure for cartel strategy, it is easy to see that the decisions made by cartel management experts in any given case may differ significantly from the theoretically optimal solution.

PRODUCTION WITH MULTIPLE PLANTS

If a firm has multiple plants, the condition for optimal allocation of output is the same as for a cartel—that is, the marginal cost of production should be the same in each plant, or total cost can be reduced by shifting output from one plant to another. Of course, many large corporations have multiple production facilities and are faced with decisions regarding how much output to place in any one facility. Sometimes these facilities are located in a single country, but in today's global economy, multinational corporations frequently have to decide how to allocate production among plants located in several countries.

The appropriate allocation method can be illustrated with a simple example. Suppose Benwag Corporation has plants for relining brake shoes in the United States, Canada, and Mexico. All output sold in the U.S. market is shipped to a distribution center in Kansas, and shipping costs from the three plants to the center do not differ significantly. Canadian and Mexican domestic sales are small compared with sales in the United States. If the plants have the marginal costs given in the table that follows, what is the optimal allocation of a total output of 14,000 units per week?

United States		Canada		Mexico	
Quantity	*Marginal Cost*	*Quantity*	*Marginal Cost*	*Quantity*	*Marginal Cost*
0		0		0	
	6.40		6.40		6.00
1,000		1,000		1,000	
	6.20		6.50		6.14
2,000		2,000		2,000	
	6.24		6.69		6.29
3,000		**3,000**		3,000	
	6.30		6.89		6.46
4,000		4,000		4,000	
	6.50		7.10		6.70
5,000		5,000		**5,000**	
	6.71		7.32		7.00
6,000		6,000		6,000	
	7.00		7.55		7.40
7,000		7,000		7,000	
	7.35		7.79		7.90
8,000		8,000		8,000	

Recall that the condition for optimal allocation, as in the cartel model, is that the marginal cost should be the same in all plants. With the given tabular data, each increment of 1,000 units of output should be allocated to the plant that can produce it at the lowest marginal cost. Thus, the first 1,000 units would be allocated to the Mexican plant, where marginal cost is $6.00. In fact, 3,000 units can be allocated to the Mexican plant before any are allocated to the U.S. or Canadian plants, since their initial marginal costs are both $6.40. Production of 4,000 units would be accomplished at least cost by producing the incremental 1,000 in either the U.S. or Canadian plant, since their marginal costs of $6.40 are below the Mexican marginal cost of $6.46 for the next increment. The optimal allocation for the required 14,000 units is highlighted in the table: 6,000 units for the U.S. plant, 3,000 for the Canadian plant, and 5,000 for the Mexican plant. The marginal costs of the last units produced in each plant are approximately the same, or about $6.70. It would not be rational to increase the output of one of the plants and decrease that of another, since for each plant, an increase beyond its current allocation would yield marginal cost greater than $6.71, the marginal cost of the last 1,000 units that were allocated to the plant in the United States.

PRODUCT MARKET STRUCTURES: RECAP AND COMPARISON

Many times in this and the preceding chapter we have used the term *market structure* to refer to the characteristics of the market where the firm sells its product. We have looked at four main product market structures: perfect competition, monopoly, monopolistic competition, and oligopoly. These differed mainly in regard to number of sellers, product differentiation, rival reactions, barriers to entry, and long-run economic profit.

Table 9-2 provides a capsule summary of the four market structures. Both perfect competition and monopolistic competition are characterized by a large number of sellers and free entry, neither of which is found in monopoly or oligopoly. In both perfect and monopolistic competition, individual firms are small and ignore the pricing behavior of others. Oligopoly, however, is characterized by few firms, rival reactions, and barriers to entry. In pure monopoly, entry is completely blocked, since there is only one firm. Entry barriers make long-run economic profit possible in both monopoly

Table 9–2 *A Comparison of Product Market Structures*

Type of Market	Number of Sellers	Product Differentiation	Rival Reactions	Barriers to Entry	Long-Run Profit Greater Than Normal
Perfect competition	Many	None	None	None	No
Monopolistic competition	Many	Some	None	None	No
Oligopoly	Few	Yes or No	Yes	Yes	Possible
Monopoly	One	Yes or No	No	Yes	Possible

and oligopoly, while the lack of barriers leads to only normal long-run profit for firms in perfect or monopolistic competition.

SUMMARY

Oligopoly Analysis and Business Behavior

In this chapter we have taken an important step from the rather simplistic analyses of the perfectly competitive and monopolistic market structures to the more complex world of monopolistic competition and oligopoly. The importance of this chapter lies in the fact that the situations we have discussed encompass many additional elements with which a majority of U.S. firms must deal in the development of their managerial strategy. These elements (product differentiation, rival reactions, price leadership, and collusion) may be significant in the decision process any time a seller's market is not characterized by perfect competition or monopoly.

We have stated that a firm in an industry structure characterized by monopolistic competition maximizes profit at a level of output where its perceived demand curve intersects its market share demand curve and $MR_d = SMC$. In the long run, a monopolistically competitive firm can expect to make only a *normal* profit because of the entry of other firms.

In the case of an oligopolistic market structure, however, there are substantial barriers to entry, and long-run economic profits are possible. Early in this chapter we discussed the duopoly theories of Cournot, Bertrand, and Edgeworth in which a firm makes naive assumptions regarding the behavior of the other firm, in spite of contradictory experiences. (Cournot indicated that each firm believes the other firm will not change its level of output, whereas Bertrand and Edgeworth assumed that each firm believes the other firm will hold price constant.)

Later in the chapter we discussed more realistic theories of oligopolistic firm behavior, each based to some extent on Chamberlin's assumption that such firms recognize their *mutual interdependence*. These theories included the kinked demand curve, price leadership, and cartel hypotheses. We have shown that what actually happens in an oligopolistic market structure is influenced to a large extent by its legal environment and by the extent to which the firms in an industry cooperate with one another.

We have only scratched the surface of the number of conceivable oligopoly situations, but we hope to have demonstrated that it is possible to apply the tools developed in earlier chapters to management's decision problems in a wide variety of oligopolistic settings. (An additional analytical device, game theory, is discussed in the next chapter.) In Chapter 11, we will continue to apply now-familiar approaches to realistic situations, analyzing a number of specific pricing problems that firms in monopolistically competitive or oligopolistic markets are likely to face.

QUESTIONS

1. What is the significance of product differentiation in a market characterized by monopolistic competition?

2. How is the kinked oligopoly demand curve related to the demand curve faced by a monopolistically competitive firm? How does the oligopolistic firm's perception of the inelastic portion of its demand curve differ from the perception of the monopolistically competitive firm regarding its demand?

3. Give some examples of product markets in your community that can be identified as monopolistically competitive. Why do you believe they fit the case?

4. Why do the nineteenth-century oligopoly models generate different conclusions about duopoly? Can you see any relationship between Chamberlin's critique of the duopoly models and the cases of price leadership discussed in this chapter?

5. Under what conditions would an oligopolistic firm facing a kinked demand curve charge a price different from the one that occurs at the kink?

6. Although General Motors is not always the price leader in the U.S. automobile industry, do you think it can be characterized as the dominant firm? Why or why not?

7. Can you state simply the rule by which a cartel should allocate output among its members to maximize profit? Why might a cartel choose to do otherwise?

8. Why can we expect that monopolistically competitive firms will tend to have only normal profits in the long run, whereas oligopolistic firms may well have greater than normal profits?

9. Gasoline stations have often been used to describe kinked demand curve oligopoly. Why do they appear to fit the case?

10. Briefly explain how a large and dominant firm's demand curve may be related to the market demand curve for its product under the assumption that smaller firms will follow its price leadership.

PROBLEMS

1. The firm in the diagram is in the short run in a monopolistically competitive market.

   a. Derive the firm's marginal revenue curve.

   b. Indicate its short-run profit-maximizing output, supplying an appropriate *SMC* curve in the diagram.

   c. Add a short-run average cost curve such that the firm has greater than normal profit.

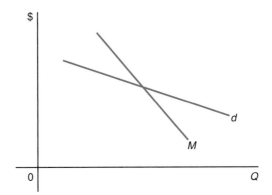

2. The monopolistically competitive firm in the following diagram is not in a long-run profit-maximizing position. Why not? What changes would have to occur for it to get to such a position? (*Hint:* Compare this diagram with Figure 9-3 in this chapter.)

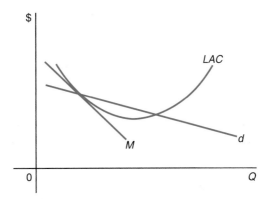

3. Suppose your favorite charity is participating in a fund-raising carnival that will run for three nights. You have been put in charge of managing the kissing booth. All labor at the carnival is voluntary, including that of the kissers, so you believe that you have a costless monopoly. Given your estimate of the nightly demand for kisses,

$$Q_k = 5{,}000 - 25{,}000\, P_k$$

   a. What price will yield the most revenue for your charity?

   b. If another charity opens a kissing booth adjacent to yours but demand remains as above (assume the product is undifferentiated), what price will prevail and how much revenue will each booth generate under the Cournot assumption?

   c. Could you improve the situation in part b through collusion? If not, why not? If so, how, and what would be the result in terms of revenue?

4. The following diagram shows a case of price leadership by a dominant firm. SMC_L is the marginal cost curve of the dominant firm, S_S is the sum of the marginal cost curves of the "follower" firms, and D_M is the market demand for the product. Find graphically the following information:

a. The demand and marginal revenue curves of the price leader.

b. The price that will be set.

c. The quantity sold by (i) the leader and (ii) the follower firms.

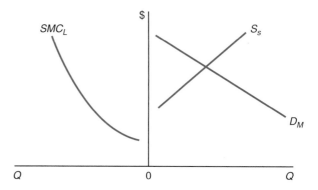

5. Suppose a large firm that is a price leader in an industry characterized also by many small, competing firms estimates the market demand for its product to be

$$Q_M = 81{,}000 - 200P,$$

and that it expects small firms in the industry to supply output according to the following function:

$$Q_S = 1{,}000 + 50P.$$

The large firm's marginal cost function is

$$MC_L = 100 + 0.014Q_L.$$

a. What price will the large firm set?

b. How much will the large firm sell?

c. What quantity will the small firms sell?

6. The two firms in the following diagram decide to form a cartel. Find graphically the following information:

a. The market price of their output.

b. The quantity each firm will sell.

c. The total profits of the cartel.

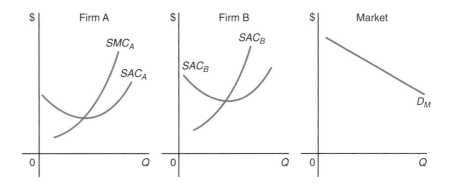

7. A cartel is maximizing profit at a price of $37.50 per barrel for its product. The demand curve for the members' product is given by the equation $Q = 200{,}000 - 4{,}000P$, so that $MR = 50 - 0.0005Q$. Suppose there are three firms in the cartel with the following respective marginal cost functions.

$$MC_1 = 2 + 0.001Q_1,$$

$$MC_2 = 1.9 + 0.0012Q_2,$$

and

$$MC_3 = 9.5 + .002Q_3.$$

How much output should be allocated to each cartel member? (Assume that Q_i is yearly output in barrels and that MC_i is marginal cost per barrel.)

8. Suppose an oligopolistic firm has the following cost and revenue data.

MR	Q	P	TR	TVC	AVC	AFC	SMC
	0	120	0	0	—	—	
	10		1150	600		60	
	20		2200		40		
	30	105	3150	900			
	40	100		1120			
	50	95			30		
	60		5400		40		
	70		5950		50	8.57	
	80		6400	4800		7.50	
	90	75		7200		6.67	

a. Fill in the blank spaces in the table.

b. What output should the firm produce? Why?

c. What price should the firm charge, and what will be its economic profit?

9. The following diagram is for an oligopoly firm that faces a kinked demand curve. Complete it by constructing the firm's marginal revenue curve and adding a marginal cost curve that is consistent with maximizing profit at the price and quantity that occur at the kink.

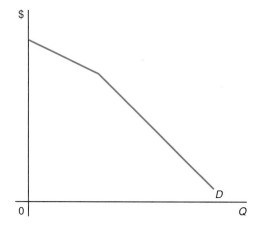

10. Suppose a monopolistically competitive firm estimates its demand curve to be $Q = 5{,}000 - 10P$ and that its market share curve is defined by the line $Q = 3{,}000 - 5P$. If the firm's marginal cost equation is $SMC = 100 + 0.2Q$, will it be at its profit maximum if it charges $400 per unit for its product? Explain.

11. A firm in noncollusive oligopoly believes that if it raises price its demand curve will be described by the equation $Q = 1{,}400 - 20P$, but that if it lowers price its demand curve will be $Q = 800 - 10P$. Management knows that the firm's average variable cost is constant at $60 per unit of output. What output should the firm produce, and what price should it charge?

The following problems require calculus.

C1. Gnoma Pest Control Company specializes in pest control services for single-family homes. Entry is easy in the local market, and a large number of local firms offer similar services. The typical contract provides whole-house service, including one interior spraying per month and a yearly foundation spray. The cost to the company can be regarded as a constant amount per unit at

$$AVC = \$5 \text{ per month per home.}$$

Advertising and image are important to pest control firms in the local market, since this method is about the only way they can differentiate what is otherwise a fairly homogeneous output. Gnoma's management advertised heavily to get the firm established but has recently cut the firm's advertising by one-half.

Management now estimates the firm's demand curve for household service to be

$$Q = 25,000 - 2,000P$$

where Q is the quantity of homes under service contract and P is the *monthly* service charge.

a. Based on management's estimate of demand, at what price and quantity sold should Gnoma be able to maximize profit?

b. If monthly fixed costs are $12,000, what will monthly profit be?

After the reduction in advertising, Gnoma's sales fell to 5,250 homes under monthly contract. A market analyst states that this drop occurred because Gnoma's market share fell when advertising expenditures were cut. The analyst further states that under conditions of the current advertising level, Gnoma should estimate its demand curve as

$$Q' = 22,000 - 2,000P.$$

The analyst states that Gnoma can either maximize profit subject to the preceding demand curve (Q') or spend an additional $5,000 per month on advertising and move back to the originally estimated demand curve, recovering its market share.

c. If Gnoma's management maximizes profit subject to

$$Q' = 22,000 - 2,000P,$$

what is the firm's optimal output and price?

d. Is the preceding profit greater or less than the profit that would be obtained by spending the $5,000 per month on advertising and returning to

$$Q = 25,000 - 2,000P?$$

e. What should Gnoma do?

C2. A firm's research department has estimated that if other firms in the industry are indifferent to changes in the price of its product, its demand curve will be

$$Q = 700 - 50P.$$

However, if other firms always charge the same price it does, the firm's demand curve will be

$$Q' = 200 - 10P.$$

a. If the firm's marginal cost equals $8.00, what output and price will maximize profit? (Assume that the other firms will not follow a price rise above $12.50 but that they will follow a price cut below $12.50.)

b. If the firm's marginal cost equals $11.50, what output and price will maximize profit?

C3. The following is a demand curve that has been estimated for an oligopolistic firm:

$$AR = P_x = 160 - (1/2)Q_x$$

where Q_x is the quantity of Product x sold per month and P_x is its price per unit. If the firm's total cost function is

$$TC = 500 + 40Q_x - 1.5\,Q_x^2 + (1/3)Q_x^3,$$

a. Determine the quantity produced (sold) that will maximize profit.

b. Indicate the dollar amount of profit for the firm at the preceding output per month.

C4. Phunny Phaucet Corporation of America (PPCA) operates in a noncollusive oligopolistic market where firms tend to base their strategies on fear of their rivals. PPCA believes that at its current price its demand curve will be $Q = 400 - 4P$ if it raises price, since it expects that other firms will not follow a price increase. For price cuts, however, it believes its demand curve is $Q = 250 - 2P$, since other firms are expected to follow a reduction in price.

a. With the above assumptions, what are PPCA's current price and quantity sold?

b. Suppose PPCA's total cost function is

$$STC = 50 + 20Q + 0.1Q^2.$$

Is PPCA maximizing its profit at the quantity and price you found in a? Explain why or why not.

c. Now suppose that PPCA has made an error in the estimate of its total cost function so that the actual total cost is

$$STC = 60 + 30Q + 0.25Q^2.$$

With this revised total cost function, what is the firm's best output and price?

C5. Aqualor Corporation is a very large producer of swimming pool electronic control valves. Aqualor typically charges a standard price for a valve that fits many different brands of swimming pool equipment. Aqualor's management realizes that smaller firms in its industry will always charge exactly the price that Aqualor sets and currently estimates the market demand curve for the valves to be

$$Q_M = 7{,}520 - 75P.$$

Aqualor's total cost function can be represented by the equation $TC = 85{,}000 + 8Q + 0.001Q^2$. In addition, it has estimated that the smaller firms' supply curve can be represented by the equation $Q_S = 120 + 25P$.

a. What price will Aqualor will charge for its valves, and how many will it sell?

b. How many valves will the smaller firms supply?

c. What will be the total profit or loss of Aqualor Corporation?

C6. Starcom Communications of America (SCA) operates in a noncollusive oligopolistic market where firms tend to base their strategies on good old-fashioned fear. SCA believes that at its current price its demand curve will be $Q = 3,000 - 20P$ if it raises price, since it expects that other firms will not follow a price increase. For price cuts, however, it believes its demand curve is $Q = 1,800 - 10P$, as other firms are expected to follow a reduction in price.

a. With the above assumptions, what are SCA's current price and quantity sold?

b. Suppose SCA's total cost function is

$$STC = 20,000 + 3Q + 0.05Q^2.$$

Is SCA maximizing its profit at the quantity and price you found in part a? Explain why or why not.

c. Now suppose that SCA has made an error in its estimate of the total cost function so that the actual total cost is

$$STC = 20,000 + 7Q + 0.08Q^2.$$

With this revised total cost function, what is the firm's profit-maximizing price, output, and total profit?

C7. Lullabye Corporation produces inexpensive baby crib mattresses that it sells to furniture manufacturers. For its segment of market demand, it currently estimates the demand curve it faces to be $Q = 3,800 - 100P$, where Q refers to monthly output. Lullabye has two plants, one located in No Hope, Arkansas, and another in Dime Box, Texas. The marginal cost in the Arkansas plant is $MC_A = 10 + 0.02Q_A$. In the Texas plant it is $MC_T = 8 + 0.03Q_T$. (In both, Q_i is monthly output.) Management believes it will maximize profit at a price of $29 per mattress. Assuming the price is correct, how much output should be allocated to each plant?

C8. Ajax Roofing Company is located in a small metropolitan area where it is one of six companies that specialize in reshingling. Management knows that basic reshingling jobs are selling in its market area for $82 per square (100 square feet.). From data on its past price increases, none of which were followed by the other firms, Ajax has estimated that its demand can be represented by the equation $Q = 1,260 - 10P$, where Q is the number of squares of replacement roofing installed per month. Its monthly total cost is $STC = \$10,000 + 34Q$, where Q is, again, the number of squares installed. Past experience shows that it is useless for Ajax to lower price below the prevailing one, since this results in a price war and almost no gain in quantity sold. (Demand at the firm level proves to be inelastic.) Is $82 the profit-maximizing price for Ajax? Explain.

SELECTED REFERENCES

Adams, Walter, and James Brock. *The Structure of American Industry,* 9th ed. Englewood Cliffs, NJ: Prentice Hall, 1995.

Borenstein, Severin. "The Dominant-Firm Advantage in Multiproduct Industries: Evidence from the U.S. Airlines." *Quarterly Journal of Economics* 106, No. 4 (November 1991): 1237–1266.

Chamberlin, Edward H. *The Theory of Monopolistic Competition.* Cambridge, MA: Harvard University Press, 1962.

Eaton, B. Curtis, and Diane F. Eaton. *Microeconomics.* Englewood Cliffs, NJ: Prentice Hall, 1995, Chapters 11 and 12.

Lipsey, Richard G., Paul N. Courant, and Christopher T. S. Ragan. *Economics.* Boston: Addison-Wesley, 1999, Chapter 12.

Mathis, Stephen, and Janet Kocianski. *Microoeconomic Theory: An Integrated Approach.* Upper Saddle River, NJ: Prentice Hall, 2003, Chapters 17–19.

Miller, Roger Leroy. *Economics Today.* Boston: Addison-Wesley, 2003, Chapter 25.

Prager, Jonas. *Applied Microeconomics.* Homewood, IL: Irwin, 1993, Chapters 13 and 14.

Shepherd, William G. "'Contestability' vs. Competition." *American Economic Review* 74, No. 4 (September 1984): 572–587.

Venkatraman, N., and John E. Prescott. "The Market Share-Profitability Relationship: Testing Temporal Stability Across Business Cycles." *Journal of Management* 16, No. 4 (1990): 783–805.

CHAPTER TEN

Games, Information, and Strategy

As the introduction to oligopoly in Chapter 9 showed, the outstanding characteristic of rivalrous market structures is that an individual firm's managers must contemplate (indeed, make assumptions about) the reactions of one or more rival firms whenever it makes a decision relating to price or some other variable that affects the firm's profit. Thus, oligopoly decision making is much like decision making in chess, football, or military operations—it involves choosing a strategy that will lead to some type of desired outcome. In a sense, oligopoly is much like a game. It should not be surprising, then, that economists have developed a branch of analysis known as **game theory** to deal with decision making in situations like oligopoly.

Another contemporary subfield of economics deals with the study of information. This has important applications to business operations, since decision makers require information to make choices. Of course, decision makers do not always have all the information they would like to have, and this presents problems, as we will see later. We begin this chapter, however, by looking at game theory.

Game theory was introduced into economic analysis by John Von Neumann and Oskar Morgenstern. Their pioneering work, *Theory of Games and Economic Behavior*, was published in 1944, and a substantial amount of additional work was done by others during the 1950s through the 1970s. Interest in game theory has waxed and waned, but it has surged strongly in recent years as economists were able to show, using both logic and experimental methods, that the approach frequently either yielded equilibrium solutions or identified certain results as very likely. Three game theorists were awarded the Nobel Prize in Economic Science, and an award-winning movie, *A Beautiful Mind,* was made about one of them.[1] Today, game theory is being used more and more by corporate and government decision makers, some of whom rely on cadres of economists and mathematicians for advice on strategic moves and countermoves.

STRATEGY AND TYPES OF GAMES

A **strategy** is a choice or sequence thereof made by a decision maker who, generally, sacrifices other alternatives in order to pursue it.

To understand game theory, we need first to consider the nature of a strategy. A **strategy** is a choice or a sequence of choices made by a decision maker when alternative choices are available. In other words, it is a game plan that a player follows. Generally, once a strategy is chosen, a sacrifice of some kind occurs. For example, if, in anticipation of what a rival will do, I choose to raise my price, I have foregone the strategies of keeping it constant or lowering it. The strategy I have chosen will have an opportunity cost, and that cost may vary depending on how my rival reacts to the choice I have made. Depending upon how the game is played, I may be able to change my strategy at some later point, but when I first make the decision, I have made a significant commitment and sacrificed other alternatives.

A **one-shot game** is a game wherein each player, acting simultaneously and without knowledge of what their rival(s) will do, has only one opportunity to pursue their chosen strategy prior to the game's end.

A *game* consists of some players, their strategies, and the outcomes that can occur from decisions the players make. Games vary in structure. For example, each player may have to make a move without knowing what the other player or players will do and without any opportunity to make subsequent moves. Such a game would be described as a single-period, simultaneous-move game, also known as a **one-shot game.** Other games can be *repeated.* Repeated games can be either infinitely repeated or repeated a finite number of times. In addition, games may involve a number of subgames if decisions are made in stages or sequentially. For many of the simplest games, possible strategies and outcomes can be described with a payoff matrix, a table showing the results of various combinations of strategies.[2]

SOME GAME THEORY EXAMPLES

The best way to understand what game theory can tell us is to put together an example. An easy first step toward understanding game theory analysis is to approach pricing in a two-firm setting using a one-shot game. Thus, we will be assuming that each firm does not know what strategy the other will

[1] The movie told the story of John F. Nash, who, along with Richard Selten and John Harsanyi, received the Nobel Prize in 1994 for contributions to game theory.
[2] This is also known as a game in *normal form.*

Table 10–1 *Payoff Matrix for Discount Game*

		FIRM B			
		Maintain		*Discount*	
FIRM *A*	Maintain	8	8	4	12^B
	Discount	12^A	4	5^A	5^B

In this game, both A and B have dominant strategies. No matter what B chooses to do, A will be best off to discount. The same is true for B, no matter what A chooses to do. There is just one Nash equilibrium, in the lower right cell, where the superscripts appear on both A's and B's choices.

choose. However, each knows what the outcome will be *if* a given choice is made by its rival. Such a game is set out in Table 10-1. In the table, data pertaining to Firm A are in color, while Firm B's data are in black. There are just two strategies: maintain price or offer a discount. In the payoff matrix, the numbers represent profit payoffs in millions of dollars, and the superscript letters indicate the choices of each firm, given the strategy of the other.

Each firm must choose between two possible strategies. It can maintain its current price, or it can discount its price in the hope of obtaining larger profits. Consider Firm A. In deciding how to play, it must analyze its rival's behavior. If Firm B chooses to maintain its current price (if it chooses the "Maintain" strategy in the left column of the matrix), the best choice for Firm A is to discount, since discounting will yield a $12 million payoff, whereas maintaining price will yield only $8 million. The superscript "A" on 12 indicates Firm A's preferred strategy if Firm B chooses to maintain its current price. However, if Firm B chooses to discount, A's best strategy is to discount too, since that yields a payoff of $5 million, which is much better than the 4 it would get if it maintained its current price. We can see that no matter which strategy B chooses, A is best off to discount. Thus, A has what is known as a **dominant strategy,** and that strategy is to discount. When a player finds that the best choice is to stick to the same strategy no matter what its rival does, the player is said to have a dominant strategy. (Alternatively, for Firm A, maintaining price is a **dominated strategy,** since maintaining yields an inferior result regardless of Firm B's strategy.)

Now consider Firm B. It does not know what Firm A will do, but it recognizes that if Firm A maintains its current price, the best Firm B strategy is to discount and receive a $12 million payoff as opposed to the $8 million it would receive if it did not discount. However, B's best choice if A discounts is to discount also, since $5 million is better than the $4 million it would receive if it maintained price. Note that B also has a dominant strategy in this game, for no matter what A chooses to do, B should discount. As explained

A **dominant strategy** is one that is best for a given player no matter the choice exercised by that player's rival(s).

A **dominated strategy** is one that will be *rejected* by a given player no matter the choice exercised by that player's rival(s).

earlier, superscripts (B) have been placed on the payoffs consistent with B's choices for the alternative A strategies. Now look at the lower right cell in the payoff matrix. It is the only cell that has a superscript on both the A and the B payoffs. There, each firm is doing the best it can given the other's strategy. No other cell has this characteristic. The result in this game is that both firms will discount, since if one discounts and the other does not, the firm that fails to discount will have a payoff of $4 million. We have an equilibrium in the lower right cell. Specifically, it is a Nash equilibrium, named for Nobelist John Nash. A **Nash equilibrium** exists when each player is doing the best he or she can, *given* the strategy of the other player. We have seen a Nash equilibrium before—in our examination of Cournot duopoly. There, each firm chose to take 1/3 of the zero-price output, given that the other would keep its output constant at the same amount. Neither could unilaterally improve its position by a change in quantity.

Although the Nash equilibrium solution to the game in Table 10-1 is where both players discount, note that if they both chose to maintain their pregame prices they would each have a larger payoff (8, 8 in the upper left cell). This solution cannot occur if each firm acts independently, since given the strategy of its rival, each will be better off with some other choice. That is, if B chooses to maintain its price, A will discount and have $12 million, rather than $8 million, as its payoff. Similarly, if A chooses to maintain price, B will choose to discount, using similar reasoning. In order to obtain the result in the upper left cell, the firms must *collude*. Clearly, the incentive to do so is there, but in the United States and many other countries, collusion to fix prices is often against the law. Furthermore, if an agreement were made, each party would have an incentive to break it, since the prospect of increasing its own payoff substantially (to 12) is very attractive.

There are many other possible one-shot, simultaneous two-player games that have a unique Nash equilibrium, and there are games with multiple Nash equilibria. Table 10-2 offers an example where data from our original

A **Nash equilibrium** is a game outcome in which each player obtains the best possible result *given* the strategy of the player's rival(s).

Table 10–2 *Payoff Matrix for Discount Game: No Dominant Strategy for B*

	FIRM B Maintain		FIRM B Discount	
Maintain (FIRM A)	8	11^B	4	10
Discount (FIRM A)	12^A	4	5^A	5^B

In this version of the discount game, there is still a Nash equilibrium in the lower right cell, even though B does not have a dominant strategy. As in the first game, collusion will yield gains for both firms.

NUMERICAL EXAMPLE

One-Shot Game

Two airlines, Air Atlantic and Trans-Global, are major rivals on routes between the United States and Europe. This year, travel has been especially slow during the spring, known as a "shoulder season" in the business—a time when traffic is moderate but far from that expected during peak periods. Both airlines are considering offering a mileage bonus to members of their frequent flyer programs for transatlantic flights taken between March 1 and May 31. The issue for each is whether to offer 5,000 bonus miles for each round-trip flight taken during that period or 10,000 bonus miles per flight. The payoff matrix for this game follows. (Payoffs are in market share as percent of total transatlantic passengers, and there are other firms that fly the routes but will not be players in the game.)

Market Share Payoff Matrix for U.S.-Europe Routes (payoffs in percent of total market)

	Air Atlantic 10,000 Bonus Miles		Air Atlantic 5,000 Bonus Miles	
Trans-Global 10,000 Bonus Miles	15^T	15^A	16^T	11
Trans-Global 5,000 Bonus Miles	11	13	12	14^A

Assuming in 1 through 3 below that play is simultaneous, answer the following and explain:

1. Does Trans-Global have a dominant strategy?
2. Does Air Atlantic have a dominant strategy?
3. Is there a Nash equilibrium in this game?
4. If play is not simultaneous, is there a first-mover advantage in this game?

Solution

1. Yes. Trans-Global has a dominant strategy, since it will choose to offer 10,000 bonus miles no matter whether Air Atlantic offers 10,000 or 5,000 bonus miles.
2. No. Air Atlantic does not have a dominant strategy. If Trans-Global offers 10,000 miles, Air Atlantic will offer 10,000 miles. However, if Trans-Global offers 5,000 miles, Air Atlantic is best off to offer 5,000 miles, too.
3. Yes. There is a Nash equilibrium in the upper left-hand cell, where both firms offer 10,000 bonus miles. This has the characteristic that both are doing the best they can *given* the other's strategy.
4. No. There is no first-mover advantage. Trans-Global has a dominant strategy, so if it moves first, it will choose to offer 10,000 bonus miles. Air Atlantic knows this, so if, instead, Air Atlantic moves first, it too will offer 10,000 miles, since offering 5,000 miles would result in a lower payoff once Trans-Global responds.

game have been changed so that Firm B does not have a dominant strategy, while Firm A's strategy is to discount as before. Analyzing B's best choices now, if A discounts, B will choose to discount as in the preceding game. However, if A chooses to maintain price, B will wish to maintain price also, since its payoff of $11 million exceeds the $10 million it would get if it discounts. Even though B does not have a dominant strategy, note that this game still has a Nash equilibrium in the same cell as before (discount, discount—lower right cell). Also, it is true as before that both firms can gain from a collusive agreement in which each maintains its pregame price. Again, this is not likely to occur for legal reasons and also because, in the case of Firm A, there would still be an incentive to break the agreement.

In the preceding example, B can decide what to do by employing an iterative dominance strategy. An **iterative dominance strategy** consists of examining the various possible outcomes and identifying dominated strategies of a rival. Thus, in Table 10-2, B can determine that maintaining price is a dominated strategy for A and, therefore, that A will not choose it. Since A will not maintain price, B's strategy will be to discount.

> An **iterative dominance strategy** is one that is chosen by examining possible game outcomes and identifying dominated rival strategies.

MULTIPLE EQUILIBRIA, SEQUENCING, AND FIRST-MOVER ADVANTAGE

We have seen two one-shot games and found that a Nash equilibrium can occur when at least one player has a dominant strategy. As mentioned above, another possibility is that of more than one Nash equilibrium. Table 10-3 shows data for two firms, Farmnet and Barnlink, that are considering expanding their rural Internet service by installing dialup "points of presence" in certain prosperous Kansas area codes. Thus, we have an entry game, where the payoffs in the table represent the firms' total profits. The first thing to note in Table 10-3 is that neither Farmnet nor Barnlink has a dominant strategy. Both are better off if only one of them enters the new market, since if they both enter, low prices will result in more modest profits. If only one enters, that firm will gain $3 million as compared to what happens if neither enters, but the other will concentrate its resources elsewhere and also gain ($1 million). As the superscripts indicate, there are two Nash equilibria, one when Farmnet enters and Barnlink does not, and the other when Barnlink enters and Farmnet does not. If we continue with our assumptions that play is simultaneous and neither player knows what the other's choice will be, we cannot really say what the result will be. Certainly, each firm has an incentive to enter but only if the other does not.

The game in Table 10-3 yields a predictable solution if we relax the assumption that play is simultaneous. That is, if one of the parties enters, we can predict what the other will do once it observes that action. For example. suppose Farmnet enters the market. Clearly, then, the best strategy for Barn-

Table 10–3 *Payoff Matrix for Entry Game: Two Nash Equilibria and a First-Mover Advantage*

	BARNLINK			
	Enter		*Do Not Enter*	
Enter	7	7	10^F	8^B
FARMNET				
Do Not Enter	8^F	10^B	7	7

This entry game has two Nash equilibria, lower left and upper right. Both firms are better off if only *one* of them enters. In addition, if the game is played sequentially, the firm that enters first obtains the greatest payoff. There is a first-mover advantage in this game.

MANAGERIAL PERSPECTIVE

Strategy in the Fast-Food Game

In 2002, the fast-food spotlight was on McDonald's, especially on the slow growth in sales that it was experiencing. It was also being criticized, along with other fast-food chains, for the nutritional deficiencies of its food and its "super-sizing" strategy, which were blamed for contributing to the obesity problem in the United States. It was clear that McDonald's needed a strategy that would address both of these issues, and, in the restaurant business, that means *menu change*.

One move made by the firm was to come up with a french fry cooked in a new oil that is very low in the type of fats linked to heart disease, and another was to add nonhamburger menu items to its main dishes. However, perhaps its most important move had to do with the menu strategy of one of its arch rivals, Wendy's. Wendy's had for several years enjoyed the success of its "99 cent" menu items. Alongside its meal deals and its regular menu, Wendy's had offered a selection of items such as baked potatoes, small "side" salads, twin-patty burgers, and chili priced at 99 cents per item. McDonald's announced in Sep-

tember 2002 that it would add a $1 menu to its offerings. Of course, Wendy's was clearly the first mover among hamburger chains in this menu game, and Wendy's had also moved first on the strategy of offering nonhamburger items on its regular menu. It seemed that McDonald's already perceived that it had been beaten to the punch on both of these strategies, so it also was pursuing another strategy—starting a chain of Mexican fast-food restaurants (Chipotle). Those new restaurant units were experiencing rapid growth in sales, and McDonald's was hoping that would begin to offset the sluggish growth of its traditional outlets.

References: "Analysts Are Skeptical of McDonald's Strategy," calendarlive, online, September 12, 2002, www.calendarlive.com/dining/cl-fimcdon12sep12.story?coll=cl-dining, September 16, 2002; "Fast-food Giants Try Value Menus," *USA Today*, online, September 11, 2002, www.usatoday.com/money/industries/food/2002-09-11-burger-king-99cents_xhtm, September 16. 2002; and "McDonald's to Reduce Bad Fat in Fries," *Detroit Free Press: Freep*, September 4, 2002, www.freep.com/features/food/fries4_20020904.htm, September 16, 2002.

link is not to enter, so the Nash equilibrium in the upper right cell will be the result. Note that Farmnet, by implementing its entry strategy before Barnlink has made a choice, not only keeps Barnlink out of the new market but also reaps the higher profits ($10 million instead of $8 million) that accrue to the entering firm when its rival does not enter. In game theory jargon, this game, when sequential rather than simultaneous, is characterized by a **first-mover advantage.** Whichever of the two firms moves first captures the new market and the higher profits that it brings when the other responds with its best strategy. Given what the first mover has done, the best strategy for the other firm is not to enter. Unfortunately, there is nothing in the data of Table 10-3 that can tell us which of the firms would decide to move first if the game were played sequentially.

A **first-mover advantage** in a sequential game is a beneficial outcome that accrues to the player who exercises the first strategic choice.

COOPERATIVE GAMES

In business, many decision strategies involve cooperative games in which two or more players make decisions collectively. Although antitrust laws frequently prohibit cooperation on matters such as pricing and market share, it may be permitted and even encouraged where product standards are concerned. An interesting example is provided by the personal computer industry, where strategic decisions have been made regarding various bus standards. (A *bus* determines the design of slots where add-in cards, such as modems and graphics accelerator cards, are installed.) Some bus standards that have been adopted by various manufacturers at different times are the ISA, PCI, and PCI-X standards. (In late 1998 Compaq, Dell, NEC, and Toshiba all announced a Mini-PCI bus specification that was subsequently endorsed by Intel.) Where competing standards are concerned, firms often must throw their weight behind a particular one in order to avoid losing their market entirely.[3] This is easy to appreciate by considering a case outside the computer industry—that of Sony Corporation and its Betamax VCRs.

When video cassette recorders for home use were introduced into the consumer market, there were two competing standards, the Sony Betamax and the VHS. Today, virtually all home VCRs are VHS machines, and Sony has lost the lion's share of the VCR market to other producers. Using hypothetical data, we can illustrate the VCR standard example as a game where cooperation benefits both players. Consider Table 10-4, which contains the payoffs in millions of dollars of profits for Sony and the rival manufacturers

---

[3] In the case of computers, when the PCI bus was developed to replace the ISA, or AT architecture, in the late 1990s, manufacturers of mainboards chose to supply them with both ISA (AT) slots and PCI slots for add-on cards, thus adopting both standards. This was a welcome strategy, since manufacturers of the accessory cards were slow to produce them for PCI slots.

Table 10–4 *Payoff Matrix for Video Format Game: Cooperation Pays*

	RIVAL MANUFACTURERS			
	Betamax		*VHS*	
SONY — Betamax	500^S	400^R	100	300
SONY — VHS	300	100	400^S	500^R

This is another game with two Nash equilibria. Both players are best off when they choose the *same* video format. Cooperation is better than noncooperation. However, Sony made a noncooperative choice (the one in the upper right cell) that yielded lower profits for it and the industry as a whole. This was not a Nash equilibrium.

of VCRs. There are two Nash equilibria in the table, one occurring when both players choose the Betamax format and the other when both choose VHS. Payoffs are much smaller for both players when they do not adopt a uniform standard, since consumers put off buying in order to see which standard survives. In the table, it does not matter for the industry as a whole whether the Beta or the VHS standard is chosen, just as long as there is *one* standard. However, the choice of format does matter to the two players, with Sony better off if the single standard is Beta and the other manufacturers better off if it is VHS.[4] Clearly, when compared with noncooperation, cooperation benefits both parties. Industry profits are only $400 million without cooperation, but they are $900 million with it. In this game, we can see that cooperation is the rational solution, but we cannot say whether a cooperative agreement would result in adoption of the Beta standard or of the VHS standard.

History tells us that in the real world Sony decided to stick with its Betamax format while the rivals continued to produce VHS machines. Our analysis indicates that this was not a Nash equilibrium solution and, further, that many consumers probably withheld purchasing a VCR because they did not know which format would prevail. In the end, VHS prevailed, but it is likely that both Sony and the industry would have been better off if Betamax had been abandoned as a home video format much earlier than it was. We should also note that Table 10-4 depicts the VCR standard game as a one-shot simultaneous game. However, Sony actually had subsequent opportunities to change its strategy, and, in fact, in 1988 it began production of VHS machines. The Beta format, which some argue was a superior technology to

---

[4] One might wonder whether the lower left cell, where Sony chooses VHS and the rivals choose Beta, constitutes a logical impossibility. However, we could imagine an extreme situation where Sony licenses its technology to the other firms but perceives that the VHS is more likely to be accepted by consumers and so chooses that technology for its own product.

VHS, is all but gone from the consumer market, though it still survives in special-purpose applications.

REPEATED GAMES

In many business settings, games are not single-period; instead, they are repeated over and over again. This is particularly the case in pricing and advertising decisions. For example, if one firm sets a low price, its rival may counter with a similar strategy. Since these strategies are likely to be self-defeating, the question arises as to the rationality of following them. Whether or not such a strategy makes sense may depend on the firm's perception regarding when the game will end. If the game is an infinitely repeated one, it is possible that the players will develop some sort of collusive agreement or that *tacit collusion* (collusion without formal agreement or illegal communication among firms) will ensue.

To illustrate an infinitely repeated game, let us set up a case involving two producers of pharmaceuticals. We will call them Smerk and Rizer. Each has a medication for blood pressure reduction, and both medications have similar properties and minimal side effects, even though they are chemically different. Thus, a physician could as easily choose to prescribe one as the other. Both medications are very well suited for their purpose, so the firms believe that neither will become obsolete. In other words, we have an infinitely repeated game, since there is always a tomorrow for both players. Table 10-5 shows the data for the two firms. As the superscripts on the payoffs (economic profits per year in millions of dollars) indicate, if we view this as a one-shot game, a Nash equilibrium occurs when both charge a low price. However, if they can agree to charge a high price, each will move from only normal profit to an economic profit of $20 million. Let's assume that they have coaxed each other into charg-

Table 10–5 *Pharmaceuticals Pricing Game: Infinite Repetition*

		RIZER		
		High Price		*Low Price*
High Price		20 20		-20 60^R
SMERK				
Low Price		60^S -20		0^S 0^R

When this game is infinitely repeated, the best strategy for both players is to avoid the Nash equilibrium in the lower right cell by colluding to maintain a high price. Such a strategy will be rational as long as the interest rate is sufficiently low to make the gains from defecting *less* than the present value of the profit stream obtained from colluding.

ing high prices, perhaps through statements made to the press or to share-holders that send a signal to each other that coexistence with high prices is "best for the industry" since both need to recover research and development expenditures as well as provide for future product development.

Examining Table 10-5, we can see that if one of the firms charges a high price, there is a substantial incentive for the other to defect from that strategy, since its profit will increase from $20 million to $60 million in the period when it defects. However, since the game is repeated, the result in the period following its defection will be that its rival will also charge a low price because it is better off to have normal profit than to continue charging a high price and lose $20 million. Thus, the defector is punished by its rival and will have normal profit forever. Whether or not defection is worthwhile in this setting depends on the interest rate. Effectively, the choice to defect is a choice to have $60 million economic profit in year one followed by normal profit forever, as opposed to having the collusive result of $20 million per year forever. At any realistic interest rate, $20 million per year forever has a much higher present value than $60 million, so defection is self-defeating.[5] The rational choice will be for both players to charge high prices.

For the pharmaceutical firms above, collusion turns out to be better than noncooperation. Furthermore, each firm can punish the other for defecting by condemning it to low prices and normal profit forever. Thus, the game involves a *threat*. In business strategy, threats are important, but a threat can only affect an outcome if it is a **credible threat.** The threat of retaliation by also cutting price in the preceding example is credible, since it is not rational for either firm to maintain its high price when the other one does not. For an example of a threat that is not credible, we can look to the airline industry. Suppose that an existing firm threatens to saturate a given market with low-fare flights when another is poised to enter it. That threat will not be credible if the threat-maker does not have sufficient aircraft to carry it out. Thus, the new entrant will go ahead with its plans. Actually, the reverse of this situation did occur in the 1980s. Investors associated with a regional carrier started a new line that paralleled a major carrier's routes along the Gulf Coast of the United States. The large carrier threatened to saturate those routes, and the rival line folded. When asked why, the CEO of the latter stated that he had only 6 planes to the large firm's more than 60. The large carrier's threat was, therefore, credible.[6]

Our pharmaceutical example assumed the game would be infinitely repeated. However, business firms also make strategic decisions that consti-

A **credible threat** is the threat of an action that a rival actually has the ability to carry out.

---

[5] Where i is the interest rate expressed as a decimal, the formula for the present value of the infinite stream of expected $20 million profits is $PV_\pi = \$20$ million $\times (1 + i)/i$. This will be greater than $60 million as long as $i < 0.5$, or as long as the interest rate is less than 50 percent. If you are not familiar with present value calculations, see Chapter 13.

[6] The story of this game was revealed in a luncheon conversation between one of the authors and one of the CEOs involved in it.

tute finite repeated games. A *finitely repeated game* may have either a known or an uncertain end period. For example, the two pharmaceutical firms of Table 10-5 would be engaged in a finitely repeated game if they expected that generic drug producers would be able to develop a close substitute for their products within, say, five years. Since they know they will reach a point where the game will terminate, each also knows that it can defect (break the cooperative agreement to charge a high price) in the last period without suffering any punishment. Thus, there is an incentive for both to defect in that period. Now consider, however, the second from the last period. If each expects the other to defect in the last period, there is no punishment from defecting in the second-to-last period either. The result is that cooperation will unravel, and both of the two firms will end up charging the low price—the same solution that would occur if the game were one-shot instead of repeated.

With an uncertain end period, however, the picture changes and is much like the infinitely repeated game. Actions will hinge on the probability that the game will end in the following period. If that probability is small, the rational solution will be to continue to cooperate, thereby reaping the net benefits from the present value of a future stream of inflows that is greater than the value received from defection. If that probability is 1.0, however, the result is, again, the one-shot game, and we can expect the same conclusion as in the finitely repeated game.

TREES AND SEQUENTIAL GAMES

Earlier, in the game presented in Table 10-3 (the two Internet service providers, Farmnet and Barnlink), we noted that sequencing of strategies would result in an equilibrium solution and that a first-mover advantage would exist. Sequential games, which may be quite complicated, are frequently analyzed using a **game tree** or *decision tree* approach. A game tree is a diagram with nodes and branches used to depict points at which decisions are made and the consequences of each decision. The branches occur at the nodes, each of which represents a decision point.

A **game tree** is a diagram that maps out a game using decision nodes and branches.

A good example of a sequential game is provided by the two dominant manufacturers of sport-utility vehicles (SUVs) in the United States, Ford and General Motors (GM). In the late 1990s, following the success of its Explorer SUV, Ford decided to develop a larger model, the Expedition. The size of the Expedition is certainly impressive, but GM was still able to boast that its Suburban, a carryall vehicle designed in the 1970s much more for hauling than for sport, was, in its 4-wheel drive version, the biggest mass-production SUV available.[7] Ford's response was to build an SUV even larger than its

---

[7] GM actually produced a Suburban as early as the 1930s. Its trucklike incarnation of the 1970s was gradually refined during the 1980s and 1990s.

FIGURE 10–1

*The GM-Ford
SUV Game*

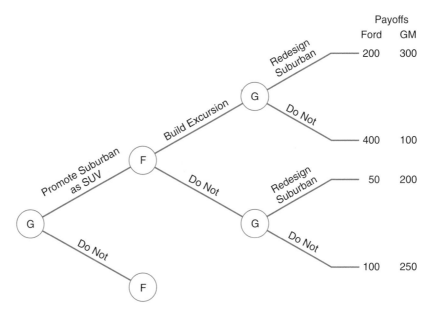

GM first decides to promote its Suburban as an SUV. Ford responds by building the Excursion. GM's response is to redesign the Suburban. The payoffs are $200 million for Ford and $300 million for GM. Backwards induction can be used to identify the best strategy for each firm.

Expedition, the Excursion, which debuted in late 1999. We can envision GM's response to this as what would occur in the third stage of a multistage sequential game that begins with GM's decision to promote the Suburban as an SUV. In Figure 10-1, the nodes are identified by decision maker (F for Ford, G for GM), and the branches indicate the strategies that can be selected at each node. The payoffs are the expected annual profits, in millions of dollars, of each firm's truck division.

The game begins when GM decides to promote the Suburban as an SUV. Ford moves next and must choose whether or not to build the Excursion. Building the Excursion moves the game along the upper branch from the "F" node. (If Ford had chosen not to build the Excursion, it would proceed along the lower branch.) There are two subsequent decision nodes for GM. Both involve whether or not it will redesign its Suburban SUV. Once Ford has chosen to build the Excursion, GM's best result ($300 million) occurs when it chooses to redesign the Suburban. For Ford, the best result occurs when it builds the Excursion and GM chooses not to redesign the Suburban. However, GM will not make this choice, since its profits will be much higher if it redesigns the Suburban than if it does not. Ford's result would be much worse, however, if it chose not to build the Excursion, which would put it on the lower branch, where its maximum payoff would be $100 million.

In this game, GM can determine its best strategy by examining the pay-offs and nodes in the game tree and observing which Ford strategies are dominated ones. GM does not have a dominant strategy. However, by working backwards through the game tree, it can determine that not building the Excursion is a dominated strategy for Ford. Since Ford will not choose that dominated strategy, GM knows the Excursion will be built. Therefore, GM will choose to redesign the Suburban.

We can conclude that confronted with this game, Ford chooses to build the Excursion (which, in reality, it did) and GM chooses to redesign the Suburban. This puts the solution at the top of the payoff columns, where Ford's payoff is $200 million and GM's is $300 million. Note that in this game the result can be readily determined by **backwards induction,** that is, starting with the best payoffs to each player and tracing backwards along the branches to determine which decisions will be made. Since the best payoffs to Ford are on the upper branches, its strategy will be to build the Excursion. Given Ford's strategy, the best payoff to GM is on the upper branch also, so GM should redesign the Suburban. In fact, GM did redesign the Suburban, and it also introduced other SUVs to compete with Ford's line. For 2003, it introduced a much redesigned Cadillac Escalade, its most luxurious SUV.

The Ford-GM example is a simple representation of what is called an **extensive form game.** Games of this type may or may not have Nash equilibria. In general, extensive form games are characterized by equilibrium strategies that involve a sequence of strategic decisions. The equilibrium strategy for GM turns out to be to promote the Suburban as an SUV and then redesign it after Ford builds the Excursion. (Ford only made one decision in Figure 10-1, but it had earlier chosen to build a smaller vehicle than the Excursion, the Expedition, a decision that preceded GM's strategy of promoting the Suburban as an SUV. This decision by Ford would have been at a node that occurred before the initial GM node in the figure.)

The examples presented above provide only a brief introduction to game theory as an analytical tool. In our games, the results of various possible plays were known to each player, and each player knew exactly what had happened when the other made a move. There are many more-complicated games where players have imperfect information or where there is uncertainty about the payoffs. Where strategies involve chance, probabilities come into play. The list of references following the problems for this chapter provides sources that discuss these more advanced types of games.

Backwards induction is the process of tracing backwards through a decision tree, starting from the best outcome for a given player, to determine that player's optimal strategy.

An **extensive form game** is a game that is characterized by sequences of decisions and may or may not have one or more Nash equilibria.

DECISION MAKING AND THE ECONOMICS OF INFORMATION

In general, the economic models presented in this and the preceding chapters have been founded on rational behavior by decision makers who have the necessary information to identify and choose strategies consistent with an optimal outcome. However, information often is neither free nor complete. For example, a consumer may have to shop around to find out whether a product is sold at very similar prices or, instead, at very different prices from one store to another. Likewise, a firm may have to engage in significant search activity to find employees it wishes to hire or to find out what constitutes a reasonable price for a material input.

Searching and Search Costs

Search costs are the economic costs incurred by individuals and/or firms associated with analyzing and making a decision to engage in a transaction.

The more a buyer shops for something, the higher are his or her **search costs**—real economic costs that might include not only the opportunity cost of time spent searching but also direct expenditures related to the search process. For a consumer, explicit search costs might include gasoline, parking, and (hopefully not) parking tickets and traffic fines. A firm, on the other hand, has explicit search costs such as advertising for and interviewing employees, sending buyers out to find merchandise, or paying brokers to secure inputs.

Our usual approach to maximizing behavior can be applied to the problem of search costs. In general, one incurs marginal benefits from additional search activities and is burdened by the marginal cost of them. Therefore, it is rational to continue searching only until one perceives that the marginal cost of additional search activity exceeds its marginal benefit. Consider a person who wishes to buy a home and is also interested in buying a camcorder. We can expect that he or she will shop a lot harder for the home than for the camcorder because the home is a high-priced item. A small percentage saved on the price of a home would outweigh any possible saving that could be obtained by intensive searching to obtain a low price on a single camcorder. The same type of argument applies to a firm in its search for employees. That is, it would be rational to spend a great deal of time and resources on recruiting for a high-level technical or professional employee but to put much less into searching for delivery persons or clerks.

We can use graphical microeconomic analysis to model the search problem. Figure 10-2 depicts the marginal benefit and the marginal cost associated with a search. Let us suppose that we are considering a consumer and that the amount of searching is measured by the number of stores searched. In the figure, marginal benefit is downward sloping because the more the consumer searches, the more she is likely to have found a price close to the lowest one that exists in the market and, therefore, the less the gain from further searching. The curve representing the marginal cost of search slopes upward because (1) additional searches become more costly as more difficult-to-obtain information is pursued and (2) the marginal disutility to the searcher rises (as in, "Boy, am I tired of this!").

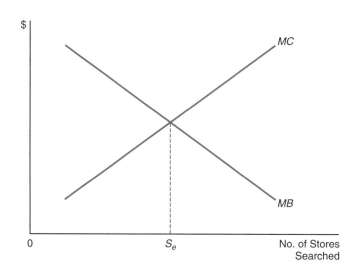

FIGURE 10–2

Applying Marginal Analysis to Searching

As the consumer increases search activity, the marginal benefit declines, whereas the marginal cost increases, since more difficult to find information is sought. The optimal level of search is S_e, where marginal benefit equals marginal cost.

Not surprisingly, the optimal amount of search activity will be determined where $MC_s = MB_s$, and further searching yields marginal benefits that are less than marginal cost. Thus, the optimal amount of search activity is S_e in Figure 10-2.

An important further consideration in analyzing search is how price variation affects the benefit from searching. We can use Figure 10-3 to examine this. Two MB curves are shown there, and MB' is higher than MB because it assumes that prices vary more from seller to seller. (The *range* of possible prices is greater.) When this happens, the benefits from additional searching are greater than they would be if prices were very similar from one seller to another. Therefore, other things equal, with a greater range of possible prices, MB' is the relevant marginal benefit curve, and the optimal amount of search activity is S_2 in the figure.

Asymmetric Information

Asymmetric information is a term applied to a situation wherein the parties to a transaction have non-identical information that may affect the outcome of that transaction.

A corollary to the proposition that information often is not free is that some individuals or firms have *better* information than others. When one party to a transaction has better information than another, we encounter a case of **asymmetric information.** In consumer goods markets, the seller frequently knows more about the product than does the buyer. A classic case of this type is the used car market, where sellers, especially an individual seller who has owned a vehicle for a sustained period of time, know much more about the car than does any potential buyer. Specifically, if the car is bad, the

FIGURE 10–3

*How Marginal
Benefit Changes
When Prices are
More Variable
Across Sellers*

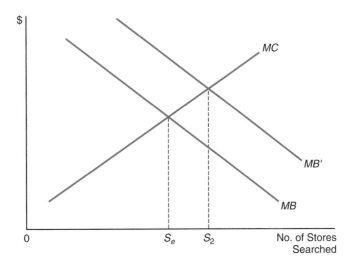

The marginal benefit of search activity increases when there is more variation in prices that sellers charge. With the *MB* curve shifted upward to *MB'*, the optimal level of search increases to S_2.

seller will know, but the buyer will not know. It is frequently argued that the result of this asymmetry will be a used car market consisting primarily (perhaps even exclusively) of cars that are bad, or *lemons*. Why? Because buyers will not be able to distinguish a lemon from a good used car and therefore will not want to pay the price that a seller offering a good car is willing to accept. Buyers will offer a price somewhere in between what a good car is worth and what a lemon is worth.

There will be two supply curves for used cars, one for lemons and one for good cars. The offers from buyers will be low relative to what most sellers of good cars are willing to part with them for, so the quantity supplied of good cars will be small. On the other hand, the in-between price offers are more than many sellers of lemons are willing to sell them for, so the quantity supplied of lemons will be great. The market will be dominated by transactions involving lemons.[8] Unless actions are taken to improve the prospects for transactions involving good cars, these changes in the quantities supplied of the two types of cars will be the expected result. In fact, that is why sellers of used cars engage in activities, such as advertising and provision of warranties, to communicate to buyers that they offer cars that are *not* lemons. Strategies like these will be analyzed in a later section.

---

[8] This is essentially the argument that was made in the following classic article: George Akerlof, "The Market for 'Lemons': Quality, Uncertainty, and the Market Mechanism," *Quarterly Journal of Economics* 84, No. 3 (August 1970): 488–500.

Adverse Selection and Guarantees Against Loss

> **Adverse selection** is a self-sorting process that occurs when the information characteristics of a transaction are such that undesirable products, services, or customers are attracted to it.

When a market has characteristics that attract undesirable products or services to it and drive away better ones, economists say that it is one where there is **adverse selection.** In the used car case, adverse selection caused increased offers of lemons and reduced offers of good used cars. The result of adverse selection is that the value of the transaction to persons on one side of the bargain is reduced. In our case, the used car purchasers pay a price above the one that a lemon would be valued at and are negatively impacted, since most of them get lemons. The selection, however, was made by the lemon sellers, who elected to place their cars on the market in advance of the actual transactions because they knew buyers could not tell whether or not the cars were good, and also by the sellers of good cars, who opted out.

To model adverse selection, we can consider the case of home mortgages. Mortgage lenders are faced with two types of borrowers: those with strong credit ratings and those with weak credit ratings. Borrowers with weak credit ratings are willing to pay high interest rates to get a loan, but people with strong credit ratings may have other avenues to finance a home purchase and will use them if mortgage rates are high. The two groups, therefore, will have different demand curves for loans.

In Figure 10-4, panel (a) shows the demand curve of borrowers with strong credit ratings, and panel (b) shows the demand curve of those with weak ratings. Note that if the interest rate is higher than i^*, borrowers with strong credit ratings will not take any mortgage loans. There will still be a positive quantity demanded of loans for the group with weak credit ratings,

FIGURE 10–4

Adverse Selection in the Mortgage Market

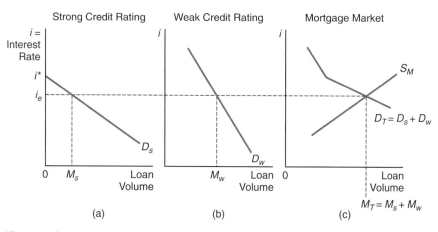

The strong borrowers in panel (a) will not take mortgages when rates are very high, since they can use other financing. Weak borrowers, like those in panel (b), will pay high rates because they do not have alternative financing. Since market demand is the sum of D_S and D_W, given the supply of loans, S_M, the result in panel (c) is a relatively high interest rate (i_e). Thus, there is adverse selection, and most borrowers are weak.

however. In panel (c), the demand curves of the two groups are summed horizontally to obtain the market demand curve for mortgage loans. With supply curve S_M, the market rate of interest is i_e, and most borrowing is done by people with weak credit ratings. Thus, there is adverse selection in this market as many very qualified borrowers use other means of financing.

The mortgage lending industry has taken steps to offset the impact of adverse selection on lenders. First-time borrowers who seek conventional mortgages and cannot make a down payment of at least 20 percent of the purchase price of their chosen home are required to buy private mortgage insurance (PMI). This insurance protects the lender when the borrower fails to make the agreed-upon payments on the loan. In the context of Figure 10-4, it lowers the cost of making loans (lower costs of default), thereby shifting the S_M curve to the right. This reduces the interest rate on home mortgages so that more borrowers with strong credit ratings take loans.

Adverse selection occurs in many markets other than those for used cars and home mortgages. The problem frequently occurs in the insurance industry. For example, consider residential fire insurance. If companies selling it base their rates on the average occurrence of fires in a large random sample of homes, they will encounter adverse selection, since the customers most interested in insurance will be those who believe they are most likely to need it. People with fire-resistant homes that have few dangerous appliances or homes that are near fire stations may choose to go without the insurance. Worse yet, the high-risk group, once they have bought insurance, may engage in riskier behaviors, since they are now "covered" for their losses if a fire does occur.

MORAL HAZARD

Moral hazard is an incentive for a party to a transaction to engage in risky or undesirable behavior (to the detriment of another party) because the transaction protects the first party against loss.

When, as a result of a transaction or agreement, a party may be encouraged to engage in risky or undesirable behavior to the detriment of another party to the agreement, a **moral hazard** occurs. With fire insurance, the moral hazard is that buyers will choose to take fire risks (pile wood beside their homes or store flammable liquids improperly) that they otherwise would not take. Moral hazard is a common problem in transactions or agreements where a participant has in one way or another secured a guarantee against loss.[9]

---

[9] The savings and loan (S&L) crisis of the 1980s in the United States is often cited as a case where a guarantee (the guarantee of accounts by the Federal Savings and Loan Insurance Corporation) led to moral hazard and subsequent risky behavior. S&L managers made many risky loans, and they knew the federal agency would bail them out or at least prevent depositor losses. Likewise, the Asian financial crisis of the 1990s has been related to risky behavior by central bankers in that region who believed the International Monetary Fund would come to the rescue in the event of a currency or banking crisis.

Moral Hazard and Business Decision Making

In Chapter 1, the *principal-agent problem* was defined as an issue that arises when one party, an agent, is entrusted to act on behalf of another (the principal) whose goals may differ from those of the first. Moral hazard can be quite important in principal-agent relationships such as those established by business contracts. For example, suppose a manufacturer signs a contract with a multi-line distributor who, in turn, markets the manufacturer's product to retailers. Although the contract may call for vigorous promotion of the product by the distributor's sales force, the manufacturer may not be able to observe how much effort the distributor's representatives are putting into selling the product. The moral hazard is that the distributor may not provide the necessary conditions or environment to obtain the result desired by the manufacturer. Indeed, the relationship between the distributor and his or her own sales representatives may also be characterized by moral hazard if the distributor cannot tell how much effort the representatives are putting forth.

Another area characterized by moral hazard is that of employee benefit programs. Suppose, for example, that a firm bargains with employees to institute a program allowing them a certain number of sick days per year. There is moral hazard because employees have an incentive to call in sick when they really are not sick. Worse yet, if the program operates on a calendar-year basis, employees who have been well all year may decide to get sick in December and use up the days they "have coming to them." This could occur at a very busy time when the impact of absenteeism is especially costly to the firm.

Managing Problems Relating to Information and Moral Hazard

We have already seen how the mortgage lending industry developed a way to deal with adverse selection. The immediately preceding example can give some insight as to the kinds of steps other parties who stand to lose because of problems related to information or moral hazard can take to address them. In the case of sick leave, an incentive *not* to use the days can be employed. One such incentive is to allow accrual of sick leave days, so that an employee can take off for a longer period of time in case of a serious health problem. Another would be a provision to compensate employees for sick leave not used when they retire or leave the firm.[10]

---

[10] Note, however, that this creates new moral hazards, since sick employees may come to work when they should not while perennially well employees may be tempted to seek a new job or retire earlier than the firm would like them to. The trick, of course, is to make the payment small enough not to entice employees to leave the firm but large enough to keep them from always using the annually awarded days.

Private information is relevant information known by the party on one side of a transaction that is not observable by the party on the other side.

Asymmetry and moral hazard often occur when one party has **private information,** that is, information relevant to the contract but not observable by the other party to it. In this case, a requirement that makes the private information available to both parties can deal with the problem. In the example of sick leave, the employee has private information because he or she knows whether or not sickness actually took place.[11] The firm, however, as part of the sick-leave agreement, may require that an employee who claims sick days bring in a form from a physician to corroborate that he or she was really ill. In the case of the manufacturer-distributor problem discussed earlier, the manufacturer may engage in monitoring the activities of the distributor by employing personnel who survey retailers to ascertain what kind of job the distributor's representatives are doing. Other steps can be taken contractually to make private information observable to both parties to the agreement. This might involve a reporting system that would track and verify the activities of sales representatives. Each of these solutions involves **monitoring costs,** expenditures to ensure that agreed-upon actions are undertaken. Of course, these become part of the total costs of the contracting firms.[12] Generally, there are alternatives to monitoring, such as **incentive contracting.** The purpose of incentive contracting is to achieve a harmonization of goals of the contracting parties. In our manufacturer-distributor case, sales bonuses might be employed to provide incentives to both the distributor firm and its representatives that would be in line with the manufacturer's desire for product promotion. Choosing between this approach and monitoring would, of course, depend on the costs and benefits of each alternative.

Monitoring costs are the costs associated with making certain the terms of an agreement are complied with.

Incentive contracting is designing agreements with incentives that harmonize the goals of the contracting parties.

Similar problems involving incentives surround the question of managing executive compensation. (How hard a CEO wants to work is private information, though screening by checking references and verifying a CEO applicant's claims can make some of that information available to those who employ the CEO. This, of course, adds to the firm's search costs.) If a CEO is hired for a high fixed salary, that person may have little economic incentive to put forth a great deal of effort for the benefit of the firm's owners. We show this in Figure 10-5, where the firm's total profit is plotted as a function of CEO effort in the upper quadrant. In the lower quadrant, the CEO's salary is an amount measured where the line R_S intersects the vertical axis.

---

[11] Private information can exist both before an agreement *(ex ante)* or after *(ex post).* The employee's knowledge of whether or not sickness actually occurred is *ex post* private information. However, even before a sick-leave program is instituted or agreed upon, an employee would probably know whether he himself, would cheat on it. That knowledge would be *ex ante* private information.

[12] Monitoring of large construction projects is frequently done from the buyer's side. For example, in the late 1990s when the College of Business Building was being constructed at the University of Texas at San Antonio, the University of Texas System had a site administrator who kept tabs on the activities of contractors.

MANAGERIAL PERSPECTIVE

Asymmetric Information and the No-Show Problem

Going to a meeting? Did you reserve a rental car? Did you reserve *three* rental cars? What about hotel rooms? How many? Have you made more than one airline reservation? Everybody in the travel industry is plagued by the problem of "no shows," people who have reservations they don't use but don't cancel either. Now, why would someone reserve three rental cars if they need only one? It could have something to do with information they have that the car rental agencies do not have: such as the possibility that the boss will also choose to come to the meeting. You are unsure about that, so you reserve a small car at a low price. You also reserve a luxury car from another agency because you know the boss would prefer to ride in something like that. In fact, for backup (let's not disappoint the boss) you reserve two luxury cars from two other agencies. Clearly, there is a problem of asymmetric information here: you know more about what you will do than any of the renters know. There is also moral haz-

ard since you, who may have nothing to lose, could impose costs on the rental agencies if you do not show up or do not take the time to cancel two of the three reservations.

The no-show problem, of course, is not limited to the car rental business, and it is not without remedies. Airlines and hotels, for the most part, have instituted no-show fees and will penalize you significantly for not showing up. The airlines, for their lower-priced fares, also will charge for changing your reservation, that is, if they are willing to change it *at all*. The rental car companies have tended to cut consumers more slack on this issue, with some charging no-show penalties only on reservations for specialty cars and vans. However, they have begun to vary their no-show policies by location, peak periods, and time of year.

Reference: "No-Shows Can Lead to Car Rental Penalties," BuyerZone.com, online, December 14, 1998, www.buyerzone.com/features/savvy_shopper/savvycarrental.html, September 16, 2002.

In Figure 10-5, the minimum effort the CEO can expend and expect to retain her job is F_1. However, she has no incentive to increase her effort beyond F_1 because her return from additional effort is zero. We can call the line R_S the CEO's *compensation curve*, which will be horizontal if she receives only a fixed salary. The firm is best off if the CEO puts forth an effort of F_2, since that corresponds with the maximum of the profit curve in the upper quadrant. The problem is how to get to F_2.

Rewarding the CEO with profit sharing based on the firm's total profit can alter her compensation curve to R_T so that the CEO's maximum return occurs at the same level of effort as the firm's maximum profit. In the figure, R_T would occur if the CEO were offered a fixed percentage of all profits in excess of $10 million. With R_T as the CEO's new compensation curve, it would appear that the profit-sharing approach to compensation harmonizes the objectives of the CEO and the firm's owners. This will be the case if the

FIGURE 10–5

Harmonizing CEO Effort with Firm Profit Maximization

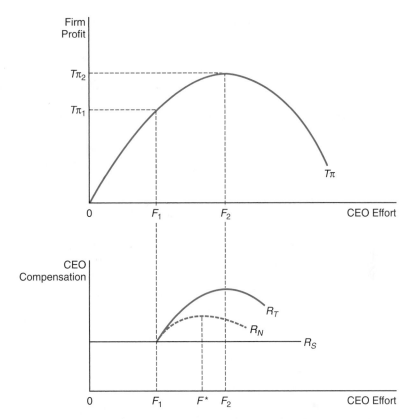

R_S is the compensation curve if the CEO is payed a fixed salary. The CEO chooses to supply only F_1 of effort based on her subjective evaluation of its marginal cost. Paying the CEO a salary plus a fixed percentage of profit above $T\pi_1$ changes the compensation curve to R_T beyond F_1, and effort is increased to F_2. If the CEO has increasing marginal opportunity cost of effort, the compensation curve could become R_N, and only F^* of effort would result.

marginal opportunity cost of effort (time given up that could be allocated to golf, family, or even more golf) is a constant.

The marginal opportunity cost of CEO effort is not likely to be constant. The more the CEO works, the greater her opportunity cost of foregone golfing and other "quality time" and the more she will value incremental amounts of sacrifice. From the decreasing slope of the R_T curve, which reflects the decreasing slope of the $T\pi$ curve, it is evident that the marginal benefit of effort to the CEO falls as more effort is expended. Furthermore, we can expect that the *net marginal benefit* (marginal benefit *minus* marginal cost) falls as the CEO devotes more time to work and less to other activities. This changes the compensation curve to R_N in Figure 10-5. (We assume that the CEO can place a dollar value on opportunity cost of effort.) The CEO will then choose to deliver F^*. When this occurs, the level of effort that maximizes the CEO's compensation is less than the one that maximizes the total profit of the firm.

The problem posed by the increasing marginal opportunity cost of CEO effort is not intractable, but it does underscore the importance of careful contract design. One way to return the CEO's optimal level of effort to F_2 is to increase the percentage of profit sharing as the profit level rises. This can offset the rising marginal opportunity cost of CEO effort, making the marginal net benefit of effort positive beyond level F^*. Indeed, offering greater marginal incentives for increased output and profit is a common approach to the problem of harmonizing shareholder and managerial objectives. (See the accompanying Numerical Example for another demonstration of this approach.)

Turning from Figure 10-5 to the real world, we should note several complications. First, the compensation plan will only harmonize the objectives of owners and the CEO if the profit sharing offsets the marginal opportunity cost of CEO effort at the level of effort that is best for owners. The owners are not likely to know what a manager's marginal opportunity cost of effort is, and, indeed, the manager herself might not know with precision. (The manager's willingness to accept a given compensation package is an indication that she expects it to be sufficient, however. See the following section, signaling). In addition, we should realize that while profit sharing can be an important tool for stimulating the desired amount of effort, it does not eliminate moral hazard. For example, managers might engage in practices that inflate the short-run profits of the firm to enhance their rewards and then move on, leaving the firm in disarray. In 2001–2002, the problems of bankrupt Enron Corporation seemed to be a case in point. Many alleged improprieties, ranging from questionable accounting practices to stock manipulation, were being investigated. The short-run vs. long-run problem can be mitigated by making the payoff for managers a long-run item. For this reason many firms that make stock options available to their managers set them up to be exercisable at some distant time in the future rather than at near term.

SIGNALING

Signaling is taking an action or set of actions that conveys otherwise unobservable information from one party in a transaction to the party on the other side of it.

We noted earlier that a CEO's willingness to consider or accept a particular compensation package might provide a sign regarding how hard he or she is willing to work. An important way to deal with private information problems is **signaling.** Signaling involves taking steps that communicate otherwise unobservable information from one party to another. (To a child, a sleeping lion may look like a huge, cute kitty, but if the lion gets up and *roars*, the child will get the message.) So, in our CEO case, the person's attitude toward a compensation proposal sends a signal to owners. For other types of employees, another case of signaling is the choice to "dress for success."

NUMERICAL EXAMPLE

CEO Compensation

A firm pays its hard-working CEO (average 50 hours per week) a fixed salary of $450,000 per year and has total annual profit of $10,000,000. Suppose the relations between CEO effort, the CEO's subjective valuation (in dollars) of the marginal opportunity cost of working more hours per week, and the firm's total profit are as follows.

CEO's Valuation of Marginal Opportunity Cost of Effort	CEO's Avg. Hours Worked per Week	Firm's Total Profit
$35,000	50	$10,000,000
45,000	51	11,000,000
70,000	52	13,000,000
100,000	53	16,000,000
140,000	54	18,000,000
	55	17,500,000

Answer the following:

1. A compensation consultant argues that if the firm offers the CEO 4 percent of additional profit over $10,000,000, the CEO will not work sufficient hours per week to maximize the firm's total profit. Is this assessment correct?

2. If you disagree with the above assessment, explain why. If you agree, discuss the marginal change in profit sharing that would provide an appropriate incentive for the CEO to increase effort to the profit-maximizing level.

Solution

1. To analyze the impact of the 4 percent incentive, it is necessary to consider the marginal benefit to the CEO as work effort is increased and compare it with the CEO's subjective valuation of the marginal opportunity cost of effort (additional hours worked per week):

CEO's Valuation of Marginal Opportunity Cost of Effort	CEO's Avg. Hours Worked per Week	Firm's Total Profit	Marginal Benefit to CEO
$35,000	50	$10,000,000	$40,000
45,000	51	11,000,000	80,000
70,000	52	13,000,000	120,000
100,000	53	16,000,000	80,000
140,000	54	18,000,000	<60,000>
	55	17,500,000	

(continues)

NUMERICAL EXAMPLE *(continued)*

Above, the marginal benefit to the CEO of additional work is 4 percent of the change in the profit column for each increment in hours worked per week. The marginal benefit exceeds the marginal cost only up to a profit level of $16,000,000, where the CEO works 53 hours per week. If the CEO works 54 hours per week instead of 53, marginal net benefit (marginal benefit – marginal cost) is $80,000 – $100,000 or –$20,000. Thus, the compensation consultant is correct.

2. The question here is how the compensation plan could be changed to both preserve the 4 percent incentive on the increases in profit up to $16,000,000 and get the CEO to supply the additional effort needed to get the profit level up to the maximum at $18,000,000. This could be done by offering a larger percentage of profit sharing after total profit reaches $16,000,000. That percentage would have to more than cover the CEO's marginal opportunity cost of $100,000. The CEO would just break even (marginal net benefit = 0), if 100,000/2,000,000 = 0.05, or 5 percent of the additional $2,000,000 profit obtainable is offered as an incentive. We can conclude that in order to make the CEO more than indifferent toward the increased effort, the step-up in the profit-sharing rate would have to exceed 1 percent, that is, to be greater than 5 percent on additional profit above $16,000,000.

Dressing appropriately for a job interview conveys to prospective employers that you are serious about working for them. One of your authors observed this some 30 years ago when interviewing a department store manager in connection with U.S. Department of Labor research on youth employment. The store manager said of a young man who was being considered for a job, "He came in to be interviewed dressed in a T shirt and dirty jeans. He seemed to be a very nice young man, but I can't put someone with judgment like that on my sales floor."

Another good example of signaling relates to the lemons case discussed earlier. In 1998–1999, two giant firms entered the used car business in the United States. Their names are easily recognizable, Auto Nation and Car Max. Their strategy was to sell used cars at relatively high prices and to signal to consumers that all of their used cars were good. The signaling involved a lot of advertising, as well as extended warranties on the cars. Auto Nation was not successful in many locations and closed 23 of its used car megastores abruptly in December 1999. It announced it would focus on the new car business, where it had become the nation's largest car retailer through acquisition of numerous local franchises.[13]

---

[13] "Auto Nation to Close Used Vehicle Megastores: Company to Take $430–$490 Million Pre-Tax Charge in Fourth Quarter," *Company News on Call,* December 13, 1999, (www.prnewswire.com)

SUMMARY

This chapter briefly considered how the game theoretic approach to economic strategy can be applied to business decisions. We began with the single-period, simultaneous-move game, known for short as a *one-shot game*. Several two-player games that employ a simple payoff matrix (normal form games) were analyzed. We noted that each player in a game takes into account both her own possible strategies and her rival's behavior. An important issue affecting the outcome of a game is whether a player has a *dominant strategy*, that is, a strategy that is the player's best choice no matter what choice a rival player makes. Strategies that yield inferior results no matter what a rival does are identified as *dominated strategies*. If a rival has a dominated strategy, one can be sure that he or she will not choose it. In our examples of one-shot games, we found that a *Nash equilibrium* exists when both players are doing the best they can, given the other's strategy. Many games do yield Nash equilibria, and a game can have a Nash equilibrium even if one player does not have a dominant strategy.

Some games may have multiple equilibria. That is, if played as a one-shot, simultaneous-move game, more than one outcome is possible, and we cannot say which will occur. However, when play is not simultaneous, some games yield a predictable solution and are characterized by *first-mover advantage*, which, as its name implies, provides a superior result to the player who makes the first strategic choice. Other types of games analyzed in the chapter include cooperative games (the VHS and personal computer bus examples), repeated games (pharmaceutical firms), and sequential games (GM and Ford SUVs). For the sequential game example, a *game tree* was employed, and *backwards induction* was used to find the outcome.

The latter part of this chapter focused on the economics of information. Beginning with an analysis of *searching and search costs,* the chapter proceeded to examine *optimal search, asymmetric information,* and *adverse selection*. We found that increased search activity makes sense when the marginal benefit from searching exceeds its marginal cost. Marginal benefit was found to be greater in markets characterized by wide price dispersion. The lemons problem in the automobile market was used to illustrate both the problem of asymmetric information (seller knows car is lemon but buyer does not) and adverse selection (low price in used car market means only lemons will be sold). Adverse selection in mortgage lending was also examined.

The final sections of the chapter dealt with *moral hazard, incentive contracts,* and *signaling.* The example of executive performance under a high fixed salary was employed to explain both moral hazard (executive might not work hard once high salary is agreed upon), and incentive contracting (profit-sharing plan provides incentive to increase executive's effort). Finally, signaling was analyzed as a means to divulge otherwise private information known by only one party to a transaction. The used car market is a case in point, where the offer of extended warranties can signal to the buyer a seller's belief that a car is not a lemon.

This chapter only scratched the surface regarding the nature of problems related to either game theory or the economics of information. The literature on these subjects is rich and growing rapidly. (A search of the ABI/INFORM database reveals over 200 articles in 2000–2001 alone.) See the Selected References for additional discussions and analyses.

QUESTIONS

1. In game theory, what is the definition of a *strategy?*
2. What is a one-shot game? What other kinds of games can you identify?
3. How can you tell if a participant in a game has a dominant strategy?
4. What is the meaning of an iterative dominance strategy?
5. In what kind of game is it appropriate to employ a tree diagram?
6. Can you give an example of a game where a player might be able to make known a credible threat to a rival?
7. What is the game theory term used to describe a situation where the player who moves earliest clearly benefits by doing so?
8. Define the following terms related to the economics of information:

   a. search costs

   b. asymmetric information

   c. adverse selection

   d. moral hazard

   e. private information

   f. monitoring costs

   g. signaling
9. It has been argued that firms that hire only employees with a college degree often do not care what a person studied in his or her college program. All that matters to them is that the person actually obtained the degree. Discuss this argument, relating your analysis to the economics of information.
10. Why is health insurance offered through employers and not through bowling leagues? Relate your answer to rational behavior and the economics of information.

PROBLEMS

1. Two wireless telephone service providers, JT&T and ACI, are entering a new market area. Each is considering two alternative strategies regarding long-distance calls. One is to offer them free with monthly service, and the other is to offer

them at reduced rates in comparison with prevailing long-distance rates for standard wire (as opposed to wireless) service. Both firms will enter at the same time, and cooperative strategies are not possible. Below are the profit payoffs, in thousands of dollars per quarter, from providing service in the new area. (Data pertaining to JT&T in color.)

	ACI			
	Free L.D.		*Reduced Rate L.D.*	
Free L.D.	400	80	450	60
JT&T				
Reduced Rate L.D.	300	100	310	90

   a. Does either firm have a dominant strategy?

   b. Determine the outcome of the game, and explain *why* it will occur.

2. Under licenses for an exclusive technology, two firms, Delta and Gamma, are introducing a new notebook computer into the market. It will sell for about one-half the price of existing comparable notebooks. Since the technology is new, both companies will have to decide whether to offer a standard warranty of one year or an extended warranty on the product. (In the industry, an extended warranty tends to be three years.) The market share percentages of the two firms for the new product will vary according to the following payoff matrix (data pertaining to Delta in color).

	GAMMA			
	Standard Warranty		*Extended Warranty*	
Standard Warranty	50	50	30	70
DELTA				
Extended Warranty	70	30	50	50

(Note that this game has the special characteristic that one firm's gains are the other's losses—the shares always add to 100 percent. This is called a *zero-sum game* since the sum of the changes in payoffs from one cell to the next is zero.)

   a. If this is a one-shot game, what is its solution? Explain.

   b. Given the payoffs, can the players obtain a net gain from cooperation? Explain.

3. Examine the following game tree for a market-entry game, and answer the questions that appear below it.

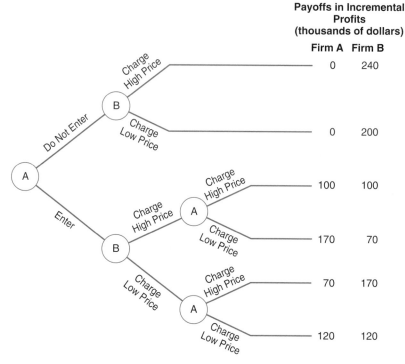

Payoffs in Incremental
Profits
(thousands of dollars)

	Firm A	Firm B
	0	240
	0	200
	100	100
	170	70
	70	170
	120	120

a. What is the optimal strategy for B? Explain.

b. What is the optimal strategy for A? Explain.

4. Two rival producers of jet planes, Embrager and Candu-Air, are considering the production of new model, small-size airliners for the regional jet market. They project their profits in delivery year 2006 from sales of the aircraft to be the figures in the following matrix (million dollars).

		EMBRAGER		
		70-Seat Plane	*50-Seat Plane*	
CANDU-AIR	70-Seat Plane	240 330	320 400	
	50-Seat Plane	260 310	220 340	

What strategy will each producer choose? Explain.

5. Two fast-food chains, McDougall's and Ashley's, are considering menu diversification to attract additional customers. From studying the strategies of other, larger firms, they have both decided that the main issue is whether or not to offer Italian food items on their menus. The payoffs, in terms of annual profit for each firm (million dollars), are shown below:

	ASHLEY'S			
	Offer Italian Items		*Do Not Offer Italian Items*	
Offer Italian Items	26	15	22	12
McDOUGALL'S				
Do Not Offer Italian Items	22	13	24	12

Determine whether there is a Nash equilibrium in this game, and discuss the game's solution.

6. You have written a book of golf jokes and have been lucky enough to find a New York publisher to produce it. They offer you a standard royalty contract of 19 percent of sales revenue. Assuming that there is a downward-sloping demand curve for the book and that the marginal cost of producing it is a constant, will the publisher want to sell the amount of books that maximizes your royalty? Explain.

7. A company that sells shoes in leased space in department stores wishes to boost its sales volume by providing a bonus to salespeople based on the number of pairs of shoes they sell per week. An employee will be subject to the following bonus schedule:

Pairs of Shoes Sold During Week	*Total Bonus for the Week (dollars)*
10	0
20	40
30	60
40	80
50	100
60	120

Suppose an employee places the following monetary values on the marginal effort required to sell an additional pair of shoes:

Pairs of Shoes Sold During Week	*Marginal Value of Effort per Pair (dollars)*
10	
20	1.00
30	1.50
40	2.25
50	4.50
60	6.90

How many shoes will the employee be willing to sell, and what will be her bonus payment for the week?

SELECTED REFERENCES

Akerlof, George. "The Market for Lemons: Quality, Uncertainty, and the Market Mechanism." *Quarterly Journal of Economics* 84, No. 3 (August 1970): 488–500.

Alm, James, and Leslie A. Whittington. "For Love or Money: The Impact of Income Taxes on Marriage." *Economica* 66, No. 263 (August 1999): 297–316.

Anders, George. "He Who Moves First Finishes Last." *FASTCOMPANY* (Consultant Debunking Unit), online, September 2000, www.fastcompany.com/online/38.cdu.html, September 16, 2002.

Bamberger, Peter A., and Linda H. Donohue. "Employee Discharge and Reinstatement: Moral Hazards and the Mixed Consequences of Last-Chance Agreements." *Industrial and Labor Relations Review* 53, No. 1 (October 1999): 3–20.

Bierman, H. Scott, and Luis Fernandez. *Game Theory with Economic Applications.* Reading, MA: Addison-Wesley, 1993.

Gardner, Roy. *Games for Business and Economics.* New York: John Wiley & Sons, 1995.

Hillier, Brian. *The Economics of Asymmetric Information.* New York: St. Martin's Press, 1997.

Katz, Michael L., and Harvey S. Rosen. *Microeconomics.* Boston: Irwin/McGraw-Hill, 1998, Chapter 16.

Landsburg, Stephen E. *Price Theory and Applications.* Cincinnati: South-Western College Publishing, 1999.

Milgrom, Paul, and John Roberts. *Economics, Organization, and Management.* Englewood Cliffs, NJ: Prentice Hall, 1992.

Mirlees, J. A. "The Theory of Moral Hazard and Unobservable Behavior." *The Review of Economic Studies* 66, No. 226 (January 1999): 3–21.

Perloff, Jeffrey M. *Microeconomics,* 2d ed. Boston: Addison-Wesley Longman, 2001), Chapter 20.

Rosenthal, Robert W. "Rules of Thumb in Games." *Journal of Economic Behavior and Organization* 22, No. 1 (September 1993): 1–13.

Salanie, Bernard. *The Economics of Contracts: A Primer.* Cambridge, MA: MIT Press, 1997.

Spence, A. Michael. "Job Market Signalling." *Quarterly Journal of Economics* 87, No. 3 (August 1973): 355–374.

Stiglitz, Joseph E. "Equilibrium in Product Markets with Imperfect Information." *Amerian Economic Review* 69, No. 2 (May 1979): 339–345.

CHAPTER ELEVEN

Topics in Pricing and Profit Analysis

In preceding chapters, our analysis of the firm and its markets has included only situations in which the firm produces and sells a single product in one market and charges a uniform price on all units sold. We have always assumed that the objective of the firm's managers is to maximize net or economic profit in both the short run and the long run. The main objective of the present chapter is to expand our analysis to take into account situations in which the firm produces more than one product, uses special pricing approaches to enhance both revenue and profit from sales of a single product, sells a single product in more than one market, or considers the level of profit to be only a secondary goal. First, however, we will look at the practice of marking up merchandise by specific proportions (percentages) to show how this simple approach to pricing is related to the economics of profit maximization.

MARKUP PRICING

Markup pricing is a pricing technique whereby a certain percentage of cost of goods sold or of price is added to the cost of goods sold in order to obtain the market price. In many industries or lines of merchandise, the experienced manager will be familiar with rules of thumb concerning the typical markup on goods sold. However, the term *markup* means different things to different people. What some would call a 50 percent markup others would define as a 100 percent markup. For example, suppose an item costs $50 to produce and is sold for $100. In some industries, this would be known as a 50 percent markup, whereas in others it would be considered a markup of 100 percent. The difference, of course, is that in the first instance the margin is a *markup on price* (the proportion of the *selling price* that represents an amount added to the cost of goods sold), whereas in the second case the markup is a *markup on cost* (the proportion of *cost of goods sold* that is added on to that figure to arrive at the selling price). In the material that follows, we will use the *markup-on-cost* approach. To avoid confusion, we recommend that when analyzing any particular industry, one begins by determining the conventional use of the term *markup* in that industry.[1]

Markup pricing has long been a traditional way of doing business for large U.S. manufacturing companies. Firms tried to set price at a level that would allow them to achieve a certain long-run target rate of return at a particular volume of production. Price cutting in periods of short-term declines in demand was not looked on with much favor. (However, especially with the availability of computer technology, which allows a firm to do market research and to maintain sophisticated cost controls more easily, target pricing is currently not being used as rigidly as it has been in the past.)

When a manager decides on a given markup for a product, the manager anticipates some specific result over the planning period in terms of quantity sold and sales revenue. To the extent that such a decision maximizes profit, the manager will have correctly estimated the elasticity of demand for the product. Alternatively, a correct estimation of the elasticity of demand for the product will allow management to determine the appropriate markup.[2]

We can demonstrate this point by examining the general relationship between marginal revenue and price elasticity of demand. We know from Chapter 2 that

$$MR = P\left(1 + \frac{1}{E_P}\right),$$

and from Chapter 7 that

$$MR = MC$$

---

[1] In the garment industry, for example, the term *keystoning* is used to mean pricing an item at twice its wholesale cost. However, in the trade, this practice is also called a "markup of 50 percent."

[2] A recent study suggests that in the presence of uncertainty, simple markup rules may perform better than rational decisions based on risky information. See Markus Pasche, "Markup Pricing and Demand Uncertainty," *Working Paper Series B,* Friedrich Schiller University Jena, Department of Economics, revised June 1, 1998.

where profit is maximized.[3] If incremental costs of production are relatively constant and average variable selling and administrative costs are immaterial, *MC* is approximately equal to *AVC*. (If the firm is a manufacturing firm, fixed manufacturing overhead per unit must also be immaterial.) Thus, at the profit-maximizing output and price,

$$P\left(1+\frac{1}{E_P}\right) = MC = AVC,$$

and

$$P = \frac{AVC}{1+\dfrac{1}{E_P}}.$$

We can simplify the right-hand side of this equation by first writing the denominator as one fraction and then inverting and multiplying as follows:

$$P = \frac{AVC}{1+\dfrac{1}{E_P}} = \frac{AVC}{\dfrac{E_P+1}{E_P}} = AVC\left(\frac{E_P}{E_P+1}\right).$$

By addition and subtraction of 1 in the numerator, we can break this last term into two terms in the following manner:

$$P = AVC\left(\frac{E_P}{E_P+1}\right) = AVC\left(\frac{E_P+1-1}{E_P+1}\right)$$

$$= AVC + AVC\left(\frac{-1}{E_P+1}\right)$$

$$= AVC + mAVC,$$

where *m* is the proportion of markup on *cost*. Of course,

$$m = \frac{-1}{E_P+1},$$

so the estimation of a profit-maximizing output and price is tantamount to estimating the elasticity of demand, E_p. Note that as long as E_p (which is nearly always negative) has an absolute value larger than 1, *m* will be *positive*. (As we showed in Chapter 2, $|E_p|$ will be greater than 1 whenever *MR* is

---

[3] See Chapter 2, footnote 28. See also Chapter 7, section on profit maximization.

positive.) Moreover, if one knows P^*, Q^*, and E_p at point Q^*, a linear equation approximating the demand curve around that point can be found.[4]

One of the most important messages to glean from the analysis of markup pricing is that the profit-maximizing markup is lower the *higher* the absolute value of the own price elasticity of demand for the good or service. Although one can easily intuit that from the fact that E_p appears in the denominator of the markup expression, some data will provide a bit more insight:

Value of Elasticity Coefficient	$100 \times -1/(E_p + 1) =$ Optimal Percent Markup on Cost
−2	100
−3	50
−4	33.3
−5	25
−9	12.5

Markups can also be expressed as a percentage of price rather than cost. That makes them seem smaller. For example, if AVC = $5 and the firm marks the product up to $10, the markup as a percent of cost is 100 percent, but as a percent of price, it is just 50 percent ($5 of the $10 price is the markup, therefore 50 percent of price). The formula relating markup on *price* to elasticity is $-1/E_p$.

Naturally, in a small business, management might not recognize the technical side of what is taking place when it determines the appropriate markup. However, the foregoing analysis makes it clear that the manager who correctly chooses the profit-maximizing markup, given the unit variable costs, either has a good feel for demand conditions in the market or has made a lucky guess.[5]

DECISIONS INVOLVING MULTIPLE PRODUCTS

Given both the large number of technologically related products sharing today's consumer markets and the trends toward merger and acquisition in the modern business world, multiproduct firms presently outnumber single-

---

[4] For example, if $P^* = 2$, $Q^* = 10$, and $E_p = (dQ/dP) \cdot P^*/Q^* = -2.0$, then $-2.0 = (2/10) \cdot dQ/dP$, or $dQ/dP = -10$. Since dQ/dP is the slope *(b)* of the linear demand curve, $Q_d = a + bP$, we know that $Q_d = a - 10P$ is the equation for a linear demand curve, given the above information. We can find the intercept term a by substituting $Q^* = 10$ and $P^* = 2$ in that equation, so $10 = a - 10(2)$, or $a = 30$. Thus, $Q_d = 30 - 10P$ is a linear approximation of the demand function at the point $Q^* = 10$, $P^* = 2$.

[5] Practical discussions of markup pricing can be found at two websites: Business Owner's Toolkit, http://toolkit.netscape.com and Canada Business Service Centers, www.infoentre-preneurs.org.

product firms in the United States and other industrialized countries. A major task of management in a multiproduct enterprise is to analyze carefully the profitability of the various final and intermediate products that compete internally for a share of the firm's resources. For example, in the mid-1980s one of America's corporate giants, General Electric Company, was reshuffling its product mix in an effort to improve its future profitability. Specifically, it had left the small-appliance field and sold off its subsidiaries that produced minerals and oil, choosing to enter markets in microcircuits, computer graphics, and radio and television broadcasting. In addition, it had moved to increase its market share in major home appliances. By 1993, GE manufactured and sold a wide variety of products ranging from jet engines to medical systems to commercial lending operations all over the world, including Europe, Japan, Mexico, India, and China. In India alone, it has factories making medical-imaging equipment, kitchen appliances, plastics, and lamps.[6]

The Gillette Company provides another good example of a firm that faces many decisions involving multiple products. Gillette's U.S. production includes razors, blades, and many other consumer items; its European subsidiary, Braun, makes more than 400 products, most of which are in the electrical appliance line. When Gillette acquired Braun, Braun's output consisted of more than 600 products; but in order to improve its profit picture, Gillette's management dictated that about one-third of the products be eliminated. Gillette also has an outstanding record in acquisitions (Duracell, Oral B) and new product development (the Mach 3 razor, 1998).[7]

Like Braun, many of today's multiproduct firms are subsidiaries or divisions of very large companies. Moreover, the affiliation between such productive units often occurs in a setting where one of the entities responsible to a firm's top management must either *supply inputs to an affiliate* or *obtain inputs from* an affiliate. Thus, the multiple-product question has two major dimensions: (1) the determination of the optimal output combination for jointly produced products and (2) the establishment of an appropriate price (known as the *transfer price*) for a product sold by one division of a firm to another division of the (same) firm. We will consider the joint product question first.

The Joint Product Problem

A multiproduct firm that has separate production facilities for each product will maximize its short-run profit by producing each product at the

---

[6] Robert Slater, *Jack Welch and the GE Way* (New York: McGraw-Hill, 1998), and William H. Miller, "General Electric," *Industry Week* 24, No. 19 (October 16, 1995): 30–32.

[7] "Build a Better Mousetrap Is No Claptrap," *Business Week*, February 1, 1999, p. 47; "Would You Spend $1.50 for a Razor Blade?" *Business Week* (April 27, 1998), p. 46; and "The Gillette Advantage," *Industry Week* 24, No. 1 (January 3, 1994): 28.

level of output where $MC = MR$, subject, of course, to the condition that MC is higher than MR at greater levels of output. Over the long run, the firm should move resources out of less profitable product lines into more profitable ones. However, if the products are produced in the same plant and they are joint products or co-products in the sense that one cannot be produced without getting some of the other (in this case one of the products might be called a byproduct), the firm will face a very special kind of problem in determining the profit-maximizing price and output combination for each product. When joint products are produced in fixed proportions, the analysis is relatively simple, but it becomes more complex when proportions can be varied.

In the former case (that is, joint products produced in fixed proportions), each increment of output, Q, consists of a certain amount of each jointly produced product. For example, if there are two products, A and B, one unit of Q might consist of one unit of Product A and one unit of Product B. Marginal revenue would in this case consist of $MR_A + MR_B = MR_J$. Marginal cost would be the increase in total cost as Q increases, and profit would be maximized where $MR_J = MC$, *provided that neither MR_A nor MR_B is negative.* The necessity for this latter qualification can be made clear by considering Figure 11-1.

FIGURE 11–1

Profit-Maximizing Output Rates for Two Joint Products Produced in Fixed Proportions

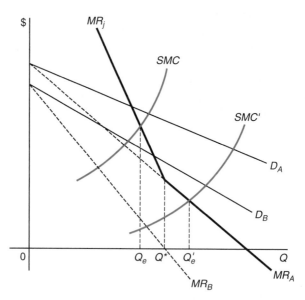

The relevant MR curve is MR_J for quantities less than Q^* and MR_A for quantities greater than Q^*. If the marginal cost curve is SMC, Q_e of both products should be sold. However, if the marginal cost curve is SMC', an amount equal to $(Q'_e - Q^*)$ of Product B should be withheld from sale.

In Figure 11-1, the demand and marginal revenue curves for Products *A* and *B* are shown, and the two *MR* curves are vertically summed (add $MR_A + MR_B$ at each level of output) between the origin and Q^* to obtain MR_J. The firm should never sell more than Q^* of Product *B*, since for larger outputs, MR_B is negative. The relevant marginal revenue curve for the firm is MR_J between the origin and Q^* and MR_A to the right of Q^*. If the firm's marginal cost curve were *SMC*, management's profit-maximizing strategy would be to sell Q_e of each product. On the other hand, it should be clear that if the firm's marginal cost curve is *SMC′*, Q_e' of Product *A* should be sold, but only Q^* of Product *B* should be put on the market. An amount of Product *B* equal to $Q_e' - Q^*$ should be withheld from the market, even though the firm has to produce it. If storage costs are not too great and demand is expected to increase, the excess output may be stored until market conditions for Product *B* are such that it is rational to sell more. Alternatively, if Product *B* is a perishable product or if its cost of storage is high, it may be rational for the firm to destroy the excess output.

One would not have to search very far in the real world to find cases that conform to the situation just described. In Canada, producers of natural gas obtain sulphur as a co-product in the process of scrubbing poisonous gases from the fuel. During the early 1970s, sulphur markets became so weak relative to world supply that the Canadian producers' stockpiles reached 10 million tons, enough to supply all U.S. industry for an entire year. The Canadian firms could not sell their natural gas without obtaining the sulphur, and there was no way to destroy the excess output. Hence, the sulphur just piled up on the ground and became an environmental problem in western Canada.[8] Processors of foodstuffs face similar problems with joint products, although disposal of excess output is usually possible. For example, pineapple packers in many instances obtain more juice than they can feasibly market, and orange juice producers are bound to wind up with a lot more rind than is likely to be marketable as a spice.

In cases where it is possible to vary the proportions in which joint products are produced, management must determine the output combination that maximizes profit. The easiest approach to this problem is to determine the various possible outputs *for each level of total cost* and identify the output that yields maximum total revenue (at least one for every level of cost). The set of profit-maximizing cost-output combinations can be determined, and the highest of these will define the firm's optimal strategy. We can employ a set of *product transformation curves* (production possibilities curves) to describe the cost-output combinations.

---

[8] See testimony of D. B. Truett before the United States Tariff Commission in hearings entitled "Elemental Sulphur from Canada," Antidumping Investigation No. AA1921-127, 1973. Sulfur has become even more abundant, and in 1998 it was reported that some Canadian producers were subsidizing sales at current prices, while others were just letting the material pile up.

NUMERICAL EXAMPLE

Joint Products Produced in Fixed Proportions

Pacific Porchposts produces fine ornamental wood columns in standard eight-foot lengths. For every column it produces, it obtains one pound of wood chips that can be sold as a byproduct. The demand for columns is estimated to be $Q_n = 1,400 - 20P_n$, while that for wood chips is $Q_w = 800 - 1,000P_w$. If its marginal cost of production for the two joint products is constant at $18, will it be able to profitably sell all of the wood chips?

Answer

The company will not be able to sell all of the wood chips. This can be easily determined by noting that for wood chips, $P_w = 0.8 - 0.001Q_w$ and $MR_w = 0.8 - 0.002Q_w$. The latter equals zero when $Q = 400$. However, if $Q = 400$, since $P_n = 70 - 0.05 Q_n$ and $MR_n = 70 - 0.1Q_n$, $MR_n = 70 - 40 = 30$. Since this is greater than MC of $18, the firm will wish to produce beyond the output where $MR_w = 0$. Thus, it will obtain more wood chips than it can profitably sell. (If you carry this example further, you will find that $Q = 520$ is the profit-maximizing production level.)

In Figure 11-2, panel (a), the contour A_1B_1 is a product transformation curve representing the possible output combinations the firm can produce with a given total cost. It is concave toward the origin because resources cannot be perfectly transferred from the production of Product A to the production of Product B. If the market prices of Products A and B are given (for example, if there is perfect competition), isorevenue lines such as TR_1 and TR_2 will show the various combinations of Products A and B that will yield a specific total revenue. With a total cost of $50, the firm could attain a total revenue of $55 by producing at R or S or at a point inside the product transformation curve on segment RS. However, if it produces at D, where the transformation curve is tangent to TR_2, the firm will attain a total revenue of $60 and thus maximize profit for the $50 level of total cost.

In panel (b) of Figure 11-2, we depict transformation curves for the $50, $60, and $100 levels of total cost. The situation is similar to one in which management would have to decide whether to operate a plant on one, two, or three shifts, given that both costs and the possible output combinations increase as we move from (transformation) curve A_1B_1 to curve A_2B_2 to curve A_3B_3. Assuming that the market prices of Products A and B remain given, the profit-maximizing output combinations for the three transformation curves are D, E, and F, respectively. Management would choose combination E as the best of these three, since here $\pi = TR_2 - TC_2 = \$15$, which is the greatest profit attainable. At point D profit is only $10, and at point F it is –$5.

FIGURE 11–2

Product Transformation Curves and Profit-Maximizing Output Combinations for Joint Products Produced in Variable Proportions

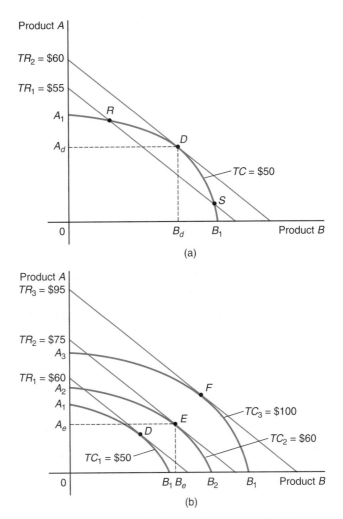

(a)

(b)

In panel (a) profit is maximized at point D, where combination A_d, B_d of the two products is produced and sold. In panel (b) the firm chooses to operate with two shifts at point E, since this strategy provides the highest profit.

The foregoing analysis seems to require that the firm's managers obtain a great deal of information in order to ascertain the exact nature of the transformation and isorevenue curves. However, in any given case, management might be able to perform a perfectly satisfactory analysis by identifying only a few feasible output combinations at each cost level, rather than trying to describe completely the product transformation curve. (Indeed, smooth transformation curves such as those of Figure 11-2 may not even exist for the firm.)

In Figure 11-3 we show a transformation "curve" for a firm in which management believes it is technologically feasible to produce Product *A* exclusively, Product *B* exclusively, or a combination consisting of 25 percent *A* and 75 percent *B*. In this case, the transformation curve consists only of the points *C*, *D*, and *F*, and the combinations represented along the dashed lines connecting these points cannot be produced. If Product *B* is relatively low priced (as expressed by isorevenue line *TR*), the firm will produce only Product *A*, operating at point *C*. If the slope of the isorevenue line is identical to that of line segment *CD*, the firm will attain its maximum total revenue at either *C* or *D*. As the isorevenue line becomes steeper than *CD*, *D* will become the revenue-maximizing output combination. When its slope is equal to that of segment *DF*, both *D* and *F* will yield the same total revenue; if steeper than *DF*, the firm's best output will occur at *F*. Thus, in the setting

---

MANAGERIAL PERSPECTIVE

Eggshells, Gun-cleaning Patches, and Thick Slop

What do eggshells, gun-cleaning patches, and thick slop have in common? All of them are joint products. Egg processing companies can generate revenue not only from providing egg products to the food industry but also from selling two co-products, shells and the membranes that line the shells. With the membranes, the shells are not very valuable, but without them, the shells are ten times as valuable since they can be used as a substitute for wood pulp in paper making. The membranes themselves contain collagen, another important co-product.

Gun-cleaning patches? Well, a Tennessee manufacturer of extra-durable women's panties and undergarments for prisons and mental institutions, where industrial-strength washing machines would ruin ordinary underwear, has found an important co-product in gun patches. The firm, called Southern Bloomer, recognized that about 20 percent of the material it bought ended up as scrap. One of the chief officers got the idea of making gun-cleaning patches from the heavy-duty cutting scraps. The gun patches have become

an important co-product, and the firm now has contracts with the Federal Bureau of Investigation, the military, and many police departments.

Thick slop? Now that's a bit of a blast from the past. It was a co-product of distilleries such as Jack Daniel in Tennessee. Farmers used it to fortify their cattle feed. The cows reportedly just loved the slop-laced feed, and one farmer said they would "stick their snoots in all the way up beyond their eyes." However, the Jack Daniel distillery switched to a process that allowed it to recover saleable grain from the slop. Thus, its co-product mix changed, much to the dismay of the locals—both farmers and cows. (The cows just mooed, but the farmers sued.)

References: "How a Panty Line Turned into Profits in the Gun Business," *Wall Street Journal* April 1, 1999, pp. A1, A8; "Turning a Gooey Mess into Gobs of Cash," *Business Week* (February 1, 1999), p. 67; and "Tennessee Cattlemen Are Suein' Jack Daniel Instead of Sippin' It," *Wall Street Journal,* February 12, 1986, pp. 1, 19.

FIGURE 11–3

*Product
Transformation
Curve When
Only One Joint
Output
Combination
Exists*

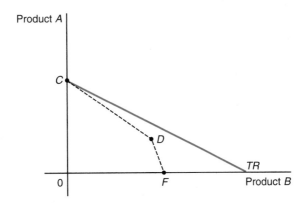

With transformation curve *CDF* and isorevenue curve *TR*, the firm would produce Product *A* only. It would produce both products when the isorevenue curve is less steep than *DF* but steeper than *CD*.

of Figure 11-3, it will be relatively easy for managers to compile a complete description of the alternatives and their profit outcomes, making an output decision based on the maximum profit attainable.

Finally, if we return to the problem of choosing whether to employ one, two, or three shifts with the kind of product transformation limitations illustrated in Figure 11-3, a complete description of the alternatives and their outcomes might be given by a table such as Table 11-1. Here, it would take an analysis of nine possible outcomes to make a decision on the best strategy in production and sale of the joint products. Under current market conditions, management would determine that profit will be maximized when two shifts are used to produce only Product *A*.

Table 11–1 *Revenue, Cost, and Profit Outcomes with
Two Products and Three Shifts*

	Output Combinations		
No. of Shifts	100% Product A	25% Prod. A 75% Prod. B	100% Product B
1	TR = 50 TC = <u>45</u> Tπ = 5	TR = 45 TC = <u>45</u> Tπ = 0	TR = 30 TC = <u>45</u> Tπ = −15
2	TR = 80 TC = <u>65</u> Tπ = 15	TR = 70 TC = <u>65</u> Tπ = 5	TR = 65 TC = <u>65</u> Tπ = 0
3	TR = 95 TC = <u>85</u> Tπ = 10	TR = 92 TC = <u>85</u> Tπ = 7	TR = 80 TC = <u>85</u> Tπ = −5

The Transfer Product Problem

Many large firms are vertically integrated, which means that at least one division of the firm produces a good that is an *input* for the product of another division. When a vertically integrated firm's top management sets out to maximize profit, it must ensure that the divisions of the firm that supply inputs produce such goods in a quantity that is consistent with profit maximization for the entire firm. The appropriate quantity, as we will see, may be less than, equal to, or greater than the needs of the division of the firm to which the inputs are transferred, depending on the state of the external market for the transferred input. To maximize firm profit, the price of the transfer product will be determined internally by the firm's management if there is no external market for the transfer product, and by the market if there is a perfectly competitive external market for the transfer product. In the event that the external market is not perfectly competitive, different internal and external prices will exist for the transfer product.

To simplify our discussion, throughout we will use as an example the case of a firm having just two divisions—a final product division and a transfer product division. Furthermore, we will consider only cases in which one unit of the transfer product is required per unit of final product output.

Where there is no external market for the transfer product, the final product division can be viewed as either a distribution division for the transfer product or a division that combines the transfer product with other inputs to produce a different final good. The marginal cost of the entire firm, MC_e (marginal cost of the enterprise), will be the sum of MC_F (the marginal cost of the final product division excluding the transfer price finally assigned to the transferred product) and MC_T (the marginal cost of the transfer product division), which is shown as follows:

$$MC_e = MC_F + MC_T.$$

The firm generates external revenue solely from the sale of the final good. If D_F is a downward-sloping demand curve for the final good and MR_F is the marginal revenue curve derived from it, the firm will maximize profit where

$$MC_e = MR_F.$$

This is shown in Figure 11-4, panel (a), at E—where Q_e is the profit-maximizing output of both the final product and the transfer product. Since $MC_e = MC_F + MC_T$, we can restate the profit-maximizing condition as follows:

$$MR_F = MC_F + MC_T.$$

Subtracting MC_F from both sides of the equation, we get

$$NMR_F = MR_F - MC_F = MC_T.$$

Net marginal revenue is marginal revenue from the sale of a firm's final product *minus* a specific portion of marginal production cost. In the case of transfer pricing, the portion of marginal production cost that is deducted from MR to obtain final product net marginal revenue (NMR) is the marginal cost of the final division, not including the cost of the transfer product.

Now, for the firm as a whole, the left-hand term above is the **net marginal revenue** (NMR_F) obtained from selling the final product after deduction of all incremental costs except that of the transfer product. The net marginal cost (NMC_F) of the *final product* is MC_T (the difference between the marginal cost of the entire enterprise, MC_e, and MC_F, the marginal cost of the final division):

$$MC_T = MC_e - MC_F = NMC_F.$$

We can restate the profit-maximizing condition as

$$NMR_F = MR_T = MC_T = NMC_F$$

In panel (b) of Figure 11-4, the preceding condition is met at E'. E' must occur directly below E, since NMC_F is MC_e reduced by MC_F and NMR_F is MR_F reduced by the same amount.

Given the preceding profit-maximizing conditions, management must develop a strategy that will ensure the following two results:

1. The transfer product division will supply Q_e of the transfer product.

2. The final product division will demand Q_e of the transfer product.

These results can be accomplished by either of two strategies. First, management might decide to let the final product division fix the price of the transfer product, giving precise information on the marginal cost curve of the division producing the transferred product and instructing the division to set the transfer price of the transfer product equal to the marginal cost of the transfer product at the optimal level of output. The final product division would then know that the price it sets will constitute the MR curve of the transfer product division, since, like a perfectly competitive firm facing a fixed price, the transfer product division will regard its situation as one in which $P = MR$. The transfer product division will profit maximize where $P_T = MR_T = MC_T$, and the final product division will have set the transfer price equal to MC_T at Q_e, the output that maximizes the firm's profit. In terms of Figure 11-4, the price would be P_T, determined by the intersection of NMC_F with NMR_F. Note that $NMC_F = MC_T$, since after accounting for all variable costs of the final product division, the remaining marginal costs will consist of those attributable to the transfer product division.

The second strategy that management might follow to ensure that Q_E of the transfer product is produced and that P_T is established as the transfer price would involve letting the transfer product division set P_T based on the

FIGURE 11–4

Optimal Production of Final and Transfer Product with No External market for the Transfer Product

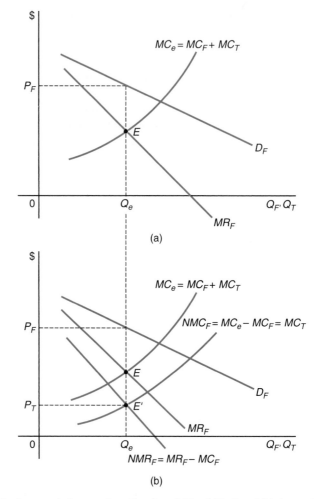

In panel (a) the firm maximizes profit at Q_e, where $MC_e = MR_F$. Panel (b) shows that with no external market for the transfer product, profit maximization is consistent with the condition $NMR_F = MC_T$.

final product division's *demand curve* for Product T. Since NMR_F in Figure 11-4, panel (b), shows the amount of Product T that the final product division would purchase when it equates a given P_T to NMR_F, it is the final product division's demand curve for Product T. With this information available, the transfer product division would be instructed to expand output up to the point at which the price that the final product division is willing to pay is exactly equal to MC_T. Again, this will occur at E' in Figure 11-4, panel (b).

Where there is a perfectly competitive external market for the transfer product, the final product division should not pay the transfer product division a price in excess of that at which the transfer product can be obtained from outside suppliers. Similarly, the transfer product division should not sell to the final product division at a price that is *less* than it can obtain in the external market. All of this leads to the conclusion that the appropriate transfer price will be the prevailing, perfectly competitive, external market price. This being the case, there is no assurance that the transfer product division will produce an amount of Product *T* equal to that demanded by the final product division when profits are maximized for the firm.

Figure 11-5 presents two situations in which there is a perfectly competitive external market for the transfer product and the output of the transfer

FIGURE 11–5

Optimal Production of Final Product and Transfer Product

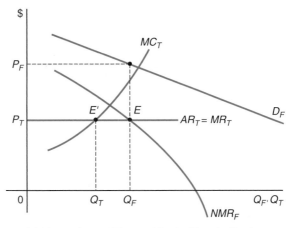

(a) Excess Internal Demand for the Transfer Product

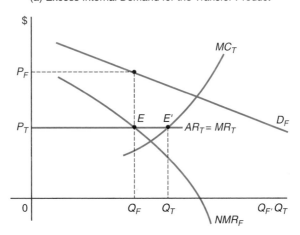

(b) Insufficient Internal Demand for the Transfer Product

In panel (a) the final product division produces Q_F and obtains $(Q_F - Q_T)$ of the transfer product from outside suppliers. In panel (b) the transfer product division sells $(Q_T - Q_F)$ to outside purchasers.

product division is not equal to the quantity demanded by the final product division when firm profits are maximized. In panel (a) the demand curve facing the transfer product division is $AR_T = MR_T$ since the price of the product, P_T, is determined in the perfectly competitive market. At the final product equilibrium quantity, P_T is also equal to NMR_F. NMR_F is obtained by subtracting MC_F from MR_F.

The final product division maximizes profit at Q_F, P_F, since this is consistent with the intersection of NMR_F with AR_T at E. In this case P_T, given by AR_T, represents the appropriate marginal cost of the transfer product to the final division. MC_T no longer gives the appropriate marginal cost of the transfer product to the final division because where $MC_T < P_T$, the firm incurs an opportunity cost if it sells the transfer product to the final product division at a price less than P_T. That is because the transfer product could be sold in the external market for P_T. On the other hand, if $MC_T > P_T$, it would not be economically sound to produce the transfer product and sell it to the final product division at a price greater than P_T, since that division could always purchase the transfer product externally at a price of P_T.

The profit-maximizing condition for the transfer product division is met at E', where $MR_T = P_T = MC_T$. Thus, only Q_T is produced by the transfer product division, and the final product division must purchase $Q_F - Q_T$ of the transfer product in the external market. Since the transfer product division cannot produce units of output beyond Q_T at a marginal cost as low as the external price, P_T, the final product division should not force the transfer product division to supply the additional amount needed to maximize firm profit.

Figure 11-5, panel (b), illustrates a situation in which firm profits are maximized when the transfer product division produces *more* output than the final product division needs when the latter is maximizing profit from the sale of the final good. In this instance, the quantity $Q_T - Q_F$ of the transfer product should be sold in the external market for P_T per unit—the prevailing market price. Such activity clearly adds to the total profit of the firm, since $MC_T < MR_T = P_T$ between Q_F and Q_T.

The transfer pricing problem, which must be confronted by many firms, has numerous dimensions. The foregoing discussion only scratches the surface of the issue. For example, the analysis becomes more complex when the transfer product can be sold in a less than perfectly competitive external market and the external price is not a given. (See Appendix 11A.)

Transfer pricing is an especially important issue in international business. If a transfer product is sold across international boundaries by a multinational corporation, management must take into account the tax consequences of accruing divisional profits in one location rather than another. In this setting, transfer prices may be manipulated to move profits out of divisions located in countries with high taxes or restrictions on capital flows and accumulate them in divisions located in lower tax areas with freer movement of capital. Some

NUMERICAL EXAMPLE

Transfer Pricing

Camgo Company makes inexpensive, fixed-focus 35 mm cameras. Its subsidiary, Focrude, Inc., makes the lenses for the cameras. The market for such lenses is highly competitive, and they can be either bought or sold at the equilibrium market price of $2. Camgo estimates the demand for its cameras to be $Q_c = 12{,}000 - 400P_c$, so that $MR_c = 30 - 0.005Q_c$. The marginal cost of manufacturing the cameras, *not* including the lenses, is constant and equal to $5. The marginal cost of the Focrude division for making the lenses is given by the equation $MC_f = 0.30 + 0.0004Q_f$. Each camera requires one lens. Will Focrude be able to both supply Camgo's required amount of mainsprings and sell profitably in the outside market?

Answer

To find out how many cameras Camgo should sell to maximize profit, set net marginal revenue from camera sales equal to the price of the transfer product:

$$\text{Definition: } NMR_c = MR_c - MC_c = 30 - 0.005Q_c - 5$$

$$= 25 - 0.005Q_c.$$

$NMC_c = 2$, because of the external competitive market. Thus,

$$25 - 0.005Q_c = 2; \text{ and } Q_c = \underline{4{,}600.}$$

The Focrude division will maximize profit where its marginal cost equals the marginal revenue of $2 from sales both inside and external to the firm. So,

$$0.30 + 0.0004Q_f = 2$$
$$0.0004Q_f = 1.70;$$

and

$$Q_f = \underline{4{,}250.}$$

Focrude will be unable to supply Camgo with enough lenses to meet its requirements, and Camgo will buy 350 of them on the external market.

---

very large multinational corporations have established divisional "profit centers" to which profits from certain designated geographical areas are transferred.[9] Needless to say, such practices may have noticeable effects on the economies of countries in which the multinational corporations operate, and

---

[9] For a good discussion of transfer pricing in multinational business, see David K. Eiteman and Arthur I. Stonehill, *Multinational Business Finance*, 5th ed. (Reading, MA: Addison-Wesley, 1989), pp. 555–561.

many nations have taken steps to curb the use of transfer pricing as a mechanism for changing the locus of profits.

PRICE DISCRIMINATION

Price discrimination is the practice of charging different prices for the same product, either by offering buyers lower prices on marginal or incremental quantities purchased or by dividing groups of buyers into separate markets. The latter is also known as **market segmentation.**

Price discrimination involves either (1) charging different prices for additional units of a good purchased by a consumer or (2) separating groups of consumers into market segments and charging different prices to each segment. In economic jargon, the former type of discrimination may be either second or first degree, while the latter is called third degree. Firms use all three types of price discrimination to increase profit.

Second- and First-Degree Discrimination

An easy way to approach price discrimination is to consider a costless monopolist as we did in the Cournot analysis of Chapter 9 and assume that we are looking at the demand curve of just one consumer. In the Cournot analysis, the monopolist simply maximized total revenue (therefore profit, since total cost was assumed to be zero) by setting price at the level where $MR = 0$. In Figure 11-6, with a demand curve $Q_X = 10 - P_X$, this would occur

FIGURE 11–6

Second-Degree Price Discrimination by a Costless Monopolist

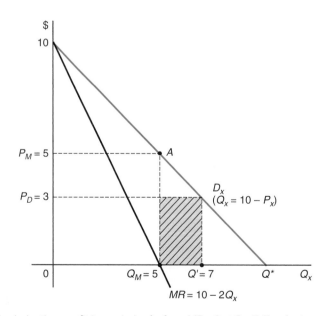

With no discrimination, profit is maximized where $MR = 0$ at $Q = 5$. Employing second-degree discrimination, a discount of $2 is offered on purchases in excess of 5 units. The consumer buys two additional units for $3 each, and profit increases by $6.

at P_M and $0.5Q^*$, or Q_M, would be sold. Could the monopolist increase the total revenue by charging the consumer *more than one price?* The answer is yes. The seller could charge the consumer P_M for the first Q_M units sold and then offer a discount of $(P_M - P_D)$ on as many additional units as the consumer will buy. Our consumer would then choose to buy $(Q' - Q_M) = 2$ additional units at price P_D, which is $3. This increases the monopolist's *TR* to the original amount (area OP_MAQ_M) plus the shaded rectangle. That rectangle adds $3(2) = $6 to the seller's total revenue. The original *TR* was $5(5) = $25, but with the discount for additional units, it rises to $25 + 6 = $31. This is a case of **second-degree price discrimination,** also known as *block pricing.* In our example, the seller employed only two price blocks. However, the more price blocks the seller establishes, the greater will be the *TR*, and the limit on *TR* will be the entire area under the demand curve. That is what is obtained if the seller charges a different price for each unit sold, a situation conforming to **first-degree price discrimination.**

Figure 11-7, with the same demand curve as Figure 11-6, illustrates first-degree price discrimination for sales of four units, where the first unit is sold for $9, the second for $8, the third for $7, and the fourth for $6. *TR* will be the entire area under the demand curve, except for the small unshaded triangles at the top, if $1 less is charged for each additional unit of output to $Q = 10$. If the firm charged a different price for each 1/2 unit (or each 1/4, or 1/8, or

Second-degree price discrimination is the practice of charging successively lower prices for bloc-type increases in quantity purchased.

First-degree price discrimination is a theoretical concept that refers to charging a different amount, specifically the maximum amount a consumer is willing and able to pay, for each unit purchased.

FIGURE 11–7

First-Degree Price Discrimination and Consumer's Surplus for Purchases of Four Units of X

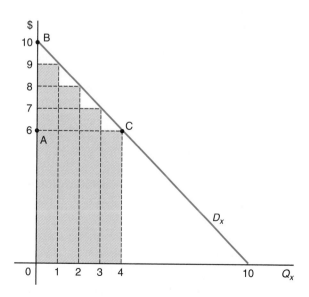

By charging $9 for the first unit, $8 for the second unit, $7 for the third unit, and $6 for the fourth, the seller obtains total revenue equal to the shaded area. By dividing the product into smaller units and increasing the number of prices charged, the unshaded triangles can also be added to total revenue.

1/16 unit), the triangles would be much smaller and the *TR* much closer to the entire area under the demand curve. That complete area is the maximum *TR* the costless monopolist could obtain if first-degree discrimination were employed.

Consumer's Surplus

Consumer's surplus is the difference between the maximum value a consumer places on a given quantity or a good he or she purchases and the money amount that is actually paid to obtain that quantity.

In economic theory, the difference between the maximum value that a consumer places on a given quantity of a good and the amount that he or she actually pays for that quantity is called the **consumer's surplus.** In Figure 11-7, the consumer values the first unit of *X* at $9, the second unit at $8, the third at $7, and the fourth at $6. If the consumer in this figure were to buy four units of *X* at $6 each, he or she would spend $24 for units of *X* valued at $9 + 8 + 7 + 6 = $30 and obtain a consumer's surplus of $6. (Note that this is equivalent to the portion of the shaded area lying within the triangle *ABC*.) Where does this extra $6 go? The answer is that it is simply additional purchasing power that the consumer can spend on other things. Part and parcel of the consumer's decision to buy four units of *X* at a price of $6 each was the consumer's understanding that the purchase yielded a surplus over the maximum he or she was willing to pay, and that the surplus could be spent on other goods and services. As a limit, this surplus approaches the area of triangle *ABC*, which, by geometry is $1/2(10 - 6) (4) = 8, but this would require that *X* be divisible into infinitely small units.[10]

What have we found out? Basically, it is that both second- and first-degree price discrimination increase the seller's total revenue and profit by capturing all or part of the consumer's surplus. First-degree price discrimination is rare, although some observers have suggested that at a market demand level something close to it occurs when automobile salespersons try to get the highest possible price from each consumer who comes in to buy a car. One individual may pay $20,000, another $19,700, and yet another $19,500 for identically equipped vehicles. Second-degree price discrimination is frequently found in water and electricity rates, where a high rate is charged for an initial amount of usage and lower rate blocks apply to additional consumption.[11]

The concept of consumer's surplus will again become important when we examine access fees, also called two-part pricing, later in this chapter.

---

[10] Technically, the consumer's surplus as given here would accurately measure the benefit from consumption of *X* only if demand for *X* were independent of income (no income effect when there is a change in P_X). However, it has been argued that this measure is useful when the proportion of income spent on *X* is small. See Robert D. Willig, "Consumer's Surplus Without Apology," *American Economic Review* 66, No. 4 (September 1976): 589–597.

[11] Recent efforts to promote conservation of water and energy have made such rate schedules less common, since penalty rates have been applied to high-volume users.

Now, however, we will turn to our remaining type of price discrimination, third degree, also known as market segmentation.

Third-Degree Price Discrimination (Market Segmentation)

Third-degree price discrimination is the practice of dividing groups of consumers into separate markets and charging a different price in each market.

In **third-degree price discrimination,** buyers are separated into distinct markets or market segments. For example, consumers of water might be segmented into a residential market and an industrial market, or airline passengers might be segmented into an advance purchase market and an unrestricted purchase market. Two economic conditions must hold for third-degree price discrimination to yield enhanced revenues and profit: (1) the market segments must be kept apart, and (2) the buyers must have different elasticities of demand for the product. The first condition ensures that buyers who purchase at a low price cannot resell to those in a higher-priced market segment, and the second is required because identical elasticities lead to a profit-maximizing solution with identical, rather than different, prices.

Third-degree price discrimination is legal in some settings but illegal in others. Briefly, in the United States, price discrimination is prohibited in interstate commerce when its effect is to lessen competition substantially or when it tends to create a monopoly. It is permitted when it can be justified on the basis of differences in grade, quality, or quantity sold; differences in transportation costs; or the lowering of price in good faith to meet competition. The prohibition against price discrimination applies only to products that will be resold; it does not apply to sales to the final consumer.[12]

Firms in many different lines of business take advantage of opportunities to increase profits by selling what is essentially the same product to different groups of consumers at different prices. Persons attending conventions get lower hotel room rates than are regularly charged. Theaters charge afternoon moviegoers a lower price than those who see the same films at night. So-called commercial rates abound in everything from electric power to rental cars. Many of the discriminations in price that occur daily in the United States have not been tested in the courts, but such testing would undoubtedly prove a large proportion of them to be justifiable. The individual firm must seek competent legal guidance in the question of pricing for multiple markets, but it must also be prepared to recognize opportunities to increase profit through acceptable forms of market segmentation.

The mechanics of increasing profit through the separation of markets are easily understood. We will use convention rates at hotels to illustrate the steps taken by management in the multiple price-setting decision. First,

---

[12] Lawrence S. Clark and Peter D. Kinder, *Law and Business: The Regulatory Environment*, 3d ed. (New York: McGraw-Hill, 1991), pp. 912–915.

management must determine whether it is actually better to establish a convention rate and a regular rate rather than charge the same rate to all occupants of rooms of a given quality. This question will depend on the *elasticity* of demand for rooms in the general market as opposed to that in the convention market. (Our definition of the general market is that in which rooms are rented singly or in small quantities, and the convention market is that in which rooms are blocked in large quantity and subsequently rented to members of a special group.) We will see that if the elasticity of demand in the general market is lower than that in the convention market, management should establish a general market room rate that is higher than the rate it charges in the convention market.

Let us say that we are looking at the multiple rate question from the standpoint of a big-city hotel that can expect to do a considerable amount of convention trade throughout the year. Management wishes to maximize daily profit from combined general market trade and convention market trade. The hotel has 1,600 rooms of equal quality that it expects to rent in the $60 to $90 per day category. Based on studies of the general and convention markets for hotel rooms in the city in which it is located and management's experience in other large cities, the demand curves for rooms in the two markets have been estimated to conform to the following equations:

$$\text{General market } R_g = 1{,}400 - 10P_g,$$

where R_g is the number of rooms rented per day and P_g is the room rate for the general market.

$$\text{Convention market } R_c = 2{,}400 - 20P_c,$$

where R_c is the number of rooms rented per day and P_c is the room rate for the convention market. These two demand curves are plotted, along with their respective marginal revenue curves, in panels (a) and (b) of Figure 11-8. The curves are drawn with solid lines only in the $60 to $90 range, where management expects to establish prices.

Now, suppose that management has estimated the total cost function for the hotel to be

$$TC = 18{,}200 + 30R_g + 30R_c$$

where R_g and R_c are, respectively, the number of general-rate and convention-rate rooms rented per day and daily fixed cost is $18,200. It should be clear from the preceding formula that the marginal cost of a room, whether rented to an occupant in the convention market or the regular market, is $30. Short-run average cost, however, will fall as the daily fixed cost is divided by an increasing quantity of rooms rented.

FIGURE 11–8

Hotel Pricing Analysis With and Without Discrimination between Convention and General Markets

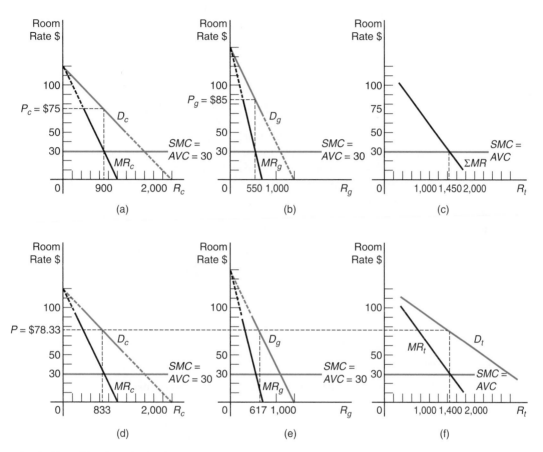

Panels (a), (b), and (c) show the hotel practicing price discrimination and charging a $75 convention rate but an $85 general rate. In panels (d), (e), and (f), there is no discrimination, and both groups of consumers are charged $78.33.

The average variable cost and marginal cost curves appear in panel (c) of Figure 11-8. The ΣMR curve in panel (c) is derived by summing the quantities that correspond to each MR level in panels (a) and (b). For example, at the $30 level of MR, MR_c corresponds to 900 rooms rented in the convention market, and MR_g corresponds to 550 rooms rented in the general market. Thus, we show the sum of these, 1,450 rooms, as the total quantity that can be rented (along ΣMR) when $MR = \$30$.

The profit-maximizing condition when selling in two markets is that marginal cost is equal to marginal revenue in both markets, or (in terms of our hotel)

$$MR_g = MR_c = SMC.$$

To understand why this must be so, consider any situation where $MR_g \neq MR_c$. For example, if $MR_g > MR_c$, the hotel can increase total revenue simply by renting one less room in the convention market and one more in the general market. As in other profit-maximizing problems, output should be increased as long as marginal cost is less than MR_g and MR_c, or up to the point where $SMC = \Sigma MR$ in panel (c) of Figure 11-8. This locates the optimum output, which for the hotel is 1,450 rooms rented per day. We satisfy the condition $MR_g = MR_c = SMC$ in panels (a) and (b) by projecting $\Sigma MR = SMC = \$30$ back to each MR curve. The price and quantity relevant to each market can then be determined as those corresponding to the intersection of $\Sigma MR = SMC = \$30$ with the individual market MR curves. For the general market, the profit-maximizing quantity is 550 rooms per day, and the rate per room is \$85. For the convention market, the optimum quantity is 900 rooms per day, and the rate per room is \$75. Mathematically, this information is expressed as follows:

(11-1)
$$P_g = 140 - 0.1R_g,$$
$$TR_g = 140R_g - 0.1R_g^2,$$
$$MR_g = 140 - 0.2R_g;$$

(11-2)
$$P_c = 120 - 0.05R_c,$$
$$TR_c = 120R_c - 0.05R_c^2,$$
$$MR_c = 120 - 0.1R_c.$$

Since SMC is constant at \$30, when profit is maximized,

(11-3)
$$30 = MR_g = MR_c,$$

(11-4)
$$30 = 140 - 0.2R_g,$$
$$R_g = 550;$$

(11-5)
$$30 = 120 - 0.1R_c,$$
$$R_c = 900.$$

From equations 11-1 and 11-2, we can then obtain $P_g = \$85$ and $P_c = \$75$. Profit is calculated as follows:

$$
\begin{aligned}
T\pi &= TR - TC \\
&= R_g(P_g) + R_c(P_c) - 18{,}200 - 30R_g - 30R_c \\
&= 550(85) + 900(75) - 18{,}200 - 30(550) - 30(900) \\
&= \$52{,}550 \text{ per day.}
\end{aligned}
$$

It can be shown that no single price could produce as much profit for the hotel as the two previous prices, given the two demand curves in panels (a) and (b) of Figure 11-8. The mathematics of this situation are somewhat complicated; however, we present a simple graphical explanation in panels (d), (e), and (f) of Figure 11-8. Panels (d) and (e) contain the same demand and *MR* curves represented in panels (a) and (b). In panel (f), instead of summing the *MR* quantities from each market, we sum the quantities demanded at each price to obtain an aggregate demand curve, D_t. This curve expresses the total amount sold at various prices subject to the condition that $P_g = P_c$. The curve MR_t in panel (f) is the marginal revenue curve relevant to D_t. Where $SMC = \$30$ intersects MR_t, we establish the optimum quantity, 1,450 rooms, and the price, \$78.33. Note, however, that when this price is applied to the demand curves in panels (d) and (e), quantities are obtained that do not correspond to the intersection of $SMC = 30$ with MR_g and MR_c. In fact, we can see that at a price of \$78.33, $MR_g < SMC$ and $MR_c > SMC$. In terms of profit, the hotel is worse off, since

$$T\pi = 1,450(78.33) - 18,200 - 30(1,450)$$

$$= \$51,879 \text{ per day.}$$

If the law permits discrimination between the two markets, the hotel's management should establish a higher rate for general market customers than for convention market customers.

Earlier we noted that when markets are segmented, the market with the lowest (in absolute value) elasticity of demand would have the highest price when profit is maximized. This can be established from the general relationship between marginal revenue and elasticity of demand, which was introduced in Chapter 2 and is expressed as follows:

$$MR = P\left(1 + \frac{1}{E_P}\right) = P\left(1 + \frac{1}{|E_P|}\right), \text{ since } E_P < 0.$$

Recall that in the two-market case, $MR_g = MR_c$ when profit is maximized. Therefore, it must also follow that

$$P_g\left(1 + \frac{1}{|E_g|}\right) = P_c\left(1 - \frac{1}{|E_c|}\right).$$

From the preceding equation we can see that when $P_g > P_c$ it must be true that $|E_g| < |E_c|$, or, in the case of our hotel, the elasticity of demand for rooms is higher in the convention market than in the general market.

Of course, in numerous cases management may be faced with a multiple-market pricing decision. We can expect the possibility of profit maximization

MANAGERIAL PERSPECTIVE

Computers and Price Discrimination

Price discrimination is becoming increasingly common in two large U.S. service industries, hotels and airlines. Travelers who use the airlines regularly are quite aware of the term *limited seat availability* that almost always appears in the fine-print footnote to air carriers' ads that trumpet special discount fares. This qualification allows the companies to switch seats from the discount market to the full-fare market when demand on a given route heats up. The discount fares are based on a specific demand estimate for each class of travel (discount, full coach, first class, etc.). With computer booking, it is feasible to track changes in demand and reduce the availability of discount seats if higher marginal revenue can be obtained from sales of nondiscounted seats. Finding the right combination of prices is extremely important to the airlines, since selling an additional seat can make the difference

between a profit and a loss on a given flight. The hotels have learned from the airlines, and now the big chains also turn to their computerized booking files to make decisions regarding the availability of advertised discount rooms when demand in the nondiscount market increases. Some state attorneys general have eyed the practice warily, fearing that consumers will be unfairly treated if sufficient numbers of the advertised rooms are not made available.

References: Terry Maxon and Suzanne Marta, "Airlines Strive to Find the Right Price," *Dallas Morning News*, May 28, 2002, pp. 1D, 8D; "Keeping the Seats Warm," *Forbes* 15, No. 1 (January 1, 1996): 62–63; and Stuart Jauncey, Sam Mitchell, and Slamet Pamudij, "The Meaning and Management of Yield in Hotels," *International Journal of Contemporary Hospitality Management* 7, No. 4 (1995): 23–26.

through price discrimination or market segmentation to exist any time that distinct groups of consumers purchase a product in different quantities, at different times of the year, or of slightly different attributes (first class vs. tourist transportation, for example). In many cases, such discrimination in pricing will be justifiable. Thus, the competent manager must be able to recognize such possibilities if the firm is to be guided to maximum profit. This is especially important when the firm deals in international trade because there may be significant differences between domestic and foreign elasticities of demand.

TWO-PART PRICING (ACCESS FEES)

Although market segmentation allows firms to enhance profits by charging different prices to distinct groups of consumers, certain other strategies that employ more than one price do not involve discrimination but can also significantly add to profits. One such strategy is to separate the price to the consumer into two parts, an access fee and a price per unit consumed. Such

FIGURE 11–9

Maximization of Profit Contribution Employing Two-Part Pricing

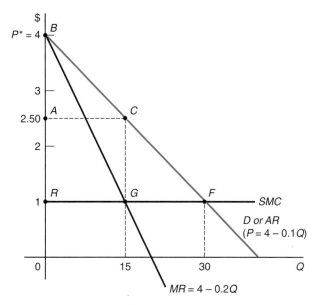

With unit pricing only, the firm would charge $2.50 and have a total profit contribution of $22.50. However, with the same unit price it could also charge an access fee equal to the area of triangle *ABC*. The maximum total profit contribution equals the area of triangle *RBF* and is obtained by charging a $1 price per unit with an access fee of $45.

Two-part pricing is a strategy that divides the amount a consumer pays for a good or service into an access fee and a price per unit.

two-part pricing is used by many firms.[13] Examples are telephone or cellular services that impose a fixed monthly fee to have a phone plus an additional charge per time unit of phone use; golf courses that charge a membership fee plus a green fee per unit of use; and amusement parks that charge an entry fee plus an additional fee for using each ride or attraction.

To understand how two-part pricing works, we will first consider the case of a market consisting of just a single consumer, and we will suppose that the marginal cost of output is constant. Let us say that the consumer's demand curve is given by the equation $P = 4 - 0.1Q$ and that $MC = AVC = \$1$. Suppose the firm charged no access fee and wanted to maximize profit contribution on sales to this one consumer. What price would it charge, and how much would its profit contribution be? Consider Figure 11-9. Here it is easy to see that profit contribution would be maximized where $SMC = MR$, so that $4 - 0.2Q = 1$. Thus, $3 = 0.2Q$ and $Q = 15$. Price would be $2.50, and total profit contribution would be $(P - AVC)\, Q = \$1.5(15) = \$22.50$.

Now let's suppose the firm decides to charge an access fee to the consumer, so that in order to buy *any* units of the product a membership or

---

[13] In economic jargon, the term *two-part tariff* is frequently used to refer to this type of pricing. When so used, "tariff" just means "price" and has nothing to do with international trade, where it usually refers to a tax on imports or exports.

entry fee must be paid. How much could the firm charge this consumer as an entry fee, assuming it charges the $2.50 price in Figure 11-9? The answer can be easily obtained from the figure if one notes that triangle ABC represents the consumer's surplus on the 15 units bought at $P = \$2.50$.[14] (Keep in mind that the demand curve tells us what the consumer values each unit of the good at, so that all units between $Q = 0$ and $Q = 15$ are worth more to the consumer than the $2.50 price that was paid for them.) What is the value of the area of triangle ABC? By geometry, it is one-half the height of the triangle multiplied by its base—that is, $(1/2)$ ($\$4 - \$2.5$) $(15) = \$11.25$. Where P^* is the price axis intercept of the demand curve, P is the current price, and Q is the quantity purchased, we can say the consumer's surplus $= (1/2)$ $(P^* - P)$ (Q). Thus, the 15 units of product bought by the consumer for $\$2.5(15) = \$37.50$ have a value to this consumer of $\$37.50 + \$11.25 = \$48.75$. This means that the firm could charge an access fee of $11.25, and the consumer would still buy the 15 units of output for $2.50 per unit since he or she values them at $48.75. The firm's profit contribution, therefore, rises by the amount of the access fee and will total the original $22.50 *plus* the access fee of $11.25, or $33.75. This is an increase in profit contribution of 50 percent, so it is easy to see why the firm might be interested in a two-part pricing strategy.

Now we must ask whether $33.75 is the most the firm can get in profit contribution from using the two-part pricing approach. The answer is no. In fact, in this case the firm's profit will be maximized by setting $P = SMC$ and charging an access fee equal to the area of triangle RBF in Figure 11-9. The consumer will then purchase 30 units of output at a price of $1 per unit. Profit contribution increases because the additional variable cost of output is covered by the unit price, while the new access fee captures both the earlier profit contribution (area $RACG$) and the previous access fee (area ABC), and adds to them the area of triangle GCF. Since price and AVC are equal, total profit contribution now consists only of the access fee (area of triangle RBF), which is $(1/2)$ ($\$3$) $(30) = \$45$. This is the maximum profit contribution obtainable.[15] The firm will therefore find it rational to charge an access fee of $45 and a price of $1 per unit.

Access Fees with Different Types of Consumers

Although the preceding analysis is fairly straightforward, two-part pricing becomes more complex if consumers have different demand curves for the product. To illustrate, let us now suppose that instead of dealing with a sin-

---

[14] Consistent with the previous discussion of consumer surplus, we continue to assume that the income effect of a change in the price of this good is negligible.

[15] It can be shown graphically that $\Delta TR < \Delta TC$ if price is dropped to a level less than SMC. You may wish to work this out for yourself.

gle consumer, the firm has to consider two types of consumers with different demand curves. Again, it plans to employ two-part pricing, but one of the two types of consumers exhibits greater demand for the product than does the other. We will retain the demand curve from the previous example for the low-demand type of consumer and introduce another for the high-demand type. In addition, the firm will *not* engage in price discrimination. The two demand curves follow.

$$P_L = 4 - 0.1Q_L \qquad \text{(low demand)}$$
$$P_H = 5 - 0.1Q_H \qquad \text{(high demand)}$$

In these expressions, the P terms are prices and the Q terms are the quantities demanded. (Although our two demand curves are not greatly different, they will suffice to illustrate the case. Moreover, if the high-demand type of consumer differs too greatly from the low-demand type, the solution will be not to sell any to the latter.)

A special problem now arises because at every possible price per unit the consumer's surplus of the high-demand type of consumer exceeds that of the low-demand type. (In our preceding equation for the area of the consumer's surplus triangle, P^* will equal 5, rather than 4, for the high-demand consumer.) This will limit the access fee the firm can charge to the amount of the consumer surplus of the low-demand type of consumer. The reason for this is that charging an amount greater than that will lead the low-demand consumer to reject purchasing *any* of the product. If F_L is the consumer surplus of the low-demand type of consumer, the firm, by charging that amount as an access fee, can collect $2F_L$ from the two types of consumers. Assuming selling to both types of consumer is more profitable than just selling to the high-demand type, we can set up a profit contribution function (where AVC stands for average variable cost) as follows:

$$T\pi_c = 2F_L + (P - AVC)(Q_L + Q_H).$$

This simply says that the total profit contribution will consist of the two access fees plus the unit profit contribution multiplied by the sum of the quantities sold in the two markets. In the preceding expression, again using the geometrical formula for the area of a right triangle, $2F_L = 2(1/2)(P^* - P)Q_L$, where P^* is the dollar axis intercept of the demand curve of the low-demand type of consumer (in this case, 4), P is the price charged per unit, and Q_L is the quantity sold in the low-demand market. Note that since both types of consumer will be charged the same unit price, $P = P_L = P_H$, so that for our given demand curves,

$$4 - 0.1Q_L = 5 - 0.1Q_H$$
$$0.1Q_H = 0.1Q_L + 1, \text{ and}$$
$$Q_H = Q_L + 10.$$

Table 11-2 *Profit Contribution Data for Example of Two-Part Pricing with Low- and High-Demand Types of Consumers*

P	Q_L	Q_H	F_L	F_H	$2F_L$	$T\pi_c$	$M\pi_c$
3.50	5	15	1.25	11.25	2.50	52.50	
							1.75
3.00	10	20	5.00	20.00	10.00	70.00	
							1.25
2.50	15	25	11.25	31.25	22.50	82.50	
							0.75
2.00	20	30	20.00	45.00	40.00	90.00	
							0.25
1.50	25	35	31.25	61.25	62.50	92.50	
							−0.25
1.00	30	40	45.00	80.00	90.00	90.00	
							−0.75
0.50	35	45	61.25	101.25	122.50	82.50	

Note: $F_L = (1/2)(P^* - P)(Q_L)$ and is the consumer's surplus of the low-demand type of consumer, where $P^* = 4$ is the price intercept of the relevant demand curve. F_H is the consumer's surplus of the high-demand type of consumer and can be calculated by the same formula where $P^* = 5$ is the appropriate demand curve intercept.

This allows us to write the total profit contribution function as

$$T\pi_c = 2(1/2)\,(4 - 4 + 0.1Q_L)\,(Q_L) + (3 - 0.1Q_L)\,(2Q_L + 10)$$
$$= -0.1Q_L{}^2 + 5Q_L + 30.$$

For prices ranging from \$3.50 to \$0.50, Table 11-2 shows the results in terms of both total and marginal profit contribution $(M\pi_c)$ along with the quantities sold, the access fee $(2F_L)$, and the respective consumer surpluses $(F_L$ and $F_H)$ for the two types of consumer. (Remember that if F_H is charged as the access fee, the low-demand type of consumer will not buy the product. Thus, charging F_H would yield a $T\pi_c$ equal to $F_H + (P - AVC)\,Q_H$, which is, at every price, *less* than the $T\pi_c$ shown in the table. You can check this for yourself.) As the table shows, the maximum profit contribution occurs when $P = \$1.50$. There, the firm will charge an access fee of \$31.25 and sell 25 units in the low-demand market plus 35 units in the high-demand market. Thus,

$$T\pi_c = 2F_L + (P - AVC)\,(Q_L + Q_H)$$
$$= 2(31.25) + (1.5 - 1)\,(60)$$
$$= 62.50 + 30 = \$92.50.$$

Note also that the firm's marginal profit contribution is positive for quantity sold less than 60 but negative for quantity sold greater than 60.[16] As a practical matter, when consumers are diverse and, therefore, have different consumer surpluses, the firm may have to do a substantial amount of experimentation to determine what combination of access fee and unit price constitutes the best two-part pricing approach. Indeed, some firms, including theme park operators such as the Disney Corporation, have decided that it is optimal to use only an access fee and not charge a price per unit for partaking of the attractions. (In these businesses, however, the pricing of food, refreshments, and souvenirs is, of course, another matter.)[17]

BUNDLING

Bundling is a strategy that offers a package deal to consumers on the purchase of two or more products.

Bundling is a pricing strategy that takes a number of forms, but its principal characteristic is that it offers the buyer a package consisting of two or more goods that is more attractive than the alternative of buying the goods separately. Like many of the other strategies we have examined, it can enhance both revenue and profit. Bundling is used by tour companies, when they offer deals that can include airfare, hotel, rental car, and even meals at one package price; by cable television companies that offer combinations of channels at package prices cheaper than the separate prices for the same channels; by computer retailers who offer package deals including a computer, software, and a number of peripherals; and even by fast-food restaurants that offer "meal deals" at prices lower than those charged for the same items bought separately.

How the firm gains from bundling is most easily demonstrated with a numerical example. Like certain other strategies, bundling is based on differing demand patterns of consumers. What is required for bundling to be attractive to the firm is a situation in which two consumers (or consumer groups) have an inverse relation between the amounts they are willing to pay for two different goods. To illustrate, let us imagine a wholesale travel company in New Orleans that advertises in selected newspaper travel pages and deals directly with consumers using a toll-free telephone number. Its research has indicated that there are basically two types of consumers in the target market. The *Type A* consumer is only mildly interested in jazz and creole cuisine but likes to take day trips to nearby attractions such as gardens,

---

[16] The calculus solution is straightforward and agrees with the table. To obtain marginal profit contribution, take the first derivative of the total profit contribution function. This yields $M\pi_C = -0.2Q_L + 5$. Setting $M\pi_C = 0$, one obtains $Q_L = 5/0.2 = 35$, and since $Q_H = Q_L + 10$, $Q_H = 35$.

[17] One of the best-known articles on two-part pricing did, in fact, deal with Disneyland. See Walter Oi, "A Disneyland Dilemma: Two-Part Tariffs for a Mickey Mouse Monopoly," *Quarterly Journal of Economics* 85 (1971): 77–96.

Table 11-3 *Maximum Amounts That Two Types of Consumers Would Pay Per Day for a Room or a Rental Car*

Consumer	Room	Rental Car
Type A	$ 85	$40
Type B	$120	$20

plantations, and beaches. The *Type B* consumer comes to New Orleans mainly for the jazz music and food but has only slight interest in the attractions of the surrounding area.

The maximum amounts that the two types of consumer would be willing to pay per day for a room and a rental car are shown in Table 11-3. The *Type A* consumer will pay up to $85 for a room and up to $40 for a rental car. The *Type B* consumer will pay up to $120 for a room but only values a rental car at $20 per day, since he or she is not terribly interested in traveling to the surrounding attractions. We can see that if more than $85 is charged for a room, the *Type A* consumer will not be interested in getting a room through this company. Similarly, if more than $20 is charged for a car, the *Type B* consumer will not be interested in booking a car through the company. If the company wishes to attract both consumers to rent a car and a room, the maximum separate prices it can charge for them is $85 for the room and $20 for the car. Then, both consumers will buy both items, and a total revenue of 2($85 + $20) = $210 will be obtained.

Now let's consider bundling the room and the car in a package deal. With the data in Table 11-3, we can see that the *Type A* consumer is willing to pay $125 per day for the combination of a room and a car, whereas the *Type B* consumer is willing to pay $140. Clearly, then, both will buy the bundle if the firm charges $125. This yields total revenue of 2($125) = $250, which is a far better result for the firm than the $210 it would obtain if the two items were sold separately at prices that would attract both types of buyers.

In the foregoing example, bundling provided a gain because the preferences of the two consumers were inversely related. That is, the *Type A* consumer was willing to pay *less* for a room but *more* for a car than was the *Type B* consumer. If the data are altered to destroy this relation, for example, by reducing the amount the *Type B* consumer will pay for a room to $84, there will be no gain from bundling. You should try this, or any other combination where one consumer is willing to pay more for both items than is the other, to prove to yourself that the inverse relation is required.

The example we have given is one known as *pure bundling*. This means that we considered only offering the two items separately or as a package and did not take into account the possibility of offering them both separately and at a special price for the bundle. The latter would constitute *mixed*

NUMERICAL EXAMPLE

Bundling

Whatsupwit U. has decided to allow beer consumption at its football games. You have been fortunate enough to secure the franchise for that operation, which is also authorized to sell hot dogs. Because you are a business school graduate, you have done some survey research that indicates the following are the maximum amounts spectators of two different persuasions would be willing to pay for those two items.

	One Hot Dog	*One Beer*
Male	$3.00	$2.50
Female	$4.00	$1.30

Your research indicates that attendance at the games will be about equally divided between males and females.

Questions

1. If the two items are priced separately, what combination of prices will yield the maximum total revenue?
2. What price would be charged if the two items are bundled, and how much would this strategy affect total revenue?

Solution

If the two items are priced separately, the firm will do best to charge $3.00 for a hot dog and $1.30 for a beer. This yields a total revenue of $8.60 from one male and one female. If hot dogs are priced above $3.00, the male will not buy any, and the female will not buy any beer if it is priced above $1.30. At the maximum prices of $4.00 for a hot dog and $2.50 for a beer, only $6.50 would be obtained from one male and one female, since the male forgoes the hot dog and the female forgoes beer.

With bundling, the firm will charge $5.30 for the two items. Both males and females will buy the package, yielding $10.60 in revenue from one male and one female. This is a $2 gain from the unbundled result.

bundling. Mixed bundling, which includes offering separate items at the same time as, perhaps, a variety of different bundles, is an appropriate strategy where there are groups of consumers with imperfectly correlated inverse preferences and where there are differential marginal costs associated with the various products or packages. In fact, many of the bundling approaches that firms use today fall into the mixed category.

ALTERNATIVES TO PROFIT MAXIMIZATION

All of the situations discussed thus far in this chapter—and indeed, throughout this book—have focused on the managerial goal of profit maximization. Although it seems reasonable to accept profit maximization as at least the long-run goal of a firm's managers, there are good reasons to question this assumption. One of the well-recognized characteristics of business in the United States today is *separation of ownership and control.*

Since modern corporations are owned by shareholders but controlled by managers who may or may not have the shareholders' interest as their prime concern, there is a possibility that profit maximization, even when desired by shareholders, will not be the objective of the firms' managers. In other words, as we noted in Chapter 1, there is an *agency problem,* since the managers are acting as agents for the shareholders. For example, a corporate manager whose goal is personal success, measured in terms of either income or prestige, might perceive that personal rewards are more closely tied to the *size of the firm* than to profitability. In this setting, the manager might wish to expand sales beyond the point of profit maximization in order to capture a larger share of the market or to give the illusion of rapid growth. The firm might then be led to operate where *sales* are maximized, subject to the constraint that profit is sufficient to keep shareholders satisfied.[18]

The preceding situation is described in Figure 11-10, where instead of operating at Q_e, the firm operates at Q^*. At output level Q^*, sales revenue is maximized, but profit is less than at Q_e. Presumably, shareholders will not complain because profit at Q^* is still greater than normal. Of course, for certain firms, appreciation of stock prices may be more closely correlated with growth than with profits during one time period or another. In such a setting, both shareholders and management might be more interested in sales increases than in maximum profit.

Although profit maximization and the conditions necessary to attain it are bound to be of importance to every manager, clearly the question of the firm's objectives includes a number of other considerations. Survival is not the least of these, and in a world characterized by oligopoly, risk aversion on the part of management could easily take precedence over profit maximization. We must also note that most profit-maximizing rules based on market demand tend to be utilized where rather short-run views of the market are estimated. As the time horizon pertinent to a management decision becomes longer, the difficulty in estimating demand increases, since more variables

---

[18] See "Course Change at Boeing," *Business Week* (July 27, 1998), p. 34; Seth Mendelson, "Market Share Vs. Bottom Line," *Supermarket Business* 5, No. 2 (February 1996): 59; and Daryl N. Winn and John D. Shoenhair, "Compensation-Based (Dis) Incentives for Revenue-Maximizing Behavior: A Test of the Revised 'Baumol Hypothesis,'" *Review of Economics and Statistics* 70, No. 1 (February 1988).

FIGURE 11-10

*Maximization of
Sales Revenue
Compared with
Profit
Maximization*

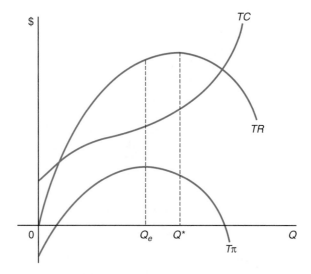

If the firm chooses to maximize sales revenue, it will operate at Q^*, even though maximum profit would be obtained at Q_e, a lower output.

are likely to become relevant. Furthermore, the possibility exists that short-run profit maximization may not be consistent with long-run profit maximization. A firm might choose in the short run to have lower profit and higher sales because over the long run or in subsequent periods, the consequences of early market penetration may have a very positive effect on profit. In other words, capturing additional markets today at rather low rates of profit may mean greatly increased profits in the future. To some extent, the capital budgeting approach to long-run planning of the firm takes into account the effects of strategies that produce differential profit outcomes over time. This approach, which is an extension of the profit-maximizing analyses we have been using all along, will be discussed in Chapter 13.

SUMMARY

Multiple Products, Segmented Markets, and Pricing Strategies

In this chapter we have discussed the firm's pricing and output decisions in more complex situations than those assumed to exist in previous chapters. At the beginning of the chapter, we examined markup pricing and found that it is not inconsistent with the conditions for profit maximization. More complex pricing problems were then discussed, beginning with the profit-maximizing behavior of firms that produce multiple products. The first case considered was that in which two products can or must be produced jointly.

If the two products *must* be produced in fixed proportions, the firm will maximize profit if it produces where the joint marginal revenue of the two products is equal to their joint marginal cost. (If the marginal revenue of one of the products becomes negative before this point is reached, some of the output of this product should be either destroyed or stored.) We also demonstrated that the situation is much more complex if the products can be produced in variable proportions.

Next we directed our attention to the case in which one division of a firm produces a product, called the *transfer product,* that is also used as an intermediate product in making the product of another division of the firm, the *final product* division. We discussed how the firm would determine the profit-maximizing quantities of the final division product and the transfer product and the appropriate price that should be charged the final product division for the transfer product. We saw that the determination of the optimal transfer price and quantities of both products differed, depending on whether or not the transfer product could be sold in an external market.

We then considered price discrimination, which occurs in various forms. We focused attention on *third-degree* price discrimination, where a firm that sells the same product in two separate markets can legally charge a different price in each market. As we saw, for price discrimination to be economically sound, customers in the two markets must have different elasticities of demand, and the firm must be able to prevent customers in the higher-priced market from buying the product in the lower-priced market.

Following the discussion of price discrimination, we developed models of both *two-part pricing,* where unit prices are supplemented by access fees, and *bundling,* where revenue and profit are enhanced by offering package deals on multiple products. Finally, we discussed alternative goals to profit maximization, such as sales maximization. Here, we noted the possibility that firm *managers* are more likely to have goals other than profit maximization if they are not also the firm's owners.

In the next chapter we return to the simpler case of the firm producing one product for one market and discuss how the firm can determine the short-run, profit-maximizing quantity of a variable input to be employed, assuming that all other inputs are fixed.

QUESTIONS

1. Under what set of circumstances would a firm that produces two joint products in fixed proportions be forced to withhold a portion of one product from the market?

2. How can a product transformation curve be employed to illustrate profit maximization with joint products produced in variable proportions? How is revenue represented in such a setting?

3. What is a transfer product? Under what circumstances might such a product be sold externally, as well as transferred?

4. State in two different ways the necessary condition for optimal production of a transfer product in the case of no external market for the transfer product.

5. What is meant by the term *consumer's surplus?* How is this concept related to both first- and second-degree price discrimination?

6. What is meant by *market segmentation* or *price discrimination?* Where a firm is selling in two separate markets, what is the condition that must be fulfilled in order to maximize the firm's profit?

7. Under what circumstances would it be useless (though not illegal) to charge different prices in two separate markets?

8. What is meant by the term *two-part pricing?* Give an example of a market where two-part pricing is frequently found.

9. What is *bundling?* Given two different types of consumers, what kind of preferences must exist for bundling to increase revenue?

10. Why might a firm's management choose to operate at a rate of output greater than the rate that maximizes profit? How can such behavior be reconciled with the profit-maximization norm?

11. Why is transfer pricing an important issue in international business?

12. Under what circumstances is price discrimination legal in the United States?

13. Name some industries in your community in which firms legally and overtly practice price discrimination.

14. What is meant by markup pricing? Has it been used by firms as a long-run or a short-run pricing strategy? Explain.

PROBLEMS

1. Given the following product transformation curve, indicate the amount of X and Y that will maximize profit for the firm if the selling price per unit of X is 1/2 the price per unit of Y.

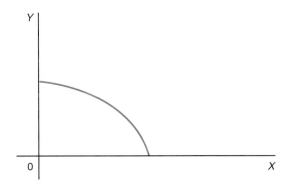

2. Sketch a product transformation curve for a firm that produces two joint products (X and Y) but has only the following input-output production possibilities:

   a. 100 percent X

   b. 75 percent X and 25 percent Y

   c. 50 percent X and 50 percent Y

   d. 25 percent X and 75 percent Y

   e. 100 percent Y

   Note: Assume that resources cannot be perfectly transferred from the production of X to the production of Y.

3. Suppose Randy Corporation is selling its product both in the United States and overseas and faces the two demand curves illustrated here. If the company's marginal cost is constant at $7.50 per unit of output, determine from the graphs what price it will charge in each market. (The United States has a large tariff on the product.)

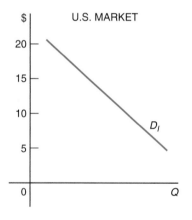

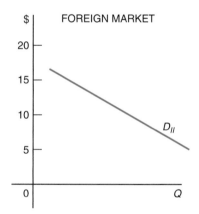

4. Suppose a company produces two products, A and B, and the production process is such that one unit of A is always obtained with one unit of B. If the demand curves for A and B are estimated to be

$$Q_A = 100 - P_A \text{ (so that } MR_A = 100 - 2Q_A)$$

and

$$Q_B = 120 - 0.8P_B \text{ (so that } MR_B = 150 - 2.5Q_B),$$

and the marginal cost of production is $MC = 4 + 1.5Q_J$, where Q_J consists of one unit of each product, how much of each product should the firm sell in order to maximize profit?

5. A company that produces plastic products by using injection molding machines has the following production and revenue alternatives for three products (*A, B,* and *C*) that are feasible to produce with the existing plant and equipment:

Product Combinations

No. of Shifts	100% A	50% A 50% B	100% B	75% A 25% B
1	TR = 200	TR = 225	TR = 275	TR = 200
2	TR = 380	TR = 410	TR = 500	TR = 400
3	TR = 490	TR = 575	TR = 575	TR = 600

TR is in thousands of dollars per month. *Total cost* for the first shift is $125,000 per month—of which $80,000 is labor, $40,000 is other variable costs, and $5,000 is fixed cost. As the number of shifts is increased, fixed cost remains at $5,000 per month while variable costs other than labor remain the same *per shift.* For the second shift, labor must be paid 1.25 times the amount paid in the first shift; for the third shift, labor must be paid 1.50 times what it receives in the first shift.

a. Determine total cost for the two-shift and three-shift alternatives.

b. Indicate the product combination and shift level that maximizes profit.

6. The Maxton Company produces a number of household appliances, including an electric coffee pot. The final product division of the company manufactures the metal pot and all plastic parts and then assembles, packages, and distributes the product. The electrical components unit of the coffee pot (consisting of a heating element, a thermocouple, and related wiring items) are produced by a separate electrical parts division of the firm.

The electrical parts division could sell the coffee pot components unit in the open market to a number of assemblers at a standard price of $2.80. There is vigorous competition in the electrical components industry, and it is unlikely that any but the going price can be obtained.

Management has determined that the demand curve for quantity sold per month of the final product is

$$Q_f = 3,000 - 125P_f \text{ (so that } MR_f = 24 - 0.016Q_f),$$

while the marginal cost of the final product, *excluding* the cost of the electrical components unit, is

$$MC_f = 0.004Q_f.$$

In addition, management has determined that the marginal cost of the transfer product division is

$$MC_t = 0.008Q_t,$$

where Q_t is the quantity of the transfer product produced.

a. At what final product price and rate of output will the firm maximize profit?

b. How much of the transfer product should be produced?

c. Should the final product division obtain *all* of its electrical components units for the coffee pot from its own components division? Why or why not?

d. Construct a diagram corresponding to the above situation. Show the equilibrium output for each division.

7. The management of Castle's Fried Chicken is planning a pricing policy based on market segmentation. M. J. Pyronic, the firm's sales manager, argues that the eat-in customer can be differentiated from the carry-out customer because the carry-out customer will generally purchase a large quantity of chicken to serve a group of people at home. Pyronic estimates that carry-out demand is more elastic than eat-in demand and states that carry-out buckets should be priced at a lower rate per serving of chicken (one wing, one drumstick, and one thigh) than the price per serving for eat-in customers.

Pyronic's estimate of carry-out demand is

$$Q_c = 10{,}000 - 2{,}000P_c \quad \text{(so that } MR_c = 5 - 0.001Q_c\text{),}$$

where Q_c is the number of carry-out orders sold per week and P_c is the price per carry-out serving. She estimates the eat-in demand per week to be

$$Q_j = 6{,}000 - 1{,}000P_j \quad \text{(so that } MR_j = 6 - 0.002Q_j\text{),}$$

where P_j is the price per eat-in serving. Marginal cost per serving is constant at $1.20.

a. Should the price per serving for the carry-out market be lower than that for the eat-in market?

b. How many servings per week should be sold in each market to maximize profit?

c. What price or prices should be charged?

d. Diagram the case showing the profit-maximizing rates of output and the average revenue.

8. Salmagam Corporation purchases video camcorder batteries from a manufacturer in Hong Kong and distributes them to retail stores throughout the United States. Salmagam's management has estimated that within the range of feasible prices for the batteries, the elasticity of demand of the retail stores for them is −3.5. If Salmagam can obtain any quantity of the batteries from the manufacturer for a fixed price of $18, answer the following:

a. What will be its profit-maximizing markup percentage?

b. What price should it charge for the batteries?

9. Smales Labs is a mail-order color film processing company. They have recently installed equipment that will allow them to expand their services to include supplying computer photodisks of customers' 35 mm and Advanced Photo System prints. Smales has identified two major types of customer—those who favor

prints *(Type P)* and those who favor photodisks *(Type D)*. The maximum amounts each type of customer would pay per roll of film (24 or 25 exposures) for prints and a photodisk appear in the following table.

Type of Customer	Prints	Photodisk
Type P	$7.50	$4.00
Type D	$5.50	$8.00

Smales is considering offering its processing only as a bundle consisting of both prints and photodisk. Given the preceding data, what price would you advise the company to charge for the bundle? Explain how this yields more revenue than unbundled pricing that would attract each type of customer to buy *both* prints and disk.

10. Water Hyperwonderland, a theme park that features dolphin shows, estimates that the typical customer who likes the shows enough to want a season discount card has an annual demand curve represented by the equation $Q = 18 - P$, where P is the price charged per admission and Q is the number of times per year the person will visit the park. The park's marginal cost per visit for any type of client is $2. Based on the foregoing demand curve, to maximize profit contribution from discount-card customers, what should be (a) the price of a season discount card and (b) the per-visit ticket price for a discount card holder?

11. Henderson-Carlton Corporation (HCC) processes and sells Jalora beans, an arid-lands bean that is the source of oils used in numerous cosmetics. A byproduct of the firm's production process is bean shells which are sold to other firms that mix goat feed. The firm estimates the current demand curve for beans to be $Q_b = 9,000 - 30P_b$, where Q_b is the number of sacks of beans sold per month and P_b is the price per sack. The production of bean shells amounts to 20 pounds per sack of beans produced. The firm estimates that its monthly demand for shells is described by the equation $Q_s = 6,000 - 800P_s$, where Q_s is a unit consisting of 20 pounds of shells. The firm's marginal cost for joint production of the two products is $50 per unit (a sack of beans plus a unit of shells). Answer the following:

   a. How much of each product should HCC produce per month?

   b. What price should HCC charge for each product?

   c. Will there be any excess output of either product?

   d. What will be HCC's monthly total profit from the sales of the two products, assuming its monthly total fixed cost is $100,000?

12. Nantucket Air flies a short-hop service between Boston and Nantucket Island. It is planning to use price discrimination to maximize profit by charging lower prices for advanced-purchase tickets than it charges for tickets purchased less than two weeks ahead of scheduled flights. It estimates that the annual demand curve for regular-price tickets is $P_r = 200 - 0.05Q_r$. For advanced-purchase tickets, the annual demand curve is estimated to be $P_a = 100 - 0.0125Q_a$. Marginal cost for the firm is $40 per passenger. What prices should it charge the respective passenger groups, and what will be its annual profit if its annual total fixed cost is $150,000?

The following problems require calculus:

C1. Schmooker Chemical Company produces bubble bath powder using a process that yields a joint product of one unit of deadly Z41 pesticide for each unit of bubble bath produced. Schmooker's demand curve for bubble bath is $Q_b = 3,800 - P_b$. Its demand curve for Z41 has the equation $Q_z = 6,000 - 5P_z$. Schmooker's total cost function for the two joint products is $TC = 500 + 20Q + 0.095Q^2$. Answer the following:

a. How much of each product should Schmooker sell?

b. What price should it charge for each product?

c. Should it withhold any of either product from the market? If so, which one (and how much) should it keep off the market?

C2. Taipei Electronics makes compact disc players under license from CRA Corporation. One of Taipei's subsidiaries, Lenscan Corporation, makes the optical stylus for the players. The total dollar cost of production of the stylus by Lenscan is

$$TC_s = 12,000 + 2Q_s + 0.0001Q_s^2.$$

Taipei's marginal cost (in dollars) for the final production of the disc players (not including the cost of the stylus) is $MC_d = 10 + 0.003Q_d$. The demand curve for the disc player is

$$Q_d = 70,000 - 400P_d, \quad \text{where } P_d \text{ is in dollars.}$$

If the optical stylus can be bought or sold in the open market at a fixed price of $5 per unit, determine the following:

a. The number of disc players Taipei should sell.

b. The price that should be charged for the players.

c. The number of optical styli the Lenscan subsidiary should produce.

d. The price that Lenscan should charge for the stylus.

C3. Down Under Products is an Australian firm that produces wine for sale to manufacturers of wine coolers. Due to spoilage in the production process, it also sells a co-product, wine vinegar. The ratio of vinegar to wine it produces is constant and equal to one case of vinegar for each case of wine produced. Down Under's current estimate of wine demand is represented by the following equation:

$$Q_w = 12,000 - 100P_w,$$

where Q_w is the number of cases of wine sold per month and P_w is the price obtained per case of wine.

Respectively, the demand curve for wine vinegar and the firm's total cost function are the following:

$$Q_v = 6,000 - 200P_v,$$

where Q_v is the number of cases of vinegar sold per month and P_v is the price per case; and

$$TC = \$100{,}000 + 4.16Q + 0.006Q^2,$$

where $100,000 is monthly fixed cost and Q represents the number of case equivalents of the two products it produces.

Down Under's present strategy is to maximize profit from the sales of the two products, given that there is no disposal cost for any excess product. Find the profit-maximizing quantities sold of the two products, their prices, the amount of excess product not sold, if any, and Down Under's total profit from sales of the two joint products.

C4. Gongalong Company makes grandfather's clocks. One of its subsidiaries, Boing, Inc., makes the mainsprings for the clocks. The market for such springs (which have many other novel uses) is highly competitive, and the going market price for them is $28.00 per unit. Gongalong estimates the demand for its clocks to be $Q_c = 14{,}000 - 20P_c$. The marginal cost of manufacturing the clocks, *not* including the mainsprings, is given by the function $MC_c = 23 + 0.12Q_c$. The marginal cost of the Boing division for making the mainsprings is $MC_s = 4 + 0.005Q_s$. There is one mainspring in each clock. Answer the following:

a. How many clocks should Gongalong produce, and what price should it charge per clock?

b. How many mainsprings should Boing, Inc., produce, and what price should it charge Gongalong per spring?

c. Will Gongalong have to buy any mainsprings from suppliers other than Boing? If not, why not? If so, how many?

C5. Peixe Louco is a Portuguese company that processes codfish. It also produces a co-product, codfish oil. Its production ratio of oil to fish is constant and equal to one gallon of oil for each case of fish produced. Peixe Louco's current estimate of fish demand is represented by the following equation:

$$Q_f = 10{,}000 - 100P_f,$$

where Q_f is the number of cases of fish sold per month and P_f is the price obtained per case of fish.

Respectively, the demand curve for fish oil and the firm's total cost function are the following:

$$Q_o = 7{,}000 - 200P_o,$$

where Q_O is the number of gallons of oil sold per month and P_O is the price per gallon; and

$$TC = \$100{,}000 + 4.06Q + 0.003Q^2,$$

where $100,000 is monthly fixed cost and Q represents the number of case and gallon equivalents of the two products it produces.

Peixe Louco's present strategy is to maximize profit from the sales of the two products, given that there is no disposal cost for any excess product. Find the profit-maximizing *quantities sold* of the two products, their *prices*, the amount of *excess product* not sold, if any, and the company's *total profit* from sales of the two joint products.

C6. Aunt Jane's Fitness Center is planning to utilize price discrimination to set its family and corporate rates. For a family membership, its estimated demand curve is

$$Q_f = 984 - 20P_f.$$

For the corporate market, its estimated demand curve is

$$Q_c = 2{,}070 - 50P_c.$$

In both equations, Q represents the quantity of members and P represents the monthly membership fee. The center's weekly total cost is

$$TC = 12{,}000 + 10Q,$$

where Q is total number of members $(Q_f + Q_c)$.

a. With price discrimination, how many memberships will be sold in each market?

b. What price will Aunt Jane's charge in each market?

c. What will be the center's monthly profit?

Problem C7 requires both partial differentiation and constrained maximization. It should be attempted only if you have covered the material in the appendix that follows Chapter 5.

C7. The Chilidome Regency Hotel is planning to use price discrimination between convention and general room rates. For a standard double room, its estimated demand curve for the general market is

$$Q_g = 4{,}344 - 20P_g.$$

For the convention market, its estimated demand curve is

$$Q_c = 5{,}800 - 50P_c.$$

In both equations, Q represents weekly quantity of rooms and P represents price per night. The hotel's weekly total cost is

$$TC = 112{,}000 + 40Q + 0.01Q^2,$$

where Q is weekly total number of rooms rented $(Q_g + Q_c)$.

a. With price discrimination, how many rooms will be rented in each market?

b. What price will the hotel charge in each market?

    c. What will be the hotel's weekly profit?

    d. Compare the results from (b) and (c), in terms of both price and profit, with what the firm could obtain if it did not practice price discrimination.

C8. The small city of Olpeson, Kansas, has a municipal golf course. For years, the golf course has been available at no charge to users. However, because of declining population and increasing costs of maintenance, the city council has decided to institute both a membership fee and a greens fee (fee charged per round played) for golf patrons. Research shows there are two kinds of patrons—city residents and persons who live in the surrounding rural area. The council believes it is not politically feasible to charge the rural users different fees than those paid by the city residents. Its research staff estimates that the typical city resident golfer's demand can be represented by the equation $Q_c = 20 - 0.4P_c$. For the typical rural golfer, the estimated demand curve is $Q_r = 18 - 0.4Q_r$. (In either equation, the P_i represents the greens fee and the Q_i represents the annual number of times it is paid.) If research estimates that the average variable cost (maintenance, fee administration, etc.) to the course of an individual's round of golf is $3.00, what combination of membership fee and greens fee will maximize the return to the city? How many rounds of golf per year will the typical city resident golfer play, and how many will the typical rural golfer play?

SELECTED REFERENCES

Beard, T. Randolph, and George H. Sweeney. "Random Pricing by Monopolists." *Journal of Industrial Economics* 42, No. 2 (June 1994): 183–192.

Carlton, Dennis W., and Jeffrey M. Perloff. *Modern Industrial Organization,* 2d ed. Boston: Addison-Wesley, 1999, Chapter 10.

Lanzillotti, Robert F. "Pricing Objectives in Large Companies." *American Economic Review* (December 1958): 921–940.

Mansfield, Edwin, and Gary Yohe. *Microeconomics: Theory and Applications.* New York: W. W. Norton, 2000, Chapters 11 and 12.

Philips, Louis (ed.). *Applied Industrial Economics.* Cambridge: Cambridge University Press, 1998.

Plott, Charles R. "Industrial Organization Theory and Experimental Economics." *Journal of Economic Literature* (December 1982): 1485–1527.

Scherer, F. M. *Industry Structure, Strategy, and Public Policy.* New York: HarperCollins, 1996.

Stiglitz, Joseph E., and Carl E. Walsh. *Economics.* 3d ed. New York: W. W. Norton, 2002, Part Three.

Transfer Pricing with a Less-Than-Perfectly Competitive Market for the Intermediate Product

In this appendix, we analyze the transfer pricing problem facing managers of a two-division, two-product firm when the transfer product can be sold externally in a market that is less than perfectly competitive. The relationship of the transfer product division to the final product division remains unchanged from the examples covered in this chapter; that is, the transfer product division knows it must price its output at marginal cost when selling to the final product division. Presumably, with an oligopolistic external market for the transfer product, T, the final product division cannot be supplied its T inputs from rival firms at a price as low as the level of the marginal cost of Product T when profit for the firm is maximized. However, if the T division has the opportunity to sell its product in such an external market, management will need to determine the combination of final and transfer product outputs that maximizes profit, as well as the profit-maximizing prices of each of the products.

In this situation, the firm's profit will be maximized when MC_T, the marginal cost of product T, is equal to the net marginal revenue of the entire enterprise, NMR_e. In the chapter, NMR_F was identified as $MR_F - MC_F$, the marginal revenue remaining after all marginal costs except that of Product T are subtracted from the marginal revenue resulting from the sale of the final product. However, with an external market for T that is less than perfectly competitive, the T division finds itself selling in what is essentially a two-market setting (internal and external) or a situation similar to the case of two-market price discrimination (also discussed within Chapter 11). From management's point of view, then, the NMR_e will consist not only of $MR_F - MC_F$, but also of MR_T—the marginal revenue obtainable from sales of T in the external market.

The firm as a whole will be able to increase profit by switching output of T from the internal market to the external market whenever $MR_T > (MR_F - MC_F)$. Note, however, that this can be accomplished only by also varying the amount produced and sold of the final product, as well as the price of the final product. Such a result follows because the amount of T supplied to the final product division cannot be reduced without also reducing the output of the final product itself.

Figure 11A-1 provides a graphical solution to the profit-maximizing problem that exists when management knows it can sell some amount of T in an oligopolistic external market. As in previous examples in Chapter 11, we depict a situation in which there is a fixed amount of T used in the manufacture of one unit of the final product. Thus the Q axis of panel (a) will measure both production of the final product, F, and utilization of T by the final product division. In panel (a) the curve $MR_F - MC_F$ is derived from D_F in the usual manner. The external market for Product T is illustrated in panel (b), where MR_T is derived from the external demand curve D_T. Finally, in panel (c) the two curves $MR_F - MC_F$ and MR_T are summed horizontally (quantities added for each level of MR) to obtain NMR_e—the net marginal revenue of the enterprise.

Profit maximization occurs in Figure 11A-1, where $NMR_e = MC_T$. By projecting the profit-maximizing level of MC_T (that is, MC_T^*) leftward to panels

---

FIGURE 11A-1

Transfer Pricing with a Less-Than-Perfectly Competitive Market for the Transfer Product

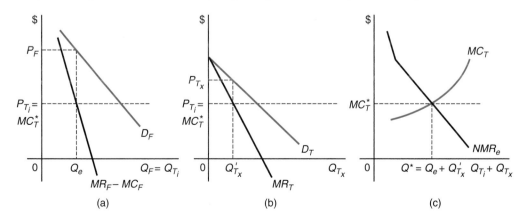

(b) and (a), we find the quantities of T sold to the final product division (Q_e) and the external market for the transfer product Q'_{T_x} such that $MC_T^* = MR_T = MR_F - MC_F$. The equality of $MR_F - MC_F$ with MR_T ensures that the firm cannot gain by switching output from the internal market to the external market, or vice versa. Since the transfer product division is instructed to set a transfer price equal to MC_T, $P_{T_i} = MC_T^*$ will be the price charged the final product division for its inputs of T. However, in the external market, a price of P_{T_x} will be charged [panel (b)]. Back in panel (a), the final product division can be seen to produce Q_e of final product F and charge a price of P_F.

The situation depicted in Figure 11A-1 is illustrative of the kind of analysis that must be done in order for managers to maximize profit where a transfer pricing decision must be made and the external market for the transfer product is not perfectly competitive. It should be clear from the preceding that sales of the transfer product to purchasers outside the firm may contribute importantly to the firm's total revenue and profit. Another way to examine this issue is to ask what would happen if the external demand for the transfer product were to increase (D_T and MR_T shift to the right). In terms of Figure 11A-1, we can verify that NMR_e would also shift toward the right, thereby intersecting MC_T at a level higher than MC_T^*. This would undoubtedly lead to increased sales in the external market for the T product—but what would happen to Q_F? If final product demand has not changed, then Q_e must fall and P_F must rise when the profit-maximizing level of MC_T rises above MC_T^*. Thus, the firm would actually be best off to reduce sales of its final product and increase the final product's price in order to be able to market more of Product T externally.

The lesson to be learned from the preceding analysis is that a change in one of the markets faced by a multiple-product, multiple-market firm can have pervasive effects on several aspects of the firm's operations. However, these effects may be predictable to some degree if the firm has sufficient information on demand and costs. Another example that could be illustrated by making some changes in Figure 11A-1 is a situation in which demand for the final product has increased [D_F shifts rightward in panel (a)] but D_T has not. The reader should be able to verify that in this setting, less of T should be sold externally and P_{T_x} should be increased.

Mathematics of
Price Discrimination[1]

The model of two-market price discrimination discussed in Chapter 11 was developed only for the case of constant marginal cost, since the mathematics of the situation is somewhat complex if marginal cost is variable. To illustrate why, we will return to the example of hotel pricing used in the chapter and use the same demand data found there with a total-cost function characterized by increasing marginal cost. The demand curves given for the hotel example were the following:

$$\text{General market } P_g = 140 - 0.1R_g$$

and

$$\text{Convention market } P_c = 120 - 0.05R_c.$$

P_g and P_c are the prices charged in the two markets, respectively, while the R terms denote the quantity of rooms demanded in each market per day.

---

[1] This material uses both partial differentiation and the Lagrangian multiplier approach to constrained maximization. It is highly recommended for students who have sufficient mathematical preparation to have been introduced to these techniques in the appendix to Chapter 5.

Whereas the original example was developed with a constant marginal cost of $30 per additional room rented, we will now suppose that the hotel has the following total and marginal cost functions:

$$TC = 18{,}200 + 4R + 0.02R^2$$

and

$$MC = 4 + 0.04R.$$

In these two expressions, R is the number of rooms rented in *both* markets. From the example in the chapter, it might appear that profit could be maximized by just setting the above MC equal to the marginal revenue equation for each market. However, this will not yield the correct answer, since the renting of an additional room in *one* of the two markets changes the marginal cost of the next room rented in *either* market.

SOLUTION PROCEDURE IF DISCRIMINATION IS PERMITTED

The usual approach to solving the price discrimination problem when marginal cost is variable is to set up a profit function where both revenue and cost depend on two independent variables, the quantities sold in each market. From the demand equations, it follows that the total revenue function for sales in both markets is

$$TR = 140R_g - 0.1R_g^2 + 120R_c - 0.05R_c^2.$$

The profit function results when the total-cost function stated earlier is subtracted from this total revenue equation. However, we restate the "R" term in the cost function as $(R_g + R_c)$:

$$T\pi = 140R_g - 0.1R_g^2 + 120R_c - 0.05R_c^2 - 18{,}200 - 4R_g - 4R_c$$
$$- 0.02R_g^2 - 0.04R_gR_c - 0.02R_c^2,$$

or, collecting terms,

$$T\pi = 136R_g - 0.12R_g^2 + 116R_c - 0.07R_c^2 - 0.04R_gR_c - 18{,}200.$$

To solve for the profit-maximizing quantities of R_g and R_c, we now take the two partial derivatives of the profit function and set each equal to zero. This will satisfy the necessary conditions for a maximum:[2]

---

[2] We will deal only with first-order conditions here. Second-order conditions are discussed in the mathematical appendix at the end of the book.

$$\frac{\partial \pi}{\partial R_g} = 136 - 0.24R_g - 0.04R_c = 0,$$

and

$$\frac{\partial \pi}{\partial R_c} = 116 - 0.04R_g - 0.14R_c = 0.$$

These two partials can be solved easily by multiplying the second equation by –6 and adding it to the first, an operation that yields

$$-560 + 0.80R_c = 0,$$
$$R_c = 700,$$

and substituting 700 for R_c in either partial,

$$R_g = 450.$$

Thus the hotel should rent 1,150 rooms, 700 in the convention market and 450 in the general market. From the demand equations for each market, it follows that the prices will be

$$P_g = 140 - 0.1(450) = \$95,$$

and

$$P_c = 120 - 0.05(700) = \$85.$$

The total daily profit of the hotel with price discrimination will be

$$95(450) + 85(700) - 18,200 - 4(1,150) - 0.02(1,150)^2 = \$53,000.$$

No other combination of prices and quantities sold in the two markets will yield a higher profit.

SOLUTION PROCEDURE IF DISCRIMINATION IS NOT PERMITTED

Using calculus, it is possible also to show that profit with price discrimination is greater than it would be if the firm were to charge a uniform price in both markets. In effect, this is a constrained maximization problem where the constraint is that the price in one of the two markets must be equal to that in the other. For the preceding case, this would mean that $P_g = P_c$, or

$$140 - 0.1R_g = 120 - 0.05R_c,$$

which can be rewritten as

$$20 - 0.1R_g + 0.05R_c = 0.$$

To solve for the quantities that will maximize profit subject to this constraint, we form the Lagrangian function as follows.

$$L\pi = 136R_g - 0.12R_g^2 + 116R_c - 0.07R_c^2 - 0.04R_gR_c - 18{,}200$$

$$+ \lambda(20 - 0.1R_g + 0.05R_c).$$

To solve for the profit-maximizing quantities of R_g and R_c, we now take three partial derivatives of the Lagrangian function and set each equal to zero. This will satisfy the necessary conditions for a maximum:

$$\frac{\partial L\pi}{\partial R_g} = 136 - 0.24R_g - 0.04R_c - 0.1\lambda = 0,$$

$$\frac{\partial L\pi}{\partial R_c} = 116 - 0.04R_g - 0.14R_c + 0.05\lambda = 0,$$

and

$$\frac{\partial L\pi}{\partial \lambda} = 20 - 0.1R_g + 0.05R_c = 0.$$

The Lagrangian multiplier, λ, can be eliminated from the first two expressions by multiplying the second equation by 2 and adding it to the first one. This yields the following:

$$368 - 0.32R_g - 0.32R_c = 0.$$

Finally, R_g, can be eliminated by multiplying the partial derivative with respect to λ by –3.2 and adding it to the preceding expression. This results in

$$304 = 0.48R_c$$

and

$$R_c = 633.33.$$

Substituting the preceding value of R_c into the constraint equation, we find that $R_g = 516.67$. Thus, to the nearest room, the profit-maximizing quantities are 633 rooms in the convention market and 517 rooms in the general market.

If this answer is correct, we should expect to find that the room rate charged is the same for both markets. To demonstrate this, we return to the unrounded values of R_g and R_c. From the demand curve equations initially given,

$$P_g = 140 - 0.1(516.67) = \$88.33$$

and

$$P_c = 120 - 0.05(633.33) = \$88.33.$$

Thus the room rate should be set at \$88.33. Note that this price is between the two prices that were charged with discrimination and that quantity has increased in the general market but decreased in the convention market. However, the total quantity of rooms rented is still 1,150 per day. Quantity will always be the same as under discrimination, since what happens when discrimination takes place is that rooms with low marginal revenue (general market) are switched for rooms with higher marginal revenue (convention market) until both of the marginal revenues are equal to marginal cost.

As we stated earlier, profit will be less with a uniform price than it was with discrimination. Recall that with discrimination, profit was calculated to be \$53,000. Without discrimination, it is

$$\$88.33(1,150) - 18,200 - 4(1,150) - 0.02(1,150)^2$$

$$= 101,579.50 - 49,250 = \$52,329.50.$$

Thus the hotel makes \$670.50 per day more with price discrimination than without. Note that total cost is the same in either case, but that price discrimination increases total revenue. This will always be the case.

PROBLEM

Trenchwich Corporation manufactures power trenching machines in the United States. It also sells them in the international market. The company spends a lot of money on lobbying and has been successful in obtaining a high tariff on competing foreign output. The annual domestic demand for its product is given by

$$Q_{us} = 30,000 - 2P_{us}.$$

Annual foreign demand for the same machine is given by the equation

$$Q_f = 50,000 - 4P_f.$$

Trenchwich's total-cost function is

$$TC = 200,000 + 2,000Q + 0.5Q^2.$$

a. Assuming the firm practices price discrimination, what will be its price per unit in each of the two markets, and how many machines will it sell in each market?

b. Calculate the firm's total profit under the preceding conditions.

c. Find the firm's profit-maximizing price, sales quantity in each market, and total profit under the assumption that it does not discriminate in pricing.

INTERNATIONAL CAPSULE II

•———————•

Markets and Pricing Strategy in International Trade

As Chapters 8 through 11 have shown, an important problem facing the firm is the *structure* of the market or markets in which it sells its product. By this we mean the nature of both consumer demand and competition from other firms. Although we cannot cover all of the possible market structures encountered in international trade in this brief capsule, a number of the situations discussed here are frequently faced by firms that deal outside their own national boundaries, and an introductory review of them will provide some food for thought regarding both the opportunities and difficulties associated with pricing strategies in world markets. We will begin with a strategy that is frequently employed by firms, that of market segmentation.

MARKET SEGMENTATION IN INTERNATIONAL TRADE

Chapter 11 showed that firms often have opportunities to employ price discrimination or market segmentation to increase their sales revenues from markets that are physically separated and characterized by different elasticities of demand. Of course, this concept carries over to the international market, as does another important maxim, the rule that it pays to sell incremental output as long as the price of that output exceeds its average variable cost.

Low-Priced Foreign Sales

Any firm that sells both at home and in a foreign market must make some determination regarding whether to charge different prices in the two outlets. How can it make the choice?

Our discussions of the determinants of demand (Chapter 2) and the impact of various market structures (Chapters 8 and 9) lead to the conclusion that the price elasticity of demand for any product is likely to be greater the larger the number of substitute goods available. Thus, if a firm sells in a largely unfettered world market where there are many substitute products, it may well maximize profit by selling at a *lower* price in the international market than at home. For many products, the world market is vastly larger and more competitive than any one country's internal market. Therefore the foreign elasticity of demand may be the greater of the two. As the hotel pricing example in Chapter 11 showed, in the case of two-market price discrimination, profit maximization dictates that the market with the higher elasticity of demand be the one that will be charged the lower price.

There are other reasons a firm may choose to sell outside its national boundaries at a price below that charged domestic consumers. First, as noted earlier, in incremental analysis it is argued that incremental sales add to profit as long as price exceeds average variable cost. A firm that has already covered all of its fixed costs from profit contribution on home country sales would be rational to sell outside the country at *any* price that is above its average variable cost. When foreign sales are viewed strictly as an incremental decision, the firm may choose to sell in the foreign market at prices that are so far below the home price that they *appear* to be unprofitable. However, such sales likely are actually adding to profit, as Figure II-1 shows. Here it is assumed that the world market is perfectly competitive with a prevailing price of P_w, that marginal cost is rising in straight-line fashion, that $P_w > AVC$ at E_f, and that the home market is insulated from foreign sellers (perhaps by a nontariff barrier). In panel (a), the firm maximizes profit on home country sales at the output where $MC = MR_h$ and charges price P_h to domestic consumers. However, in panel (b) it sells an additional amount, $0Q_w$, to foreign purchasers at the world market price. The addition to its profit from the foreign sales is triangle $P_w ZE_f$, which measures the difference between MR and MC on the $0Q_w$ units sold. (Note that this is a price discrimination problem that differs from those discussed in Chapter 11 in that the firm itself sets only one of the two prices, and the firm has not obtained the maximum possible profit, since $MR_w > MR_h$ at Q_h. Thus the firm would be better off to switch output from home to foreign sales until it reaches a combination where $MR_h = MR_w$.)

Thus far we have seen that both price discrimination and incremental analysis support the possibility that a firm might charge a lower price internationally than at home for the same product. There is another reason,

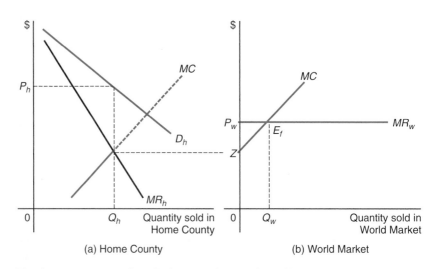

FIGURE II-1

One Rationale for a Low Foreign Price

(a) Home County

(b) World Market

This firm maximizes profit in the home market and then sells an additional amount, $0Q_w$, in the world market until $MC = MR_w$. While this strategy adds to profit, the firm is not maximizing profit since $MR_w > MR_h$. To maximize profit, it must sell less at home and more in the world market.

also related to the discussion of Chapter 11, that could account for selling at a low price to foreign purchasers. Suppose a firm produces two joint products. If there is limited domestic demand for one of them, foreign sales might provide an outlet that is cheaper than paying for disposal of unwanted product at home. In fact, if a firm bases its production quantity of two joint products strictly on the domestic demand for them, and one product is produced in excess quantity, it will be rational to sell an amount in the foreign market equal to the excess *plus* any amount of domestic sales for which domestic marginal revenue is below foreign marginal revenue. Here again, there may be a strong incentive to sell outside the home market at a very low price.

High-Priced Foreign Sales

While we have emphasized foreign market prices that are below home market prices, we should realize that firms also have opportunities to maximize profit by charging *higher* prices in the foreign market than at home. After all, price discrimination just says that the higher price should be charged where demand is less elastic; it does not say home demand is always less elastic than foreign. What kinds of situations might conform to a lower foreign demand elasticity than at home? Again, our earlier observation about market size gives a hint. If the foreign market is small in comparison with the home market, it may pay to charge a higher price on foreign sales. This may be the case for luxury goods that are in common use in the market of a highly developed country such as the United States but would be purchased by only a small proportion of consumers in many less-developed countries. Keeping in mind that demand is a "willing and able" concept, we note that in some countries

many consumers are willing but *not* many are able to buy certain types of goods. Within the markets of those countries, goods exported from the industrialized countries may command very high prices, and the demand of the small consuming group for such goods will likely be less elastic than that found in the industrialized countries. In addition, less developed countries are characterized by both limited and uncertain domestic production of many types of manufactured goods, and these characteristics on the supply side of such markets can also lead to higher prices than those found elsewhere.

THE PROBLEM OF DUMPING

The term "dumping" has a very specific meaning in international trade. It refers to the practice of selling in a foreign market at a price that is lower than the home market price.[1] Since we have seen that there are a good number of reasons for a firm to charge foreigners a low price, it should be no surprise that dumping often occurs. In some cases, the main result of dumping is just that some consumers get a bargain price on foreign goods. However, there are laws regulating dumping that can cause serious difficulties for a firm, particularly if its managers are unaware of how a foreign government may react. If consumers in the country where goods are dumped get them at bargain prices, what is the issue? The problem is that producers in the same country may

---

[1] Some of the laws that regulate dumping state that it occurs when the foreign price is below the home cost of production. These laws usually are difficult to administer, since precise data on home cost are not easily obtained and definitions of cost vary. Note that if the definition of cost is average variable cost, a firm that is dumping is doing so for negative incremental profit.

view dumping as a form of unfair competition. After all, to remain in business they must generate sufficient revenues to cover both variable and fixed costs. The firm that is dumping in a foreign market probably has already covered its fixed costs from home sales and, as we have already noted, can sell profitably to foreigners at any price above average variable cost.

To keep foreign firms from damaging domestic firms through dumping, national governments have enacted antidumping laws that may deal rather harshly with foreign firms. The United States has one of the most actively used antidumping laws in the world—the Antidumping Act of 1921. Under this act, as modified by later legislation, the U.S. Treasury Department is required to initiate an investigation whenever a U. S. firm or group of firms files a complaint alleging that it is being "injured" by competition from foreign goods dumped in the U.S. market. If Treasury investigators do find dumping, the next step is hearings before the United States International Trade Commission (ITC), which must make a determination regarding the question of injury. In the event the ITC does find injury, antidumping duties may be assessed against the U.S. firms that *purchased* the dumped merchandise, and the foreign exporters' shipments may be subject to surveillance for several years. Although antidumping duties may be substantial, in many cases the litigation costs of defending an antidumping charge far exceed the penalties.[2]

A U.S. firm that exports its goods to a foreign country may find that it faces a similar situation to that faced by foreign firms that dump in the United States. Dumping in the foreign market could not only disrupt its export activities but also lead to substantial foreign legal expenses.[3]

WEBB-POMERENE AND EXPORT TRADING COMPANIES

In 1918, largely as a response to German cartels that were set up before World War I, the U.S. Congress passed the Webb-Pomerene Act, which allows U.S. firms to form export trade associations to market their products abroad. In effect, it permits for export trade purposes a number of practices—such as price fixing and division of markets—that in domestic trade are in violation of the antitrust laws (see Chapter 16). What this means for U.S. firms is that they need not compete in the international market and have the alternative of taking a cartel approach to pricing and division of markets in foreign trade.

Historically, the U.S. export trade associations have been most important in certain natural-resource-based industries such as

---

[2] New provisions against dumping are also included in the Uruguay Round of negotiations of the General Agreement on Tariffs and Trade accord. See "Trade Pact Is Set by 117 Nations, Slashing Tariffs, Subsidies Globally," *The Wall Street Journal*, December 16, 1993, pp. A3, A13; and other articles in that same issue on pages A12–A13.

[3] We should note also that in the United States the antidumping law has sometimes served as a nontariff trade barrier. By this we mean that U.S. firms that are *not* in danger of significant injury from imports file antidumping complaints simply to discourage foreign competition of any kind. Part of the job of the International Trade Commission is to fend off groundless complaints so that the U.S. market will not be unduly restricted. Antitrust authorities from the Federal Trade Commission frequently attend the ITC hearings and give testimony when they believe a U.S. industry is using the antidumping law as a market weapon to restrict competition.

minerals and forest products. The associations have had a checkered past, since they have at times engaged in anticompetitive practices that may have had an adverse impact on the domestic market in the United States as well as on foreign markets. For example, in the 1930s the Sulphur Export Corporation suppressed a newly discovered Norwegian process for sulphur production by purchasing a patent to ensure that no one outside Norway would ever be able to employ it without their consent.[4] Further, throughout the Great Depression, U.S. domestic prices of sulphur were quite stable and differed from the export price by only $2 per ton. In the 1960s the Phosphate Export Corporation sold phosphate rock to Korea for an export price substantially above the U.S. domestic price. It was later discovered that the phosphate was purchased with U.S. aid money and that the U.S. government (and its taxpayers) had been charged the foreign price.

Despite the less than satisfactory results of the Webb-Pomerene Act, there has been much interest in the establishment and promotion of new U.S. export trading companies. The reason for this development is the great success of Japanese export trading companies in world markets. These companies have specialized in representing broadly based consortia of corporations, in league with banking interests, to market a very large number of different products. In 1982, the U.S. Congress passed the Export Trading Companies Act (PL 97-290), which amended the Webb-Pomerene Act and provided for active government promotion of export trading companies. The new law allowed a variety of financial institutions to invest in export trading companies and authorized the Export-Import Bank (a government institution) to provide loan guarantees to trading companies. With regard to the antitrust laws, it clarified the position of U.S. firms that formed trading companies and set up a certification procedure for establishing limited antitrust immunity.

Although there has not been a rush to take advantage of the new law, the apparatus is now in place to allow U.S. firms to harmonize their international pricing through the trading company approach. This could have far-reaching consequences in the future.

THE EFFECTS OF TRADE RESTRICTIONS ON PRICES

As indicated in our first international capsule, tariffs and other trade restrictions may be important considerations affecting a firm's prospects for selling abroad. Clearly, if the tariff wall surrounding a given foreign market is so high as to be totally prohibitive, export sales to that market will not be possible. However, we should ask what happens when a new tariff that is not prohibitive is levied on an export product of a firm. In general, economic theory shows that the foreign market price will rise by *less* than the amount of the tariff if the foreign supply elasticity is not infinite. In other words, if the country imposing the tariff is large enough that its purchases will impact the world market price, its domestic price will rise by less than the amount of the tariff. This happens because there is a drop in the quantity of foreign goods purchased after imposition of the tariff, which means sellers will move down their supply curves and thereby absorb some of the tariff in a lower supply price.

We can illustrate this for a two-country case as follows. Suppose the exporting

---

[4] U.S. Federal Trade Commission, *Report of the Federal Trade Commission on the Sulphur Industry and International Cartels* (Washington, D.C., 1947), p. 56.

industry is in the United States and the amount its producers are willing to supply abroad is represented by the export supply curve SX_{US} in Figure II-2. S is the supply curve of producers in the foreign country, and SS is the horizontal sum of the two supply curves. SS is the curve that will define equilibrium in the country's internal market when both imported and internally produced output are available. Imposition of a per-unit import tariff equal to t will shift SS to SS' and move the importing country's equilibrium point from E to E', raising its internal price from P to P'. However, note that the amount of the price increase is less than t, since t is the vertical distance between the old supply curve and the new one and is larger than $(P' - P)$. Thus the price U.S. producers receive for their exports will fall (to level P_S on the supply curve). Any U.S. firm

that is exporting this product can expect to sell less *and* realize a lower price after the tariff is imposed.

Of course, import tariffs are not the only type of trade restriction that may affect prices or sales volume in foreign markets. Import quotas and other types of quantitative restrictions will have similar effects. This is true because any reduction in quantity of exports sold will be accompanied by a fall in price if the supply curve of those exports is upward sloping. While the type of analysis we have been employing here does not give an exporting firm a way to predict *when* trade restrictions will be imposed, it does help to show what the effects of such restrictions will be when and if they are imposed. Given that trade restrictions are a fact of life in many foreign markets (particularly in less-developed countries, where they are used to

FIGURE II-2

Price Effect of a Per-Unit Import Tariff

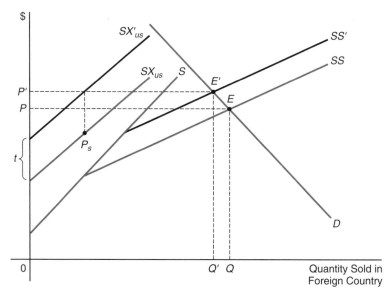

Imposition of a per-unit tariff equal to t (the vertical distance between SX_{us} and SX'_{us}) causes price to rise to P' in the foreign country, while quantity sold falls. The price increase $(P' - P)$ is less than the amount of the tariff. The price received by producers after the tariff is shown by P_s.

promote industrialization), it is useful to have some idea of how to analyze their impact on a firm's exports and the prices it receives for them.

INTERNATIONAL TRANSFER PRICING

Our final topic in this brief survey is transfer pricing, a subject that is significantly more complicated in the international marketplace than in a single country. As Chapter 11 showed, the optimal transfer price within divisions of a firm that do not trade across international boundaries is argued to be a price equal to the marginal cost of the transfer product. While a situation *could* exist in international trade where a transfer product is exchanged between two units of the same firm at a price equal to its marginal cost, a number of factors make this unlikely.

When products are transferred internationally, they move from one country with one set of laws, regulations, tax codes, and financial institutions to another country with different laws, regulations, taxes and financial institutions. Thus the transfer prices may be employed as a device to obtain a wide variety of results, given the objectives of the firm. For example, suppose a firm in the U.S. has a subsidiary in a developing country where the tax rate on corporate income is 20 percent. Suppose the U.S. corporate tax rate is higher, say 40 percent. In this case the firm can benefit in terms of total profit after taxes by establishing a high transfer price for goods shipped from the subsidiary to the U.S. parent company. The following table provides hypothetical data for such a case.

In the table, note that the total revenue of the subsidiary from selling to the parent appears as cost of goods sold on the income statement of the parent. Since the amount

International Transfer Pricing Example with Differences in Taxation of Corporate Income (million dollars)

Low Transfer Price	Foreign Subsidiary	U.S. Parent	After-Tax Income Subsidiary + Parent
Total Revenue	2,000 ┄┄┄	3,800	
Cost of Goods Sold	1,200 ┄┄┄►	2,000	
Other Costs	300	400	
Earnings Before Taxes	500	1,400	
Taxes (20%/40%)	100	560	
After-Tax Income	400	840	**1,240**

High Transfer Price	Foreign Subsidiary	U.S. Parent	After-Tax Income Subsidiary + Parent
Total Revenue	3,000 ┄┄┄	3,800	
Cost of Goods Sold	1,200 ┄┄┄►	3,000	
Other Costs	300	400	
Earnings Before Taxes	1,500	400	
Taxes (20%/40%)	300	160	
After-Tax Income	1,200	240	**1,440**

paid for the transferred goods is a cost to the parent, the high transfer price policy reduces before-tax income of the parent but increases it for the subsidiary. Total after-tax income of the two-unit firm is $200 million higher with the high transfer price than with the low one.

While the high transfer price strategy seems attractive from the standpoint of the firm's total tax bill, if remittances of profits from the subsidiary to the parent are restricted by regulations of the subsidiary's host government, the firm may choose to charge a low transfer price and and put up with higher total taxes in order to shift profits out of the host country.[5] Our example

assumed that the U.S. parent did not have to pay import tariffs on the goods shipped from the subsidiary. It would be further complicated if tariffs were a consideration.[6] Finally, firms sometimes use transfer pricing to "dress up" financial statements, and this, too could lead to results different than that predicted by either standard economic analysis or the impacts of income taxes or tariffs.

[5] It is not surprising that many countries have enacted laws regulating transfer pricing in an attempt to thwart such activity.

[6] For discussion of this and other transfer pricing issues, see Alan C. Shapiro, *Multinational Financial Management*, New York: John Wiley and Sons, 1999, Chapter 14, or Kirt C. Butler, *Multinational Finance*, Cincinnati: South-Western College Publishing, 2000, Chapter 8.

QUESTIONS AND PROBLEMS

1. Explain how each of the following strategies discussed in earlier chapters is related to pricing problems firms frequently encounter in international trade.

   a. Incremental profit analysis

   b. Price discrimination

   c. Pricing of joint products

2. Discuss the problem of dumping in international trade. Under what circumstances might a firm be likely to have legal problems if it dumped in a foreign market?

3. What is an export trading company? How is it related to recent U.S. interest in more permissive laws regulating business?

4. Suppose a firm sells in only two markets, its home market and one foreign market. Its total

cost function is $TC = 200,000 + 120Q$. Suppose its home demand curve has the equation $Q_h = 10,000 - 20P_h$ and the foreign market demand curve has the equation $Q_f = 7,500 - 12.5P_f$.

   a. Will the prices in the two markets be the same, assuming no trade barriers in the foreign market? Explain, and calculate the price(s) the firm will charge as well as its profit from sales in the two markets.

   b. If the importing country imposes an import tariff of $10 per unit, what price will be charged in that country after the tariff? Calculate the firm's profit after the tariff.

5. How does transfer pricing in international business differ from that in firms that do not operate across national boundaries?

SELECTED REFERENCES

Cateora, Phillip R., and John Graham. *International Marketing.* 11th ed. Boston: Irwin McGraw-Hill, 2001, especially Chapter 18.

"EEC Acts on Japanese Dumping," *Business Europe* (January 25, 1985), p. 31.

Eun, Cheol S., and Bruce G. Resnick. 2nd ed. *International Financial Management,* Boston: Irwin McGraw-Hill, 2000.

Exporter's Encyclopedia. Dunn & Bradstreet, Inc., New York (annual).

Salvatore, Dominick. *International Economics,* 7th ed. New York: John Wiley and Sons, 2001.

CHAPTER TWELVE

Factor Markets and Profit-Maximizing Employment of Variable Inputs

As the new millennium dawned, the U.S. economy marked a record—the longest expansion in its history. By January 2000, the unemployment rate was down to 4 percent (a 30-year low), indicating that almost everyone who seriously wanted a job was employed. However, labor shortages had become troublesome in a number of sectors of the economy, and the long boom had also led to materials shortages in construction (drywall, bricks, insulation, lumber) and other industries.[1] Information technology specialists were acutely scarce as electronic commerce and increased business reliance on computer information systems grew faster than the supply of professionals seeking work in the field. Some of the steps taken by firms to attract and retain these workers included signing bonuses, accelerated reviews for salary increases, and implementation of profit-sharing plans.[2] Even industries like food service that employ low-skilled workers were finding that attracting and keeping personnel required higher wages, better working conditions, and more benefits.[3]

---

[1] "Economy Continues Torrid Pace—Fed Survey Shows Inflation in Check, Tight Labor Market," *Wall Street Journal,* January 20, 2000, p. A2, and "Materials Scarce, Price Hikes Abound," *Professional Builder* (August 1999): 15–18.

[2] "Stretched to the Limit," *InformationWeek,* December 20–27, 1999, pp. 22–24.

[3] "The Millennium: A Foodservice Odyssey—Labor," *Nations Restaurant News,* September 14, 1998, pp. 134–40.

The recession of 2001, as well as the aftermath of the 9/11 terrorist attacks and the corporate scandals of 2001–2002, led to layoffs and higher unemployment rates. However, low interest rates fueled a boom in construction, and labor shortages persisted in that sector of the economy. In addition, with the aging of the population in the United States and in other industrialized countries, shortages of essential workers were being predicted in many other sectors.[4]

The shortages and price increases associated with the 1990s–2000 boom and those anticipated for the near future contrast sharply with the economic milieu of the early 1980s, when workers in major industries such as automobile manufacturing were willing to accept wage cuts to save their jobs. A common thread in these economic changes, however, is that they require firms to make adjustments in the employment of inputs in order to maintain or increase profits, or even minimize losses. The procedure for determining a least cost combination of inputs was examined in Chapter 5. However, the question of how input *prices* are determined was deferred, and that chapter discussed only briefly how a firm can identify the profit-maximizing level of employment of a short-run variable input. These matters will be the central focus of the present chapter.

The firm with a goal of profit maximization wishes to produce at its optimal level of output and to do so at the lowest possible cost, given the market structures within which it operates. To accomplish this goal, managers must make economic judgments with regard to how much of each input to use and, often, corresponding decisions with regard to the prices paid for inputs or for their services. We will begin this chapter with a discussion of how the profit-maximizing quantity of a variable input is determined, and then relate this analysis to the determination of the demand curve for an input and the equilibrium price and quantity of the input.

As we stated in Chapter 5, the least cost combination of inputs L and K associated with a given level of output requires that

$$\frac{MP_L}{P_L} = \frac{MP_K}{P_K}$$

as long as the firm cannot affect P_L and P_K. However, we also stated that in the short run the firm may not be able to achieve the least cost combination of inputs for its optimal level of output because the amounts of some of its inputs may be fixed. The relevant question in such a situation becomes this:

---

[4] "Builders See Labor Shortage on Horizon," *The Salt Lake Tribune,* online, January 17, 2002, www.sltrib.com/2002/jan/0172002/business/ business/htm, September 12, 2002; and "Retirement Trends Foster Global Stagnation," Center for Strategic and International Studies (press release), online, April 5, 2002, www.csis.org/press/pr02_19.htm, September 14, 2002.

How can the firm maximize profits in the short run by utilizing the inputs that are variable?

PROFIT-MAXIMIZING EMPLOYMENT OF ONE VARIABLE INPUT

Consider the plight of a local soda-pop bottler. It has $1 million worth of capital equipment and another $1 million invested in the building and land. The equipment, building, and land are relatively fixed in the short run. The only decisions the firm's management needs to make regarding them are in the nature of long-range planning decisions. What management must determine now is how much labor (of various types) should be employed and what level of output should be produced to maximize profits, given the plant and equipment.

Directly related to the managerial decisions involving the bottler's labor force and level of output will be decisions regarding raw materials and intermediate goods, such as concentrated soda mix, aluminum for cans, and empty bottles. In the real world, the amounts of raw materials and intermediate products could vary widely per unit of output produced (and sold), as workers are more or less careless (and drink more or less of the product) while on the job. However, we will assume for the sake of simplicity that such inputs are used in fixed proportions to the level of output produced. We will also assume that when the firm decides on the level of its labor force and, correspondingly, its level of output, it will have automatically decided on the required amounts of the raw materials and intermediate-good inputs. How does the bottler determine the optimal labor force and level of production in the short run? To some extent, the minimum number of workers necessary to operate the plant will influence its decision. However, the plant could operate and function well with many different quantities of labor above the minimum required. So how is the profit-maximizing quantity determined?

To employ one variable factor of production (labor, in this case) in a manner so that profits will be maximized, the firm should follow the same type of marginal rule as it does with respect to output: *Continue using additional units of the input until the last unit just pays for itself.* (That is, continue employment of additional units of a factor of production until the additional revenue resulting from employment of one more unit of the input is just equal to the amount the input adds to the costs of the firm.) If we (the authors) have done our job well, such a decision rule should seem obvious at this point. We emphasize again that the situation we are considering is one in which the firm has the problem of trying to decide how much of one particular variable input to use, *given* certain fixed inputs and a fixed quantity of raw materials and intermediate goods required for each unit of output.

To phrase our rule—*continue to employ an input until the last unit just pays for itself*—in the language of economists, we state that the firm should continue to employ an input until its marginal revenue product is equal to the input's marginal cost. Thus, the manager of the bottling company should employ labor until the marginal revenue product of the last person hired is just equal to that person's marginal cost—both with respect to some specific time period, of course, such as per hour, day, or week.

We have already defined the marginal revenue product of an input in Chapter 5, but we will do so in greater depth here to ensure that its meaning is understood. The *arc* **marginal revenue product of input L** (MRP_L) is defined as the arc net marginal revenue the firm can obtain by selling an additional unit of output produced by input L multiplied by the number of additional units of output produced per additional unit of input L. (As we stated in Chapter 5, input L's **marginal product,** MP_L, equals $\Delta Q/\Delta L$.) The *arc* **net marginal revenue** *(NMR)* the firm can get from selling one more unit of output produced by input L is the addition to total revenue that the sale of one more unit of output will bring in—or arc marginal revenue of the output $(\Delta TR/\Delta Q)$—*less* the cost of raw materials and the intermediate goods required for each additional unit of output.[5]

$$NMR \equiv MR - MC_M,$$

where MC_M is the marginal cost of raw materials and intermediate goods per unit of output. Obviously, we cannot consider *all* of the additional revenue going to the bottler as a result of the sale of another case of soda produced by the last person hired as being solely the result of that person's efforts, since the firm still had to contribute additional raw materials for the soda and the packaging materials. Thus, if the sale of an additional case of soda would bring in additional revenue of $2 and the additional mix and other materials needed cost $0.50 per case, the arc net marginal revenue, *NMR*, would be equal to $1.50 per case of soda.

We need a little more information, however, to find the arc marginal revenue *product* of input L. The net marginal revenue of input L and its marginal revenue product are usually *not* equal because an additional unit of input L frequently does not produce *exactly* one additional unit of output during the time frame of reference the firm is using. For example, suppose the last worker hired enabled the firm to produce four more cases of soda per hour. The arc marginal revenue product, or the additional revenue per hour that

The **marginal revenue product of input L** is equal to the net marginal revenue of input L multiplied by marginal product of input L: $MRP_L = NMR_L \times MP_L$.

The **marginal product of input L** is the additional output that the firm can produce by adding one more unit of input L: $MP_L = \Delta Q/\Delta L$.

Net marginal revenue is marginal revenue from the sale of a firm's final product *minus* a specific portion of marginal production cost. In determining the optimal amount of a variable input, net marginal revenue is defined as marginal revenue minus marginal cost of components.

---

[5] In calculus terms, the marginal revenue product of input L equals net marginal revenue times the marginal product of L, or

$$MRP_L \equiv NMR \cdot MP_L \equiv \left(\frac{dTR}{dQ} - \frac{d \text{ materials cost}}{dQ} \right) \cdot \frac{\partial Q}{\partial L}.$$

the worker would bring in for the firm, would be the net marginal revenue of $1.50 per case *multiplied by* the four cases per hour added to production, or $6.00. Thus, in this case,

$$MRP_L \equiv MP_L \times NMR = 4 \times \$1.50 \equiv \$6.00.$$

At last we are in a position to restate our profit-maximizing rule for employing input L: Employ input L until its arc marginal revenue product equals its marginal cost, or until

$$MRP_L (\equiv NMR \times MP_L) = MC_L.$$

MC_L is the change in a firm's total costs as a result of using another unit of input L.[6]

The marginal cost of an input is the increase in the firm's total cost from employing one more unit of the input $MC_L = (\Delta TC / \Delta L)$. If the price of an input is constant, the marginal cost of the input is equal to its price.

If the price of input L is *constant*, the **marginal cost of an input** is equal to its price. In our soda-pop bottling company example, if the marginal revenue product of the *last* person hired was $6.00 per hour and the additional worker *cost* the firm $6.00 per hour, the bottler would maximize profit by holding its employment of labor at that level. If the worker cost the firm $7.00 per hour, that person should be let go (a gentle phrase for "fired"). If the worker cost the firm only $5.00, the firm manager should consider hiring another worker, as the additional worker might bring in additional profit after all additional costs were subtracted from additional revenue. (In this case, the last person hired would have added $1 per hour to the total profit of the firm.)

Unfortunately, the process of finding the optimal amount of an input is usually a bit more complicated in the real world than we have made it appear up to this point. One reason is that the marginal product of an input usually does not stay constant as more units of the input are added (remember the law of diminishing returns). A second reason is that marginal revenue may also change—usually in a downward direction, since many firms have to lower price to sell larger quantities of output.

Moreover, once we acknowledge the fact that the marginal product of an input may first increase and then decrease, we must recognize the possibility that the *MRP* of an input may also first rise and then fall. In this case we must add another condition to our **profit-maximizing rule for employing a variable input:**

The profit-maximizing rule for employing a variable input, say input L, is to employ that input until its marginal revenue product is equal to the marginal cost of the input; that is, to where $MRP_L = MC_L$, and at higher levels of output $MRP_L < MC_L$.

> Employ the input up to the point where its *MRP* is equal to its marginal cost, *as long as the marginal cost of the input would be at least equal to or above the MRP of the input for a greater quantity of the input.*

Thus, if the last soda-pop bottler hired had an *MRP* of $6.00 and a marginal cost of $6.00, but the *next* person to be hired would have an *MRP* of $7.00

---

[6] This decision rule is mathematically derived in Appendix 12, found at the end of this chapter.

NUMERICAL EXAMPLE

Profit-Maximizing Input Use

Complete the following table and find the profit-maximizing level of use of input L. Assume that L is the only variable input, that its price (P_L) is \$110 per unit, that there are no components costs, and that total fixed cost *(TFC)* is \$350.

Arc MP_L	L	Q	P	TR	Arc MR	Arc MRP_L
	0	0	22	0		
10					20	200
	2		20	400		
					14	
	4	60	16	960		
15					7	
	6	90	13	1,170		
					2	
	8	110	11	1,210		
6					0.8	4.80
	10		10	1,220		

Answer

The missing MP_L values are 20 and 10, each obtained by calculating $\Delta Q / \Delta L$. The missing Q values are 20 and 122, each obtained by multiplying the relevant MP by ΔL and adding on the ΔQ to the preceding Q value. The missing MRP_L values are 280, 105, and 20, each calculated as $MR(MP_L)$.

Profit is maximized where $P_L = MRP_L$ but for an increase in L, $P_L > MRP_L$. This occurs at $L = 4$, since increasing L to 6 would result in $P_L = 110$, but $MRP_L = 105$. Profit is $TR - TC = 960 - L(P_L) - TFC = \$960 - 440 - 350 = \underline{\$170}$.

and a marginal cost also of \$6.00, then the firm should continue to hire workers until there were no further opportunities to hire a worker whose *MRP* was above marginal cost. This is another way of saying one should employ the input until the last unit just pays for itself, but additional units of the input will cost more than the additional revenue they would bring to the firm.

For example, in Table 12-1 we give revenue and labor productivity data for the manufacturer of a black-and-white portable television. Arc marginal revenue is obtained by finding $\Delta TR / \Delta Q$, and *NMR* is obtained by subtracting the \$20 components cost from *MR* at each level of output. The marginal product of labor is obtained by finding $\Delta Q / \Delta L$. The MRP_L is then found by multiplying *NMR* by MP_L. If the wage rate is fixed at \$9.00, then the price of

Table 12-1 *Revenue, Labor Productivity, and Cost Data for a Manufacturer of Black-and-White Televisions*

Quantity Produced per Hour	Price (P)	Total Revenue (TR = P·Q)	Arc Marginal Revenue $\left(MR = \frac{\Delta TR}{\Delta Q}\right)$	Components Cost (per Unit)	Arc Net Marginal Revenue (NMR = MR – Marginal Components Cost)	Quantity of Labor (L)	Arc Marginal Product of Labor $\left(MP_L = \frac{\Delta Q}{\Delta L}\right)$	Arc Marginal Revenue Product of Labor $(MRP_L = NMR \cdot MP_L)$	Hourly Wage Rate	Arc Marginal Cost of Labor $\left(MC_L = \frac{\Delta TC}{\Delta L}\right)$
0	$240	$0		$20		0				
			$230		210		.5	$105.00	$9.00	$9.00
5	230	1,150		20		10			9.00	9.00
			200		180		1.0	180.00		
15	210	3,150		20		20			9.00	9.00
			150		130		1.5	195.00		
30	180	5,400		20		30			9.00	9.00
			100		80		1.0	80.00		
40	160	6,400		20		40			9.00	9.00
			64		44		.8	35.20		
48	144	6,912		20		50			9.00	9.00
			38		18		.5	9.00		
53	134	7,102		20		60			9.00	9.00
			24		4		.2	.80		
55	130	7,150		20		70			9.00	9.00

MANAGERIAL PERSPECTIVE

Profit and Chocolate-Loving Cows

Dairy farmers, just like other people involved in production, must make choices about the inputs they use to produce their product. Naturally, the type of cow they choose is important, since some breeds are better milk producers than others. After that, their main concern related to the cattle themselves is what kind of feed mix to use. This is a very different mix from that employed by farmers raising cattle for beef, rather than feeding them for milk production. Milk prices that processors pay to dairy farmers vary depending on the butterfat content of the milk. So, the farmers must pay close attention to how much fat content the feed mix has and to the prices of inputs that supply the fat. They "fortify" the mix to increase fat in the milk.

In the northeastern United States, producers have found a great source of fat close to their home turf. It is Hershey Corporation, of Hershey, Pennsylvania. Farmers buy broken (therefore rejected) chocolate bars from Hershey and fortify their dairy cattle feed with it. According to Pennsylvania State University (2001), the fat content of the chocolate bars far exceeds that of alternative concentrates that can be fed to the cattle. For example, the proportion of fat in chocolate bars is 48.7 percent. The next closest feed concentrate to that would be *donuts* at 25.6 percent. After that, it's no contest, unless alternative concentrates

have very low prices. "Candy product" (waste candy other than chocolate) only offers 15 percent fat, and shell corn and canola, less than 5 percent.

Some years ago farmers found that chocoholic cows were the way to go. Then, the price of the chocolate bars was $60 per ton. Feeding a cow about 6 pounds per day of the bars mixed with hay and grain raised the fat content of the milk they produced by 0.4 percent. Milk processors would pay an additional 5.12 cents per gallon for the output above the standard price for milk with normal butterfat content. Of course, farmers determine the optimal amount to feed based on the addition to revenue of a pound of chocolate (its marginal revenue product) compared to its addition to cost of production (the input's marginal cost). The determination of the optimal amount of chocolate in the feed mix would also depend on its price, the prices of alternative inputs (donuts, candy, corn, etc.), and the price of milk.

References: Virginia Ishler, John Tyson, and Peter Tozer, "Use of Commodity Ingredients for Dairy Cattle," Publication DAS 01-25, Pennsylvania State University, Department of Dairy and Animal Science, 2001; Randy D. Shaver, "By-Product Feedstuffs in Dairy Cattle Diets in the Upper Midwest," University of Wisconsin, Department of Dairy Science, 1999; and "Now the Question Is: How Do You Get Rid of a Cow's Pimples?" *Wall Street Journal*, June 1, 1988, p. 25.

labor also equals the MC_L. In this case, the firm maximizes profits (assuming labor is the only variable input besides the components) where *output* is between 48 and 53 television sets per hour and the firm's *labor force* is between 50 and 60 people. Between 48 and 53 units of output, the $MRP_L = 9.00 and $MC_L = 9.00. Between 53 and 55 units of output, the $MRP_L = 0.80 and $MC_L = 9.00. Thus, 70 workers would clearly be too many to employ in order to maximize profits, since workers 61 through 70 would each bring in an average of $0.80 net revenue per hour but would each cost $9.00 per hour.

Finally, if more inputs than one are variable, changes in the quantity utilized of one will affect the productivity of the others *if* the inputs are *related,* thereby changing their optimal levels. The resulting changes in those inputs will in turn affect the optimal level of the first input. In this kind of situation, we define related inputs as being either substitutes or complements. Two inputs are *substitutes* if utilizing more of one *decreases* the marginal product of the other. Two inputs are *complements* if utilizing more of one *increases* the marginal product of the other. Two inputs could be substitutes or complements, depending on the situation. For example, a painter's use of a paint sprayer would probably reduce the marginal product of a paint roller. However, a research institution's use of a computer might well increase the marginal product of an employee engaged in research. In the first example, the paint sprayer and the paint roller are substitutes. The paint sprayer might also be a substitute for an additional painter with a brush. In the second example, the computer and the employee are complements. We will leave further consideration of related inputs to a more advanced text. It is sufficient at this point to be aware of the possibility (and probability) of relatedness among inputs and to take that possibility into account when determining the optimal levels of variable factors of production for the firm.

DETERMINATION OF EQUILIBRIUM PRICES FOR INPUTS: PERFECT COMPETITION IN THE INPUT MARKET

In the opening section of this chapter, we concentrated on developing a profit-maximizing decision rule for a business firm to use in employing inputs. There, we assumed that the firm knew what the price—and consequently the marginal cost—of another unit of the input would be. Now we turn to the question of what factors determine the market price of an input. As you might expect from the discussion of the profit-maximizing price and output in the product markets, the *structure* of an input market is an important factor affecting the determination of its price. We consider first the case of perfect competition in the input market.

As in the output market, if *perfect competition* exists in the market for an input, there are many buyers and sellers of that input, and an individual firm considers the price of the *input* to be "given." Since the amount demanded of an input by an individual firm is too small relative to the total market demand and supply of the input to influence its price significantly, the marginal cost of a unit of the input is constant and equal to its price. When we considered the case of a firm *selling its output* in a perfectly competitive market, we said (1) that the firm considered the price it received for its *output* to be given, (2) that the *demand curve* for its product was a horizontal line, and (3) that *output price was equal to marginal revenue.* On the other hand, when a firm is *buying an input* in a perfectly competitive market, it accepts (1) that the input price is given, (2) that the *supply curve* of the input *to the firm* is horizontal, and (3) that the *input price equals the input's marginal cost* (as was the case in the example in Table 12-1).

In this situation, therefore, the firm's profit-maximizing condition for utilizing input L is to employ input L up to the point where the *marginal revenue product of L is equal to its price,* which (as we have just said) is equal to its marginal cost:[7]

$$MRP_L = P_L = MC_L.$$

We need to add one more qualification to this decision rule: the firm should employ input L up to the point where $MRP_L = P_L$ as long as MRP_L is decreasing. Thus, the firm's *demand curve* for input L is given by the portion of the marginal revenue product curve for input L where MRP_L is decreasing. This part of the MRP_L curve is the demand curve for input L because it indicates the quantity of input L the profit-maximizing firm will employ at each price.[8]

---

[7] If the firm also *sells* its *output* in a perfectly competitive market, marginal revenue equals price and *NMR* = price minus marginal materials cost. In this case economists also call MRP_L the *value of the marginal product of L,* or VMP_L.

[8] However, the output price must also be sufficiently high to cover *AVC,* or the firm will at least temporarily shut down. With *more than one variable input,* a change in the amount used of one input, say input L, may affect the *MRP*(s) of the other variable input(s), which will change the profit-maximizing quantity(ies) of the other input(s). A change in the quantity(ies) utilized of that input (those inputs) will cause the MRP_L to shift because the MP_L will change. Whether the MRP_L shifts rightward or leftward will depend on whether input L is being increased or decreased in the first step. For example, if the inputs are substitutes, then the use of more of input L will decrease the marginal product of the other variable input(s) and the quantity used of it (them) will decrease. This decrease, in turn, will cause the MP_L to *increase,* shifting the MRP_L curve to the right. If the inputs are complements, then an increase in the use of input L will increase the marginal product of the other input(s) and the quantity used of it (them) will increase. This increase will also cause the MP_L to *increase,* again shifting the MP_L curve to the right. The demand curve will consist of points where $MRP_L = P_L$, but each point will be on a different *MRP* curve, as shown below:

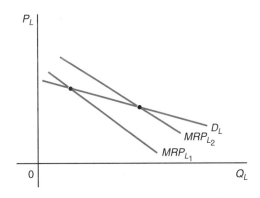

FIGURE 12–1

*Optimal
Employment of
an Input in a
Perfectly
Competitive
Input Market*

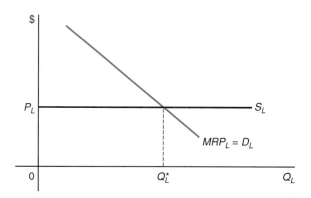

The marginal revenue product curve for input L, MRP_L, is the firm's demand curve for input L.
The supply curve of the input to the firm is a horizontal line, S_L, at the market-determined
price of P_L. The firm will maximize profit by employing Q_L^* units of input L at price P_L.

In Figure 12-1 we have shown the firm's demand curve for input L, the
supply curve for input L, and the profit-maximizing quantity of L (Q_L^*) for
the firm to employ. In the case of the television manufacturer discussed in
the previous section, Q_L is approximately equal to 55 and P_L = \$9.00 (see Fig-
ure 12-2). We say that Q_L is approximately equal to 55 because we are using
arc values for MRP_L, which gives an *average* value for a particular interval
(such as L = 50 to L = 60). We must plot such figures at the midpoint of the
interval.

We now understand the process by which a firm manager determines
how much of an input the firm should employ to maximize its profit, *given
the price of the input.* However, how is the price of the input determined? The

FIGURE 12–2

*Demand and
Supply Curves
of Labor for a
Television
Manufacturer*

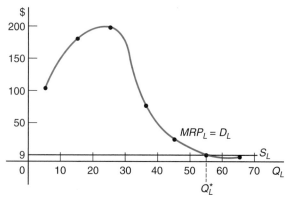

In this case, the supply curve of workers to a television manufacturer is a horizontal line at \$9
per hour. The firm will employ workers up to the point where the MRP_L = \$9, at Q_L^* = 55,
approximately.

FIGURE 12-3

Demand and Supply Curves for Input

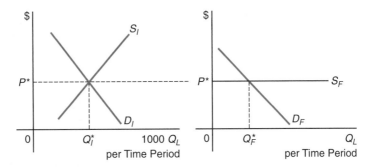

In panel (a) the industry supply and demand curves for input L determine the input's price, P^*, and the total quantity sold of input L, Q_I^*. In panel (b) an individual firm accepts the price of input L, P^*, as given (S_F is horizontal). The firm employs Q_F^* units of input L at a price of P^*, where D_F intersects S_F.

answer is that in perfectly competitive input markets, the input price is determined by the total market demand for and supply of the input. A rough approximation to the *market demand* for the input is obtained by summing the quantity of the input that each firm that utilizes the input will demand at each price.[9] Thus, we obtain the *market demand* curve for an *input* in a perfectly competitive input market much as we determined the market *supply* curve in a perfectly competitive *output* market. The market supply curve of the *input* merely reflects the quantity of the input that will be supplied at each price. We will assume, as is generally realistic, that the market supply curve for an input is upward sloping, which means that more of the input will be supplied at higher prices.

We have drawn the *market* demand and supply curves for input L in Figure 12-3, panel (a), and a *firm's* demand and supply curves for input L in Figure 12-3, panel (b). Note that the horizontal axis of panel (a) is in *thousands* of units per time period, whereas that of panel (b) is in single units per time period. The equilibrium price and total quantity of input L utilized are determined in panel (a) to be P^* and Q_I^*. The individual firm considers P^* to be fixed and employs Q_F^* of input L.

The determination of the price of an input when the market for its services is imperfectly competitive is a little more complicated, as we will now see.

---

[9] This horizontal summation of firm demand curves for inputs is only an approximation to the market demand curve for an input because as all firms in an industry expand, the market price and marginal revenue for a firm's product may fall more than is indicated by an individual firm's demand and marginal revenue curve. For example, the horizontal demand curve of a perfectly competitive firm is drawn under the assumption that only the individual firm is changing its level of output and therefore that price will not be affected. The market demand curve for an input must take into account the effects on the price and marginal revenue of the firm's product caused by factors external to the firm.

DETERMINATION OF EQUILIBRIUM PRICES FOR INPUTS: MONOPSONY IN THE INPUT MARKET

A **monopsony** is a market with one buyer.

Monopsony is the label we attach to a market structure that is characterized by one *buyer* of some particular product or service. In this case, we will use the term *monopsony* to refer to the situation where there is one firm that demands the services of an input. You will recall that we used the term *monopoly* to describe the situation where there is only one firm that *supplies* a product, *oligopoly* where there are a few suppliers of a product, and *monopolistic competition* where there are many suppliers of a differentiated product. In a similar fashion, we also use the terms **oligopsony** to describe the market structure where there are a few *buyers* of a product and **monopsonistic competition** where there are many buyers of a differentiated product. We will discuss only the case of monopsony in the input market in this book, but the profit-maximizing decision rule discussed here applies to oligopsony and monopsonistic competition as well. In this section, we will further assume that the *suppliers* of the input are perfectly competitive in the sense that they do not organize and attempt to affect the price received for the services of the input.

An **oligopsony** is a market with a few buyers, or a few dominant buyers.

A market characterized by **monopsonistic competition** has many buyers of a differentiated product.

In a monopsonistic input market, the firm *buying* the input knows that the price of the input will be determined by the quantity of the input that it purchases. In this case, changes in the quantity of an input demanded by the firm will appreciably affect the input's price because we have assumed that the market supply curve of the input is upward sloping, meaning that a greater quantity of the input will be supplied only at a higher price. Since there is only one *buyer* of that input, changes in the quantity demanded of the input by that buyer will noticeably affect the input's price.

In this situation, the profit-maximizing firm that is utilizing the input will still follow the decision rule stated earlier in this chapter: *Employ the input until its marginal revenue product is equal to its marginal cost.* Unlike the case of perfect competition in the input market, however, for the monopsonistic firm the price of an input is (theoretically, at least) *not* equal to its marginal cost. The marginal cost of another unit of an input is greater than its price because it is assumed that the monopsonistic firm has to pay a higher price to get an additional unit of the input per time period. It is also assumed that if a firm pays a higher price for one more unit of the input, it must pay the same price for *all units* of the input.

Consider the following situation, which the only garage in a small town might face if it wishes to hire another mechanic. The garage has three mechanics currently working for it at $10.00 an hour and can hire a fourth mechanic for $12.00 an hour. If it hires the fourth mechanic for $12.00 an hour, the firm will find that the first three mechanics will be unhappy unless their wage rates are also raised to $12.00 per hour. In fact, their dissatisfaction may cause their productivity to decline unless their salaries are raised. In this case, the marginal cost of the fourth mechanic is $18.00 per hour, which is $12.00 for the fourth mechanic's wage plus $2.00 per hour for each

Table 12–2 *Supply and Marginal Cost Schedules of Mechanics to a Garage*

Number of Mechanics	Hourly Wage Rate	Marginal Cost of Labor (MC_L)
0	$ 4.00	
1	6.00	$ 6.00
2	8.00	10.00
3	10.00	14.00
4	12.00	18.00
5	14.00	22.00

of the other three mechanics. The supply and marginal cost schedules of mechanics to the garage are given in Table 12-2, and the corresponding curves are drawn in Figure 12-4.

The profit-maximizing garage should now follow the decision rule stated at the beginning of this chapter: Employ an input up to the point where its marginal revenue product is equal to its marginal cost. Therefore, the *profit-maximizing rule for employment of a variable input in a monopsonistic input market* is to employ that input until its marginal revenue product is equal to its marginal cost. In this case, the price of the input will be less than its marginal cost.

FIGURE 12–4

Supply and Marginal Cost of Mechanics to a Garage

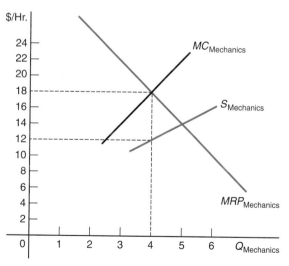

Here, the supply curve of mechanics to a garage is upward sloping, which means that the marginal cost of another mechanic to the firm, given by $MC_{Mechanics}$, also increases as the number of mechanics employed increases. In this case, the firm will employ mechanics up to the point where the $MRP_{Mechanics} = MC_{Mechanics}$, at 4 mechanics and an hourly wage of $12.00.

In Figure 12-4, the *MRP* of mechanics is just equal to the marginal cost of mechanics when the garage hires four mechanics. Note that whereas the marginal cost of the fourth mechanic is $18.00 per hour, all of the mechanics are actually being paid only $12.00 per hour. Since the garage is the only buyer of this input, the number of mechanics it employs to maximize profits will determine both the total number of mechanics employed in this town and their wage rate. Thus, $12.00 per hour is the market wage rate, at least in this limited market for mechanics.

In the next section, we will discuss a third extreme case involving an input market—the situation of bilateral monopoly in which there is only one buyer and *one seller* of an input.

DETERMINATION OF EQUILIBRIUM PRICES FOR INPUTS: BILATERAL MONOPOLY IN THE INPUT MARKET

Bilateral monopoly in the input market means that there is one buyer and one seller of the input.

Bilateral monopoly in the input market means that there is *only one buyer* and *one seller* of an input. Admittedly, we are talking about an extreme case, but bilateral monopoly may more nearly approximate the market structure between "big business" and "big labor" in industries such as automobiles and steel than does any of the other cases we have described.

Since both the seller of the input and the buyer of the input are the sole businesses involved on their respective sides of the market, the *seller* of the input may wish to behave as a monopolist and the *buyer* may wish to behave as a monopsonist. Suppose all of the potential mechanics in the small town in the example earlier in the chapter form a union and bargain as a group with the owner of the garage. In Figure 12-5 we have redrawn Figure 12-4 and added one more curve, which indicates the marginal revenue to the *supplier* from selling another unit of the *input* under the assumption that the buyer could be forced to pay a wage rate equal to the marginal revenue product of the input.

In this situation, the old supply curve of mechanics is now not really their supply curve *if* their union behaves as a profit-maximizing monopolist. It merely indicates what quantities they would be willing to supply at each wage rate *if* they thought they had to accept whatever wage rate the garage offered them *or* not work as mechanics. If their old supply curve in some sense measures their marginal cost of supplying labor, the mechanics will maximize their group profit by selling their services up to the point where the marginal cost *to themselves* of their services is equal to the marginal revenue brought in by those services. At point *A* the marginal revenue brought in by the mechanics' services is just equal to the marginal cost to the mechanics of supplying their services, and the mechanics' union would like to have three people employed at a wage rate of $22.00.

FIGURE 12–5

*A Case of
Bilateral
Monopoly*

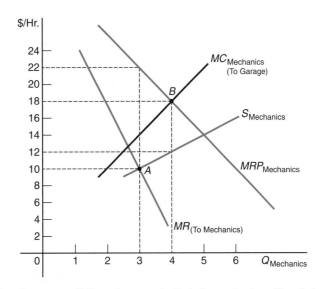

This figure describes a case of bilateral monopoly. Both the mechanics selling their services and the firm buying their services have some monopoly power. As in Figure 12–4, the marginal cost of mechanics increases as the quantity of mechanics employed increases, and $MC_{\text{Mechanics}}$ is above $S_{\text{Mechanics}}$. The marginal revenue to mechanics from selling their services is given by $MR_{(\text{To Mechanics})}$. The firm will wish to employ 4 mechanics at a wage rate of \$12 per hour, where $MRP_{\text{Mechanics}} = MC_{\text{Mechanics}}$. Mechanics will wish to offer their services up to the point where $MR_{\text{Mechanics}} = S_{\text{Mechanics}}$, at an hourly wage of \$22 for 3 workers. The final result will depend on the relative bargaining strength of the firm and of the mechanics.

It would be quite a feat, however, for the mechanics' union to get three people hired at a wage rate of \$22.00 because when a seller gets a buyer to pay the *maximum* price the buyer would be willing to pay for that particular quantity of the product (or input) in question, the buyer usually assumes that any monopsony power previously held has been lost in bargaining for a lower price. Such a case should not occur here. The garage should perceive that it has some monopsonistic power, and it would like (as we indicated in Figure 12-4) to employ four workers at a wage rate of \$12.00. That is because at point *B* the marginal revenue product of mechanics is equal to their marginal cost to the firm, at least if we consider $S_{\text{Mechanics}}$ to be the supply curve of mechanics. In this situation where bilateral monopoly exists, presumably the mechanics and the garage owner will bargain, and the wage rate agreed upon will be somewhere between \$12.00 and \$22.00. The level at which the wage rate is finally established will depend on the relative persuasiveness of the mechanics' union and the garage owner.[10]

---

[10] An alternative theory regarding this situation is based on a joint profit maximization model, which yields a determinate level of employment of the input and a corresponding determinate level of final product output and price. See A. L. Bowley, "Bilateral Monopoly," *The Economic Journal* (December 1928): 651–659; Roger D. Blair, David L. Kaserman, and Richard E. Romano,

(footnote continues)

The Age of Agrimation

Robots in the factory are now an everyday fact of life, but their use in agriculture has been much less prevalent. However, if researchers at a number of universities and countries around the world are successful, the age of agrimation is not far away.

Through automation, the direct labor cost of most items manufactured by mass production methods has been reduced to 5 to 15 percent of their selling price. However, direct labor costs may be as much as 30 percent of the selling price of agricultural products, and proponents of agrimation contend that robots could reduce costs significantly in the production of agricultural goods. Take fruit, for example. These researchers state that a worker hired to harvest fruit could pick approximately 1,000 pieces of fruit per hour during six- to eight-hour working days. However, one-armed robots have already been developed that can pick fruit almost as quickly as a person, and two-armed robots are under consideration. In one laboratory test, a one-armed robot picked 15 oranges per minute, while an experienced human picker picked 20 oranges per minute. French manufacturers have developed an apple-picking robot that technicians believe will be able to pick 30 apples a minute, more than double that of a skilled apple picker. The apple-picking robots handle the fruit far more gently than the old mechanical pickers, which shook the trees or blasted them

with air to force the fruit to fall to the ground, often bruising it in the process. The robots can pay for themselves in three seasons. Also in France, tractor guidance systems have been developed to robotically steer cultivating machinery through grape fields at Chateau Mouton-Rothschild. These machines can put in 24-hour days so that both cultivating and picking can be done on an optimal schedule.

Dairy farms have used milking machines for many decades. However, more recently, in both the Netherlands and Great Britain, "cowbots" have been developed that will feed dairy cows, hook them up to the milking machines, and later clean the equipment. Cowbots have just recently made their way to the United States. Such helpers could save dairy farmers more than four hours each day.

These new technologies force farmers to consider the productivity and cost of human labor compared with that of robots. In turn, farm workers may be forced to consider ways to increase their productivity. Alternatives will be working for lower wages or finding new careers.

References: "Let Your Robot Do the Milking," *USA Today*, online, March 1, 2002, www.usatoday.com/life/cyber/tech/2002/03/01/cows-robots.htm, July 20, 2002; "Robots Take Toil From the Vineyard," *Design News*, August 3, 1998, pp. 68–71; and "Researchers Bring Outer-Space Robotics to the Farm," *Resource*, January 1997, p. 4.

(footnote continued from previous page)

"A Pedagogical Treatment of Bilateral Monopoly," *Southern Economic Journal* 55, No. 4: 831–841; and Dale B. Truett and Lila J. Truett, "Joint Profit Maximization, Negotiation, and the Determinacy of Price in Bilateral Monopoly," *Journal of Economic Education* 24, No. 3: 260–270. The limiting cases of the input price described in the Blair, Kaserman, and Romano model depend, however, on the assumption that the dominant firm can force the other firm to purchase (or sell) a quantity of the input that is not consistent with the usual marginal profit requirements for profit maximization. However, an equilibrium input price would exist at the joint profit-maximizing quantity where the *MRP* of the input is equal to the marginal cost of supplying it.

SUMMARY

Profit Maximization and Employment of Inputs

In this chapter we have discussed the decision rule that a firm must follow in order to determine the *quantity* of a variable input that it should utilize to maximize profit: Employ a variable input, input L, up to the point where $MRP_L = MC_L$. If P_L is constant for all levels of input L employed by the firm, $MC_L = P_L$, and the firm should utilize the input until $MRP_L = P_L$.

We have also discussed input *price* determination under three types of market structures: (1) where both the firms buying the input and the suppliers of the input are perfectly competitive, (2) where there is only one buyer of the input (monopsony) but the suppliers view the market as perfectly competitive, and (3) where there is only *one* buyer and *one* seller of the input (bilateral monopoly). In the case of a perfectly competitive market for an input, the market price and equilibrium quantity are determined by market demand and supply. In the case of a monopsonistic input market, the market price and equilibrium quantity are determined by the quantity of the input utilized by the one buyer of the input. This firm employs an input (for example, input L) until $MRP_L = MC_L$. Finally, in the case of bilateral monopoly, the market price and equilibrium quantity of an input are determined through a bargaining process.

It is fairly easy to find an approximation to a perfectly competitive (buyer and seller) type of market structure for an input—the market for unskilled, nonunion labor in a large metropolitan area is one example. It is somewhat more difficult to find an example of a monopsonistic firm that is faced with quite the situation we described earlier—that is, facing a perfectly competitive market on the supply side for an input. Recall that such a firm was forced to pay a higher price for *all* units of that input that it employed in order to obtain additional units of the variable input. Consider the case of the finance department in a university where the university is the only institution of higher education in a given area. The university will probably find that to get an *additional* finance professor, it may have to pay *that professor* more than the salary paid to comparable professors already working for the institution. However, to the extent that the university has monopsony power in the area in regard to the employment of finance professors, it may not have to *increase* the salaries of the professors it is currently employing but has hired previously. We have observed such a phenomenon first-hand numerous times in academic departments. Only when faculty members who were hired earlier are *willing* and *able* to accept jobs elsewhere in lieu of a raise at their present university must the university also raise the pay of the current employees to correspond to that of the new employee in order to keep the department intact. To have any clout with the university, the current employees must have alternative job opportunities elsewhere that they have convinced the university they are willing to accept—a situation meaning that the firm was not a monopsonist after all. (However, the market for these professors is still imperfectly competitive.) It is illegal to price discriminate purely on the basis of race or sex, but it is not illegal to price discriminate solely on the basis of when someone was hired. To the extent that a firm can do such discriminating with regard to wages paid employees, the marginal cost of another employee will still be that employee's *wage rate,* even though that wage rate is greater than the wage rate of employees hired previously.

Finally, concerning bilateral monopoly, we suggest that in the case of big labor and big business—for example, the UAW and the automakers—our wage-determination model may be somewhat inappropriate to the extent that the labor union involved does not behave as a profit-maximizing monopolist. The union must be concerned about the level of employment of its members, *as well as* their wage rate(s); thus, the assumption that the goal of a union is profit maximization may be neither meaningful nor realistic. The bilateral monopoly model might be realistic in a situation where the U.S. government was purchasing some classified military equipment from a firm that had the sole patent for the product. Even in this situation, however, we would have to assume that the Department of Defense behaved as a profit-maximizing monopsonist.

Still, none of the foregoing comments alters our basic decision rule for a firm interested in employing the profit-maximizing quantity of a variable input: *Employ the input until its marginal revenue product equals its marginal cost.*

QUESTIONS

1. What is meant by the profit-maximizing employment of one variable input?

2. What is the general decision rule for determining the profit-maximizing employment of one variable input?

3. Compare the general decision rule for determining the profit-maximizing employment of one variable input when its price is fixed and when its price is variable.

4. How are the market price and equilibrium quantity of a variable input determined when the input is sold in a perfectly competitive market?

5. How are the market price and equilibrium quantity of a variable input determined when the input is sold in a monopsonistic market?

6. How would your answer to Question 5 change if the input were sold in a market characterized by bilateral monopoly?

7. Compare the decision rule for the least cost combination of inputs and that for profit-maximizing employment of one variable input. What does each tell the firm? How are they different? Under what circumstances should each be used?

PROBLEMS

1. The following table shows worker, quantity of output, and output price information for a sweatshirt manufacturer. The cost of materials used in each sweatshirt is $0.50.

   a. Complete the table below.

Workers per Hour	Quantity Total Product per Hour	Price of Output	Total Revenue	Arc Marginal Revenue	Arc Net Marginal Revenue	Arc Marginal Product of Labor	Arc Marginal Revenue Product of Labor
0	0	$2					
1	10	2					
2	25	2					
3	45	2					
4	60	2					
5	70	2					
6	77	2					
7	81	2					
8	84	2					
9	85	2					

   b. How many sweatshirts should the company produce to maximize profits if the wage rate is $4.50 per hour? Why?

2. Shown in the following table is the relationship between the number of workers per hour and the total product per hour for a tire company. The relationship between output produced per hour and the price at which it can be sold is also given. Assume that the cost of materials in tires is $6.50.

Number of Workers	Quantity Total Product per Hour	Price of Output	Total Revenue	Arc Marginal Revenue	Arc Net Marginal Revenue of Labor	Arc Marginal Product of Labor	Arc Marginal Revenue Product of Labor
0	0	$50.00					
10	200	40.00					
20	300	35.00					
30	350	32.50					
40	380	31.00					
50	400	30.00					
60	410	29.50					

a. Complete the table.

b. If the wage rate is $5 per hour, how many workers should this firm hire to maximize profits? Why?

3. Suppose the workers in Problem 2 organize, form a union, and succeed in bargaining the wage rate up to $9.50 per hour. How many workers should the tire company employ now? Does your answer to this question indicate a reason why a labor union would not necessarily want to bargain for the highest wage rate it might achieve? Why or why not?

4. Wizard, Inc., produces electronic business calculators. Revenue and labor productivity data are given in the following table. The components cost for one calculator is $20. The wage rate is constant and equal to $7.00 per hour.

Price of Output	Number of Calculators per Hour	Quantity of Labor	Total Revenue	Arc Marginal Revenue	Arc Net Marginal Revenue	Arc Marginal Product of Labor	Arc Marginal Revenue Product of Labor
$100.00	0	0					
						1.0	
95.00	10	10					
						2.0	
85.00		20					
						1.5	
77.50		30					
						1.0	
72.50		40					
						.5	
70.00		50					
						.2	
69.00	62	60					

a. Complete the table.

b. How many workers should Wizard employ? Why?

c. How much output per hour should Wizard produce and what price should it charge?

d. What is the marginal cost of a calculator at this point? (You should be able to determine this figure using relationships discussed in Chapter 6.)

5. The bar in a small town is faced with the situation depicted in the table on the following page in regard to revenue per night from the sale of drinks, the number of bartenders working per evening, and the wage rate paid the bartenders. The average cost of ingredients in one drink is $0.50. The average price of one drink varies with the number of customers because more people patronize the bar as more "specials" are offered on various drinks.

a. How many bartenders should this bar employ, and what should be the average price of drinks in order to maximize profit? Why?

b. What is the equilibrium wage rate?

Table for Problem 5

Number of Drinks Sold per Hour	Number of Bartenders	Average Price of One Drink	Total Revenue per Hour	Arc Marginal Revenue	Arc Net Marginal Revenue	Arc Marginal Product of Bartenders	Arc Marginal Revenue Product	Hourly Wage Rate	Arc MC of Bartenders
0	0	$5.00						—	
20	1	4.00						$4.00	
50	2	3.40						5.00	
70	3	3.00						6.00	
85	4	2.70						7.00	
95	5	2.50						7.75	
100	6	2.40						8.50	

6. Vinox Company makes portable copying machines. Demand and labor productivity data per month are given in the table below. The components cost per machine is $200. The average monthly cost of labor is $1,800.

Quantity of Labor	Quantity of Copiers	Price	Total Revenue	Arc Marginal Revenue	Arc NMR	Arc MP_L	Arc MRP_L
0	0	$1,000					
10	100	900					
15	200	800					
25	300	700					
45	400	600					
70	500	500					

a. Complete the table.

b. What is the profit-maximizing number of copiers to be produced monthly, price, and number of workers for Vinox? Why?

c. If Vinox tried to produce and sell 100 more copiers than it does at the profit maximum you identified, what will be the arc marginal cost per copier over this range? Explain how the profit-maximizing number of copiers that you found in part b is consistent with the $MR = MC$ condition for copiers.

7. Rio Grande Fitness Machines, Inc., makes muscle toner exercise machines. Daily production and revenue data and corresponding labor requirements for the machines are given in the following table. The daily cost of one worker is $80. The cost of components for each exercise machine is $30.

Quantity of Labor (L)	Quantity of Machines (Q)	Price of a Machine (P)	Total Revenue (TR)	Marginal Revenue (MR)	Net Marginal Revenue (NMR)	Marginal Product of Labor (MP_L)	Marginal Revenue Product of Labor (MRP_L)
0	0	$200					
10	20	190					
15	40	180					
19	60	170					
24	80	160					
29	100	150					
35	120	140					
43	140	130					
53	160	120					
68	180	110					
88	200	100					

a. Complete the table above.

b. What is the profit-maximizing number of exercise machines for Rio Grande to produce, the corresponding price of an exercise machine, and the quantity of labor to employ? Why?

c. What is the marginal cost of producing another exercise machine at the point found in your answer to part (b)?

The following problems require calculus.

C1. Suppose the total product (per hour) of labor for a restaurant is given by $TP_L = 38L - 2L^2$.

a. Find the MP_L function.

b. How many workers should the restaurant employ if the wage rate is $4, the average price of a meal is $6, and the average cost per meal of the food ingredients is $2? Why?

C2. In Problem C3 of Chapter 5, a firm was said to have the following short-run total product curve:

$$TP_L = Q = 48L + 4L^2 - (1/3)L^3,$$

where labor, L, is the only variable input and TP_L is the total output produced per day. Suppose the firm faces a fixed price of $2 per unit for its output.

a. If the firm must pay a market-determined wage rate of $78 per day for each unit of labor hired, how much labor should it employ?

b. If the firm's daily fixed costs total $250, what will be its total profit per day?

C3. A firm uses a single variable input, L, in its production process.

Its total product function for daily output in the short run is given by the equation

$$Q = 200L - L^2,$$

where L is the number of workers employed per day. The firm sells its output in a perfectly competitive market for $2 per unit.

a. Make a sketch of the firm's labor demand curve.

b. Suppose that labor is bought in a perfectly competitive market and that the going wage is $40 per day. Determine the amount of labor the firm will employ. (Show calculation.)

c. Now suppose the market wage rises to $52. Determine how much labor the firm will employ.

SELECTED REFERENCES

Browning, Edgar K., and Mark A. Zupan. *Microeconomic Theory and Applications*, 6th ed. Reading, MA: Addison-Wesley, 1999, Chapter 15.

Landsberg, Stephen E. *Price Theory and Applications,* 4th ed. Cincinnati: South-Western, 1999, Chapter 15.

Lazear, Edward P. *Personnel Economics for Managers.* New York: John Wiley & Sons, 1997.

Mansfield, Edwin, and Gary Yohe. *Microeconomics: Theory and Applications,* 10th ed. New York: W. W. Norton, 2000, Chapter 14.

Pindyck, Robert S., and Daniel L. Rubinfeld. *Microeconomics,* 5th ed. Upper Saddle River, NJ: Prentice-Hall, 2001, Chapter 14.

Varian, Hal. *Intermediate Microeconomics,* 6th ed. New York: W. W. Norton, 2002, Chapter 26.

Mathematics of Profit-Maximizing Input Use When There Are Materials Costs

Consider a firm that has two variable inputs (K, L) and also has given materials costs per unit of output. Mathematically, it can be shown that the profit-maximizing level of input use occurs where the marginal revenue product of each input equals that input's marginal cost to the firm. First, if $TR = P \cdot Q$, where $P = f(Q)$, the production function is given by $Q = Q(K,L)$, and the total cost is given by $TC = (P_K \cdot K) + (P_L \cdot L)$, then the total profit function is

$$T\pi = [P \cdot Q(K,L)] - (P_K \cdot K) - (P_L \cdot L).$$

A firm manager who wishes to find the quantities of inputs K and L that will maximize profits must find the first partial derivatives of $T\pi$ with respect to inputs K and L and set them equal to zero, so that

(12A-1)

$$\frac{\partial T\pi}{\partial K} = P \cdot \frac{\partial Q}{\partial K} + Q \frac{dP}{dQ} \frac{\partial Q}{\partial K} - P_K - \frac{dP_K}{dK} \cdot K$$

$$= \left(P + Q \frac{dP}{dQ}\right) \frac{\partial Q}{\partial K} - \left(P_K + \frac{dP_K}{dK} \cdot K\right) = 0,$$

and

$$\frac{\partial T\pi}{\partial L} = P \cdot \frac{\partial Q}{\partial L} + Q \frac{dP}{dQ} \frac{\partial Q}{\partial L} - P_L - \frac{dP_L}{dL} \cdot L$$

(12A-2)

$$= \left(P + Q\frac{dP}{dQ}\right)\frac{\partial Q}{\partial L} - \left(P_L + \frac{dP_L}{dL} \cdot L\right) = 0.$$

The term $[P + Q(dP/dQ)]$ is the marginal revenue to the firm from selling the output. It follows that $[P + Q(dP/dQ)]\,(\partial Q/\partial K)$ and $[P + Q\,(dP/dQ)]\,(\partial Q/\partial L)$ are the marginal revenue products of inputs K and L, respectively, if there are *no* marginal materials costs. If there *are* marginal materials costs $(= MC_M)$, these must be subtracted from $[P + Q(dP/dQ)]$ to get *net* marginal revenue, so

$$NMR = P + Q(dP/dQ)) - MC_M,$$

$$MRP_K = \left[P + Q\,(dP/dQ) - MC_M\right]\left(\frac{\partial Q}{\partial K}\right),$$

and

$$MRP_L = \left[P + Q\,(dP/dQ) - MC_M\right]\left(\frac{\partial Q}{\partial L}\right)$$

Notice that as long as dP/dQ is negative and/or MC_M is positive, NMR is less than P.

The terms $[P_K + (dP_K/dK) \cdot K]$ in equation 12A-1 and $[P_L + (dP_L/dL) \cdot L]$ in equation 12A-2 measure the marginal costs of inputs K and L, respectively. Thus equations 12A-1 and 12A-2 state that for profit maximization of inputs K and L,

(12A-3)

$$MRP_K - MC_K = 0$$

and

(12A-4)

$$MRP_L - MC_L = 0.$$

We could rewrite equations 12A-3 and 12A-4 as

(12A-5)

$$MRP_K = MC_K$$

and

(12A-6)

$$MRP_L = MC_L.$$

If both inputs are variable, *both* equations 12A-5 and 12A-6 must be satisfied.

We can find a more general condition for obtaining the least cost combination of inputs than developed in Chapter 5 by dividing equation 12A-5 by equation 12A-6 and rearranging terms:

(12A-7)
$$\frac{MRP_K}{MRP_L} = \frac{MC_K}{MC_L},$$

and

(12A-8)
$$\frac{MRP_K}{MC_K} = \frac{MRP_L}{MC_L}.$$

Dividing both sides of this equation by *NMR*, which is equal to $[P + Q(dP/dQ) - MC_M]$, we obtain the more general form of the least cost combination of inputs rule:

(12A-9)
$$\frac{MP_K}{MC_K} = \frac{MP_L}{MC_L}.$$

If the firm cannot significantly affect P_K or P_L by using more or less of input *K* or input *L*, dP_K/dK and $dP_L/dL = 0$, $MC_K = P_K$, $MC_L = P_L$, and equation 12A-9 becomes

(12A-10)
$$\frac{MP_K}{P_K} = \frac{MP_L}{P_L},$$

our previous rule for the least cost combination of inputs. In this case equations 12A-5 and 12A-6 become

(12A-11)
$$MRP_K = P_K$$

and

(12A-12)
$$MRP_L = P_L.$$

This is the solution consistent with perfect competition in the input markets for both *K* and *L*.

German-American Metals Corporation[1]

German-American Metals Corporation (GAMC) is an affiliate of a Stuttgart firm that uses a patented process to recover lead and other nonferrous metals from very fine-sized mixed metallic scrap. The process used by GAMC is based on thermal separation of metals in a smelter. The smelting plant consists of a drying system, a lead-smelting separator, separating equipment for other nonferrous metals, and an exhaust purification system with related utility devices. GAMC uses natural-gas-fired burners to generate heat for the smelter, and it currently has a long-term contract guaranteeing it natural gas at $4 per 1,000 cubic feet for the next two years.

GAMC's overall production is dependent on the lead segment of its operations, since its source material contains predominantly lead scrap. The company has two primary outlets for the lead it recovers. First, there is the general market for lead ingots, an oligopolistic market in which GAMC must follow the price leadership of a large, established domestic firm. Its

---

[1] This case is based on research conducted in Germany. We wish to thank the officers and management of Texas Shredder Parts, Inc., as well as their German counterparts, for their help in making it possible for us to carry out our investigation.

second outlet is sales to one of its own U.S. subsidiaries, Southern Electrical Devices, Incorporated, a producer of lead battery plates for large industrial batteries.

A forecast prepared by GAMC's planning department indicates that the lead component of its scrap purchases next year will cost $0.15 per pound. On the surface this appears to management to be a favorable development, since lead ingot is expected to sell for $520 per short ton (2,000 lbs.). GAMC has been studying its recovery plant data to come up with reasonably accurate cost projections in the light of high but stable energy prices. The firm's engineers have indicated that, given the quality of scrap available, 20,000 cubic feet of gas must be burned to recover a short ton of lead. Fixed overhead and fixed labor costs comprise most of the remaining costs of lead recovery. However, because of pollution control expenses, marginal cost is expected to rise by $.02 per ton of lead recovered up to GAMC's capacity of 8,500 tons per year.

GAMC's subsidiary, Southern Electrical Devices (SED), may choose to purchase lead ingot either from GAMC or from other outside suppliers. Not including the expected price of lead ingot for next year, SED's total cost function for the production of battery plates has been estimated to be the following:

$$TC_B = 4,000,000 + 80Q_B + 0.1Q_B^2,$$

where total cost (TC_B) is in dollars, and Q_B is the number of tons of battery plates produced. The SED plant makes efficient use of all the lead it purchases, so that one ton of ingot yields one ton of battery plates. SED's management is not certain whether to plan to purchase lead from outside suppliers next year or to restrict its production of battery plates to those it can make from GAMC's total lead output. Its marketing department has estimated a statistical demand function for the battery plates such that

$$Q_B = 131,720.0 - 80.0P_B + 255.5P_n + 0.5I,$$

where Q_B is the number of tons of battery plates produced, P_B is the sales price per ton of plates, P_n is an index number of regional industrial production, and I is regional per-capital income. SED has contracted with an economic forecasting firm that regularly supplies it with forecasts of a large set of economic variables relating to output, prices, and income levels. For next year the forecasters have estimated that the average value of the regional production index will be 210 and that regional per-capita income will average $13,250.

QUESTIONS

Given the foregoing data, answer the following questions.

1. What strategy will maximize the joint profits of GAMC and its SED subsidiary?

2. For the two products (lead and battery plates), what will be the prices and outputs consistent with a profit-maximizing strategy during the coming year?

3. For next year should SED plan to restrict its output to that which can be produced from the ingot output of GAMC? Why or why not?

Bonco, Incorporated: A Firm in Transition

B onco, Incorporated, produces a patented surgical device known as the *incis-a-matic*. The device has been sold successfully in the U.S. market, but it has been produced in two of the company's outdated plants, in Columbus, Ohio, and in Cincinnati, Ohio.

Barry Cosgrove, a young economist hired to assist management in making decisions regarding the future of incis-a-matic production and marketing strategies, has been developing cost and revenue data relevant to next year's operations.

His boss, Mary Thompson, has argued that for next year, the company should plan to duplicate this year's annual output of 2,400 units and raise price from $10,000 to $12,000 per unit. Thompson's reasoning is that the company plans to build a new plant that will begin operating year after next and has arranged to dispose of its two old plants. She believes they should simply mark time as far as output is concerned (in the old facilities), but raise price to cover some anticipated overall inflation in the economy.

Cosgrove's data for the two plants are as follows:

Columbus Plant		Cincinnati Plant	
Output per Month	Arc MC	Output per Month	Arc MC
0		0	
	$4,000		$3,000
100		100	
	7,000		5,000
200		200	
	9,000		7,200
300		300	
	11,000		9,200
400		400	
	13,000		11,000
500		500	

From the company's chief accountant, Cosgrove has learned that total fixed costs per month will be $700,000 in the Columbus plant and $600,000 in the Cincinnati plant. He has discovered that no one in the company has ever attempted to estimate a demand curve for the incis-a-matic and that Thompson has always based her pricing and output recommendations on her general impressions about the state of the economy. In order to estimate the demand for the incis-a-matic, Cosgrove performed a survey of hospital administrators and department chiefs. The result was the following demand schedule:

Price per Unit	Quantity Sold per Month
$16,000	0
14,000	100
12,000	200
10,000	300
8,000	400
6,000	500
4,000	600

QUESTIONS

Given Cosgrove's demand data, answer the following questions.

1. What should Cosgrove recommend regarding next year's total output and price per unit of the incis-a-matic?

2. How should next year's total output be allocated between the two plants? Why?

3. What will be next year's profit from sales of the incis-a-matic if Cosgrove's data are accurate and his recommendations are followed?

4. How does the Cosgrove recommendation compare with Thompson's strategy in terms of profit?

   Beginning year after next, Bonco will be operating in its new plant, where a constant marginal cost of $5,000 per unit can be achieved over the 200- to 1,200-unit-per-month output range. Cosgrove has been asked to study the prospects for both U.S. and foreign sales of the incis-a-matic once the new plant is operational. For two years from now, based on analysis of surgical data for foreign hospitals and projections of U.S. demand, Cosgrove has estimated the following demand curves:

$$AR_f = 20,000 - 15Q_f$$
$$AR_{us} = 21,000 - 20Q_{us,}$$

where

AR_f = average revenue from foreign sales,

Q_f = quantity sold per month in the foreign market,

AR_{us} = average revenue from sales in the U.S. market, and

Q_{us} = quantity sold per month in the U.S. market.

In addition, preliminary data on the new plant indicate that in the first year of operation, total fixed costs will be $800,000 per month.

   Given the data on costs and on U.S. and foreign demand, answer the following questions for the first year of operations in the new plant.

5. What price should be charged in the U.S. market?

6. What price should be charged in the foreign market?

7. What will be the amount sold in each market if the preceding prices are charged?

8. What will be the maximum profit obtainable from incis-a-matic sales for the year?

A Hare-Raising Decision

In 2002, media magnate Ted Turner was reported to have owned 10 percent of all buffalo (American bison) in the U.S and to have opened a restaurant chain, *Ted's Montana Grill*, specializing in buffalo dishes. Many ranchers bought into a buffalo craze during the 1990s, but virtually all lost huge sums when consumers showed little interest in buffalo meat. An Indiana firm, Rex Rabbit, with 42 rabbit ranches, tried a similar move during the 1980s, but, apparently, with little success. The rabbit restaurant venture was initiated to develop a market for byproduct rabbit meat. The following case was suggested by the Rex Rabbit undertaking, but all of the data are hypothetical and not intended to be an exact representation of any firm, hopping or dead.[1]

Wonder Bunny, Incorporated, raises rabbits and sells their pelts to manufacturers of fur hats and accessories. For the past 10 years, it has also sold a by-product, unprocessed rabbit meat, to packinghouses that use it as an ingredient in canned pet foods. Chico Saltar, a production manager for Wonder, has noted that the company has recently encountered disposal problems

---

[1] Scott Kilman, "Buffalo is a Hard Sell and Lots of Ranchers Are Biting the Dust," *Wall Street Journal*, July 12, 2002, pp A1, A5; and "Firm Hopping into Fast-Food Bunny Trade," *San Antonio Express*, January 24, 1983, p. 3-D.

with the rabbit meat, due to a tapering off in packinghouse demand for the product. As a result, Wonder has had to pay a waste disposal firm to haul away and destroy the excess meat. Currently, disposal costs are running $0.30 per unit on all unsold meat (production of one rabbit pelt yields one unit of meat). For the foreseeable future, Chico does not expect a recovery in packinghouse demand for the meat.

His current estimate of this demand is represented by the following equation:

$$Q_m = 12{,}000 - 5{,}000 \, P_m,$$

where Q_m is the number of units of meat sold per quarter and P_m is the price obtained per unit of meat. Respectively, he has estimated the demand function for pelts and the firm's total cost of production to be

$$Q_f = 3{,}600 - 4{,}000P_f + 1{,}000P_s + 1.8I,$$

where Q_f is the number of rabbit pelts sold per quarter, P_f is the price per rabbit pelt, P_S is the price of squirrel pelts, and I is household income; and

$$TC = \$38{,}000 + 1.8Q + 0.0001Q^2,$$

where $38,000 is quarterly fixed cost and Q represents the number of rabbits processed or production of one pelt *and* one unit of the by-product meat. Wonder's present strategy is to maximize profit from the sales of the two products, given the disposal cost per unit applicable to any amount of excess meat.

Mariel Hutch, a financial consultant for Wonder, has come to the company with a proposal that it stop selling rabbit meat to packing houses and process the meat for sale to a new market, fast food restaurants specializing in rabbit dinners. She has estimated that Wonder's demand curve for sales in this market is given by the equation

$$Q_r = 18{,}500 - 5{,}000 \, P_r,$$

where Q_r is the number of units of meat sold per quarter and P_r is the price charged for a unit of meat. (The unit of meat remains the amount obtained with the production of one pelt.) While this demand clearly exceeds Chico's current estimate of demand in the packinghouse market, the changeover would require an increase in fixed costs of $14,000 per quarter as well as additional marginal costs of $0.28 per rabbit to process the meat to specifications of the new market. The cost increases will be applicable to all production of pelts and meat, because of once-over changes that will have to be made in the processing line. In other words, the new costs cannot be allocated to meat production alone. Moreover, it would not be feasible for Wonder to sell in both the restaurant market and the packing house market, since the decision to interrupt sales to the latter would likely cause a permanent loss of customers there. In the event that all of the meat cannot be sold in the restaurant market it will still be possible to use the waste disposal alternative described above.

Wonder must make a decision regarding the two by-product market possibilities within the next few weeks. As far as the pelt market is concerned, the company believes that the demand function variables other than the rabbit pelt price will remain constant. The current price of squirrel pelts is $3.20, and household income is $18,000. Given this additional information, what should Wonder do?

Hint: It is rational for Wonder to accept negative marginal revenue from meat sales as long as the negative MR per unit is less than the disposal cost per unit.

Omega Distributing Company II

(Note: This case is a continuation of the analysis done in Integrating Case 1B, Omega Distributing Company I, which is found at the end of Part I. A review of that case would be helpful for understanding this one.)

Duncan Haynes, a member of the team that developed a demand function for Omega Distributing Company's Blast fabric softener, has been assigned the task of determining whether the price of the product should be changed. (Duncan had earlier suggested changing price, since the results of a regression analysis of demand indicated that the company had been pricing the product in the inelastic range of its demand curve.) The demand function for Blast from the earlier analysis is

$$Q = -820 - 689P_b + 1{,}972P_c + 18A.$$

Q is denominated in hundreds in the equation and refers to the number of hundreds of units of Blast sold per week.

Duncan has decided that the pricing decision can best be analyzed by assuming that the price of the competing brand of softener, Cloud (P_c in the preceding equation), remains at its average recent value, $1.42 per unit, and that his own company cuts its advertising expenditure on Blast (A in the equation, denominated in ten thousands) to $20,000 per week ($A = 2.0$). This leaves only P_b, the price per unit of Blast, as an unknown in the preceding equation.

Duncan knows that Omega pays the manufacturer of Blast $0.875 and that Omega's unit variable cost for the product is equal to 112 percent of the amount it pays the manufacturer. Given that the price of Blast and that of Cloud in the estimated demand function are denominated in dollars, what sales price per unit should Duncan recommend? What impact on profit would these changes in price and advertising have as compared to the profit Blast would generate with the average price and advertising levels determined in Integrating Case 1B (P_b = $1.37, P_c = $1.42, and A = 3.86)? Should Omega be cautious about instituting the price increase that Duncan's demand curve calls for? Why or why not?

CHAPTER THIRTEEN

Fundamentals of Project Evaluation

In many of the preceding chapters, our primary emphasis was on the way a firm's managers identify a profit-maximizing rate of output and its corresponding price under various types of market situations. Over the short run, as we defined it, a significant proportion of the firm's inputs was envisioned as fixed (plant and equipment, for example), and the issue of investment in new capacity did not arise. Generally, when we considered the long run, the firm remained in a given industry or product line, even though it might change the size of its plant. Moreover, product differentiation or an adjustment in the share of output of joint products did not constitute a change in the type of activity undertaken by the firm.

Now, we shift our emphasis to the question of management's analysis of investment opportunities, which include wholly new undertakings of the firm. Such ventures range all the way from the expansion of capacity in a given line of activity to entry into a new and different industry. In today's industrial society, firms typically have many investment opportunities before them. As the firms grow, their managers must be prepared to determine not only how and when to expand existing operations but also whether to steer the firm toward new types of activities in which profitable investments can be made. The large U.S. and European business conglomerates are an obvious case in point. Many of these giant corporations, such as Eastman Kodak, Olin Industries, 3M, and Mannesmann, are characterized by divisions that produce totally unrelated types of output. The managers of these large firms must constantly review the expansion alternatives before them. In a given firm, viable alternatives may range from developmental expenditures in space technology to the introduction of a new pastry snack into the consumer market.

A recent example of a firm faced with vexing investment alternatives is General Electric Corporation, which had to choose what path to take in developing an engine for the new Boeing 777 jumbo jet. GE's competitors, Pratt & Whitney and Rolls-Royce PLC, each spent about $750 million to modify existing engine designs. General Electric instead decided to spend more than $2 *billion* to develop a totally new engine, a decision that was particularly difficult because demand for new plane engines within both commercial aviation and the defense industry was depressed at the time. The new engines were introduced in 1995. By early 1996, however, a price war had developed among the three engine makers, and it was estimated that the engines were selling for only about half their full cost, including allocated development costs. Further adding to GE's problems were delays in completing Federal Aviation Administration certification of the engine. It was estimated that the program would not break even for at least 10 years, twice as long as GE had originally anticipated. In fact, a GE manager stated, "It's a 30-year business."[1] By 2002, the engine had proved itself on many 777 aircraft, and GE's sales were boosted when KLM Airlines selected it for its new fleet of extended-range 777s.[2]

Even the venerable Walt Disney Productions is not exempt from the need to evaluate investment projects carefully. For example, the company invested $4 billion to build Euro Disneyland near Paris. The park opened in April 1992, and Disney soon found that its earlier estimates of attendance—as well as the amount of money that each visitor would spend once inside the park—were far too optimistic. The park lost $905 million in its second fiscal year, and Euro Disney stated that it needed to restructure its finances. In 1995, Euro Disney finally had its first profitable year—a profit of 114 million French francs, including 112 million francs from a buyback of convertible bonds, compared with a loss of 1.8 *billion* francs the previous fiscal year. In 1999, however, Disney's theme parks experienced a substantial increase in operating income while the company's net income dropped by an equal percentage, and Disney launched another theme park venture, Animal Kingdom. After the 9/11 terrorist attacks, Disney parks suffered from the general decline in tourism. The company also suffered financially from its television

---

[1] "Defying the Law of Gravity," *Business Week* (April 8, 1996), pp. 124–125.
[2] "KLM Selects GE Engines to Power Widebody Aircraft in $250 Million Engine Order," PRdomain.com, online, June 26, 2002, www.prdomain.com/companies/g/ge/news_releases/200206june/pr_ge_nr_20020626.htm, September 13, 2002.

network, ABC, which lost almost 20 percent of its viewers in 2001. In 2002, the company and its board were being scrutinized by disappointed investors who for a number of years had criticized its corporate governance.[3]

CAPITAL BUDGETING AND PROJECT ANALYSIS

Capital budgeting is the analysis of alternative investment opportunities by a firm.

The analysis of alternative investment opportunities is the focus of a subject area known as **capital budgeting,** which encompasses both economics and finance. We can view capital budgeting as the process by which a firm's managers determine how to allocate investment expenditures among alternative projects. The projects that are the subject of analysis usually include only those that will yield dollar returns to the firm for periods longer than one year. *Capital project analysis* is a major part of the capital budgeting process, providing managers with the data necessary to carry out capital budgeting decisions. Accordingly, we will first consider the analysis of a single undertaking (investment project) and later turn to the question of deciding which of a number of alternative investment projects should be accepted.

COSTS IN NEW UNDERTAKINGS

From our earlier analysis of the firm, we know that any operation of a given size (plant) normally has both fixed and variable costs of production. Thus, to analyze a specific capital project, it is necessary to determine such costs and compare them with the revenues the project will generate. However, a *new* undertaking has one-time costs associated with obtaining and organizing the resources necessary to bring it into existence, and project analysis must also take these costs into account. For convenience we will call this latter set of costs the *price* or *initial cost outlay* of the project. A capital project's price includes initial outlays for land, buildings, and equipment, as well as developmental costs for both the undertaking itself and the product it is intended to produce. Another item that should be included in a project's price is the cost to the firm of any increase in working capital requirements attributable to the project. Finally, if the project involves replacement of existing capital goods, the after-tax salvage value of the old equipment should be deducted from the project's price.

---

[3] "Activist in Bid to Rally Disney Dissenters," *Financial Times,* September 12, 2002, p. 13; "Desperate for a Hit, ABC Is Refocusing on Middle America," *Wall Street Journal,* September 13, 2002, pp. A1, A12; "Walt Disney Earnings Decline by 12% as Consumer-Products Unit Plays Role," *Wall Street Journal,* July 23, 1999, p. B4; "Euro Disney Posts First Annual Profit, Stock Slides 14%," *Wall Street Journal,* November 16, 1995, p. A17; "Mickey's Trip to Trouble," *Newsweek* (February 14, 1994), pp. 34–39; and "The Mouse Isn't Roaring," *Business Week* (August 24, 1992), p. 38.

Capital budgeting puts managers into an accept-or-reject framework with respect to the individual capital project. The following general rule for acceptance of a single project is simple:

A project should be accepted as long as the *present value* of the expected *net receipts* it generates *equals or exceeds its price* (the net outlay required).

In other words, worthy investments are those that yield returns at least equal to their costs, where the costs include a normal or target rate of return on invested capital. *Returns* from the project are defined as the present value of net receipts, or a discounted stream of *net cash flows.* Such a concept will be familiar to students who have had a course in finance, but others should give it particular attention. The following section provides a summary of how to calculate the discounted stream of net receipts. More detailed information on the use of discounting and compounding methodologies appears in the appendix to this chapter.

STREAM OF RECEIPTS OR RETURNS

In general, capital projects have a finite life, even though the project analyst does not always know how long a given venture might be expected to yield net operating returns to the firm. Even if the life of a particular project were viewed as indefinitely long or infinite, it would be possible to calculate just what one would be willing to pay today in order to obtain an infinite stream of annual receipts of a given amount per year. In approaching this problem, we would quickly find out that we would not be willing to pay very much for an amount that we would not receive until many, many years in the future. To understand this point, ask yourself what you would be willing to pay for a piece of paper that guarantees you will receive $50 exactly 30 years from today. Not much! The exact answer, assuming no inflation, would depend on the interest rate.[4]

To examine the effect of interest rate considerations on management's evaluation of net receipts from a capital project, let us suppose a firm's project analysts are reasonably certain that a given project will generate net receipts for the firm for the next 10 years. Specifically, let us suppose that in terms of today's prices (this means that inflation is adjusted out of all calculations), $100,000 will be generated each year. We will assume that the first annual receipts of the project are received at the end of one year's time from comple-

---

[4] We use the term *interest rate* very loosely at this point. In general, when we employ the term, we are referring to the rate of return expected from alternative uses of funds. If we are certain that the funds paid out for the guarantee of receiving $50 30 years from now can be placed in a risk-free account paying 6 percent interest compounded annually, we could ascertain that $8.71 placed in such an account would reach a value of $50 in 30 years. Therefore we would not want to pay more than $8.71 for the paper guaranteeing $50 at the end of 30 years.

tion of the project, and we will treat the project's net outlay as a current value (paid immediately, at time-period zero). Thus, the first $100,000 is received at the end of year one, the second $100,000 at the end of year two, and so forth.

The **present value** of a future payment or series of payments represents the amount received today that would be equivalent in value to the future payment or payments.

The **future value** of a sum of money held today is the amount that would be accumulated at some future date if we invested that sum of money now at a particular rate of interest.

Compounding is the process of computing the value of a current sum of money at some future date.

Discounting is the process of computing the present value of sums of money to be received in the future.

The **discount rate** is the rate of interest used to compute present values.

The value at the time of project completion of $100,000 of receipts that will be earned at the end of, say, year three is not $100,000 but something less. In particular, it is the amount of money that would *accumulate* to $100,000 at the end of year three if it were invested today at some specific rate of interest per year. This is the case because the firm at project completion and initiation of production is in the same position as the person who is promised a given sum of money at some future time. The current value, or **present value,** of that promised amount is something less than the future amount itself. If the interest rate is 6 percent, the present value of $100,000 received at the end of year three is $83,961.93. Alternatively, if we receive $83,961.93 *now* and put it into an account paying 6 percent interest per year, at the end of this year we will have ($83,961.93)(1.06) = $88,999.64. If we do not remove any of the funds from the account, at the end of year two we will have ($88,999.64)(1.06) = $94,339.62; and at the end of year three we will have ($94,339.62)(1.06) = $100,000.00. Thus, we can say that if the interest rate is 6 percent, $83,961.93 in our hands today is *equivalent* to $100,000 received at the end of year three. Similarly, both of the foregoing are equivalent to $94,339.62 received at the end of year two. The process by which we have determined the amount or **future value** that the $83,961.93 will accumulate to is called **compounding.** In the foregoing example, 6 percent interest was compounded at the end of each year. This means that at the end of each year, the interest for that period was added to the amount that was in the account at the beginning of the year. Therefore, the 6 percent interest is paid on a larger amount the next year.

The proposition that discounted future amounts are equal to a certain present amount is known as the *concept of equivalency.* The process by which we determine the present value of an amount to be received at some time in the future is called **discounting,** and the interest rate we use in determining the present value is called the **discount rate.**

The farther out in time a future amount is received, the lower its present value. Returning to the previous project with a $100,000 annual net receipts figure, we find that for year ten the present value of $100,000 is only $55,839.47 if a discount rate of 6 percent is applied. Such a present value is found by the formula

(13-1)

$$PV = \frac{FV_n}{(1+r)^n}$$

where

PV = present value,

FV_n = future value at the end of year n,

r = applicable discount rate, and

n = number of periods (years) until the amount is received.

In the preceding case, n would be 10 and r would be 0.06. We can derive the present value formula by further examining the concept of equivalency previously discussed. We have already seen that when r = 0.06, $100,000 received at the end of year three is equal to a present value of $83,961.93. Note that the $100,000 received at the end of year three is equal to an initial amount of $83,961.93 increased by 6 percent at the end of year one to $88,999.64, compounded at 6 percent again at the end of year two to $94,339.62, and compounded at 6 percent at the end of year three to $100,000.00. So we have the following:

Amount at the end of

year one: ($83,961.93)(1.06) = $88,999.64

year two: ($83,961.93)(1.06)(1.06) = $94,339.62

                                 = ($83,961.93)(1.06)^2

year three: ($83,961.93)(1.06)(1.06)(1.06) = $100,000.00

                                 = ($83,961.93)(1.06)^3

or for each year,

(13-2)
$$FV_n = PV(1.06)^n,$$

where FV is received at the end of n periods in the future. If we divide both sides of the preceding expression by $(1.06)^n$, we get

(13-3)
$$PV = \frac{FV_n}{(1+.06)^n}.$$

Since 0.06 is the discount rate, r, we have

(13-4)
$$PV = \frac{FV_n}{(1+r)^n},$$

which is identical to equation 13-1.

We can also state equation 13-4 as

(13-5)
$$PV = FV_n \, (PVF \; r, n),$$

where $(PVF \; r, n) = 1/(1+r)^n$ is the *present value factor*. Tables have been developed for the value of the PVF (also known as the present value of $1) for

Table 13-1 *Present Value of $100,000 per Year Stream of Net Receipts Discounted at 6 Percent per Year*

Period (n)	FV = Future Value (At End of Period)	PV Factor (PVF 6%, n)	Present Value (FV × PVF)
1	$100,000	0.9434	$ 94,340
2	100,000	0.8900	89,000
3	100,000	0.8396	83,960
4	100,000	0.7921	79,210
5	100,000	0.7473	74,730
6	100,000	0.7050	70,500
7	100,000	0.6651	66,510
8	100,000	0.6274	62,740
9	100,000	0.5919	59,190
10	100,000	0.5584	55,840
		PV of 10-year stream =	$736,020

given rates of interest and numbers of periods in the future. In Appendix B at the end of the text, Table B-3 gives the values of the *PVF*. To find the present value of $100,000 received at the end of the third year for the preceding project, we simply multiply $100,000 times the present value factor from the table, which for $n = 3$ and $r = 0.06$ is 0.8396. (Read down the 6 percent column of Table B-3 to $n = 3$.) Thus

$$\$100,000 \ (PVF \ 6\%, 3) = \$100,000(0.8396) = \$83,960.$$

which corresponds closely to the $83,961.93 in the previous example. The slight difference in the result is due to the rounding of the *PVF*, which is more precisely given by 0.83962.

To evaluate our example of $100,000 per year stream of annual net receipts for 10 years, we construct Table 13-1, using the 6 percent present value factors from Appendix B, Table B-3. Each of the 10 annual $100,000 amounts is multiplied by its respective 6 percent present value factor, and the present values in the fourth column are then summed to obtain the present value of the entire 10-year stream of receipts. From Table 13-1, we can see that the present value of the 10-year flow of $100,000 in net receipts per year is $736,020—the sum of the *discounted* future values where the applicable discount rate is 6 percent.

This result can be obtained more easily by multiplying $100,000 times the present value factor for an annuity (PVF_a) of 10 years discounted at 6 percent. Defined briefly, an *annuity* is a constant amount payable at the end of each year for a specified number of years. In the case of our current example, if we let $A = \$100,000$, then PV_a (the present value of the 10-year stream of $100,000 per year) is

(13-6)
$$PV_a = \frac{A}{(1+r)^1} + \frac{A}{(1+r)^2} + \cdots + \frac{A}{(1+r)^n},$$

where $n = 10$. Factoring out the A, we obtain

(13-7)
$$PV_a = A\left[\frac{1}{(1+r)^1} + \frac{1}{(1+r)^2} + \cdots + \frac{1}{(1+r)^n}\right].$$

The present value factor for the annuity is the term in brackets in the preceding equation, or

(13-8)
$$PVF_a = \left[\frac{1}{(1+r)^1} + \frac{1}{(1+r)^2} + \cdots + \frac{1}{(1+r)^n}\right],$$

The **net present value (NPV)** of an investment is the present value of its net cash inflows minus the present value of its cost outlays. An investment project is acceptable if its *NPV* is greater than or equal to zero.

so that we can state $PV_a = A(PVF_a$ r, n). A table of present value of annuity factors also appears in Appendix B. For a discount rate of 6 percent and 10 periods (PVF_a 6%, 10), the present value factor is 7.3601.[5] Thus, in the case of our example, we have

$$PV_a = \$100,000 \ (PVF_a \ 6\%, 10) = \$100,000(7.3601) = \$736,010.$$

In round numbers, then, we have determined that the present value of the net receipts stream anticipated from our example project is \$736,000. This assumes, of course, that management has determined that 6 percent per year is an appropriate rate of discount to apply.

The **net cash flow** of a project is equal to any increase in revenues brought about by the project less any increase in operating expenses and depreciation multiplied by (1 – T), where T is the firm's marginal income tax rate. The incremental depreciation associated with the project is then added to the above sum.

According to the general rule stated in the preceding section, the project should be accepted as long as its price (the net outlay) is not more than \$736,000. Another way of stating this requirement is to say that the **net present value (NPV)** of the project must be *nonnegative* (zero or greater). The net present value of a project is the difference between the discounted stream of expected **net cash flows** from the project and the project's price, or

(13-9)
$$NPV = \sum_{i=1}^{n} \frac{(TR_i - TC_i)(1-T) + D_i}{(1+r)^i} - C_p,$$

where *TR* is total revenue, *TC* is total operating cost (short run and including depreciation for the project), *T* is the firm's marginal income tax rate, *D* is

---

[5] The PVF_a factor can be calculated by the following formula, which is a simplified version of equation 13-8:

$$PVF_a = \frac{1 - \left[\frac{1}{(1+r)^n}\right]}{r}$$

The Saturn: A Product Made in Heaven?

"All-new aluminum engine, fail-safe sophisticated marketing research and highly automated assembly technique … a revolutionary change from a company and industry that heretofore have stressed slow, evolutionary change." These words could have been used to describe General Motors' Saturn, a new small car introduced in the fall of 1990, but *The Wall Street Journal* was actually quoting them from J. Patrick Wright's 1979 book, *On a Clear Day You Can See General Motors*. And where did Wright pick these words up? From General Motors' claims for the Vega, a car introduced in 1970. An indication of the Vega's success, or lack thereof, can be gleaned from a comment by Richard LeFauve, the boss at General Motors' Saturn subsidiary, who admits: "We've had many letters from people saying, 'Don't let this be another Vega.'"

Work on the Saturn began in 1983, and General Motors spent $4.5 billion to bring the car to market. The Saturn was envisioned as a top-quality small car that would be more technologically advanced than competing Japanese cars. The Spring Hill, Tennessee, plant that manufactures the new cars cost $1.9 billion, with an initial capacity of 240,000 cars a year. However, Thomas G. Manoff, Saturn's vice-president of finance, calculated that plant capacity would have to double if Saturn were to become profitable.

General Motors began the Saturn project by attempting to design a plant that would be so automated that very little human labor would be required. Later, however, the company had to modify that plan because comparable equipment in other General Motors facilities was not performing as well as had been hoped.

In contrast, Honda began developing a U.S. plant in 1982 in Marysville, Ohio, at a cost of about $2 billion. Initially, the degree of automation at the plant was relatively low, but Honda gradually added sophisticated equipment as workers became more adept at using it. The company also added capacity as demand for the car expanded. Although the plant began by building an existing model of the Accord, by 1985 it had introduced a new Accord model. For approximately the same cost as General Motors' Saturn project, Honda got two assembly plants with a total annual capacity of 510,000 cars as well as a factory capable of building nearly all of the engines, transmissions, and related parts needed by its auto assembly plants plus a motorcycle plant.

GM originally created the Saturn to compete with Japanese automobiles. The company hoped that once people discovered that GM could deliver Japanese-quality cars, customers graduating to larger-sized vehicles would be willing to purchase other GM cars. Unfortunately, many customers still purchased Hondas and Toyotas when they wanted bigger automobiles, although market research indicated that 75 percent of Saturn customers would not have originally purchased other GM products. As the economy improved and gasoline prices dropped in the late 1990s, Saturn sales decreased as people bought bigger cars from other companies. In response, in late 1999 GM introduced a larger L-series sedan with the Saturn brand name. However, this car is built at an existing GM plant in Wilmington, Delaware, rather than the Saturn plant at Spring Hill. In 2001, it introduced the Saturn Vue sport utility vehicle built at Spring Hill. However, with two years of Saturn division annual losses in the neighborhood of $850 million, and plant upgrades costing $1.5 billion, Saturn as a capital investment project was still looking far from stellar.

References: David Kiley, "Huge Losses Could Jeopardize Future of GM's Saturn," *USA Today,* April 24, 2001, online, July 20, 2002, www.usatoday.com/money/autos/2001-04-24-saturn.htm; "Saturn Expands Brand in New Campaign," *Wall Street Journal,* June 28, 1999, p. B8; "GM's Saturn Division Plans to Build a Midsize Car to Keep Customers Loyal," *Wall Street Journal,* August 6, 1996, p. B5; "GM Confirms Plan for Midsize Saturn, Available by 1999," *Wall Street Journal,* August 7, 1996, p. C18; "GM's Plan for Saturn, to Beat Small Imports, Trails Original Goals," *Wall Street Journal,* July 9, 1990, pp. A1, A12.

depreciation, and C_p is the price or net outlay for the project. Equation 13-9 indicates that we should determine the *net* receipts for each time period *(i)* and discount such receipts at the rate *r* for all time periods for one through *n;* then we should sum them (the Greek letter Σ, sigma, indicates that we should sum all items with an *i* subscript from $i = 1$ to $i = n$) and subtract the price of the project to obtain the *NPV.*

If the *NPV* in equation 13-9 turns out to be zero, the project will yield a return identical to the return that would be received if an amount equal to C_p were put into an account paying $(r \times 100)$ percent interest compounded annually. Where *NPV* is greater than zero, the project yield will exceed the discount rate, *r.*

In fact, it is possible to determine the net annual percentage yield of a project (its **internal rate of return** or **IRR**) when its price and annual dollar receipts are known by setting *NPV* equal to C_p and solving for *r* in equation 13-9. Thus, we find *r* such that

The **internal rate of return *(IRR)*** of a project is the discount rate that will result in a net present value of zero for the project.

$$\sum_{i=1}^{n} \frac{(TR_i - TC_i)(1-T) + D_i}{(1+r)^i} = C_p.$$

The *r* value can be found by trial and error or by interpolation. There is no simple formula for finding it, and not all financial calculators have this capability. However, there are computer programs available for determining the internal rate of return.[6] Later in this chapter, an example of trial-and-error determination of a project's internal rate of return will be introduced.

A SIMPLE CAPITAL PROJECT ANALYSIS

Any investor, whether a large corporation or an individual, must go through an analysis similar to that outlined previously in order to make an appropriate accept-or-reject decision on a capital project. For the large enterprise contemplating a major undertaking, the process of enumerating project costs and returns may be very tedious and expensive. For an individual or a small business, however, the procedure may be relatively simple.

Let us consider as an example the case of a small firm, Clickwash, Inc., which operates a chain of coin laundries in a given area. The firm's managers are quite experienced in the construction and operation of such facilities but

---

[6] As long as the project cash flows follow the pattern of negative cash flows in the first few periods and positive cash flows thereafter, there will usually be only one positive-valued solution for the *IRR* (the others are negative or imaginary). However, if there is a mixture of positive and negative cash flows during future periods, it is possible to have more than one positive-valued solution for the *IRR*. In such cases, one reverts back to the *NPV* method to determine the acceptability of the project in question.

are now considering opening a coin-operated car wash in a location that appears to be desirable. A car wash franchising company owns the site and has offered Clickwash an attractive ground lease in exchange for a franchise fee of 30 percent of sales revenue.

According to our prior discussion of project analysis, Clickwash's management will have to determine the following:

1. The price or net outlay of the project,
2. Anticipated annual sales revenues from the project,
3. Annual operating costs of the project, and
4. A salvage value at the end of the project's life.

Based on its experience with coin laundries, management has determined that five years is an appropriate project life, since the machinery receives rather rough use and leases on suitable locations can seldom be negotiated for a term greater than five years. The car wash will have seven bays made of structural steel and aluminum siding. The bays and washing equipment can be dismantled and sold or moved at termination of the project. However, driveway pavement, the concrete slab on which the bays rest, and plumbing placed in the slab will all be abandoned when the project is over. The initial cost of the bays and washing equipment is $159,000. They can be sold at the end of the project for $66,500. The paving, slab, nonsalvageable plumbing, and plant installation cost an additional $20,000. The management of Clickwash thus knows that the price or net outlay of the project will be $C_p = \$179,000$.

The next step for management is to calculate the annual net receipts from the project and determine the present value of the five-year receipts stream. Suppose they have the following information:

1. The car wash will operate an average of 360 days a year.
2. There will be an average of 36 car washes per day at each of the seven bays.
3. The average receipts for a single wash are $0.875. This result is based on an assumption that the average wash will yield $1.25 in revenues (some people will spend four quarters per wash and others six) but that 30 percent of that amount belongs to the franchising company ($0.375).
4. Variable costs per wash are as follows:

Utilities and water	$0.08
Soap and supplies	0.04
Maintenance of machinery	0.02

5. Fixed costs per month are as follows:

Rent	$ 750.00
Utilities (fixed portion)	90.00

Site maintenance	80.00
Labor	190.00
Administrative expense	100.00

6. Depreciation is $22,500 per year.

7. The company is in the 34 percent income tax bracket.

From 1, 2, and 3, it can be determined that annual receipts from sales will be

$$7 \text{ bays} \times 36 \text{ washes} \times 360 \text{ days} \times \$0.875 = \$79,380.$$

Based on the preceding cost information, management can determine the annual cost of the car wash project as in Table 13-2. Our format in Table 13-2 is a hybrid of the economic and accounting costs discussed in Chapter 6. At this point, we do not take into account the opportunity cost to the firm of using its own funds for the project. However, the discount rate applied to the future net receipts and the criterion that the present value of such receipts be greater than the price of the project do account for the opportunity cost of investing the funds in another way.

Table 13-3 presents a worksheet for the project itself. Here, the anticipated receipts from sales are reduced by the annual cost of operations from Table 13-2 and by federal income taxes, which are 34 percent of net income before taxes. In order to obtain the annual net inflow of cash from the project, the firm's managers must add back the yearly depreciation figure, since depreciation is charged against current receipts but not paid to anyone else

Table 13-2 *Annual Operating Cost of Car Wash Project*

Variable Costs:		
Utilities and Water (0.08 × 90,720 washes per year)	$7,258	
Maintenance of Machines (0.02 × 90,720 washes per year)	1,814	
Soap and Supplies (0.04 × 90,720 washes per year)	3,629	
		$12,701
Fixed Costs:		
Utilities (fixed portion, $90 per month)	$1,080	
Rent ($750 per month)	9,000	
Site Maintenance ($80 per month)	960	
Labor ($190 per month)	2,280	
Administrative Expense ($100 per month)	$1,200	
		14,520
Depreciation		22,500
Total Annual Operating Cost of Project		$49,721

Table 13–3 *Worksheet for Car Wash Project NPV Analysis*

Annual Receipts from Sales		$ 79,380
Less:		
Annual Cost of Operations	$49,721	
Net Income Before Taxes		29,659
Less:		
Income Tax	10,084	
Net Income		19,575
Plus:		
Depreciation	22,500	
Annual Net Inflow from Project		$42,075
PV of Five-Year Net Inflow[a]		$ 159,498
Salvage Value of Equipment		
$66,500		
PV of Salvage Value[b]	41,290	
GPV of Project		200,788
Price of Project (C_p)		(179,000)
NPV of Project		$ 21,788

[a] This amount is $42,075(PVF_a \ 10\%, 5) = \$42,075(3.7908)$. See the discussion of PVF_a earlier in the chapter, and consult Table B-4 in Appendix B.
[b] This amount is $66,500(PVF \ 10\%, 5) = \$66,500(0.6209)$. See Table B-3 for PVF.

outside the firm.[7] As Table 13-3 shows, after this adjustment the annual net inflow from the project is $42,075. Then management applies a discount rate of 10 percent to analyze the project. (The question of choosing the appropriate discount rate will be discussed later in this chapter.)

The present value of a cash inflow of $42,075 for five years when discounted at 10 percent is $159,498, a figure substantially lower than C_p, the price of the car wash project ($179,000). However, we must recall that management estimates the equipment to have a salvage value of $66,500 at the end of the five-year project life, and the present value of that salvage amount (discounted at 10 percent) is $41,290.[8] This gives a gross present value (*GPV*) figure for the project of $159,498 + $41,290 = $200,788. Since C_p is only $179,000, the project is acceptable. Alternatively, Table 13-3 shows that the net present value of the project is $21,788. Since the net present value is greater than zero, the project meets the general rule for acceptability.

---

[7] Depreciation expense is an accounting concept employed to reflect the using up of certain fixed assets (that is, having them wear out or become obsolete) in the production process of the firm. On the firm's income statement, depreciation is an expense, but no cash is paid out. As a result, the firm's *net flow of cash benefits* will exceed net income. Therefore, we must add the depreciation back to the net income to account for its contribution to the benefits stream.
[8] In this example, the salvage value is exactly equal to the book value of the equipment at the end of five years. If these two values were not equal, the income tax due (saved) on the gain (loss) as a result of the sale of the equipment would have to be considered.

PROJECT YIELD OR RATE OF RETURN

Management will also be interested to know the return that is generated by the project in terms of a percentage yield or rate of return on the $179,000 of invested capital. Logically, the project has a return of more than 10 percent per year, since its *NPV* is greater than zero. If the *NPV* were zero, the net inflows from the project discounted at 10 percent per year would exactly equal $179,000. In financial analysis, the *internal rate of return (IRR)* of a project is its yield. As explained earlier in the chapter, the *IRR* can be defined as the discount rate that will just equate the present value of the stream of net receipts with the price of the project. To estimate the *IRR* in the context of our car wash project, we would want to find a discount rate such that the five-year stream of $42,075 in net receipts per year plus the present value of the salvage amount (*PV* of $66,500) is just equal, in present value terms, to C_P, or

$$\$42{,}075 \; (PVF_a \; IRR\%, \; 5) + \$66{,}500 \; (PVF \; IRR\%, \; 5) = \$179{,}000.$$

Mathematically, solving for the *IRR* is a difficult process. However, it is quite easy to estimate a project's *IRR* using an ordinary financial calculator or a set of present value tables and employing a trial-and-error method. In the preceding case, we know that the *IRR* is greater than 10 percent. We can calculate the present value of the stream of annual receipts plus the salvage amount at discount rates of 12 and 14 percent and see which most closely approximates $179,000. The following are the *PV*s of the five-year stream of $42,075 per year, plus the salvage value for the preceding rates of discount.

Discount Rate	PV of $42,075/yr. + $66,500
(IRR)	*(n = 5)*
12%	$189,404
14%	$178,987

The *PV* for 12 percent is too high, indicating that the *IRR* exceeds 12 percent. In fact, the *IRR* must be about 14 percent. For 14 percent, if we calculate the *PV* of an annual net inflow of $42,075 for five years plus the *PV* of the $66,500 salvage value, we get $178,987, which is very close to the project price. Thus, we can conclude that Clickwash's management will enjoy a yield of approximately 14 percent on its investment in the car wash project. Since this yield is greater than the 10 percent discount rate, the project should be undertaken. This analysis provides a new and slightly different statement of the accept-reject rule: An individual project is acceptable if its *IRR* equals or exceeds the discount rate.[9]

---

[9] Some exceptions to this rule exist, particularly when there are multiple positive-valued solutions for the *IRR*. For more information on this topic, see J. Fred Weston, Louis C. Gapenski, and Michael Ehrhardt, *Financial Management,* 9th ed. (Fort Worth, TX: Dryden Press, 1999), Chapter 11.

PROJECT RANKING IN CAPITAL BUDGETING ANALYSIS

We have shown how to determine whether a single given project is acceptable from an investment standpoint. However, we have not yet developed any rules for ranking alternative projects in terms of their relative acceptability. In the context of our hypothetical firm, Clickwash, this issue would emerge if management had to decide not only whether a car wash would be an acceptable investment but also whether such an investment would be *better* than several other alternatives that have the same initial price and project life.

For example, Clickwash might be faced with whether it should build the car wash, take over an existing pizzeria, build a donut shop, add another laundromat to its chain, or build an automobile muffler shop—each of which would entail an outlay (project price) of $179,000 and have a planned project life of five years. Under these circumstances, there is little difficulty choosing the most desirable project. In this case, the appropriate procedure for choosing among the projects is simply to go through the *NPV* analysis for each of the five projects and select the one with the highest *NPV.* Furthermore, if the firm had enough funds to undertake four of the five projects, management could decide which one to reject by determining which had the lowest *NPV.*

If the projects were of different size (price) but the same planned life, the *NPV* approach to ranking them could be applied, but management would have to take into account the possibility that various *combinations* of projects might generate different aggregate *NPVs.* Thus, management would end up ranking various feasible *packages* of projects, rather than each project individually. Returning to the example of Clickwash, suppose that the five projects previously stated are analyzed and the following results are obtained:

Project	Price	*NPV*
Car wash	$179,000	$21,788
Pizzeria	100,000	15,200
Donut shop	70,000	10,150
Coin laundry	80,000	10,800
Muffler shop	181,000	18,100

All of the projects meet the general rule for acceptability, since each has an *NPV* greater than zero. Suppose that the firm has only $360,000 to allocate for new investments. Management will then have to devise a plan for *capital rationing*—that is, decide which of the numerous projects to undertake, given the limited capital budget of $360,000. Management's objective should be to select the combination of projects that provides the greatest aggregate *NPV* for an outlay of $360,000 or less.

Table 13–4 *Clickwash, Inc., Project Array in Rank Order by Price*

Project	Price	NPV
1. Muffler Shop	$181,000	$18,100
2. Car Wash	179,000	21,788
3. Pizzeria	100,000	15,200
4. Coin Laundry	80,000	10,800
5. Donut Shop	70,000	10,150

Our first step is to rank-order the projects by price, as in Table 13-4. This provides a way to determine both the minimum and maximum number of projects that can be accepted. From Table 13-4 we can see that the minimum number of projects is two (Projects 1 and 2, which exhaust the $360,000). Furthermore, all combinations of two projects require $360,000 or less and thus could be undertaken. However, it is easy to see that no other two-project combination will yield as much as the combination 1,2. We illustrate this with a complete enumeration of the possible two-project combinations in Table 13-5. Since none of the two-project combinations has an *NPV* greater than combination 1,2 or greater than $39,888, we can drop all two-project combinations other than 1,2 from consideration.

Mathematics would indicate that there are also 10 possible three-project combinations from the list of Table 13-4, since

$$C_b^a = \frac{a!}{b!(a-b)!}$$

Table 13-5 *Clickwash, Inc., Analysis of Possible Two-Project Investment Combinations*

Project Combination	Price	NPV
1,2	$360,000	$39,888
1,3	281,000	33,300
1,4	261,000	28,900
1,5	251,000	28,250
2,3	279,000	36,988
2,4	259,000	32,588
2,5	249,000	31,938
3,4	180,000	26,000
3,5	170,000	25,350
4,5	150,000	20,950

Table 13–6 *Clickwash, Inc., Analysis of Possible Three-Project Capital Budgeting Combinations*

Project Combination	Price	NPV
1,2,3	$460,000	$55,088
1,2,4	440,000	50,688
1,2,5	430,000	50,038
1,3,4	361,000	44,100
1,3,5	351,000	43,450
1,4,5	331,000	39,050
2,3,4	359,000	47,788
2,3,5	349,000	47,138
2,4,5	329,000	42,738
3,4,5	250,000	36,150

is the formula for the number of combinations of *a* things taken *b* at a time. In Table 13-6 we enumerate all three-project combinations, showing their respective aggregate *NPV*s and prices. Note that only six three-project combinations fall within the capital budget constraint of $360,000. Of these, combination 2,3,4 has the greatest aggregate *NPV*—$47,788. This particular combination of projects has a total *NPV* that exceeds that of the best two-project combination—combination 1,2 (aggregate *NPV* of only $39,888). The conclusion is that combination 2,3,4 (the car wash, the pizzeria, and the coin laundry) should be undertaken.

In the preceding analysis, all the alternative projects had the same planned project life (five years). Obviously, firms can be faced with making accept-reject decisions on capital undertakings of unequal project life. The problem of unequal project life in capital budgeting analysis can be handled in several ways. One approach is to set up "replacement chains," which would extend the capital budgeting analysis to the number of years divisible by the respective project lives. For example, if we are comparing two projects—one that has a life of two years and one that has a life of three years—we could use six years as our period for comparison, assuming that we would repeat the first project three times over the period and the second project twice over the period. This would be a reasonable approach to use in a case such as the evaluation of two machines, one of which is more durable than the other. Employing such an approach, management could decide whether to use a less durable machine that would be replaced every two years or a more durable one that would be replaced every three years.

Where alternative projects have rather long lives (30 to 40 years or more), it might be reasonable to compare them using some arbitrary point (say, 30 years), which is set as the "life" of each alternative. This is so because as the flow of project returns is extended into the more distant future, not only does the present value of far-off receipts fall, but also the uncertainty of their occurrence increases.[10]

COST OF CAPITAL AND THE DISCOUNT RATE

As our example of Clickwash, Inc., has shown, the discount rate is an extremely important item in conducting a capital project analysis. Thus far, we have not discussed how a firm determines the discount rate used to calculate the present value of project cash flows. In its most basic form, this rate represents the cost to the firm of obtaining new funds to invest. It is called the **marginal cost of capital.**

The **marginal cost of capital** *(MCC)* is the discount rate which represents the marginal cost of investment funds to the firm. It is calculated as a weighted-average of the after-tax-cost of funds from each source.

Generally, firms have two principal sources of investment funds—debt and equity. In other words, they can obtain new financing either by borrowing or by using owner-supplied funds. (Owner-supplied funds can be generated internally or raised by issuing new stock.) Since interest paid on borrowed funds is tax deductible, it is the after-tax cost of debt that is relevant to estimating the effect of debt on the firm's overall marginal cost of capital. Its marginal cost of capital at any point in time will then be the weighted average of its cost of debt and cost of equity.

To illustrate, let's assume that the interest rate on new bonds issued by the firm is 12 percent and that the firm's owners expect a return of 14 percent on funds that they invest. Let's further assume that the best capital structure for the firm is 60 percent debt and 40 percent equity.[11] If the corporate income tax rate *(T)* is 34 percent, the firm's marginal cost of debt will be the interest rate on borrowed funds *(bond rate)* multiplied by the quantity $(1 - T)$, or $0.12(1 - 0.34) = 0.0792$. Its marginal cost of capital will be this rate multiplied by the proportion of debt in its capital structure *plus* the expected rate of return on equity (14 percent) multiplied by the proportion of owner-supplied funds in the capital structure. For the preceding numbers, the marginal cost of capital *(k)* is calculated as follows:

$$k = 0.0792(0.6) + 0.14(0.4) = 0.0475 + 0.056 = 0.1035.$$

---

[10] Another technique used to evaluate projects with unequal lives is that of the equivalent annual annuity approach, which essentially assumes that the replacement chains extend to infinity for each project. For more information on comparing projects with unequal lives, see Eugene F. Brigham and Phillip R. Daves, *Intermediate Financial Management*, 7th ed. (Cincinnati: South-Western, 2002), Chapter 12.

[11] By *best* or *optimal capital structure*, we mean the combination of debt and equity that will minimize the weighted average cost of capital for the firm, all other factors remaining the same. For a more thorough discussion of this issue, see Brigham and Daves, *Intermediate Financial Management*, Chapters 9 and 11.

FIGURE 13–1

Determination of the Firm's Capital Budget and Marginal Cost of Capital

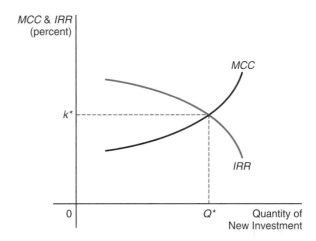

As the quantity of new investment undertaken increases, the firm's marginal cost of capital rises. However, the internal rate of return falls because less and less attractive new investments are undertaken. At k^*, where $MCC = IRR$, the optimal size capital budget and the firm's MCC are determined.

Ordinarily, as a firm expands the amount of its new investment at any point in time, the marginal cost of capital will rise. This occurs because the firm must turn to more and more expensive means of financing as the total amount of investment funds to be raised is increased. Thus, a curve relating the marginal cost of capital to the size of the capital budget will look something like the MCC curve in Figure 13-1. Similarly, one can construct a curve that relates the internal rates of return of available investment alternatives to the amount of investment undertaken. This is done by rank-ordering capital projects in decreasing order of internal rate of return. The IRR curve of Figure 13-1 reflects the decrease of the internal rate of return as less and less profitable projects are undertaken.

If we recall the rule that states that a project is acceptable as long as its internal rate of return exceeds the firm's discount rate, we can find both the equilibrium size of the capital budget and the firm's MCC in Figure 13-1. This occurs where the rising MCC curve intersects the falling IRR curve. Beyond Q^*, the return on additional projects is less than the firm's marginal cost of capital, so these projects will not be undertaken. Thus, k^* is the firm's marginal cost of capital for the given MCC and IRR curves.

Of course, firms generally have to choose among investment alternatives that not only are risky but also vary in riskiness. Therefore, it is necessary to modify capital project analyses to take explicit account of the problem of risk. In Chapter 14, several approaches to handling the problem of decision making under risk will be discussed.

The Leverage Roller Coaster

"They Shopped—Now They've Dropped." That is how *Business Week* writers characterized the fate in 2002 of firms that went shopping for acquisitions during the high-rolling 1990s. With high market capitalizations yielding strong borrowing power, many chose the leveraged buyout (LBO)—the purchase of a company typically by management primarily through the use of borrowed money as their acquisition strategy.

Borrowed money became a popular means of financing corporate takeovers because *if* a company is highly profitable, the after-tax cost of debt is typically cheaper than the cost of equity financing. For example, if a corporation is in the 34 percent income tax bracket and borrows money at an 8 percent annual rate of interest, the after-tax cost of debt is $(1 - 0.34) \times 8\% = 5.28\%$. The return that stockholders will require to keep their money invested in the firm will depend on the level of interest rates in the economy and the risk associated with a particular company's stock, together with the riskiness of the stock market as a whole. The rate of return on a long-term (10-year) U.S. government bond, considered virtually risk-free in terms of default risk, was around 4 percent on an annual basis in 2002. The added-on amount, called the market risk premium, associated with general market riskiness, has historically ranged from 4 percent to 7 percent per year. If an individual company's stock is perceived to be riskier than the market as a whole, an additional risk premium will be required as well. Thus, since it is not tax deductible, the cost of equity capital can easily exceed 10 percent on an annual basis.

Although debt may be a relatively inexpensive source of funds for a firm, it may increase the risk of bankruptcy. If a company's stock does not yield the rate of return required by the stockholders, the price of the stock will likely fall, but this situation does not force a firm into bankruptcy. (The risk premium attached to the stock of an individual company will increase as the percent of the value of the company financed by debt increases, all other factors remaining the same.) On the other hand, if a company cannot meet the required payments for its debt, holders of the firm's debt can force it to resort to a declaration of bankruptcy.

One recent example of a company that has a troubled history connected with leveraged buyouts is Formica Corporation, maker of Formica, a laminated material, and Surell, a substitute for Corian, a synthetic marble. The company has been through three LBOs, including one in 1998. Although the investors in these buyouts actually made a high rate of return on their money, the frequent ownership changes and concerns over the amount of debt have taken a toll on the company.

Other companies whose growth strategies for the 1990s went sour in the 2000s include Georgia-Pacific, which spent $17 billion to acquire other pulp and paper makers in recent years. In 2002, in the middle of a sharp downturn in its markets, the Georgia-Pacific Group was grappling with $12 billion in debt and the possibility that it would have to sell off assets to keep its commitments to lenders. In the financial services industry, Conseco Inc., which had spent $7.6 billion to buy Green Tree Financial, was also reported to be struggling with its debt.

Although a high amount of corporate leverage may result in a lower cost of capital and substantially higher earnings per share for stockholders, it frequently also means "betting the company." A successful future for a highly leveraged company requires astute management at the very minimum and, for certain, much better luck than the markets dealt out in 2001–2002.

References: "They Shopped, Now They've Dropped," *Business Week* (February 25, 2002), pp. 36–37; "How Formica Got Burned Out by Buyouts," *Business Week* (March 22, 1999), pp. 82–84; and "All That Leverage Comes Home to Roost," *Business Week* (September 10, 1990), pp. 76–77.

SUMMARY

Project Analysis and Capital Budgeting

In this chapter we have examined the application of interest and discount rate methodologies to managerial decisions concerning capital projects or new investments. We defined *capital budgeting* as the process by which a firm's managers determine how to allocate investment expenditures among alternative projects. The evaluation of individual investment undertakings, or *capital project analysis,* was shown to be a major part of the capital budgeting process.

The concept of *equivalency* was introduced to show that a present amount of money is equal in value to a discounted future amount. The present value of an amount received *n* years in the future, we saw, can be found by the formula

$$PV = \frac{FV_n}{(1+r)^n},$$

where *r* is the applicable discount rate (a target yield or rate of return on similar alternative investments). Tables of *present value factors* were introduced to simplify the mathematics of the discounting process.

Application of the preceding concepts led us to the conclusion that the present value of an anticipated stream of net receipts generated by a capital project is something less than the additive amount of such receipts. In particular, the present value is the discounted value of the stream. We argued that a given capital project is *acceptable* when adjustments are made for depreciation and salvage value as long as such a *discounted stream of net cash flows is at least equal to the price of the project.* The *net present value (NPV)* of the project (*PV* of net receipts minus project price) would thus be equal to or greater than zero. This criterion was related to an alternative statement: namely, that the yield on the project's price, or its *internal rate of return (IRR),* should be at least equal to the marginal cost of capital for the firm. A simple capital project analysis involving a coin-operated car wash (Clickwash, Inc.) was introduced as an example of the steps management must go through to make an accept-or-reject decision on a new undertaking.

Later in the chapter we discussed the *capital rationing* aspect of the capital budgeting process. We examined the special problem of allocating a limited amount of investment dollars to various feasible combinations of capital projects. The net present value approach was extended to this setting, and a methodology for identifying the combination of projects producing the greatest aggregate *NPV* was developed. The simple methodology we employed is usable for projects with different prices and equal planned project lives but must be modified somewhat if projects with unequal lives are being analyzed.

Finally, we introduced the notion of the firm's *marginal cost of capital* and its marginal cost of capital curve. The equilibrium quantity of investment and marginal cost of capital was defined by the intersection of the firm's *MCC* curve with its *IRR* curve.

This chapter did not deal with the problem of differences in the risk associated with dissimilar capital projects. For example, in the case of our hypothetical firm, Clickwash, we treated the flows of returns from investments in endeavors (muffler shop, pizzeria, donut shop) unfamiliar to the firm as being either risk free or equal in risk to undertakings (an additional laundromat) that are thoroughly covered by management's prior experience. It is unlikely that managers would take such a view in real-world capital budgeting situations. Generally, managers will attempt to take into account differences in the risks associated with alternative capital projects. In Chapter 14, we will examine some methodologies that allow for comparison of projects with unequal risk.

QUESTIONS

1. From an economist's point of view, would you characterize capital budgeting decisions as long- or short-run decisions? Why?

2. Which of the following would you include as part of the price of a capital project undertaken to expand a company's production of minicomputers? (For each item you *exclude,* give a brief explanation of why it should not be considered a part of the project price.)

   a. Production labor for minicomputers

   b. Product development costs

   c. Interest on construction loan for new building to house project

   d. Components for assembly of minicomputers

   e. Architectural fees for new building

   f. Present value of expanded working capital requirements

   g. Cost of fuel to heat new building

   h. New machine tools for manufacture of minicomputer parts

3. What is the definition of the net present value *(NPV)* of a capital project? What *NPV* rule should be followed in classifying capital projects as acceptable or unacceptable?

4. How would you define the internal rate of return of a capital project?

5. A certain capital project has anticipated net cash receipts of $180,000 per year for 10 years and a salvage value of $20,000. What is the maximum price a firm should pay for this project if the appropriate discount rate is 12 percent?

6. If a capital project has estimated net receipts of $8,000 per year and a life of 15 years with no salvage value, what would be its *NPV* if its price were $54,487 and the applicable discount rate were 9 percent?

7. What is the *IRR* (internal rate of return) of the preceding project?

8. Briefly explain how a firm's managers can use the *NPV* approach to allocate a limited capital budget among a number of acceptable capital projects, each having the same life and price.

9. Suppose a firm has a given-size capital budget. Explain how the best combination of a number of acceptable capital projects with *different* prices but the *same* lives can be determined using the *NPV* approach.

PROBLEMS

1. A project has an anticipated stream of annual net receipts of $23,500. Its life is 12 years. No salvage value is expected at the end of the 12 years. Compute the net present value of the project if its price is $130,000 and the applicable discount rate is each of the following:

   a. 6 percent

   b. 9 percent

   c. 12 percent

2. Gretna Corporation is about to sell some used equipment to Allied Leasing. Allied has offered the following two payment schemes:

   a. $100,000 now and $250,000 at the end of five years.

   b. $100,000 now, $50,000 at the end of two years, and $215,000 at the end of eight years.

   If the appropriate discount rate for either transaction is 6 percent, which would be the better of the two alternatives for Gretna? Why? Show your work.

3. In the preceding problem, what would you advise Gretna's management to ask for if it desired to settle the transaction this year for a single cash payment?

4. Jayne Corporation has decided to undertake a capital project that has a life of eight years and estimated annual net inflows of $27,460. At a discount rate of 6 percent, what is the present value of the eight-year receipts stream?

5. Hamstrung, Inc., is contemplating an investment in a new food processing plant. Management's best estimate of the project's price is $620,000. The plant will have an indefinite life, but management expects to divest it at the end of 12 years at an estimated after-tax salvage value of $273,000. Annual net inflows from operations are expected to be $60,000. Is the project acceptable at a discount rate of 9 percent? Why or why not? What would happen if a discount rate of 6 percent were applied to the project?

6. Pickadilly Peppers is trying to decide whether to invest in a new cannery, to set up a wholesaling operation that would eliminate intermediaries currently selling its product, or to computerize several older plants. All three alternatives are viewed as having the same project life of 15 years. However, different project prices are applicable to each, and each has a different expected stream of annual net inflows. The firm's managers believe that a discount rate of 6 percent is appropriate for evaluating the alternatives. Data are as follows:

Project		Price	Annual Net Inflows
A	New Cannery	$190,000	$20,000
B	Wholesale Operation	168,000	18,000
C	Plant Computerization	159,000	17,000

After examining the project prices, management finds it has a sufficient capital budget to undertake two of the projects. Assuming that the cash flows from the projects are independent of one another (i.e., that undertaking one of the projects will have no effect on the returns from another), which two projects should be undertaken?

7. All of the following projects have an initial cost (project price) of $87,500. Which are acceptable at a discount rate of 9 percent?

   a. Purchase of a vintage car that can be sold for $120,000 at the end of five years.

   b. Investment in a restaurant partnership that will return you a net inflow of $5,000 per year for 10 years and will provide a buyout of your share for $100,000 at the end of 10 years.

   c. Purchase of a piece of machinery that will generate net inflows of $18,000 per year for eight years and have an after-tax salvage value of $7,000 at the end of the period.

8. The following is a list of four projects that Capital Corporation must choose from for the coming year:

Project	Project Price	Annual Net Inflows	Internal Rate of Return
A	$700,000	$118,861	11%
B	670,000	109,039	10%
C	184,000	32,549	12%
D	273,000	48,305	12%

John Smart, a junior vice-president of the company, has argued that Projects A, C, and D should be accepted, since they all have higher internal rates of return than Project B and their prices sum to less than the capital budgeting constraint of $1,700,000. Jane Cranston, a consultant to the company, politely suggests that Smart is not so smart and that Projects A, B, and D should be undertaken. If the appropriate rate of discount for all four projects is 9 percent and each has a life of 10 years, who is right—Smart or Cranston? (Assume no salvage values.)

9. The managers of Zeron Corporation have determined that their firm's optimal capital structure is 40 percent debt financing and 60 percent equity. The current interest rate is 14 percent for borrowers like Zeron, and the company's shareholders expect a return on equity of 16 percent. The company's corporate income tax rate is 40 percent, and interest is a deductible expense.

   a. What is Zeron's marginal cost of capital?

   b. If Zeron is considering an investment project with a life of 10 years, an annual net flow of benefits of $470,000, a project cost of $2,500,000, and no salvage value, what advice would you give to management?

10. Lagrange Chicken Farm is considering the installation of new automated chicken feeders. The feeders are more efficient and will reduce wastage of chicken feed. The new feeders will cost $160,000 and will have an expected life of five years with a salvage value of $10,000. They are expected to result in a cost savings of $30,000 a year. The old feeders were purchased five years ago at a cost of $65,000 and have been depreciated on a straight-line basis with an expected life of 10 years and a salvage value of $5,000. Their current market value is $40,000. The firm's marginal cost of capital is 12 percent, and its marginal tax rate is 40 percent. The firm will also be able to get an investment tax credit equal to 5 percent of the cost of the new feeders. (Do not adjust the cost basis of the feeders to reflect the tax credit when calculating depreciation.)

    a. What is the initial cash outlay required for the new machine?

    b. What are the annual after-tax cash flows from the new feeders in years one through four?

    c. Should the company purchase the new feeders? Why or why not?

    d. Suppose that the cost saving on the new feeders will be $30,000 the first year but will increase by 10 percent a year each year for the next four years. What is the *NPV* of the new feeders now?

11. Transcendental Research Laboratories is considering replacing its old super-computer with a new terraflops computer. TRL believes that the new computer would enable the company to increase the sales revenues from research projects by $8,500,000 per year with a corresponding increase in operating costs (not including depreciation) of $500,000 per year. The new computer will cost $42,500,000 and will have an expected life of 10 years. It will be depreciated using straight-line depreciation, with an assumed salvage value of $2,500,000. The old supercomputer was purchased five years ago for $22,500,000 and depreciated on a straight-line basis with an expected life of 15 years and no salvage value. The current market value of the old computer is $10,000,000 (before any tax consequences of the sale are considered). The marginal cost of capital is 12 percent, and the marginal income tax rate is 40 percent.

    a. Calculate the net outlay that would be required for TRL to purchase the new computer. This net outlay figure should consider the sale proceeds from the old machine and all initial tax consequences of the sale of the old computer and the purchase of the new one.

    b. Calculate the net present value of replacing the old computer with the new one. Do you recommend that TRL purchase the new computer? Why or why not?

SELECTED REFERENCES

Block, Stanley B., and Geoffrey A. Hirt. *Foundations of Financial Management,* 7th ed. New York: McGraw-Hill, 2003.

Brigham, Eugene F., and Phillip R. Daves. *Intermediate Financial Management,* 7th ed. Cincinnati: South-Western, 2002.

"Divisional Hurdle Rates and the Cost of Capital." *Financial Management* 18, No. 1 (Spring 1989): 18–25.

Flannery, Mark J., Joel F. Houston, and Subramanyam Venkataraman. "Financing Multiple Investment Projects." *Financial Management* 22, No. 2 (Summer 1993): 161–172.

Gitman, Lawrence J. *Principles of Managerial Finance,* 10th ed. Boston: Addison-Wesley, 2002.

Mao, James C. T. *Corporate Financial Decisions.* Palo Alto, CA: Pavan, 1976, Chapters 7 and 8.

Moyer, R. Charles, James R. McGuigan, and William J. Kretlow. *Contemporary Financial Management,* 8th ed. Cincinnati: South-Western, 2001, Chapters 4, 8, and 9.

Mukherjee, Tarun K., and Vineeta L. Hingorani. "Capital Rationing Decisions of *Fortune 500* Firms: A Survey." *Financial Practice and Education* 9, No. 1 (Spring/Summer 1999): 7–15.

Pohlman, Randolph A., Emmanuel S. Santiago, and F. Lynn Markel. "Cash Flow Estimation Practices of Large Firms." *Financial Management* 17, No. 2 (Summer 1988): 71–79.

Roubi, Raafat R., Richard T. Barth, and Alex Faseruk. "Capital Budgeting Use in Canada: Sophistication and Risk Attributes." *Journal of Applied Business Research* 7, No. 4 (Fall 1991): 83–89.

Compounding and Discounting

COMPOUND INTEREST

The process of determining the amount to which a given sum will accumulate over a specified number of time periods at a stated rate of interest per period is known as *compounding*. An example of a compound interest problem would be the determination of the amount to which a $1,000 savings deposit will accumulate in 10 years if 6 percent interest is added to the account at the end of each year. We can analyze this problem as follows:

		Account Balance	Interest Earned = .06 × Previous Account Balance
Initial Deposit:		$1,000.00	
Amount at End of Year:	1	1,060.00	$ 60.00
	2	1,123.60	63.60
	3	1,191.02	67.42
	4	1,262.48	71.46
	5	1,338.23	75.75
	6	1,418.52	80.29
	7	1,503.63	85.11
	8	1,593.85	90.22
	9	1,689.48	95.63
	10	1,790.85	101.37

If the account is left untouched and each year's interest is compounded on the previous year's ending balance (including interest), the 10-year result will be $1,790.85. Each entry in the "Interest Earned" column is .06 times the previous year-end balance; for example, year 5 will yield $75.75 = .06 × $1,262.48, the ending balance for year 4.

It is easy to derive a formula for the amount that the $1,000 will accumulate to at the end of year 10. Denote *FV* (future value) as the account balance at the end of a given period. For the end of year 1, we have

$$FV_1 = PV(1.06),$$

where *PV* is the initial deposit (a present value). At the end of year 2, *FV* will be increased by 6 percent so that

$$FV_2 = FV_1 (1.06) = [PV(1.06)] (1.06) = PV(1.06)^2.$$

At the end of year 3, we will have

$$FV_3 = FV_2(1.06) = [PV(1.06)^2] (1.06) = PV(1.06)^3.$$

For each period that we compound the interest, the exponent of the above expression will rise one digit. Thus for 10 years we have

$$FV_{10} = PV(1.06)^{10},$$

or

$$FV_{10} = \$1,000(1.06)^{10} = \$1,000 (1.7909) = \$1,790.90,$$

a rounded-off version of the answer we obtained in the preceding calculations.

Compound interest tables are commonly used to determine future values, as stated previously. Such tables contain the values of the term $(1 + r)^n$ where *r* is the rate of interest and *n* is the number of periods the interest is compounded. In the preceding example, $(1 + r)^n = (1 + .06)^{10} = 1.7909$. The number 1.7909 is called a compound interest factor, *CIF,* and it is the amount to which one dollar will accumulate in 10 years with interest annually compounded at 6 percent. To find the future value of $1,000 compounded at 6 percent for 10 years, we simply multiply the *CIF* for a 6 percent interest rate and 10-year term (*CIF* 6%, 10) times the present amount (*PV* = $1,000):

$$FV_{10} = PV(CIF\ 6\%, 10)$$

$$= \$1,000(1.7909) = \$1,790.90.$$

Table B-1 in the Interest Factor Tables at the end of the book provides compound interest factors. To use the table, simply look up the *CIF* for the number of periods that interest will be compounded and multiply the factor times the principal or present value. The result will be the future amount. Thus, if we wished to determine the future value of $25,000 compounded at 9 percent annually for 18 years, we would find

$$FV_{18} = \$25{,}000 \; (CIF \; 9\%, \; 18)$$

$$= \$25{,}000 \; (4.7171) = \$117{,}927.50.$$

PRESENT VALUE AND DISCOUNTING

The present value of some amount to be received at a specific future date is equal to the present amount that would accumulate to the future amount by the date in question at some appropriate rate of interest. The rate of interest applied to such calculations is called the *discount rate,* since the present value will be smaller than the future value by a specific percentage per year.

Discounting, then, is the reverse of compounding. To understand this, ask how much you would be willing to give for $1,790.90 received 10 years from now if you expect you can easily make 6 percent interest per year on any present amount you have on hand. From our above discussion of compounding, it is clear that $1,000 will accumulate to the sum of $1,790.90 in 10 years if 6 percent interest is compounded annually. Thus the discounted value of $1,790.90 received 10 years from now is $1,000.00, and 6 percent is the discount rate.

Alternatively, from our formula for compounding, we know

$$FV_{10} = PV(1 + r)^{10}.$$

Therefore,

$$PV = \frac{FV_{10}}{(1+r)^{10}} = FV_{10}\left[\frac{1}{(1+r)^{10}}\right].$$

The term in brackets is the *present value factor, PVF.* For the preceding problem, we can write

$$PV = FV_{10} \; (PVF \; 6\%, \; 10),$$

where, for the term in brackets, $r = .06$ and $n = 10$. This factor appears in Table B-3 in the Interest Factor Tables and its value is 0.5584. Thus, for a future value of $1,790.90, we have

$$PV = \$1{,}790.90 \; (0.5584) = \$1{,}000.04 \approx \$1{,}000.$$

The slight error is due to the rounding of the present value factor, which is more accurately 0.558394.

The notion of present value is extremely important in managerial economics and finance, since project decisions generally involve evaluations of benefits or receipts that are generated at some future date or over some period of years in the future. For further discussion of this point, see the relevant sections within this chapter.

ANNUITIES

An annuity is a fixed sum received at the end of each period for some specified number of periods in the future. The *compound* or *future* value of an annuity is the amount to which such period-end payments would accumulate if each payment were left in an account at a specified rate of interest compounded annually. For example, if you are to receive an annuity of $1,000 for 10 years and you leave all of the payments in an account with 6 percent interest compounded annually, at the end of the tenth year you will have $13,180.80. The compound value is determined as follows, where A is the amount of each period-end payment and n is the number of periods:

Year 1	Year 2	Year 3	Year 10
$FV_a = A$ or $FV_a =$ $A(1+r)^0$	$A + A(1+r)$ or $A[(1+r)^0$ $+ (1+r)^1]$	$A + [A + A(1+r)](1+r)$ or $A[(1+r)^0 + (1+r)^1$ $+ (1+r)^2]$	$A[(1+r)^0 + (1+r)^1$ $+ \ldots + (1+r)^9]$

Therefore the general formula is

$$FV_a n = A[(1+r)^0 + (1+r)^1 + \ldots + (1+r)^{n-1}].$$

Again, tables have been developed for the term in brackets, which is the compound value factor for an annuity, CVF_a. For 6 percent and 10 years, CVF_a 6%, 10 equals 13.181 (see Appendix B, Table B-2). For our $1,000 annuity, we can write

$$FV_a 10 = \$1,000 \, (CVF_a \, 6\%, 10)$$

$$= \$1,000 \, (13.181) = \$13,181.$$

The *present value of an annuity* is the amount that, if received today, would accumulate to the same amount as an annuity received for a specified number of periods with interest compounded at the end of each period. With a 6 percent interest rate, the present value of the $1,000 per-year annuity discussed previously is $7,360.27, which is its future compound value, $13,181, discounted at the given rate of interest. From our formula for the compound value of an annuity, we derive the formula for the present value of an annuity, PV_a, in the following way.

We know that the present value of the annuity is the same as the PV of $13,181 received 10 years from now, or

$$PV_a = \frac{FV_a}{(1+r)^n} = \frac{A[(1+r)^0 + (1+r)^1 + \ldots + (1+r)^{n-1}]}{(1+r)^n}$$

$$= A\left[\frac{(1+r)^0}{(1+r)^{10}} + \frac{(1+r)^1}{(1+r)^{10}} + \cdots + \frac{(1+r)^9}{(1+r)^{10}}\right]$$

$$= A\left[\frac{1}{(1+r)^{10}} + \frac{1}{(1+r)^9} + \cdots + \frac{1}{(1+r)}\right].$$

The term in brackets in the last expression is the present value factor for an annuity, and its general formula is

$$PVF_a(r\%, n) = \left[\frac{1}{(1+r)^n} + \frac{1}{(1+r)^{n-1}} + \cdots + \frac{1}{(1+r)}\right].$$

Table B-4 in the Interest Factor Tables contains such factors for up to 60 payment periods. For the present problem, we have PVF_a (6%, 10) = 7.3601. Therefore PV_a = $1,000 ($PVF_a$ 6%, 10) = $7,360.10, which is the same (except for rounding) as the present value of $13,181 received 10 years in the future where the discount rate is 6 percent.

In capital project analysis, the present value of an annuity approach can be used to determine the present value of project benefits or inflows when a certain fixed dollar return per period is expected to be generated by the project for a specified number of periods in the future. For a direct application of this method, review the case of Clickwash, Inc., in Chapter 13.

PROBLEMS

1. To what amount will $20,000 left untouched in an account accumulate at the end of 13 years if 9 percent interest is added to the account at the end of each year?

2. What is the present value of a single payment of $187,000 received eight years in the future if the discount rate is 12 percent?

3. Suppose your company puts $2,000 per year into an annuity for you at the end of each year and you are guaranteed to receive 6 percent per annum interest on all funds left in your annuity account. How much will your account balance be at the end of six years if you are not permitted to make any withdrawals?

4. A retiring executive of Pygmalion Enterprises has offered to sell her 20-year annuity back to the company for cash. She or her survivors were to receive $18,000 per year at year-end over the 20-year period. If the company normally applies a 6 percent discount rate to such transactions, how much will it be willing to pay for the annuity?

5. Barclay Concrete Company owes its supplier, Ace Cement, $172,000 for trade credit extended to Barclay's account for cement purchases. Barclay has had cash flow problems and cannot pay off the account with current revenues. Ace's management has offered to convert the account to a long-term debt, extending a 10-year balloon note at 9 percent compound interest per year. If the principal and interest are not due until the end of the 10 years, how much will Barclay have to pay Ace when the note comes due?

6. A given investment project is expected to yield $10,000 in net receipts per year for each of 10 years following its undertaking. If the discount rate is 12 percent, what is the present value of the net receipts stream?

7. You are offered a risk-free investment that you can sell at the end of three years for $14,000. You know that you can easily and safely earn 6 percent interest on your funds. What is the maximum amount you would be willing to pay for the investment?

CHAPTER FOURTEEN

Risk in Project Analysis

Chapter 13 introduced some tools for the analysis of capital projects or alternative investment possibilities. Throughout that chapter we assumed that the decision maker was certain about the outcome of each project that was evaluated. We also assumed that combinations of projects could be compared without considering the possibility that the success of a given undertaking might depend on whether it was combined with a related project. In short, we assumed away the problem of *risk* in project analysis. In this chapter we address that remaining issue.

CERTAINTY VERSUS RISK

A situation is certain when there is absolutely no doubt as to its outcome. Most people would regard the purchase of a certificate of deposit (CD) at a bank as an investment characterized by certainty. The decision maker who has made the purchase knows that a given return will be received if the CD is held to maturity. A situation is characterized as *risky* when there is some doubt as to its outcome. Thus, a person who invests in a restaurant may expect to receive a given return from the investment if the restaurant is successful in attracting enough customers and if costs of operation do not change. Clearly, this type of investment is different from the purchase of a

CD. It is a risky alternative because the decision maker is faced with some doubt about the outcome of the decision.

RISK IN ECONOMIC ANALYSIS

To analyze risk from an economic point of view, we must first make a behavioral assumption about the decision maker who is confronted with alternatives of unequal risk. In project analysis, the assumption usually made is that the decision maker is **risk averse.** Simply stated, this means that the decision maker will prefer a situation that promises a guaranteed or certain return of a given amount of money to a situation in which the receipt of the same amount of money is less certain. From our preceding example, a risk averter would choose to invest, say, $5,000 in a certificate of deposit rather than in a restaurant if both investments were expected to yield a net return of $2,000 at the end of five years. That is because the return from the CD is certain and the return from the restaurant is not.

Economic theory also recognizes the possibility that a decision maker may be a risk seeker or have a neutral attitude toward risk. If the decision maker in the previous example were a **risk seeker,** the restaurant investment would be chosen, even though the money return expected from it was the same as that for the CD. A **risk-neutral** decision maker would be indifferent between the two alternatives.

A **risk-averse investor** is one that given a choice between two investments with the same expected return will always prefer the less risky one.

A **risk seeker** is an investor that given the choice between two investments with the same expected return will prefer the riskier one.

A **risk-neutral investor** is indifferent between two investments with the same expected return, regardless of their risk.

RISK-RETURN INDIFFERENCE CURVES

A risk-return indifference curve shows combinations of risk and return that are equally attractive to a given investor. Figure 14-1 illustrates two risk-return indifference curves. We assume that risk is measurable and that it increases along the vertical axis. For the moment we will use the numbers 1, 2, 3, and 4 to indicate increasing levels of risk. The horizontal axis of the diagram shows money returns expected by the investor. A single risk-return indifference curve traces out combinations of risk and expected money return that will make the investor equally happy. Consider curve I_5 in Figure 14-1, for example. It indicates that the investor would be indifferent between combination A (which consists of zero risk and a return of $1,000) and combination B (which consists of a risky return of $1,750). The risk-return indifference curve slopes upward to the right because the risk-averse investor will be indifferent toward higher risk only if he or she expects a greater return to be associated with it. The curvature of the indifference curve reflects one further assumption—that as risk increases, progressively larger increments in expected return will be required to offset given increments in risk (in order to keep the investor equally happy).

FIGURE 14-1

*The Risk-Return
Indifference
Curve Concept*

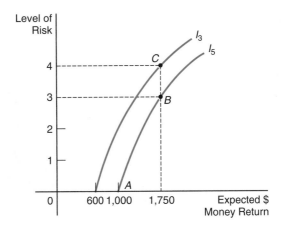

Risk-return indifference curve I_3 is less desirable to the investor than I_5, since each combination of risk and return on I_3 is equal to a certain return of only $600, which is much less than the certain return of $1,000 associated with I_5 combinations.

In Figure 14-1, combinations of risk and return that lie on risk-return indifference curve I_3 are less satisfying to the investor than those that lie on I_5. Why? Clearly, it is because the combinations of risk and return on I_3 all involve either a higher risk for any given return or a lower return for any given level of risk. For example, point C, which corresponds to a return of $1,750, is less satisfying to the investor than is point B. This is because the return associated with C is the same as with B, but B is on a lower level of risk.

In general, for a risk-return indifference curve diagram such as Figure 14-1, we view the quadrant as being filled with indifference curves such as I_5 and I_3, all of which are nonintersecting. Return decreases and risk increases as we move toward the northwest area of the quadrant, so that less desirable indifference curves lie to the northwest of any given point (risk-return combination), whereas more desirable indifference curves lie to the southeast. The risk-return indifference curve is a concept similar to the equal-output isoquants employed in production analysis (Chapter 5). However, risk-return indifference curves are concave toward the X or "return" axis, since at the margin the decision maker's willingness to accept additional risk for an additional dollar's worth of return diminishes.

If we consider a whole family of risk-return indifference curves for a given investment decision maker, we can conclude that for any amount of expected money return, the risk averter will be less happy the greater the level of risk. This is shown in Figure 14-2. Note that the investor regards point A on I_5 as a risk-return combination equivalent to a certain return of $1,000. If, however, we consider a combination involving more risk than level 4 for a $1,300 return, the investor is seen to be on a lower risk-return

FIGURE 14–2

A Family of Risk-Return Indifference Curves

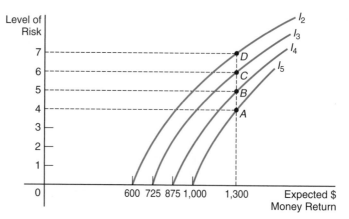

Assuming the investor is risk averse, higher risk levels associated with a given expected return yield less and less satisfaction. Thus, for an expected return of $1,300, the investor's satisfaction decreases progressively from point *A* through points *B, C,* and *D*.

indifference curve (the *certain return,* which is viewed as equally desirable to the risky return, *falls*). Thus, points *B, C,* and *D* represent successively less desirable risk-return combinations for an expected money return of $1,300.

If we retain the assumption of risk aversion, then, we can conclude that the economic nature of risk is that its presence *lessens the desirability* of a given undertaking or investment project. Furthermore, the more risky a given undertaking, the less desirable it will be in comparison to other alternatives having the same expected money outcome.

PROBABILITY AND UNCERTAINTY

To measure risk in a meaningful way, we must apply *probability analysis.* In probability analysis, the term *event* is used to designate an outcome. The probability of a particular event is a numerical value measuring the uncertainty that the event will occur. More specifically, it is the proportion of times under identical circumstances that the event can be expected to occur, or

$$P(E) = \frac{\text{number of times event occurs}}{\text{number of times situation is repeated}}.$$

If an event is certain to occur, its probability is one; if it can never occur, its probability is zero. An event's probability can be viewed as the *odds* that the event will occur or the percentage of times it will take place when a given set of circumstances is repeated many times. Running an experiment where a situation is repeated many times is a way to determine empirically the probability of a specific event. However, it is also possible to determine an event's probability deductively if enough information is available. For this, we need a few more definitions.

Each event in a listing of all the possible outcomes of a given situation is called an *elementary event*. For example, in picking a card from a deck of 52 cards, each card is an elementary event. A *composite event* consists of a number of elementary events, and an *event set* consists of all the elementary events that satisfy a particular outcome. Thus, we can restate our formula for the probability of an event as

$$P(E) = \frac{\text{number of elementary events in event set}}{\text{number of equally likely elementary events}} .$$

From the preceding, we can see that the probability of picking a two of spades from a deck of 52 cards is 1/52, but the probability of picking a deuce is 4/52, since the event set includes the four elementary events: two of spades, two of hearts, two of diamonds, and two of clubs. For a deck of 52 cards, the sum of the probabilities of all the cards (elementary events) is one (there are 52 elementary events, each having a probability of 1/52). In general, any time a listing of all possible events includes every conceivable outcome—one of which *must* occur—the sum of the probabilities of all the elementary events will be one.

In many situations, probabilities can be ascertained empirically or through experimentation. The card-picking examples are cases in point. For the composite event "pick a deuce," a deck of cards can be shuffled and a card picked. This can be repeated a very large number of times, and the more the experiment is run, the closer the ratio of deuces picked to the total number of cards picked will approach 4/52. It is also true that in many cases probabilities can be ascertained logically. Again, card picking suffices as an example. Since we know there are 52 possible elementary events, four of which constitute the event set "pick a deuce," the odds (or probability) of picking a deuce equal 4/52.

When the probability of events in an uncertain situation cannot be ascertained either empirically or logically, we enter the realm of *subjective probability*. A subjective probability is simply a probability value *assigned* to an event by an investigator. It is a judgmental estimate rather than strictly an empirical one. Subjective probability is used in the analysis of investment projects, since decision makers frequently must rely on expert opinion (their own personal judgment, perhaps) regarding the likelihood of any particular event. For example, the decision maker may be able to estimate how successful in terms of dollar return a project will be, *given* various rates of growth in personal income for a particular region or state. However, there may be a great deal of uncertainty about the occurrence of each possible rate of growth in income. An approach that employs the subjective probabilities of the possible rates of growth in income may be used to determine both a weighted average outcome for the project and a measure of its riskiness. In the following section, we provide an example of the probability approach to project analysis under risk.

APPLICATION OF PROBABILITY ANALYSIS TO RISK

Statistical analysis of risk becomes quite complicated when the time horizon for a payoff or return from an investment is long or when alternatives consisting of multiple-project combinations are being considered. However, we can gain considerable insight into the application of probability to risk situations from a simple example involving a choice between two investments—each of which has a single cash payoff that is received one year in the future. To illustrate, we choose an example from real estate investment.

Suppose the Texland Corporation has obtained similar tracts of land in Houston and Dallas at identical cost and is considering subdivision and marketing alternatives for next year. Management has information indicating that the cost of subdividing and marketing the land will be the same in each city and that under even the most pessimistic assumptions, either project will yield a positive net present value. However, the firm's financial condition and resource base are such that it cannot develop both tracts in the coming year.

From past experience, Texland's managers are confident that the returns from either project will depend on the rate of growth of personal income in Texas during the year. Their estimates of the cash inflow generated by each alternative appear in Table 14-1. Texland's managers do not believe that the rate of income growth in the state will fall below 6 percent or exceed 14 percent, but they are uncertain about the probabilities of occurrence of various growth rates within this range. As the table shows, the potentially higher payoffs associated with the Dallas project are attractive, but it is clear from the payoff estimates that the Dallas alternative will yield less than the Houston alternative if the rate of growth of personal income is relatively low.

Table 14–1 *Cash Flow Estimates for Two Land Development Projects*

Percentage Rate of Growth in State Personal Income	Estimated Cash Inflow	
	Dallas Project ($1,000)	*Houston Project* ($1,000)
6	$ 600	$770
8	700	790
10	800	800
12	900	810
14	1,000	830

To help analyze the growth rate problem, Texland has employed an economist from Austin Commerce College who has provided the following subjective probabilities for the growth rates in Table 14-1.

Rate of Growth in State Personal Income	Probability of Occurrence
6%	0.15
8%	0.20
10%	0.30
12%	0.20
14%	0.15

Texland's management then used the preceding probabilities to construct the payoff tables shown in Table 14-2. For each project an **expected value** is calculated. The expected value is a weighted average of the possible outcomes, and it is obtained by multiplying each outcome by the probability associated with it and then summing the individual outcome values (sum of

*The **expected value** of an investment is found by multiplying each possible outcome by the probability that it will occur, then summing these values.*

Table 14–2 *Payoff Tables for Land Development Projects*

(a) Dallas Project

Percentage Rate of Growth in State Personal Income (Event)	Subjective Probability (P_i)	Cash Flow Payoff (X_i) ($1,000)	X_iP_i ($1,000)
6	0.15	$ 600	$ 90
8	0.20	700	140
10	0.30	800	240
12	0.20	900	180
14	0.15	1,000	150
		$\bar{X}$ = Expected Value = ΣX_iP_i =	$800

(b) Houston Project

Percentage Rate of Growth in State Personal Income (Event)	Subjective Probability (P_i)	Cash Flow Payoff (X_i) ($1,000)	X_iP_i ($1,000)
6	0.15	$ 770	$115.5
8	0.20	790	158.0
10	0.30	800	240.0
12	0.20	810	162.0
14	0.15	830	124.5
		$\bar{X}$ = Expected Value = ΣX_iP_i =	$800.0

the fourth column of each payoff table). In effect, each payoff is associated with an event (rate of growth in personal income) that has a subjective probability. Weighting the payoffs by their respective associated probabilities and summing the weighted values, one obtains the expected value of the project. It is this kind of weighted average that appears on the "return" axis of the indifference curve diagrams in Figures 14-1 and 14-2.

As Table 14-2 shows, Texland found that the expected values of the two alternatives were exactly the same. We will see, however, that this does not mean there is no basis for choosing one project over the other. To complete the analysis, we must consider the risk of each alternative; in fact, the information given in Table 14-2 does provide a means for quantifying risk and differentiating between the two projects.

An acceptable way to measure risk is to examine the *probability distribution* of the possible outcomes of a given situation. A probability distribution may be represented by a rod graph relating the probability of each growth rate (event) to its outcome in terms of cash inflow. For the data of Table 14-2, probability distributions are constructed in Figure 14-3. In each panel of Fig-

FIGURE 14–3

Rod Graphs of Probability Distributions of Returns from Two Land Development Alternatives

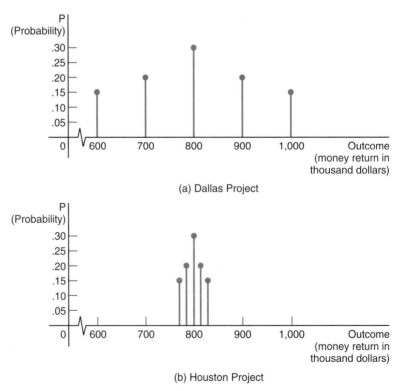

(a) Dallas Project

(b) Houston Project

The rod graphs above show that the Dallas project is riskier than the Houston project, since the expected money outcomes associated with the Dallas project display greater dispersion.

FIGURE 14–4

A Continuous Probability Distribution

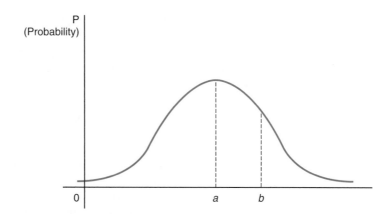

A continuous probability distribution that is normal will plot as a bell-shaped curve. The cumulative probabilty of obtaining a result between *a* and *b* above is equal to the area under the curve between *a* and *b*.

ure 14-3, the payoffs associated with each possible growth rate appear on the horizontal axis, and the probability value associated with each payoff appears on the vertical axis.

The probability distributions of Figure 14-3 are called *discrete* probability distributions because they do not include information on the probabilities associated with payoffs that might occur at growth rates in between those of Table 14-2. (For example, we do not have any information on the probability of a growth rate between 8 and 10 percent.) A *continuous* probability distribution would be represented by a line rather than a bar graph and would contain information on the probability values associated with a wide range of possible payoffs. It might look like Figure 14-4. If we added up all of the probability values associated with the outcomes in Figure 14-4 (i.e., in calculus terms, if we "integrated the area under the probability distribution"), we would get a value of one for their *cumulative* probability. In other words, we would say that it is certain that one of the outcomes will occur. Similarly, we could ascertain the probability of obtaining a result between *a* and *b* by integrating the area under the curve between these two values. A particularly useful continuous probability distribution is the *normal* distribution, which is symmetrically shaped about its *mean* or expected value (the value at point *a* in Figure 14-4). We will use such a distribution here to help interpret the results of the risk analysis of Texland's Dallas and Houston projects.

Returning to Figure 14-3, note that the distribution of outcomes along the horizontal axis is much wider for the Dallas project than for the Houston project. In statistical terms we would say that the *range* of the Dallas outcomes is greater or that there is more *dispersion* of the possible outcomes about the mean (expected) value, $800,000. The **variance** of a given set of data is a statistic that measures the dispersion about the mean of the set of probable outcomes or payoffs. It is calculated by squaring the difference between each probable outcome and the weighted average (mean or expected value) of the outcomes, multiplying each such squared value by its associated probability, and summing these multiplied values. In other words we have

$$\text{variance } = \sigma^2 = \sum_{i=1}^{n} (X_i - \overline{X})^2 P_i,$$

The variance of the possible returns of a project is found by subtracting the expected value of the project from each possible outcome, squaring each of these values, multiplying each squared deviation by the probability of each respective outcome, and summing the resulting products. The variance, a measure of the dispersion of possible project outcomes, is one indicator of risk.

where σ^2, a standard notation for variance, is read "sigma squared"; the X_i are the outcomes; $\overline{X}$ is the expected value; and the P_i are the respective probabilities associated with the outcomes.

In project analysis, the variance of the distribution of probable returns (payoffs or cash inflows) is often employed as a measure of risk. Generally, the higher the variance of the distribution, the greater the risk. In Table 14-3, variance calculations are shown for the Dallas and Houston tract development projects of Texland Corporation. The variance is frequently an

Table 14–3 *Variance Calculations for Two Land Development Projects*

(a) Dallas Project

Percentage Rate of Growth in State Personal Income	P_i	$(X_i - \overline{X})$ ($1,000)	$(X_i - \overline{X})^2$ ($1,000)	$(X_i - \overline{X})^2 P_i$ ($1,000)
6	0.15	$-200	$40,000,000	$ 6,000,000
8	0.20	−100	10,000,000	2,000,000
10	0.30	0	0	0
12	0.20	100	10,000,000	2,000,000
14	0.15	200	40,000,000	6,000,000
			Variance = σ^2 =	$16,000,000
			Standard Deviation = σ =	$ 126,490

(b) Houston Project

Percentage Rate of Growth in State Personal Income	P_i	$(X_i - \overline{X})$ ($1,000)	$(X_i - \overline{X})^2$ ($1,000)	$(X_i - \overline{X})^2 P_i$ ($1,000)
6	0.15	$- 30	$ 900,000	$ 135,000
8	0.20	− 10	100,000	20,000
10	0.30	0	0	0
12	0.20	10	100,000	20,000
14	0.15	30	900,000	135,000
			Variance = σ^2 = $	310,000
			Standard Deviation = σ = $	17,610

extremely large number, since it expresses dispersion in terms of original units (dollars, in this case) squared. For the Dallas project, we obtain a variance of $16 billion, whereas the variance for Houston is only $310 million.

It is sometimes quite useful to calculate the square root of the variance,

$$\sqrt{\sigma^2} = \sigma = \sqrt{\sum_{i=1}^{n}(X_i - \overline{X})^2 P_i},$$

The **standard deviation,** another measure of risk, is the square root of the variance.

which is called the **standard deviation** of the probable outcomes (payoffs). The standard deviation is also used as a measure of risk. For the Dallas project, $\sigma = \$126,490$, whereas for the Houston project, it is $17,610.

Whether the variance or the standard deviation is used as a measure of risk, it is clear from the preceding calculations that the Dallas project is riskier than the Houston project, since both statistics are higher for Dallas than for Houston. Using the standard deviation as a risk measure, we can carry the analysis one step further if we are willing to assume that the distribution of probable returns in each case is normal or forms a symmetrical, bell-shaped curve (such as that in Figure 14-4) around the expected value. This assumption may be acceptable if the outcomes constitute values of a continuous random variable, which means a variable that is measured on a continuous scale (dollars, heights, weights, etc.), and the outcomes have values determined by chance only after the experiment (project) is over.

Statistics tells us that for a normal distribution, approximately 68 percent of the distribution (its *area*) lies within plus or minus *one* standard deviation about the mean, and that approximately 95 percent of the distribution lies within *two* standard deviations of the mean. In the case of the Dallas project, this would mean that we expect only a 5 percent probability that we would get a cash inflow outside the range

$$\$800,000 \pm 2(\$126,490),$$

or that there is a 95 percent probability of a cash inflow between $547,020 and $1,052,980. However, with the Houston project, our 95 percent probability is between $764,780 and $835,220. If Texland's managers are risk averters, they will choose the Houston project.

Now we can return to the concept of risk-return indifference curves to complete our analysis of the Texland decision. Figure 14-5 is very similar to Figure 14-1. As we noted in our earlier discussion, the assumption of a risk-averse decision maker assures a preference structure in which less desirable combinations of risk and expected money return lie on indifference curves that are, in general, successively further toward the northwest area of the indifference curve map. Alternatively, indifference curves representing less and less desirable combinations of risk and return will have successively lower intercepts on the expected-money-return axis (the intercept being the

A Gamble on Tigers, Dolphins, and a Volcano

What do tigers, dolphins, a volcano, and beds have in common? They are all part of the Mirage casino and hotel in Las Vegas. The hotel, opened in the early 1990s, was the brainchild of developer Stephen Wynn and had an initial estimated cost of $620 million to over $700 million. Its features include a five-story volcano that erupts with gray smoke every five minutes, a lobby displaying white tigers behind a glass wall and several sharks in a 20,000-gallon aquarium, dolphins in a tank near the pool, and a $37 million golf course containing 10,000 transplanted pine trees. Moreover, the annual hotel operating costs included such things as $11.5 million for magicians.

At the time it opened, the Mirage was the largest hotel in Las Vegas, with 3,056 rooms. Industry analysts estimated then that the Mirage would have to generate $1 million *per day* to break even; Wynn himself put the daily breakeven revenue at $800,000. Of all the casino-hotels in Las Vegas, only Caesar's Palace did that kind of volume. Nevertheless, in its first two years of operation, the Mirage turned out to be a profitable gamble, and Wynn's Mirage Corporation subsequently built the Treasure Island and New York, New York casino hotels.

The Mirage touched off a boom in Las Vegas hotel building that resulted in the addition to the famous hotel "Strip" of names like the Stratosphere, the MGM Grand, the Luxor, the Mandalay Bay, and the Bellagio. Although at least five older casino-hotels went bankrupt during the influx of luxury hotels and even some of the new ones have experienced financial difficulties, the demand for upscale Las Vegas hotel rooms has

remained strong. After a huge dip following the 9/11 terrorist attacks in 2001, tourists began returning in great numbers in summer 2002. Given an earlier estimate by an MGM Grand executive that only 15 percent of Americans had ever visited Las Vegas, and the city's transformation into both a resort destination and a retirement community, long-run prospects for the casino hotels looked very good.

As for Wynn, although he left the Mirage Corporation in 2000 when it was sold to MGM Grand (now MGM/Mirage), he filed an SEC registration in June 2002 for his Le Reve ("The Dream") resort project to be built on the site of the now defunct Desert Inn. The price tag: $1.83 billion for a 2,700-room structure with an eight-story, man-made mountain, a three-acre lake, and an on-site Ferrari/Maserati dealership. Wynn's IPO was expected to raise over $400 million, and most of the rest of his financing was taken by banks through a consortium that included Deutsche Bank Securities, Bear Stearns, and Banc of America Securities. Undoubtedly, that group did not view the project as excessively risky.

References: Jeff Simpson, "Wynn Unveils Plan for $1.83 Billion Resort," *Las Vegas Review-Journal*, June 18, 2002, online, July 21, 2002, www.lvrj.com/lvrj_home/2002/Jun-18-Tue-2002/news/; "Las Vegas Hotel Boom Begins Paying Off," *Wall Street Journal*, April 20, 1999, pp. B1, B4; "Roller-Coaster Ride of Stratosphere Corp. Is a Tale of Las Vegas," *Wall Street Journal*, October 29, 1996, pp. A1, A6; "MGM's Grand Ambition," *Business Week* (September 23, 1996), pp. 87, 90; "Newest Mega-Resort Set for Vegas Debut," *San Antonio Express-News*, June 15, 1996, p. 1E.

risk-free equivalent dollar value of the risky returns that lie on a given indifference curve).

As Figure 14-5 shows, the risk-return combination for the Dallas project must correspond to a lower risk-free return and lie on a less desirable indifference curve than the Houston combination, since both have the same expected value and the Dallas combination has higher risk (a larger σ). Again, we must conclude that if Texland's managers are risk averters, they will choose the Houston project.

One final observation can be made about Figure 14-5 as it applies to decisions involving more than two projects. Even if we do not know the shape of I_5, the Houston project will be preferred over all other projects that have any of the following: (1) a lower expected money return but an identical σ; (2) a higher σ but an identical expected money return; or (3) a lower expected money return *and* a higher σ. Thus, graphically we can say that the Houston project is preferred not only to the Dallas project but also to any project that falls in the shaded area of the indifference curve diagram. In more advanced analysis of decision making under risk, this notion (which is called *dominance*) provides a means of defining an efficient set of risk-return alternatives.

An **efficient portfolio** is a project or a combination of projects or investments that have the lowest risk for a given rate of return. In other words, no other investment has the same expected return but lower risk. A risk-averse investor would prefer such a portfolio to any other portfolio with the same expected return and higher risk. The **efficient set** is the set of all efficient portfolios.

> An **efficient portfolio** is a project or a combination of investments that will involve the least risk for a given rate of return.
>
> The **efficient set** is the set of all efficient portfolios.

FIGURE 14–5

Risk-Return Combinations for Two Land Development Projects

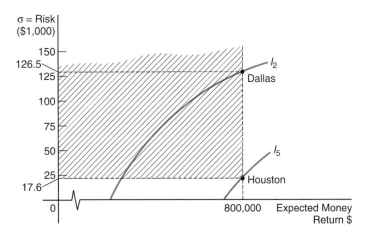

Risk-return indifference curves for the Dallas and Houston land development projects show that the Dallas project is less desirable, since both projects have an expected return of $800,000 and the standard deviation of the return is much higher for Dallas.

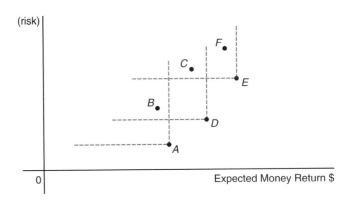

FIGURE 14–6

The Concept of Dominance in Risk Analysis

A risk-return combination will dominate other combinations of either equal risk and lower return or greater risk and the same return. Thus, combination *A* dominates *B*, combination *D* dominates *B* and *C*, and combination *E* dominates *C* and *F*. Among combinations *A*, *D*, and *E*, none dominates.

Thus, many portfolios (and projects) can be systematically rejected because they lie outside the efficient set. In Figure 14-6 we provide an example. Here, points *A*, *D*, and *E* dominate points *B*, *C*, and *F*, respectively. Therefore, points *B*, *C*, and *F* lie outside the efficient set. However, among points *A*, *D*, and *E*, none clearly dominates either of the others. The optimal portfolio (or project) among those in the efficient set is determined for each investor by his or her preferences regarding risk and expected return.

EVALUATING RISKY STREAMS OF RECEIPTS

Unlike the preceding Texland example, many project analyses deal with more than one expected return per project. Where an individual project has a number of periodic returns, such as a flow of annual receipts over a number of years, there will be a probability distribution of payoffs for each year. In such cases, the standard deviation of the entire stream of discounted receipts must be calculated in order to measure the project's risk.

The procedure for determining the expected present value of a stream of risky returns is summarized in the following formula:

$$E(PV) = \sum_{t=1}^{n} \frac{\overline{X}_t}{(1+r)^t},$$

where

$$\overline{X}_t = \text{expected value of net receipts in period } t,$$
$$r = \text{the appropriate discount rate, and}$$
$$t = \text{the time period.}$$

The formula simply says to sum up the discounted expected values of the future net cash inflows.

If the future cash flows are independent of one another (that is, if the cash flow outcome in time period one has no effect on the cash inflows in subsequent periods), then for *each period,* the standard deviation is:

$$\sigma_t = \sqrt{\sum_{i=1}^{m}(X_{it} - \overline{X}_t)^2 P_i} \, ,$$

where P_i is the probability associated with the *i*th net cash inflow. For the entire project, the standard deviation is as follows:

$$\sigma = \sqrt{\sum_{t=1}^{n}\frac{\sigma_t^2}{(1+r)^{2t}}} \, .$$

Although derivation of the preceding three formulas is beyond the scope of this text, some of the selected references at the end of this chapter provide more detail for the interested student.

If cash flows are *interdependent* (in other words, if the net cash flow in one time period has some relationship to that in another time period), the calculation of expected value and variance for the stream of receipts becomes more complicated. In such a case (and many projects will necessarily fit this case), the *covariances* of the probable returns must also be taken into account. Defined briefly, the covariance of one probable return with respect to another is a measure that reflects the degree to which the first return is correlated with the second. To the extent that two returns are positively correlated, when a high value occurs for the first, a high value will also occur for the second. In general, other things being equal, the greater the degree of correlation between a project's cash flows, the greater the standard deviation of the expected present value of the project. Thus, it is important to recognize the existence of interdependence between individual period cash flows in the stream of receipts.

PROBABILITY APPROACH TO MULTIPLE PROJECT ALTERNATIVES

The analysis of our previous chapter culminated with a discussion of methodologies for selecting the optimal combination of projects under conditions of certainty. As we have indicated, the probability approach to risky investment alternatives can be extended to encompass the evaluation of alternative combinations *(portfolios)* of projects. For each portfolio, such a procedure involves an analysis of the degree of interdependence of cash flows over time. Thus, the analyst of alternative portfolios would have to calculate the expected present value or expected return of each portfolio, taking into account not only the interdependence of cash flows in each single project but also the interdependence of cash flows *between* projects in each alternative combination of projects. Once the expected present value of each portfolio is determined and its variance or standard deviation is calculated, the dominance approach described earlier can be applied to define the efficient set of portfolios. Again, the optimal portfolio will be determined by the investor's preferences regarding risk and expected return.

The portfolio approach to multiple-project alternatives is usually modified when it is applied to capital budgeting situations for a variety of reasons. First, the approach was developed for application to the question of analyzing portfolios of securities, primarily common stock.[1] It is possible to divide a common stock portfolio into almost any combination of available stocks. However, the share of a total capital budget allocated to a given physical capital undertaking often is not divisible. Such projects must be either accepted or rejected in total, and the possibility of undertaking, say, one-half of one project and one-fourth of two others just does not exist. In addition, the covariances and correlation coefficients that are needed to analyze interdependent projects are much more difficult to obtain for capital projects than for common stocks. Finally, there is the problem of identifying the risk-return preferences of a firm. For any given firm, management may consist of a group of decision makers, each group member having his or her own preference set (set of risk-return indifference curves). Furthermore, the preferences of managers, either singly or in the aggregate, may not reflect the wishes of the owners (shareholders) of the firm.

ACCEPTABLE SHORTCUTS TO RISK ANALYSIS

Although the portfolio approach outlined in the preceding section is generally viewed as a theoretically correct approach to risk evaluation and project selection problems, some shorter methodologies that directly adjust present values for perceived differences in project riskiness are widely used. These methodologies are (1) the risk-adjusted discount rate approach and (2) the certainty equivalent approach.

---

[1] One interesting result obtained from portfolio theory supports the old adage about not putting all of one's eggs in the same basket. In particular, it can be shown that adding new projects to a portfolio can reduce its overall risk (standard deviation) as long as the projects are not perfectly positively correlated. In the literature of finance, such risk reduction through diversification of investments is known as the *portfolio effect*.

Risk-Adjusted Discount Rate

The risk-adjusted discount rate approach simply alters the standard present value formula by substituting a higher discount rate, k, for the risk-free rate, r, that was employed in Chapter 13. Thus, we would have

$$k = r + \rho,$$

where ρ (the Greek letter *rho*) is called the *risk premium.* The present value formula would then be

$$PV_{|k} = \sum_{t=1}^{n} \frac{\overline{X}_t}{(1+k)^t}.$$

Since k is larger than r, the effect of the risk-adjusted discount rate is to lower the value of PV for a risky future return. The higher the risk premium, the more risky the project and the lower the risk-adjusted PV for each future cash inflow.

For two projects of equal size (cost), equal lives, and approximately equal subjective risk, the selection procedure is simply to choose the one with the higher risk-adjusted net present value. If the risks of the two projects differ, then it is appropriate to apply a higher discount rate to the project judged to be riskier. The selection of the discount rate may be a subjective matter, a point that will be discussed further in the following section.

If we were to apply the preceding methodology to the Texland example, management would evaluate the Dallas project using a higher discount rate than the one applied to the Houston project. Suppose that instead of one-year lives, the land development alternatives were expected to have four-year net cash inflows of $200,000 per year and suppose that each alternative had a price of $550,000. If management chose to apply a 12 percent discount rate to the Dallas project and a 9 percent rate to the Houston project, the result would be as follows:

Dallas Project
NPV $| k_\text{D}$ = $200,000 ($PVF_\text{a}$ 12%, 4) – $550,000 = $57,460

and

Houston Project
$NPV | k_\text{H}$ = $200,000 ($PVF_\text{a}$ 9%, 4) – $550,000 = $97,940.

Clearly, the Houston project would be the better choice.

Certainty Equivalent Approach

Continuing with the question of evaluating two mutually exclusive projects with uncertain cash flows, we turn now to the certainty equivalent approach.

This approach relates closely to the risk-return indifference curve tradeoff we discussed in connection with the portfolio approach. It adjusts the present value of an uncertain return through the numerator of the present value formula as follows:

$$PV_{|\alpha_t} = \sum_{t=1}^{n} \frac{\alpha_t \overline{X}_t}{(1+r)^t}$$

where α_t is a "certainty equivalent adjustment factor" and r is the risk-free discount rate. For all but completely certain returns, $0 < \alpha_t < 1$. Thus, $\alpha_t = 1$ would indicate that the tth return (X_t) was certain, whereas $\alpha_t = 0$ would indicate that the probability of the tth return was zero. Thus, very risky projects will have low α_t's, whereas less risky ones will have α_t's closer to one.

It is argued that the certainty equivalent approach is superior to the risk-adjusted discount rate approach when project returns do not become increasingly risky over time. Still, the risk-adjusted discount rate approach is more frequently used because (1) it is easier to calculate *NPV* and (2) the two approaches, it can be shown, will yield the same result whenever

$$\alpha_t = \frac{(1+r)^t}{(1+k)^t} = \frac{PVF \, k,t}{PVF \, r,t}.$$

That is, the two approaches yield identical results whenever the certainty equivalent adjustment factor for each future period equals the ratio of the present value factor (including a risk premium) to the risk-free present value factor. It follows that if far-off returns are viewed as increasingly less certain, the risk-adjusted discount rate approach will frequently be chosen.

EXTERNALITIES AND THEIR NATURE

Studies reveal that many business managers have a cautious attitude toward new capital projects and tend to apply what might seem to be excessive risk-adjusted discount rates to project inflows. In some cases, this may be a sign of prudence rather than paranoia. A hint about the problems underlying such behavior is found in the possibility that project analysts may have overlooked certain elements of cost, such as federal requirements concerning facilities for the handicapped. The tendency in project evaluation is to analyze first and foremost the estimated revenue and operating cost components of the flow of annual benefits and to compare the discounted net amount of those two figures with project price. However, the operating cost item directs attention to nuts-and-bolts aspects of annual cost that are very much *internal* to the firm. In other words, the emphasis is on those cost items over which the firm has direct control through management's ability to plan and organize the process of production.

For any given project, there are likely to be elements of cost markedly affected by changes in data that are *externally* determined—that is, over which management has no control. Changes in input prices are perhaps the most obvious of such external factors. A firm may be faced with rising input prices because it is in an industrial sector where many rapidly expanding firms are bidding against one another for relatively scarce resources. Thus, costs may rise for an individual firm even though no changes have occurred in its production function. Such externalities, which economists have called *pecuniary externalities,* are occasionally overlooked by project evaluators. More likely to be overlooked are certain other types of externalities, particularly those associated with what have come to be known as *public goods.*

A public good is a good that is jointly consumed by many people, and, once it is made available, the marginal cost of increased consumption is zero. A highway bridge provides a good example. Once the bridge has been built, it can handle any amount of traffic up to the capacity per unit of time of the roadway. If it is being used at one-half its capacity, and an additional user wishes to cross it, the additional user will be able to do so at zero addition to the cost of the bridge. Theoretically, no price should be charged for using the bridge, since marginal cost equals zero. Therefore, the perfectly competitive $P = MC$ market solution is price equals zero. The users of public goods who benefit from but do not pay for them through market transactions enjoy what are known as *third-party benefits.*

The cost of operation of an investment undertaking in the private sector is seldom affected by such public goods as a bridge, although we could certainly imagine circumstances where it might be. (In an underdeveloped country or region, the roads, bridges, and electric power plants often are externalities on which successful private capital projects ultimately depend.) However, over the past few decades we have come to the realization that clean air, clean water, the preservation of wildlife, and a relatively quiet environment are public goods that have often been neglected in our economic calculus. This neglect has provided the business sector an array of public-good externalities, such as free water, zero-cost dumping of pollutants, and the prerogative to increase noise and temperature levels at will.

The recent awakening of both the general public and governmental authorities to the fact that much private sector output is produced in a setting where external costs are imposed on third parties has caused business decision makers to be wary about regulatory changes and penalties that might well *internalize* such costs.

Of course, firms may also try to capture potential external benefits. One of the best historical examples of an attempt to internalize the potential third-party benefits of a capital project is Walt Disney World in

Florida.[2] When Walt Disney Productions constructed the original Disney-land in California, the Disney interests purchased only enough land to provide for the amusement park and a few related activities. The result was that the project supplied tremendous external benefits to the owners and users of surrounding property in the development boom that the area experienced after Disneyland opened. In planning the Florida Disney World project, the corporation ensured its own capture (internalization) of many of the potential external benefits that it would create by purchasing 6,000 acres of land, thereby assuring control over nearby related activities. There were still some spillover benefits to third parties who owned land or set up businesses on the perimeter of the Disney World tract, but the distance of these sites from the park itself much reduced external benefits and enhanced the long-run profitability of the Disney project. The moral is clear: Successful investors take into account opportunities to internalize project-related external benefits. If at first they do not, they will indeed *learn* to do so!

SUMMARY

Risk and Risk Adjustment in Capital Projects

In this chapter, we extended our analysis of capital projects to include situations involving risk. Our basic behavioral assumption throughout the chapter was that the decision maker is a *risk averter.* This means that the decision maker will be willing to accept a risky project over one that is less risky but involves the same initial outlay (project price) *only if* the risky alternative yields a sufficiently greater net present value to more than offset its added risk. To illustrate this point, the concept of risk-return indifference curves was introduced and eventually related to a probability approach to risk analysis.

We showed in this chapter that the riskiness of various investment alternatives can be evaluated by examining the probability distribution of payoffs of each alternative. For each alternative, a weighted average or expected value is calculated, and this is used, along with the distribution of probable outcomes, to obtain two measures of riskiness—the *variance* and the *standard deviation* of net project returns. For projects with equal prices, lives, and expected values, we showed that a risk-averse decision maker will choose

---

[2] This example has been used previously elsewhere. See Richard B. McKenzie, *Economics* (Boston: Houghton Mifflin, 1986), p. 689. Later it was argued that by creating increased demand for public services, Disney World resulted in external costs to the citizens of Florida. See "A Sweet Deal for Disney Is Souring Its Neighbors," *Business Week* (August 8, 1988), pp. 48–49.

the alternative with the lowest variance. In addition, the *normal distribution* was utilized to make some inferences about the probability of payoffs outside a specified range.

One result of applying the probability approach to project analysis is the attention it directs toward the question of interdependence of cash inflows. In particular, we noted that the cash flow in a given time period might in some way be correlated with that in another time period. Thus, a thorough analysis of a project's risk using the probability approach would have to take into account the covariance between project inflows. This increases the information requirements of the approach and complicates the calculation of variance. When combinations or portfolios of projects are evaluated, it becomes necessary to consider not only the interdependence of cash flows within each individual project but also the problem of interdependence of cash flows *between* projects.

The last part of this chapter described and evaluated some shortcuts to risk analysis. Specifically, we examined the *risk-adjusted discount* rate concept and its application. Use of the risk-adjusted discount rate is viewed as a practical and acceptable approach as long as the project analyst understands its shortcomings. Its primary shortcoming, the fact that it treats project cash flows as becoming increasingly risky over time, can be offset by using a related method, the *certainty equivalent approach,* in which each future cash flow is separately adjusted for risk and a risk-free discount rate is applied to the present value calculation.

Finally, we considered issues relating to externalities. We noted that it would be wise for capital project analysts to review carefully the external costs and benefits related to each project and to assess the probable consequences of internalization of such costs and benefits.

This chapter has dealt almost entirely with the more obvious quantitative aspects of project evaluation under risk. However, many capital projects have both inflows of benefits and elements of cost or price that might easily escape analysis if the firm's managers or project evaluators take a strictly private or internal point of view. In the next chapter, we extend our discussion not only to such externalities—and, in some cases, nonquantitative considerations—but also to the question of project evaluation in the public sector.

QUESTIONS

1. What is the economic nature of risk? How can risk be described using a tradeoff concept?

2. What is meant by the term *expected return?*

3. What is the usual assumption regarding the risk attitude of decision makers in economic theory? What other kinds of attitudes toward risk exist? Describe each attitude in terms of the decision maker's behavior in a risk situation.

4. What is a probability distribution of returns? How can it be related to the risk associated with a given capital project?

5. Suppose two projects have the same lives and prices but that one of them (Project A) has an expected value that is greater than that of the other (Project B). Can you determine from this which project should be selected? Why or why not?

6. Explain how the concept of the standard deviation of probable returns from a capital project relates to that of risk-return indifference curves.

7. What problem in project analysis arises from the possible interdependence of cash flows in a project or a portfolio of projects?

8. What is a risk-adjusted discount rate? Explain how it is used and discuss the problems inherent in its application to project analysis.

9. What is a certainty equivalent adjustment factor? Why do some experts argue that use of the certainty equivalent adjustment factor is a better approach than the risk-adjusted discount rate method.

PROBLEMS

1. Using a set of risk-return indifference curves for a single decision maker, describe a case in which the decision maker would prefer a risky investment returning an expected $1,500 to a less risky one with an expected return of $1,000. Explain how an increase in the perceived riskiness of the project with the $1,500 expected return might cause the decision maker to reject it and to choose the less risky project with the $1,000 expected return instead.

2. Suppose a one-year project has the following probable returns in relation to the percentage growth in population for a given region:

Percent Growth in Population	Net Cash Inflow of Project
1.0	$150,000
1.5	185,000
2.0	210,000
2.5	275,000

The following are the subjective probabilities of occurrence of the preceding population growth rates:

Percent Growth in Population	Subjective Probability (P_i)
1.0	0.25
1.5	0.50
2.0	0.20
2.5	0.05

What is the *expected value* of the cash inflow from the project?

3. Construct a rod graph showing a discrete probability distribution of the cash inflows from the project in Problem 2, and then determine the variance and standard deviation of the inflows. What could be said about the relation of the standard deviation to the expected value of the cash inflow if the true probability distribution of the cash inflows were normal?

4. Given the following data on two one-period capital projects, calculate (1) the expected value of each project's cash flows and (2) the standard deviation of probable cash flows from each project. Indicate which of the two projects would be chosen by a risk-averse decision maker if their prices were the same and they had similar lives.

Net Cash Flows

Project A	Project B	Subjective Probability (P_i)
200	190	0.05
240	250	0.25
250	260	0.40
290	270	0.25
300	290	0.05

5. Belco Corporation has been evaluating two possible alternative locations for a small oil refinery. One of the locations is in the United States, and the other is in a nearby Latin American republic. The cost will be $22 million if the project is built in the United States, but because of lower land and labor costs it will be only $19 million if the project is built in the Latin American country.

   Recent uncertainties in the oil and gas industry have convinced Belco's managers that the lives of such projects should not be treated as longer than seven years. Management doubts that the project will have any salvage value if it is undertaken in Latin America, but it is willing to attach a $7 million after-tax salvage value to the U.S. alternative.

   The estimated net annual cash inflows, which are believed to be independent, are $5 million per year if the project is located in the United States and $5.2 million per year if it is located in Latin America. Because of the inherent risk of changes in government regulations in the Latin American republic, Belco's managers have decided to apply a risk-adjusted discount rate of 22 percent to the inflows from the foreign alternative, whereas their risk-adjusted discount rate for the U.S. project will be 16 percent. Which project will they choose? (*Note:* PVF_a 22%, 7 = 3.4155; PVF_a 16%, 7 = 4.0386.)

6. Develop a set of certainty equivalent adjustment factors from the following information on a decision maker's preferences:

Certain Return	Equivalent Risky Return
$120,000	$160,000
170,000	210,000
250,000	300,000
325,000	400,000
500,000	625,000

7. Given the following set of risk-return indifference curves, calculate the certainty equivalent adjustment factors for an expected return of $1,400,000.

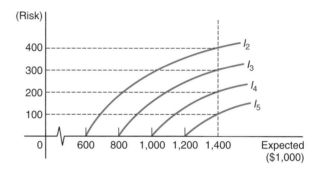

8. International Cosmographics, a small corporation in the printing industry, is considering expanding into the greeting card market. Its managers have hired two consultants to evaluate an investment project that involves both an addition to factory space and the purchase of new printing equipment. Consultant *A* has suggested that the company adjust its expected annual cash inflows using a risk-adjusted discount rate approach. Consultant *B* argues that such an approach is inappropriate and that what should be used is a certainty equivalent approach that takes into account the fact that after the first two years risk will decline because a market share will have been established.

   Consultant *B* has estimated that the following certainty equivalent adjustment factors should be applied to the cash inflows from the project, assuming a risk-free discount rate of 6 percent.

Year	Certainty Equivalent Adjustment Factor
1	0.9464
2	0.8957
3	0.9197
4	0.8944
5	0.8698
6	0.8458
7	0.8225
8	0.7999

Consultant *A* argues that the risk-adjusted discount rate approach is simpler and equally applicable, since a risk-adjusted discount rate of 12 percent for the first two years of project life should be applied and 9 percent should be used for the remaining six years. The annual inflows (before risk adjustment) follow. They should be treated as being independent.

Year	Net Cash Inflow
1	$100,000
2	175,000
3	200,000
4	200,000
5	200,000
6	200,000
7	200,000
8	200,000

If both risk-adjustment methodologies are applied to the preceding inflows, what difference in present value will the two approaches yield? Explain the difference you find.

9. Using a set of risk-return indifference curves, explain how the concept of dominance makes it possible in theory to eliminate certain risk-return combinations from the "efficient set" of project portfolios.

10. American Astrotronics Corporation is evaluating two new investment projects for possible undertaking in the next fiscal year. One is the short-term operation of a cleaning franchise that will yield a net after-tax cash flow of $42,000 per year for the next three years. The second is the short-term operation of a parking lot that will yield net after-tax cash flows of $36,000 for each of two years and $56,000 for the third and final year of operation. Neither project has a salvage value, and either can be acquired for a present outlay of $90,000.

   a. Evaluate the two projects using a risk-adjusted discount rate of 18 percent per year.

   b. If the company can undertake only one of the two projects, which should it choose? Why?

11. Garfield just won $2 million in the California lottery. Since he knows that many long-lost cat relatives will want to share in his good fortune, Garfield is trying to find the optimal place to invest his funds. At the present time, he is considering two options. The first is a real estate investment trust that is purchasing repossessed property in Texas. The second is a well-diversified mutual fund with a return closely approximating that of the market. The possible returns on the real estate investment trust, R_T, the market, R_M, and their associated probabilities, P_i, are given in the table. The risk-free rate of return, R_F, is .06.

% Growth in Real GNP	P_i	R_{T_i}	R_{M_i}
–1%	0.05	–0.40	–0.10
1%	0.3	0.30	0.10
2%	0.5	0.30	0.20
3%	0.15	0.40	0.30

a. Calculate the expected rate of return for the real estate trust and for the market.

b. Calculate the standard deviation of the returns for the real estate trust and for the market.

c. With no other information regarding alternative investment opportunities, how would Garfield choose whether to invest in the real estate investment trust, the mutual fund, or a risk-free asset?

SELECTED REFERENCES

Brigham, Eugene F., Louis C. Gapenski, and Michael C. Ehrhardt. *Financial Management: Theory and Practice,* 9th ed. Fort Worth, TX: Dryden Press, 1999, Chapters 5, 6, and 13.

Brightman, Harvey J. *Statistics in Plain English.* Cincinnati: South-Western, 1986, Chapters 2 and 3.

Butler, J. S., and Barry Schachter. "The Investment Decision: Estimation Risk and Risk Adjusted Discount Rates." *Financial Management* 18, No. 4 (Winter 1989): 13–22.

Chan, Louis K. C., and Josef Lakonishok. "Are the Reports of Beta's Death Premature?" *Financial Management* 19, No. 4 (Summer 1993): 51–62.

Finnerty, John D., and Dean Leistikow. "The Behavior of Equity and Debt Risk Premiums." *Financial Management* 19, No. 4 (Summer 1993): 73–84.

Fuller, Russell J., and Kent A. Hickman. "A Note on Estimating the Historical Risk Premium." *Financial Practice and Education* 1, No. 2 (Fall/Winter 1991): 45–48.

Gitman, Lawrence J. *Principles of Managerial Finance,* 9th ed. Reading, MA: Addison-Wesley, 2000, Chapters 10 and 11.

Grundy, Kevin, and Burton G. Malkiel. "Reports of Beta's Death Have Been Greatly Exaggerated." *Journal of Portfolio Management* 22, No. 3 (Spring 1996): 36–44.

Haugen, Robert A. "Finance from a New Perspective." *Financial Management* 25, No. 1 (Spring 1996): 86–97.

Moyer, R. Charles, James R. McGuigan, and William J. Kretlow. *Contemporary Financial Management,* 8th ed. Cincinnati: South-Western College Publishing, 2001, Chapters 10 and 11.

Sick, Gordon A. "A Certainty-Equivalent Approach to Capital Budgeting." *Financial Management* 15, No. 4 (Winter 1986): 23–32.

"The New Rocket Science." *Business Week* (November 2, 1992): 131–135.

INTERNATIONAL CAPSULE III

Project Analysis in a Multinational Setting

Chapters 13 and 14 provided a brief introduction to the subject of capital projects and their evaluation. There the emphasis was on comparison of alternative investment opportunities available to the firm over the long run. As we saw, the procedures normally followed in project evaluation take into account the price tags attached to various undertakings and the stream of benefits the firm expects to receive from each of them. The methodology of determining the net present value *(NPV)* of the alternatives is fairly straightforward and involves the use of pro-forma income statements based on discounted future revenues and costs for some specified project life. But a number of complexities enter the analysis when capital budgeting techniques are applied to international projects.

INTERNATIONAL DIMENSIONS OF PROJECT ANALYSIS

Today, the most common setting for international capital budgeting decisions is one in which a large firm is evaluating whether or not to set up a subsidiary in a foreign country, or, perhaps, whether or not to add to the fixed assets of an existing foreign subsidiary. In multinational finance, the country where a

foreign subsidiary is located is commonly called the *host country*, the firm that owns the subsidiary the *parent firm*, and the country where the parent firm is located the *home country*. The basic framework for analysis of foreign capital projects is the same as that used for domestic projects. However, in the case of international projects, the evaluation is complicated by a number of factors that do not enter the picture in home country capital project analysis. Some of the more important considerations follow.

1. Should the capital budgeting analysis be conducted from the viewpoint of the parent company, that of the foreign subsidiary, or both?

2. Will remittances of profits from the foreign operation be restricted by the host country of the subsidiary?

3. What will be the income tax treatment of subsidiary earnings by the host government and parent company income by its home government?

4. Will there be differential rates of inflation between the home country and the host country of the subsidiary?

5. How will net flows of income to the parent company be affected by changes in foreign exchange rates between its currency and that of the subsidiary?

6. What are the political risks associated with investment in the host country?

7. What additional factors will affect the cost of capital and therefore the discount rate applicable to the project?

From this list, it should be apparent that many of the differences between domestic and international capital projects call for quantitative adjustments that will affect either the discounted cash flows or the rate of discount for any given international investment undertaking. In addition, a firm planning a significant foreign investment project will have to ascertain whether or not there are unusual elements that may increase or decrease the initial amount of investment (project price). For example, a government may require that a firm undertake certain ancillary investments (worker housing, medical clinics, etc.) along with its investment in plant facilities, or it may provide subsidies to foreign firms that invest in certain types of activities deemed essential for economic growth.

Parent vs. Subsidiary

While a thorough analysis of a foreign capital project might include a capital budgeting analysis from the point of view of the subsidiary as an independent firm operating in the foreign country, it is widely argued by financial experts that the overriding consideration in analyzing a foreign capital project is whether or not the project is acceptable when analyzed from the viewpoint of the parent company. The two viewpoints may produce different results because of limitations on the amount of profits that can be transferred to the parent and because of the tax treatment of such flows. If the objective of the firm is to maximize shareholder wealth, then it is the cash flows to the par-

ent that are available to pay dividends and use for reinvestment purposes that will determine whether or not a foreign project is acceptable.[1]

Adjustment of Project Cash Flows

Cash flows into a projected foreign subsidiary are estimated as in any capital budgeting analysis on the basis of anticipated annual sales revenues, operating costs, and depreciation, as well as the salvage value that may occur from disposition of fixed assets at the end of the project. These calculations usually are made in the currency of the country where the subsidiary is located (local currency).

If the subsidiary is destined to sell only in the local market, an analysis of local demand will be required for the revenue estimates. This may not be an easy matter for the parent company, since the determinants of local demand may differ from those used to analyze demand in the home country. Operating costs may differ in the foreign country for a variety of reasons, ranging from labor union practices to such cost items as those associated with locally purchased materials and parts and local charges for insurance, utilities, and government-provided services.

---

[1] Contemporary research on international capital budgeting shows that many firms do use the subsidiary's point of view rather than that of the parent. This is partially explained by the historical evidence that remittances are seldom permanently blocked and that firms can use transfer pricing and other techniques to get around restrictions on remittances of earnings. See, for example, Vinod B. Bashevi, "Capital Budgeting Practices at Multinationals," *Management Accounting* (August 1981), pp. 32-35; and Marjorie Stanley and Stanley Block, "An Empirical Study of Management and Financial Variables Influencing Capital Budgeting Decisions for Multinational Corporations in the 1980s," *Management International Review*, Vol. 23, No. 3 (1983), pp. 61–71.

Moreover, both cost and revenue estimates may have to be adjusted for anticipated inflation. Finally, the net cash flow of the subsidiary will depend also on the host country's laws regarding income taxes and allowable depreciation.

Once the net cash inflow to the subsidiary is determined, a number of additional adjustments must be made in order to arrive at the net inflow to be received by the parent company. First, the funds remitted annually by the subsidiary must be converted into the currency of the parent. This is not a simple matter, since the exchange rate applicable to one time period may differ substantially from that applicable to another. While forecasting exchange rates is difficult, any tendency for a rate to move in a predictable direction should be taken into account. With the flows to the parent now expressed in its own currency, the next adjustment would be for income taxes owed by the parent to the home country. In general, the United States tax laws have provided that a parent company may credit any foreign income taxes paid against the U.S. tax liability on remittances. Thus, the tax on earnings transferred annually to the parent from the subsidiary is reduced by the amount of foreign income taxes already paid. There may be a final inflow to the parent due to transfer of funds from the sale of the entire project or some of its assets at the end of the project's life. A home country tax liability may be incurred, depending on the relation between the sale price and book value of the assets sold.

Risk and the Discount Rate

It is widely recognized that risk in foreign capital projects may differ from risk in home country capital projects. Besides exchange rate risk, there are important elements of political risk that can affect anticipated project inflows. For example, if the host country has an unstable government, flows into the subsidiary may be interrupted by economic or social disorder. There is also the possibility that the host country may expropriate or confiscate foreign businesses. Clearly, the evaluation of a foreign capital project must take these additional types of risk into account.

There is a temptation to argue that the firm can allow for the additional risks associated with foreign projects by applying a higher discount rate than that used in home country analyses. In fact, many firms do take this approach.[2] However, it is argued that doing so is too simplistic and overlooks such possibilities as the fact that a fall in the value of the foreign currency, for example, may either decrease or increase the net inflows, depending on where output is sold and the sources of inputs. A high discount rate may also penalize early inflows excessively and not penalize distant inflows enough.

Because of these complications, many analysts argue that, wherever possible, adjustment for the foreign risks of a project should be handled by adjusting its forecasted cash flows. Then, when the cash flows to the parent are determined, they are discounted at a rate that reflects only overall business and financial risk. In effect, this is the same rate used for home country projects. However, if the firm's presence in a country with extremely high foreign risk increases its overall risk of bankruptcy, this would likely drive up its cost of obtaining funds and thus also the discount rate.

---

[2] See David K. Eiteman and Arthur I. Stonehill, *Multinational Business Finance,* 5th ed. (Reading, MA: Addison-Wesley, 1989), p. 524.

EXAMPLE OF A FOREIGN PROJECT

Perhaps the best way to understand how foreign capital project analysis differs from analysis done for investments at home is to consider an example of such a project. In our example, we will follow the pattern used for the capital project study in Chapter 13 (Click-wash), indicating where specific steps are taken to adjust for foreign operations. The name of our parent firm will be MacWash, Incorporated, and its product line will be washing machines. MacWash is considering an investment in a plant in a developing country, Lavaria, where the sales of modern laundry detergents have been growing rapidly. The company has developed a hand-operated washing machine that takes advantage of the new detergents and can be used in areas where electricity is not widely available. It believes Lavarians will respond dramatically to the introduction of this product, especially if it is produced in their country.

MacWash will have to set up a subsidiary that is incorporated in Lavaria. The initial investment (project price) will be $4,800,000. Studies indicate that the subsidiary can be expected to have annual gross sales receipts amounting to 12,000,000 units of local currency. In Lavaria, the local currency is the Elsie, abbreviated $L\rlap{/}c$. Annual operating costs including depreciation are estimated to be $L\rlap{/}c 7,200,000$. The income tax rate in Lavaria is 25 percent, and the subsidiary will have allowable straight-line depreciation of $L\rlap{/}c 800,000$ per year. The Elsie is a stable currency and is expected to remain at $L\rlap{/}c 1 = \$0.30$ throughout the life of the project, which MacWash knows will be six years. At the end of the six years, the Lavarian Development Bank will pay MacWash $L\rlap{/}c 11,200,000$ (the book value of the project) and take over the

plant. The U.S. tax rate is 34 percent. MacWash has decided to use a risk-adjusted discount rate of 14 percent for the project, even though it currently uses only a 12 percent rate on domestic investments. Finally, Lavaria does not restrict remittances or assess additional taxes against them.

Table III-1 is a worksheet for the MacWash project. The top portion of the table shows the project's net cash inflows in local currency. This is what the subsidiary in Lavaria would receive as a firm incorporated there. The bottom half of the sheet continues the analysis to determine the net present value *(NPV)* of the project from the viewpoint of the parent. Here the annual net cash inflows to the parent are converted to U.S. dollars, and the additional U.S. tax liability is deducted. The present value of the net after-tax inflows for the six-year period is then added to that of the net after-tax inflow from the development bank payment occurring at the end of the six years to obtain the present value *(PV)* of the net cash inflows to the parent. Finally, the *NPV* of the project is obtained by subtracting its price from the *PV* of the net cash inflows. Since the *NPV* is positive, the project should be accepted.

Although our MacWash example is greatly simplified, it does call attention to three of the important foreign variables that must be considered in any analysis of this type—taxes, exchange rates, and political risk. A different tax treatment of income or remittances by Lavaria or of foreign source income by the United States might possibly yield a negative *NPV* for the project. This is one reason why it would not be prudent to evaluate the project from the standpoint of the subsidiary alone. A weakening of the Elsie would present additional problems, since the $L\rlap{/}c$ earnings of the subsidiary might not translate into a sufficient net cash inflow to the parent to make the project feasible.

Table III–1   Worksheet for MacWash Foreign Capital Project

Annual Gross Receipts from Sales		LĊ12,000,000
Less:		
Annual Cost of Operations		LĊ7,200,000
Net Income Before Taxes		
		LĊ4,800,000
Less:		
Income Tax (Lavaria, 0.25)		LĊ1,200,000
Net Income		LĊ3,600,000
Plus:		
Depreciation		LĊ800,000
Annual Net Inflow from Project		LĊ4,400,000
Annual Net Inflow to Parent (LĊ = $0.30)		$1,320,000
Less:		
U.S. Income Tax	$489,600[a]	
Credit Local Tax	(360,000)	
		$ 129,600
Parent Net Annual Inflow After Taxes		$1,190,400
PV of 6-Year Net Inflow [PVF_a (14%, 6) = 3.8887]	$4,629,108	
PV of Development Bank Purchase		
Payment [LĊ11,200,000 × .30] = $3,360,000		
Times PVF (14%, 6) =	$1,530,816	
PV of Net Inflow to Parent		$6,159,924
Project Price		($4,800,000)
NPV of Project		$1,359,924

[a][.34 × LĊ4,800,000 × .30 = .34 × $1,440,000]

Finally, this project is acceptable with the end payment from the Lavarian development bank but would not be acceptable without it. If the Lavarians were to delay this payment very much, its PV would fall and likely make the project unacceptable.

In practice, capital budgeting analyses of projects such as this one can become extremely complex. Since a project of this type is often fraught with uncertainties, it is not uncommon to simulate a number of scenarios, including a worst-case possibility, before making a final decision on it. However, despite the difficulties involved and the additional risks that confront a firm when it operates on foreign turf, the widespread success of multinational corporations suggests that the rewards are often well worth the effort.

QUESTIONS AND PROBLEMS

1. How is foreign capital project analysis similar to home country project analysis? How is it different? Identify specific considerations the firm must take into account in foreign project analysis that do not exist in home country analysis.

2. Do firms ever employ a higher risk-adjusted discount rate for foreign than for domestic cap-

ital budgeting? Why or why not? Discuss the use of such a rate as opposed to the adjustment of project flows as an approach to foreign capital project analysis.

3. Reevaluate the MacWash project of Table III-1 on the assumption that the Lavarian Elsie will have the following values over the life of the project:

Year	Dollar Value of One Elsie
1	$0.30
2	0.34
3	0.32
4	0.28
5	0.28
6	0.28

4. Garibaldi Pizza Machine Corporation (a U.S. firm) is evaluating an investment project in Blutonia. The government of Blutonia is anxious to establish a capital goods industry and believes pizza machines would be a good place to start, since Blutonians prefer high-calorie foods. The plan calls for Garibaldi to set up a subsidiary in Blutonia at an initial outlay cost of $5.2 million (U.S.) It will be allowed to operate the subsidiary for four years and return all the profits to the United States each year. At the end of the four years, the subsidiary must be turned over to the Blutonian government, which will sell it to local private investors and retain all proceeds from the sale.

The local currency is the Bluto. At the inception of the project, the value of one Bluto is $0.50 U.S. It is projected that the before-tax earnings of the subsidiary will be:

Year	Earnings Before Taxes (Blutos)
1	2,000,000
2	4,000,000
3	6,000,000
4	6,000,000

The subsidiary will have a cash inflow from allowable depreciation of 200,000 Blutos per year. The Bluto is expected to remain stable. The corporate income tax rate in Blutonia is 20 percent, while in the United States it is 38 percent. Garibaldi currently uses a risk-adjusted discount rate of 12 percent for international projects.

a. What will be the estimated after-tax net cash inflows to the parent?

b. Should Garibaldi accept the project?

SELECTED REFERENCES

Booth, Laurence D. "Capital Budgeting Frameworks for the Multinational Corporation," *Journal of International Business Studies* (Fall 1982), pp. 114–123.

Eiteman, David K., and Arthur I. Stonehill. *Multinational Business Finance*, 5th ed. (Reading, MA: Addison-Wesley, 1989), especially Chapters 16–18.

Lessard, Donald R. "Evaluating Foreign Projects: An Adjusted Present Value Approach," In D. R. Lessard (ed.), *International Financial Management*, (New York: Wiley, 1985).

Madura, Jeff. *International Financial Management*, 2nd ed. (St. Paul: West, 1989), especially Chapters 15–16.

Weston, J. Fred, and Bart W. Sorge. *Guide to International Financial Management* (New York: McGraw-Hill, 1977).

A "Guaranteed" Foreign Investment

Western Consolidated Industries, a diversified manufacturing firm, has been negotiating with the government of a large Latin American country regarding a proposal to install and operate a packaging equipment plant in a new industrial park located outside the nation's capital city. The foreign government's current offer would allow Western Consolidated to operate the plant for a period of six years and to transfer its after-tax profits to the United States each year. The foreign tax rate on corporate profits is 46 percent, a higher rate than the existing United States tax rate. Therefore, under United States tax laws, no additional income tax would be due on remittance of profits. Presently, there are two variations of the project that would be acceptable to the foreign government.

PROPOSAL I

Western Consolidated would install a plant with facilities for manufacturing two types of packaging machines: Type *A*, a light-duty machine commonly used by small packaging firms, and Type *B*, a heavy-duty machine capable of handling larger jobs and faster rates of output. The government would guarantee the following quantities sold and prices for the six years that Western Consolidated is permitted to operate the plant:

	Type A			Type B	
Year	Price	Quantity Sold		Price	Quantity Sold
1	$12,000	50		$22,000	20
2	13,000	50		24,000	20
3	14,000	60		26,000	40
4	16,000	60		28,000	40
5	18,000	60		30,000	60
6	20,000	60		32,000	60

At the end of the six years of operation, the government would buy the plant from Western Consolidated at U.S. book value, thereby returning the remainder of invested capital to the company with no gain on the sale and therefore no U.S. tax due.

Western Consolidated's management estimates that the initial outlay to install the plant will be $1,200,000 and that the book value of the plant to be returned at the end of the sixth year will be $960,000. Annual fixed costs, including depreciation, will be $200,000 for the first year of operation and will increase 10 percent each year over the remaining five years. For any one year, the average variable cost of each type of unit is expected to be constant, but AVC will have to be adjusted upward for rising input prices. The AVC estimates by year for the two types of machines are as follows:

Year	AVC_A	AVC_B
1	$9,600	$15,500
2	10,400	17,100
3	11,200	17,940
4	12,000	19,320
5	14,400	20,250
6	16,000	21,500

The Latin American government has agreed to make all guaranteed payments in U.S. dollars, so that Western Consolidated will run no exchange-rate risk. Management normally uses a discount rate of 12 percent for its U.S. investments, and it has been argued that the same rate should be applied to this foreign project, since the government guarantees will minimize risk.

PROPOSAL II

Under this alternative, Western Consolidated would install a somewhat less flexible plant with facilities for producing only the Type B packaging machine. The initial outlay on the plant installation would be only $960,000, but the book value that would be returned at the end of six years would also be less: $768,000. Annual total fixed costs for this type of plant will be only $180,000 in the first year of operation, but will increase by 10 percent each year. The prices guaranteed for the Type B machine would be the same as those stated for each year in Proposal I. In addition, the above data on AVC for the Type B machine, would continue to be applicable. However, the guaranteed quantity sold of the Type B machine, when it is the only kind produced, would be as follows:

Year	Quantity Sold of Type B
1	50
2	60
3	60
4	80
5	100
6	100

The tax rate of 46 percent on profits will apply as in Proposal I, and the purchase of the plant at book value will ensure that no capital gains taxes will be due on the amount received when the government takes over the operation at the end of six years. Finally, the company's management will use a 12 percent discount rate in the evaluation of this alternative, again because of the low level of risk assured by government guarantees.

QUESTIONS

(Hint: When evaluating project inflows, be sure to reduce annual gross profits by the amount of foreign profits taxes paid.)

1. Is Proposal I an acceptable capital project? Why or why not?

2. Is Proposal II an acceptable capital project? Why or why not?

3. If the discount rate is raised to 14 percent, would either proposal be acceptable?

4. What kinds of information about the projects or the environment of the country might lead to a decision to employ an even higher discount rate to evaluate inflows?

Shanghai Magnificent Harmony Foundry II

Happy Mr. Fei! His manhole cover project (Case 2B, "Shanghai Magnificent Harmony Foundry I," following Chapter 7) has been deemed a smashing success, since he was able to obtain U.S. trade preference status and iron ore prices did not increase. The Central Management Committee is so impressed with Fei's handling of the matter that they now want him to search out other types of simple cast-iron products that could be exported to the United States.

On a trip to the United States, Mr. Fei discovered that the health and fitness boom has created dramatic increases in demand for all types of exercise equipment. Cast-iron weights for body-building programs at fitness centers and gyms seemed to be selling very well in the U.S. market. Mr. Fei realized that it would be a simple matter for Shanghai Magnificent Harmony Foundry (SMHF) to cast the circular weights used on lifting bars, but producing the bars themselves would present an additional problem.

To be competitive with other producers of weight-lifting equipment, Mr. Fei will have to provide lifting bars to the U.S. firms that would distribute the cast-iron weights. These bars must be of forged metal, and they are normally machined and chromium-plated to improve their appearance and deter rust. While SMHF has sufficient idle capacity in forging to manufacture the bars, it has no facilities for machining and chrome plating and will have to invest in both types of equipment to realize the new project.

The cost of the equipment is estimated to be 1,600,000 Renminbi Yuan, or 200,000 U.S. dollars at the official exchange rate applicable to both offshore sales and valuation of capital investments.

Because of a slowdown in China's shipbuilding industry, SMHF will be able to release some casting capacity to Mr. Fei for export-oriented production of the weights. This is estimated to be 500 short tons per year (2,000 lb. = one short ton) over the next five years.

Mr. Fei has been told that the weight-lifting equipment undertaking must be evaluated with a five-year project life, since management expects it will have to reallocate the casting capacity to parts for shipbuilding as demand recovers in that sector. If casting capacity increases due to government allocation of investment funds, exports of the new product would be continued, but there is certainly no guarantee of this.

Given the success of his previous project, Mr. Fei is certain that no tariff will have to be paid on the weight-lifting equipment. For every pound of weights sold, 0.25 lb. of lifting bars (straight bars, curling bars, and dumbbell bars) will be sold. The simple cast-iron, weights will have to be sold at the world market price of cast iron, which comes to $0.48 per lb. delivered to U.S. West Coast ports. His net price for both weights and bars will have to be reduced by $0.06 per lb. for freight. The landed price of the bars will be double that of the weights. Mr. Fei estimates that the forging, machining, and chrome plating processes will increase the cost of the bars by 75 percent in comparison with ordinary cast-iron products. Further, he believes that all of the 500-ton output can be sold each year.

Fei has been instructed to evaluate the weight-lifting equipment project over the five-year time horizon using a risk-adjusted discount rate of 18 percent per year. The Central Management Committee has chosen not to require this project to carry any allocated fixed costs. Variable cost per pound of product will be the same as for manhole covers (see SMHF I), with appropriate adjustment for the production of the lifting bars. The bars and weights must sum to the available capacity allocated to the project. Mr. Fei has been told not to assume any salvage value for the equipment. Assume that the project will not be assessed income taxes, and therefore that Mr. Fei will not be able to achieve any tax savings from depreciation of the new equipment.

QUESTIONS

1. From the data given in this case, will the project be acceptable given the investment that must be made to do the plating of the bars?

2. Calculate the impact that the following would have on the project:

   a. A reduction in the risk-adjusted discount rate to 15 percent per year.

   b. A shortening of the project life to four years, given the original (18 percent per year) risk-adjusted discount rate.

CHAPTER FIFTEEN

Economics of Public Sector Decisions

In this chapter and the next, we direct attention to the economic interrelationships between business firms and government. We begin at an operational level, adapting the optimizing decision rules discussed in previous chapters to problems of public sector decision making. We will find that many of the economic principles developed in the context of the profit-maximizing firm can be carried over to certain types of public managerial problems. However, the nature of much of the public sector's product is such that some new tools of analysis must also be developed.

This chapter deals primarily with managerial decisions concerning the supply of goods and services by the public sector. In Chapter 16 we address the matter of the effects of one of the public sector's products, laws and regulations, on private firms and their managers.

MICRO- VERSUS MACROECONOMICS IN PUBLIC SECTOR ANALYSIS

In the United States, public sector purchases of goods and services amount to about 29 percent of GDP (gross domestic product, the nation's total output of final goods and services). Much of our national economic policy focuses on the *macroeconomic* variables (aggregate consumption expenditures, gross private domestic investment, total government expenditures, taxes, and the money supply) that determine the level of employment and activity in the economy. In a very broad and general sense, the GDP is an indicator of the well-being of the nation's citizens, and increases in real GDP (i.e., GDP adjusted for changes in the purchasing power of the dollar) can be interpreted as improvements in the overall standard of living, as long as they are not outstripped by population increases and the picture is not distorted by shifts in the distribution of income among individuals or groups.

The way in which government utilizes resources is another important factor affecting the well-being of a society. The federal government, through its budgetary processes and its management of monetary policy, attempts to make the decisions necessary to move toward attaining an overall goal of full employment and relatively stable prices. However, in the process of managing the federal budget and the activities subsumed under it, literally thousands of *microeconomic* decisions must be made each day in the agencies and the bureaus that are responsible for the particular uses to which government-obtained resources are put.

Administrators working in public bureaus and agencies (whether local, state, or federal) frequently occupy slots not unlike those held by business managers. Therefore, the decision analyses developed for profit-maximizing firms can prove very useful to such administrators, even if the objective of their agency seems remote from the notion of economic profit. To apply managerial economics to the problems of public sector microeconomic decisions, we must first take a close look at the nature of public sector output and the objectives of its production. In the balance of this chapter, we emphasize the techniques used in making public sector decisions relating to governmental output of specific goods and services.

THE PUBLIC SECTOR'S PRODUCT

The public sector (for our purposes, federal, state, and local government) produces an output of goods and services that consists mainly of public goods and *mixed goods* (goods that are partly public). In Chapter 14 we noted that an essential characteristic of a public good is that it provides benefits to parties who do not engage in a market transaction to obtain it. We also called these benefits *external benefits* or *third-party benefits.*

Perhaps the most obvious example of a public good is national defense. The benefits to all members of our society as a result of "consuming" national defense are generally considered to be significant. However, we do not individually engage in market transactions to purchase national defense, and the amount any given consumer would be willing to pay for defense would probably be zero if the consumer thought that the defense would be supplied whether or not he or she paid anything for it.

A **pure public good** is a product or service that is indivisible and nonexcludable.

Economists say that a good is a **pure public good** if it is *indivisible* (if one person cannot consume a unit of it apart from other units) and *nonexcludable* (if it is difficult or impossible to keep it from consumers who do not pay for it). Aside from national defense, other examples of public goods are scenic views, lakes and rivers, food and drug regulation, criminal justice, and "free" radio and television. Clearly, not all public goods are produced by the public sector—God or NBC may be the supplier of some of them.

The public sector also produces a large quantity of mixed goods that provide third-party benefits, as well as private benefits, to users who pay (perhaps not the full cost) for the privilege of using them. Postal service, public housing projects, state and federal parks, and toll roads are all examples.

Finally, the public sector does produce certain goods that are almost purely private. For example, the Tennessee Valley Authority (TVA), which was set up primarily to control floods and provide rural electricity, produces fertilizer that is sold to farmers in the marketplace alongside similar products made by private industry. In this case, however, it can be argued that an important reason for the public sector's production of such a divisible and excludable good as fertilizer is that such production results in social benefits that exceed the private benefits to farmers from their use of the product. For example, excess or off-peak generating capacity can be used in fertilizer production rather than left idle, and the TVA is able to conduct research on the production and use of fertilizer in depressed agricultural areas. Thus, even when an element of the public sector's output takes on the appearance of a private good, its character can be expected to be mixed because of external benefits related to its production.

Although we have so far characterized public and mixed goods by focusing on external benefits that accompany their production, it should be noted that the production of many goods (including public, mixed, and private goods) also entails external costs. As we will see in the following section, both external costs and external benefits raise serious problems regarding the extent to which a free market system can achieve an economically efficient allocation of resources.

RESOURCE ALLOCATION AND THE SUPPLY OF PUBLIC GOODS

If government undertakes to supply a particular good or service, it must withdraw resources from the private sector, usually by purchasing them in the market. Since a reallocation of resources and a change in the economy's output follow, it is important that government decision makers ascertain whether these products result in an increase in the general well-being of the citizenry as a whole. There are really two parts to this question. First, will the government activity result in a more efficient allocation of resources? And second, will the distribution of income be altered in a way that is likely to improve the general well-being? The second question is necessary, since the provision of certain types of public sector output may involve taking income from one group of citizens and transferring it to another. At this point, however, we will concentrate on answering only the first of the two questions.

The resource allocation question applies both to privately produced goods and to public sector output. In theory, the amount of any good that should be supplied at a point in time is the quantity that *equates the marginal social cost of the good with its marginal social benefit.* We need a few definitions to understand this concept.

First, the marginal *private* economic cost of a good includes all explicit and implicit costs of its production that are borne by the producer. A product's **marginal social cost** differs from its marginal private cost by the amount of external costs (third-party costs) that accompany the production of an incremental unit of output. This cost includes the value to consumers of any alternative product or products whose production is reduced or eliminated. If there are no external costs, marginal social cost and marginal private cost will be identical at each level of output.

In similar fashion, we can define **marginal social benefit** as the sum of marginal private benefits and marginal external or third-party benefits. The private benefits accrue to those who directly pay a price for the good, whereas the external benefits are enjoyed by either the purchasers and/or nonpurchasers but are not accounted for in the product's market price. Where there are no external benefits, marginal social benefit and marginal private benefit will be identical at each level of output.

If we argue that all sorts of benefits and costs can be given a dollar value, we can proceed very straightforwardly to the rationale behind the assertion that a good should be provided up to the quantity where marginal social cost equals marginal social benefit. Actually, this principle is a simple extension of the profit-maximizing decision rule for a firm: that the firm should produce up to the point where its marginal revenue equals its marginal cost. Where the decision-making unit is a governmental unit rather than a firm, we merely substitute "social benefit" for revenue and "social cost" for private cost:

> To maximize the **net social benefit** received from a good or service, it should be produced up to the point where its marginal social benefit is equal to its marginal social cost. The net social benefit of a good is equal to its total social benefit less its total social cost.

In Figure 15-1, we illustrate a total social benefit curve and a total social cost curve, both of which are increasing functions of the quantity of public good X. Net benefits are maximized at Q_x^*, where marginal social cost equals marginal social benefit. In the lower panel, the marginal social cost curve intersects the marginal social benefit curve at Q_x^*, and the slopes of the two

The **marginal social cost** of a good is equal to the marginal private cost of producing it plus any marginal external costs imposed on third parties by its production. The marginal social cost of a good reflects the value of resources used in its production.

The **marginal social benefit** of a good is equal to the marginal private benefits the good provides plus any additional external or third-party benefits.

The **net social benefit** of a good is equal to its total social benefit less its total social cost.

FIGURE 15–1

*Maximization of
Net Social
Benefits*

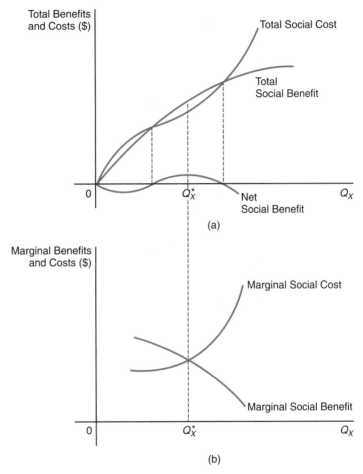

(a)

(b)

The optimal quantity of a public good is produced where the marginal social benefit of the good equals its marginal social cost. At Q_x^*, net social benefit—the difference between total social benefit and total social cost—is maximized. Production beyond Q_x^* would add more to social cost than to social benefit.

curves ensure that for levels of output greater than $Q_{x'}^*$, additions to social cost will exceed additions to social benefit. Thus, $Q_{x'}^*$, is the amount of output that will maximize society's net benefit from production of this good.

A theoretically optimal allocation of society's resources exists when for all goods the condition that *MSB* = *MSC* is attained. We can further examine this principle by looking at a two-goods case, where X and Y are the goods, where both costs and benefits are measured in dollars, and where initially we have

(15-1)
$$MSB_X = MSC_X = 20,$$

and

$$MSB_Y = MSC_Y = 40.$$

Thus, the social cost of producing the marginal or last unit of X is $20, while that of producing the marginal unit of Y is $40. Obviously, it is also true that

(15-2)
$$\frac{MSB_X}{MSC_X} = \frac{MSB_Y}{MSC_Y} = 1.$$

Now assume that the following conditions exist:

1. All resources are fully employed.
2. Marginal social benefit *falls* as the quantity of each good produced is increased.
3. Marginal social cost is constant at $20 per unit of X and $40 per unit of Y.

What will happen to equation 15-2 if one more unit of Y is produced? First of all, a marginal social cost of $40 will be incurred; this means *two* units of X production must be forgone. Since MSB_X will *rise* as the quantity of X is reduced, and MSB_Y will *fall* as the quantity of Y is increased, the result must be

(15-3)
$$\frac{MSB_X}{MSC_X} > 1 > \frac{MSB_Y}{MSC_Y}.$$

For example, we might have

(15-4)
$$\frac{22}{20} > 1 > \frac{38}{40}.$$

What are these ratios saying? The answer is much the same as the one we derived in the theory of production with regard to the substitution of inputs in the long run. In particular, for the new output combination, the social *benefit gained* from a *dollar's worth of expenditure* on product X is $22/$20 = $1.10, whereas the social *loss* from spending a *dollar less* on resources to produce Y is $38/$40 = $0.95. Clearly, resources are *misallocated* in the new position [equation (15-4)]. The production of Y should be reduced and that of X increased until the original position is again attained and $MSB_X/MSC_X = MSB_Y/MSC_Y = 1$.

Finally, we should note that marginal social *cost* is likely to *increase* as production of a good increases and decrease as production falls. This more realistic assumption would not change the directions of the inequalities in equations 15-3 and 15-4, since MSC_X would be less than 20 and MSC_Y would be greater than 40. Our case would simply be reinforced by having both marginal social benefits *decrease* and marginal social costs *increase* as the output of a good expands.

We can now summarize the implications of the preceding discussion. First, for a given income distribution, efficient resource allocation will take place when, for *n* goods,

(15-5)
$$\frac{MSB_a}{MSC_a} = \frac{MSB_b}{MSC_b} = \cdots = \frac{MSB_n}{MSC_n} = 1.$$

This condition simply means that a dollar's worth of social benefit is received for an additional dollar spent on the production of each good. Any

---

MANAGERIAL PERSPECTIVE

The $5 Billion Mistake

Long Island Lighting Company (LILCO) had a problem on its hands—a $5.3 billion problem. Its Shoreham nuclear plant, completed at the end of 1983, had not received a license to operate and was not likely to receive one. The reason was that nearby communities were not satisfied with LILCO's emergency evacuation plan.

Finally, then New York governor, Mario Cuomo, decided that the plant must not start up. After a great deal of negotiation, the state of New York agreed to take the plant off LILCO's hands for $1. However, the $1 price included an agreement to dismantle the plant and haul away the pieces, at least when someone came up with a safe way to dispose of the radioactive core. Moreover, the state guaranteed LILCO annual rate increases of 5 percent for at least three years and perhaps as long as 10 years. As a result, LILCO customers would have to pay for part of LILCO's expensive white elephant. The state guarantee made it possible for LILCO to raise its rates repeatedly, and in 1996, they were the highest in the continental United States. By raising its rates, LILCO was able to continue paying dividends

to its investors and retain its ability to borrow. Needless to say, this was a much better deal for LILCO's investors than for consumers.

By 1998, it was evident that ratepayers had seen enough and that LILCO was unlikely to survive. In May, it was taken over by a state corporation formed for the purpose of liquidating it. Then it was revealed that just days before the takeover, LILCO had awarded its top executives over $67 million in severance packages, including $42 million to its CEO. The New York attorney general wanted to recover these funds but found that the the severance package included "ironclad corporate indemnification agreements and other provisions holding the executives harmless from any cost liability, or legal expense relating to their conduct as officers and directors of Lilco."

References: Office of the New York State Attorney General, "Report Finds Lilco Payout Irretrievable" (press release), April 29, 1999; Charles M. Studness, "LILCO: The Ultimate Failure of Regulation," *Public Utilities Fortnightly* (March 1, 1996), pp. 33–36; and "The $5 Billion Nuclear Waste," *Time* (June 6, 1988), p. 55.

The **incremental benefit-cost ratio (MSB/MSC)** of a project is equal to the marginal social benefit divided by the marginal social cost of an incremental unit of the project. The net benefit obtained from a project or activity will be maximized by increasing the size of the project or scope of the activity up to the point where the incremental benefit-cost ratio, *MSB/MSC,* is equal to 1.

The **benefit-cost ratio (B/C)** for an activity or project is equal to the present value of its benefits divided by the present value of its cost. A project is acceptable from a social welfare point of view if and only if its *B/C* is greater than or equal to 1.

Cost-benefit analysis is an extension of capital project analysis to public sector project decisions that attempts to take into account the economic criteria for an optimal allocation of society's resources.

deviation from this condition will result in a situation where too much of some good (or goods) and too little of some other good (or goods) is produced.

Furthermore, we can make the following important statement:

No incremental activity (j) should be undertaken where $MSC_j > MSB_j$.

Where the production of public goods is concerned, therefore, it is justifiable to increase output only where $MSB_j/MSC_j \geq 1$—that is, when the incremental social benefit exceeds or equals the incremental social cost of the activity.

The fraction MSB/MSC is called the **incremental benefit-cost ratio;** in cost-benefit analysis it is employed to determine the optimal *size* of a given public sector activity or project. In the following section, we will contrast this ratio with the ratio of *total* benefits to *total* costs, *B/C*, a concept frequently utilized to identify worthwhile projects and rank-order them. The ratio *B/C* is often called the **average benefit-cost ratio,** or simply the **benefit-cost ratio.**

COST-BENEFIT ANALYSIS: A PROCEDURAL OUTLINE

Cost-benefit analysis is simply the extension of capital project analysis, described earlier in Chapters 13 and 14, to public sector microeconomic decisions. It proceeds from the notion that the aggregate output of government or any subsector thereof consists of an array of alternative projects, each having costs and benefits and each of which can be undertaken at various sizes or operated at various levels of output. To the extent that each of these projects is carefully screened, their aggregate is likely to have the most beneficial effect on national well-being.

The steps usually taken in the construction of a cost-benefit analysis for a government undertaking are as follows:

1. Specify objectives and identify constraints.

2. Formulate alternative means of meeting objectives.

3. Estimate costs of each alternative.

4. Estimate benefits attributable to each alternative.

5. Select the best alternative.

Every item in the preceding list poses a substantial problem or set of problems for the decision maker. First, the objectives of a public expenditure project are often easy to state in general terms but are difficult to quantify. If, for example, our objective is to improve mass transit services in a given metropolitan area, how can we state it specifically? Do we just want to move a given number of people in less time? Should *more* service be available to a broader range of potential users? What kind of service should we offer (buses, streetcars, subway)? What about passenger comfort? Will the project impose environmental costs or perhaps reduce them?

Some of the preceding questions will be unanswerable until the study is completed, since each of the possible outputs will have a social cost that might exceed its social benefit. In addition, the constraint structure will help to identify feasible characteristics of the preliminary planning objectives. For example, it might be clear at the outset that the metropolitan government can afford to consider only projects with an initial capital outlay of $24 million or less. Thus, no combination of services requiring a larger outlay could be considered. There may also be technological constraints. (For example, if the city is located near sea level, a subway might be an impossibility.) Finally, existing political or institutional constraints or barriers may limit the way in which the undertaking can be designed. For example, if a separately incorporated area that is opposed to a metropolitan transit system lies in the way of one possible alternative route, then the route may not be feasible.

Once the objectives and the constraints are well understood, alternative proposals for the undertaking can be formulated. The next step is to delineate the costs and benefits for each alternative. Then a dollar value estimate must be obtained for each item of cost and benefit. This is not a simple procedure, since a correct analysis of the alternatives must consider *all* economic costs and benefits attributable to each.

In the calculation of costs and benefits, items are usually categorized as *direct* or *indirect* costs or benefits. **Direct costs** of an undertaking include research and planning outlays, initial capital outlay, and maintenance and operating expenses over the project's life. Some items of direct cost will be difficult to estimate because they are implicit. For example, the cost of using government-owned resources (perhaps land) in the project would be estimated using an opportunity cost approach. In the case of land, the cost would be estimated by ascertaining its present value in its next best use.

Indirect costs of a project are generally those costs related to externalities that are outputs of the project not accounted for in outlays of the government for project components. For example, if streets must be dug up to construct a subway, the resulting disruption of traffic and business activity will have real costs to society. These kinds of costs are always difficult to estimate because of their partly nonmarket nature. Nonetheless, they must enter into the analysis; indeed, a good part of the literature on cost-benefit analysis is directed precisely toward issues of measurement. The one maxim that writers on the subject universally mention is to estimate such costs using the closest possible approximation to the market value of their

The **direct costs** of a project or activity are the costs directly associated with the project or activity.

The **indirect benefits and costs** associated with a project or activity are external, or third-party, benefits and costs.

negative effects. For example, one might use the average value of a working motorist's time to estimate the cost of disruption caused by public works construction.

On the benefits side, **direct benefits** generally accrue to *users* of the project's facilities or primary outputs. In passenger transportation, for example, the main direct benefits accrue to riders of the transportation system. Direct benefits may also accrue to persons employed in the construction and/or operation of the facilities if such persons were previously unemployed. Otherwise, employment associated with the project may simply reflect changes in the distribution of employment, which may produce little or no net social gain.

The **direct benefits** of a project or activity are the benefits obtained by the users of the project or activity.

Much like indirect costs, **indirect benefits** stem mainly from externalities. Thus, a system of public mass transit may eliminate congestion for nonusers of the system, and it may enhance the environment by reducing exhaust fumes. A roundabout means of estimation may be necessary to come up with a figure for the dollar value of such benefits. Indeed, the elusiveness of indirect benefits, and especially of their estimation, is one of the major dangers in cost-benefit analysis. This point will be discussed further in a following section.

Since some costs and virtually all benefits will be flows occurring over time, it will be necessary to discount the dollar value of such streams. In the final analysis, the evaluation of each alternative undertaking will rest on the tradeoff between the present value of project cost and the present value of benefits. For the field of public investment, the matter of the appropriate discount rate (the **social rate of discount**) has been the subject of much controversy. At this point, it is sufficient for us to note that it is generally a lower rate than that used in the private sector, since government can usually borrow at low rates of interest (for example, the low rates usually paid on municipal bonds). In a subsequent discussion, we will provide an example of the effect of changes in the discount rate on project acceptability.

The **social rate of discount** is the discount rate appropriate for evaluating public sector projects.

In capital project analysis in Chapter 13, we saw that a project was acceptable as long as its net present value was greater than or equal to zero. Similarly, a public project or activity is acceptable as long as its net benefit is greater than or equal to zero or, equivalently, as long as its benefit-cost ratio is greater than or equal to 1. Moreover, an increase in the size of a project or activity will increase the net benefit associated with the project as long as its incremental benefit-cost ratio *(MSB/MSC)* is greater than 1. The net benefit of a project will therefore be maximized by increasing the project size until *MSB/MSC* is equal to 1. This condition implies that *MSB = MSC* at the optimal point for the production of a project, the social welfare maximization rule discussed earlier in this chapter.

With the preceding general notions about benefit and cost estimation in mind, we now turn to an illustrative application of cost-benefit analysis.

MANAGERIAL PERSPECTIVE

Valuing a Sea Otter, Asthma Attacks, and Fishing Trips

We have stated that valuing indirect costs and benefits has presented public officials and economists involved in cost-benefit studies with estimation problems. Recently, however, natural resource economists have been increasingly in demand to do just that with respect to the environment. In the past, for example, cost-benefit studies of air pollution controls have usually included reduced medical costs among the benefits. Now a recent study has shown that people might be willing to pay as much as $10 per day to avoid the discomfort of coughing and eye irritation caused by pollution.

When the New Bedford Harbor in Massachusetts was found to be polluted by PCBs, the calculated damages included not only the loss to commercial lobster fishers, but also $11 million in damages to beach-goers. Similar calculations were done with respect to lost recreational opportunities as a result of contamination of the Eagle River in Colorado from mining operations. Both Exxon Corporation and the state of Alaska have employed economists to estimate the damages to wildlife (such as sea otters) and recreational users as a result of the oil spill in Prince William Sound. In one recent case, a court ruling held that those responsible for dumping oil or toxic chemicals must either restore the environment to its original condition or pay compensation for the total value of the damages, including the loss of nonmarket benefits.

Many of these estimates of nonmarket damages involve asking people how much they would be willing to pay in higher taxes to maintain some natural resource. Some examples of values placed on intangibles include $73 per household per year for fishing trips on the Eagle River, for an aggregate annual value of $0.5 million; $10 per household per year for preserving the bald eagle in Wisconsin, for a total annual value of $30.0 million; and $25 per household for one less asthma attack per year, for an aggregate annual value of $175 million. Although such figures are still often disputed, it is becoming clear that these nonmarket or intangible costs of pollution are quite real to those who incur them.

References: "The Value of Nature," on *To the Best of Our Knowledge*, Wisconsin Public Radio, March 30, 1997; "Putting a Price Tag on Nature," *Montana Business Quarterly* (Summer 1995): 8–10; and "How Much Is a Sea Otter Worth?" *Business Week* (August 21, 1989), pp. 59–62.

An Application to Urban Mass Transit

Perhaps the best way to illustrate steps taken in reaching a decision through the cost-benefit approach is to look at an application to a specific problem. Let us suppose that we are preparing a cost-benefit analysis of proposed improvements in the transportation system of one of the nation's 15 largest metropolitan areas. It is widely agreed that the current public transportation system, consisting solely of buses and airport limousines, is woefully inadequate. A countywide metropolitan transit authority has been set up to deal with the problem.

The transit authority has engaged our firm to prepare a cost-benefit analysis of the metropolitan problem. A rough dollar constraint has been established for a number of possible improvement alternatives to be financed by a 20-year bond issue. The maximum amount of funds available for the improvements, which will be completed within 18 months of the sale of the bonds, will be $24 million. Throughout our analysis, we will be able to use this figure (or a lower one) as the present value of the project price, even though as many as two years will be required to complete improvements to the system, since the metropolitan authority can earn interest on the unexpended portion of the funds raised at about the same rate as it pays bondholders.[1]

Project Design: The Alternatives

Obviously, in an urban mass transportation project, one of the main items that will determine the possible configurations of services is the demand of the users and potential users. In the present case, we know that existing bus service is considered to be inadequate and that some specific type of service between the airport and certain other points is warranted. Undoubtedly, the existing transit system will have records providing information on routes and passenger utilization of services. It may even have survey data on passenger opinions regarding new routes and types of service. If not, one of the tasks of the project analysts will be to conduct such surveys. In addition, nontransit objectives (such as pollution control, noise abatement, and general aesthetics) will be items of interest to both the community and the decision makers in the transit authority. To the extent that there are such secondary objectives of the project, they must be made as explicit as possible, and the effects of different alternative solutions on these objectives (the indirect costs and benefits of each alternative) must enter into the overall project calculations.

Let us suppose that in consultation with local authorities, a set of planning objectives is generated. Let us also suppose that based on these objectives and some preliminary estimates of passenger demand, the following alternatives are chosen for evaluation:

1. Modernize and expand the existing bus fleet and continue airport limousine service (initial capital outlay: $4,000,000).

2. Combine bus modernization with helicopter service to the airport and minibus service around the central shopping area (initial capital outlay: $6,000,000).

3. Modernize the existing bus fleet and utilize an existing railway right-of-way to provide commuter train service between the airport, nearby

---

[1] This is possible because the bonds would be tax exempt and might therefore bear a rate of interest no higher than that earned on large-size time deposits.

points, and the central business district (initial capital outlay: $11,000,000).

4. Modernize the bus fleet and construct a subway line linking the central business district with the airport and intermediate points (initial capital outlay: $17,000,000).

5. Modernize the bus fleet and construct a monorail train line from the airport and nearby points to the central business district (initial capital outlay: $22,000,000).

With the project alternatives thus set out, the next step is to determine the cost of each alternative. In the present case, each alternative will in theory have an optimal size. That size can be expressed in dollar terms as the level of cost that is consistent with provision of service up to the point where marginal social cost equals marginal social benefit. Thus, using alternative 1 as an example, we know there is a limit beyond which additions to the bus fleet and limousine service will likely increase social cost more than they will increase social benefits. However, this does not mean that a change to another type of service, such as the types described in alternatives 2, 3, 4, and 5, would have no potential for net additions to social benefit. We are merely establishing the level of operation of alternative 1 that will provide the maximum net benefit from its employment.

Since there is already a transit system in operation, the relevant cost of each improvement alternative is the present value of the *differential* in cost between the alternative and operation of the existing system *without* modification. Such costs will consist primarily of the initial outlay (from the bond issue) on new capital equipment or modernization of old equipment, the present value of the difference in operating costs over the project life, and any indirect or external costs associated with undertaking and operating the new project—over and above those generated by continued operation of the existing system.

Measurement of the preceding cost items is relatively straightforward, except in the case of indirect or external costs. For example, if we consider alternative 4 or alternative 5, there will be external costs of disruption of traffic caused by the construction of subway or monorail facilities. Indeed, construction of such facilities may require some permanent adjustment in street routes (some may be blocked off by the rapid transit lines and become dead ends), which imposes external costs on motorists in a given area. These costs will by nature be more difficult to estimate than will direct capital costs or operating expenses.

Once the present value of the cost differential for each alternative has been estimated, the calculation of benefits begins. Again, the relevant measure is the differential between benefits generated by each new alternative and benefits that would occur if the existing system were continued over the time period identified as the project life.

Turning our attention now to the question of benefits, we expect that most of the incremental benefits will accrue to passengers who use the transit system and pay a fare for the service. However, public transportation is a mixed good that in almost all circumstances generates external benefits. For example, we can expect that nonusers of the transit system will benefit from reduced congestion if the system attracts riders who formerly drove their cars to destinations served by mass transit. In addition, businesses may benefit from reduced expenditures on employee parking facilities or company-subsidized car pool arrangements. Obviously, in this and in almost all public investment projects, we are dealing with a *flow* of benefits over time. Thus, the appropriate measure of benefits will be the present value of the differential benefits generated by each alternative.

In Table 15-1 we show an enumeration of the differential costs and benefits attributable to alternative 1. As mentioned previously, the direct cost items are generally the easiest to estimate. The indirect cost items, pollution and noise, are difficult but not impossible to estimate. One well-known procedure is to ascertain the effects of pollution and noise on land values and then use this figure as a proxy for external cost. Obviously, where diesel fumes become noxiously thick, land values are likely to suffer. Fortunately,

Table 15–1 *Present Value of Differential Costs and Benefits of Mass Transit Improvements: Alternative 1[a]*

Differential Costs	
(a) Direct:	
1. Initial capital outlay	$ 4,000,000
2. *PV* of operating cost differential	2,900,000
(b) Indirect:	
1. *PV* of additional pollution and noise	600,000
Total Differential Costs *(PV)*	$ 7,500,000
Differential Benefits	
(a) Direct:	
1. *PV* of time saved by users	$ 2,500,000
2. *PV* of motor fuel saved by users	3,000,000
3. *PV* of other automobile-operating expenses saved by users	2,000,000
(b) Indirect:	
1. *PV* of reduced congestion to motorists	2,000,000
2. *PV* of parking and car pool savings of businesses	1,000,000
Total Differential Benefits *(PV)*	$10,500,000

[a] The project life is assumed to be 20 years, and the discount rate is 5 percent. The $3,500,000 *PV* of future differential costs is a discounted stream of $280,847 per year. The $10,500,000 *PV* of future differential benefits is a discounted stream of $842,541 per year.

data on the effects of pollution and environmental decay on land values can frequently be obtained.

In the benefits portion of Table 15-1, we see the estimation problem in a different light. To some extent, the direct benefits can be estimated by ascertaining the price that users of the service would be willing to *pay* to ride the system at the optimal level of operation. In fact, this is the theoretically correct way to estimate private benefits to users. However, it may be somewhat difficult to estimate, *ex ante*, the fare that will yield the optimal level of use (the passenger volume consistent with $MSC = MSB$). Nevertheless, surveys can be used to determine approximately the number of people who would use the new service, given various prices.

As far as indirect benefits are concerned, the *PV* of reduced congestion to motorists can be estimated by calculating the amount of time that would be saved and then multiplying that figure by an appropriate dollar value per hour. The *PV* of savings to businesses from reduced expenditures on parking facilities and car pool arrangements can be estimated from data supplied by firms.

Once estimation problems have been surmounted, an enumeration such as Table 15-1 is prepared for each alternative. From these enumerations of costs and benefits, data for selecting the best alternative are calculated. Note that from Table 15-1, we have for alternative 1 a ratio of total differential benefits to total differential costs of $10,500,000/$7,500,000 = 1.40. Since the differential benefits exceed the differential costs, or the average benefit-cost ratio is greater than 1, alternative 1 is an acceptable project. In fact, any alternative that has an average benefit-cost ratio greater than 1 is acceptable, since it generates *net* social benefits.

Table 15-1 has been prepared using a discount rate of 5 percent to calculate the present values of future costs and benefits (operating costs, indirect costs, and all of the differential benefits). At this point we provide no rationale for the use of the 5 percent rate and proceed as though the rate itself were not an issue, but the effect of changing the discount rate will be examined later in this chapter.

In Table 15-2 we present summary data on the five alternative projects. Using the average benefit-cost ratio as an accept-reject criterion, we see that all five of the projects are acceptable, since $B/C > 1$ for each one of them.

In Table 15-2 the projects have been listed in order of *ascending cost*. This is a convenient format for our next step—the selection of the optimal project. What we need to know in order to select the best alternative is whether the additional costs incurred when going from a smaller project to a larger one are offset or more than offset by the additional benefits attributable to the larger project. The *incremental benefit-cost ratio*, $\Delta B/\Delta C$, answers this question. A move from a smaller undertaking to a larger one (in terms of total differential costs) is warranted as long as $\Delta B/\Delta C > 1$. Thus, according to Table 15-2, alternative 2 should be selected, since it yields net benefits above alternatives 1 and 3,

Table 15–2 *Cost-Benefit Comparison of Five Alternative Metropolitan Mass Transit Projects*[a]

Alternative No.	PV of Differential Costs (C)	PV of Differential Benefits (B)	B/C	$\dfrac{\Delta B}{\Delta C}$	Net Differential Benefits (B-C)
1	$7,500,000	$10,500,000	1.40		$3,000,000
				1.56	
3	12,000,000	17,500,000	1.46		5,500,000
				1.18	
2	17,500,000	24,000,000	1.37		6,500,000
				0.74	
5	27,000,000	31,000,000	1.15		4,000,000
				0.71	
4	34,000,000	36,000,000	1.06		2,000,000

[a] All future differential costs and benefits are discounted at a rate of 5 percent per annum for 20 years. See Table 15-3 for division of costs between capital outlay and discounted future flows, as well as annual benefit inflows.

whereas selecting either alternative 5 or alternative 4 over alternative 2 would add more to differential costs than to differential benefits.[2]

The preceding procedure is simply a way to approximate the condition $MSB = MSC$ where data are discrete or "lumpy" rather than continuous and smooth. From our earlier discussion of profit maximization and its relation to benefit-cost analysis, it should be evident that net benefits will be maximized when the project selected is the largest one for which $\Delta B/\Delta C > 1$. Indeed, the last column of Table 15-2 substantiates this result, since net differential benefits are largest for alternative 2.

PUBLIC INVESTMENT AND THE DISCOUNT RATE

Although the discount rate was assumed not to be an issue in the foregoing example, it has been the subject of much concern in public investment projects for two reasons. First, there has been a long debate among economists

---

[2] The student should note that if alternative 3 had yielded an incremental cost-benefit ratio less than 1, it would have been appropriate to compare alternative 2 with alternative 1 rather than with alternative 3. For example, if the *PV* of differential costs for alternative 3 had been $15,500,000 instead of $12,000,000, its $\Delta B/\Delta C$ would have been $7,000,000/$8,000,000 = 0.88. We would then check $\Delta B/\Delta C$ between alternative 1 and alternative 2. We would find for this increment that $\Delta B/\Delta C = $13,500,000/$10,000,000 = 1.35. Accordingly, our rule should be that when projects are listed in ascending order of costs, each successively larger project should be compared with the last project for which $\Delta B/\Delta C > 1$ to determine whether or not it should be undertaken. To test your understanding, show that alternative 5 would be the best choice if the *PV*s of differential costs for alternatives 3 and 2 were $15,500,000 and $21,500,000, respectively.

on how to determine the appropriate discount rate for public capital projects. Second, the choice of the discount rate in many cases affects the decision as to which of several alternative projects is optimal. In fact, we will see shortly that our decision in the urban transit example will be altered if a sufficiently higher discount rate is applied to the future streams of benefits and costs. Before we examine the effects of various discount rates on project selection, however, it will be useful for us to consider the question of the *theoretically* correct rate.

The "Appropriate" Discount Rate

The rate of discount that in theory should be applied to public investment projects is called the *social rate of discount* by economists. Since public investment usually involves a reallocation of resources from private to public sector use, many economists argue that the opportunity cost, in terms of rate of return, for the private sectors from which the public undertaking would draw its resources constitutes the appropriate rate of discount. Returns from public sector activities are not taxed; therefore, the before-tax rate of return for the forgone private output should be used as the discount rate. Finally, analysts also want to take into account the full social costs and benefits of the forgone private output when calculating the rate of return, since this is the procedure they would normally use in estimating the costs and benefits associated with the alternative public use of the resources.[3]

Where *neither externalities nor risk* are viewed as materially affecting the opportunity-cost rate of return, the social rate of discount can be viewed as the riskless market rate of return, adjusted for federal income taxes. Thus, if a business can place its funds in riskless government bonds yielding 6 percent interest tax-free, and if the tax rate on its corporate income is 46 percent, its required before-tax rate of return on a riskless project that will generate taxable income will be

$$\frac{0.06}{1 - 0.46} = 11.11\%$$

If a business were to place \$10,000 in a 6 percent, tax-free bond, at the end of the year it would receive a return of \$600 = \$10,000 (0.06). However, at the 46

---

[3] See U.S., Executive Office of the President, Office of Management and Budget, *Memorandum for the Heads of Departments and Agencies, Subject: 2002 Discount Rates for OMB Circular No. A-94* (Mitchell E. Daniels, Jr., Director), January 29, 2002, and *Guidelines and Discount Rates for Benefit-Cost Analysis of Federal Programs (Circular No. A-94)*, October 29, 1992. Also see David F. Bradford, "The Choice of Discount Rate for Government Investments," in Robert H. Haveman and Julius Margolis (eds.), *Public Expenditure and Policy Analysis*, 3d ed. (Boston: Houghton Mifflin, 1983), Chapter 6.

percent income tax rate, we can see that an 11.11 percent taxable return would yield the same after-tax income, since

$$\$10,000 \ (0.1111) = \$1,111$$
$$1,111 \ (-0.46) = \underline{\ \ -511}$$
$$\text{Net Yield} = \$ \ \ 600$$

In practice, analysts of public sector capital projects have seldom attempted to estimate a social rate of discount that reflects the opportunity cost of resources withdrawn from private use. Historically, many federally funded projects have been evaluated using a very low discount rate that was thought to be appropriate because it approximated the cost to the Treasury of borrowing funds.

In the final analysis, the best estimate of the appropriate social rate of discount may be the discount rate that reflects the cost of funds for a project of similar length and riskiness in the private sector. Public projects do take resources from the private sector, and the fact that a government may be able to borrow money more cheaply than a private firm because of the tax laws seems irrelevant when one is attempting to value these resources. Therefore, it seems reasonable to argue that the private sector cost of funds reflects the opportunity cost of funds used by the public sector for a similar project.

Effect of Changing the Discount Rate

In the preceding discussion, we asserted that changes in the discount rate can markedly affect the outcome of a capital project evaluation. Clearly, the *higher* the discount rate, the *lower* the value of a project's net inflow of benefits, since most of these occur over long periods of time. Moreover, different projects will likely have different ratios of present costs to future costs. Where a project's costs are in large part *future* costs, the present value of total cost may fall dramatically as the discount rate is increased. We can return to our urban transit alternatives to demonstrate how project choice may be affected by higher discount rates.

Table 15-3 reviews the five mass transit projects described earlier in this chapter, and their future costs and benefits are discounted at rates of 5, 7, and 9 percent per year. The 5 percent result is identical to that in Table 15-2, from which we determined that alternative 2 would be optimal. Note the difference in the average and incremental benefit-cost ratios for the higher rates of discount. At a discount rate of 7 percent, alternative 2 is still the project to select, since the incremental benefit-cost ratio between it and the next smallest project is 1.02. Also, its net benefits of $3,876,000 are the highest that can be obtained from any of the alternative when the discount rate is 7 percent. If the discount rate is increased to 9 percent, alternative 2 is no longer the best choice, since the incremental benefit-cost ratio between it and the next small-

Table 15–3 Effect of Different Discount Rates on Cost-Benefit Comparison of Five Alternative Metropolitan Mass Transit Projects[a]

Alternative	Discount Rate (r)	Initial Capital Outlay	PV of Future Differential Costs	PV of Total Differential Costs (C)	PV of Total Differential Benefits (B)	B/C	$\frac{\Delta B}{\Delta C}$ r = 5%	$\frac{\Delta B}{\Delta C}$ r = 7%	$\frac{\Delta B}{\Delta C}$ r = 9%	Net Differential Benefits (B-C)
1	5%	$4,000,000	$3,500,000	$7,500,000	$10,500,000	1.40				$3,000,000
	7%	4,000,000	2,975,000	6,975,000	8,926,000	1.28				1,951,000
	9%	4,000,000	2,564,000	6,564,000	7,691,000	1.17				1,127,000
3	5%	6,000,000	6,000,000	12,000,000	17,500,000	1.46	1.56			5,500,000
	7%	6,000,000	5,101,000	11,101,000	14,877,000	1.34		1.44		3,776,000
	9%	6,000,000	4,395,000	10,395,000	12,818,000	1.23			1.34	2,423,000
2	5%	11,000,000	6,500,000	17,500,000	24,000,000	1.37	1.18			6,500,000
	7%	11,000,000	5,526,000	16,526,000	20,402,000	1.23		1.02		3,876,000
	9%	11,000,000	4,761,000	15,761,000	17,579,000	1.12			0.89	1,818,000
5	5%	17,000,000	10,000,000	27,000,000	31,000,000	1.15	0.74			4,000,000
	7%	17,000,000	8,501,000	25,501,000	26,353,000	1.03		0.66		852,000
	9%	17,000,000	7,325,000	24,325,000	22,706,000	0.93			0.60	(1,619,000)
4	5%	22,000,000	12,000,000	34,000,000	36,000,000	1.06	0.71			2,000,000
	7%	22,000,000	10,201,000	32,201,000	30,603,000	0.95		0.63		(1,598,000)
	9%	22,000,000	8,790,000	30,790,000	26,368,000	0.86			0.57	(4,422,000)

a Assumes the following annual inflows and costs for a period of 20 years:

Alternative	Annual Inflow of Differential Benefits	Annual Differential Costs
1	$ 842,547	$280,849
3	1,404,245	481,456
2	1,925,822	521,577
5	2,487,520	802,426
4	2,888,733	962,911

est project (alternative 3) falls to 0.89. Given the 9 percent discount rate, however, *alternative 3* has an incremental benefit-cost ratio of 1.34 in comparison with alternative 1, so alternative 3 is the best choice. Note that at the 9 percent discount rate, the net differential benefits of $2,423,000 for alternative 3 are the highest for any of the projects.

From the preceding illustration, we can conclude that the choice of the discount rate is important in project selection. However, our mass transit example still gives no clue as to which discount rate we should choose. Obviously, proponents of alternative 2 will not want to accept the results of the analysis at 9 percent, even if we, as consultants, argue that the 9 percent discount rate is the appropriate one. The final decision is thus likely to be a political one, but it will at least be tempered by a realistic attempt to measure what the public is getting from the various alternatives.

COST-BENEFIT ANALYSIS AND DIVERGENT PUBLIC OBJECTIVES

We have focused thus far on the selection of an optimal project from an array of alternatives, each of which serves approximately the same objective. However, public funds often must be allocated among alternative programs or investments that have greatly different objectives. For example, a city commission may have to decide whether to allocate funds from a bond issue to mass transit improvements, expansion of hospital facilities, development of new parks and recreation facilities, or improvements of streets and sewers. In such a setting, cost-benefit analysis can again be useful.

Economists generally argue that more efficiency is obtained from public expenditures *the greater the benefit per dollar spent*. Benefit per dollar of expenditure is what we measure with the average benefit-cost ratio, *B/C*. Thus, where alternatives involve roughly the same outlay of public funds, those with the highest *B/C* ratios are viewed as the best choices.

Table 15–4 *Average Benefit-Cost Ratios and Ranking of Widely Divergent Public Investment Alternatives*

Alternatives	Description	B/C (Average Benefit-Cost Ratio)	Project Rank
A	Mass Transit Improvements	1.17	2
B	Hospital Facilities Expansion	1.02	4
C	Development of Parks and Recreation Facilities	1.05	3
D	Improvement of Streets and Sewers	1.35	1

In Table 15-4 we show a list of widely divergent public investment alternatives along with the *B/C* ratio for each. Assuming that approximately the same dollar amount is required to fund each alternative, their rank order in terms of efficiency is *D, A, C,* and *B*. That is, they are ranked such that the alternative with the highest *B/C* ratio is the most desirable, followed by that with the second highest ratio, and so forth.[4] Naturally, this is the point at which competing public agencies and citizens' interest groups are most likely to attack the results of a cost-benefit analysis. There is likely to be no shortage of persons who will argue that improved medical facilities are more important than better streets and sewers, regardless of what the benefit-cost ratios show.

Public outcry against the results of cost-benefit analyses and related types of economic impact analyses (environmental impact studies, for example) is not to be taken lightly. Indeed, the history of cost-benefit analyses in the United States is a very checkered one; economists themselves disagree on issues of cost and benefit measurement, as well as on the appropriate method of determining the social rate of discount. We investigate these problems further in the following section.

PITFALLS OF COST-BENEFIT ANALYSIS

Historically, the reputation of cost-benefit analysis as a policy tool has been severely damaged by over-eager users of the approach who have seldom failed to justify their pet projects in terms of stated economic benefits and costs. The Bureau of Reclamation is a federal agency that is often criticized for its questionable application of cost-benefit analysis to project evaluation. The economics literature contains cases too numerous to cite where such branches of government as the Army Corps of Engineers, the Department of Agriculture, the Department of Labor, and many state and local authorities or their consultants have produced project studies involving unsound cost-benefit analyses that served mainly to foster bureaucratic ends. The saving grace of some of these documents is that they also ignited the flames of public opinion against both the projects and their sponsors. One example of such a case is the Cross-Florida Barge Canal, a long-term pet project of the Army Corps of Engineers.

The Corps of Engineers has one of the longest histories of use and abuse of cost-benefit analysis in U.S. public works. The Corps has employed cost-benefit analysis to evaluate its waterways projects since 1900.[5] The Cross-Florida Barge Canal was first proposed by President John Quincy Adams, and nine

---

[4] If the required outlays for the various projects are *not* equal, the social welfare will be maximized if officials select that *group* of projects that yields the highest total net social benefit and still satisfies the budget constraint under which the governmental authority must operate.

[5] David N. Hyman, *The Economics of Governmental Activity* (New York: Holt, Rinehart, & Winston, 1973), p. 136.

studies of its feasibility were made by the government during the period from 1826 to 1930. Some digging was done in 1930, but the project was abandoned.

Congress authorized construction of the canal as a war measure in 1942, but it took another 20 years to appropriate any funds for the project. The Corps resumed work on the canal in the early 1960s; by 1970, it had completed roughly 25 miles of the waterway and had spent about $50 million in the process. The canal was finally scuttled by President Richard Nixon in 1971 after environmental groups waged a successful campaign against it.[6]

Throughout the period that the Cross-Florida Canal was under consideration, the Corps never failed to justify the project from a cost-benefit standpoint. A 1965 article surveying how cost-benefit analysis has been used compares a Corps of Engineers estimate of the canal's benefits with that of the railroad lobby to show a glaring example of self-serving benefit-cost studies. Whereas the Corps had come up with a benefit-cost ratio of 1.20 for the project, the railroad interests estimated the ratio to be 0.13. The Corps attributed a large share of total benefits to transportation savings, an item that was much disputed by the railroads. In addition, the Corps included indirect benefits from flood control, recreational boating, fishing, and enhancement of land values in its estimate. In the railroads' study, each of these items was valued at zero! The authors of the survey article concluded:

> To what extent the divergence is due to the facts that the Corps likes to build canals and that the consultants were retained by the railroads, and to what extent it is due to the intrinsic impossibility of making accurate estimates is left entirely to the reader to decide![7]

In 1984, environmentalists in Florida won another victory over the Corps of Engineers when the South Florida Water Management District initiated a project to fill in a part of the Kissimmee River Channel, a 20-year-old Corps project that had dried up vast areas of marshlands and damaged the complex ecology of South Florida. It was reported that the Water Management District might spend as much as $65 million to undo the alleged damage caused by the channel.[8] By 2002, substantial damage from the canal project still remained, and Florida environmental groups were struggling to have the Ocklawaha River ecosystem, which was damaged by the Corps in 1968, restored as a wildlife reserve and recreational area.[9]

In 1985, the Corps celebrated the completion of another southern dredging project, the Tennessee-Tombigbee Waterway. Bigger than the Panama

---

[6] See "Florida Sets Out to Restore Wetlands by Refilling a Canal Inadvisably Dug," *Wall Street Journal,* July 5, 1990, p. A10; and "The Environment: Blocking Florida's Big Ditch," *Newsweek* (February 1, 1971), p. 55.

[7] A. R. Prest and R. Turvey, "Cost-Benefit Analysis: A Survey," *The Economic Journal* (December 1965): 718.

[8] Now You See It, Now You Don't," *Time* (August 6, 1984), p. 56.

[9] Florida Defenders of the Environment, *Why Restore the Ocklawaha River Ecosystem?* http://polk-county.com/audubon/rodman.shtml, October 13, 2002.

Canal and with a price tag of $1.8 billion, this was widely recognized as the granddaddy of pork-barrel projects. Shortly after its opening, it was reported that barge traffic on the waterway was running at only about 5 percent of the optimistic projections that had been prepared by its proponents.[10] Fifteen years later, it appeared that the waterway was used primarily for logging and recreation and had done little to foster economic development of the region it passed through.[11]

The use and misuse of cost-benefit analysis are not likely to go away. The possible pitfalls of cost-benefit analysis are summarized in the following three points:

1. *Estimation,* particularly of *indirect benefits,* is not governed by strict standards, so an analysis can be "cooked" to show what its sponsors wish to show.

2. The opportunity-cost approach to the *social rate of discount* may bias the analysis against many worthwhile public undertakings.

3. The sheer *cost* of performing a credible cost-benefit analysis makes the approach unfeasible for many public investment decisions.

A good deal of research has been done on the estimation problems in cost-benefit studies, and, in general, it suggests that the estimation of direct benefits can be adequately accomplished by careful application of the market value or opportunity-cost approaches. Extension of such valuation techniques to the estimation of indirect benefits is questionable and may be unnecessary in many cases. In fact, the current trend seems to be toward leaving all but the most obvious indirect benefits out of cost-benefit calculations and including a discussion of their existence and probable extent in the nonquantitative part of project studies or reports. What is being recognized is that the opinions or values of public decision makers and their constituencies regarding nonmarket benefits (and costs) of a given public undertaking might best be expressed by the decision makers themselves rather than by professional economic analysts. Indeed, the nature of many indirect benefits is so elusive that the professional literature on them has taken to referring to them as "intangibles," "irreducibles," and "incommensurables." Thus, from the analyst's standpoint, the best prescription would seem to be to provide a very careful estimate of direct and clearly measurable costs and benefits in public investment studies but to call intangibles by their proper name and make their existence clear to public decision makers.

---

[10] "Rivaling Cleopatra, A Pork-Barrel King Rides the Tenn-Tom," *Wall Street Journal,* May 31, 1985, pp. 1, 10.

[11] Manuel Torres, "Boon or Boondoggle: The Debate Continues," *Tombigbee Country,* online, January 1999, www.ccom.ua.edu/Tombigbee/boon.html, September 13, 2002; and "House Passes Aqua-Pork Bill," *foe.org,* online, April 29, 1999, www.foe.org/pressreleases/aqua-pork/, September 13, 2002.

Turning to the discount rate dilemma, we wish to make two points. First, research on the issue reveals that many studies have been made using questionably low rates of discount for future streams of benefits. Certainly, proponents of the opportunity-cost approach would argue as much. Second, and perhaps of more importance, is the question of whether public investment undertakings should be measured using the same criterion, in terms of the rate of return, as that used in the private sector. A minority of analysts and policymakers argue that such projects should not. As a member of Congress once put it, the view that the appropriate discount rate for evaluation of public investment is one that reflects the opportunity cost rate for resources withdrawn from the private sector leads to the conclusion that society would benefit more from a new gadget than from the construction of a new school or sewerage system because the financial return was 5.5 percent on the gadget and only 5 percent on the school or sewerage system.[12] Nevertheless, one could respond that an economic problem would not occur in such cases if the social benefits from each project were estimated with a reasonable degree of accuracy.

Finally, we are left with the pitfall of the *cost* of cost-benefit studies. Much was learned about this problem during the administration of President Lyndon B. Johnson, when the Bureau of the Budget (now called the Office of Management and Budget) implemented an approach to government expenditure analysis known as the Planning, Programming, and Budgeting System (PPBS). Under PPBS, agencies were expected to conduct a yearly review of all of their programs, using the cost-benefit technique. The idea was that each agency would rank its projects internally and that the Bureau of the Budget would oversee the process from above, making appropriate recommendations to the Executive Branch regarding interagency allocation of funds.

Although PPBS proved useful in the internal evaluation processes of the agencies, it failed as a *system*, since it proved to generate more information (in terms of sheer information volume) than the Budget Bureau could handle. Indeed, in 1969 it was reported to Congress that 1,145 positions were added to 21 agencies just to support PPBS activities.[13] Not only was PPBS costly, but Congress itself made little use of the output produced by the system and went about business as though PPBS scarcely existed. In any event, the PPBS experience suggested that, although cost-benefit analysis could prove quite useful in the evaluation of individual projects, its use would have to be tempered by consideration of the cost of the studies themselves and the ability of the decision-making apparatus to comprehend and absorb cost-benefit information.

---

[12] The statement was made by Senator William Proxmire and is cited in H. H. Liebhafsky, *American Government and Business* (New York: John Wiley & Sons, 1971), p. 561.

[13] U.S. Congress, Joint Economics Committee, *Analysis and Evaluation of Public Expenditures: The PPB System,* Vol. 2 (Washington, DC: U.S. Government Printing Office, 1969), p. 636.

Toronto's $400 Million SkyDome

The city of Toronto, Canada, has a domed stadium that opened in 1989 and reportedly cost about $600 million to build. Originally, city managers forecasted that it would turn a profit. SkyDome officials expected the stadium to generate a cash flow of $20 million its first year. This projection was accepted despite the fact that the Superdome in New Orleans, built for less than $180 million 14 years earlier, still typically was recording annual operating losses in the millions.

The SkyDome was designed as a multiple-use facility that included a restaurant center, a hotel, and a retail mall in the center of Toronto. Financing for the initial outlay came from a variety of sources: bank loans, corporate investors, presold boxes and seats, the Ontario government, metro-Toronto governments, a public stock sale, and the sale of advertising rights. The stadium has had its critics, however. Some of them argued early on that too much was given to the corporations in return for their investment. In 1994, the Ontario provincial government sold its share of the dome to a group of private investors (some of them the same ones originally involved in the project) for $194 million. It was reported that the sale resulted in a $262 million loss for taxpayers.

In late 1998, the private owner, SkyDome Corporation, announced that it would seek court protection under the Companies' Creditors Arrangement Act while it reorganized its finances. The company also stated that it expected to lose about $3 million during the year because of declining revenues. The decrease in revenues was blamed partly on problems connected with baseball and partly on the expansion of the adjacent Metro Convention Centre.

Not all public projects turn out so badly, however. One apparently highly successful project is Boston's Central Artery/Tunnel Project, informally known as the Big Dig. This project, with a cost of nearly $12 billion, was initially considered to be a federal boondoggle. Partially opened by 2002, it was viewed as a model for reviving dying downtowns and addressing urban highway problems in spite of the fact that it was the most expensive public works project in U.S. history.

References: "Dig Deep: Tunnel Tour a Sign That Completion Is Near for Boston Highway Megaproject," *Buildings.com*, August 7, 2002, http://204.118.37.25/siteware/output/buildings/2002/08/07/krtbn/0000-0287-GL-BIG-DIG.asp, October 13, 2002; "Skydome Fiasco, A Sign of Things to Come? *Bread Nor Circuses* online, December 12, 1998, www.breadnotcircuses.org/skydome.html October 13, 2002; "The New Stadium Fallacy," *The Imbalance Sheet,* online, April 12, 2001, www.baseballprospectus.com/news/20010412imbalance.html, October 13, 2002; Tim O'Brien, "Skydome Sold for $111 Million," *Amusement Business* (March 28–April 3, 1994) p. 11; and "After Skydome, Stadiums Will Never Be the Same," *Business Week* (March 20, 1989), pp. 136–138.

THE FUTURE OF COST-BENEFIT ANALYSIS

As a policy tool, cost-benefit analysis has been heavily sold by economists in the past 30 years or so. Despite the demise of PPBS, cost-benefit analysis has unquestionably survived and will continue to be an important policy evaluation tool. From the material presented in this chapter, the appropriate conclusion to draw is that judicious application of the approach is probably the closest economic analysis can get to a straightforward evaluation of the overall consequences of public investment decisions. In addition, cost-benefit analysis has had enough public exposure to make it a familiar tool to many public sector managers. Fortunately, such exposure has also bared its abuses and shortcomings, so the ability of unscrupulous users to misguide policy-makers is somewhat limited. Certainly, many public investment decisions can be reviewed adequately using the cost-benefit approach if the pitfalls discussed here are avoided.

SUMMARY

Managerial Decisions in the Public Sector

In this chapter we have attempted in a selective way to discuss some of the issues surrounding the application of managerial economics to micro-level decisions in the public sector. We noted that one of the primary characteristics of many goods and services supplied by the public sector is that *external benefits* accrue to persons or groups who do not pay a direct charge for what they receive. The same was also shown to be true for some private sector production. We also found that both types of output (public and private sector) might be accompanied by *external costs*. To the extent such costs and benefits could be measured, it was shown that the optimal allocation of a society's resources at a given point in time would occur if each product or service were supplied up to the point where its *marginal social benefit equaled its marginal social cost*.

The chapter also provided a survey of *cost-benefit analysis,* an approach for evaluating public capital projects that attempts to take into account the economic criteria for an optimal allocation of society's resources. We applied cost-benefit analysis to five alternative proposals for improving a metropolitan area's mass transit system and related the concepts of the *average benefit-cost ratio (B/C)* and the *incremental benefit-cost ratio ($\Delta B/\Delta C$)* to the acceptability of projects and the determination of the optimal project size. Finally, our discussion turned to some of the problems associated with cost-benefit analysis, and we noted that application of the technique must be tempered in the light of *estimation difficulties, discount rate questions,* and the *expense* involved in preparing such studies.

We concluded that cost-benefit analysis is a tool that will likely be applied to public managerial questions in the future. In Chapter 16 we consider the interrelationships between the public and private sectors in matters of law and business regulation.

QUESTIONS

1. How can you distinguish between the micro- and macroeconomic decisions of public sector managers? In what sense do some public sector managers occupy positions similar to those of managers of private firms?

2. What is the importance of externalities in the analysis of public goods? Do market prices of privately produced goods usually reflect externalities? Why or why not?

3. Theoretically, what principle determines the optimal amount supplied of a public good? Explain why this principle applies equally to privately produced output.

4. What are the procedural steps that are usually taken in the preparation of a cost-benefit analysis? How is the analysis similar to a private capital project evaluation? How is it different?

5. What is the importance of the *incremental* benefit-cost ratio in making a decision based on cost-benefit analysis? What is the importance of the *average* benefit-cost ratio? Are projects with high average benefit-cost ratios necessarily more desirable than those with lower ones? Explain.

6. Why is the discount rate a more complex issue in public managerial decision making than in private sector analysis? What problems have analysts found in the use of discount rates by federal agencies?

7. What are the main pitfalls of cost-benefit analyses? How can some of them be avoided?

8. Do you think cost-benefit analysis can prove useful in a setting where decision makers must choose between widely different projects? Why or why not? How might the average benefit-cost ratio be utilized in such a case?

PROBLEMS

1. Illustrate graphically how the socially optimal amount of a public good is determined in economic theory. Provide an appropriate verbal explanation for what you show, and discuss why the market is unlikely to provide an acceptable solution to the optimal amount problem.

2. City Councillor Foghorn has argued that a new sports stadium should be constructed, since it would provide the city annual lease receipts of $900,000 per year for the next 20 years. The capital outlay for the stadium is $15,000,000. Normally, the City Planning Department employs a discount rate of 6 percent per year in its evaluation of capital projects. It is expected that revenues from food and drink concessions will offset the city's annual operating and maintenance costs for the stadium. Given this information, do you agree with Councillor Foghorn? Why or why not?

3. Which of the following projects would be acceptable from a benefit-cost standpoint if the applicable discount rate were 9 percent per year?

Project	Project Life (Years)	Annual Differential Benefits	Annual Differential Costs	Capital Outlay
A. Flood Control	20	$100,000	$30,000	$700,000
B. Street Paving	15	40,000	5,000	250,000
C. Playground Eqpt.	12	10,000	1,000	75,000
D. Rat Control	5	30,000	20,000	40,000
E. Street Lighting	20	20,000	7,000	100,000
F. Alarm System	20	80,000	10,000	500,000

4. Although the projects in Problem 3 are not comparable in size or scope, you have been asked to rank those that are acceptable. In what order would you rank the projects based solely on the given information? Explain why.

5. The Board of County Commissioners is attempting to choose one project from among the following drainage control alternatives:

Drainage Control District	Capital Outlay	Annual Differential Costs	Annual Differential Benefits
Northeast	$180,000	$17,000	$34,000
Northwest	160,000	20,000	33,000
Central	175,000	22,000	32,000
Southeast	150,000	16,000	33,000
Southwest	165,000	20,000	35,000

If the appropriate discount rate is 6 percent per year and such projects are normally viewed as having a 20-year life, which project should the commissioners choose?

6. How would your response to the preceding change if the appropriate discount rate were 9 percent per year instead of 6 percent per year?

7. The City Parks and Recreation Department is considering the expansion alternatives shown in the following table for the next fiscal year. Projects *A* and *D* are located in high-crime areas. Therefore, the city council has instructed the Parks and Recreation Department to add a 10 percent premium to the annual differential benefits given for each of these projects. Evaluate the five alternatives based on the table, the council's adjustment for Projects *A* and *D*, and a standard city policy of utilizing a life of 20 years and a discount rate of 6 percent for capital projects.

Project	Initial Capital Outlay	Annual Differential Operating Expense	Annual Differential Benefits
A. Build New Swimming Facility at Royer Park	$110,000	$10,000	$20,000
B. Improve J.F.K. Park Playground Area	70,000	4,000	8,500
C. Build Tennis Center at G. W. Park	120,000	12,000	21,000
D. Install Lighting at Thorp Track & Field Facility	80,000	5,000	13,000
E. Add 2,000 Seats to Memorial Gym	105,000	6,000	17,000

SELECTED REFERENCES

Baumol, William J. "On the Discount Rate for Public Projects." In Robert H. Haveman and Julius Margolis (eds.), *Public Expenditure and Policy Analysis.* Chicago: Rand-McNally, 1977, pp. 161–179.

Boardman, Anthony E. (ed.). *Cost-Benefit Analysis: Concepts and Practice,* 2d ed. Upper Saddle River, NJ: Prentice-Hall, 2000.

Fromm, Gary, and Paul Taubman. *Public Economic Theory and Policy.* New York: Macmillan, 1973, especially Chapters 1–5.

Fuguitt, Diana, and Shanton J. Wilcox. *Cost-Benefit Analysis for Public Sector Decision Makers.* Westport, CT: Quorum Books, 1999.

Gramlich, Edward M. *A Guide to Benefit-Cost Analysis,* 2d ed. Prospect Heights, IL: Waveland Press, 1997.

Haveman, Robert H., and Julius Margolis (eds.). *Public Expenditure and Policy Analysis,* 3d ed. Boston: Houghton Mifflin, 1983.

Hinrichs, Harley H. "Government Decision Making and the Theory of Benefit-Cost Analysis." In Harley H. Hinrichs and Graeme M. Taylor (eds.), *Program Budgeting and Benefit-Cost Analysis.* Pacific Palisades, CA: Goodyear, 1969), pp. 9–20.

Prest, A. R., and R. Turvey. "Cost-Benefit Analysis: A Survey." *The Economic Journal* (December 1965), pp. 683–735.

Stine, Jeffrey K. *Mixing the Waters: Environment, Politics, and the Building of the Tennessee-Tombigbee Waterway.* Akron, OH: University of Akron Press, 1994.

Zerbe, Richard O., Jr., and Dwight D. Dively. *Benefit-Cost Analysis in Theory and Practice.* New York: HarperCollins, 1994.

CHAPTER SIXTEEN

Legal and Regulatory Environment of the Firm

Businesses do not operate in a legal vacuum, and infractions of laws designed to regulate their activities can prove costly both to firms and to individual managers or officers of a firm. The mind-boggling Enron and MCI/Worldcom bankruptcies of 2001–2002 are well-documented cases of how firms can do themselves and the general public damage by adopting illegal or unethical practices. A Brookings Institution study released in late 2002 estimated that the fallout from the scandals at these two firms would cost the U.S. economy between $37 and $42 billion in terms of reduced GDP.[1] Moreover, not only were both companies in bankruptcy, but their executives faced federal investigations that could result in criminal prosecution.

Although the Enron and MCI/Worldcom debacles were huge, there is no shortage of other examples of firms where managers have made bad choices with equally bad repercussions. Indeed, in 2001, headlines were made when Alfred Taubman, chairman of Sotheby's auction house, was charged and convicted of price fixing involving Sotheby's supposed chief rival, Christie's. Taubman had to pay fines of $7.5 million and was sentenced

---

[1] Brookings Institution, "Brookings Study Details Economic Costs of Recent Corporate Crises," online, July 25, 2002, www.brook.edu/comm/news/20020725graham.htm, September 15, 2002.

to a one-year jail term.[2] In 1999, two vitamin companies agreed to pay a total of $725 million in fines for fixing the prices of vitamins. The $500 million fine assessed F. Hoffmann-LaRoche was apparently the largest federal *criminal fine* ever imposed.[3] That same month Toys 'R' Us agreed to pay $50 million in toys and cash to settle a lawsuit by states attorneys general contending that the company had kept toymakers from selling Barbie dolls, Mr. Potato Head, and other toys to discount stores. A few months earlier, a federal judge approved a $1.03 billion settlement of a class-action civil lawsuit against brokers of Nasdaq-listed stocks for alleged damages as a result of price fixing by brokers. This sum was stated to be a record high for a *civil* suit.[4] In 1996, 11 major drug producers, including such well-known firms as Merck, Pfizer, and Bristol Meyers-Squibb, agreed to pay $351 million to settle a civil suit charging that they had fixed prices by charging drugstores higher prices than they charged managed-care groups and mail-order pharmacies.[5] In that same year, Archer-Daniels-Midland Company agreed, with two Japanese firms, to a $45 million settlement stemming from charges they had conspired to fix prices for lysine, an amino acid that promotes rapid growth in chickens and hogs.[6] In 1993, Miles, Inc., maker of S.O.S. steel wool pads, agreed to plead guilty to price fixing and to pay a $4.5 million fine.[7] Between 1983 and 1985, investigations of price-fixing conspiracies in the electrical contracting industry yielded jail sentences for at least 14 executives, and 33 companies paid fines, damages, and legal expenses totaling more than $20 million.[8]

Although jail sentences are not common in cases involving violations of business practices or antitrust laws, over the past two decades some judges have argued that managers simply will not obey the law if they suffer no personal consequences for their actions. A significant number of judges now believe that fines and damages payments are insufficient deterrents to corporate lawbreaking, since some firms just view them as a cost of doing business.

The question of purposeful lawbreaking in business management has deep ethical dimensions. Some laws that adversely affect businesses are poorly designed and deserve to be challenged. Others are well designed to foster business competition and to protect consumers. Managers who break

---

[2] "Alfred Taubman to Serve Time," *Brown Daily Herald*, April 24, 2002, p. 1; and "Sotheby's Chief Is Convicted of Price Fixing," *Wall Street Journal*, December 6, 2001, pp. B1, B4.

[3] "Vitamin-Fix Fine History's Largest," *San Antonio Express News*, May 21, 1999, pp. 1E, 2E.

[4] "Price-Fix Penalty Is a Record," *San Antonio Express-News*, October 10, 1998, pp. 1F, 2F.

[5] "Settlement Cleared in Pharmacies' Suit over Price Fixing, but Debate Lingers," *Wall Street Journal*, June 24, 1996, p. B5.

[6] "Judge Approves $45 Million Pact in Civil Suit on ADM Price Fixing," *Wall Street Journal*, July 22, 1996, p. B5.

[7] "S.O.S. Pad Maker Agrees to Pay Fine for Price Fixing," *Wall Street Journal*, October 1993, p. B3.

[8] "Busting a Trust: Electrical Contractors Reel under Charges They Rigged Bids," *Wall Street Journal*, November 29, 1985, pp. 1, 5.

any law relating to their responsibilities within a firm are courting trouble, especially if the law involves well-established maxims of business behavior. Moreover, even in the case of bad or ill-conceived laws, civil disobedience can be viewed only as a measure of last resort.

Many businesses find themselves in costly legal proceedings because of *mistakes* made by managers rather than because of intentional lawbreaking. Such mistakes are frequently the result of ignorance of the law on the part of a specific decision maker or group, but the old saying that "ignorance of the law is no excuse" can make legal mistakes very costly indeed. The typical manager is not a lawyer and cannot be expected to have a very complete knowledge of all the legal ramifications of business decision making. In general, the best that can be expected is that managers have a broad conception of the purview of business law and government regulations, so that they will know when to seek legal advice and thus avoid some of the pitfalls that laws and regulations hold for the firm. In addition, a competent manager should be able to recognize the possibility that a rival firm or group of firms might be damaging his or her firm through illegal business practices.

In this chapter, we attempt to provide an overview of the legal and regulatory environment in which firms operate in the United States. We emphasize those areas of regulation that bear on the economic decisions of managers whose objective is to maximize the firm's value over the long run. We look first at the nature of business law and the types of laws that apply to the firm, and then we turn to a very specific part of business regulation: the antitrust laws. The major facets of antitrust law are discussed, followed by an examination of administrative agencies that both create and enforce laws affecting business. A later section deals with the specific problem of regulated industries, such as public transportation and utilities. Finally, we return to the question of the behavior of managers in the context of what we have said about the legal and regulatory environment in the United States and provide a general prescription for including legal and regulatory variables in the short- and long-run decision processes of the firm.

MANAGERS AND THE LAW

In the preceding chapter, we noted that one of the most important "products" of the public sector is laws and regulations. Rules of the game are necessary to attain and secure both social and economic order. Indeed, countries and societies where rules of the game are ill defined or cast aside by an oligarchy are often plagued by civil strife. The need for a system of rules is obvious, but the extent to which economic regulations should supplant market-determined solutions to a society's problems of production and distribution of output has long been a burning issue.

From the standpoint of the manager of a business firm, government regulations are a very mixed bag. Much of the conventional wisdom of the private sector leans toward the idea that "that government is best that governs least," but it seems clear that if government did not regulate business, many firms could not survive. For example, small firms could easily be destroyed by the predatory pricing strategies of large firms if government failed to make such practices illegal or to enforce sanctions against such activities. Thus, from the business firm's private point of view, most managers today are sufficiently enlightened to realize that government regulations produce both costs and benefits; that is, some of the regulations have positive effects on the firm, and others affect it adversely.

In the United States, private sector managers have only recently been made aware of an apparently new potential cost of decision making—that of *personal liability.* Historically, the corporate form of organization has caused penalties for breaking business rules and regulations to be exacted in the form of monetary payments (fines and/or damage settlements) from the firms that break the law. In cases where culpability could be traced to specific managers, their fines were usually paid from corporate coffers. As a result, many managers viewed the costs of lawbreaking in the business sector as just another business expense. The Department of Justice has taken a very dim view of this attitude and recently has begun to demand that judges mete out prison sentences to executives who knowingly break antitrust laws. The electrical contractors' case cited previously is one example.

TYPES OF LAW AFFECTING THE FIRM

Criminal law pertains to acts that are viewed as offenses against a federal, state, or local government.

Tort law deals with injuries sustained by private parties as a result of nonperformance of a duty created by law.

Contract law pertains to the establishment of contractual obligations and to wrongful acts in breach of contract.

Setting aside for the moment the special areas of antitrust laws, business practices laws, and the regulations of administrative agencies, we may divide the laws affecting the firm into basically three types: criminal law, the law of torts, and the law of contracts. All three types have their bases partly in English common law, civil law (Roman law), and statutory law (that law produced by local, state, or federal legislative bodies). In all three types of law, procedures are set up to determine who is a wrongdoer (person or corporation) and what should be done about a wrongful act. **Criminal law** deals with wrongful acts that are viewed as offenses against the state or government. **Tort law** has to do with injuries sustained by private parties because of a wrongful act involving the breach of a duty created by law. **Contract law,** of course, deals with the establishment of contractual obligations (agreements between parties) and wrongful acts in breach of contract. A single wrongful act can simultaneously be a crime, a tort, and a breach of contract. For example, suppose that a firm enters into a conspiracy to divide markets, which causes it to break a contractual agreement with one of its distributors and to interfere with contracts made between other suppliers and *their* distributors. In such a case, the firm will have not only violated the antitrust laws (a crime) and broken a contract, but also intentionally interfered with contracts of a third party (a tort).

Business Crime

Criminal wrongdoing in business is seldom the result of a managerial mistake. Often it involves some willfully wrong act such as receiving stolen goods, embezzlement, arson, false labeling, swindling, or obtaining goods through false pretenses. Mistakes are more likely to result in violations of state and federal antitrust laws or fair business practices laws, although in some cases such violations do constitute crimes. For example, many supplier firms in the franchise food business require franchisees to enter into tying agreements whereby all types of food inputs must be bought from the franchiser. Such contracts are often unwittingly drawn in a manner that places both parties in violation of federal antitrust laws. Although criminal penalties are not likely to be assessed against managers in such a case, the fact remains that the breaking of the federal antitrust sanction against such behavior is viewed as an offense against the state. We will return to this problem in the section on antitrust violations.

Torts

In today's business environment, the largest volume of tort cases occurs in the area of *negligence.* We can define negligence as failure to exercise reasonable care in performing a duty created by law. Underlying the whole negligence field is a concept known as the "duty of care," which in its simplest terms is the duty of a person or firm to act prudently or carefully so as not to harm other persons or things. The notion extends all the way from industrial accidents to product liability and rests on the idea of a "reasonable person" concept. That is, all steps that a reasonable person would take to avoid injuring other persons or things within his or her zone of influence should be adhered to. It is a variable standard that can be applied to all sorts of cases, and in any given case its precise definition rests with the jury.

In cases of negligence, three major determinations must be made: (1) Was the defendant negligent? (2) Was there contributory negligence on the part of the plaintiff or plaintiffs? and (3) What is the extent of injury to the plaintiff or plaintiffs? The injury phase of many legal proceedings can be both involved and costly, since expert analysis and testimony may be necessary. Frequently, parties on both sides of an injury case will hire expert witnesses (physicians, economists, engineers) to estimate damages and testify in court. The value of life itself becomes an issue when the tort involves a wrongful death.

Besides negligent acts or omissions that result in personal harm or damage to property, other common business torts are invasion of privacy; slander; trespassing on land; interference with contracts between others; and infringement of copyrights, patents, or trademarks.

Contracts

A *contract* is a binding agreement between two or more parties (persons, corporations, partnerships, government entities), wherein one of the parties is obliged to do or refrain from doing a specific act and the obligation incurred is recognized or enforced by law. Most business activities involve a contract of one kind or another.

For example, a person or a firm agrees to sell something to another party for a specified amount, or a firm agrees to purchase raw materials from a supplier at a stated price. For a contract to exist, an offer must be made by one party (the offeror) and accepted by another party (the offeree). A typical written contract will include the date of the agreement, the name and address of each party to the contract, a statement of the agreement or *promise* made by each party, the *consideration* received or to be received by each party as the price of the respective promise, and the signature of the parties.

Contracts can, of course, be very intricate, and our only purpose here is to make several important points about them and about contract law. Clearly, in the case of a large corporation, legal counsel will be available for the preparation of contractual agreements normally and regularly used, as well as for special types of contracts regarding capital projects, mergers, acquisitions, and so forth. Small businesses will also obtain legal expertise when entering into complex agreements or contracts involving large undertakings. However, many everyday transactions involve contracts that are not prepared by an attorney and in some cases are not even in writing.

A good general rule regarding agreements intended to be contractual is that they should be *written*. Nonetheless, oral contracts can be valid and enforceable; thus, it is important to understand that an oral agreement may be a contract. Furthermore, every state has certain kinds of contracts that cannot be enforced unless they are evidenced by a writing. The Uniform Commercial Code (UCC), which has been adopted in whole or in part by all 50 states, provides that sales contracts for goods where the price is $500 or more are not enforceable (with certain exceptions) unless there is some writing sufficient to indicate that a contract for sale has been made between the parties and signed by the party against whom enforcement is sought or by a qualified agent or broker. Other agreements that generally must be evidenced by a writing (not necessarily a contract, but perhaps just a memorandum or a note) are those involving a duty that cannot be performed within one year of the date of contract, those involving the sale or transfer of real estate, and those involving a promise to pay the debt of another party.

Remedies for *breach of contract* (failure to keep the promise as originally stated) include the following: (1) rescinding the contract, (2) suing for specific performance, and (3) bringing an action for damages. The injured party may have the option to rescind the contract—that is, to treat it as discharged, provided the entire contract is rescinded and the party in breach is restored, as far as possible, to its original position (the one that existed before the contract). The rescinding party may still recover the value of any performance rendered or money paid. *Specific performance* (wherein the party in breach of contract is compelled by the court to carry out the terms of the contract) is generally available as a remedy to the injured party only in cases involving the purchase of real estate, the purchase of personal property having a unique value (works of art, old relics), or the purchase of stock essential for control of a closely held corporation.

When there is a breach of contract, the injured party is always entitled to sue for damages. The award of economic damages to the plaintiff is the most common remedy in cases involving breach of contract and, of course, may be a very costly occurrence for the party or the firm that is at fault. Ordinarily, the injured party can be compensated only for actual loss sustained as a result of the breach of contract and cannot be awarded *punitive damages* (excess damages sought in order to punish the wrongdoer). However, actual loss can include such items as the difference between a contract price and the price a purchaser had to pay to obtain goods not delivered due to breach of contract, interest expenses incurred because of a breach, and loss of *actual* and *future* profits attributable to a breach of contract. Where the future profits of an injured party are affected, damages can sometimes be quite substantial. In addition, the costs of litigation for a case involving such a claim often mount up, since it is likely that expert witnesses may be hired to estimate the damages. Estimation of damages suffered by injured parties can be a substantial portion of the litigation of cases involving violations of the antitrust laws, a subject to which we now turn.

Antitrust laws are laws regulating any business practices and agreements that intensify monopoly power or otherwise restrict trade.

Price fixing is the practice of a group of firms agreeing to set the price of a final or intermediate product at a specific level.

A trying agreement occurs when a firm agrees that goods sold or leased will be used only with other goods of the seller or lessor.

Exclusive dealing refers to a situation where a firm buying or leasing the goods of one firm agrees not to deal with competing suppliers.

ANTITRUST AND BUSINESS PRACTICES LAWS

Both the federal government and the states have enacted laws to preserve competition and prevent concentration of economic power in one or a few firms (antitrust laws) and to prevent deceptive and otherwise unscrupulous business methods (business practices laws). The objectives of such laws are both to protect individual firms from the wrongful acts of other firms and to provide consumer protection from such evils as monopoly control of prices, price discrimination, deceptive advertising, and the sale of adulterated or otherwise unfit products.

With respect to such acts as monopolization, price fixing, tying agreements, boycotts or exclusive dealing, and price discrimination, the principal body of statutes in the United States is the federal **antitrust laws. Price fixing** is the practice of a group of firms agreeing to set the price of a product at a specific level. **Tying agreements** occur when a buyer of certain goods agrees to purchase certain other goods only from that same seller. **Exclusive dealing** refers to a situation in which a firm buying or leasing the goods of one firm agrees not to deal with competing suppliers. As explained in Chapter 11, *price discrimination* is the practice of charging different buyers different prices for the same or similar products or services, where the price differentials cannot be justified by differences in the cost of supplying them.

The antitrust laws primarily include the Sherman Act of 1890, the Clayton and Federal Trade Commission Acts of 1914, and the Robinson-Patman Act of 1936. The original Sherman Act declared in very broad terms that contracts, combinations, and conspiracies in restraint of trade are illegal, and it provided criminal penalties for persons or firms guilty of the acts of "monopolizing, attempting to monopolize" and "combining or conspiring to monopolize." The act also provided for actions in equity (damage suits) on behalf of parties injured by such illegal acts. Under the act, as amended, injured parties are to be awarded treble damages (an amount paid by the wrongdoers to the injured parties that is three times the amount of the actual economic loss).

Because the Sherman Act lacked specificity regarding the types of business conduct to be considered illegal and because inadequate provision had been made for enforcement of its antitrust sanctions, Congress passed the Clayton Act and the Federal Trade Commission Act in 1914. The primary effects of these two Acts were as follows: (1) to identify some specific wrongful acts that would be punishable as antitrust violations; (2) to embody the common law approach of trial, error, and precedent into the development of the rules of antitrust; and (3) to create a federal commission (the Federal Trade Commission) with far-reaching authority to regulate business practices.

With the growth of chain stores in the 1920s and the 1930s, the Federal Trade Commission (FTC) recommended to Congress that more precise prohibitions in the area of price discrimination were needed. The result was the Robinson-Patman Act of 1936, which forbade price discrimination between buyers of like commodities purchased under like conditions and broadly prohibited price discrimination where its effect was to injure, destroy, or prevent competition. The broad nature of the act reaffirmed that the rules of antitrust would be developed on a case-by-case basis through the judicial process.

Today, the federal antitrust laws are developed to the point that it is clear that certain acts or practices will be viewed as wrongful "in and of themselves." In technical jargon such acts are called *per se violations* of the antitrust laws. The list of *per se* violations includes the following:

1. Price fixing

2. Division of markets

3. Group boycotts

4. Tying agreements

From a managerial point of view, any agreement that appears on its face or could be construed to be one or more of the preceding violations deserves careful scrutiny.

The fact that the preceding are *per se* violations of federal law does not mean that contracts between firms are unlikely to include any of them in their provisions. To the contrary, since state laws sometimes do not forbid the same acts or practices and since not all lawyers who prepare contracts are well versed in antitrust law, many contracts are written that are in violation of federal antitrust sanctions if an effect on interstate commerce can be shown. Furthermore, the trend in the federal courts has been that an effect on interstate commerce is easily demonstrated.

As we mentioned in the introductory section of this chapter, penalties for violation of the antitrust laws can be quite severe—fines ranging up to $1 million per violation for firms and fines and/or prison sentences for individuals. In addition, the provisions that allow recovery of treble damages by injured parties further punish offenders and also constitute a strong incentive for aggrieved parties to file antitrust actions. The money damages paid by defendants often amount to many times the fines levied by the court. In 1985, for example, it was reported that MCI Communications Corporation had agreed to accept an offer by American Telephone & Telegraph to settle two antitrust suits for damages payments and other considerations valued at well above $113 million. MCI would not disclose the exact amount of the settlement, but it was publicly known that a jury had awarded $113 million in the first of the two suits. MCI's original claim was for $5.8 billion, and at one point a jury had awarded it $1.8 billion, but that decision was overturned in a new trial. The litigation between MCI and AT&T (including the regional Bell companies) went on for 11 years.[9] AT&T also had its problems with the Justice Department, which spent six years trying to break up the company's telephone monopoly before a federal judge finally came up with a plan that did just that. The estimated costs of defending the suit over the six years were said to have been $350 to $500 million.[10] Even for small firms involved in private antitrust suits, litigation costs can be quite substantial. Moreover, if a defendant firm loses such a suit, its costs are further escalated by the requirement that it pay the plaintiff's costs of suit, including a reasonable attorney's fee.

Many cases that involve a probable antitrust violation do not end up in the federal courts. One reason is that most states have some form of antitrust legislation under which complaints can be pursued. Another is that once a federal court agrees to hear a case, it may never reach the trial stage because the plaintiff and defendant settle the damages issue in an out-of-court nego-

---

[9] "MCI Says It Settled Two Antitrust Suits Against AT&T, Former Bell Companies," *Wall Street Journal*, November 19, 1985, p. 2.
[10] "Antitrust Grows Unpopular," *Business Week* (January 12, 1981), pp. 90–93.

tiation. Finally, minor violations that are in restraint of trade may be settled through the actions and authority of an administrative agency, such as the FTC, which is empowered to take regulatory steps to restrain persons or firms from using unfair methods of competition or deceptive or predatory practices.

Recent Developments in Antitrust

During the period 1980–1988, under the administration of President Ronald Reagan, the federal government took a permissive attitude toward many business deals that in earlier years would probably have been viewed as questionable from an antitrust viewpoint. A rash of merger and acquisition activity seemed to have the potential of substantially lessening competition in a number of important industries (airlines, food and beverages, radio and television communications).

Perhaps in response to the federal government's less active stance, state attorneys general became much more aggressive in enforcing state antitrust laws and consumer protection laws during the second half of the 1980s. In some cases, the attorneys general from several states combined forces to combat what they perceived were antitrust violations.[11] Moreover, the George H.W. Bush administration followed a gradual policy of increasingly vigorous enforcement of the antitrust laws.[12] When the Clinton administration took over (1993), Anne K. Bingaman was appointed assistant attorney general for antitrust. Under her guidance, the Justice Department focused on sectors that were expected to be increasingly important in the U.S. economy during the twenty-first century: computers, telecommunications, financial services, and health care. The Department moved to block acquisitions, such as Microsoft's bid for Intuit, an important firm in the personal finance market, when it believed competition would be stifled.[13]

Bingaman's successor, Joel I. Klein, was known as a pragmatist with respect to anticompetitive issues and markets. In 1997, Klein and FTC chairman Robert Pitofsky issued new guidelines that would allow companies to argue that a merger that enabled them to charge lower prices or improve their product or service could have benefits that offset anticompetitive concerns. It was argued that the new guidelines were closer to those of Europe and Canada and that they would have the greatest impact where significant economic efficiencies would result from the merger and the potential anticompetitive problems were modest. For example, the FTC allowed a merger

---

[11] "Attorneys General Flex Their Muscles," *Wall Street Journal*, July 13, 1988, p. 21.

[12] "FTC's Hard Line on Price Fixing May Foster Discounts," *Wall Street Journal*, January 11, 1991, pp. B1, B6; "Psst! The Trustbusters Are Back in Town," *Business Week* (June 25, 1990), pp. 64–67; and "Putting the 'Anti' Back in the Antitrust Division," *Business Week* (June 19, 1989), pp. 64–70.

[13] "The Cops Are Coming," *Business Week* (June 10, 1996), pp. 32–33.

between Boeing and McDonnell Douglas, even though the result would be only one U.S. manufacturer of commercial aircraft. In this case, the regulators considered the relevant market for commercial aircraft to be global and believed that the combined company would be better able to compete with Europe's Airbus. Also, judges have recently tended to not ask whether a merger *might* lessen competition but, rather, whether it *will* actually do so.[14]

Klein, Pitofsky, and the FTC's chief trustbuster, William Baer, continued to vigorously pursue mergers and activities that they believed were unduly anticompetitive and, in some cases, set new precedents. For example, in the Toys 'R' Us case mentioned at the beginning of this chapter, Baer argued that Toys 'R' Us had violated antitrust laws by dictating terms to toy manufactures, even though the company only had a 30 percent market share. Previously, an 80 percent market share was considered the standard for bringing predatory-conduct suits. The FTC also sued Intel and reached an agreement that, according to Pitofsky, represented "an essential balance between protecting the incentives for smaller firms to produce innovations and Intel's right to conduct its own business." In another case, the FTC challenged a proposed merger between Staples and Office Depot, even though the combined companies would have only a 5 percent market share. The FTC argued that although the companies might have only a 5 percent share of the total market for office supplies, they would have a 75 percent share of the office superstore market and would, therefore, be in too powerful a position. In this case, the FTC argued that the relevant market was local and that prices would increase by 5 to 10 percent if the merger were allowed. A federal court issued an injunction against the merger, and the companies later dropped their request to merge.

The Justice Department also has been active in the area of international price-fixing. For example, in 1998, UCAR International agreed to pay a $110 million fine for participating in price-fixing in the international market for graphite electrodes. In the 1999 Archer-Daniels-Midland case mentioned earlier, three former executives of the firm were given prison sentences and two were assessed $350,000 fines for their roles in the global price-fixing conspiracy for lysine.[15] Also in 1999, authorities issued a preliminary report that accused Coca-Cola Co. and its bottlers in Italy of violating antitrust laws through efforts to eliminate competitors by offering discounts, bonuses, and exclusive deals.[16] The Justice Department continued its scrutiny of interna-

---

[14] "Antitrust Enforcers Drop the Ideology, Focus on Economics," *Wall Street Journal,* February 27, 1997, pp. A1, A8; "New Antitrust Rules May Ease Path to Mergers," *Wall Street Journal,* April 9, 1997, pp. A3, A4; "Boeing, McDonnell Douglas Deal Gains U.S. Antitrust Clearance," *Wall Street Journal,* July 2, 1997, p. B4; and "But Nary a Trust to Bust," *Newsweek* (June 2, 1997), pp. 44–45.

[15] See "3 Sentenced in Price-Fixing Plot at Archer Daniels," *Los Angeles Times* (July 10, 1999), pp. C1, C3; and "Justice's Cartel Crackdown," *Business Week* (July 27, 1998), pp. 50–51.

[16] "Coke, Bottlers Violated Antitrust Laws in Italy, A Preliminary Report States," *Wall Street Journal,* August 13, 1999, pp. A3, A6.

tional firms during the George W. Bush administration, and in a 2001 lawsuit, Akzo Nobel Chemicals (Netherlands) pled guilty to price fixing and was fined $12 million. In addition, an Akzo executive was required to serve a three-month jail term in the United States.[17]

The role of the Baby Bells in the information networks, the behavior of firms in the broader high-tech industry, and the pricing practices of the airlines were among the continuing antitrust issues in the courts during the 1990s and on into the 2000s. In 2002, the federal government's case against Microsoft regarding its behavior with respect to the Windows operating system and Internet Explorer was, for the most part, settled. Many observers argued that Microsoft's market power was hardly curtailed, but both the firm and the federal government had spent millions on four years of litigation.[18]

ADMINISTRATIVE AGENCIES AND THE LAW

Today, it is well recognized in the United States that government administrative agencies have both legislative and judicial powers. In general, Congress and the courts have delegated such authority to the agencies because of the difficulty inherent in making judgments and setting up rules and regulations where the problems and information involved are of a highly technical nature. We have already mentioned the FTC, an agency that takes direct action outside the courts in matters involving competition and business practices. Other federal agencies that operate similarly in various fields of administration affecting business are the Federal Energy Regulatory Commission, the Consumer Product Safety Commission, the Internal Revenue Service, the International Trade Commission, the Environmental Protection Agency, the Federal Maritime Commission, and the Federal Communications Commission.[19]

A consent decree is a statement of certain provisions agreed to by both the government and the defendant.

Typically, an administrative agency develops standards and rules, as well as the means for dealing with violations of such regulations. The latter include fines, confiscation of property, informal settlements, and **consent decrees** (agreements by wrongdoers to adjust their behavior along lines specified by the agency), as well as procedures for investigating possible wrongful acts and providing a remedy. An action is usually initiated by a *complaint,* which may be filed by an alleged injured party or initiated by the agency itself. The complaint is served on the alleged wrongdoer, who is

---

[17] "Akzo Nobel Pleads Guilty to Fixing Prices of Industrial Chemical," *Wall Street Journal,* June 28, 2001, p. B11.

[18] "U.S. Settlement With Microsoft Is Opposed by Top Economists," *Wall Street Journal,* January 28, 2002, p. B2.

[19] We have mentioned only a few of the 120 or so federal government departments, bureaus, and agencies that implement regulatory programs.

MANAGERIAL PERSPECTIVE

Some Legal Aspects of Retail Pricing

Friction frequently arises between manufacturers of a product, company-authorized retailers who do not discount the price of the product below the manufacturer's suggested retail price, and retailers who do offer the product at a lower price. Retailers who wish to sell at discounted prices believe that it should be their right to sell their products at any price at which they can make a profit. Those sellers who refuse to discount the price and would like to have other retailers prevented from doing so argue that the discounters are able to offer the products at a lower price because they do not provide the customer service that the nondiscounting firms do. For example, the list-price stores contend that potential customers visit their showrooms to learn about the features of the various products, using the services of their sales personnel, and then actually purchase the goods through a mail-order discount house or similar establishment that offers little or no customer service other than supplying the product ordered.

There were a number of court decisions involving these issues during the twentieth century. For example, in 1911 the Supreme Court ruled that "agreements between manufacturers and independent retailers fixing the retail price of goods are so likely to be anticompetitive that they automatically violate antitrust law." In such a case, the existence of the agreement *in itself* would be a violation of the law, regardless of whether it could be shown to have been anticompetitive in nature or to have resulted in injury to another party. In later years, the courts issued differing rulings in cases where agreements between manufacturers and retailers could possibly affect prices but were not direct price-fixing agreements.

In 1988, the Supreme Court reached a noteworthy decision on this issue involving Sharp Corporation and Business Electronics Corporation, a discounter in the Houston area. Sharp stopped supplying Business Electronics with its product after another firm complained about Business Electronics' low prices. The Court held that the fact that a company stops

given time to answer it. The agency may then proceed with a hearing, and the administrator (generally a panel or a commission) makes a decision either dismissing the complaint or requiring the wrongdoer to take certain actions or refrain from doing certain things. The order of an administrative agency may not be self-enforcing, and the law generally provides that either the administrator may turn to the courts for enforcement or the wrongdoer may appeal the administrator's ruling through the courts. The phase involving investigation of the complaint may be quite detailed and may require that the alleged wrongdoer supply a great deal of business information to federal or state investigators. The modern tendency is for prehearing investigations to become very long and involved.

As an example of the actual procedures of a regulatory agency and the effects of its activities on individual firms, we will review briefly a case that was heard by the U.S. International Trade Commission (ITC) in 2002. A com-

doing business with a discount retailer after receiving complaints from other full-price retailers does not in and of itself constitute a violation of the antitrust laws. Justice Antonin Scalia stated that manufacturers should be able to refuse to do business with discounters who take unfair advantage of the services offered by nondiscount stores. Thus, the impact of the Court decision seemed to be that agreements between manufacturers and retailers were illegal only if they involved explicit efforts to fix prices.

In a more recent case, the Supreme Court held that a competing firm does not *automatically* have the right to sue a distributor or manufacturer for setting *maximum* retail prices, although setting maximum retail prices may violate the antitrust laws. Predatory pricing, or setting prices so low that they preclude making a profit and are designed to drive competitors out of business, is illegal. However, the Court decision indicated that for a competing firm to bring a successful suit in a situation where a manufacturer set a maximum retail price, it would be necessary to show that the firm was in fact damaged by prices that were sufficiently low to be predatory in nature. The decision did not prevent individual retailers of the merchandise or customers from bringing suits challenging the prices. (For example, dealers could argue that the maximum prices were so low that they could not offer adequate customer service, and customers could contend that the maximum prices were in fact a price-fixing scheme designed to limit competition.)

The history of these decisions by the Supreme Court shows that relationships between manufacturers and retailers and those between different retail firms may involve complex legal issues. A responsible business firm manager must be aware of potential problems in such dealings and be willing to seek legal advice.

References: "States Allege Antitrust Violations by Salton, Inc., on 'George Foreman Compact Grills,'" Iowa Attorney General press release, online, September 6, 2002 www.state.ia.us/government/ag/latest_news/releases/ sept_2002/Salton_GF.html, September 14, 2002; "You'll Charge What I Tell You to Charge," *Business Week* (October 6, 1997), pp. 118–120; Arthur Golden, Ronan Harty, Joel Cohen, and Arthur Burke, "United States," in *International Corporate Law* (Competition Law Supplement, April 1995), pp. 1087–1089; and "Justices' Antitrust Ruling to Help Firms Crack Down on Retailers That Discount," *Wall Street Journal*, May 3, 1988, p. 4.

plaint involving stainless steel bar imports was brought to the ITC in late 2000 by five U.S. producers.[20] The U.S. firms alleged that producers of stainless steel bar located in France, Germany, Italy, South Korea, and the United Kingdom were selling stainless steel bar in the United States at less-than-fair value, a practice that violated the federal Antidumping Act. The Act provided that imported goods could not be sold in the United States at prices below their adjusted home market price (fair value) if the effect of such sales was to injure competing U.S. producers.

The immediate effect of the complaint was to set off a Commerce Department investigation of the *fact* of less-than-fair-value sales (dumping)

---

[20] "ITC Rules On Stainless Injury," *Steel News,* online, February 20, 2002, www.steelnews.com/north_american/feb02/trade02.htm, September 15, 2002.

by the foreign firms. Federal investigators demanded to see the firms' relevant records. The firms were compelled to supply the data, since the U.S. government could direct its customs officials to withhold shipments of their products at U.S. ports of entry in the event of noncompliance. After several months of investigation, the Commerce Department reported to the ITC that the fact of less-than-fair-value sales had been established and that the margins of dumping (differences between actual and fair-value prices) were from 1.7 to 126 percent.

The Commission then weighed the Commerce Department's findings and voted to assess antidumping duties against the products of the producers named in the complaint. Thus, for a specified number of years in the future, the foreign firms would have to pay duties on their goods entered into the United States and be subject to monitoring by U.S. authorities.

Although this case may suggest that the foreigners got their just deserts, one should also consider that U.S. firms that *buy* stainless steel bar have a very different perspective from those that produce it. They are interested in competitive prices, and the ITC's findings no doubt raised their production costs. In addition, although none of the foreign firms in this case were subsidiaries of U.S. companies, antidumping actions in the past have involved such subsidiaries. In other words, some U.S. companies have filed complaints about the foreign subsidiaries of *other* U.S. companies.

We can conclude that the power and reach of federal administrative agencies is strong and pervasive. Although parties adversely affected by their decisions do have appeal rights, the courts seldom rule against the agencies if they are willing to admit an appeal at all. The courts tend to reverse administrative agency decisions only when they are contrary to law or when it can be proved that the administrators' exercise of authority was "arbitrary and capricious." The latter charge is rarely argued successfully.

THE REGULATED INDUSTRIES

Some administrative agencies deal exclusively with specific industries that provide public services under conditions of monopoly or near monopoly. For example, electric and gas utilities are broadly subject to regulation by the Federal Power Commission, and their retail pricing within each state is usually governed by a state public utilities commission. Other economic sectors characterized by regulation of conditions of service and price are transportation and communications.

Firms in these sectors are often described as **natural monopolies** for two primary reasons. First, it is a matter of public convenience that within a given market area, a large number of sellers of a public utilities type of good are not allowed to operate. (Imagine what it would mean to have, for example, four competing natural gas sellers digging up the streets of a given town

A natural monopoly is present where economies of scale are sufficiently large that if two or more firms were to be involved in the production of the industry output, unit cost would be higher than for a monopoly.

to install pipelines!) Second, the fixed capital investment of public utilities suppliers is usually very large, since there are economies of scale in the production of their output and since variations in demand between peak-load periods and slack periods require that they have a capacity far in excess of *average* output. The result is that although the marginal cost of output may be very low and may even fall as output increases, average costs (particularly AFC) will be very high when output is well below capacity. With too many firms in a given market area, each one would have a strong incentive to cut price and increase output. Only the largest and strongest would survive. In fact, the only way smaller firms could continue to exist would be through a policy of price regulation that would maintain the high prices necessary for them to cover their inordinately high fixed costs. The onerous consequences for consumers in such a setting are obvious.

Without some type of regulation, natural monopoly will lead to a market with only one firm. That firm will be a price maker and will charge a price consistent with profit maximization. That price very likely could be one that would generate greater than normal profit in the long run, a clear signal that more resources should enter the industry. With entry blocked, those resources will not move, and price will be higher than it would otherwise be. It is not surprising, then, that regulation enters the picture.

Price Regulation in Theory

Government, having determined that monopoly or partial monopoly is inevitable in certain economic activities such as public utilities, has taken on the task of regulating the prices that such monopolies can charge. Economic theory has provided some guidelines on this problem, and we can summarize the theoretical case briefly with the help of Figure 16-1.

Figure 16-1 depicts a monopoly firm that is assumed to be a public utility. Of course, one of government's options in such a situation is simply to allow the firm to make its own pricing decisions, in which case the firm would charge price P_a for each unit of its output and supply quantity Q_a to its customers. From a social point of view, this has two undesirable consequences. First, the firm will have greater-than-normal profits (equal to the area of rectangle $C_aP_aAC'_a$), which can persist indefinitely, since no other firms can enter its market. Second, if price is regarded as a measure of the marginal social benefit of the output to consumers and the firm's marginal cost approximates marginal social cost, the socially optimal output is Q_b, which is consistent with marginal social benefit equaling marginal social cost.

From a resource allocation point of view, it has been argued that a policy of marginal cost pricing, in which the regulators establish price P_b and price becomes the marginal revenue curve of the firm up to Q_b, would provide the socially optimal result. At Q_b, marginal social benefit would be equal to marginal social cost. Furthermore, the firm could do no better than to produce

FIGURE 16–1

*Marginal Cost
vs. Average Cost
Pricing for a
Regulated Public
Utility Firm*

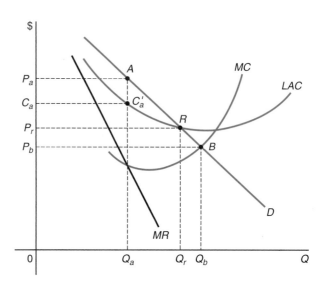

The unregulated profit-maximizing monopoly would produce where $MR = LMC$ (at Q_a) and charge a price of P_a. In this case, economic profit is equal to $(P_a - C_a) \times Q_a$. If the government were to follow a marginal cost pricing policy and set a ceiling price of P_b (where LMC intersects demand curve D), the firm would produce Q_b units of output if it produced at all. However, the firm would be incurring an economic loss at Q_b, so it would leave the industry in the long run. If the government were to follow a policy of average cost pricing, it would set a ceiling price of P_r, where LAC intersects D. In this situation, the firm would produce Q_r units of output and receive a normal profit.

Q_b, since for smaller outputs, $P_b = MR > MC$. For larger outputs, the original marginal revenue curve once again depicts the correct marginal revenue value, and $MR < MC$.

   The problem with price P_b is that it will not cover the firm's long-run average cost of production. For the firm to stay in business at Q_b, a subsidy will have to be provided. The lowest price on the given demand curve that *will* cover LAC is P_r, which occurs at the intersection of the firm's LAC curve with the market demand curve. Setting the regulated price at P_r is known as *average cost pricing,* and, as we will see, this approach is similar to the one that regulatory agencies pursue in practice. Although average cost pricing assures that profit will be only normal and increases the quantity of output (from Q_a to Q_r in Figure 16-1), it does not ensure that the socially optimal output will be produced.

   Another alternative for the regulatory agency is to allow the utility to employ price discrimination in a way that increases the quantity of output and the firm's profit. In Figure 16-2, we show the same firm as in Figure 16-1. This time, however, the regulators have instructed the firm to use *price dis-*

FIGURE 16–2

Use of Price Discrimination to Increase Output and Profits of a Regulated Utility

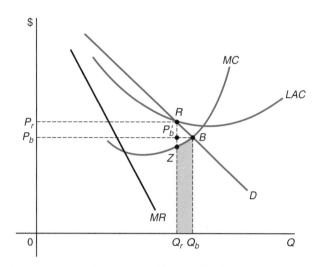

This graph illustrates government regulation with a combined average cost and marginal cost pricing policy. Here, the government sets a ceiling price of P_r on the first Q_r units of output (average cost pricing). Then, the regulators instruct the firm that it may practice price discrimination and charge a lower price, such as P_b, for additional units. If the firm establishes a price of P_b on incremental units beyond Q_r, it will sell an additional $Q_b - Q_r$ units. The firm would receive incremental revenue equal to the area $Q_r P_b' B Q_b$ on these units and incur an incremental cost given by the shaded area within $Q_r Z B Q_b$. The firm, therefore, would receive an incremental profit on these units equal to $Z P_b' B$, and the public would benefit from the opportunity to buy the additional units at the lower price.

crimination or *block pricing* and to sell Q_r of output at price P_r and an additional amount, $Q_r Q_b$, at price P_b. (The firm can accomplish this by providing each customer with a reduced rate on consumption over and above a specified amount, a practice regularly followed by electric utilities.) On amount Q_r of the total quantity sold, $TR = TC = OP_r R Q_r$, and profit is only normal. On the additional quantity sold at P_b, amount $Q_r Q_b$, total revenue is equal to area $Q_r P_b' B Q_b$; however, the additional cost the firm incurs is equal to the shaded area under the marginal cost curve (an amount obtained by summing all the individual MCs of the units of output between Q_r and Q_b). Since the incremental cost of the output sold for P_b is less than the incremental revenue (by an amount equal to area $Z P_b' B$), the firm will be quite happy to oblige the regulators.

Price Regulation in Practice

Although economic analysis has provided some useful tools for studying regulatory pricing, it must be conceded that, in practice, price regulation employs the method of trial, error, and precedent in much the same fashion as is used in antitrust and other regulatory matters. Typically, the rates set by regulatory

MANAGERIAL PERSPECTIVE

The Cost of Regulation Can Make a Hospital Sick

Most people know that government regulation imposes costs as well as benefits on society, but sometimes the magnitude of the cost is far greater than is generally recognized. A 430-bed nonprofit hospital in the San Francisco area illustrates this point. The hospital estimates that the annual cost of dealing with various regulatory bodies and government-mandated paperwork is about $7.8 million.

The current average daily census of patients in the hospital is the same, 250 people, as it was in 1966, but the hospital staff is 75 percent larger (from 448 to 734 people) Part of this increase can be accounted for by a greater number of people treated on an outpatient basis as well as by a greater proportion of seriously ill inpatients.

Nevertheless, complying with the governmental requirements requires a staff of 140 full-time employees, plus many hours on the part of physicians as they cooperate with government-mandated audits and utilization review programs. For example, four full-time and one part-time employee spend all their time reviewing patient records. Another nine or ten people investigate the appropriateness of hospitalization.

The Federal Peer Review Act requires that all government-reimbursed hospital care be reviewed by an independent agency employed by the Health Care Finance Administration. It takes 20 employees just to supply the information needed for these audits. In addition, to obtain Medicare funds, the hospital must also be audited by the Joint Commission on Accreditation of Health Care Organizations. The hospital has added four people to the medical staff office to assist physicians with completing paperwork. An additional three data processors are also required.

The point of this story is not that all government regulation is bad, but that it all costs society in terms of resources that could be used elsewhere. Thus, the benefits and costs of each government regulation must be evaluated if the welfare of society is to be maximized. On the other hand, sometimes deregulation may lead to increased costs. For example, administrative costs of medical benefit plans were expected to increase 2 to 3 percent as a result of the deregulation of hospital prices in New York state.

It is clear that a business firm cannot ignore the cost of government regulations in its long-term planning. To do so would substantially underestimate the firm's costs and could lead to unprofitable investment.

References: "Health Reform in New York Triggers Taxes," *Wall Street Journal,* December 31, 1996, p. 9; "One Hospital Tells the Cost of Regulation," *Wall Street Journal,* June 26, 1990, p. A18; and Richard L. Clarke, "Tame the Healthcare Paperwork Monster," *Healthcare Financial Management* (April 1993): 12.

authorities are the result of hearings in which accounting data on costs, equity capital, and sales revenues substitute for the cost and revenue *functions* necessary for the solutions familiar to economic theorists. The result is that emphasis is placed on ensuring the regulated firm a "fair rate of return" on its investment, subject to the provision of an acceptable level of service to consumers.

The notion of a fair rate of return is similar to the theoretical concept of average cost pricing. That is, if we define total costs in their economic sense as including a return to entrepreneurship or investment that is sufficient to keep industry output at or near the socially desirable level in the long run, then when price equals long-run average cost ($P = LAC$), such a return is assured. However, our model of Figures 16-1 and 16-2 showed that such a rate of return is not necessarily consistent with the $P = MC$ socially optimal level of output.

Accordingly, public utilities have been permitted to employ price discrimination to push output beyond the level that would likely be supplied with a single-rate approach. Discrimination has been of both the rate-block type, or "second degree discrimination," and the segmented-market type, or "third degree discrimination" (see Chapter 11 for an example). In the latter case, separate rates have been established for commercial, industrial, and residential users. Some studies have shown that the result of these practices in public utilities pricing has been to favor commercial and industrial users at the expense of the residential consumer.[21]

WHOSE INTERESTS DO REGULATORS SERVE?

From the preceding discussion, it should be clear that in the case of public utility rate setting, one of the jobs of regulators is to make sure that privately owned utility firms are profitable. Many analysts have suggested that in public utilities (and even more so in transportation, communications, and banking), the regulators have represented producer interests much better than they have those of the public in general. A study published in 1971 summed up the situation as follows:

> the regulatory agencies have become the natural allies of the industries they are supposed to regulate. They conceive their primary task to be to protect insiders from new competition—in many cases from any competition.
>
> The Civil Aeronautics Board prevents qualified airlines from entering markets they desire to serve. The Interstate Commerce Commission keeps new motor carriers from competing with existing carriers. The Comptroller of the Currency and the Federal Reserve Board prohibit new banks from opening. In none of these fields is there any natural barrier to entry. There may be neither technical nor valid economic reasons for such decisions. Instead, the primary purpose often seems to be nothing more nor less than the protection of the "ins" from new competition by the "outs."[22]

---

[21] See Paul W. MacAvoy, ed., *The Crisis of the Regulatory Commissions: An Introduction to a Current Issue of Public Policy* (New York: W. W. Norton, 1970); James Miller III and Bruce Yandle, eds., *Benefit/Cost Analysis of Social Regulation* (Washington, DC: American Enterprise Institute, 1979); and George C. Eads and Michael Fix, eds., *The Reagan Regulatory Strategy: An Assessment* (Washington, DC: Urban Institute, 1984).

[22] Morton Mintz and Jerry S. Cohen, *America, Inc.: Who Owns and Operates the United States?* (New York: Dial Press, 1971), p. 103.

As many writers have indicated, the trucking industry provides an outstanding example of the protection of established interests by government regulatory agencies. Trucking in interstate commerce was, until the 1980s, regulated by the Interstate Commerce Commission (ICC). The ICC was established in the nineteenth century to regulate the railroads, which had been engaging in discriminatory rate wars that had proved detrimental to both themselves and their customers. As trucking developed in the twentieth century, the ICC first attempted to protect the railroads from the competing motor carriers. Eventually, its role changed to that of protector of large established trucking companies from the competition of smaller firms. The result was a maze of regulations that stifled competition and a licensing policy that blocked entry through elaborate and expensive procedural requirements.

For example, in his book *Economic Concentration: Structure, Behavior, and Public Policy,* John M. Blair cites the case of a small trucking firm in the mid-South that petitioned the ICC to obtain approval to extend its routes to two small Alabama towns not served by any large carrier. After more than *four years* of proceedings, the Commission granted the firm limited approval to serve only one of the two towns. Another writer reported in 1975 that ICC regulations caused a carrier to detour 800 miles out of its way and waste 160 gallons of fuel on a trip from Dallas to San Diego.[23] In 1978, *Newsweek* reported that independent trucking was about to die because of continued ICC restrictions on routes and "certificates of authority" (licenses).[24] However, a crack appeared in the facade of protection and restriction that the regulatory agencies had constructed over the years.

Alfred E. Kahn, a respected economist in the fields of regulation and antitrust who had been appointed chairman of the Civil Aeronautics Board (CAB) by President Jimmy Carter, began to dismantle the system of fare regulation that for many decades had determined the prices charged by airlines. Kahn allowed the firms much freer rein in the area of price competition and permitted entry of firms into certain key markets where access had been restricted. The immediate result was a flurry of fare reductions and a tremendous increase in passenger traffic (an indication of highly elastic demand for the service).[25] Eventually, the CAB was eliminated from the roster of federal agencies, and its duties, which no longer included setting fares, were transferred to the Department of Transportation.

In the wake of air fare deregulation, the federal government took action to reduce legal restrictions and thus—it was hoped—increase competition in

---

[23] See John M. Blair, *Economic Concentration: Structure, Behavior, and Public Policy* (New York: Harcourt, Brace, Jovanovich, 1972), p. 397; and Mark Frazier, "Highway Robbery—Via the ICC," *Readers' Digest* (January 1975), p. 72.

[24] "The Joy of Truckin'," *Newsweek* (February 20, 1978), p. 68.

[25] "The Double Standard of CAB Enforcement," *Business Week* (August 14, 1978), p. 26.

two other important economic sectors, banking and trucking. The Depository Institutions Deregulation and Monetary Control Act, passed by Congress in 1980, was designed to put savings banks and credit unions on a more-or-less equal footing with commercial banks, particularly by relaxing restrictions on the types of loans that could be made and allowing widespread use of interest-bearing checking accounts. Although competition increased, so did the cost of borrowing. Thus, the final impact on consumers was difficult to assess.

Steps toward deregulation of the trucking industry were spelled out in the Motor Carrier Act of 1980. Specifically, the Act made entry into the industry much easier and provided for the removal of numerous geographical and commodity restrictions that had plagued independent truckers. According to one report, the ICC approved 2,700 restriction-removal applications filed during the first five months of 1981.[26] The same source noted that service seemed to be qualitatively better, while both shipping rates and profits had fallen off.

Nevertheless, problems remained with *intrastate* regulation of trucking. In 1992, *Business Week* reported that Procter & Gamble saved 26 percent of the total shipping cost of restocking Tide detergent in San Antonio, Texas, by hauling it from Alexandria, Louisiana, rather than from Dallas, although the Dallas location was 30 miles closer. Shipping from Raleigh, North Carolina, to Richmond, Virginia, a distance of 146 miles, cost $204. However, a similar shipment from Danville, Virginia, to Richmond, also 146 miles, cost $539. Such discrepancies between intrastate and interstate trucking rates existed in many other states as well.[27] By 1995, however, intrastate trucking was virtually deregulated as an offshoot of airline deregulation, since carriers such as Federal Express and United Parcel Service that have combined air and ground service could not be regulated by state authorities.[28] Meanwhile, Congress in 1994 had phased out the ICC.

The Federal Communications Commission (FCC) is another agency that has taken numerous steps to reduce regulation in the past decade or so. The FCC is in charge of overseeing the telecommunications and broadcasting industries. In the wake of the breakup of American Telephone & Telegraph Company (1984), the FCC chose to allow smaller nonmonopoly phone companies to change prices or add services without approval and instituted lotteries as a method of distributing licenses for new services such as cellular mobile telephones. In regard to broadcasting, it relaxed regulations on tele-

---

[26] James C. Miller III, "First Report Card on Trucking Deregulation," *Wall Street Journal*, March 8, 1982, p. 22. (Miller was chairman of the FTC when this article was written.)

[27] At that time, 42 states regulated intrastate trucking. See *Business Week* (April 6, 1992), p. 30.

[28] "Courts Block Attempts to Restore Intrastate Trucking Regulation," *Traffic Management* (April 1995): 25; and Michael Totty, "Trucking Deregulation Shifts into High," *Wall Street Journal*, April 13, 1994, p. T1.

vision programming aimed at children, loosened guidelines requiring programming on community issues, eliminated time and frequency limits on television commercials, and relaxed rules limiting economic concentration in station ownership.

With the passage of the Telecommunications Act of 1996, the FCC entered a new era. The Act was aimed at promoting efficiency through further deregulation of the communications sector and the intermingling of telephone, broadcasting, and Internet services. Regarding implementation of its provisions, *Business Week* noted that "Congress booted many of the thorny details to the FCC."[29] For example, under the Act new firms that enter local telephone service are provided access to the networks of existing firms. However, the fees that existing carriers can charge for use of their equipment are not clearly defined, and the FCC will have to develop the rules for them. In 1999, the FCC gave the Baby Bells more pricing flexibility with respect to their special, high-capacity access lines in some markets.[30] In the cable TV industry, the FCC is now charged with defining "effective competition," a condition that will determine when rate regulation can be ended in a local market. Numerous competitive issues have arisen with respect to the Internet.[31]

REGULATION OF "UNREGULATED INDUSTRIES"

The relationship between many businesses and the regulatory agencies they must deal with is quite different from that enjoyed by firms in the so-called regulated industries (public utilities, communications, transportation). In manufacturing, for example, such agencies as the Occupational Safety and Health Administration (OSHA), the Environmental Protection Agency (EPA), and the Equal Employment Opportunity Commission (EEOC) are often viewed as unwelcome interlopers who both limit and *add costs* to the process of production.

Actually, the costs of regulation are borne by everyone in several ways. First, if the regulations implement policies that affect the production (and cost) functions of the firms they oversee, the likely result will be lower output and higher prices for the products of the regulated firms. Such a result would follow any time the marginal cost curve *(MC)* of a firm shifts upward. If the shift merely represents internalization of costs that were formerly borne (via externalities) by third parties, based on our earlier analysis of

[29] See "BT-MCI Merger Reshapes Telecom Industry," *Wall Street Journal,* November 5, 1996, p. B1; and "Showtime for the Watchdog: Now, the FCC Must Set the Rules for Reform," *Business Week* (April 8, 1996), p. 86.

[30] "Baby Bells Expected to Get Price Flexibility," *Wall Street Journal,* August 4, 1999, p. B6.

[31] For example, see "Federal Judge Says 'You Have Mail' Is Not Just AOL's," *Wall Street Journal,* August 17, 1999, p. B6.

social costs and benefits in Chapter 15, we know that the resultant adjustment in output and price may be a socially acceptable result.

Of course, managers of profit-oriented firms are unlikely to take kindly to regulatory internalization of costs, even when the objective of such internalization is one with obvious social merit, such as pollution control or noise control. Installation of equipment that has no effect on the final product but involves substantial investment and adds to both fixed and variable costs of production is not the sort of change that managers can be expected to welcome. Often, regulatory standards call for strict policing of the production process. The costs of such monitoring have frequently been shifted away from the regulatory agency to the firms themselves, necessitating the hiring of "compliance officers" and cadres of specially trained personnel.

From the point of view of the consuming and taxpaying public, it is not always clear that the course of regulatory agencies leads to social gains. The great debates over such regulatory innovations as cars that will not start when seat belts are unfastened and the use of saccharin as a sugar substitute are cases in point. Furthermore, some regulatory agencies have tended to duplicate the activities of others or to proliferate their rules and reporting requirements to an absurd degree. OSHA, which has been in existence since 1971, provides a splendid example of the latter. In 1978, it was reported that OSHA had decided to repeal 1,100 of the more than 10,000 rules it had generated since its inception.[32] Moreover, an earlier study reported that OSHA had placed in the Code of Federal Regulations about 140 standards pertaining to wooden ladders used on construction jobs.[33]

After 1980, many of the regulatory agencies became less aggressive under the leadership of Reagan appointees. This certainly occurred at OSHA, which began its retrenchment by backing off on numerous "nuisance" regulations. Between 1981 and 1985, OSHA produced only two standards on toxic substances. In 1985, it was reported that the AFL-CIO viewed the agency as nearly "irrelevant" in the effort to control workplace hazards. Business firms, which at first had criticized OSHA for excessive regulation, were reported to have become tired of waiting for OSHA to come up with standards for such dangers as chemical exposure. Some had resorted to setting strict standards on their own.[34] Their incentive was fear of litigation brought against them by workers and the general public. Both business and labor argued that OSHA needed to be revamped, but for different reasons. The debate on OSHA has continued, and it has been suggested that the agency shift its emphasis from enforcement and penalties to helping firms

---

[32] "The Regulation Mess," *Newsweek* (June 12, 1978), p. 86.

[33] Richard B. McKenzie and Gordon Tullock, *Modern Political Economy* (New York: McGraw-Hill, 1978), p. 330. Also see Robert Stewardt Smith, *The Occupational Safety and Health Act: Its Goals and Its Achievements* (Washington, DC: American Enterprise Institute for Public Policy Research, 1976), p. 11.

[34] "The Pressure on OSHA to Get Back to Work," *Business Week* (June 10, 1985), pp. 55–56.

design appropriate health and safety programs. Businesses, in particular, hope for reductions in the monitoring of firms with good safety records and additional relief from nuisance regulations.[35]

In general, deregulation has apparently been good for the U.S. economy. Competition in many industries is vigorous, in some cases even where the number of firms has declined because of failures, mergers, or acquisitions. According to one estimate, the costs imposed by economic regulations in the United States fell from about 0.9 percent of GDP in the early 1980s to less than 0.4 percent of GDP in recent years.[36] However, a report released by the Small Business Administration in 2001 calculated the cost to small businesses (fewer than 20 employees) of federal regulations to be $6,975 *per employee.* This was 56 percent higher than the per employee cost in large businesses.[37]

Where deregulation has increased the concentration of economic power, lawmakers, regulators, and the courts will have to decide whether new policies need to be developed. In addition, some observers argue that regulation is still imposing substantial burdens on U.S. consumers. For example, a University of North Carolina researcher has reported a finding that only 13 of 33 key safety regulations succeeded in saving lives at a cost below $4 million per individual saved. He also found that regulations on wood preservatives adopted in 1990 impose costs of $6.3 trillion per life saved. Other researchers have argued that the annual costs to the economy of federal government regulations of all kinds is on the order of $500 to $650 billion.[38] This compares with total federal spending for all purposes of $1.5 trillion in 1995 and almost $2 trillion in 2001. Clearly, government regulation is costly, but there is virtually no chance that all of it could be eliminated, and very few people would argue that all of it should. Probably the healthiest outcome of the deregulation trend is that we now tend to look at regulation more carefully and to ask critical questions about the impact of specific existing regulations or proposed new ones.

LAWS, REGULATIONS, AND THE FIRM'S STRATEGY

Regulatory changes can produce both costs and benefits for the firm. In the short run, when a regulatory change causes an adjustment of the firm's mar-

---

[35] Kenneth Silverstein, "OSHA Reform," *Adhesives Age* (July 1996): 6.

[36] "The Costs Imposed by Economic Regulation Are Falling," *New Economy Index,* online, www.neweconomyindex.org/section3_page13.html, September 14, 2002.

[37] Karen Kerrigan, "Burdensome Regulation a Drag on Recovery," online, December 17, 2001, www.bizjournals.com/extraedge/consultants/small_business_briefing/2001/.../column96.htm, September 15, 2002.

[38] "Tomorrow's Economic Argument," *Economist* (July 27, 1996), pp. 19–21; and Murray Weidenbaum, "Getting Our Economic House in Order," *Vital Speeches of the Day* (September 1, 1996), pp. 703–704.

ginal cost or marginal revenue function, profit maximization will likely require a change in either output or price, or both. At a minimum, the firm's managerial strategy should include evaluation of the impact of current or expected regulatory changes on its short-run price-output decision. Other short-run strategies may include efforts to influence the regulatory process itself through participation on government advisory committees, support of trade organizations, and lobbying efforts. However, it is in the firm's long-run planning that analysis of the legal and regulatory environment often is of major importance.

From Chapters 13 and 14, we know that the present value of the firm's activities depends on what new undertakings it chooses to pursue and how these projects contribute to its future stream of profits. Obviously, when a firm's managers analyze a new investment venture, they may find that legal or regulatory variables could substantially affect the venture's outcome. A decision to accept or reject a project could easily depend on anticipated costs attributable to laws or regulations or merely uncertainty regarding the regulatory environment.

What questions should management ask regarding legal and regulatory variables in the process of capital project evaluation? The following are some of the more obviously important ones:

1. What *currently existing laws and regulations* have particular bearing on the project's outcome?

2. What are the *anticipated changes* in laws or regulations that will affect the project?

3. What *regulatory agencies* have jurisdiction over the proposed project?

4. Do rival firms enjoy *regulatory privileges,* and how will they react to a new entrant into their territory?

5. Are firms that *supply inputs* for the projected activity or that *purchase* its *output* subject to peculiar regulatory constraints?

6. Will a successful undertaking of the project require substantial expenditures on *litigation* or *representation* before regulatory agencies?

7. In general, to what extent do regulatory uncertainties add to the project's *risk?*

Once a thorough survey of the possible regulatory impacts on a given capital project is completed, the net present value *(NPV)* of the project can be appropriately adjusted for regulatory variables. This can be accomplished in a number of ways. For example, regulatory costs can be deducted from the project's annual flow of receipts if they recur each year, or they can be added to the price of the project if they are relevant only to getting it started. Anticipated future benefits from regulation can be added to project inflows. Finally, the matter of regulatory risks can be handled through adjustment of the discount rate. The important point is to make certain that legal and regulatory impacts are not overlooked, since they often can make or break a given business venture.

SUMMARY

The Legal Environment and Managerial Economics

In this chapter we have emphasized how the legal and regulatory environment affects the economic decisions made by managers of business firms. Our major focus has been the avoidance of mistakes that may occur because of indifference toward or ignorance of the firm's obligations under the law. We briefly surveyed the types of laws affecting the firm in its everyday relationships with other firms, with individual persons, and with the various levels of government. *Antitrust law* was reviewed, with emphasis on some of the kinds of business activities that constitute *per se violations* of the federal law (price fixing, division of markets, group boycotts, and tying agreements).

The last half of this chapter dealt with the important issue of *administrative or regulatory agencies* and their relation to the firm. We noted that such agencies both make and enforce laws and that the expertise of their administrators is seldom overturned by the courts. From the historical record of the so-called regulated industries (public utilities, transportation, communications), we found that the relationship between private business and the regulators is not always an adversarial one and that, in fact, regulatory agencies may have actually promoted the concentration of economic power in many sectors of the economy.

A feature of our discussion of the regulated industries was the extension of the monopoly model to the question of *price-setting by regulatory commissions,* a common approach in public utilities management. In general, we found that such commissions emphasize a *fair return on investment* in public utilities capacity and allow price discrimination in the rate schedules of public utilities firms.

The final sections of this chapter dealt with the effects of miscellaneous regulatory measures on the operations of firms outside the regulated industries. The impact of such measures on production and prices was discussed, and we questioned whether *regulatory costs* might exceed the social benefits gained from some recent rules and standards. The chapter closed with a discussion of *strategies* the firm might employ to bring regulatory variables into the decision process. It was argued that in the short run the firm's managers should pay special attention to the *effects of regulation* on *marginal cost* and *marginal revenue,* being prepared to alter price and output in order to maximize profit under changing constraints. Our prescription for the firm's long-run strategy was that *regulatory variables should be explicitly included in capital project analyses* through adjustment of project prices, inflows, and discount rates.

QUESTIONS

1. What is the difference between a crime and a tort? Give some examples of business activities that may result in litigation because a tort has occurred.

2. What kinds of contracts must generally be evidenced by a writing? Are oral agreements ever recognized as contracts? What are the usual remedies for breach of contract?

3. What are the principal antitrust laws of the United States, and what kinds of activities do they prohibit?

4. For what kinds of penalties do the federal antitrust laws provide? Is it possible to find corporate executives guilty of crimes when the antitrust laws are violated?

5. Do government administrative agencies have legislative or judicial powers? What is the relationship of Congress and the courts to administrative agencies and their activities?

6. What means can administrative agencies use to enforce their regulations? How is action against violations of business regulations initiated in cases where administrative agencies have jurisdiction?

7. Explain why firms such as electric utilities are viewed as natural monopolies.

8. What is marginal cost pricing? Use a diagram to explain why a marginal cost pricing policy might make subsidization of a public utility firm a necessity.

9. What is average cost pricing? How is average cost pricing related to the regulatory concept of a fair rate of return?

10. What kinds of price discrimination are used by public utilities? Why do regulators permit the utilities to discriminate?

11. Why does the imposition of new regulations often result in reductions in output and increases in the prices charged by firms? Use a diagram to explain how the profit-maximizing output of a single firm would change because of the imposition of new costs related to regulation.

12. Discuss some of the steps that managers of firms can take to ensure that regulatory variables are taken into account when long-run decisions are being made.

SELECTED REFERENCES

Adams, Walter, and James Brock. *The Structure of American Industry,* 9th ed. Englewood Cliffs, NJ: Prentice Hall, 1995.

Adams, Walter, and James Brock. *The Tobacco Wars.* Cincinnati: South-Western College Publishing, 1999.

Areeda, Phillip, and Louis Kaplow. *Antitrust Analysis: Problems, Text, Cases,* 3d ed. New York: Aspen Publishers, 1998.

Blair, Roger D., and James M. Fesmire. "The Resale Price Maintenance Policy Dilemma." *The Southern Economic Journal* 60, No. 4 (April 1994): 1043–1047.

Carlton, Dennis W., and Jeffrey M. Perloff. *Modern Industrial Organization,* 3d ed. Boston: Addison-Wesley, 1999.

Crandall, Robert W. "Surprises from Telephone Deregulation and the AT&T Divestiture." *The American Economic Review* 78, No. 2 (May 1988): 323–327.

Khan, Alfred E. "Surprises from Deregulation." *The American Economic Review,* 78, No. 2 (May 1988): 316–321.

Kleit, Andrew N., and Malcolm B. Coate. "Are Judges Leading Economic Theory? Sunk Costs, The Threat of Entry and the Competitive Process." *The Southern Economic Journal* 60, No. 1 (July 1993): 103–118.

Kwoka, John E. Jr., and Lawrence J. White, eds. *The Antitrust Revolution: The Role of Economics.* New York: HarperCollins, 1994.

Mann, Richard, and Barry Roberts. *Business Law and the Regulation of Business,* 7th ed. Cincinnati: South-Western College Publishing, 2001.

Peltzman, Sam. "The Economic Theory of Regulation after a Decade of Deregulation." *Brookings Papers on Economic Activity: Microeconomics,* 1989.

Schiller, Bradley R. *The Economy Today,* 8th ed. New York: McGraw-Hill, 2000, Chapter 27.

Bayville Convention Center

The Board of Supervisors of the city of Bayville is faced with a dilemma. For a number of years, there has been an undercurrent of community interest in building a convention center on a large downtown tract of land that has remained vacant since dilapidated public housing was torn down. (The former tenants were relocated to new facilities in a less-congested area.) Several older downtown hotels recently have undergone renovation, and two new luxury hotels have been built. Presently, there is excess capacity in downtown hotel rooms. Although the central city's commercial and financial districts have undergone a renaissance, population has shifted to the suburbs, and downtown retail trade has declined. Finally, the downtown area has had a long-term drainage and flood control problem that recently has been improved by large public investment in several runoff canals.

The community is divided over the convention center proposal. Naturally, the hoteliers and downtown commercial interests favor construction of the convention center. They have enlisted the help of the Economic Development Alliance (EDA), a group of industrialists with a progrowth stance, to further public sector consideration of the project. The EDA, at its own expense, has prepared a feasibility study for the center. Initially, the Board of Supervisors welcomed this gesture, since city funds for such an effort were severely limited. However, when the study was released, certain civic groups and some members of the board began to criticize it. In general, they argued that the EDA had painted an overly optimistic picture of the convention center project.

The EDA investigated four possible sizes for the convention center. In their study they assumed a useful life of 20 years and no salvage value, since this approach is generally used by the city planning department. The sizes, estimated construction costs, and estimated operating costs of the alternative convention centers follow:

Convention Center Size (sq.ft.)	Construction Cost (dollars)	Annual Operating Cost (dollars)
130,000	$23,000,000	$ 900,000
160,000	30,000,000	1,500,000
210,000	43,000,000	2,000,000
240,000	50,000,000	2,700,000

The EDA projected *annual* operating revenues from the center to be $2,400,000 if the 130,000-square-foot structure were built. Revenue was expected to increase by 37.5 percent if the size of the center were increased to 160,000 square feet. The 210,000-square-foot center would provide 25 percent more operating revenue than would the 160,000-square-foot alternative, and an increase in size from 210,000 to 240,000 square feet would yield a further increment of 12 percent in annual operating revenue. Indirect benefits, attributable primarily to expenditures of conventioneers in the local economy, were also estimated for each size center. The indirect benefit estimates follow:

Convention Center Size (sq.ft.)	Annual Estimated Indirect Benefits (dollars)
130,000	$1,800,000
160,000	2,475,000
210,000	3,625,000
240,000	4,027,000

The EDA and downtown business interests have taken a strong position, advocating that the 240,000-square-foot center should be built, since it would yield net benefits to the community at discount rates of both 6 and 9 percent per annum. The EDA has argued that there is no use to building any of the smaller proposed centers when the largest one proves to be a viable alternative.

A. L. Tella, chairperson of a citizens group called the Bay Area Council of United People (BACUP) has led the opposition to the center and has appeared before the supervisors to criticize the EDA study. Tella has argued that the study has several shortcomings. Among them, Tella has listed the following:

1. The EDA is promoting too large a project, given the alternatives, particularly if the 9 percent discount rate is appropriate.

2. The 9 percent discount rate is too low for present conditions, since BACUP estimates the opportunity cost of resources withdrawn from the private sector to be approximately 12 percent.

3. The EDA's study is lopsided because it considers only the indirect benefits from the center and does not identify any indirect costs. BACUP has demanded that the Board of Supervisors employ a consultant to evaluate the EDA's study and to indicate what modifications would be necessary to provide a more accurate assessment of the convention center proposal.

QUESTIONS

Suppose you were hired as a consultant to evaluate the EDA study. Using only the data given in the case, answer the following questions:

1. How would you assess the EDA's choice of the 240,000-square-foot center?

2. What would you say about the impact of using a 12 percent discount rate, rather than a 9 percent one, to evaluate the alternative projects?

3. What would be your approach to the criticisms regarding the handling of indirect costs and benefits?

Mathematical Appendix

It is very important that a student of economics understand what a functional relationship is and how it can be depicted graphically. Therefore, we begin this appendix with a brief review of functions and graphs. Moreover, it is helpful, though *not essential*, for a student of managerial economics using this text to have an understanding of the fundamental techniques of differential calculus and optimization. Accordingly, we review these procedures in this appendix so that those students who have had no previous formal training in calculus can achieve a working knowledge of the mathematical tools that are helpful in understanding basic economic theory.

FUNCTIONS AND GRAPHS

If we say that *y is a function of x*, we mean that some variable y depends upon the value of another variable x. For each value of x, there is *one and only one* value of y. We call x the *independent variable* and y the *dependent variable*. We can write this relationship in mathematical notation as

$$y = f(x).$$

Table A–1 *Some Values for Total Cost and Quantity When TC = 1,000 + 200Q*

Q	TC
0	$1,000
5	2,000
10	3,000
15	4,000
20	5,000

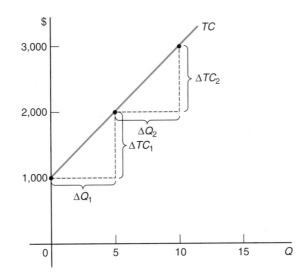

One function commonly used in economics is the total cost function. An example of one that has constant average variable cost is

$$TC = 1,000 + 200Q,$$

where TC is total cost per week and Q is quantity produced per week. Table A-1 gives some corresponding values for TC and Q. These values are plotted in Figure A-1.

An example of a total cost function with first decreasing and then increasing unit cost is

$$TC = 50 + 20Q - 15Q^2 + 5Q^3.$$

Some values of TC and Q that satisfy this function are presented in Table A-2 and are plotted in Figure A-2.

Table A-2 *Some Values for Total Cost and Quantity When TC = 50 + 20Q − 15Q² + 5Q³*

Q	TC	Average Cost
0	$50	—
1	60	$60.00
2	70	35.00
3	110	36.67

FIGURE A-2

A Total Cost Function, TC = 50 + 20Q − 15Q² + 5Q³

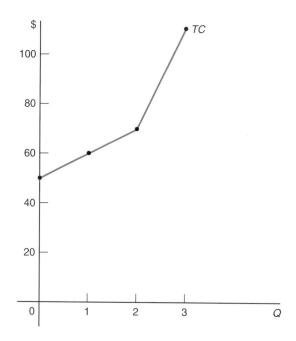

The *slope* of a function $y = f(x)$ that can be graphed as a straight line is given by the change in y divided by the change in x, $(\Delta y / \Delta x)$. Technically, as we will see later, the slope of *any* function $y = f(x)$ is given by the derivative dy/dx, which is only approximated by $\Delta y / \Delta x$ if $y = f(x)$ *cannot* be graphed as a straight line. In Figure A–1 we observe that $\Delta TC_1 / \Delta Q_1 = \Delta TC_2 / \Delta Q_2 = 1{,}000/5 = 200$. Note that for our example and for any straight line (*linear*) function, the average rate of change $\Delta y / \Delta x$ of a function $y = f(x)$ is the slope of that function and is the *coefficient* of the x variable. Thus, a function of the form $y = a + bx$ can be graphed as a straight line with the slope equal to b and an intersection with the y axis at a. To discuss the slope of a function such as that sketched in Figure A–2, which cannot be graphed as a straight line (*is nonlinear*), we must first define the concepts of *limit* and *derivative*.

LIMITS

The concept of the limit of a function is fairly simple. Specifically, it refers to the value, if any, that the dependent variable approaches as the independent variable approaches infinitely close to—but does not reach—a given value. Since any particular value (except $+\infty$ or $-\infty$) can be approached from either the positive or negative direction, we can define both right-hand and left-hand limits. The left-hand limit of a function $f(x)$ as x approaches some number x_0 is the value that $f(x)$ approaches as x approaches x_0 from the negative or left-hand direction and is denoted by $\lim_{x \to x_0^-} f(x)$. The right-hand limit refers to the value that $f(x)$ approaches as x approaches x_0 from the positive or right-hand direction and is denoted by $\lim_{x \to x_0^+} f(x)$.

These concepts can be illustrated with the function defined as follows and drawn in Figure A–3:

$$f(x) = 1, \text{ when } x < 2$$

$$f(x) = 2, \text{ when } x = 2$$

$$f(x) = 3, \text{ when } x > 2.$$

FIGURE A–3

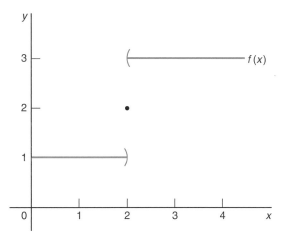

Graph of the Function $y = f(x)$

where $f(x) = 1$, when $x < 2$,
    $f(x) = 2$, when $x = 2$, and
    $f(x) = 3$, when $x > 2$

Consider $\lim\limits_{x \to 2^-} f(x)$. The value of $f(x)$ approaches 1.0 as x approaches, but does not equal, 2.0 from the left-hand side. However, the value of $f(x)$ approaches 3.0 as x approaches (*but does not equal* 2) from the right-hand side, so $\lim\limits_{x \to 2^+} f(x) = 3$. Note that the right-hand and left-hand limits of this function are not equal as x approaches 2.0.

We are now in a position where we can define the overall limit of a function $f(x)$ as x approaches x_0 as $\lim\limits_{x \to x_0} f(x) = \lim\limits_{x \to x_0^-} f(x) = \lim\limits_{x \to x_0^+} f(x)$. This limit exists only when the left-hand and right-hand limits both exist and are equal to each other. To illustrate the concept of an overall limit, we will redefine the function given previously, so that

$$f(x) = 1, \text{ for } x \gtrless 2$$

$$f(x) = 2, \text{ for } x = 2,$$

and it is graphed in Figure A–4. In this case, $\lim\limits_{x \to 2^-} f(x) = 1 = \lim\limits_{x \to 2^+} f(x)$; therefore, $\lim\limits_{x \to 2} f(x)$ exists and is equal to one. Note that $\lim\limits_{x \to 2} f(x)$ does *not* equal $f(2)$ in this case. However, $\lim\limits_{x \to x_0} f(x)$ *may* equal $f(x_0)$.

FIGURE A–4

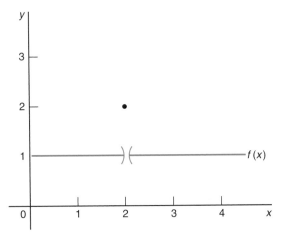

Graph of the Function $y = f(x)$
where $f(x) = 1$, when $x \gtrless 2$, and
$f(x) = 2$, when $x = 2$

DIFFERENCE QUOTIENT

Before we proceed any further, we must develop the concept of the difference quotient. The different quotient, $\Delta y / \Delta x$, of some function $y = f(x)$ is equal to $\dfrac{f(x_0 + \Delta x) - f(x_0)}{\Delta x}$ over some x interval $(x_0, x_0 + \Delta x)$ and gives the *average rate of change* of the function over that interval. We also indicated above that $\Delta y / \Delta x$ gives the slope of a linear function. For example, let us use the function $y = f(x) = 2x + 1$ and examine the difference quotient where $x_0 = 1$ and $\Delta x = 2$. (See Figure A–5.)

At $x = 1$, the value of $f(x) = 3$. At $x = 1 + \Delta x$, or 3, $f(x) = 7$. Thus, over the interval (1,3) for x, $\Delta y / \Delta x = \dfrac{f(x_0 + \Delta x) - f(x_0)}{\Delta x} = \dfrac{7 - 3}{2} = 2.$

THE DERIVATIVE

We are now ready to examine the concept of the derivative of a function. The derivative dy / dx of a function $y = f(x)$ at x_0 is defined as

$$\frac{dy}{dx} = \lim_{\Delta x \to 0} \frac{\Delta y}{\Delta x} = \lim_{\Delta x \to 0} \frac{f(x_0 + \Delta x) - f(x_0)}{\Delta x}.$$

FIGURE A–5

Graph of the Function $y = 2x + 1$

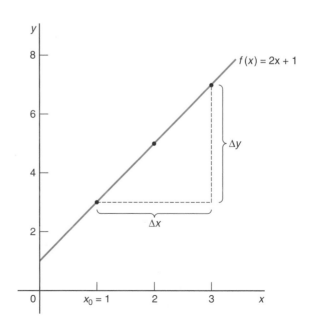

What we are saying is that the derivative dy/dx at x_0 is the limit of the difference quotient as the change in x approaches zero. Note here that it is *not* the limit of the *function $f(x)$ at x_0* with which we are concerned, but rather the *limit of the difference quotient, $\Delta y/\Delta x$.*

Examine once more the function used in Figure A–5, which is redrawn in Figure A–6. The derivative, dy/dx, of $f(x)$ where $f(x) = 2x + 1$ at $x = 1$ is thus the $\lim\limits_{\Delta x \to 0}$ of $\dfrac{f(1+\Delta x) - f(1)}{\Delta x}$, which is equal to $\lim\limits_{\Delta x \to 0}$ $\dfrac{2(1) + 2\Delta x + 1 - 3}{\Delta x} = 2.$ In fact, we can easily demonstrate that for any x_0 we pick, the derivative of this function at that point equals 2, or $\lim\limits_{\Delta x \to 0}$ $\dfrac{f(x_0 + \Delta x) - f(x_0)}{\Delta x} = \lim\limits_{\Delta x \to 0} \dfrac{2x_0 + 2\Delta x + 1 - 2x_0 - 1}{\Delta x} = 2.$ In this case, dy/dx will equal $\Delta y/\Delta x$, since $f(x)$ is linear and its slope is constant. The derivative is, then, the *instantaneous* rate of change of a function at a point ($x = x_0$), whereas the difference quotient is the *average* rate of change over some interval ($x_0, x_0 + \Delta x$). Again, we emphasize that the difference quotient and the derivative are equal in the previous example because $f(x)$ was a straight line and, therefore, its slope did not change. (The instantaneous rate of change and the average rate of change of the function are, therefore, equal in this case.)

FIGURE A–6

Graph of the Function y = 2x +1, Showing a Constant Difference Quotient

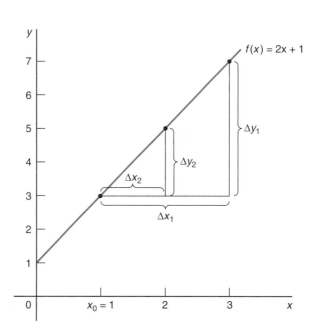

FIGURE A–7

The Derivative
Δy/Δx and the
Difference
Quotient Δy/Δx
for a Nonlinear
Function, y =
10x −x²

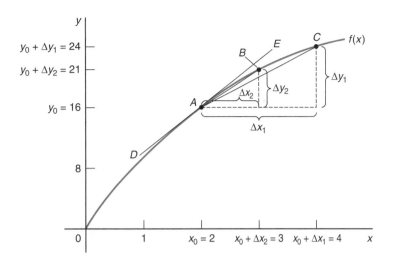

We can further illustrate the relationship between the derivative dy/dx and the difference quotient $\Delta y/\Delta x$ by contrasting the slope of a line tangent to a curve at a point with that of a line connecting two points on the curve, as done in Figure A–7 for the function $y = f(x) = 10x - x^2$.

Line segment DE is tangent to $f(x)$ at point A, and its slope is equal to the value of the derivative dy/dx at point A because the tangent to $f(x)$ at point A must have the same slope or rate of change as $f(x)$ at that point. Segments AC and AB have slopes equal to $\Delta y_1/\Delta x_1$ and $\Delta y_2/\Delta x_2$, respectively. We can see that as the length of a line segment joining point A and another point on $f(x)$ gets shorter and shorter, the slope of such a line segment approaches that of the tangent DE. For example, $\Delta y_1/\Delta x_1 = 8/2 = 4$, and $\Delta y_2/\Delta x_2 = 5/1 = 5$. The derivative dy/dx at $x = 2$ is given by the

$$\lim_{\Delta x \to 0} \frac{10(x+\Delta x)-(x+\Delta x)^2-10x+x^2}{\Delta x}$$

$$= \lim_{\Delta x \to 0} \frac{10x+10\Delta x-x^2-2x\Delta x-\Delta x^2-10x+x^2}{\Delta x}$$

$$= \lim_{\Delta x \to 0} \frac{10\Delta x-2x\Delta x-\Delta x^2}{\Delta x} = 10-2x = 6 \text{ at } x = 2.$$

We should pause here to note the conditions required for the derivative dy/dx of $f(x)$ at x_0 to exist, which are as follows:

1. $\lim_{x \to x_0} f(x)$ must exist.
2. $\lim_{x \to x_0} f(x) = f(x_0)$. This condition requires that $f(x)$ be continuous; that is, it must not have a "hole" at $f(x_0)$. The function in Figure A–4 is *not* continuous at $x = 2$.
3. The function $f(x)$ must have no "sharp corners" at x_0, so that the slope of a line tangent to $f(x)$ at $x = x_0$ is defined. An example in which conditions 1 and 2 are met but the slope of the tangent is not defined at $x = x_0$ is shown in Figure A–8. The reason that the slope of the tangent is not defined at $x = x_0$ in Figure A–8 is that we could draw an infinite number of lines, each with a different slope, tangent to $f(x)$ at that point.

RULES FOR DIFFERENTIATION

It would be possible to derive all of the following formulas for finding the derivative dy/dx of a function $y = f(x)$ by using the definition of a derivative and finding the limit as Δx approaches zero of the difference quotient $\Delta y/\Delta x$ for each function, as we did for the functions $f(x) = 2x + 1$ and $f(x) = 10x - x^2$ earlier. However, it is sufficient that students using this text be able to understand and to apply these rules, so we will not prove them here.

1. *Constant Rule*
   If $y = f(x) = C$, a constant, then $dy/dx = 0$.
   Example: If $y = 100{,}000$, then $dy/dx = 0$.
   This rule is easy to comprehend if one recalls that the graph of a constant function is a horizontal line, which has a zero slope.
2. *Power Function Rule*
   If $y = f(x) = Cx^n$, then $dy/dx = nCx^{n-1}$.

   Examples: If $y = x$, then $dy/dx = 1x^0 = 1$.
   If $y = 2x^{10}$, then $dy/dx = 10(2)x^9 = 20x^9$.
   If $y = 15x^{-3}$, then $dy/dx = -45x^{-4}$.
   If $y = ax^{50}$, then $dy/dx = 50ax^{49}$.

FIGURE A–8

Graph of a Function $y = f(x)$ That is Not differentiable at x_0

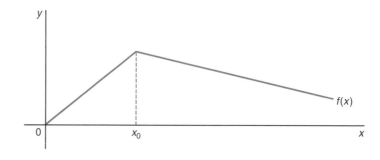

3. *Sum-Difference Rules*

    a. If y equals the sum of two functions, $y = f(x) + g(x)$, then

    $dy/dx = f'(x) + g'(x)$, where $f'(x) = \dfrac{df(x)}{dx}$ and $g'(x) = \dfrac{dg(x)}{dx}$.

    Example: If $y = 10x^2 + 5x$,
    $$dy/dx = 20x + 5.$$

    b. If y equals the difference of two functions, $y = f(x) - g(x)$, then
    $dy/dx = f'(x) - g'(x)$.
    Example: If $y = 4x - 10x^2$,
    $$dy/dx = 4 - 20x.$$

    Note that these rules can be extended to the sum or difference of any number of functions.

4. *Product Rule*

    If y is the product of two functions, $y = f(x) \cdot g(x)$, then $dy/dx = f'(x) \cdot g(x) + g'(x) \cdot f(x)$.

    Example: If $y = (2x + 6)(3x^4 + 1)$,
    $$dy/dx = 2(3x^4 + 1) + 12x^3(2x + 6)$$
    $$= 6x^4 + 2 + 24x^4 + 72x^3$$
    $$= 30x^4 + 72x^3 + 2.$$

5. *Quotient Rule*

    If y is a quotient of two functions, $y = f(x)/g(x)$, then $dy/dx =$

    $$\frac{f'(x) \cdot g(x) - g'(x) \cdot f(x)}{[g(x)]^2}.$$

    Example: If $y = \dfrac{5x}{2x+1}$,

    $$dy/dx = \frac{5(2x+1) - 2(5x)}{(2x+1)^2} = \frac{5}{(2x+1)^2}.$$

6. *Chain Rule or Function-of-a-Function Rule*

    If $y = g(z)$, where $z = f(x)$, then $dy/dx = \dfrac{dy}{dz} \cdot \dfrac{dz}{dx} = g'(z) \cdot f'(x)$.

    Intuitively, the chain rule makes sense, for it indicates that a change in x will product a change in z, which will, in turn, produce a change in y. Thus, dy/dx, or the rate of change of y with respect to x, is given by the rate of change of z with respect to x, dz/dx, multiplied by the rate of change of y with respect to z, or dy/dz.

    Example: $y = 4z^2$, where $z = 3x^5 + 5$
    $$dy/dx = 8z \cdot 15x^4 = 8(3x^5 + 5) 15x^4$$
    $$= 120x^4(3x^5 + 5) = 360x^9 + 600x^4.$$

7. *Inverse Function Rule*

    If $y = f(x)$ defines a one-to-one mapping between x and y such that y is steadily increasing *or* steadily decreasing as x increases and if the derivative dy/dx exists, then the derivative dx/dy of the inverse function $x = f^{-1}(y)$ exists and $dx/dy = 1/(dy/dx)$. Note that here f^{-1} refers to the *inverse* function, *not* $1/[f(y)]$.

Example: If $y = 5x + 2$, then

$$x = \frac{1}{5}y - \frac{2}{5},$$

and

$$\frac{dx}{dy} = \frac{1}{5} = \frac{1}{dy/dx}.$$

OPTIMIZATION

Much of economics deals with optimization, or the maximization or minimization of something. For example, one important variable that firms would usually like to *maximize* is *profit*. Firms normally wish to *minimize costs*, subject to the requirement that a specific level of production is maintained.

The First Derivative Test

The derivative is quite useful as a tool in optimization—a procedure that involves finding a maximum or minimum value of some function, as indicated previously. To understand how the derivative can be helpful in locating such points, observe the functions $y = f(x)$ in Figure A–9, panel (a), and $y = g(x)$ in Figure A–9, panel (b). Note that $f(x)$ reaches a (relative) maximum at x_1 and that $g(x)$ reaches a (relative) minimum at x_2. Also, note that the slope of $f(x)$ at $x = x_1$ equals the slope of $g(x)$ at $x = x_2$, which equals zero. Since the derivative dy/dx, also denoted by $f'(x)$ and $g'(x)$, respectively, gives the slopes of these functions (different for each function), then dy/dx also must equal zero at x_1 for $f(x)$ and at x_2 for $g(x)$. In fact, if dy/dx exists at such points, it is *necessary* that $dy/dx = 0$ for any function $y = f(x)$ to be at a maximum or a minimum. This result makes sense if we reflect that the function is not changing at minimum or maximum points (as long as the function is differentiable); thus, the function has a slope equal to zero at those points. That $dy/dx = 0$ at a possible maximum or minimum point is called the *first derivative test*. The graphs of $f'(x)$ for $f(x)$ in Figure A–9, panel (a), and $g'(x)$ for $g(x)$ in Figure A–9, panel (b), would appear similar to those drawn in Figure A–10, panels (a) and (b), respectively.

However, $dy/dx = 0$ is not a *sufficient* condition to ensure that $f(x)$ is at a maximum or minimum value at that point. To see why this is so, consider the

FIGURE A–9

FIGURE A–9

Graph of a Function with a Maximum and a Function with a Minimum

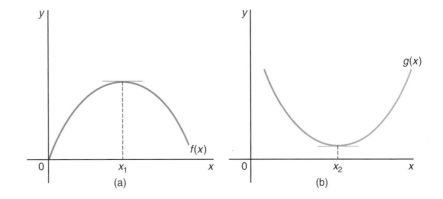

function in Figure A–11. At $x = x_0$, the slope of the function (dy/dx) equals zero, but $f(x_0)$ is neither a relative maximum or minimum and is an example of an *inflection point*. An inflection point of a function $y = f(x)$ occurs at a point where the derivative dy/dx reaches a maximum or minimum. If we were to graph dy/dx for the function $y = f(x)$ in Figure A–11, it would look similar to the curve in Figure A–12.

We emphasize that while $dy/dx = 0$ at x_0 is a *necessary* condition for the function $y = f(x)$ to be at a relative *maximum* or *minimum* at x_0, it is *not* a necessary condition for an *inflection point*. This fact is illustrated in Figure A–13. At x_0, dy/dx is at a maximum, and hence, $f(x_0)$ is an inflection point. However, dy/dx is not equal to zero at x_0.

If $dy/dx = 0$ for some $x = x_0$, one way of discriminating between an inflection point and an extreme point (maximum or minimum) of $f(x)$ is to examine the sign of dy/dx for points on either side of x_0. If dy/dx *changes signs*

FIGURE A–10

The First Derivative of Each of the Functions in Figure A–9

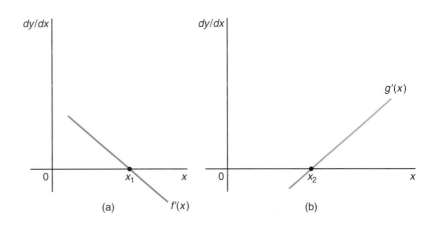

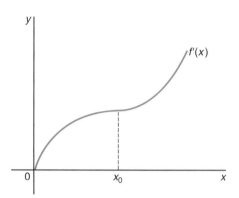

at x_0, the function $f(x)$ reaches an extremum (maximum or minimum) at $f(x_0)$. If dy/dx does not change signs, then $f(x)$ has an inflection point at x_0. This point can be grasped by examining Figures A-9, A-10, A-11, A-12, and A-13. However, a more convenient test is discussed in the next section.

The Second Derivative Test

While the condition that $dy/dx = 0$ at x_0 is a necessary condition for $f(x_0)$ to be a relative maximum or minimum point, we have seen that it is not a sufficient condition. We need an additional condition, convenient to apply that, when met, will ensure the presence of a relative extremum of $f(x)$ at x_0. It would be helpful if our additional condition could also discriminate between a maximum or minimum.

Fortunately, such a condition does exist and can easily be grasped by again observing Figures A-9, A-10, A-11, A-12, and A-13. Notice from Figures A-9 and A-10 that dy/dx is *decreasing* when $f(x)$ reaches a *maximum* and

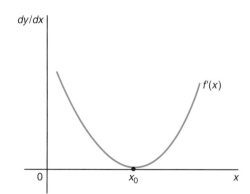

Graph of a Function y = f(x) and Its Derivative dy/dx Showing an Inflection Point

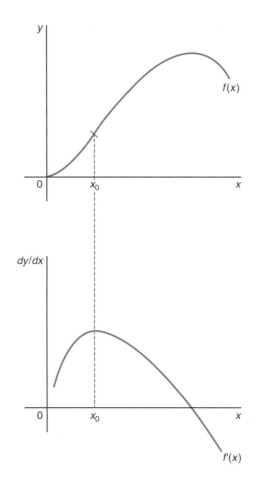

is *increasing* when $g(x)$ is at a *minimum*. However, as noted previously, dy/dx *itself* reaches an extreme value at an inflection point. This information suggests the usefulness of a *second derivative test*.

The second derivative of a function $y = f(x)$, denoted by $f''(x)$ or d^2y/dx^2, gives the instantaneous rate of change or the slope of the *first* derivative, $f'(x)$. It is found by taking the derivative of $f'(x)$ in the same manner as one finds $f'(x)$ by taking the derivative of $f(x)$. For example, if $y = 3x^3 - 4x^2 + 5$, then $f'(x) = 9x^2 - 8x$, and $f''(x) = 18x - 8$.

The second derivative test asserts that the function $y = f(x)$ reaches a *maximum* at some point $x = x_0$ if $f'(x_0)$ is equal to zero *and* $f''(x_0)$ is negative, which indicates $f'(x)$ is decreasing at x_0. Similarly, $f(x)$ reaches a *minimum* at x_0 if $f'(x_0)$ equals zero and $f''(x)$ is positive. We have graphed $f''(x)$ and $g''(x)$ for Figure A–9, panels (a) and (b), respectively, in Figure A–14, panels (a) and (b).

FIGURE A–14

*The Second
Derivative of
Each of the
Functions in
Figure A–9*

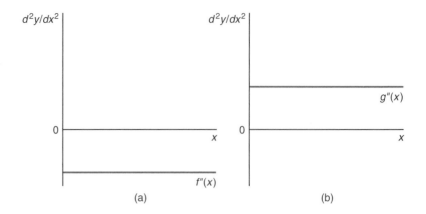

(a)   (b)

Example: $f(x) = x^3 - 6x^2 + 10$
$f'(x) = 3x^2 - 12x$
$f'(x) = 0$ when $x^2 - 4x = 0$ or $x = 0, 4$
$f''(x) = 6x - 12$
At $x = 0, f''(x) = -12$ and $f(0)$ is a relative maximum value.
At $x = 4, f''(x) = 12$ and $f(4)$ is a relative minimum value.

The second derivative test is inconclusive, however, if both $f'(x_0)$ *and*
$f''(x_0)$ equal zero. Such a result may indicate an inflection point, as would be
the case for the functions in Figures A–11 and A–13. However, it may also
indicate a relative extremum. For example, at $x = 0$ for the function $f(x) =$
$Cx^4, f'(x_0) = f''(x_0) = 0$, but $x = 0$ is a minimum point of $f(x)$.

TOTAL, AVERAGE, AND MARGINAL RELATIONSHIPS

In economics, we deal with many total, average, and marginal relationships—
such as total, average, and marginal cost and total, average, and marginal
profit. Since the total, average, and marginal functions for all of these variables have basically the same relationships with each other, we will briefly
discuss those relationships here. The total function states the relationship between an independent variable and the total amount of some other variable,
such as output to total dollar cost of production, output to total dollar profit
of a firm, or the amount of an input to the total output of the firm. The average function is obtained by dividing the total function by the independent
variable. The marginal function is obtained by taking the derivative of the
total function with respect to the independent variable. Graphically, the value
of the *average* function for some value of the independent variable is given by

the *slope of the line drawn from the origin of the graph of the total function to the corresponding point on the total function*. The value of a *marginal* function for some value of the independent variable is given by the *slope of the total function at that point*. When the average function reaches a maximum or minimum, the line drawn from the origin to the corresponding point on the total curve is tangent to the total curve at that point, and the value of the average function is thus equal to the value of the marginal function at that point. Examples of the relationships among total, average, and marginal product of an input and those among total, average, and marginal cost are shown in Figure A–15 and Figure A–16, respectively.

Note that when the average function is *decreasing*, the marginal function, whether decreasing or increasing, is taking on values *smaller than* those of the average function. This relationship is necessary for the average function to diminish. Similarly, if the average function is *increasing*, the marginal function, whether increasing or decreasing, must be taking on values *larger than* those of the average function. If the average function is not changing in value, it must be at a maximum, a minimum, or an inflection point; and the marginal function must be at a value equal to that of the average function.

FIGURE A–15

Relationships Among Total Average, and Marginal Product Functions

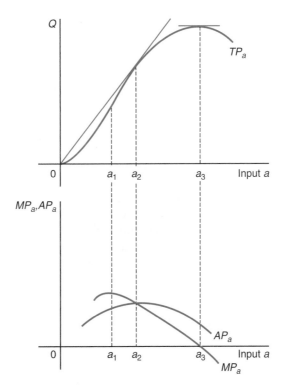

FIGURE A–16

Relationships Among Total Average, and Marginal Cost Functions

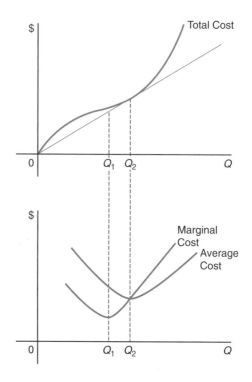

A student can easily grasp the nature of the relationship between a marginal function and an average function if grade point averages (GPAs) are considered. Consider your current semester GPA to be a marginal function and your cumulative GPA to be an average function. It is a well-known fact among students that if the GPA achieved during the current semester (say, 2.50) is smaller than the cumulative GPA (say, 3.00 up to that semester), the cumulative GPA will have fallen at the end of the current semester. The cumulative GPA will *still fall* at the end of the next semester if the GPA for that semester rises (say, to 2.60) but is still below the cumulative GPA at the beginning of that semester. On the other hand, if the current semester GPA (say, 3.70), is greater than the cumulative GPA (say, 3.00), the cumulative GPA will rise at the end of the semester. Only when the current semester's GPA is equal to the cumulative GPA will the cumulative GPA remain the same.

PARTIAL DERIVATIVES

We will conclude this appendix with a brief discussion of partial derivatives and optimization conditions for a function with two independent variables and a few remarks about the total differential. We are interested in a partial derivative when we have a dependent variable that is a function of two or more independent variables, and we wish to know the individual effect that a change in one independent variable (while the other is held constant) will have on the dependent variable. To find a partial derivative, take the derivative of the function with respect to the variable in question, treating the other independent variable or variables in the same manner as a constant. Several examples of the procedure follow:

Example 1:

$$\text{If } y = f(x,z) = x^3 + 5x^2z + 3xz^2 + 10z^3 + 10, \text{ then}$$

$$\partial y/\partial x = 3x^2 + 10xz + 3z^2, \text{ and}$$

$$\partial y/\partial z = 5x^2 + 6xz + 30z^2.$$

Example 2:

$$\text{If } y = \frac{6x^2}{z}, \quad \text{then}$$

$$\frac{\partial y}{\partial x} = \frac{12x}{z}, \quad \text{and}$$

$$\frac{\partial y}{\partial z} = \frac{-6x^2}{z^2}. \quad \left(\text{Use the quotient rule for } \partial y/\partial z.\right)$$

Example 3:

$$\text{If } Q = f(K,L) = 15K^{2/3} L^{1/3}, \text{ then}$$

$$\partial Q/\partial K = 10K^{-1/3} L^{1/3}, \text{ and}$$

$$\partial Q/\partial L = 5K^{2/3} L^{-2/3}.$$

If $Q = f(K,L)$ is a production function with inputs capital (K) and labor (L), then $\delta Q/\delta K$ and $\delta Q/\delta L$ can be interpreted as the marginal products of capital and labor, respectively.

OPTIMIZATION CONDITIONS WITH TWO INDEPENDENT VARIABLES

The optimization conditions for a function with two independent variables are similar to those with one independent variable. The *first-order* condition for a maximum or a minimum of a function $y = f(x,z)$ is that

$$\partial y/\partial x = f_x = 0, \text{ and}$$
$$\partial y/\partial z = f_z = 0.$$

The *second-order* condition for a *maximum* is that

$$\frac{\partial(f_x)}{\partial x} = f_{xx} < 0,$$

$$\frac{\partial(f_z)}{\partial z} = f_{zz} < 0,$$

and

$$f_{xx} \cdot f_{zz} > \left[\frac{\partial(f_x)}{\partial z}\right]^2 = (f_{xz})^2.$$

The *second-order* condition for a *minimum* is that

$$f_{xx} > 0,$$
$$f_{zz} > 0,$$

and

$$f_{xx} \cdot f_{zz} > (f_{xz})^2.$$

The condition that $f_{xx} \cdot f_{zz}$ be greater than $(f_{xz})^2$ ensures (assuming the other conditions are met) that the point in question is a relative maximum or minimum rather than a *saddle point*, which is roughly the three-dimensional counterpart of an inflection point. Again, satisfaction of the second-order conditions is not *necessary* for an extremum to exist at a point, but their satisfaction together with that of the first-order conditions ensures that a relative extremum *does* exist at that point.

For example, consider the function $y = f(x,z) = x^2 - 4x - 2xz - 8z + 2z^2$. Then

$$f_x = 2x - 4 - 2z, \text{ and}$$
$$f_z = -2x - 8 + 4z.$$

To find a maximum or minimum point(s), we first set f_x and f_z equal to zero and solve the two equations simultaneously, as follows:

$$2x - 2z - 4 = 0$$
$$-2x + 4z - 8 = 0$$
$$2z - 12 = 0$$
$$z = 6.$$

Solving for x from the first equation, we find

$$2x - 2(6) - 4 = 0,$$
$$2x - 12 - 4 = 0,$$
$$2x - 16 = 0, \quad \text{and}$$
$$x = 8.$$

To check the second-order conditions for the point $f(x,z) = f(8,6)$ we find

$$f_{xx} = 2,$$
$$f_{zz} = 4, \quad \text{and}$$
$$f_{xz} = -2.$$

Since f_{xx} and f_{zz} are greater than zero and $f_{xx} \cdot f_{zz} > (f_{xz})^2$ or $2(4) > 4$, $f(x,z) = f(8,6)$ is a *minimum* point.

TOTAL DIFFERENTIAL

We will close with a brief discussion of the total differential. The total differential of a function attempts to measure the change in the value of a function as a result of infinitely small changes in all independent variables. If $y = f(x,z)$, the total differential, dy, is defined as

$$dy = f_x dx + f_z d_z,$$

where dx and dz represent infinitely small changes in x and z, respectively. The total differential can be approximated at a specific point by using discrete (but small) changes in x and z as

$$\Delta y = f_x \Delta x + f_z \Delta_z.$$

Example 1:

If $Q = 15K^{2/3} L^{1/3}$, then
$$dQ = 10K^{-1/3} L^{1/3} \, dK + 5K^{2/3} L^{-2/3} \, dL.$$

Example 2:

If $Q = K^2 + 10KL$, then
$$dQ = (2K + 10L) \, dK + 10K \, dL.$$

We can approximate dQ at $K = 10$ and $L = 5$ by substituting in those values for K and L in the preceding equation for dQ and substituting $\Delta K = \Delta L = .01$ for dK and dL, respectively. Thus we obtain

$$\Delta Q = [2(10) + 10(5)]\ (.01) + 10(10)(.01)$$
$$70(.01) + (100)(.01) = 1.7.$$

Such a procedure can be useful, for example, in estimating the effect that changes in the quantities of factors of production will have on total output produced by the firm. In fact, in the preceding example, $\Delta Q = 1.7$ could be interpreted as the *estimated* change in total output if capital and labor were to be changed from 10 and 5 to 10.01 and 5.01 units, respectively.

SELECTED REFERENCES

Dowling, Edward T. *Schaum's Outline Introduction to Mathematical Economics* (New York: McGraw-Hill, 2000).

Klein, Michael W. *Mathematical Methods for Economics* (Boston: Addison Wesley, 2001).

Soper, Jean. *Mathematics for Economics and Business: An Interactive Introduction* (Oxford: Blackwell Publishers, 1999).

Takayama, Akira. *Mathematical Economics* (Cambridge: Cambridge University Press, 1994).

Interest Factor Tables

Table B–1 *Compound Amount of $1 (CVF)*

Period	1%	2%	3%	4%	5%	6%	7%	8%	9%	10%	12%
1	1.0100	1.0200	1.0300	1.0400	1.0500	1.0600	1.0700	1.0800	1.0900	1.1000	1.1200
2	1.0201	1.0404	1.0609	1.0816	1.1025	1.1236	1.1449	1.1664	1.1881	1.2100	1.2544
3	1.0303	1.0612	1.0927	1.1249	1.1576	1.1910	1.2250	1.2597	1.2950	1.3310	1.4049
4	1.0406	1.0824	1.1255	1.1699	1.2155	1.2625	1.3108	1.3605	1.4116	1.4641	1.5735
5	1.0510	1.1041	1.1593	1.2167	1.2763	1.3382	1.4025	1.4693	1.5386	1.6105	1.7623
6	1.0615	1.1262	1.1941	1.2653	1.3401	1.4185	1.5007	1.5869	1.6771	1.7716	1.9738
7	1.0721	1.1487	1.2299	1.3159	1.4071	1.5036	1.6058	1.7138	1.8280	1.9487	2.2107
8	1.0829	1.1717	1.2668	1.3686	1.4774	1.5938	1.7182	1.8509	1.9926	2.1436	2.4760
9	1.0937	1.1951	1.3048	1.4233	1.5513	1.6895	1.8385	1.9990	2.1719	2.3579	2.7731
10	1.1046	1.2190	1.3439	1.4802	1.6289	1.7908	1.9671	2.1589	2.3673	2.5937	3.1058
11	1.1157	1.2434	1.3842	1.5395	1.7103	1.8983	2.1048	2.3316	2.5804	2.8531	3.4785
12	1.1268	1.2682	1.4258	1.6010	1.7958	2.0122	2.2522	2.5182	2.8126	3.1384	3.8960
13	1.1381	1.2936	1.4685	1.6651	1.8856	2.1329	2.4098	2.7196	3.0658	3.4522	4.3635
14	1.1495	1.3195	1.5126	1.7317	1.9799	2.2609	2.5785	2.9372	3.3417	3.7975	4.8871
15	1.1610	1.3459	1.5580	1.8009	2.0789	2.3965	2.7590	3.1722	3.6424	4.1772	5.4736
16	1.1726	1.3728	1.6047	1.8730	2.1828	2.5403	2.9522	3.4259	3.9703	4.5949	6.1304
17	1.1843	1.4002	1.6528	1.9479	2.2920	2.6927	3.1588	3.7000	4.3276	5.0544	6.8660
18	1.1961	1.4282	1.7024	2.0258	2.4066	2.8543	3.3799	3.9960	4.7171	5.5599	7.6899
19	1.2081	1.4568	1.7535	2.1068	2.5269	3.0256	3.6165	4.3157	5.1416	6.1158	8.6127
20	1.2202	1.4859	1.8061	2.1911	2.6533	3.2071	3.8697	4.6609	5.6043	6.7274	9.6463
21	1.2324	1.5157	1.8603	2.2788	2.7859	3.3995	4.1405	5.0338	6.1087	7.4002	10.8038
22	1.2447	1.5460	1.9161	2.3699	2.9252	3.6035	4.4304	5.4365	6.6585	8.1402	12.1003
23	1.2571	1.5769	1.9736	2.4647	3.0715	3.8197	4.7405	5.8714	7.2578	8.9542	13.5523
24	1.2697	1.6084	2.0328	2.5633	3.2250	4.0489	5.0723	6.3412	7.9109	9.8496	15.1786
25	1.2824	1.6406	2.0938	2.6658	3.3863	4.2918	5.4274	6.8485	8.6229	10.8346	17.0000
26	1.2952	1.6734	2.1566	2.7725	3.5556	4.5493	5.8073	7.3963	9.3990	11.9180	19.0400
27	1.3082	1.7069	2.2213	2.8834	3.7334	4.8223	6.2138	7.9880	10.2449	13.1098	21.3248
28	1.3213	1.7410	2.2879	2.9987	3.9200	5.1116	6.6488	8.6271	11.1669	14.4208	23.8838
29	1.3345	1.7758	2.3565	3.1186	4.1160	5.4183	7.1142	9.3172	12.1719	15.8629	26.7498
30	1.3478	1.8113	2.4272	3.2434	4.3218	5.7434	7.6122	10.0626	13.2674	17.4491	29.9598
35	1.4166	1.9999	2.8138	3.9461	5.5159	7.6859	10.6765	14.7853	20.4135	28.1019	52.7994
40	1.4888	2.2080	3.2620	4.8010	7.0398	10.2855	14.9743	21.7244	31.4085	45.2583	93.0506
45	1.5648	2.4378	3.7816	5.8412	8.9847	13.7643	21.0022	31.9203	48.3257	72.8888	163.9868
50	1.6446	2.6915	4.3838	7.1067	11.4670	18.4197	29.4566	46.9013	74.3549	117.3878	289.0005
55	1.7285	2.9716	5.0821	8.6463	14.6350	24.6496	41.3143	68.9134	114.4037	189.0539	509.3174
60	1.8166	3.2809	5.8915	10.5196	18.6784	32.9867	57.9454	101.2563	176.0238	304.4724	897.5906

Period	14%	15%	16%	18%	20%	24%	28%	30%	32%	36%	40%
1	1.1400	1.1500	1.1600	1.1800	1.2000	1.2400	1.2800	1.3000	1.3200	1.3600	1.4000
2	1.2996	1.3225	1.3456	1.3924	1.4400	1.5376	1.6384	1.6900	1.7424	1.8496	1.9600
3	1.4815	1.5209	1.5609	1.6430	1.7280	1.9066	2.0972	2.1970	2.3000	2.5155	2.7440
4	1.6890	1.7490	1.8106	1.9388	2.0736	2.3642	2.6844	2.8561	3.0360	3.4210	3.8416
5	1.9254	2.0114	2.1003	2.2878	2.4883	2.9316	3.4360	3.7129	4.0075	4.6526	5.3782
6	2.1950	2.3131	2.4364	2.6995	2.9860	3.6352	4.3980	4.8268	5.2898	6.3275	7.5295
7	2.5023	2.6600	2.8262	3.1855	3.5832	4.5077	5.6295	6.2748	6.9826	8.6054	10.5413
8	2.8526	3.0590	3.2784	3.7588	4.2998	5.5895	7.2057	8.1573	9.2170	11.7034	14.7579
9	3.2519	3.5179	3.8030	4.4354	5.1598	6.9310	9.2234	10.6044	12.1665	15.9166	20.6610
10	3.7072	4.0455	4.4114	5.2338	6.1917	8.5944	11.8059	13.7858	16.0597	21.6465	28.9254
11	4.2262	4.6524	5.1173	6.1759	7.4301	10.6571	15.1115	17.9215	21.1988	29.4392	40.4955
12	4.8179	5.3502	5.9360	7.2875	8.9161	13.2148	19.3428	23.2979	27.9825	40.0373	56.6937
13	5.4924	6.1528	6.8858	8.5993	10.6993	16.3863	24.7587	30.2873	36.9368	54.4508	79.3711
14	6.2613	7.0757	7.9875	10.1472	12.8392	20.3190	31.6912	39.3734	48.7566	74.0531	111.1195
15	7.1379	8.1370	9.2655	11.9736	15.4070	25.1956	40.5647	51.1854	64.3587	100.7122	155.5673
16	8.1372	9.3576	10.7480	14.1289	18.4884	31.2425	51.9228	66.5410	84.9535	136.9685	217.7942
17	9.2764	10.7612	12.4676	16.6721	22.1861	38.7407	66.4612	86.5033	112.1385	186.2770	304.9116
18	10.5751	12.3754	14.4625	19.6730	26.6233	48.0384	85.0703	112.4541	148.0229	253.3367	426.8760
19	12.0556	14.2317	16.7765	23.2142	31.9479	59.5676	108.8900	146.1903	195.3902	344.5378	597.6267
20	13.7433	16.3664	19.4607	27.3927	38.3375	73.8638	139.3791	190.0474	257.9150	468.5715	836.6768
21	15.6674	18.8214	22.5744	32.3234	46.0050	91.5912	178.4052	247.0614	340.4475	637.2573	
22	17.8608	21.6446	26.1863	38.1416	55.2060	113.5730	228.3587	321.1794	449.3909	866.6689	
23	20.3613	24.8913	30.3761	45.0070	66.2472	140.8306	292.2991	417.5330	593.1960		
24	23.2119	28.6249	35.2363	53.1083	79.4966	174.6298	374.1428	542.7930	783.0186		
25	26.4615	32.9187	40.8741	62.6677	95.3958	216.5408	478.9026	705.6304			
26	30.1661	37.8565	47.4139	73.9478	114.4750	268.5107	612.9951	917.3188			
27	34.3894	43.5349	55.0001	87.2584	137.3700	332.9531	784.6340				
28	39.2039	50.0652	63.8002	102.9649	164.8440	412.8621					
29	44.6924	57.5749	74.0082	121.4985	197.8128	511.9485					
30	50.9493	66.2111	85.8495	143.3682	237.3754	634.8164					
35	98.0982	133.1740	180.3130	327.9907	590.6653						
40	188.8793	267.8601	378.7190	750.3613							
45	363.6697	538.7612	795.4382								
50	700.2131										
55											
60											

Table B–2 *Compound Amount of an Annuity of $1 (CVF$_a$)*

Period	1%	2%	3%	4%	5%	6%	7%	8%	9%	10%	12%
1	1.0000	1.0000	1.0000	1.0000	1.0000	1.0000	1.0000	1.0000	1.0000	1.0000	1.0000
2	2.0100	2.0200	2.0300	2.0400	2.0500	2.0600	2.0700	2.0800	2.0900	2.1000	2.1200
3	3.0301	3.0604	3.0909	3.1216	3.1525	3.1836	3.2149	3.2464	3.2781	3.3100	3.3744
4	4.0604	4.1216	4.1836	4.2465	4.3101	4.3746	4.4399	4.5061	4.5731	4.6410	4.7793
5	5.1010	5.2040	5.3091	5.4163	5.5256	5.6371	5.7507	5.8666	5.9847	6.1051	6.3528
6	6.1520	6.3081	6.4684	6.6330	6.8019	6.9753	7.1533	7.3359	7.5233	7.7156	8.1152
7	7.2135	7.4343	7.6625	7.8983	8.1420	8.3938	8.6540	8.9228	9.2004	9.4872	10.0890
8	8.2857	8.5830	8.8923	9.2142	9.5491	9.8974	10.2598	10.6366	11.0284	11.4359	12.2997
9	9.3685	9.7546	10.1591	10.5828	11.0265	11.4913	11.9780	12.4875	13.0210	13.5794	14.7756
10	10.4622	10.9497	11.4639	12.0061	12.5778	13.1808	13.8164	14.4866	15.1929	15.9374	17.5487
11	11.5668	12.1687	12.8078	13.4863	14.2067	14.9716	15.7836	16.6455	17.5602	18.5311	20.6546
12	12.6825	13.4121	14.1920	15.0258	15.9171	16.8699	17.8884	18.9771	20.1406	21.3842	24.1331
13	13.8093	14.6803	15.6178	16.6268	17.7129	18.8821	20.1406	21.4953	22.9532	24.5226	28.0291
14	14.9474	15.9739	17.0863	18.2919	19.5985	21.0150	22.5504	24.2149	26.0190	27.9748	32.3925
15	16.0968	17.2934	18.5989	20.0236	21.5784	23.2758	25.1290	27.1520	29.3607	31.7723	37.2796
16	17.2578	18.6392	20.1568	21.8245	23.6573	25.6724	27.8880	30.3242	33.0031	35.9495	42.7532
17	18.4303	20.0120	21.7615	23.6975	25.8402	28.2127	30.8401	33.7501	36.9734	40.5444	48.8835
18	19.6146	21.4122	23.4143	25.6454	28.1321	30.9055	33.9989	37.4501	41.3010	45.5988	55.7496
19	20.8107	22.8404	25.1168	27.6712	30.5387	33.7598	37.3788	41.4461	46.0180	51.1587	63.4395
20	22.0188	24.2972	26.8703	29.7780	33.0656	36.7853	40.9953	45.7618	51.1596	57.2746	72.0522
21	23.2390	25.7831	28.6763	31.9691	35.7189	39.9924	44.8650	50.4227	56.7639	64.0020	81.6985
22	24.4713	27.2988	30.5366	34.2479	38.5048	43.3919	49.0055	55.4566	62.8727	71.4021	92.5023
23	25.7160	28.8447	32.4527	36.6178	41.4300	46.9954	53.4359	60.8931	69.5311	79.5423	104.6026
24	26.9732	30.4216	34.4263	39.0825	44.5015	50.8151	58.1763	66.7645	76.7889	88.4965	118.1549
25	28.2429	32.0300	36.4591	41.6458	47.7265	54.8640	63.2487	73.1057	84.6998	98.3461	133.3335
26	29.5253	33.6706	38.5528	44.3116	51.1128	59.1558	68.6761	79.9541	93.3227	109.1806	150.3335
27	30.8205	35.3440	40.7094	47.0841	54.6684	63.7051	74.4834	87.3504	102.7217	121.0986	169.3735
28	32.1287	37.0509	42.9306	49.9675	58.4017	68.5274	80.6972	95.3385	112.9666	134.2085	190.6983
29	33.4499	38.7919	45.2186	52.9661	62.3218	73.6390	87.3459	103.9655	124.1335	148.6292	214.5821
30	34.7844	40.5677	47.5751	56.0848	66.4378	79.0573	94.4601	113.2827	136.3054	164.4921	241.3319
35	41.659	49.994	60.461	73.651	90.318	111.432	138.234	172.314	215.705	271.018	431.658
40	48.886	60.402	75.401	95.026	120.797	154.758	199.630	259.052	337.872	442.580	767.080
45	56.479	71.891	92.718	121.027	159.695	212.737	285.741	386.497	525.840	718.881	1358.208
50	64.461	84.577	112.794	152.664	209.341	290.325	406.516	573.756	815.051	1163.865	2399.975
60	81.670	114.05	163.05	237.99	353.58	533.12	813.52	1253.2	1944.7	3034.8	7471.6

708

Period	14%	15%	16%	18%	20%	24%	28%	30%	32%	36%	40%
1	1.0000	1.0000	1.0000	1.0000	1.0000	1.0000	1.0000	1.0000	1.0000	1.0000	1.0000
2	2.1400	2.1500	2.1600	2.1800	2.2000	2.2400	2.2800	2.3000	2.3200	2.3600	2.4000
3	3.4396	3.4725	3.5056	3.5724	3.6400	3.7776	3.9184	3.9900	4.0624	4.2096	4.3600
4	4.9211	4.9934	5.0665	5.2154	5.3680	5.6842	6.0155	6.1870	6.3624	6.7251	7.1040
5	6.6101	6.7424	6.8771	7.1542	7.4416	8.0484	8.6999	9.0431	9.3983	10.1461	10.9456
6	8.5355	8.7537	8.9775	9.4420	9.9299	10.9801	12.1359	12.7560	13.4058	14.7986	16.3238
7	10.7305	11.0668	11.4139	12.1415	12.9159	14.6153	16.5339	17.5828	18.6956	21.1261	23.8533
8	13.2327	13.7268	14.2401	15.3270	16.4991	19.1229	22.1634	23.8576	25.6782	29.7315	34.3947
9	16.0853	16.7858	17.5185	19.0858	20.7989	24.7124	29.3691	32.0149	34.8952	41.4349	49.1525
10	19.3372	20.3037	21.3214	23.5212	25.9586	31.6434	38.5925	42.6193	47.0617	57.3514	69.8135
11	23.0444	24.3492	25.7328	28.7550	32.1503	40.2378	50.3984	56.4050	63.1214	78.9979	98.7388
12	27.2706	29.0016	30.8501	34.9309	39.5804	50.8948	65.5099	74.3265	84.3202	108.4372	139.2343
13	32.0885	34.3518	36.7861	42.2184	48.4965	64.1096	84.8527	97.6244	112.3027	148.4745	195.9280
14	37.5808	40.5045	43.6719	50.8177	59.1958	80.4959	109.6114	127.9117	149.2395	202.9253	275.2991
15	43.8421	47.5802	51.6594	60.9649	72.0349	100.8149	141.3026	167.2851	197.9961	276.9783	386.4185
16	50.9800	55.7172	60.9249	72.9385	87.4419	126.0104	181.8673	218.4705	262.3547	377.6904	541.9856
17	59.1172	65.0748	71.6728	87.0674	105.9303	157.2529	233.7901	285.0115	347.3081	514.6589	759.7798
18	68.3935	75.8360	84.1405	103.7395	128.1164	195.9936	300.2512	371.5146	459.4465	700.9358	
19	78.9686	88.2113	98.6029	123.4125	154.7396	244.0320	385.3213	483.9687	607.4692	954.2725	
20	91.0241	102.4430	115.3794	146.6267	186.6875	303.5996	494.2112	630.1589	802.8594		
21	104.7675	118.8094	134.8401	174.0194	225.0250	377.4634	633.5901	820.2063			
22	120.4348	137.6308	157.4145	206.3428	271.0298	469.0544	811.9951				
23	138.2957	159.2754	183.6008	244.4843	326.2356	582.6274					
24	158.6570	184.1667	213.9769	289.4912	392.4827	723.4578					
25	181.8689	212.7916	249.2132	342.5994	471.9792	898.0874					
26	208.3304	245.7103	290.0872	405.2668	567.3750						
27	238.4966	283.5667	337.5010	479.2146	681.8499						
28	272.8857	327.1016	392.5010	566.4729	819.2197						
29	312.0896	377.1665	456.3010	669.4377	984.0637						
30	356.7817	434.7412	530.3091	790.9360							
35	693.552	881.152	1120.699	1816.607							
40	1341.979	1779.048	2360.724	4163.094							
45	2590.464	3585.031	4965.191	9531.258							
50	4994.301	7217.488									
60	18535.	29219.									

Table B–3 *Present Value of $1 (PVF)*

Period	1%	2%	3%	4%	5%	6%	7%	8%	9%	10%	12%
1	0.9901	0.9804	0.9709	0.9615	0.9524	0.9434	0.9346	0.9259	0.9174	0.9091	0.8929
2	0.9803	0.9612	0.9426	0.9246	0.9070	0.8900	0.8734	0.8573	0.8417	0.8264	0.7972
3	0.9706	0.9423	0.9151	0.8890	0.8638	0.8396	0.8163	0.7938	0.7722	0.7513	0.7118
4	0.9610	0.9238	0.8885	0.8548	0.8227	0.7921	0.7629	0.7350	0.7084	0.6830	0.6355
5	0.9515	0.9057	0.8626	0.8219	0.7835	0.7473	0.7130	0.6806	0.6499	0.6209	0.5674
6	0.9420	0.8880	0.8375	0.7903	0.7462	0.7050	0.6663	0.6302	0.5963	0.5645	0.5066
7	0.9327	0.8706	0.8131	0.7599	0.7107	0.6651	0.6228	0.5835	0.5470	0.5132	0.4523
8	0.9235	0.8535	0.7894	0.7307	0.6768	0.6274	0.5820	0.5403	0.5019	0.4665	0.4039
9	0.9143	0.8368	0.7664	0.7026	0.6446	0.5919	0.5439	0.5002	0.4604	0.4241	0.3606
10	0.9053	0.8204	0.7441	0.6756	0.6139	0.5584	0.5084	0.4632	0.4224	0.3855	0.3220
11	0.8963	0.8043	0.7224	0.6496	0.5847	0.5268	0.4751	0.4289	0.3875	0.3505	0.2875
12	0.8875	0.7885	0.7014	0.6246	0.5568	0.4970	0.4440	0.3971	0.3555	0.3186	0.2567
13	0.8787	0.7730	0.6810	0.6006	0.5303	0.4688	0.4150	0.3677	0.3262	0.2897	0.2292
14	0.8700	0.7579	0.6611	0.5775	0.5051	0.4423	0.3878	0.3405	0.2992	0.2633	0.2046
15	0.8614	0.7430	0.6419	0.5553	0.4810	0.4173	0.3624	0.3152	0.2745	0.2394	0.1827
16	0.8528	0.7285	0.6232	0.5339	0.4581	0.3936	0.3387	0.2919	0.2519	0.2176	0.1631
17	0.8444	0.7142	0.6050	0.5134	0.4363	0.3714	0.3166	0.2703	0.2311	0.1978	0.1456
18	0.8360	0.7002	0.5874	0.4936	0.4155	0.3503	0.2959	0.2502	0.2120	0.1799	0.1300
19	0.8278	0.6864	0.5703	0.4746	0.3957	0.3305	0.2765	0.2317	0.1945	0.1635	0.1161
20	0.8196	0.6730	0.5537	0.4564	0.3769	0.3118	0.2584	0.2145	0.1784	0.1486	0.1037
21	0.8114	0.6598	0.5376	0.4388	0.3589	0.2942	0.2415	0.1987	0.1637	0.1351	0.0926
22	0.8034	0.6468	0.5219	0.4220	0.3419	0.2775	0.2257	0.1839	0.1502	0.1228	0.0826
23	0.7955	0.6342	0.5067	0.4057	0.3256	0.2618	0.2109	0.1703	0.1378	0.1117	0.0738
24	0.7876	0.6217	0.4919	0.3901	0.3101	0.2470	0.1971	0.1577	0.1264	0.1015	0.0659
25	0.7798	0.6095	0.4776	0.3751	0.2953	0.2330	0.1843	0.1460	0.1160	0.0923	0.0588
26	0.7721	0.5976	0.4637	0.3607	0.2812	0.2198	0.1722	0.1352	0.1064	0.0839	0.0525
27	0.7644	0.5859	0.4502	0.3468	0.2679	0.2074	0.1609	0.1252	0.0976	0.0763	0.0469
28	0.7569	0.5744	0.4371	0.3335	0.2551	0.1956	0.1504	0.1159	0.0896	0.0693	0.0419
29	0.7494	0.5631	0.4243	0.3207	0.2430	0.1846	0.1406	0.1073	0.0822	0.0630	0.0374
30	0.7419	0.5521	0.4120	0.3083	0.2314	0.1741	0.1314	0.0994	0.0754	0.0573	0.0334
35	0.7059	0.5000	0.3554	0.2534	0.1813	0.1301	0.0937	0.0676	0.0490	0.0356	0.0189
40	0.6717	0.4529	0.3066	0.2083	0.1420	0.0972	0.0668	0.0460	0.0318	0.0221	0.0107
45	0.6391	0.4102	0.2644	0.1712	0.1113	0.0727	0.0476	0.0313	0.0207	0.0137	0.0061
50	0.6081	0.3715	0.2281	0.1407	0.0872	0.0543	0.0339	0.0213	0.0134	0.0085	0.0035
55	0.5786	0.3365	0.1968	0.1157	0.0683	0.0406	0.0242	0.0145	0.0087	0.0053	0.0020
60	0.5505	0.3048	0.1697	0.0951	0.0535	0.0303	0.0173	0.0099	0.0057	0.0033	0.0011

Period	14%	15%	16%	18%	20%	24%	28%	30%	32%	36%	40%
1	0.8772	0.8696	0.8621	0.8475	0.8333	0.8065	0.7813	0.7692	0.7576	0.7353	0.7143
2	0.7695	0.7561	0.7432	0.7182	0.6944	0.6504	0.6104	0.5917	0.5739	0.5407	0.5102
3	0.6750	0.6575	0.6407	0.6086	0.5787	0.5245	0.4768	0.4552	0.4348	0.3975	0.3644
4	0.5921	0.5718	0.5523	0.5158	0.4823	0.4230	0.3725	0.3501	0.3294	0.2923	0.2603
5	0.5194	0.4972	0.4761	0.4371	0.4019	0.3411	0.2910	0.2693	0.2495	0.2149	0.1859
6	0.4556	0.4323	0.4104	0.3704	0.3349	0.2751	0.2274	0.2072	0.1890	0.1580	0.1328
7	0.3996	0.3759	0.3538	0.3139	0.2791	0.2218	0.1776	0.1594	0.1432	0.1162	0.0949
8	0.3506	0.3269	0.3050	0.2660	0.2326	0.1789	0.1388	0.1226	0.1085	0.0854	0.0678
9	0.3075	0.2843	0.2630	0.2255	0.1938	0.1443	0.1084	0.0943	0.0822	0.0628	0.0484
10	0.2697	0.2472	0.2267	0.1911	0.1615	0.1164	0.0847	0.0725	0.0623	0.0462	0.0346
11	0.2366	0.2149	0.1954	0.1619	0.1346	0.0938	0.0662	0.0558	0.0472	0.0340	0.0247
12	0.2076	0.1869	0.1685	0.1372	0.1122	0.0757	0.0517	0.0429	0.0357	0.0250	0.0176
13	0.1821	0.1625	0.1452	0.1163	0.0935	0.0610	0.0404	0.0330	0.0271	0.0184	0.0126
14	0.1597	0.1413	0.1252	0.0985	0.0779	0.0492	0.0316	0.0254	0.0205	0.0135	0.0090
15	0.1401	0.1229	0.1079	0.0835	0.0649	0.0397	0.0247	0.0195	0.0155	0.0099	0.0064
16	0.1229	0.1069	0.0930	0.0708	0.0541	0.0320	0.0193	0.0150	0.0118	0.0073	0.0046
17	0.1078	0.0929	0.0802	0.0600	0.0451	0.0258	0.0150	0.0116	0.0089	0.0054	0.0033
18	0.0946	0.0808	0.0691	0.0508	0.0376	0.0208	0.0118	0.0089	0.0068	0.0039	0.0023
19	0.0829	0.0703	0.0596	0.0431	0.0313	0.0168	0.0092	0.0068	0.0051	0.0029	0.0017
20	0.0728	0.0611	0.0514	0.0365	0.0261	0.0135	0.0072	0.0053	0.0039	0.0021	0.0012
21	0.0638	0.0531	0.0443	0.0309	0.0217	0.0109	0.0056	0.0040	0.0029	0.0016	0.0009
22	0.0560	0.0462	0.0382	0.0262	0.0181	0.0088	0.0044	0.0031	0.0022	0.0012	0.0006
23	0.0491	0.0402	0.0329	0.0222	0.0151	0.0071	0.0034	0.0024	0.0017	0.0008	0.0004
24	0.0431	0.0349	0.0284	0.0188	0.0126	0.0057	0.0027	0.0018	0.0013	0.0006	0.0003
25	0.0378	0.0304	0.0245	0.0160	0.0105	0.0046	0.0021	0.0014	0.0010	0.0005	0.0002
26	0.0331	0.0264	0.0211	0.0135	0.0087	0.0037	0.0016	0.0011	0.0007	0.0003	0.0002
27	0.0291	0.0230	0.0182	0.0115	0.0073	0.0030	0.0013	0.0008	0.0006	0.0002	0.0001
28	0.0255	0.0200	0.0157	0.0097	0.0061	0.0024	0.0010	0.0006	0.0004	0.0002	0.0001
29	0.0224	0.0174	0.0135	0.0082	0.0051	0.0020	0.0008	0.0005	0.0003	0.0001	0.0001
30	0.0196	0.0151	0.0116	0.0070	0.0042	0.0016	0.0006	0.0004	0.0002	0.0001	0.0000
35	0.0102	0.0075	0.0055	0.0030	0.0017	0.0005	0.0002	0.0001	0.0001	0.0000	0.0000
40	0.0053	0.0037	0.0026	0.0013	0.0007	0.0002	0.0001	0.0000	0.0000	0.0000	0.0000
45	0.0027	0.0019	0.0013	0.0006	0.0003	0.0001	0.0000	0.0000	0.0000	0.0000	0.0000
50	0.0014	0.0009	0.0006	0.0003	0.0001	0.0000	0.0000	0.0000	0.0000	0.0000	0.0000
55	0.0007	0.0005	0.0003	0.0001	0.0000	0.0000	0.0000	0.0000	0.0000	0.0000	0.0000
60	0.0004	0.0002	0.0001	0.0000	0.0000	0.0000	0.0000	0.0000	0.0000	0.0000	0.0000

Table B–4 *Present Value of an Annuity of $1 (PVF_a)*

Period	1%	2%	3%	4%	5%	6%	7%	8%	9%	10%	12%
1	0.9901	0.9804	0.9709	0.9615	0.9524	0.9434	0.9346	0.9259	0.9174	0.9091	0.8929
2	1.9704	1.9416	1.9135	1.8861	1.8594	1.8334	1.8080	1.7833	1.7591	1.7355	1.6901
3	2.9410	2.8839	2.8286	2.7751	2.7233	2.6730	2.6243	2.5771	2.5313	2.4869	2.4018
4	3.9020	3.8077	3.7171	3.6299	3.5460	3.4651	3.3872	3.3121	3.2397	3.1699	3.0373
5	4.8534	4.7135	4.5797	4.4518	4.3295	4.2124	4.1002	3.9927	3.8897	3.7908	3.6048
6	5.7955	5.6014	5.4172	5.2421	5.0757	4.9173	4.7665	4.6229	4.4859	4.3553	4.1114
7	6.7282	6.4720	6.2303	6.0021	5.7864	5.5824	5.3893	5.2064	5.0330	4.8684	4.5638
8	7.6517	7.3255	7.0197	6.7327	6.4632	6.2098	5.9713	5.7466	5.5348	5.3349	4.9676
9	8.5660	8.1623	7.7861	7.4353	7.1078	6.8017	6.5152	6.2469	5.9953	5.7590	5.3282
10	9.4713	8.9826	8.5302	8.1109	7.7218	7.3601	7.0236	6.7101	6.4177	6.1446	5.6502
11	10.3677	9.7869	9.2526	8.7605	8.3064	7.8869	7.4987	7.1390	6.8052	6.4951	5.9377
12	11.2551	10.5754	9.9540	9.3851	8.8633	8.3839	7.9427	7.5361	7.1607	6.8137	6.1944
13	12.1338	11.3484	10.6350	9.9856	9.3936	8.8527	8.3577	7.9038	7.4869	7.1034	6.4235
14	13.0038	12.1063	11.2961	10.5631	9.8987	9.2950	8.7455	8.2442	7.7862	7.3667	6.6282
15	13.8651	12.8493	11.9380	11.1184	10.3797	9.7123	9.1079	8.5595	8.0607	7.6061	6.8109
16	14.7180	13.5778	12.5611	11.6523	10.8378	10.1059	9.4467	8.8514	8.3126	7.8237	6.9740
17	15.5623	14.2929	13.1661	12.1657	11.2741	10.4773	9.7632	9.1216	8.5437	8.0216	7.1196
18	16.3984	14.9921	13.7535	12.6593	11.6896	10.8276	10.0591	9.3719	8.7557	8.2014	7.2497
19	17.2261	15.6785	14.3238	13.1339	12.0854	11.1582	10.3356	9.6036	8.9502	8.3649	7.3658
20	18.0457	16.3515	14.8775	13.5903	12.4623	11.4700	10.5940	9.8181	9.1286	8.5136	7.4694
21	18.8571	17.0113	15.4151	14.0292	12.8212	11.7641	10.8355	10.0168	9.2923	8.6487	7.5620
22	19.6605	17.6581	15.9369	14.4511	13.1631	12.0416	11.0613	10.2007	9.4425	8.7716	7.6446
23	20.4559	18.2923	16.4436	14.8568	13.4887	12.3034	11.2722	10.3711	9.5803	8.8832	7.7184
24	21.2435	18.9140	16.9356	15.2470	13.7987	12.5504	11.4694	10.5288	9.7067	8.9848	7.7843
25	22.0233	19.5235	17.4132	15.6221	14.0940	12.7834	11.6536	10.6748	9.8226	9.0771	7.8431
26	22.7953	20.1211	17.8768	15.9828	14.3753	13.0032	11.8258	10.8100	9.9290	9.1610	7.8957
27	23.5597	20.7070	18.3270	16.3296	14.6431	13.2106	11.9867	10.9352	10.0266	9.2373	7.9425
28	24.3166	21.2813	18.7641	16.6630	14.8982	13.4062	12.1371	11.0511	10.1162	9.3066	7.9844
29	25.0659	21.8444	19.1884	16.9837	15.1412	13.5908	12.2777	11.1584	10.1983	9.3696	8.0218
30	25.8078	22.3965	19.6004	17.2920	15.3726	13.7649	12.4091	11.2578	10.2737	9.4269	8.0552
35	29.4087	24.9987	21.4872	18.6646	16.3743	14.4983	12.9477	11.6546	10.5669	9.6442	8.1755
40	32.8349	27.3555	23.1147	19.7927	17.1592	15.0464	13.3317	11.9246	10.7574	9.7791	8.2438
45	36.0948	29.4902	24.5186	20.7199	17.7741	15.4559	13.6056	12.1084	10.8813	9.8628	8.2825
50	39.1964	31.4237	25.7297	21.4820	18.2560	15.7620	13.8008	12.2335	10.9617	9.9148	8.3045
55	42.1476	33.1749	26.7743	22.1084	18.6335	15.9906	13.9400	12.3186	11.0141	9.9471	8.3170
60	44.9555	34.7610	27.6754	22.6233	18.9293	16.1615	14.0392	12.3765	11.0481	9.9672	8.3240

Period	14%	15%	16%	18%	20%	24%	28%	30%	32%	36%	40%
1	0.8772	0.8696	0.8621	0.8475	0.8333	0.8065	0.7813	0.7692	0.7576	0.7353	0.7143
2	1.6467	1.6257	1.6052	1.5656	1.5278	1.4568	1.3916	1.3609	1.3315	1.2760	1.2245
3	2.3216	2.2832	2.2459	2.1743	2.1065	1.9813	1.8684	1.8161	1.7663	1.6735	1.5889
4	2.9137	2.8550	2.7982	2.6901	2.5887	2.4043	2.2410	2.1662	2.0957	1.9658	1.8492
5	3.4331	3.3522	3.2743	3.1272	2.9906	2.7454	2.5320	2.4356	2.3452	2.1807	2.0352
6	3.8887	3.7845	3.6847	3.4976	3.3255	3.0205	2.7594	2.6427	2.5342	2.3388	2.1680
7	4.2883	4.1604	4.0386	3.8115	3.6046	3.2423	2.9370	2.8021	2.6775	2.4550	2.2628
8	4.6389	4.4873	4.3436	, 4.0776	3.8372	3.4212	3.0758	2.9247	2.7860	2.5404	2.3306
9	4.9464	4.7716	4.6065	4.3030	4.0310	3.5655	3.1842	3.0190	2.8681	2.6033	2.3790
10	5.2161	5.0188	4.8332	4.4941	4.1925	3.6819	3.2689	3.0915	2.9304	2.6495	2.4136
11	5.4527	5.2337	5.0286	4.6560	4.3271	3.7757	3.3351	3.1473	2.9776	2.6834	2.4383
12	5.6603	5.4206	5.1971	4.7932	4.4392	3.8514	3.3868	3.1903	3.0133	2.7084	2.4559
13	5.8424	5.5832	5.3423	4.9095	4.5327	3.9124	3.4272	3.2233	3.0404	2.7268	2.4685
14	6.0021	5.7245	5.4675	5.0081	4.6106	3.9616	3.4587	3.2487	3.0609	2.7403	2.4775
15	6.1422	5.8474	5.5755	5.0916	4.6755	4.0013	3.4834	3.2682	3.0764	2.7502	2.4839
16	6.2651	5.9542	5.6685	5.1624	4.7296	4.0333	3.5026	3.2832	3.0882	2.7575	2.4885
17	6.3729	6.0472	5.7487	5.2223	4.7746	4.0591	3.5177	3.2948	3.0971	2.7629	2.4918
18	6.4674	6.1280	5.8178	5.2732	4.8122	4.0799	3.5294	3.3037	3.1039	2.7668	2.4941
19	6.5504	6.1982	5.8775	5.3162	4.8435	4.0967	3.5386	3.3105	3.1090	2.7697	2.4958
20	6.6231	6.2593	5.9288	5.3528	4.8696	4.1103	3.5458	3.3158	3.1129	2.7718	2.4970
21	6.6870	6.3125	5.9731	5.3837	4.8913	4.1212	3.5514	3.3198	3.1158	2.7734	2.4979
22	6.7430	6.3587	6.0113	5.4099	4.9094	4.1300	3.5558	3.3230	3.1180	2.7746	2.4985
23	6.7921	6.3988	6.0442	5.4321	4.9245	4.1371	3.5592	3.3253	3.1197	2.7754	2.4989
24	6.8352	6.4338	6.0726	5.4510	4.9371	4.1428	3.5619	3.3272	3.1210	2.7760	2.4992
25	6.8729	6.4642	6.0971	5.4669	4.9476	4.1474	3.5640	3.3286	3.1220	2.7765	2.4994
26	6.9061	6.4906	6.1182	5.4804	4.9563	4.1511	3.5656	3.3297	3.1227	2.7768	2.4996
27	6.9352	6.5135	6.1364	5.4919	4.9636	4.1541	3.5669	3.3305	3.1233	2.7771	2.4997
28	6.9607	6.5335	6.1520	5.5016	4.9697	4.1566	3.5679	3.3312	3.1237	2.7773	2.4998
29	6.9831	6.5509	6.1655	5.5098	4.9747	4.1585	3.5686	3.3317	3.1240	2.7774	2.4998
30	7.0027	6.5660	6.1772	5.5168	4.9789	4.1601	3.5692	3.3321	3.1242	2.7775	2.4999
35	7.0701	6.6166	6.2153	5.5386	4.9915	4.1644	3.5708	3.3330	3.1248	2.7777	2.5000
40	7.1051	6.6418	6.2335	5.5482	4.9966	4.1659	3.5712	3.3332	3.1249	2.7778	2.5000
45	7.1232	6.6543	6.2421	5.5523	4.9986	4.1664	3.5714	3.3333	3.1250	2.7778	2.5000
50	7.1327	6.6605	6.2462	5.5541	4.9994	4.1666	3.5714	3.3333	3.1250	2.7778	2.5000
55	7.1376	6.6636	6.2482	5.5549	4.9998	4.1666	3.5714	3.3333	3.1250	2.7778	2.5000
60	7.1401	6.6651	6.2491	5.5553	4.9999	4.1666	3.5714	3.3333	3.1250	2.7778	2.5000

Answers to Selected Odd-Numbered Problems

Chapter 1

1. a. demand would increase.   **b.** cream demand would decrease.
c. demand for mopeds would increase, since they use less fuel than cars.   **d.** demand for the players would increase.

3. a. $35 per bushel.   **c.** quantity demanded would exceed quantity supplied, so price would rise.

5. a. The missing quantities demanded are 400 (at $P = 40$) and 100 (at $P = 100$). Missing values of $(Q_s - Q_d)$, going down the column, are –600, –400, and 0.   **b.** $P = 60$, $Q = 300$.
c. a shortage; a surplus.

Chapter 2

1. c. $E_p = -4.33$; $E_p = -0.45$.

3. b. Marginal revenue would equal price; marginal revenue would be less than price.

5. a. $Q_2 = 23,590$.   **b.** $\Delta TR = +\$87,200$.

7. a. 56,000 stuffed animals.   **b.** Total revenue would increase by $48,000.

9. 7,600 cars.

13. a. $TR = 240Q - 0.1Q^2$, $MR = 240 - 0.2Q$.
b. $TR = 360Q - 0.2Q^2$, $MR = 360 - 0.4Q$

C1. $TR = 120Q - 1.5Q^2$; $MR = 120 - 3Q$; $AR = 120 - 1.5Q$.

C3. a. $AR = P = 142 - .05Q$; $TR = Q(P) = 142Q - .05Q^2$; $MR = dTR/dQ = 142 - 0.1Q$.   **b.** max. $TR = \$100,820$.   **c.** Inelastic; $|E_p| = 0.78$.   **d.** $E_p = -1.70$; TR will increase if price is cut, since $|E_p| > 1$.

C5. a. 0.72.   **b.** Normal; $E_I > 0$.   **d.** –10.   **e.** Elastic; $|E_p| > 1$.

C7. a. $Q_x = 1{,}228 - 20P_x$.   **b.** Complements, since the coefficient of P_y is negative.   **c.** −4.39.
d. Total revenue will be maximized at $Q_x = 614$; $P_x = \$30.70$, and total revenue will be
$\$18{,}849.80$.

Appendix 3

1. a. The slope, b, is −237.84 and the intercept, a, is 287.57.   **b.** $R^2 = .97$.   **d.** $147.26 < Y <$
190.04.   **e.** The estimates should be more reliable in a large sample since both $\hat{\sigma}_a$ and $\hat{\sigma}_b$
become smaller as the sample size becomes larger.

Chapter 5

1. a. The robots are more productive per dollar spent and probably should be bought.
b. $96/P_L = 0.25; 0.25P_L = 96; P_L = 96/0.25 = \$384$.   **c.** Does she expect any change in the wage
rate of artists or in the operating costs of robots? Either or both will affect her decision.

3. Use more capital, less labor, since $\dfrac{MP_K}{P_K} > \dfrac{MP_L}{P_L}$.

5. Purchase the machine.

7. a. Constant returns to scale; doubling the inputs results in a doubling of the level of output.   **d.** This is not a least-cost combination because output per additional dollar spent is greater for capital.

9. d. 30 units and 20 units of input a, respectively.   **e.** Immediately after $a = 20$ units.

11. Robot, because additional output per additional \$1 is greater for the robot.

C1. a. $100 = 4KL + 3L^2 - (1/3)L^3$.

   b. $dQ = 4L\ dK + (4K + 6L - L^2)dL = 0$,
     $-4L\ dK = (4K + 6L - L^2)dL$,

$$\frac{dK}{dL} = \frac{4K + 6L - L^2}{-4L}.$$

This expression can also be derived using

$$\frac{dK}{dL} = -\frac{MP_L}{MP_K}$$

$$MP_L = \frac{\partial Q}{\partial L} = 4K + 6L - L^2,$$

$$MP_K = \frac{\partial Q}{\partial K} = 4L, \text{ so}$$

$$\frac{dK}{dL} = \frac{-(4K + 6L - L^2)}{4L}.$$

   c. From (b), $MP_L = 4K + 6L - L^2$.
      When $K = 5$, $MP_L = 20 + 6L - L^2$.

   d. $L = 3$.

C3. a. $Q = 576$.   **b.** $L = 6$.   **c.** $Q = 234.67$ at $L = 4$.

C5. a. $Q = 2{,}258.67$.   **b.** $L = 10$.   **c.** $Q = 1{,}106.67$.   **d.** $AP_L = 119$.

Appendix 5

  1. $Q = 55{,}200$ units; $K = 10$; $L = 190$; $\lambda = 96$.

Chapter 6

  3. a. \$900.   **b.** \$3.00.   **c.** 400.   **d.** \$700.   **e.** \$3.50.

  5. b. Between 40 and 100 units of output; between 40 and 100 units of output and 2 and 4 units of labor.

  9. a. *LAC* will decrease since there are increasing returns to scale.
     b. Combination is least cost, since $MP/P = 2.5$ for both inputs.
     c. In the table, $TFC = Z(P_z) = 48$, and $TVC = Y(P_y) = Y(14)$.

  11. b. $AFC = \$504/180 = \$2.80$.   **c.** $P_b = \$42$.

  13. a. $TVC = 10Q + 4Q^2$,   **b.** If $Q = 2$, $TVC = 36$; if $Q = 4$, $TVC = 104$; if $Q = 6$, $TVC = 204$; if $Q = 8$, $TVC = 336$; if $Q = 10$, $TVC = 500$.   **d.** The slope of TVC increases, so marginal cost rises.   **e.** $SMC = 10 + 8Q$

  C1. a. $SMC = 240 - 8Q + Q^2$; $AVC = 240 - 4Q + (1/3)Q^2$; $SAC = (1{,}000/Q) + 240 - 4Q + (1/3)Q^2$
      b. $Q = 4$.   **c.** $Q = 6$.

  C3. a. $AFC = 800/20 = 40$.   **b.** $Q = 10$.   **c.** $Q = 15$; $AVC = 26.25$.

  C5. a. Home plant: \$30.50; Foreign plant: \$29.00.   **b.** Home plant: \$30.00; Foreign plant: \$25.00.

Chapter 7

  1. Profit-maximizing price = \$14.67; output = 6.

  3. Profit-maximizing price = \$3.50; output = 50; profit = \$50.

  5. Profit-maximizing price = \$600; output = 60; profit = \$10,000.

  7. b. Profit-maximizing price = \$140; output = 6,000.

  9. a. 30,000 cases per month.   **b.** Yes, because the net increase in profit contribution is \$144,000.

  11. a. $Q = 20$; $P = \$290$.   **b.** Profit = \$1,333.33.

  C1. a. $Q = 10.5$.   **b.** $Q = 6$.   **c.** Profit = \$66.

  C3. a. $P = 220 - Q$; $TR = 220Q - Q^2$.   **b.** $Q = 14$; $P = \$206$.   **c.** Profit = \$437.33.

  C5. $Q = 40$; $P = \$1{,}240$; Profit = \$14,666.67.

  C9. a. $C = 170$; $I = 245$.   **b.** Profit = \$10,670.   **c.** $\lambda = 22.7$.

Appendix 7

1. a. 500,000 raw pineapples and 2,500,000 cans of pineapple.   **b.** $725,000.

3. Minimize $C = 300V_1 + 500V_2 + 540V_3$

Subject to: $2.0V_1 + 2.5V_2 + 3.0V_3 \geq 4,000$

$2.0\ V_2 + 2.0V_3 \geq 3,000.$

Also, $2.0V_1 + 2.5V_2 + 3.0V_3 - L_M = 4,000$

$2.0V_2 + 2.0V_3 - L_T = 3,000$

a. V_1, V_2, and V_3, for each input, the additional profit contribution that could be obtained by relaxing the respective constraint by one unit.

b. $C = 300\ (0) + 500(\$1000) + 540(\$500) = \$770,000.$

c. $V_1 = 0$ implies marginal opportunity cost of one more hour of power train capacity is zero, since there is excess capacity in this input. $V_2 = \$1,000$ and $V_3 = \$500$ are the approximate increases in profit contribution from one more hour of capacity, respectively, for the paint/trim and body assembly inputs. $L_M = L_T = 0$ indicates opportunity cost of resources used in producing the two items is equal to their respective profit contributions. $C = \$770,000$ indicates total opportunity cost of the fixed inputs equals their maximum profit contribution.

Chapter 8

3. Total profit = –$6,160, so by producing, the firm will lose more than the $4,000 fixed costs. It should shut down.

7. a. $Q = 56$ is optimal output.   **b.** Profit = –$468, a loss minimum.

11. a. $Q = 450$.   **b.** Yes $P > SAC$.   **c.** Entry will occur; price will fall; profit will eventually be just normal.

C1. $127.50.

C3. a. $Q = 480$; $P = \$60.80$.   **b.** Profit = $16,780.

C5. a. $Q = 100$; $P = \$195$.   **b.** $2,450.

C7. a. $Q = 30$.   **b.** $T\pi = \$2,200$.   **c.**   **i.** $LAC = 660 - 9Q + 0.05Q^2$.   **ii.** $Q = 90$; $P = LAC = \$255$; $T\pi = 0$.

Chapter 9

3. a. $.10.   **b.** Price = $.07. Each booth will sell 1,667 kisses and earn $116.69.

c. Yes, if firms cooperated, each could produce 1,250 kisses at a unit price of $.10.

5. a. $280.   **b.** 10,000 units.   **c.** 15,000 units.

7. Firms 1, 2, and 3 should be allocated 23,000, 19,250, and 7,750 barrels per year, respectively.

11. $Q = 100$, $P = 65$.

C1. a. $P = \$8.75$; $Q = 7,500$ homes.   **b.** $\$16,125$.   **c.** $P = \$8.00$; $Q = 6,000$ homes.
   d. Profit is decreased by $\$5,125$ when advertising expenditures are cut by $\$5,000$.
   e. Restore advertising to its original level.

C3. a. $Q = 12$.   **b.** $\$508$.

C5. a. Large firm will maximize profit at $Q = 3,000$ and charge a price of $\$44$.   **b.** Small firms'
   quantity supplied will be 1,220.   **c.** For Aqualor, profit will be $\$14,000$.

C7. $Q_A = 500$; $Q_T = 400$.

Chapter 10

1. a. dominant strategy for both is to offer free long distance.
   b. both offer free long distance.

3. a. Firm B will charge a low price.   **b.** Firm A will also charge a low price.

5. "Offer Italian Items" is a Nash equilibrium. Both will do so, though it is a dominant strategy for Ashley's only.

7. Sells 30 pairs. Bonus, $\$60$.

Chapter 11

5. b. Profit is maximized with two shifts, producing 100% B.

7. a. Yes.   **b.** 3,800 carryout servings; 2,400 eat-in servings.   **c.** Price for carryout is $\$3.10$,
   and price for eat-in is $\$3.60$.

C1. a. $Q_z = 2,000$; $Q_b = 1,900$.   **b.** $P_z = \$800$; $P_b = \$1,900$.

C3. The firm should produce 3,620 units of the joint products but sell only 3,000 units of vinegar. $P_w = \$83.80$; $P_v = \$15$; Profit = $\$154,670.40$.

C5. $Q = 3,690$; $P_f = \$63.10$; $P_O = \$17.50$; $T\pi = \$138,259.30$. There is excess codfish oil of 190.

C7. a. $Q_g = 1,340$; $Q_c = 820$.   **b.** $P_g = \$150.20$; $P_c = \$99.60$.   **c.** Profit = $\$37,884$.   **d.** Price will
   be $\$114.05$ in both markets. $Q_g = 2,063$; $Q_c = 97$; Profit is $\$1,292$.

Chapter 12

1. The firm should produce 84 sweatshirts because at that point, the $MRP_L = \$4.50 = MC_L =$
   the wage rate.

3. Forty workers should be employed. Because employment of its members would likely
   decrease, a union would not necessarily bargain for the highest wage.

5. a. Four bartenders should be employed, and the average price of one drink should be set
   at $\$2.70$.   **b.** $\$7.00$/hour.

C1. $L = 9.25$, so use 9 workers.

Chapter 13

1. a. $67,019. **b.** $38,276. **c.** $15,568.

3. The greatest present value in Problem 2 = $286,825.

5. The project is not acceptable at a discount rate of 9% as the *NPV* is –$93,306. At a discount rate of 6%, the *NPV* is $18,709 so the project is acceptable.

7. a. Not acceptable. **b.** Not acceptable. **c.** Acceptable.

9. a. About 13%. **b.** Since the *NPV* is $50,314, management should be advised to accept the project (assuming there is no further adjustment of the discount rate for risk).

Appendix 13

1. $61,316.

3. $13,951.

5. $407,124.

7. $11,754.

Chapter 14

3. Variance = σ^2 = 835,687,500.

Std. Deviation = σ = 28,908.26.

5. Belco will choose the U.S. refinery. The Latin American project has a negative net present value.

7.

Level of Risk (σ)	Certainty Equivalent Adjustment Factor (α)
400	0.4286
300	0.5714
200	0.7143
100	0.8571

11. a. $E(R_T)$ = 0.28; $E(R_M)$ = 0.170. **b.** σ_T = 0.16; σ_M = 0.09. **c.** He would choose in accordance with his preferences regarding risk and return.

Chapter 15

3. Projects *B*, *E*, and *F* are acceptable. The others are not acceptable.

5. The Southeast project has the highest *B/C* and net differential benefits. Also, $\Delta B/\Delta C$ is less than 1.0 for higher cost projects. Therefore the Southeast project should be chosen.

7. Project *D* has the highest benefit-cost ratio, so it would be ranked first. The other two acceptable projects, *A* and *E*, have approximately the same *B/C* ratios, so they would be ranked equally behind project *D*.

Glossary

A

adverse selection: A self-sorting process that occurs when the private information characteristics of a transaction are such that the attributes or behavior of those on one side of the transaction reduce the value of it to the party on the other side.

antitrust laws: Laws regulating any business practices and agreements that intensify monopoly power or otherwise restrict trade.

arc marginal product: An approximation to marginal product over some range of output; is equal to the change in total product divided by the change in the variable input.

arc marginal revenue: The average rate of change of total revenue with respect to quantity sold over some range of output.

asymmetric information: Relative holdings of information when parties to a potential or actual agreement or transaction have different private information relevant to the outcome.

average fixed cost: Fixed cost per unit of output in the short run. Equal to total fixed cost divided by level of output.

average/marginal relationship: The average cannot rise unless the related marginal value is above it; the average cannot fall unless the corresponding marginal value is below it; the average value must equal the marginal value when the average is at a maximum or a minimum.

average product (of a variable input): Total output divided by the number of units of the input in use. It gives output per unit of input.

average profit: Profit per unit of output. Average profit is found by dividing total profit by quantity of output. It is also equal to price minus average cost.

average revenue: Revenue per unit sold. Average revenue is equal to total revenue divided by quantity sold, and as long as only one price is charged, is equal to price.

B

backwards induction: In game theory, process of working backwards through a series of decisions to determine the choices that lead to the solution of a game.

barometric forecasting: Forecasting techniques that involve the use of current values of certain variables, called *indicators,* to predict future values of other economic variables.

barriers to entry: Conditions that make it difficult for new firms to enter an industry or market where existing firms have long-run interests.

benefit-cost ratio (*B/C*): The present value of the benefits divided by the present value of the cost of a project. A project is acceptable from a social welfare point of view if and only if its *B/C* is greater than or equal to one.

bilateral monopoly: A market structure characterized by having only one buyer and one seller of a particular good or service.

bundling: A strategy that offers a package deal to consumers on the purchase of two or more products.

C

capital budgeting: The process by which a firm determines how to allocate investment expenditure among alternative projects.

cartel: A group of firms that have joined together to make agreements on pricing and market strategy.

change in demand: A shift in a demand curve for a good or service caused by a change in some variable other than the price of the given good or service.

change in quantity demanded: A change in the amount of a good or service that consumers are willing to purchase over some time period, which is caused by a change in the price of the good or service.

complementary goods: Products or services that are usually used with one another and have a negative cross price elasticity of demand.

compounding: The process of computing the value of a current sum of money at some future date.

consent decree: A statement of certain provisions agreed to by both the government and the defendant.

consumer's surplus: The difference between the maximum value a consumer places on a given quantity of a good he or she purchases and the money amount that is actually paid to obtain that quantity.

consumption spending: Expenditures by individuals for newly produced goods and services (excluding housing).

contestable markets: Oligopolistic markets characterized by free and costless entry and exit and by a lack of rival reaction on the part of existing firms.

contract law: Laws that pertain to the establishment of contractual obligations and to wrongful acts in breach of contract.

cooperative game: Strategic situation in which players make credible commitments, and binding agreements can take place.

cost-benefit analysis: An extension of capital project analysis to public sector project decisions that attempts to take into account the economic criteria for an optimal allocation of society's resources.

cost elasticity: The percentage change in long-run total cost from a 1 percent change in output.

credible threat: The threat of an action that a rival actually has the ability to carry out.

criminal law: Laws that pertain to acts that are viewed as offenses against a federal, state, or local government.

cross price elasticity of demand: The cross price elasticity of demand for Product X with respect to the price of Product Y is a measure of the relative responsiveness of quantity demanded of X to changes in P_y.

cross-section data: Observations of a particular variable at a single point in time.

cyclical factors: Factors related to fluctuations in the general level of economic activity.

D

demand curve: Graphical representation of the relationship between the quantity demanded of a good and its price.

demand function: Relates the quantities of a product that consumers will purchase during some specific period to the variables that influence their decisions to buy or not to buy the good or service. Examples of such variables include the price of the good or service, prices of related goods or services, and income of potential consumers.

determinants of demand: Those variables other than a good's own price that affect the amount of the good buyers are willing and able to buy at some point in time. Some examples are income, prices of related goods, tastes, and advertising.

determinants of supply: Those variables other than a good's own price that affect the amount of the good sellers are willing and able to sell at some point in time. Some examples are input prices, technology, and various kinds of taxes.

direct benefits: The benefits obtained by the users of a project or activity.

direct costs: The costs directly associated with a project or activity.

discount rate: The rate of interest used to compute a present value.

discounting: The process of computing the present value of a sum of money to be received in the future.

diseconomies of scale: Technological and organizational disadvantages that accrue to the firm as it increases output in the long run. Diseconomies of scale increase long-run average costs.

dominant strategy: A strategy that is always strictly better than every other strategy available to a given player no matter what strategy is chosen by other players.

dominated strategy: A strategy that is always strictly worse than every other strategy available to a given player no matter what strategy is chosen by other players.

E

economic region of production: The range in an isoquant diagram where both inputs have a positive marginal product. It lies inside the ridge lines.

economies of scale: Technological and organizational advantages that the firm encounters as it increases output in the long run. Economies of scale reduce long-run average costs.

economies of scope: Occur when the average cost of undertaking two or more activities together is less than the sum of the costs of each activity separately.

efficient portfolio: A project or a combination of investments that will involve the least risk for a given rate of return.

efficient set: The set of all efficient portfolios.

equilibrium price: The price at which the quantity demanded by consumers of a product is equal to the quantity supplied by sellers of a product.

exclusive dealing: A situation wherein a firm buying or leasing the goods of one firm agrees not to deal with competing suppliers.

expansion path: The line connecting all of the least-cost combinations of input points for a particular ratio of input prices.

expected value: A weighted average of the possible outcomes, which is obtained by multiplying each outcome by the probability associated with it and then summing the resulting values.

explicit costs: Those costs of production that involve a specific payment by the firm to some person, group, or organization outside the firm. Also known as *historical costs*.

extensive form game: Presentation of a game that maps out its sequence using decision nodes and branches to analyze the moves made by players.

F

first-degree price discrimination: A theoretical concept that refers to charging a different amount, specifically the maximum amount a consumer is willing and able to pay, for each unit purchased.

first-mover advantage: Benefit gained by a player in a game that accrues to that party by virtue of having made the first strategic choice.

fixed costs: Those costs that cannot be eliminated in the short run.

forecasting: The process of analyzing available information regarding economic variables and relationships and then predicting the future values of certain variables of interest to the firm or to economic policymakers.

free entry: The absence of barriers to entry into a market. In a market characterized by free entry, profit serves the function of drawing new firms into the industry when greater than normal.

future value: The amount that would be accumulated at some future date if a sum of money held today were invested now at a particular rate of interest.

G

game: A model of strategic choice that consists of a set of players, order of play, body of information, set of actions, outcome(s), and payoff(s).

game theory: Approach to modeling social or economic phenomena that sets out, in detail, information, order of decisions, strategic behavior, possible actions, and outcomes in situations requiring choice.

game tree: Diagram, consisting of decision nodes and branches, that sets out the order of play of a game.

GATT (General Agreement on Tariffs and Trade): The mechanism set up by the market economies after World War II to reduce barriers to international trade. It had over 100 member countries in 1993, and many former Eastern Bloc nations were hoping to join the group.

government expenditures: Expenditures for newly produced goods and services, including government investment expenditures, by all levels of government.

gross domestic product: The market value of all final output produced within the geographical area of a country during a given time period (generally one year).

gross national product: The market value of final goods and services produced with factors of production owned by residents of a country during some time period, usually one year.

H

historical costs: Costs of the firm for which explicit payment has been made sometime in the past or for which the firm is committed in the future. Also known as *explicit costs*.

I

implicit (opportunity) costs: Costs that do not involve actual payment by a firm to factors of production but nevertheless represent cost to the firm in the sense that in order to use certain inputs in the production process, the firm has had to abandon opportunities to use them elsewhere.

incentive contracting: Contracting approach that attempts to harmonize the goals of the contracting parties.

income elasticity of demand: A measure of the relative responsiveness of the quantity demanded of a product to the changes in income.

incremental benefit-cost ratio: The change in total benefits divided by the change in total costs, obtained by moving to the project with the next higher level of price or initial outlay.

incremental cost: The additional costs that will be incurred by the firm if it undertakes a new project or produces an additional batch of output.

incremental profit: Incremental revenue minus incremental cost resulting from an activity of a firm.

incremental revenue: The additional revenue that a firm will receive by undertaking a particular project.

indirect benefits: External, or third party, benefits associated with a project.

indirect costs: External, or third party, costs associated with a project.

inferior good: A product or service with a negative income elasticity of demand.

internal rate of return *(IRR)*: The net annual percentage yield of a project, obtained by solving for the discount rate that will cause the net present value of the project to be equal to zero.

investment spending: (GNP definition) All purchases of capital goods—including buildings, equipment, and inventories—by private businesses and nonprofit institutions. Includes all expenditures for residential housing.

isocost line: Gives all combinations of two inputs that can be used for a given dollar cost to the firm, assuming given and fixed input prices.

isoprofit curve: Indicates the different combinations of two products that will result in equal profit for the firm.

isoquant: Indicates the various combinations of two inputs that would enable a firm to produce a particular level of output.

iterative dominance strategy: A strategy or sequence of decisions that is selected by a process of eliminating the dominated strategies of a given player in a game.

K

kinked demand curve: Occurs when rival firms will not follow the price increase of a single firm in an oligopoly but will cut prices when another firm does so. Such a demand curve is relatively elastic for prices above the going market price and much less elastic for lower prices.

L

law of demand: Proposition that price and quantity demanded of a given good or service are inversely related, so that consumers are willing and able to buy more of the good at lower prices than they are at higher prices.

law of diminishing returns: A technical proposition which asserts that if equal increments of one variable input are added while the amounts of all other inputs remain fixed, total product may increase, but after some point, the *additions* to total product will decrease.

least-cost combination of inputs: That input combination that will enable a firm to produce a given level of output at the lowest possible cost or to produce the greatest output for a given dollar cost.

linear programming: A mathematical technique whereby a firm can make optimizing decisions in a situation where the function to be maximized or minimized is linear and subject to linear constraints that are in the form of inequalities.

long run: Time period sufficiently long that all inputs are variable.

long-run average cost: Long-run total cost divided by the level of output. Measures cost per unit of output when all inputs are variable.

long-run marginal cost: The rate of change of long-run total cost as the level of output changes.

long-run total cost: The minimum economic cost of producing each possible level of output when the time period is sufficiently long to change all inputs of the firm's production function.

M

macroeconomics: The branch of economic analysis that deals with aggregate economic variables such as the economy's total output, central government spending and tax policy, and money supply and interest rates.

marginal cost of an input: The rate of change of a firm's total cost with respect to a change in the amount of an input. *Arc* marginal cost of an input is given by the change in a firm's total cost divided by the change in the input.

marginal cost of capital *(MCC)***:** The discount rate that represents the marginal cost of investment funds to the firm. Calculated as a weighted average of the after-tax cost of funds from each source.

marginal or **incremental analysis:** Examines how changes in certain economic variables affect other economic variables; for example, how a change in the output of a firm affects both sales revenue and cost or how an increase in household income affects savings.

marginal product (of a variable input): The rate of change of total output with respect to changes in the variable input—other inputs kept fixed. *Arc* marginal product is an approximation to marginal product and is given by the change in the total product divided by the change in the variable input.

marginal profit: The rate of change of total profit with respect to changes in the level of the firm's output. *Arc* marginal profit is found by dividing the change in total profit by the change in quantity of output. Marginal profit is also equal to marginal revenue minus marginal cost.

marginal rate of (technical) substitution of two inputs (MRS): Indicates the rate at which two inputs can be substituted for each other while a constant level of production is maintained. The marginal rate of substitution is equal to minus one times the slope of an isoquant.

marginal revenue: The rate of change of total revenue with respect to quantity sold. Marginal revenue indicates to a firm how total revenue will change if there is a change in the quantity sold of a firm's product. An approximation to marginal revenue is the change in total revenue divided by the change in quantity sold. We call this value *arc marginal revenue.*

marginal revenue product of an input: The rate of change of total revenue with respect to change in the variable input. The marginal revenue product of an input is equal to the marginal product of the input multiplied by the net marginal revenue.

marginal social benefit: The marginal private benefit of a good or service (usually measured by its price) plus any marginal external or third-party benefits.

marginal social cost: Marginal private cost plus marginal external cost.

market segmentation: See *price discrimination.*

market share curve: Shows the amounts the firm can actually sell at various prices as all firms in the industry adjust price together.

markup pricing: A pricing technique whereby a certain percentage of cost of goods sold or of price is added to cost of goods sold, in order to obtain the market price.

microeconomics: The study of individual economic units such as consumers, business firms, or specific government agencies.

monitoring costs: The costs associated with making certain that the terms of an agreement are complied with.

monopolistic competition: A market structure characterized by the existence of many firms in the industry (but with an element of product differentiation so that each firm has some control over price) and by free entry into and exit from the industry.

monopoly: A market structure characterized by the existence of only one firm in the industry. For a firm to retain monopoly control, there must be complete barriers to entry into and exit from the industry.

monopsonistic competition: A market with many buyers of a differentiated product.

moral hazard: Potential for *ex post* behavior that is contrary to the actions required or desired under an agreement or after the establishment of a policy.

N

Nash equilibrium: Outcome from which no decision maker or player of a game would want to deviate, given the behavior of the other players.

natural monopoly: An industry where the existence of only one firm is a matter of public convenience and allows for the maximum benefits of economies of scale.

net cash flow: Any increase in revenues brought about by the project less any increase in operating expenses and depreciation, multiplied by $(1 - T)$, where T is the firm's marginal income tax rate. The incremental depreciation associated with the project is then added to the preceding sum.

net exports: Value of newly produced U.S. goods and services purchased by foreigners (exports) less the value of newly produced foreign goods purchased by the United States (imports).

net marginal revenue: Marginal revenue from the sale of a firm's final product *minus* a specific portion of marginal production cost. In the case of transfer pricing, the portion of marginal production cost that is deducted from MR to obtain final product net marginal revenue (NMR_F) is the marginal cost of the final division, not including the cost of the transfer product. In determining the optimal amount of a variable input, net marginal revenue is defined as marginal revenue minus marginal cost of components.

net present value *(NPV)*: The present value of the net cash inflows minus the present value of the cost outlays of an investment. An investment project is acceptable if its NPV is greater than or equal to zero.

net social benefit: The total social benefit less the total social cost of an activity.

noncooperative game: Strategic situation in which decision-making parties act independently and do not enter into binding agreements or credible commitments.

normal form game: A game where strategies and payoffs are described in a table or matrix showing the various possible decisions and their results.

normal good: A product or service with a positive income elasticity of demand.

O

oligopoly: A market structure characterized by the existence of a few dominant firms in an industry (each of which recognizes their mutual interdependence) and by substantial barriers to entry into the industry.

oligopsony: A market with a few buyers, or a few dominant buyers.

one-shot game: A game, played only once, in which all players make decisions at the same time (also known as a single-period, simultaneous-move game).

opportunity cost: Cost as measured by the next best alternative given up when a choice is made.

P

payoff: The effect of the outcome of a game on a given player.

perfect competition: A market structure in which (a) the firm takes market price as given, since an individual firm produces only a small fraction of total industry output; (b) the products of all firms are undifferentiated; (c) there is freedom of entry into or exit from the industry; (d) there are no artificial interferences with the activities of buyers and sellers; and (e) all buyers and sellers have perfect knowledge of market conditions.

present value: The value today of a stream of receipts to be received in the future. Present value is obtained by discounting the stream of receipts using an appropriate discount rate.

price discrimination: The practice of charging different prices for the same product, either by offering buyers lower prices on marginal or incremental quantities purchased or by dividing groups of buyers into separate markets. The latter is also known as *market segmentation.*

price elasticity of demand: A measure of the relative responsiveness of quantity demanded of a product to a change in its price. The price elasticity of demand indicates how total revenue will change as a result of a change in price.

price fixing: The practice of a group of firms agreeing to set the price of a product at a specific level.

price leadership: Occurs when a firm in an oligopoly sets a price that subsequently determines what other members of the industry will charge for their products.

principal-agent problem: This occurs when one party is entrusted with making a decision on behalf of another party in a setting where the goals of the two may differ.

private costs of a firm: The sum of the explicit and implicit costs that the firm incurs.

private information: Information affecting the value of an agreement or other mutual activity that is known to the party(ies) on one side of the agreement but unobservable to the party(ies) on the other side.

product differentiation: A wide variety of activities, such as design changes and advertising, that rival firms employ to attract customers by distinguishing their product from competitors' products.

production function: A mathematical statement of the way that the quantity of output of a product depends on the quantities used of various inputs or resources.

profit maximization: Making the greatest economic profit possible.

profit-maximizing rule: Produce up to the point where marginal revenue is equal to marginal cost and at higher output levels marginal revenue is less than marginal cost, as long as price is greater than or equal to average variable cost in the short run or long-run average cost in the long run. Also known as *loss-minimizing rule.*

pure public good: A product or service that is indivisible and nonexcludable.

Q

quantity supplied: Along a supply curve, the amount that producers will make available for purchase at a specific price.

R

repeated game: Game in which players repeatedly engage in strategic interactions (may be either finitely or infinitely repeated).

returns to scale: Refers to how output changes when all inputs are increased by the same multiple (e.g., doubled or tripled).

ridge lines: The lines connecting the points where the marginal product of an input is equal to zero (one line for each input) in the isoquant map and forming the boundary for the economic region of production.

risk averse investor: An investor who, given a choice between two investments with the same expected return, will always prefer the less risky one.

risk neutral investor: An investor who is indifferent between two investments with the same expected return, regardless of their risk.

risk seeker: An investor who, given a choice between two investments with the same expected return, will always prefer the riskier one.

S

search costs: The economic costs of obtaining information relevant to making a decision.

seasonal factors: Factors connected with a specific season of the year.

second-degree price discrimination: The practice of charging successively lower prices for block-type increases in quantity purchased.

semivariable costs: Costs that are fixed over some ranges of output and variable over others.

sequential game: A game where all players make their decisions in a sequence, one after another.

short run: A time period sufficiently short that at least one input is fixed.

short-run average total cost: The cost per unit of output in the short run. Equal to short-run total cost divided by the level of output. Also equal to average fixed cost plus short-run average variable cost for each level of output.

short-run average variable cost: The variable cost per unit of output produced in the short run. Equal to short-run total variable cost divided by the level of output.

short-run marginal cost: The rate of change of *either* short-run total cost or short-run total variable cost as the level of output changes in the short run.

short-run total cost: All of the private economic costs of the firm in the short run. Equal to total fixed cost plus short-run total variable cost.

short-run total variable cost: The sum of all private economic costs of the firm that vary with its level of output in the short run.

signalling: Activity that communicates otherwise unobservable information about a party to others who are actual or potential participants in a mutual activity.

social costs of a firm: The costs that society in general incurs because of a firm's activities. Social costs include private costs plus any additional costs that the firm imposes on society but for which it does not pay.

social rate of discount: The rate of discount appropriate for evaluating public sector projects.

strategy: A complete plan of play for a game, consisting of a choice or sequence thereof made by a decision maker who, generally, sacrifices other alternatives in order to pursue it.

substitute goods: Products or services that can be substituted for one another and that have a positive cross price elasticity of demand.

T

third-degree price discrimination: The practice of dividing groups of consumers into separate markets and charging a different price in each market.

time series data: Observations of a specific variable over a number of time periods.

tort law: Laws that deal with injuries sustained by private parties as a result of nonperformance of a duty created by law.

total fixed cost: Total dollar amount of costs that do not vary with the level of output.

total product function (of a variable input): Indicates the maximum output that can be obtained from different amounts of one variable input, while all other inputs are kept fixed.

total profit: Total revenue minus total costs, including opportunity costs. Also known as *economic profit.*

total revenue: Total dollar sales volume of a firm, which is equal to price times quantity sold.

trend analysis: A forecasting technique that relies primarily on historical data to predict the future.

trend factors: Factors related to movements in economic variables over time.

two-part pricing: A strategy that divides the amount a consumer pays for a good or service into an access fee and a price per unit.

tying agreement: Occurs when a firm agrees that goods sold or leased will be used only with other goods of the seller or lessor.

V

variable costs: Those costs that vary with the level of a firm's output.

variance: One measure of the dispersion about the expected value or mean of a set of data or possible outcomes of a project.

Index